SPORTS AND ATHLETICS PREPARATION, PERFORMANCE, AND PSYCHOLOGY SERIES

SPORTS AND ATHLETICS PREPARATION, PERFORMANCE, AND PSYCHOLOGY SERIES

HANDBOOK OF SPORTS PSYCHOLOGY

CALVIN H. CHANG
EDITOR

Nova Science Publishers, Inc.
New York

For permission to use material from this book please contact us:
Telephone 631-231-7269; Fax 631-231-8175
Web Site: http://www.novapublishers.com

NOTICE TO THE READER

The Publisher has taken reasonable care in the preparation of this book, but makes no expressed or implied warranty of any kind and assumes no responsibility for any errors or omissions. No liability is assumed for incidental or consequential damages in connection with or arising out of information contained in this book. The Publisher shall not be liable for any special, consequential, or exemplary damages resulting, in whole or in part, from the readers' use of, or reliance upon, this material. Any parts of this book based on government reports are so indicated and copyright is claimed for those parts to the extent applicable to compilations of such works.

Independent verification should be sought for any data, advice or recommendations contained in this book. In addition, no responsibility is assumed by the publisher for any injury and/or damage to persons or property arising from any methods, products, instructions, ideas or otherwise contained in this publication.

This publication is designed to provide accurate and authoritative information with regard to the subject matter covered herein. It is sold with the clear understanding that the Publisher is not engaged in rendering legal or any other professional services. If legal or any other expert assistance is required, the services of a competent person should be sought. FROM A DECLARATION OF PARTICIPANTS JOINTLY ADOPTED BY A COMMITTEE OF THE AMERICAN BAR ASSOCIATION AND A COMMITTEE OF PUBLISHERS.

LIBRARY OF CONGRESS CATALOGING-IN-PUBLICATION DATA

Handbook of sports psychology / editor, Calvin H. Chang.
    p. cm.
Includes index.
ISBN 978-1-60741-256-4 (hardcover)
1. Sports--Psychological aspects. I. Chang, Calvin H.
GV706.4H3713 2009
796.01--dc22
                2009033369

Published by Nova Science Publishers, Inc. ✦ *New York*

CONTENTS

PREFACE

Sport psychology is the scientific study of people and their behaviors in sport contexts and the practical application of that knowledge. Sport psychologists identify principles and guidelines that professionals can use to help adults and children participate in and benefit from sport and exercise activities in both team and individual environments. Sport psychologists have two objectives in mind: (a) to understand how psychological factors affect an individual's physical performance and (b) to understand how participation in sport and exercise affects a person's psychological development, health and well-being. This new and important book gathers the latest research from around the globe in the study of this dynamic field and highlights such topics as: gender role conflict among female rugby players, stress in young athletes, sport and spirituality, supplementation in bodybuilding, performing under pressure, measuring sport spectators' coping strategies, and others.

Chapter 1 - Explanatory styles are a predictor factor about the quality of sport practice motivation and the performance level reached by an athlete (Seligman et al, 1990). The possibility of using stability, globality and internality dimensions in order to analyze athletes' explanatory styles and help them to interpret their own failure and success experiences in a more adaptive way, give to this research area a great applied potential. However, sport psychology literature about attributional processes shows how theoretical models and available analysis tools don't ensure an exhaustive comprehension of the real way in which these processes really develop in the sportive context and the intervention methods that result from these scientific assumptions don't always result as useful (Rees et al., 2005).

This contribution, starting from a critique analysis of the literature about explanatory styles in sport psychology, has the aim to identify the critical aspects, some of which already detected by researchers (Rees et al., 2005), and to propose a method of qualitative analysis which allows to find out more factors that could help us understand exhaustively attributional processes in sport.

According to important sport psychology works (Grove & Pargman, 1986; Biddle et al., 2001; Gordon, 2008), the qualitative analysis of a wide sample of texts reporting athletes' descriptions about their own success/failure experiences suggested to us the opportunity to recover the dimension of control and to consider other categories of analysis such as: the level of complexity of the causal explanations (see also the concept of "explanatory flexibility" in Fresco et al. 2007), the level of rigidity with which these explanations are made and the timing of the attributional process.

The approach the authors used to make the qualitative analysis is mainly based on the theoretical model on Perceptual and Cognitive Linguistic Indicators (Bongelli & Zuczkowski, 2008a, 2008b) which offers many cues deriving from linguistic elements information about the cognitive state of the speaker. In this chapter a set of comparisons made through this approach are presented by highlighting important differences regarding the way in which athletes explain their owns successes and failures. These differences, detectable through the new categories of the proposed analysis system, did not emerge through the traditional content analysis like CAVE (Peterson et al, 1992), and they seem potentially able to moderate the predictor power of explanatory styles. This suggests the opportunity to study attributional processes in their complexity. The authors propose an interpretation of the results of this study according to important theoretical models of motivational processes (Csíkszentmihályi, 1990), Artificial Intelligence (Castelfranchi, 1998) and mental control (Wenzlaff and Bates, 2000; Singer, 2000)

Chapter 2 - Gender role conflict theory proposes that female athletes experience role conflict because they are expected to enact both feminine and masculine gender roles, which reflect very discrepant expectations for a female athlete's behavior. Understanding these conflicting expectations for gender role behavior can lead to greater options for resolution and thereby remove some obstacles to sport participation for female athletes. This chapter presents findings from a qualitative study exploring how female rugby players negotiate gender role expectations and conflict, as women participating in a traditionally masculine sport. Eleven Caucasian female rugby players between the ages of 25 and 38 were interviewed regarding expectations for their behavior and gender expression, experiences of distress and conflict, and strategies for resolution. The results indicate that participants perceived numerous discrepant gender role expectations related to their appearance, physical activity and durability, sexual orientation, level of aggressiveness and assertiveness, and social behavior. Participants also described three different types of gender role conflict: conflict regarding being feminine enough, conflict about being too feminine to play the sport, and concerns about how gender role behavior affects perceptions of their sexual orientation. In keeping with previous findings, participants perceived more conflicting expectations for their behavior than they reported to experience conflict problems. It also appears that the level of distress as the result of gender role conflict appears to be minimal. Participants displayed great resiliency and utilized numerous active coping strategies in the resolution and negotiation of discrepant expectations, which has not been documented in previous research. Coping strategies utilized include influencing the source of the expectations, resolving conflict internally and accommodating gender role expectations. Coping strategies will be discussed in detail so as to provide clinical resources for counseling and sport psychology practitioners in their work with female athletes. Additionally, the identification of different types of gender role conflict has implications for gender role conflict theory.

Chapter 3 - This chapter evaluates the psychological concept of exercise addiction from a scholastically multidisciplinary perspective. The most recent developments in the area of investigation are evaluated with reference to theory and critical analysis of extant research. The chapter summarizes the current knowledge about the psycho-physiological nature of exercise addiction. Further, it presents the conceptual hegemony in addressing the problem of exercise addiction within the scientific community. The characteristic and most prevalent symptoms of the disorder are discussed alongside the modes of risk-assessment. Subsequently, the underlying motives and several theoretical models of exercise addiction are reviewed. Finally, the research on exercise addiction is evaluated and directions for future research are suggested. Difference is made between primary exercise addiction in which the exercise behavior is the problem and secondary exercise addiction in which exercise is used as a means in achieving another objective, like weight loss. The chapter concludes with two brief sections summarizing plainly what we know today and what we still need to know about exercise addiction.

Chapter 4 - It is difficult to think of a subject of greater bearing to our understanding of sport than the effect of emotions on sport performance. Researchers interested in exploring emotions among youth athletes have a unique opportunity to examine their thoughts, feelings, and behaviors in a rich and dynamic natural laboratory. Despite this opportunity, our understanding of emotional experience among young athletes is relatively uncharted territory in pediatric sport psychology. Stress and enjoyment have well developed and integrated literatures and provide a solid base for further emotion research among youths in sport (Scanlan, Babkes, & Scanlan, 2005). Current research, however, is beginning to address other issues in different contexts with emotion as a central element such as coping (Holt & Mandigo, 2004; Nicholls, 2007; Raedeke & Smith, 2004), burnout (Hill, Hall, Appleton, & Kozub, 2008) and perfectionism (Appleton, Hall, & Hill, 2009) illustrating that many intrapersonal, situational and significant other sources of positive and negative emotion exist. This chapter reviews the literature on stress and anxiety among young athletes with an emphasis on burnout, perfectionism and coping.

Chapter 5 - Recently, sport psychology has given increasing attention to the role of religion and spirituality in sport. Much of this research examines the prominence and similarities between sport and religion as well as disparate religious beliefs and practices athletes incorporate in their sport participation. However, this research lacks an overarching conceptual framework grounding sport and religion in sound theory amenable to empirical observation. This chapter provides a critique of the literature on sport and religion from various fields of study. It begins by examining research comparing sport and religion as social institutions. It then turns to research from sport psychology, which examines the role of religion and spirituality in the lives of athletes, including their athletic performance. Next, borrowing from the psychology of religion, the constructs of spirituality and sanctification are presented as a framework for understanding the convergence between sport and religion. These theoretically driven and empirically supported constructs address the limitations of previous research and provide an original perspective for understanding how athletes integrate their sport and spirituality. Finally, future directions addressing the inherent vicissitudes of sport are suggested.

Chapter 6 - To manage the stressors they face in competitive settings athletes must develop a range of cognitive and behavioural coping skills. Athletes who use maladaptative coping strategies or fail to interpret sport-related events accurately and to react in a rational manner, will experience chronic stress that frequently leads to reduced performance quality and, eventually, to burnout and sport dropout. Therefore, athletes who participate in competitive sports need to employ effective psychological skills and coping strategies in order to satisfy their expectatives and to improve their performance. Although different questionnaries aimed to identify coping strategies used by athletes have been developed in the last few years, establishment of the most adequate instruments to determine under which situations cognitive and behavioral coping strategies reach its optimal efficacy is still required.

Chapter 7 - Bodybuilders pursue a muscular physique through a specific programme of weightlifting and nutrition. The sport is growing rapidly in popularity, especially amongst young males in the Western world.

Ever since the development of bodybuilding as an athletic pursuit there has been a market for nutritional supplements. These purport to increase the participant's ability to attain a hitherto unobtainable physique through such means as increasing strength or decreasing body fat. The promotional strategies for such supplements tap directly into men's insecurities about their bodies and most assertions about efficacy are not supported by scientific evidence.

For most individuals bodybuilding remains a healthy pastime that forms a balanced part of an active lifestyle. However, evidence is growing that for a number of men bodybuilding has facilitated the emergence of a unique disturbance of eating, exercise behaviour and body image termed muscle dysmorphia.

In this chapter the author provides an overview of the bodybuilding subculture and discuss the development of the supplement industry. Existing literature on the prevalence of supplementation amongst bodybuilders is reviewed, together with data on the type of products marketed to consumers. The physiological validity of the claims made by purveyors of such preparations is assessed in light of existing evidence. The author highlights the use of cynical marketing strategies that target vulnerable individuals and link such behaviour to the rise of muscle dysmorphia amongst male bodybuilders. Existing regulatory frameworks in the United States and the European Union are outlined and these are considered in the context of concerns about potential physical and mental ill effects. Future directions for research in this field are discussed, including an urgent need to obtain an up to date assessment of current trends in nutritional supplements and a pressing requirement to assess the physical and mental consequences of long-term supplementation.

Chapter 8 - Background: Research suggests that coach-athlete interactions with can be a stressful aspect of competitive sport (Horn, 2008). Perceptions of autonomy support, structure, and involvement have been advocated by Deci and Ryan (2002) within the framework of Self-Determination Theory (SDT) as key elements of interpersonal support during most interactions that can invoke adaptive (or debilitative) responses.

Purpose: The purpose of this study was (a) to review the evidence concerning the role of interpersonal support provided by coaches to athletes using SDT as a framework, and (b) test the psychometric properties of an instrument (Interpersonal Supportiveness Scale-Coach; ISS-C) designed to assess perceived autonomy support, structure, and involvement experienced by athletes from coaches.

Summary: The wealth of evidence suggests that interactions between competitive athletes and coaches have been examined mainly with reference to perceived autonomy support experienced by competitive athletes from their coaches. In comparison, substantially less evidence is available concerning the role of perceived structure and involvement as they relate to athlete-coach interactions within sport. Results of the psychometric analyses provide initial albeit limited support for the structural validity and internal consistency reliability of ISS-C responses although concerns regarding discriminant validity were evident. Overall, the results of this study suggest perceived structure and involvement could be assessed with the ISS-C in athletes and warrant consideration in future sport research embracing SDT as a conceptual approach.

Chapter 9 - The aim of this study was to test the predictions of attentional control theory (Eysenck et al., 2007) in a sporting environment. The authors adopted a basketball free-throw task and examined the gaze behavior of participants during the occlusion period (when the ball and arms block the target as the ball is raised). Previous research (Vickers, 1996) has shown that skilled performers fixate on the target early in the aiming phase (the quiet eye) but do not look towards the target when their hands and the ball enter their field of view. This attentional control strategy was termed the location suppression hypothesis by Vickers (1996) and it is suggested that such suppression of visual processing prevents interference from the moving hands and ball in the visual field, preserving the aiming commands derived from the quiet eye. Skilled players suppress their vision during the occlusion period by blinking or directing their gaze to other locations, rather than try to maintain a fixation on the occluded target. The authors propose that anxiety may alter this optimal strategy, as attentional control theory suggests that anxious individuals have less efficient *negative* attentional control and are less able to inhibit attentional capture from distracting stimuli.

Ten basketball players took free-throws in two counterbalanced experimental conditions designed to manipulate the anxiety they experienced. Point of gaze was measured using an ASL Mobile Eye tracker and gaze behavior during the occlusion period (including blinks, fixations to other locations and fixations to the ball) was determined using frame-by-frame analysis. The manipulation of anxiety resulted in significant reductions in suppressed vision and free-throw success rate, thus supporting the predictions of attentional control theory. Anxiety impaired goal directed attentional control (suppressed vision) at the expense of stimulus-driven control (longer duration of fixations to the ball and hands). The findings suggest that attentional control theory may be a useful theoretical framework for examining the relationship between anxiety and performance in visuomotor sport skills.

Chapter 10 - The purpose of this study was to investigate the self-regulation strategies employed by elite kitesurfers during self-paced training. It was hypothesized that declared self-regulation strategies could predict athletes' involvement in training and performance in future competitions. The participants were seventy-five male kitesurfers, chosen based on their performances in previous, European, French and international kitesurfing competitions. In order to enhance content validity, researchers used interviews with kitesurfers. A discriminant analysis tested construct validity, and Cronbach's Alpha coefficients were calculated to test the reliability of each sub-scale. Multiple regressions showed that self-regulation strategies could predict training involvement (R^2=.26). Training involvement is quite a good predictor of performance (R^2=.11). These results should be attested external validity for the SRSPTQ (Self-Regulation Strategies in Self-Paced Training Questionnaire). The procedure allowed us to propose 13 sub-scales with satisfactory psychometric properties. Self-regulation strategies in kitesurfing were identified using the SRSPTQ.

Chapter 11 - Performance, coping and anxiety are critical ingredients for the consultant in working with athletes at all levels. Consultation in sport requires competency and specificity. The greater the specificity of the service in terms of offering information and training that will assure athletes can adapt to both the known and unknown factors that will operate to pose threats to their career should be the primary goal (Miller, Ogilvie,. Branch, 2008). In consultation with agents or coaches, appealing to individual athletes who could benefit from any aspect of sports consultation requires each having an empirical basis to the consultation services. New recruits whether to a college or pro team will confront a number of issues within the purview of the sports consultant when signing a contract. As a consultant, it is essential to emphasize to agents and others within college or professional organizations why it is imperative that an extensive psychometric study be utilized for the benefit of both athlete and coaching staff. Individual assessment helps to diagnose potential problems and will be instructive for the organization in understanding enhancing the individual's probability of making and completing effectively in the athletic arena.

Chapter 12 - Developmentally disabled children and their families face numerous challenges throughout their lives. The focus of this chapter is to provide health care professionals with models that may be beneficial in the care and treatment of children with a spectrum of disabilities. Attention to both physical and psychological aspects of their involvement in sport activities will be explored as well as their ability to perform, coping mechanisms, and anxiety that may be experienced. Decreasing maladaptive behaviors with these children will be explored, including necessity for redirection to task and inappropriate communication. The clinical assessment of disabled children prior to their participation will be discussed in detail, as well as how to match a sport with a child. Existing contemporary models of sport involvement such as the "Miracle League" model will be examined (Miracle League 2008). This program is specifically designed for children with developmental disabilities and may include programs in baseball, basketball, swimming, martial arts and other sport activities. The importance of future clinical research will be discussed.

The opportunity for sports participation among individuals with disabilities has grown dramatically in recent decades. A thorough understanding of the issues involved as well as the how to address the concerns is paramount for anyone who works with disabled individuals. The benefits of sports participation for the disabled are numerous. Nationally, rates of obesity in the general population are increasing, and the disabled tend to have lower levels of fitness and higher rates of obesity than their nondisabled peers. There is a growing body of literature demonstrating improved outcomes in multiple health measures with fitness programs and sports participation. In addition, sports participation helps develop a healthy self-concept, builds confidence, and improves overall quality of life. Sports also provide children with special needs with valuable social interactions, both with other disabled individuals, as well as their nondisabled peers.

Chapter 13 - Parents play important roles in the lives of young athletes, both in terms of facilitating their initial involvement in sport and influencing their on-going participation and development (Côté, 1999). But whereas parents often play a positive role in youth sport, inappropriate parental involvement can negatively influence child-athletes' experiences (Gould, Lauer, Rolo, Jannes, & Pennisi, 2008). Inappropriate involvement includes parents' holding excessive expectations for their children, criticising children during competitions, and exerting too much pressure on them to perform (Gould, Tuffey, Udry, & Loehr, 1996). There is little research examining *why* parents may engage in inappropriate behaviours in youth sport contexts. One promising line of research to help uncover more information about parents' behaviour in sport examines the *stressors* parents themselves experience (e.g., Harwood & Knight, 2009a). Therefore, the purpose of this chapter is to examine stressors parents may experience in relation to their children's sport involvement. Main issues discussed are: (a) general parenting stressors; (b) sport-related parenting stressors; (c) potential relations between sport parents' stressors and their behaviours; and (d) directions for future research.

Chapter 14 - Introduction: As athletes train for competition, volume load and training intensity are specifically manipulated in an attempt to elicit gains in performance. The Theory of Periodization states that the planned manipulation of training variables over time can "peak" an athlete for competition while minimizing fatigue and preventing accommodation to training and/or overtraining. Overtraining can be defined as any increase in volume load and/or training intensity in which adaptation does not occur and results in long-term performance decrements. A milder form of overtraining, known as overreaching, can occur on a short-term basis in which athletes can easily recover over the course of a few days of reduced training. Daily manipulation of training variables can elicit changes either toward or away from a state of overtraining. If training and recovery periods have been planned correctly, a delayed increase in performance can occur upon the resumption of normal training. This delayed training effect should occur within approximately 2-5 weeks following the resumption of normal training.

Purpose: To determine the effects of a short-term planned period of overreaching on weightlifting performance and compare the training variables (volume load, total sets, total repetitions) performed during the overreaching stimulus and the taper week immediately following the stimulus to normal training.

Methods: Members of a weightlifting team participated in a week-long training camp, in which volume load was double that which the athletes typically experience during normal training. At the completion of the training camp, athletes took part in a weightlifting competition. The results of the competition were compared to the athletes' self-reported best snatch and clean-and-jerk using a paired t-test, to determine the effects on weightlifting performance.

Results: Seven members of the weightlifting team were used in final analyses (age: 21y; height: 173.8cm; weight: 88.5kg; bodyfat: 15.2%; lean body mass: 74.7kg; systolic BP: 130.9mmHg; diastolic BP: 71.4mmHg; resting heart rate: 76.6bpm; weightlifting experience: 3.1y). Snatch performance following the overreaching stimulus was not significantly altered (Pre-camp = 103.9kg; Post-camp=99.6kg; -4.1%; p=0.27). A trend was noted in the clean-and-jerk following the overreaching stimulus, such that performance was reduced 5.25% (Pre-camp: 135kg; Post-camp=127.9kg; -5.25%; p=0.08). Training variables were also reduced 50%-80% during the taper week immediately following the week of overreaching.

Discussion: The results of this study indicate that weightlifting performance during a competition is not affected immediately following an overreaching stimulus. This work supports previous studies in which performance of a weightlifting-specific test battery in a group of junior weightlifters was not significantly affected by an overreaching stimulus. However, this study extends previous studies on the effects of short-term overreaching by analyzing the effects of the stimulus during an actual weightlifting competition.

Chapter 15 - Sport spectators' reactions to their favourite team's (athlete) defeat is a well studied phenomenon and several strategies used by sport spectators to cope with it have been previously identified in the literature. However, the conceptual distinctions between these strategies have not been empirically tested and no measure of spectators coping strategies has been elaborated so far. The current brief research attempted to fill this void. Based on the framework of the Social Identity Approach (Haslam, 2004) which postulated different categories of identity management strategies (i.e., individual mobility, social competition, and different social creativity strategies), the authors of this research developed a preliminary version of the Sport Spectator Identity Management (SSIM) scale which is made up of four subscales, and an empirical investigation was then conducted with one hundred and twenty spectators. Results of an exploratory factor analysis confirmed the four factors structure of the scale which accounted for 73.37% of the overall variance and revealed satisfying levels of internal reliability. In line with past research about this topic, the criterion related validity of the SSIM scale showed, as expected, that amount of identification with the team is significantly and positively related to all subscales. Finally, the study also supported a rather traditional picture of *rioters*: The spectators who demonstrate the highest levels of aggressive coping strategy are young males and tend to have the lowest socioeconomic status. Future directions to improve this instrument and to better track the condition of identity management strategy choices are discussed.

Chapter 16 - New possibilities for research and training in sport could be offered thanks to virtual reality simulations. The literature is examined, analysing the advantages and properties of current simulators. This paper aims to present an original experiment in virtual reality simulation design based on autonomy, interaction and evolving concepts. Our main suggestion is that believability of simulation for the user needs both regularity and surprises (in terms of virtual agents' behaviour). A naturalistic approach was used to study experts' decision-making processes in soccer settings. The decision-making model represented a guideline for choosing and implementing computational models. The advantages of virtual reality simulation are discussed in relation to training and research in sports science.

Chapter 17 - Anxiety and depression were the major mental health disease in worldwide (Zoeller, 2007). The prevalence of anxiety and depression in children and adolescents were accelerating at an alarming rate. Previous studies reported that 5.7% to 17.7% children were suffering form anxiety and 2% to 5% of them with diagnosed depression. Anxiety might lead to serious impairment to individual daily lives and depressed individuals were more likely to suffer from other chronic disease (i.e. diabetes, cardiovascular disease), health risk behaviors (i.e. drug abuse and alcoholism) and committed suicide.

Growing body of research indicated that physical activity (PA) was a protective factor of anxiety and depression and adopted it as a non-pharmaceutical for treating anxiety and depression in adults. However, issue in respect to the effectiveness, mechanism and the application of PA in the treatment and prevention of childhood anxiety and depression is still equivocal. Therefore, this chapter provided an overview on 1) the effect of PA in the treatment and prevention of anxiety and depression in children; 2) the mechanism of PA on anxiety and depression, and 3) PA recommendation for treating and preventing anxiety and depression treatment and prevention in children.

Chapter 18 - In this paper, changes of subjective sleep quality and state anxiety prior to a final sport exam have been investigated. Subjective sleep quality and state anxiety were psychometrically recorded from a group of high-school students one month prior, one week prior and the night before the exam. The high-school students showed higher state anxiety in the morning of the sport exam and for the night they reported less sleep quality, prolonged sleep latency and a higher number of nocturnal awakenings in comparison to the baseline measurement. Furthermore, a correlation between the feeling of being refreshed in the morning, cognitive state anxiety and self-confidence was found for the morning of the exam. It seems plausible that poor sleep quality and/or a feeling of not being refreshed in the morning might interfere with the performance during the sport exam. Future studies should correlate sleep parameters with performance to corroborate this assumption.

Chapter 19 - Relaxation-enhanced, cognitive-behavioral coping methods (CBM) were taught to an Olympic athlete in mental skills training. In a controlled setting, salivary cortisol and mood were assessed in parallel at 4-minute intervals as the athlete repeatedly viewed a distressing competition video. After a baseline orientation (8-minutes) and mood provocation (12-minutes, immediately following baseline), the athlete was instructed to use CBM (8-

minutes). Subjective distress was assessed together with cortisol secretion in a time sequence with eight saliva samples, collected over 28-minutes. Not until the final stage when the subject managed his subjective distress did mood and cortisol covary as commonly reported in the literature: During the CBM phase of the study, as the athlete reported reduced distress, his cortisol levels also reduced. It is suggested that in the case of negative mood, salivary cortisol secretions be assayed as an adjunct to psychometric assessment in multi-dimensional tracking during CBM training.

Chapter 20 - To date, research in sport psychology has predominantly used quantitative methods to understand coping, performance, and anxiety. For example, questionnaire scales are prevalent and readily available that measure anxiety -e.g. CSAI-2- (Martens et al., 1990), emotions -e.g. Sport Emotion Questionnaire- (Jones et al., 2005), and coping -e.g. Modified COPE- (Crocker and Graham 1995). Further, there have been calls for more work on quantitative methods. For instance, as Hanton, Neil, and Mellalieu (2008) put it in their erudite review of coping and anxiety work in sport psychology, future research should develop a measure that considers the stressors, appraisals, emotions and orientations, and behavior of the athlete "within the competitive environment. In the meantime, researchers should not tire of furthering our knowledge of the stress process through the adoption of a reductionist approach by combining instruments or rephrasing participant instructions to respond to specific demands".

In: Handbook of Sports Psychology
Editor: Calvin H. Chang
ISBN: 978-1-60741-256-4
©2009 Nova Science Publishers, Inc.

Chapter 1

ATTRIBUTIONAL PROCESSES BEFORE, DURING AND AFTER COMPETITIONS: A QUALITATIVE ANALYSIS APPROACH TO UNDERSTAND EXPLANATORY STYLE STARTING FROM ATHLETES' WORDS

Giorgio Merola

University of Roma Tre, Rome, Italy and University of Macerata, Macerata, Italy

ABSTRACT

Explanatory styles are a predictor factor about the quality of sport practice motivation and the performance level reached by an athlete (Seligman et al, 1990). The possibility of using stability, globality and internality dimensions in order to analyze athletes' explanatory styles and help them to interpret their own failure and success experiences in a more adaptive way, give to this research area a great applied potential. However, sport psychology literature about attributional processes shows how theoretical models and available analysis tools don't ensure an exhaustive comprehension of the real way in which these processes really develop in the sportive context and the intervention methods that result from these scientific assumptions don't always result as useful (Rees et al., 2005).

This contribution, starting from a critique analysis of the literature about explanatory styles in sport psychology, has the aim to identify the critical aspects, some of which already detected by researchers (Rees et al., 2005), and to propose a method of qualitative analysis which allows to find out more factors that could help us understand exhaustively attributional processes in sport.

According to important sport psychology works (Grove & Pargman, 1986; Biddle et al., 2001; Gordon, 2008), the qualitative analysis of a wide sample of texts reporting athletes' descriptions about their own success/failure experiences suggested to us the opportunity to recover the dimension of control and to consider other categories of analysis such as: the level of complexity of the causal explanations (see also the concept of "explanatory flexibility" in Fresco et al. 2007), the level of rigidity with which these explanations are made and the timing of the attributional process.

The approach we used to make the qualitative analysis is mainly based on the theoretical model on Perceptual and Cognitive Linguistic Indicators (Bongelli & Zuczkowski, 2008a, 2008b) which offers many cues deriving from linguistic elements information about the cognitive state of the speaker. In this chapter a set of comparisons made through this approach are presented by highlighting important differences regarding the way in which athletes explain their owns successes and failures. These differences, detectable through the new categories of the proposed analysis system, did not emerge through the traditional content analysis like CAVE (Peterson et al, 1992), and they seem potentially able to moderate the predictor power of explanatory styles. This suggests the opportunity to study attributional processes in their complexity. We propose an interpretation of the results of this study according to important theoretical models of motivational processes (Csíkszentmihályi, 1990), Artificial Intelligence (Castelfranchi, 1998) and mental control (Wenzlaff and Bates, 2000; Singer, 2000)

1. INTRODUCTION

The people's natural tendency to search for explanations about personally experienced events, identifying their possible causes, as an attempt to better understand how the world goes and to have more control over it (Heider, 1944; 1958), assumes a major role in a sport context, in which the athletes often feel the necessity to understand the reason of their athletic successes or failures. Paraphrasing White (1959), we could say that by explaining the causes of good or poor performances, athletes create an understanding that they take with them into future competitions/sport experiences, and this helps them develop mastery over their agonistic career.

The fact that this understanding accompanies an athlete in future situations means that the attributions will influence the behaviours he will have and the performances he will obtain afterwards.

"The issues for sport psychology are how people explain performances and pinpoint the root cause of them, and what impact an in-depth search for these causes has on future emotions, expectations and performance" (Rees et al., 2005, p.190).

Sport psychology, starting from the 80s, interested itself in the study of the causal attributions athletes make regarding their performances (Bukowski & Moore, 1980; Brawley & Roberts, 1984; Biddle, 2001) and of the explanatory styles (Seligman et al. 1990), optimistic or pessimistic, which emerge from the way they usually explain their successes and failures to themselves.

As noted by Biddle (1993), "the majority of sport-related attribution research has used a Weinerian perspective" (p. 439). According to Weiner et al.'s (1971) and Weiner's (1979) perspective, explanations could be assigned to a combination of three attribution dimensions: locus of causality, stability and controllability (this dimension was identified only in Weiner, 1979): the locus of causality is internal or external depending on whether the subject links the event to himself or to external causes; the stability dimension defines if the cause goes on in time or if it can be eliminated; the controllability refers to whether the cause be perceived as controllable or uncontrollable.

Kelley's Co-variation Model (1967), which represents an evolution of Heider's (1958) and Jones'and Davies'(1965) work, predicts that, in order to interpret events and situations through causal attributions, people use the information of consistency, distinctiveness e consensus. That is, they ask themselves if the cause has already occurred or has a good chance of occurring again (consistency), if the consequences it determined are totally or partially negative or positive (distinctiveness), if also other people experienced similar situations or are likely to experience them (consensus).

Abramson et al.'s (1978), by a reformulation of the learned helplessness hypothesis (Maier & Seligman, 1976), suggested to consider the dimensions of locus of causality, stability and globality.

The research on the explanatory style (Peterson, 1991; Peterson & Seligman, 1984), by studying the way people usually explain bad or good events (Peterson, 2000; Peterson & Steen, 2002), defines as optimistic the person who usually attributes the positive events to internal, stable and global causes (the cause will have consequences on many aspects of the person's life) and the negative events to external, instable and specific causes. On the contrary, pessimistic subjects and especially depressed ones, tend to attribute the negative events to internal, stable and global causes, and the successes to external, temporary and contingent causes.

As Seligman explains (1990), this approach is different from Weiner's because the explanatory styles represent the explanatory habits and not the single explanation the person links to a specific failure. Secondly, while Weiner referred to two dimensions of explanation - stability and internality- researchers of the explanatory styles consider instead the globality of it. Another difference between the two theories concerns the fact that, while Weiner was interested in the success, the studies on explanatory styles started off to better understand the mental disease and the possible therapeutic remedies.

1.1 Effects of Attributional Style on Athletic Performance

Brawley (Brawley & Roberts, 1984), starting from an organizational model that summarizes the principal attributions theories, explains that two research categories in sport psychology can be identified: the first ones, in largest number, inspired mostly to Weiner's theory (1974), investigated on antecedents of attributive processes (information, reasons, memory processes, beliefs, social climate); the second ones concentrated on the relation between attributions and consequences on a behavioural, affective, cognitive (expectations) and motivational level.

Yukelson, Weinberg, West, and Jackson (1981), basing on Kukla's model (1972), examined the effects of causal attributions on the performance considering the achievement motive as a moderator factor. These authors demonstrated that the attribution to unstable causal factors, such as the effort, leads the subjects to the perception of being able to modify their performance and actually improve it, while the attribution to stable causes leads them to less positive expectations and performances.

Coherent with other authors (Carver & Scheier, 1982), Brawley (Brawley & Roberts, 1984) points out that the effect of attributions on the performance could be mediated by the expectations.

McAuley, Russell and Gross (1983), studying the relation between causal dimensions and affective reactions in table tennis players, demonstrate that attributions are related to affects especially when wins and defeats are attributed to internal causes.

Vallerand's studies(1987) demonstrate that causal attributions are an antecedent able to influence the affect of esteem (that constitute a moderator factor) and to modify the intrinsic motivation (consequence).

McAuley and Gross (1983), by using the Causal Dimension Scale (CDS), revealed that among college students playing table tennis, the attributions of winning players were more internal, stable, and controllable than those of losers.

The great part of the studies on attributional causes in sport pointed out that athletes of success tend to identify internal and stable causes with successes, while less performing athletes tend to attribute failures to internal factors.

Several researches showed a positive linear relation between optimism and performances in employment (Corr & Gray, 1995; Seligman & Schulman, 1986), academic (Schulman, 1995) and athletic situations (Rettew & Reivich, 1995; Seligman, Nolen-Hoeksema, Thornton & Thornton, 1990). In particular, Rettew & Reivich (1995) noticed a relation between optimism and performance in baseball and basket players and college swimmers and observed how the pessimistic athletes are more likely to carry out poor performances.

Seligman (1990) reports several researches that, through different methodology procedures, demonstrate that:

teams, and not only individuals, have a significant and measurable explanatory style; the explanatory style predicts a team's performance apart from its effective play ability; optimism predicts the winning on field; pessimism predicts defeat on field; the explanatory style predicts a team's performance in situations of high tension, following a defeat or in the last game phase of a final.

It is exactly in difficult situations that explanatory styles play a determining role to predict what the player's reactions will be and the results of their future performances.

About this, Seligman describes the methodology of the tests carried out with the swimmers of Barkeley: in these tests the athletes, who had previously answered to the items of the Attributional Style Questionnaire, were told wrong about their performances during practice, so that their timing would result much worse than the real one realized, and were then invited to try again. This was to see how optimistic and pessimistic athletes would differ in the way they reacted to defeat situations determined by these false counter-performances.

From the test it resulted clearly that optimistic athletes, after this kind of defeat, reacted, reaching timing even better than the ones they really obtained; on the other hand the pessimistic ones were discouraged and obtained much worse performances, even worse than the false timing they had been told before.

The ecological validity of these studies has been confirmed in that the athletes who resulted optimistic from this kind of evaluation (ASQ), other than during the test, actually carried out better performances also in following competitions and especially in situations of great pressure or difficulty.

Through the Content Analysis of Verbatim Explanation (CAVE), Seligman and his collaborators (Seligman, 1990) collected and analyzed, during entire athletic seasons, many statements that appeared on newspapers and magazines of the main american basket and baseball teams. Also in the case of team sports, a positive relation emerged between optimistic explanatory styles and the percentage of success or improvement from one year to the other. This way the author demonstrated how it was possible to anticipate what the efficiency of a team would be during the year, based on how the players commented their successes and, most of all, the suffered defeats.

Seligman (1990) states that the reason why someone who has a more optimistic explanatory style wins repeatedly depends on the ability to engage himself and to persist, especially after a defeat: the optimism characterizing a team becomes decisive especially in moments of difficulty or great disadvantage in a game's score, because it activates resilient behaviours. Prapavessis and Carron (1988) found that table-tennis players who, following defeats, referred to internal, stable and global causes, besides presenting disadaptive patterns from the motivational, cognitive and emotional point of view, were judged as less persistent by their coaches.

About this, Martin-Krumm et al. (2003), interested in studying the relation between optimism and resilience, conducted a research to understand why some athletes recover after sport failures and others react negatively. The authors confirmed the results of other studies (Prapavessis & Carron, 1988; Rettew & Reivich, 1995; Seligman et al., 1990) in respect to the fact that participants with a more optimistic explanatory style obtained better performances after receiving failure feedback, while the pessimists didn't obtain any improvement.

The interesting fact showed by Martin-Krumm et al.(2003) consists however in having identified moderator factors between the explanatory style and such resilient behaviours conducting to an improvement of performance in the optimistic. They found, in fact, that the explanatory style influences other two factors, one of cognitive nature and one of affective nature: the expectations of success and the state of anxiety.

In other words, the positive effects that optimism generates on the performance depend on the fact that they increase expectations of success and reduce the state of anxiety, while pessimism, that is the perception that one's own failures derive from stable and global causes, leads to greater reactions of stress and correlates positively with anxiety (Mineka net al., 1995; Helton et al., 2000; Jackson, Sellers & Peterson, 2002), because the lack of control over negative events is perceived as difficult to modify (exactly because the causes are stable and global).

Martin-Krumm and collgues (2003) conclude inviting the researchers working in the tradition of learned hopelessness to measure"not only explanatory style and helplessness outcomes, but also expectations, and state anxiety level which seem to deserve attention, as well as other potential mediators, maybe like irrational thinking (e.g. Ziegler & Hawley, 2001).

From the reviewed studies results evident the applicative relevance of the research on explanatory styles. Seligman (1990; 2006), in his text Learned optimism, concludes the chapter dedicated to sport reaffirming the usefulness of studying the explanatory styles to positively intervene in the sportive context. The practical implications deriving from the results of the researches to which Seligman refers to, concern: the fact that optimism is not a factor which can be known instinctively, because often the judgement of the trainers on the athletes' explanatory style is not realistic; the possibility to base on the athletes' optimism to choose the most proper players to various situations, limiting for example the use of pessimistic athletes in situations of advantage or following victories; the opportunity to consider also optimism when selecting and recruiting athletes with the same talent; the possibility to teach the athletes how to become optimistic.

Regarding this last point, Rees et al. (2005), in an attempt to underline the importance of a greater congruence between theory, research and practice, refer to the technique of attributional retraining (Forsterling, 1988) trying to suggest to sport psychologists some guidelines to structure their work with athletes. For example, if the theoretical framework of reference is Kelley's (1967) Co-variation Model,

> "Using consistency information, the psychologist might ask about other times the player performer well. Using distinctiveness information, psychologist might ask about aspects of her performance that were good, even thug she lost the match. Using consensus information, the psychologist might ask whether other players have been in a similar situation, had similar feelings, but pulled through. The psychologist can use all three types of information (or just one or two, depending on the most important aspect to work on) to help the performer develop a clearer and potentially more adaptive and functional way of thinking." (Rees et al., 2005, p. 190).

With a direction referring instead to the theory of explanatory styles, the psychologist will help the pessimistic athlete by leading him towards explanations of his failures as due to causes less stable in time, less pervasive and not linked to the athlete himself.

Taking into consideration Vallerand's (1987) intuitive-reflective appraisal model of emotion in sport, Rees et al (2005) believe that it is important to help the athletes to go beyond their intuitive appraisals to think in a way that is not usual to them. The psychologists should encourage athletes to develop reflective evaluations (appraisals), and to pose questions bringing them to challenge the usual attributive thought reaching more realistic and adaptive explanations.

The importance that Rees and collegues recognize to the dimension of controllability brings them to consider the perception of control on the performance the main goal of the interventions of attributional re-training.

Also Gordon (2008) reports studies confirming the usefulness of working on the dimension of control. For example, Orbach et al. (1997) in basketball, and Orbach et al. (1999) in tennis, demonstrated that it is possible and appropriate to change the attributions about failures by referring to controllable and instable causes. Through the attributional retraining the athletes can increase their persistence to the task and even obtain sensibly better performances (Orbach et al, 1997). However, Gordon (2008) underlines that not all the studies led to such encouraging results about works of attributional retraining and, with Rees (2005), we can suppose that the reason coincides with the presence of a mismatch between the research and the practice in sport psychology. In other words, the theory is not always able to develop models guiding effective interventions for the real requirements of athletes and the psychological dynamics characterizing their agonistic career.

1.2 Dimensions of Attributive and Explanatory Processes

Rees, Ingledew, & Hardy (2005), going through the main studies on causal attributions and explanatory styles, retain that between the 5 main dimensions emerging from literature (locus of causality; controllability; stability; globality and universality-this a dimension similar to the one of consensus in Kelley, indicating if a person considers a cause as common to everyone or, on the contrary, thinks that it regards only himself-) the most important one is the perception of control.

Several authors (Rees et al, 2005) support the advantage for an athlete to attribute the failure to controllable causes or, more in general, to factors subject to change in time. In particular, the opportunity, in terms of adaptability, to attribute the failure to the lack of effort from the athlete and, on the other hand, the negative consequences deriving from attributions referring to the lack of ability, have been emphasized.

However this emphasis on the importance of effort was criticized (Covington & Omelich, 1979; Robinson, 1990; Biddle, 1993; Biddle et al., 2001) because if the athlete continues to fail even though he increases the effort, he can be discouraged and react with a dramatic increase attributions to the lack of ability.

The importance of the dimension of controllability is well explained by Anderson (1983) who makes clear:

> "Any attempt to modify a person's attributions assumes that the problem situations *can* be controlled, and the person can learn from failures, can improve with practice, and can reach an acceptable level of success. But in many cases, failure is guaranteed, either by particular ability deficits or by the setting of unrealistic goals. In such cases, maintaining high-motivation levels may be more maladaptive than is recognising the hopelessness of the situation and giving up that particular goal" (p.1146).

Actually, people try to identify the causes of the events specifically to increase their control over the environment: to attribute an event to controllable causes leads to expectations of control about future events.

Based on these observations, some authors (Anderson, 1983; Biddle, 1993; Biddle et al., 2001; Clifford, 1986; Curtis, 1992; Hardy & Gould, 1996; Holschuh, Nist, & Olejnik, 2001; Sinnott & Biddle, 1998) conclude that the most adaptive causal attributions are those referring to strategies used in practice or in competition. In fact, in many cases the explanation of a failure that happened even though the athlete put great effort in it, could be determined really by non functional strategies.

The attribution to this factor in explaining one's own failure has the advantage of moving the attention on the strategic characteristics of the task, of creating expectations of improvement linked to the acquisition of more efficient strategies and of bringing to actually better performances.

The theory of explanatory styles (Abramson et al., 1978), deriving from a reformulation of the learned hopelessness model (Maier & Seligman, 1976), considers 2 of Weiner's model dimensions (locus of causality and stability) and suggests the one of globality, that is the degree in which the causal factor attributed by the subject can produce consequences on more relevant aspects of his life.

Because the theory of learned hopelessness developed based on laboratory experiments in which the subjects (initially animals) reacted to situations in which the perception of non-controllability was induced, the theory of explanatory styles wants to identify the causal attributions deriving from this perception of lack of control, analyzing them in terms of locus of causality, stability e globality, but not considering if the causal factors are controllable or not.

Many authors criticized this aspect of the explanatory styles' theory, because the perception of control, at least in respect to the dimensions of locus of causality, seems to play an even more determining role for the motivation and realisation of performances. In fact, stable and non-controllable attributions will negatively affect the self-efficacy, left aside if they refer to internal or external elements (locus of causality).

The necessity to focus the attention of the research on the dimension of control was underlined by sport psychologists as well: differently from Weiner's model supporters, they even believe that it plays a more important role than stability in determining the expectations of future success. Grove and Pragman (1986) think that the reason why the dimension of stability often resulted as the key factor to predict future expectations depends on the fact that most of the researches considered non-competitive contexts.

They report a series of experimental results, explainable on the basis of a greater saliency of the dimension of controllability. According to them, the uncertain nature of competitive situations in real world (characterized by dynamic and changeable interactions with the adversaries, weather and physical conditions, playgrounds and external factors of various nature) suggests the necessity to focus on attributions of controllability more than on those of stability.

Recent contributions of sport psychology (Gordon, 2008), confirm this necessity stating that, for example, to attribute negative results to external factors could be adaptive if these factors are susceptible to change, but disadaptive if perceived as stable and non-controllable. Such consideration reviews the predictive value of the theory of explanatory styles which, as we said, defines as optimistic style the one characterized, between others, by external attributions in case of failure.

Another critical element, emerged from literature, on causal attributions in sport psychology (Ross et al., 2004), concerns the importance of considering the situations in which people identify more than one cause to explain themselves a result or relate a single cause to several consequences.

It is relevant that the questionnaires and interviews usually used to indentify the explanatory styles and attributions don't allow to catch how the athletes, left free to talk about their performances, can differ from each other in the way they relate results and causal factors.

Concerning this, we cite the concept of "integrative complexity", described by Lee e Peterson (1997) but not explicitly put into relation with the study of explanatory styles and that therefore is not taken into consideration by the system of analysis proposed by the second author (Peterson et al., 1992) of which we will talk about in the next paragraph. The integrative complexity describes the complexity of thought with which a person interprets the events and derives from the differentiation, that is the ability of taking different perspectives in front of the events, and from the integration, which refers to the ability to see connections between these diverging perspectives.

Even if underlining the predictive value of the integrative complexity in respect to vulnerability and resilience, thus being a factor linked to the answer to stress given by the individuals, the authors limit their statement: " Although conceptually distinct, both concepts"- the causal attributions and the integrative complexity- "reflect how individuals categorize and interpret complex issues and events".

From this approach, not thoroughly studied by Lee and Peterson, results however reasonable to identify in the integrative complexity an important element to understand the individual differences in attributive processes which, as Ross et al. (2004) underlined, often give space to different ways of linking events and causal factors.

The dimension of explanatory flexibility recently proposed by Fresco et al. (Fresco et al. 2006; Moore and Fresco, 2007) if on one side it catches people's tendency to interpret events in a more or less flexible way, showing a greater or smaller variability in the degree of internality, stability and globality of the causes to which they attribute their successes and failures, it doesn't on the other hand catch the spontaneous tendency to refer to a greater or smaller amount of causes.

In fact, the "explanatory flexibility" was operationalized as the standard deviation of a person's answers to the items of globality and stability regarding negative events reported in the Attributional Style Questionnaire (ASQ; Peterson et al. 1982). A small standard deviation is conceptualized as a rigidity measure, while a great standard deviation is interpreted as flexibility measure.

Confirming the predictive value of this individual variability, the scholars (Fresco et al. 2006) demonstrate that, if the explanatory styles are equal, people with greater explanatory flexibility develop less depressive symptoms: the explanatory flexibility together with the coping flexibility both represent factors that mediate the effects of explanatory styles on the development of depressive symptoms.

Two elements that surely emerge from this brief review and that result relevant for the research we are presenting in the following paragraphs concern: on one side, the opportunity to recover the dimension of control abandoned by theorists of the explanatory style and that, instead, appears to be determining in the sportive context and, on the other side, the opportunity to consider other elements such as explanatory flexibility and integrative complexity, which take into account the complexity of the attributive processes.

This complexity emerges also from Rees at al. (2004) considerations suggesting to consider thoughts linked to attributive processes in a similar way as those characterizing the coping strategies: "Like the conceptualisation of coping (Lazarus & Folkman, 1984), one might consider the process of attributional thought as a dynamic, transactional process over time, with attribution affecting responses, responses affecting future appraisal of environment, and appraisal leading to altered attributions".

On the other hand the theoretical suppositions supporting the relevance of certain dimensions guide the applicative organization with which sport psychologists operate, trying to cognitively restore the athletes' attributions in order to make them more adaptive.

In fact, as explained by Den Boer et al. (1991): " It should be clear that is not attribution itself which is important, but the perception subjects have of the (dimensionality) of these attributions. It is this perception of the dimensions that is responsible for the effect of attributions on expectation of success, emotion and behaviour" (p. 243).

Seen the necessary congruence between theory and practice, the systems of analysis, being just the reflex of determined theoretical premises, must be able to show the main elements characterizing the athletes' explanatory styles and making them more or less adaptive. In the next paragraph we will refer to the main assessment systems of the explanatory and attributive styles by describing in particular the CAVE technique that is the most used system of content analysis in this area of investigation and that, coherently with the theory of explanatory styles does not consider the dimension of controllability nor the dimensions of explanatory flexibility and integrative complexity.

1.3 Main Criteria of Analysis of Explanatory Styles

In the sportive context, the most used scales for the assessment of the athletes' attributive styles, are those developed starting from Weiner's model. The most widespread instrument is the Causal Dimension Scale II (CDS II) representing an evolution of the CDS created by Russel in 1982 and involves soliciting open ended attributions from participants and then instructing them to rate these on 9 point Likert-type scales (Likert, 1932) along the attributional dimensions of locus of causality, stability and controllability.

Sport psychologists have also used the Performance Outcome Survey (Leith & Prapavessis, 1989), a modified version by Prapavessis & Carron (1988) of the Attributional Style Questionnaire (ASQ: Peterson et al., 1982), the Sport-attributional Style Scale (SASS: Hanrahan, Grove & Hattie, 1989) and the Benson's 5- Attributional Dimension Scale (5-ADS, Benson, 1989) that, because of psychometric limits , was less frequently used. All these instruments share the limit of eliciting attributions compared to predefined results (events) and the one of inviting the athlete to put into relation single causes to single events. Both these limits make poorer the ecologic validity of such instruments that are not able to record the people's tendency, present in greater or smaller measure, to search more causes about a single performance. For example, people tend to spontaneously engage themselves in attributive reasoning and to search for a greater number of causes following failures, while they do it in smaller measure when they win (Ross et al., 2004). Rees et al (2005), basing on writings about coping (Lazarus & Folkman, 1984; Tennen, Affleck, Armeli, & Carney, 2000), suggest about this the opportunity to use alternative methods of assessment, as for example the one of the analysis of samples of experiences (Csikzentmihalyi & Larson, 1984), that allow a much more detailed observation of the attributions naturally developing in time, in interaction with the environment and bringing to re-attribution processes.

In order to obtain valid results on the ecological side, Ross et al. (2004) propose a semi-structured interview, that doesn't plan direct questions on attributions, and a qualitative analysis of the answers that is an adaptation of the LACS (Leeds Attributional Coding System of Stratton et al., 1988; Munton et al., 1999) used to classify attributions in discussion in a setting of family therapy. The LACS is used to analyze attributions occurring spontaneously during conversations, through the codification of the participants' answers, basing on the attributive dimensions.

Through this technique, the authors identified the presence of various structural forms: consequences and causes can be linked in many different ways by the athletes.

The implication is that the athletes must be free to "provide more than one cause for an outcome; provide more than an outcome for a cause; use "dual" statements for both purposes and use statements as cause or outcome irrespective of their subject matter" (Ross et al., 2004, p. 11).

The technique of Content Analysis of Verbatim Explanation (CAVE) was proposed by Peterson et al. (1983) to identify the explanatory styles of persons and characters to which, for different reasons, the questionnaire ASQ was impossible to submit.

Moreover, differently from ASQ, this technique has the advantage not to refer to hypothetical situations but to really occurred events, regarding which people spontaneously make attributions of cause. With this system of analysis it is in fact possible to study interviews, letters, diaries, newspaper articles, school essays, in which there are descriptions of events that generally include indicators of the causal explanations the person gives.

Zullow and coll. (1988) talk about an approximate average of one indicator every 100 words.

The CAVE technique is composed of two phases: first the causal explications in the examined document are extracted, then they are evaluated in a 7 points scale concerning their stability, globality and internality.

Extraction of the causal explications: In order to identify the causal statements, references to positive and negative events are searched for in the perspective of the subject in exam.

Adler and coll. (2006) refer to 3 criteria:

1) a specific event or an experience with defined beginning and end must be described;
2) the event involves the Self and was experienced in some non-desirable way;
3) a causal statement is made about an event, that can be identified by the use of one or more sentences with "because", "since", "as a result of", this led to", "due to", etc. Using these criteria, the agreement between independent judges reaches up to more than 90% of the times in which a causal explanation is present.

Once an event is located, an attribution factor co-variable with the event is sought. Sometimes the explanation is clear and transparent, while other times it is necessary to refer it to the sentence, for example beginning with "because…" "as a result of" "this led to" and so on. Once identified, the causal explication and the event they refer to are extracted and copied.

Afterwards these event-explication units are mixed with many other units concerning other subjects and other sources and 3 or 4 independent judges evaluate each unit in the 3 dimensions.

Evaluation of causal explanations:

The scale used to evaluate attributions about the dimension internality-externality doesn't constitute a measure of responsibility taking or control perception, but explains if the cause implies the person's(7) or situation(1) characteristics.

The stability-instability dimension is useful to distinguish if the cause attributed to the event persists in time (7) or is temporary (1). It is important to remember that what is evaluated is the stability of the cause and not the stability of the event. The main indicator of the stability of the cause is determined by the tense of the sentence in which the causal explanation is expressed: present tense if the cause is stable , past tense if it's unstable. They follow the probability of recurrence, the continuity vs intermittence of the cause and the cause's nature concerning personality traits vs behaviours. A score of 1 is reserved to explanations based on something that happened in the past, a sporadic event that has no possibility of repeating itself and concerns more the behaviour than the person's permanent manners. On the contrary, a score of 7 is attributed when the explanations are in the present, they have a great probability of persisting and concern continuous manners in time.

The globality-specificity dimension refers to the level in which the cause produces consequences on more aspects of the person's life (global=7) or instead if it involves to a limited extent some specific domains (specific=1).

This dimension is often considered the most difficult one to evaluate because generally there is not enough information to give the wideness of the cause's effects and which are the domains having importance for the person in study. For example, for an accountant the mathematical abilities could be very important and influence his own life in a much more evident way than what would happen to a painter, while the quality of friendship could have consequences on more fronts for someone socially orientated rather than for a workaholic. It is for this reason that, in absence of information about it, scholars of explanatory styles using this technique suggest to reason on the impact a cause can have on the purposes of a person with a normal life, regarding the two main categories of achievement and affiliation, each including many sub-categories (achievement: occupational or academic success, accumulation of knowledge or skills, sense of individuality or independence; economic or social status; affiliation: intimate relationships, sense of belongingness, sex, play, marital or family health).

The cause is considered from more or less specific to global if, in order, conditions only one situation, part of a category, an entire category or both categories.

It can be useful to consider the event to evaluate a cause's globality, because the event is an effect in the whole of possible effects. However, it is important not to evaluate the reported event only but to consider how many and which other ambits the cause is able to condition. The authors suggest to consider the event only after having evaluated the globality of the cause in itself.

The CAVE technique was used for different researches in sportive context and it came out to be able to evaluate the athletes' and teams' optimism and to predict their performance during entire agonistic seasons (Seligman, 1990).

However, how it emerged from the brief bibliographic review on the study of attributive processes in sport presented in the first paragraphes , this technique, as the model of learned hopelessness from which it derives, does not consider the possibility to pick some aspects (as the controllability dimension, the explanatory flexibility, the integrative complexity, the dynamicity of the attributive process in time) showed by the literature on causal attributions on one side and the contributions of sport psychology referring to practical applicability of theoretical suppositions on the other.

Rees et al. (2005), at the end of a brief review on the main assessment systems about causal attributions, propose the possibility to consider other qualitative methods such as the categorical-content analysis (Lieblich, Tuval-Mashiach, & Zilber, 1998), the paradigmatic analysis (Polkinghorne, 1995), the conversation analysis (Faulkner & Finlay, 2002) and the narrative analysis (Crossley, 2000; Sparkes, 1999), which can contribute to understand attributive processes in their complexity and dynamic nature.

In the next paragraph we are going to describe the qualitative analysis of a corpus of texts regarding athletes' speeches, which constituted the first step of a research we are still working on and that has the aim to structure a system of analysis allowing to catch some aspects of attributive processes and that can be integrated with the already existing systems.

2. TOWARDS A SYSTEM OF LINGUISTIC ANALYSIS FOR THE UNDERSTANDING OF EXPLANATORY STYLES: DESCRIPTION OF THE THEORETICAL APPROACH AT THE BASE OF THE RESEARCH

Aim of the here presented research was to propose a method of analysis able to integrate with the already existing ones, allowing to collect more information about explanatory styles and attributive processes. In order to obtain this aim we thought appropriate to use the theoretical contributions regarding the study of the relation between language and psychological processes(Shinzato, 2004; Papafragou et al., 2007; Zuczkowski, 1995; Bongelli e Zuczkowski, 2008 a, 2008b).

Several attempts are reported in literature in order to identify the psychological value of the speaker's linguistic choices in order to deduct mental and emotional states or personality features also with diagnostic or therapeutic purposes (Pennebaker et al., 2002).

The first step to identify categories of analysis useful to understand the attributive processes and explanatory styles consisted in analyzing 2 corpora constituting of: 1) 120 records of athletes' reports concerning their best and worst performances; 2) 80 contributions of athletes describing their sport performances in a forum of sport psychology in order to gain help and advice from experts.

More specifically, the first corpus made up of 70 texts relative to the oral expositions of 35 athletes of different sports which were requested to talk about their own best and worst performances and of 50 texts written by other 25 athletes who did the same task in writing during a lesson of a course on Sport Psychology at the University of Educational Science in Rome. We asked them to do an exhaustive description of their competition, trying to identify the possible causes determining their success or failure. Differently, the texts collected by the forum represent totally spontaneous interventions because we selected a sample of texts in which athletes described their performances in order to gain advice and spontaneously referred to causal factors.

The approach used to carry out the qualitative preliminary analysis of the records, which enabled us to identify these new categories, was inspired mostly to recent writings about the analysis of PaCLIs (Perceptual and Cognitive Linguistic Indicators), offering many cues to get information on the cognitive state of the speaker from linguistic elements.

The PaCLIs, the study of which is inserted in the ambit regarding what literature calls markers of knowledge, epistemic indexes, mind markers, cognitive attitudes, propositional attitudes, etc. (Bertuccelli-Papi 1987, 2001; Huspek 1989; Thompson, Mulac 1991; Tsui 1991; Venier 1991; Cacciari, Levorato 1992, 1999, 2003; Givón 1993; Persson 1993; Stein, Wright 1995; Traugott 1995; Anderson 1996; Chafe 1996; Chafe, Nichols 1996; Kärkkänen 1996; Simon-Vandenbergen 1996, 1997, 1998a,1998b, 2000; Aijmer 1997; Sperber 1997; Sholl, Leslie 1999; Weizman 1999; Ifantidou 2001; Mushin 2001; Nuyts 2001; Carston 2002; Fetzer 2002, 2004, 2007; Aikhenvald 2004; Croft, Cruse 2004; Cappelli 2005, 2007a, 2007b, 2007c; Pennebaker, Slatcher, Cindy 2005; Poggi 2006; Berlin 2007) are those linguistic indicators revealing which is the perceptual or cognitive attitude that the speaker or reader has about what he says or reads, that is the perceptual or cognitive system he activates when he talks or writes (Bongelli & Zuczkowski, 2008 a, 2008b).

The analysis made to understand the perceptual or cognitive attitude of the speaker regarding the conveyed information are of lexical and morpho-syntactic nature and bring to identify PaCLIs present in the linear manifestation of the texts which are then analysed from a semantic and pragmatic point of view.

The reference theory from which writings on PaCLIs derives is the "Text Structure - World Structure Theory" by J. S. Petöfi (1973, 1980, 1981, 2004; Nicolini, 2000; Zuczkowski, 1995, 2006). This author proposes a model of deep structure or Atomic Text constituted by three propositions hierarchically ordered:

- - the modal-performative proposition (mpp) represents the particular illocutionary act that the speaker does in saying what he says (Austin, 1962);
- - the world-constitutive proposition (wcp) represents the particular perceptual or cognitive process by which the speaker has access to the state of affairs s/he describes, that is the specific world of his perceptual and cognitive experience to which belongs the communicated state of affairs;
- - the descriptive proposition (dp) represents that part of the statement describing a state of affairs (occurring, quality, action, etc.) and constitutes the real nucleus of communication:

Alex is on the beach

- <u>mmp:</u> Here and now I say to you that
- <u>wcp</u>: here and now I remember /think/see, etc, that
- <u>dp:</u> Alex is (would be) on the beach

From a psychological point of view, the world-constitutive proposition offers the most important information regarding, besides the perceptual or cognitive system from which the speaker has access to the state of affairs communicated in the descriptive proposition, also the degree of certainty the speaker attributes to the contents of his statements. For example, the presence of mental verbs like "think", "believe", "retain" with world-constitutive function, indicates that the description of the state of affairs doesn't refer to sure knowledge, but instead derives from suppositions and inferences of the speaker, while verbs like "see", "know" and "remember" give the idea of certainty.

The world-constitutive proposition has this name because the meaning of the verb or the verbal expression that can be part of it 'constitutes', and therefore indicates, a particular 'perceptual or cognitive world' of the speaker/writer, exactly that to which belongs the state of affairs communicated in the descriptive proposition (Bongelli & Zuczkowski, 2008 a, 2008b).

The world-constitutive proposition, as the modal-performative one, is characterized by the verb in the first person of the present tense and indicative tense and, besides, it expresses if the speaker in that precise moment is seeing, listening, remembering, thinking, imagining what he is talking about.

The expression Here and Now, the present tense and indicative tense characterize then both the linguistic act and the perceptual or cognitive process, and also indicate the simultaneity of 'saying' (declaring/asking/ordering, etc.) and of 'experience' (seeing/remembering/thinking, etc.) in relation to the time and place where the communication takes place. The Ego places emphasis on the subjectivity of the speaker in this double and contemporary cognitive and communicative function (idem).

The speaker, however, can refer to his cognitive and perceptual states not related to the moment in which he is speaking, but to the situation of There and Then being described. In this case, as in the following example, the function of the verb is descriptive and this will therefore be expressed in a different tense than present or with a different person than the first singular person:

I saw that Peter was at home
- mpp: Here and now I say to you that
- wcp: Here and now I remember that
- dp: There and then I saw that (descriptive use)
- dp: Peter was at home

The psychological relevance of the world-constitutive proposition concerns also, how we were saying, the degree of certainty with which the speaker makes his statements.

Normally the declarative sentences in the present indicative and past not containing a world- constitutive proposition communicate the Knowledge, that is what the speaker knows, remembers, sees, hears, etc. When it is not specified through a world-constitutive proposition the perceptual and cognitive system with which the speaker enters the information he is reporting, the listener takes this information as known.

The world-constitutive proposition, if present also in the surface structure, communicates the Knowledge when it is characterized by perceptual and cognitive verbs like see, remember, hear, know, while it communicates the Belief in presence of verbs like think, believe, retain/reckon, imagine, hypothesize, etc. expressed in affirmative or negative form.

The Unknown is instead indicated by the negation of the verbs of Knowledge (I don't know, don't remember, don't see, don't hear).

Besides the presence of verbs with world-constitutive use in the surface structure of the sentence, there are other lexical and morpho-syntactic PaCLIs offering indications on the Epistemic Categories.

In fact the Unknown can be showed also through the use of interrogative literal sentences that can be linked down to the deep structure "I don't know dp (descriptive proposition) and I expect you to tell me dp". The Belief can be indicated by verbs in conditional, subjunctive or future tense, which, differently from verbs in the present indicative or past, refer to the world of Possible. Moreover, also the adverbs probably, maybe, etc. indicate that what is communicated represents a belief, while the adverbs certainly, surely, etc. are used by the speaker to underline that he is sure about what he is saying in the descriptive proposition and therefore refer to the category of the Knowledge.

Besides framing the information of the speaker in the different Epistemic Categories, the survey of PaCLIs contained in a text offers information about the perceptual or cognitive worlds characterizing the speaker's experience: the prevailing in a text of verbs like do, go, have, etc., referring to behaviours, facts, events, etc., everything that is considered, principally, directly accessible to everyone from a perceptual point of view and therefore inter-subjectively shareable collocates the text in what Zuczkowski (2006) metaphorically calls Body Semantic Category; verbs like see, listen, think, believe, imagine, referring to perceptual and cognitive processes, belong to the Mind Semantic Category; finally, verbs denoting feelings, moods, emotions, affections, etc. having to do with the so called internal world, belong to the Heart Semantic Category.

The fact that a text belongs mostly to a Semantic Category represents an aspect of the so called Textual Linguistic Focus (Zuczkowski, 1995). Another aspect concerns the prevalence of personal pronouns referring to the speaker ("I"), the listener (you), the speaker and someone else (we), to a third person or object (he, she, they, etc.): the prevalence of verbs and pronouns in the first singular person indicates a Focus on the Subject, while the prevalence of pronouns and verbs in the third person indicates a Focus on the Object.

The approach of PaCLIs, guiding the qualitative analysis that constitutes the first step of a research that is still in progress and finalized to the study of explanatory processes, seemed to offer reading criteria of the relation between language and mental processes useful to mark out some aspects of verbal communication able to convey information on how people explain their successes and failures. We retained namely that the detecting of PaCLIs and other linguistic elements in texts containing the athletes' causal explanations of their own performances, could represent a method that, integrated with the traditional ones like, for example, the CAVE technique, would allow to understand the attributive processes in their complexity.

This is why the qualitative analysis we preliminarily conducted to identify the linguistic indicators mostly informative on the side of causal attributions from which to derive a grid of analysis, was made inspired by PaCLI method of analysis proposed by Bongelli & Zuczkowski (2008a, 2008b).

As an example we propose here an analysis of two records concerning an athlete's report about his best and worst performance. In this analysis, the attention was put on the relevance of linguistic indicators implying the mental state of the speaker and his attitude towards the reported event, and it showed the presence of many PaCLIs and others indicators that are informative about the attributions and explanatory style of the athlete.

3. EXAMPLE OF QUALITATIVE ANALYSIS

We propose the analysis of two reports referring, respectively, to the best and worst performance of a sprinter, with the aim to show all those linguistic elements that can be relevant to understand the attributive process made by the athlete.

Best Performance

A competition, in which I felt many sensations, some very nice. From the beginning, the tension was very high, then at the start shot I sprinted out very well and from there I felt right away a nervous sensation of well-being. Little by little, going forward, I had in mind the fact that I had to finish and to finish well, in the best possible way. But the...let's say the best sensation I felt was when coming out of the curve: I came out of the curve and I felt psychic sensations, let's say the nervous impulses to the whole body: a wonderful sensation where it really seemed that my body was swinging towards...swinging, going further and further towards the finishing line.

And from there I thought in those moments to free the mind from all those things and to live only, be concentrated only in that specific moment of the competition I was living, without thinking about who was ahead or behind me: to live that situation ,to free the mind and concentrate only on what I was living. Then at the finish line, at the finish line I don't remember anything else, because I arrived, from there on I lost all those sensations. It's as if I had lived this competition in another world, in another dimension, that is not the human dimension in which I can notice many small things: in that competition I noticed this one…first of all to feel good with myself. But then the sensation of swinging and going on, made it, made it possible that inside me a perfect balanced would be reached, of which I dream since in every competition, I dream to have it, because it isn't the first time that this sensation occurs: it happened other times, but rarely. And then I did my personal record, at 39, on the 200…and this made me think also that in an athlete's life nothing is impossible and it's not said that in adult age one gets worse, it's not always said because it's here (points at the head), it's in our mind that there are abilities we don't even imagine, but they are there. And in an athlete's competition, in MY competition, sometimes, when I'm concentrated and when I am able to feel in harmony with myself these abilities develop themselves…it is a question of instants, not even seconds, of instants: when you feel good with yourself. See, this sensation is worth more than 100 medals because it's the sensation one has of feeling good, of well-being. And mine, let's say, goal, the motivation for which I still continue to run it's exactly this one: to find these energies, these abilities I have inside me, to develop them, to feel good…

We will now try to propose an interpretation of the athlete's explanatory style analyzing the PaCLIs that mostly give information about this.

Semantic Categories

As a first criteria of analysis we use the one referring to the Semantic Categories because we hypothesize it to be important, to understand a mental process as the one of causal attributions, to identify the athlete's cognitive attitude at the moment of reporting and at the moment of the competition he is describing, that is understanding if the athlete reports mostly events and facts characterized by observable behaviours (Body Semantic Category), thoughts and cognitive actions (Mind Semantic Category) or emotions and sensations (Heart Semantic Category).

Already from the first sentence, the athlete introduces the experience he is about to tell and refers also to the perceptual world through which he lived it, and through which he will report it that is the world of pleasant physical and psychological sensations (Heart).

In fact, the PaCLI-verbs and the PaCLI-non-verbs referring to sensations (Heart Semantic Category) are 16 ("I felt" + "sensation/s" 4 occurrences; "sensations" -6 occurrences-; "tensions"; "to feel good" - 4 occurrences- to feel in harmony;) , those referring to cognitive thoughts or actions (Mind Semantic Category) are 11 ("I had in mind"; "it seemed"; "I thought"; "to free the mind" -2 occurrences- ; "to be concentrated"; "without thinking"; "concentrate it"; "I remember"; "it made me think"; "I'm concentrated"), while the verbs that can be collocated in the Body Semantic Category are 9 ("I came out" -2 occurrences-; "I went on"; "conclude"; "swinging"; "advancing"; "was before"; "I arrived"; "I did my personal") of which 2 refer to only thought actions (I had in mind…to have to conclude"; "without thinking about who was before me") and 2 to body movements the athlete had only the sensation to have ("sensation...it seemed my body was swinging...going on"). The speaker uses the verb feel with descriptive function as he will do also in the rest of the report in which he will not explicate his current cognitive state (verbs with world consititutive function) if not referring to the difficulty to remember ("I don't remember anything else").

The psychological verbs (among them "to feel"), if used in a world-constitutive way, have a meta-narrative function, because they concern the speaker's mental attitude in the Here and Now with which he sees and evaluates the situation (the competition) of the There and Then he is talking about, while the descriptive use allows to convey mental processes lived during competition and in case lived again at the time of reporting (and anyhow not expressed in the present). Therefore the fact that the verb to feel is used in a descriptive way and that the sensations of There and Then are mentioned several times give the idea that the experience was lived mostly through sensations.

The athlete doesn't use verbs describing his attributive process, neither at the time of reporting nor at the time of competition.

Also the mental verbs with which the athlete describes the cognitive processes characterizing this agonistic experience don't refer to attributive reasoning nor to expectations of the pre-competition or evaluations on himself or the competition situation, though they are conditioned by the convictions of the attributive kind. On the contrary, these verbs refer to the athlete's intention and attempt to concentrate and focus on the competition.

Epistemic Categories

The prevailing Epistemic Category of the report is the one of Knowledge, also referring to the only causal explanation clearly expressed: this explanation even assumes the form of a generalization of the causal relation between concentration and the development of the abilities leading him to success ("when I'm concentrated and when I am able to feel in harmony with myself these abilities develop themselves").

However, the presence of the verb to seem and of the PaCLI as if plus the subjunctive I had lived, indicate a reference to the impressions and to the epistemic category of the Belief (cfr. Bongelli & Zuczkowski, 2008b about the continuum between Knowledge and Belief[1]) with which the athlete describes the harmony of his body's movement that seemed to swing and underlines the peculiarity of the sensations during competition, that makes them belong to another world and dimension. This way, the speaker makes the passage from the memory of the sensations to the one of "evoked worlds", that is, the swinging of the body, through the verb "it seemed". The verb used in the past tense explains that the analogy refers to a sensation lived during competition: it is during competition that the athlete had the impression (he was brought to believe) that his body was swinging.

---

[1] "The appearance is the place immediately near to the Knowledge and is characterized by a very first epistemic uncertainty and of doubt level, simplified by impressions, that is by appearances about which many of our subjects have written using prevalently the verb to seem. The region spatially more distant from Knowledge on the contrary constitutes the place of imaginations, fantasies, dreams, castles in the sky etc, that is of everything that progressively goes away, until it becomes distant at maximum, from what the subjects consciously live as certain, real and reachable. Between appearances and non real fantasies are located the conjectures, the hypothesis, the plans etc, lived as reachable, about which there are no complete certainties: hypothesis and plans , in fact, on one side are based on data of reality, on the other side they take into consideration the fantasy, imaginary functions." p.106

Also the verb "to dream" referring to the wish to reach again the perfect balance he lived in this situation ("a perfect balance...I wish to have") is collocated in the epistemic category of the Belief, because the athlete doesn't know with certainty if he will actually see this dream fulfilled.

Relevant Linguistic Elements and Considerations on the Attributive Processes

From the analysis of PaCLIs, we can observe how the main modality of access to the world (Semantic Categories), during the best competition, is the one of sensations (to the point that when the competition is over, the athlete doesn't "record" anything else: "at the finish line I don't remember anything because...I've lost all those sensations").

If from this analysis it emerges the athlete's tendency to report especially the sensations felt in competition (therefore, probably, to have lived it –or remembered it- mostly through this perceptual modality), from a overall study of the text we can understand how such sensations represent not only the means through which he achieves the optimal performance, but also the ultimate goal he aims to ("this sensation is worth more than 100 medals").

This helps us to understand the scale of causal relations identified by the athlete to explain his success: the sensation, in fact, is sometimes considered the cause determining an effect (on the psychological side the concentration possibility coming after, and finally, on the behavioural side, the good performance obtained) and sometimes the ultimate consequence, the goal to be reached. This means that, in this last case, what the athlete considers as success, the reaching of it explained by causes, coincides with the sensations themselves, while what he considers failure (that still needs to be explained referring to other factors) coincides with the absence of such beautiful sensations.

The only causal explanation in explicit form traced in the record is towards the end, when the athlete's words suggest that the positive event (that, exactly, he puts together with the positive sensation that "is worth more than 100 medals") is determined by concentration and ability to feel in harmony: "when I am concentrated (cause)...when I am able to feel in harmony with myself, these abilities develop (positive event)".

This causal explanation (if I concentrate I will feel nice sensations/I will succeed) is coherent with the athlete's conscious attempt during the run to control his thought made explicit in the report through PaCLIs: " I thought (...) to free the mind (...) and (...) to be concentrated (...)without thinking (...) to free the mind and concentrate it only in what I was living". The use of the verb "I thought" is to understand again as a reference to a conscious and voluntary mental action[2].

In other words, the athlete, judging the concentration as a possible cause of success, during the run makes an effort to concentrate and reports it in the story using the mental verbs which describe this cognitive process of planning (exactly:" I had in mind the fact that I needed to finish; I thought to free the mind, etc.).

The causal explanation proposed by the athlete comes from a later evaluation (about the Here and Now of the report and anyway not about There and Then) of the competition which

---

[2] Onishi (1997) reports how in Japanese there are two different words to indicate the thought meant as analytic and conscious process or a spontaneous and involuntary process

leads him to a generalization of a principle no more valid for him only but for the category he represents (an athlete): this made me think also that in an athlete's life nothing is impossible(…) when I'm concentrated (…) these abilities develop themselves…"

This temporal placement of the causal explanation in the Here and Now is confirmed by the athlete's mental attitude in competition which was characterized by living it through sensations and by using the thought in its planning function (and not evaluating) as it is demonstrated by the verbs we referred to before (I had in mind that I needed to finish; I thought to free the mind (…) to live only, be concentrated only): this is a mental attitude of total involvement in the competition, that doesn't leave space to interfering thoughts such as, for example, attempts of causal explication that will be made instead later[3].

From an attributional point of view, the reference to voluntary and conscious thoughts regarding the attempt to concentrate give the idea of perception of control: if the athlete tries to concentrate it could be because he thinks that this can be an advantage for his performance and because he knows he can do it.

The cause to which the athlete attributes success (concentration) is an internal cause, because it coincides with his mental operation, basically instable and rather pervasive (it is useful both for the achievement and, in minor measure, for the affiliation). However, having to give a CAVE score from 1 to 7 to the dimension stability-instability, it is a difficult task because, considering only this report, we are not able to define if the expression when I'm concentrated refers to frequent situations where the athlete realizes his ability (psychological ability) or to less frequent situations in which this state of grace occurs[4] : concentration meant as mental action is instable (as a behaviour) but the degree of ability to concentrate makes such action more o less probable, therefore the more or less stable cause.

The athlete makes us understand that the ability to reach this mental state is not a stable ability but a temporary one (when I can be in harmony with myself…).

Two especially interesting linguistic indicators giving a clear indication about the non complete perception of control that the athlete has concerning the reaching of these sensations (which though derive from his behaviour, that is, the concentrating act), coincide with the verbs dream to have and it happens: one dreams of something when it is difficult to achieve and something happens leaving aside our will and actions.

In the report there are other indicators of causal explanations (markers as from there) that show better what we said before concerning the hierarchy of causes and consequences proposed by the athlete.

For example: "(…) I sprinted out very well and from there I felt right away a nervous sensation of well-being." In this case it seems that he identifies the cause of this beautiful sensation in having been able to start well. This cause has immediate consequences (right away). Afterwards this sensation becomes itself cause or better condition that allows the athlete to concentrate:" A beautiful sensation (…)and from there I thought in those moments to free the mind(…) be concentrated(…)to free the mind and concentrate (…).

---

[3] In an additional interview proposed to the athlete regarding which were the main emotions (and mental states) associated to the competition he reported, coherent with this attitude of involvement in the competition, all emotions lived during it: well-being, harmony, freedom and concentration.

[4] We will see that this doubt will be partly solved analysing the report of the negative performance, where the state of concentration is not reached and the athlete doesn't report even the attempt of reaching it probably because blocked from other stronger causes.

Therefore, summarizing, in the perception of the athlete, the attempt to free the mind DERIVES from the condition of well-being that itself DERIVES from having sprinted out well at the shot. This confirms that concentration is sometimes seen by the athlete as subordinate to the sensation of well-being that elsewhere is by him indicated as ultimate goal (reached thanks to concentration).

Worst Performance

This is a competition, my worst competition I have in memory, in which I already started defeated. I'll explain myself better. I already started before with the idea that I didn't want to do it. Also because previously I had lived an unpleasant situation with some team-mates, a situation that gave me perturbation, a lot of perturbation. And therefore I have a strong sensitivity, very developed and this made it possible that all the energies that I had to concentrate for competition didn't come out. And then I saw myself in a situation of discomfort where I didn't want to run that competition and I didn't want to have, I didn't want to feel good with myself because actually I wasn't feeling good with myself. And therefore the bad part of, the trouble of an athlete is when he doesn't feel good with himself and there are some external situations influencing him. So I did this competition without will, I came out of the curve already far behind and at the end of the curve I had already stopped running because I said "I don't feel like, I don't feel like because I have too much tension, too many external tensions conditioning me and that don't allow me to be myself, don't make me live well, don't make me feel well." The balance of an athlete is a very delicate balance because when the athlete feels good, is in condition of feeling good, of making a good competition without being conditioned, then surely the competition will turn out well. If the athlete is instead conditioned by some conditions that preclude even his will of doing well, surely that competition will turn out bad and not only will it be bad, but it'll come out the worst way. The negativity of an athlete is shown exactly there when he doesn't feel good with himself. Every champion if he's not motivated to do well is half a champion, a champion cut in half. So I, reviving that competition, I re-live it after two years with an internal anger and I ask me: "but why is it like that?": because if well-being brings joy, brings peace, brings freedom, the situation of discomfort brings regret, brings pain. And this is reflected everywhere in an athlete's life and especially in competition. That is, an athlete like me lives on a very delicate balance and this, and every athlete I think lives on a very delicate balance because not all competitions can go well. And so it's a matter of maintaining this balance , trying then to revive afterwards those sensations lived before by an athlete when the competition went well. But if it goes wrong unfortunately it has its traces, it has its traces that stay exactly in an athlete's life anyway. In my opinion one must not detach the life of the athlete from the person, those are two aspects essentially united. When a balance is reached though, I think that with 39 I did reach the balance, it's easier to have good successes than failures.

Semantic Categories:

Also in this second report the PaCLIs are mainly collocated in the Heart Semantic Category (15 references to athlete's internal world: "I didn't want to do it"; "I didn't feel like doing it"; "gave me perturbation"; "I have a very strong sensitivity"; "I didn't want to run"; "I didn't want to have"; "I didn't want to feel good"; "I wasn't feeling good"; "I don't feel like"; "without will"; "I have too much tension"; "they don't make me live well"; "internal anger";

"regret"; "pain"), while the Mind Semantic Category (the expressions "I saw myself" and "I had to concentrate" that refer to the competition, and the world-constitutive propositions "think" and "in my opinion" that appear in the end of the text where the speaker does general considerations) and the Body one ("I came out of the curve"; "I already stop") are scarcely represented. However, differently than in the first report's, PaCLIs of the Heart Semantic Category denote almost all a state of discomfort and lack of motivation defining a process of rumination (Zullow et al., 1988). Moreover, differently than in the first report, the speaker uses many references to the mental states characterizing the moments preceding the competition (started defeated, idea of not wanting to do it, I didn't feel like doing it, I felt a sensation, it gave me perturbation) and to his psychological predispositions (I have a very strong sensitivity) that interacted in making the situation unfavourable.

With the expression "I saw myself in a situation of discomfort", collocated in the Mind Semantic Category, the athlete refers to a mental operation of self-evaluation of the own mental state made before starting ("I didn't want to run", "I didn't want to feel good with myself").

After this self-evaluation, the speaker opens a parenthesis in which he generalizes on the negativity of his experience using an impersonal form "therefore (…) the trouble of an athlete is when he doesn't feel good with himself and there are external situations influencing him" connectable to the world of Knowledge. The choice of the third person (with the subject "an athlete") in the present tense preceded by the adverb "when" meaning "every time that" is made to give the idea of a generic consideration that, as specified through the adverb "therefore" is a logic consequence of (or is a demonstration of) what the athlete just said about himself (in first person). [Something like that is done in the previous report when the protagonist becomes "an athlete": "(what I experienced) made me think also that in an athlete's life nothing is impossible and it's not said that in adult age one gets worse, it's not always said because it's here (he points at the head), it's in our mind that there are abilities we don't even imagine, but they are there. And in an athlete's competition…". In this case as well then the speaker abandons the first singular person and the past tense in which the experience took place to reach conclusions concerning mental processes that characterize the athletes in general].

Epistemic Categories

From the point of view of the Epistemic Category, the prevalence of the Knowledge characterizing the athlete's causal conviction, is partly mitigated by the use of the PaCLIs "I believe", "In my opinion" and "I think" that don't refer to attributive reasoning though but to other generic considerations.

The speaker's linguistic behaviour after the generic considerations is interesting. For the first time he starts to talk truly about competition, going back first to the "emotive framework" characterizing it , that is the lack of will: "I came out of the curve already far behind and at the end of the curve I already stopped running because I said "I don't feel like", I don't feel like because I have too much tension, too many external tensions conditioning me and that don't allow me to be myself, don't make me live well, don't make me feel well." The speaker refers to a couple of actions, through verbs linked to the Body Semantic Category (I came out of the curve, I stopped running), that he interprets as caused ("because") by what he was thinking at that time and that he reports right after ("I said I don't feel like, I don't feel because I have too much tension"). The speaker actually refers only to a very small fragment of competition (the moment when he comes out of the curve and stops running) when still the prevailing perceptual world was the one of thought, of reflecting about his own tensions and about what these tensions imply. If, talking about the best performance the athlete reports the sensations accompanying it and that brought him the perception to test "another dimension", talking about the worst performance he only proposes again the reasoning he made during that experience.

The linguistic focus is moved in some cases to the Object, because the athlete becomes victim of external elements therefore the subjects of the sentences become: the situation "bringing perturbation"; the energies that "didn't come out"; the external situation influencing him (the athlete); the external tensions "conditioning me", that "don't allow me to be myself", "don't make me live well", "don't make me feel well"; etc.

Main Relevant Linguistic Indicators and Attributional Processes

In this second report, it emerges right away how the athlete refers to two main causal elements he thinks might have compromised his performance: the delusion deriving from his team-mates' behaviour and his strong sensitivity.

It seems therefore an attribution of cause to internal (the strong sensitivity) and external (the team-mates' behaviour) interacting factors, of which the athlete shows to have no perception of control, as demonstrated by the complete absence of mental verbs or relative to actions about a planning attitude during competition.

The athlete's sensitivity is a stable non controllable and pervasive cause that enhances the negative consequences of the instable non controllable and less pervasive cause constituted by the team-mates' behaviour.

Also other indicators confirm this perception of poor control on what happened during competition: the energies that didn't come out become subject of the sentence.

Through the expression I saw myself in a situation of discomfort, the speaker gives the idea of the cognitive dysfunctional reading that he applies DURING competition and that reflects his explanatory reasoning he will express further on:" If the athlete is conditioned by some conditions that preclude even his will of doing well, surely that competition will turn out bad and not only will it be bad, but it'll come out the worst way".

During this competition, the thought is one of noticing a situation that will bring to negative consequences (predictable on the base of the explanatory reasoning reported by the athlete) and not one of planning just as in the best competition: I said: "I don't feel like", I don't feel like because I have too much tension…"

Already during the run the athlete is engaged in a process of causal explanation, differently than what happens in the report of the positive competition where he refers to sensations felt during the run and to planning thoughts (what he needs to do) and only later he proposes a causal explanation.

In the rest of the text a tendency of externalization of the event is to be noted: the situation is posed as subject of an action suffered by the athlete "gave me perturbation"; the expression I saw myself, that as said identifies the auto-evaluating attitude of the athlete during competition, at the same time implies a detachment from the situation (he is observer of his own acting).

The use of the verb to influence (and, later, to condition), having as subject the external situations and as object an athlete, demonstrates further the passivity of the athlete: this verb is per definition a causal verb and the fact that the athlete is not the subject of the phrase in which it is used emphasizes the external polarity of the attribution. The fact that it refers to an athlete demonstrates the speaker's conviction that such explanatory principle can be generalized to all athletes (this makes the conviction even more solid and strong).

Always near the passive attitude (and therefore of powerlessness about the external and not controllable cause) are the expressions: don't make me feel good with myself; don't make me be myself; didn't come out.

More than that, all the mental states reported being passively suffered are not, on a verbal level, mediated by the reference to sensations: the athlete doesn't say "I felt perturbation" just as, in the previews report, he said I felt many sensations; I felt right away a nervous sensation of well-being.

The presence of the evaluating element about the tensions of the competition, judged There and Then as too many, brought the athlete to a lack of will that, from its side brought him to stop running fast: I had stopped running because I said "I don't feel like", I don't feel like because I have too much tension, too many external tensions conditioning me and that don't allow me to be myself, don't make me live well, don't make me feel well.

Actually, in this case as well, as for the best performance, the athlete starts this reasoning after evaluating his efficiency up to that moment: I came out of the curve already far behind (in the best competition he refers to having come out well from the curve, that brought him to feel positive sensations).

The difference lies in the fact that in the report of the worse competition such evaluating process (negative) seems to re-start or find confirmation after the slow start compared to the adversaries, while in the other report it's about a much less present process (probably non conscious):

The athlete limited himself to referring to the good start and then paused exclusively on the good sensations that such a positive start had on in him.

In the worst competition the self-evaluating and of causal reasoning operation is much more present and the continuous reference to negative elements gives the idea of the process of rumination (Zullow et al., 1988)

During the worst competition the athlete is concentrated on what he has already done wrong and on what already hasn't worked and not on what he has to do.

The strongest and more generalized causal explanation takes place half way through the report: "The balance of an athlete is a very delicate balance because when the athlete feels good, is in condition of feeling good of making a good competition without being conditioned, then surely the competition will turn out well. If the athlete is instead conditioned by some conditions that preclude even his will of doing well, surely that competition will turn out bad and not only will it be bad, but it'll come out the worst way".

From this explanation four considerations emerge:

1.   the athlete speaks in absolutistic terms: he refers to an athlete; he proposes the causal relation when (…) then using the adverb surely, that is referring to the inevitability of the

negative event; the use of the verb preclude (because referring to an impossibility of action) confirms such perception of inevitability;

2.   the athlete refers to the gravity of the consequences: it'll come out the worst way. This expression seems to give indications not as much on the pervasiveness of the cause (it doesn't tell us in fact which areas of the athlete's life will be compromised) but as the strength of the action of this causal factor (the situation);

3.   the athlete confirms to perceive poor control: is in conditions of being able to do well. This means that if such conditions do not occur the possibility to use the resource (cause) "concentration", to which he referred to about the best competition, is cancelled. Therefore the cause "conditions" is stronger than the cause "concentration" to the point that the athlete, in presence of negative conditions (conditions that preclude his will), doesn't even try to concentrate (in the text verbs referring to this attempt are missing). The will to do well is precluded in such conditions.

4.   It seems that the state the athlete considers of default is the one of being conditioned; in fact, even referring to the situation in which an athlete feels good, he underlines the necessity of not being conditioned.

So, if we take both texts into account, one can suppose that the athlete identifies in the presence/absence of conditions (external situations mediated by his sensitivity) the main cause of his successes and failures. The conditions are considered previously also on a temporal basis compared to concentration, to wanting to do a nice competition, to feeling positive or negative sensations.

This suggests the presence of a possible bias in the athlete's thought, regarding the implicit conviction that the possibility to put into act the concentration attempt is subordinated to internal conditions (perturbation) deriving from the interaction of external events (team-mates' behaviour) with psychological dispositions (strong sensitivity).

If the negative situation occurs, the rigid attributive process the athlete tends to formulate is released: because I'm sensitive, external influences will start off a series of effects which will determine my failure. Otherwise the cause (of success) will coincide with the non presence of the failure's cause (the external influences). The strong sensitivity makes the occurrence of negative external situation a salient factor able to determine the outcome of the competition.

The athlete's cognitive-behavioural process DURING competition seems to be structured as follows: Negative situation and sensitivity determine perturbation (regret, anger, delusion), no will to do it and not feel good with himself; the athlete is then involved in an observation of such negative mental state (I saw myself in a situation of discomfort) and put into act dysfunctional behaviours (I had stopped running) that bring him to failure.

It seems to emerge a high rigidity of the athlete's causal thought, concerning the inevitability of the link between external negative conditions and counter-performance. The strength he attributes to the interaction between the negative situation and his sensitivity make it impossible any attempt of concentration before the competition. When an athlete feels a negative emotion he tends to confirm it with his actions and interpretations of reality[5] .

---

[5] Regarding the cognitive behavioural treatment, Linehan (1993) talks about *mood congruity effect* referring to the constant interaction between cognitions and emotions and to the incapacity to handle an emotive state when this has started off (see the athlete's expression *I already started*

In the following tables (figures 1,2) the relevant linguistic aspects present in the reports are summarized to interpret the athlete's attributive processes.

Best Performance

High frequency of references to sensations felt during competition using the past tense (*I felt many sensations, etc*), reference to planning thoughts through mental verbs (*I thought...to free the mind... and to...be concentrated... without thinking about who was ahead or behind me: ... to free the mind and concentrate ...*) and absence of verbs which indicate cognitive evaluations and causal explanations made in the There and Then of competition	The athlete *lived* competition without leaving room for reasoning on what was going wrong and that would have led to unpleasant consequences (based on his explanatory style). Verbs referring to conscious and voluntary thought (of planning) link to a certain perception of control (that will turn out to not be so solid)
From there	Indicator of causality
Right away	Immediacy of the consequences due to the cause
I dream to have	Indicator of scarce perception of control over the achievement of such sensations and state of concentration
It happens	Indicator of the fact that this state of grace does not depend on the athlete
When I'm concentrated...these abilities develop	Indicator of the instability of the cause (he is not always concentrated as comes out clearly by the presence of *when*). Explicit causal relation between concentration and performance.

Figure 1. Relevant linguistic aspects present in the best performance report

defeated and the interpretations he works out during competition, confirming such a mood). It is often explained to the athletes that the performance comes to take part in this cognitive model and this is why it is negatively conditioned.

Worst Competition

Started defeated	The double past participle summarizes the rigidity of the causal explanations the athlete gives (already before starting and realizing the outcome) about the event. The implicit thought could be: I started with such a negative mental attitude (caused by external agents) that the negative consequence (defeat) was inevitable.[6]
Already	Reference to the anticipation of thoughts compared to facts.
Because previously	Indicator of the causal relation between the *team-mates* behaviour and the scarce will.
The situation gave me perturbation	Externality of the cause
Strong sensitivity, very developed	Evaluation of the degree of presence of the factor "sensitivity ", exactly because it is "very strong" it assumes a causal power.
I saw myself	Self evaluation in the There and Then of competition
The trouble of an athlete is when	Generalization of the causal reasoning
External situations	Clear reference to the externality of the cause
influencing; conditioning	Verbs indicating the causal action of the external factors on the athlete's thoughts and behaviours
Then	Causal connection
I had stopped running because	Behavioural consequence (I had stopped running) and causal connection
Too many	Evaluation of the degree of presence of the causal factor
External tensions don't allow me/make me+verb	The external factors become the grammatical subjects of the sentence indicating the athlete's passivity, who suffers them losing the possibility to do something
"the balance of an athlete…"	Generalization through the reference to the category to which the speaker belongs
Surely	Adverb of certainty (*Epistemic Category of Knowledge*) indicating the rigidity of the causal reasoning
Preclude	Verb that underlines the athlete's powerlessness in which his will is cancelled by the causal strength of the external conditions, leading to inevitable consequences.
In the worst way	The superlative is indicator of the STRENGHT of the cause
"Why is it like that?"	Interrogative thought through which the athlete refers to the world of UNKNOWN, searching for causal explanations of the negative event.[7]
Is reflected everywhere	This expression confers pervasivity to the causal explanation

Figure 2. Relevant linguistic aspects present in the worst performance report

---

[6] The participle *defeated* gives the idea of the mental attitude of evaluation that should be made afterwards and that instead is part of the athlete's thoughts during competition. During competition he has the mental attitude he should have after it. That's why he can't operate any control, he feels like a victim of his negative interpretations and of the reading in absolutistic terms of the relation between the external negative event (his team-mates' behaviour) and the negative outcome of competition (mediated by the internal cause *sensitivity*).

[7] this kind of attitude is evident in many athletes who cannot explain to themselves the causes of unforeseen failures.

4. STRUCTURE GRID OF ANALYSIS

Our analysis of the above mentioned descriptions of 200 athletes about their performances has brought us to point out relevant aspects useful to understand the attributive processes: they can be integrated with those traditionally studied in this research field.

Coherent with what emerged in recent sport psychology contributions (Gordon, 2008), it was noticed the opportunity to recover the dimension of control and to consider other categories of analysis such as the causal explanations degree of complexity, the rigidity level with which these explanations are made, the temporal collocation of the attributive process, that will be described in this paragraph.

A first analysis of the material on which we focused on the survey of the PaCLIs showed how many of these offer useful information to locate the explanatory processes.

Each category includes therefore a series of PaCLIs and verbal expressions present in the texts, that imply specific perceptual or cognitive operations relevant to define the athletes' explanatory styles.

A grid was constructed to collect data that would allow to calculate values for each category in exam, these determined by the presence of the corresponding PaCLIs

The grid was used to analyse two corpora of transcripts with the same characteristics of those used for the preliminary qualitative analysis: one corpus is constituted by reports of 30 athletes concerning their best and worse performances; the other one by the interventions of 20 athletes at a Sport Psychology Forum, in which they told about their performances and the difficulties met in receiving advise from experts in their activity.

Dimensions of Grid

Attributional complexity: the athletes differentiate in the level of complexity of the explanations they structure to identify the causes of their successes and failures. Some of them give very simple and linear explanations, in which they precisely refer to what they believe to be the cause of their performance. They often do it using the indicative and not using adverbs that would moderate the level of certainty of their statements.

Moreover, these simple explanations are not preceded by particular mental verbs used as world-constitutive propositions that specify the epistemological nature of the information conveyed by the speaker. In other words, it is not explicated from where the knowledge expressed in the attributional explanation comes from (from the speaker's thought?).

Other athletes demonstrate to take into consideration more than one element, to have difficulty to reduce attribution to only one causal factor gathering more the complexity of the events, they make explicit the mental process that leads them in the reasoning, referring to specific cognitive states/actions given to the use of particular mental verbs. These athletes often report some reflections that brought them to modify the attributions made close to the competition, proposing interpretations of wider view and showing maybe to have caught a teaching from this sport experience.

It's about a sort of cognitive restructuring carried out independently that leads to read the failure/success under another point of view and considering other causal factors ("in that moment I thought I had been unlucky, now I understand that I didn't correctly follow the advice of the trainer, who was right").

Based on the above mentioned observations, the subcategories on which we organize the definition of the attributive complexity, characterizing the causal explanations of each athlete, concern: 1) the presence or not and the frequency of multi-causal factors; 2) the use of explanatory verbs (for example:" I explained to myself the event X on the base of Y"; " I attribute the cause to Y") or of expressions indicating a mental process of causal reasoning (also posed as question:" How come it happened?") 3) the presence and frequency of mental verbs that attenuate the absoluteness of the explanatory statements ("I think the cause could be X" instead of "the cause is X") explicating the inferential, hypothetical ("I hypothesise"; "I retain/reckon"; "I believe") nature of the reported knowledge (relative to the identification of the causal factor) that belongs therefore to the Epistemic Category of BELIEF; 4) the presence of changes of perspective deriving from a cognitive restructuring of the interpretation of event's cause. The change of perspective probably implies the passage from what Vallerand (1987) calls intuitive evaluation to the one defined as reflective that as we saw in paragraph 1.1. constitutes an objective of attributional retraining interventions.

From our point of view, two athletes resulting just as much pessimistic from an analysis of their reports with the CAVE method, could remarkably differ in the degree of attributive complexity, and this factor could mediate the negative effects on the performance: for example, A, following a defeat, even if referring to a mostly stable, global and internal cause, does not result more pessimistic than B who attributes his defeat to a definitely stable, internal and global cause but at the same time to another cause evidently more external, contingent and unstable.

Actually B, exactly because of this wider view and of this more complex reading of the event, shows, at least in theory, a greater inclination to adopt an optimistic view, he is more willing to consider a functional explanation of the event, he has in mind an alternative hypothesis.

This consideration is coherent with the recent studies on depression and anxiety (Fresco et al., 2006) that suggest how individuals demonstrating a tendency to approach stressful situations contextually and with flexibility have more probability to find more adaptive solutions compared to people who tend to look at negative events as deriving from indistinct causes and who respond with a smaller range of coping strategies.

As we have seen in paragraph 1.2. , the authors studying the explanatory styles (Fresco et al. 2006; Moore and Fresco, 2007), have recently proposed a dimension. similar to this of attributive complexity, called explanatory flexibility and that was operationalized as the standard deviation of an individual's answers to the items of globality and stability concerning negative events, reported in the Attributional Style Questionnaire (ASQ; Peterson et al. 1982).

The concept of explanatory flexibility and the one of integrative complexity (Peterson, 1992) of which we talked about in paragraph 1.2. and that has not been put into relation with attributive processes, like the one here proposed of attributive complexity suggest to go beyond the distinction between pessimists and optimists, hypothesizing that the persons distinguish themselves also by the major or minor variability with which they interpret the failures (and the successes in the case of attributive complexity) in terms of stability and globality of the causes to which they attribute them. The necessity to propose the concept of attributive complexity comes though from the observation that, in the athletes' descriptions, a spontaneous tendency to bring in more or less factors and to assume a more or less reflexive and analytic attitude can be noticed, trying to interpret the events.

Instead, the explanatory flexibility, basing on the variability with which a person interprets 6 negative events, does not take into consideration different interpretations of the same event and most of all does not distinguish the persons in respect to the spontaneous tendency to bring in more factors.

Another theoretical proposal that showed the opportunity to consider the number of causal factors identified by the athletes to explain their successes and, most of all, their failures, is the one we talked about in paragraph 1.2., of Ross et al. (2004), who have identified 4 possible kinds of structures with which attributions present themselves: 1) one single causal statement linked to one single statement of result (it was raining and therefore I didn't play well); 2) a single causal statement linked to more statements concerning the consequences (it was raining therefore I didn't play well and then the game was interrupted); 3) more causal statements linked to one single statement concerning one consequence (I was tired and was playing away, therefore I lost); 4) more causal statements linked to more statements on the effects (It was raining therefore I didn't play well and as a consequence I feel miserable).The authors propose a scoring calculated by dividing the number of statements on the consequences by the number of causal statements used to explain them.

Attribution types 3 and 4 are those that have more to do with what we called attributive complexity, while attributions of type 2 are more indicative of the presence of rigidity that is the dimension we are going to describe in the next paragraph.

Rigidity: another element diversifying the explanations reported by the athletes and their explanatory styles is the degree of rigidity of thought that characterizes their attributive processes.

We believe that two causal statements considered identical by traditional models can, using the PaCLI criteria of analysis, assume very different meanings depending on if they describe cause-effect mechanisms in a deterministic and absolute way, thus offering an idea of inevitability of success/failure given the cause X, or if referring to less rigid relations between causal factors and consequences.

Especially in case of pessimistic attributions an explanatory process excessively rigid can aggravate the negative relapses on the performance creating or reinforcing vicious circles ("if X happens then inevitably a failure will follow").

The same authors proposing the concept of explanatory flexibility (Fresco, 2007) operationalize the rigidity as a reduced standard deviation in the answers to the items of stability and globality for the negative events described in ASQ: rigidity, with this meaning, is the opposite of explanatory flexibility.

Here a wider meaning of the term is proposed, including the subjects' tendency to communicate their causality interpretations as if they were unquestionable, to believe that these cause-effect relations between factors identified as causes and consequences on performance (negative or positive events) can be generalized to other situations and can always be valid, that the causal factors have the power to produce particularly important consequences. Moreover, rigidity of attributions, as we here intend it based on what emerged from the qualitative analysis of the wide sample of reports, has a direct effect on the expectations grown close to competition, in case the causal element to which great predictive power is attributed occurs. For example, athletes who are convinced that a sensation of nervousness before competition inevitably compromises their performance, often report expressions like "I started defeated" referring to competitions where actually they felt this sensation that led them to have highly negative expectations just before the start. From our point of view, this kind of expressions, even if concerning expectations, offer information on the rigidity of the attributive processes the athlete usually puts into act: he is so convinced of the causality relation between nervousness and counter-performance that , in the moment in which he feels nervousness, he creates a rigid expectation of failure. The rigidity of the expectation reflects the rigidity of the explanatory reasoning.

Moreover, because the behaviours the athlete reports to have put into act to reach a good result reflect his causal reasoning (for example, practice causes success, therefore I practice), we believe that another element offering information about the rigidity of the athlete's explanatory thought is the use he makes of verbal expressions like "have to" referring to the perceived necessity to put in act pre-performance behaviours: "I had to stay relaxed"(the failure cause is surely linked to not being relaxed, therefore I have to stay relaxed), "I had to feel those sensations", etc.

This consideration comes as well from the preliminary qualitative analysis of many transcripts showing how athletes often report reasoning of this kind that associate to other elements of attributive rigidity.

Summarizing, the sub-categories we enclosed in the grid of analysis to evaluate the athletes' explanatory rigidity concerns: the presence of the expressions "I have/had to", "I must" ("I had to stay relaxed"; "I had to start as first"), the presence of generalizations ("when a team doesn't start well looses a match"), the prevalence of the epistemic category of KNOWLEDGE (absence of lexical PaCLIs or, if present, verbs of the KNOWLEDGE expressed in the first singular person of the indicative present as I know, see, remember, hear; declarative sentences in the present or past indicative : "I know that every time X occurs Y happens" "(I know that) the cause of my counter-performance was...") ; the presence of adverbs or locutions of certainty (surely, certainly etc. indicating rigidity, in contrast with probably, maybe, according to me, in my opinion, etc. indicating minor rigidity); the reference and emphasis reserved to the seriousness of the consequences given through the use of superlatives (it will come out the worst way; the fact of being de-concentrated brought me to reach an awful result, to arrive last, etc.) or to the absolute value of the causal action ("it compromises the result") reflecting somehow the force of cause; the description of expectations referred with a rigidity denoted by the presence of Knowledge, that mirrors the one of the linked attributive process ("started defeated" "I knew I had no chances- because cause X occurred-; "when I face the year's competition it's a sure flop").

Rigidity, parallel to attributive complexity, could be a mediation element between the explanatory style and the quality of the obtained performances (in terms of success/failures), we believe however, on a purely intuitive level, that, in the sense in which we intended it, it doesn't represent necessarily a limit to the performance: probably a person firmly (rigidly) retaining that the merit of his own success is undoubtedly his(internal cause) and depends on his intelligence (stable cause), coherently with what previewed by Seligman's model will tend to obtain the same successes (or even more) of who is as much optimistic but proposes reasoning in less absolutistic terms.

Rigidity can maybe represent instead another complication factor for pessimistic people who risk to enter vicious circles self-perpetuating (coherently with Brosschot & Thayer, 2004; Johnsen et al, 2003; etc.).

Control: The authors who studied the explanatory styles in the sport psychology field suggest the importance to recover the dimension "perception of control", absent in Seligman's model, because it is a factor that plays a mediation role between the optimistic disposition and success in sport (Grove & Pragman, 1984, 1986; Gordon, 2008).

Also the qualitative analysis that guided us in constructing the grid we are presenting, seen the evident individual differences emerged about this factor, confirms such an opportunity. Besides taking into consideration the nature of the causal factor mentioned by an athlete that can refer to controllable causes (effort) or uncontrollable (talent), we noticed other elements that offer useful indications to understand how much the athlete perceives to have control on the outcomes of his performances. In fact, for example, concentration itself is a controllable causal factor, but not easily, this leading to the athletes sometimes describing it as a state of grace realized thanks to a series of circumstances and factors, not all of them controllable.

Starting from the application of the concept of Textual Linguistic Focus to the analysis of texts proposed by Zuczkowski (1995), we narrowed the meaning of this concept, obtaining the parameter indicating if the speaker mostly refers to himself as subject making the actions and living the emotions or as causal object determining certain effects, feelings or thoughts in him .

In the writings one could often observe that athletes, even if referring to partly controllable causes, tell them as if they were not such because they grammatically organize their statements putting the causal factors as subject or expressing themselves in the passive form ("thoughts invaded my mind and this has compromised my concentration and therefore my result"; "I was pervaded by thoughts that compromised my concentration and therefore my result" instead of "I couldn't concentrate…"): We interpreted the "Focus on the object" in the statements revealing athletes' attributions of cause as a possible indicator of scarce perception of control.

Another fact we believe can be included in the category of control analysis is the tendency to describe the lived competition as a sort of de-personification ("My legs didn't oppose any strength and made me stay still…I was swimming, but was moving in slow-motion"; "the other two attempts was the other side of me who made them, the one that has fun to emerge only in the most important occasions so as to create in me a strong belief of impossibility of success" " I was only the pale reflection of myself" "it wasn't me throwing but my skeleton of a few years ago"…). Not necessarily the causal factor becomes the grammatical subject of the statements but there is anyway reference to incontrollable strengths or to metaphors with which the athletes describe their body or their actions as other than self that, independently from the speaker's will prevail and determine the failure (or, more rare, the success).

Associated to the focus on the object is the use of verbs in passive form (sensation X led me to run badly; it brought me perturbation, etc.), while verbs expressing athlete's wishes referred to future performances (I dream of reviving those sensations that brought me to win) could indicate how he doesn't perceive full control on the causal factors. In the same way verbs like "happen" "occur" "take place" (" it isn't the first time it happens to me to remain concentrated for the whole competition") give the idea that the athlete doesn't feel to have determined himself the result.

Sometimes verbs or words are present referring to emotions lived by the athlete after competition, that give valuable indications on which are the causes to which he attributes his success/failure in case these are not already explicit or there are contradictions in his words. For example an athlete who refers to feel responsible for the result unlikely attributed the failure to incontrollable elements (see Weiner, 1979).

Often athletes, in proposing their causal reasoning, more than identify causes they exclude others, getting to the conclusion of not perceiving control on the performance any more: "I practiced a lot but it was of no use at all"; "it can't have been my poor concentration to determine my failure…" "even if I make an effort in thinking positive the result doesn't change".

Through these statements the athletes take off the responsibility from themselves limiting the power of controllable factors, or anyway asking themselves if there are other controllable factors on which to aim to improve the performance.

The sub-categories present in the grid, through which we want to analyse the control factor, therefore are: 1) Focus on the Subject ("I didn't concentrate"); on the Object ("my concentration was not tuned with…); on the relation between Subject and Object ("that sensation didn't make me concentrate"); 2) presence of de-personification ("I was only a pale reflection of myself"; "the other side of me that has fun to emerge"; "my body was empty, light , motionless…the legs didn't oppose any strength and made me stay still…"; 3) verbs of passivity (the situation brought me perturbation"; " these things don't make me feel good with myself"); 4)desiderative verbs (I dream of reviving this sensation" "I hope to start well also the next time"); 5)verbs like to occur/ happen (the strangest thing was what was happening in my mind"); emotion verbs or words (control: "I'm proud"; "I'm disappointed by myself"; no control: "frustrated"); 6) negations of controllable causes (I practiced a lot but it was of no use", "it's not a matter of effort"; "even if I face the competition positively the result doesn't change"); 7) nature of the cause (controllable or not controllable).

Temporal collocation: The attributive process is a mechanism that activates following the evaluation of a performance outcome with the adaptive function of identifying the causes that determined it, allowing a person to recreate the conditions that led him to a success and avoid that the causal factors determining failure occur.

We believe that some causal reasoning in order to keep their adaptive power, even if deriving from a system of convictions well consolidated in the athlete's mind (if an athlete attributes the cause of his failure to scarce practice it is because he believes that practice allows to obtain good results), should be made or activated "cold", at the end of a competition and not during it. Sometimes, as we could see during the preliminary qualitative analysis, athletes report thoughts they had during competition, in which seeing that a causal factor they retain decisive happened or not happened, they put into act the causal reasoning because X (or non X), therefore I will lose.

In this sense we thought it was important to consider all those elements which are retraceable in the analyzed texts, that would give information on the temporal collocation of the attributive process: this attributive process reported by the athlete is an operation made after the Here and Now or did it come into act in the There and Then of the competition?

A statement of this kind: "At the moment of competition I see that if I had correctly done training I would surely have had better results and I impose myself to prepare well for the next one, but the story repeats itself cyclically" describes a reasoning produced in the There and Then of com petition that exactly because of the temporal collocation comes out to be dysfunctional. In fact, to attribute failure to the correct training is an absolutely functional attributive attitude (internal but behavioural cause, therefore instable and non pervasive, and controllable) because it prepares the athlete to put more effort looking at the next competition. The problem comes out when this reasoning takes place during competition when there is nothing to do any more about training and it determines an attitude of mental rigidity (because X -the training-didn't occur, Y-the failure- will follow) in which other controllable factors are not taken into consideration and it reduces itself to a self-fulfilling prophecy.

Some of the criteria of analysis studied by Bongelli & Zuczkowski (2008b) in order to identify the PaCLIs, result particularly relevant to obtain information about the temporal collocation of attributions. For example, the use of mental verbs (already considered in the attributive complexity category) in a world-constitutive way (Petöfi, 1973), i.e. in the indicative present with the I of the speaker as subject, referred to the attributive process("I think that the cause was X"; "I believe that the scarce practice brought me to the defeat", etc.) indicates that the attribution occurs in the Here and Now of the report. When, instead, these mental verbs are used in a descriptive way (always in the first person but in the past) they refer to a mental operation of There and Then ("seen the bad start, I thought I wouldn't make it").

Another criteria of analysis , taking hint from Bongelli & Zuczkowski's approach, and that allows to get information to establish the attribution's temporal collocation, is to consider the Semantic Categories ("Body", "Mind", "Heart") of which the verbal predicates used by the speaker are part.

For the purpose of our analysis, we are mostly interested in finding out which of the semantic categories prevails in the description of competition. In fact, from the transcripts analyzed for the construction of the grid, it seemed to us that the athletes involved in the attributive process in the There and Then went back mainly to the semantic category of Mind referring to the experience of the competition itself "I thought I could do it"; "I saw myself in difficulty"(in an evaluative sense).

On the contrary, athletes reporting attributive reasoning in the Here and Now don't refer at all to thoughts in competition apart when referring to what they were planning There and Then in order to give their best, that is thoughts concerning the immediate future (they were concentrated on task, on the action). These athletes often use predicates belonging to the Heart Semantic Categories (many references to the sensations felt There and Then; to emotions, etc.) and Body Semantic Categories(There and Then: I surpassed an adversary; I scored, etc.).

The presence of an evaluative attitude about the current performance is coherent with the activation of an attributive reasoning in the There and Then of competition ("I saw myself in difficulty" "I thought I didn't start well enough to be able to win"; "I had the sensation to be too heavy" ;etc.).

A last indicator we inserted in the grid in order to give the temporal collocation of attribution concerns the presence of statements linked to the expectations built during competition or right before it (" I had bad sensations, I started defeated").

Summarizing then the categories taken into consideration to evaluate the temporal collocation of attribution concern: the distinction between the world-constitutive use and the descriptive use of mental verbs referred to the attributive process (if one refers to thoughts with mental verbs in the present, in first person-and not in a direct form- he probably refers to an attributive process of the Here and Now; if there is use of past tense or present but in an indirect form, the athlete refers to an attributive process made There and Then); the prevalence of verbs belonging to the Heart, or to the Mind, or finally to the Body Semantic Category; the presence of verbs referring to evaluative operations made in the There and Then on competition; the building of expectations before or during competition.

Rumination: Kuhl (1981) and Zullow (Zullow & Seligman 1988) define rumination as the tendency to refer to negative events. This verbal and mental behaviour is often associated to the pessimistic explanatory style.

From the qualitative analysis a pessimistic attitude of the athletes often emerged, even when they didn't explicitly refer to causes.

5. EXAMPLE OF APPLICATION OF THE GRID

In this paragraph we are going to suggest an example of analysis of a text taken from the corpus of interventions on a sport psychology forum. A girl who does track and field asks the experts for help because on one side she cannot explain to herself her failures having seen the positive premises and the attempts she says to have made in order to solve the problem, on the other side she cannot find a strategy allowing her to face the competitions with greater success.

We propose first an analysis of the text pointing out the most relevant PaCLIs concerning our research target and, afterwards, an analysis using the before described grid.

> Doctor, I believe to be a complex case, I do 1500, 3000 (meters) and, starting this year, also the 800, because to do a nice 1500 one needs to be able to do a nice 800! Anyway, in January I changed coach, because the previous one didn't supervise me well and consequently I lost confidence…let's get to the new coach…perfect! Very skilful, available, doesn't put pressure, he supervises me very well we decided together some goals and he looks for me to reach them…in brief everything is too good to seem true!
>
> The day of the first competition arrives, it goes bad…another one, goes bad…anther one even worse than the others…I suffer the competition a lot, I can't bring in well…my coach says that depending on how I run during practice I should make a wonderful timing, instead during competition I get stuck…I think about all the negative ones…that I'm not able, I can't, etc; and I even arrived to make a 3000 in competition 1 minute slower than the one tried in practice a few weeks before!
>
> Then I try to change there comes another 3000, I try to have confidence in me, I try to think of nothing negative and convince myself that it would go well, because practice should be a perspective of competition …start, good sensations, anxiety still under control…we start, I'm calm, and everything goes the way it has to go...until the other girls make a little sprint and there is again the mental block...I don't react…I don't think of anything… I just can't make it, and I retire! a big disappointment…also for my coach! All this to tell you that starting with a positive or negative thought the result of my competitions doesn't change! I'm afraid of not being able to really express myself as I should…help me, because I don't know what to think or do any more!

PaCLI- verbs with world-constitutive use: The athlete uses PaCLI-verbs in the first singular person of the present indicative to refer to There and Then perceptions and thoughts of the competitions (temporal collocation) also when they are used in world-constitutive way ("I think…that I am not able, I can't, etc").

In fact she reports the competition as if she were reviving it (prevailing of present tense). The only exception is I believe because this verb refers to an evaluation of the Here and Now other than the There and Then of competition. There is instead no use of mental verbs with world-constitutive function that have to do with the attributive process made in the Here and Now of the report (see the attributive complexity reported in figure 3).

Other relevant verbs: there is a frequent use of the verb to try that conveys the cognitive attempt of control that fails

PaCLI-non verbs: we notice the absence of adverbs or locutions (like "in my opinion, to me") denoting the degree of certainty with which the athlete makes his statements or moderating the absoluteness of these (low level of attributive complexity and high level of rigidity). Statements like "as if + subjunctive" are absent.

Morpho-syntactic PaCLIs: the presence of conditional sometimes moderates the rigidity of reasoning . However the epistemic category of KNOWLEDGE prevails as demonstrated by the prevalence of the indicative mode.

The verbs "to have to, to need to" ("to do a nice 1500 one needs to be able to do a nice 800"; "goes the way it has to go") should convey athlete's rigid conviction of "obligatory", "duty", "necessity". Sometimes it is present a generalization of the reasoning ("to do a nice 1500 one needs to be able to do a nice 800"; "practice should be a perspective for competition"), while the use of the expression "should make" in the reasoning "depending on how I run during practice I should make a wonderful timing" gives rigidity and absoluteness to the statement, only relatively moderated by the use of conditional. In this case it is a rigid expectation.

Semantic category: it emerges a wide reference to the Semantic Category of the MIND through the many mental verbs describing the athlete's thoughts in the There and Then of competition.

We now propose an analysis of the text using the grid described in the previous paragraph.

Dimension	Value	Sub-categories of analysis					
Attributive complexity	low	Multi-causalF	Explanatory v.	Mental v.	Change of perspective		
		No: cause 1 (+ negation other causes)					
Rigidity	Very high	"Need" "Have to" verbs	Generalizati on	Epistemic category	Adverbs of certainty	Force cause	Expectat ions (E)
		("<u>one needs to </u>be able to do..." "it has to go")	("<u>one needs to </u>be able to do...";)	Prevalence KNOWLEDGE		"I arrived to make 1 minute slower "	"Depend ing on...I should do"

Figure 3. Continued on next page.

Dimension	Value	Sub-categories of analysis					
		Focus	Depersonif.	"passivity" verbs	Desiderative verbs	"to happen" verbs	Emotion. verbs
Control	Very low (unknown "I don't know what to think any more; negation controllable cause; emotion "fear")	48% Ego; 26% object; 20% impers (3rd pers; infinitives and gerunds) 4% you; 4% we					Fear no to make it; I suffer
Temporal collocation		World Constitutive vs descriptive	Semantic Category	Evaluations (verbs/ adjectives)	Expectations before/ during		Tense
	There and Then	Descriptive and World Costitutive but referring to the There and Then;	MIND (There and Then)	I think I can't make it (There and Then)			Prevalence of present but referring to the There and Then of competition (revived)
Rumination	Present, preceded by list of positive elements						

Figure 3. Grid of analysis

This is the key to reading the grid (figure 3):

In the first column are the dimensions we decided to use for the analysis; in the second one a value is indicated (from very low to very high) deriving from what emerges in the following columns that refer to the sub-categories of analysis about each dimension. Considering the definitions and criteria of analysis suggested in the previous paragraph, in fact, we propose to evaluate the attributive complexity based on the presence or not of con-causes, explanatory and mental verbs and changes of perspective; the rigidity based on the presence of "have to" verbs, of linguistic forms linking to generalizations of the attributive reasoning, of adverbs of certainty, of prevalence of the Knowledge Epistemic Category, of linguistic expressions emphasizing the strength of the factor to which the cause is attributed, and the presence of rigid expectations linking to attributive convictions just as rigid; the perception of control depending on the Linguistic Focus in the meaning proposed in the previous paragraph, on the presence of Depersonifications characterized by a total loss of the athlete's power of action, on verbs indicating the passivity of the subject about the actions taken from external elements, on verbs expressing wishes or that, instead, refer to happenings independent from the athlete's will and, finally, on words referring to emotions coherent with the perception of control or the absence of it; the value of temporal collocation, differently from what occurs in other dimensions, refers to the distinction between collocation of the attributive process in the Here and Now or in the There and Then of competition. As we explained in the previous paragraph, we obtain the information that bring us to give the temporal collocation based on: the use of the verbs referring to cognitive processes concerning the attributive reasoning, and that can be descriptive or constitutive of world; the prevalence of one of the 3 Semantic Categories; the presence of evaluations expressed through adjectives or verbs, or of expectations implying explanatory beliefs; the used tense.

In the end, the presence of many words referring to emotions, lived facts and negatively associated thoughts indicate the presence of an episode of Rumination.

We propose now the analysis of this text and a series of considerations deriving from it, based on the dimensions that in this case result more significant.

The text shows a poor attributive complexity because the only factor to which the athlete more or less explicitly seems to attribute a causal value about the counter-performances is the mental block.

Instead the athlete only lists some factors that potentially could have brought her to success but that instead didn't have any positive effect or change on the performance. This way the athlete excludes the causal power of these elements and convinces herself further that the performance is determined by incontrollable factors. The tendency to restrict the number of possible interpretations is accompanied by the absence of reflections bringing the athlete to consider other possible explanations taking another perspective. The impression is that the athlete's attributive operation is guided more by an attempt to get hurriedly to an explanation than by the will to make a more complex reading of the happening that gives space for example to possible changes of perspective in time. The nature of the superficial attributive route made by the athlete is confirmed by the absence of explicit references to her cognitive route because there are no explanatory verbs. Moreover, her statements are not mediated by mental verbs attenuating the degree of certainty, this especially about the conviction concerning what one should be in order to reach good results. This conviction takes in it a causal explanation that, coherent with what White (1959) said about attributive processes, the athlete takes with him/her in every competition.

The reference through the verb to need to express the necessity that some premises take place in order to obtain the wished consequences (to make a nice 1500 one needs to able to make a nice 800) indicates the rigidity degree of these convictions that are proposed almost like some general law.

In fact the athlete generalizes the causal relation between quality of performance in the 800 and quality of performance in the 1500 using the impersonal form.

The drastic effect of the consequences of the cause identified in the "mental block" is emphasized by the expression "I arrived to make 1 minute slower" indicating how much power the athlete attributes to such factor, that is how high is what we called the "force of cause".

Also the athlete's expectations that, as we hypothesized in the previous paragraph about the description of the grid , can be a reflex of the made causal attributions , show high levels of rigidity, as emerges by the use of another recourse to the verb "to have to": the expressions "depending on how I run during practice I should…"and "practice should be a perspective for the com petition" indicate that for the athlete it should be a certain and unquestionable fact that the factor "practice" constitutes a cause of good performance. It is exactly because this conviction is not confirmed by the reported facts that the athlete asks herself what other factors don't work and what could explain the continuous failures, introducing the Category of the Unknown.

Also the inefficiency of the attempts of facing the competition with positive thought as a possible remedy is questioned in an absolute way. The statement "starting with the positive or negative thought the result of my competitions doesn't change" recalls the epistemic category of KNOWLEDGE from which the athlete seems to derive her convictions and rigidly excludes the possibility of a productive change in the mental attitude during future competitions.

The drastic re-dimensioning of the power of causal factors that intuitively and EVIDENTLY could have led to positive consequences (practice and positive thought) brings the athlete to move the cognitive state on the epistemic world of the UNKNOWN and state "I don't know what to think any more".

This expression of the UNKNOWN, so as the exclusion of controllable causes, the reference to the "fear of not succeeding in it" and the use of a passive verb "to suffer" explicating the sense of powerlessness felt by the athlete, concur to give the idea of her poor perception of control on the events.

The athlete's report is characterized by a tendency to rumination as testified by many words with negative meaning and by the use of many references to fear or to perception of not succeed and verbs indicating her negative mental attitude (it goes bad…another one, goes bad…anther one even worse than the others…I suffer the competition a lot, I can't bring in well in competition I get stuck…I think of all the negative…that I can't, I'm not able to, etc; …I arrive to make a 3000 in competition 1 minute slower..! there is again the mental block… there it is again the mental block…I don't react...I don't think of anything…just I can't make it, and I retire! a big disappointment…also for my coach! I'm afraid of not being able to really express myself as I should…help me, because I don't know what to think or do any more!).

Moreover, this mental attitude doesn't only characterize the reading the athlete makes afterwards of the negative event, but her happening itself in the There and Then of competition.

The general interpretation of the text, considering the various categories analysed with the grid , suggests that the athlete has very strict convictions about what should guarantee a good performance (practice and then positive thought) and expects that the attempt to act on these factors always and right away leads to results. It is probably consequently to this rigidity of thought that the athlete doesn't seem willing to persist in her attempts and to consider other factors on which to act.

6. EXAMPLES OF ANALYSIS AND CONFRONTATIONS

We now propose a series of confrontations between report's extracts in which the dimensions of the grid allow to point out some differences in explanatory styles not differentiated by internality, stability and globality: each couple of confronted reports is characterized by relevant differences in one of the dimensions of analysis of the grid proposed by us. We therefore suggest an example of analysis for each dimension.

6.1. Comparison between Causal Explanations Differentiating by Level of Attributive Complexity and Rigidity

The following extracts concerning causal explanations of two tennis payers following their respective defeats are to be considered:

1) Today was a bad game: everything depended on the fact that it went on too long (optimism) and I can't put effort (pessimism) in a task for too long, I don't like the strain beyond certain limits.

2) The defeat derived from a series of con-causes: I think that probably my emotionalism (high pessimism) played a bad trick on me, but it is not to underestimate also the fact that I was not at top (low pessimism) due to cancelled practice (medium-low pessimism) nor that I faced an adversary who evidently has technically grown a lot in the last year (optimism). More than that I lost 2 decisive points sending the ball out for a nothing: that's bad luck!

The difference between the two extracts concern mostly the different level of complexity characterizing the causal explanations proposed by the two athletes. Athlete I gives a very simple explanation in which he identifies the cause of failure in the interaction between the length of the game and the incapacity, or poor will ("I don't like the strain") he recognises in himself about putting effort during long terms. From the point of view of the Epistemic Categories, the athlete suggests the causal inferences as statements of well known facts, using the indicative present and without using any verb with world-constitutive use expressing the inferential nature of the conclusions he reaches about causal attributions: "everything depended on..". Also his inability to put effort and the little will to work hard beyond certain limits are presented as stable traits and, especially, as facts.

In the report of athlete II, instead, the prevalence of the epistemic Category of Belief, underlined by the mental verb "I think, I believe" specifying the hypothetical nature of the causal explanation, and by the adverb "probably", both used with a world-constitutive function, besides the use of subjunctive, demonstrates that the athlete reports less rigid beliefs inserted in a more complex and flexible interpretation of the event. Referring to a series of con-causes, the athlete seems to explicate his reflection of evaluation of which were the most determining factors when he uses the expression " it is not to underestimate also the fact...".

The two athletes, based on the dimensions of internality, stability and globality, do not differentiate much in terms of optimism. In fact both consider more internal, stable and global causes (I:"I can't put effort"; II "emotionality") and also external, temporary and contingent causes (I: "game too long"; II: "an adversary who evidently has technically grown a lot"), however we believe that the noticed differences make the attitude of athlete II more adaptive about the fact that he is able to give a more complete reading of the event, which can preserve him from self-fulfilling prophecy mechanisms.

A. I questioned myself right away on the reason of this bad performance: if at first I interpreted the defeat as the demonstration that, even if I love it very much, I don't have the talent for this sport, then I considered other possible explanations. For example I'm realizing that before a competition of this kind that requests great resources on the nervous level I have to avoid making too many trials both in practice and during warm up. Moreover I believe that the sensations of poor brilliance I perceived exactly because I was not ready on a nervous level, brought me to distraction losing the right concentration for competition. We need to add that I'm probably also too emotional.

B.   When there are important occasions is an assured flop: I can't stand the anxiety.

Athlete A and athlete B evidently show different explanatory styles. Even if it's an extrapolation and being necessary to consider the athletes' reactions to a wide number of events in order to correctly infer the explanatory habits, already from this example we can notice that while the first athlete makes a reading of the event able to catch in a greater way the complexity and the nuances, and proposes it as an hypothesis, athlete B interprets the defeat in only one direction attributable to his own difficulty to stand anxiety in important events. Analyzing the two attributive processes in terms of internality, stability and globality, A would result even more pessimistic than B, because he refers to ability ("I don't have the talent for"), to concentration and to emotionality, which are internal causes, with high levels of stability (ability and emotionality) with exception of concentration, and of high globality (concentration, emotionality and poor ability in a sport considered important by the athlete will probably affect in great measure on his possibilities to succeed also in other contests). These factors, even if balanced by less stable and global factors (too many trials determining the poor nervous charge and poor brilliancy) make an hypothetical average CAVE scoring relatively high, showing the picture of a generally pessimistic reading from the athlete's side. Athlete B refers to a cause that has to do with the interaction between an individual disposition and an external factor (importance of the event) and it's therefore averagely internal (as CAVE guidelines suggest: "ratings in the 2-6 range apply to explanations in which the cause shares both internal and external elements and is an interaction between self and another person or between self and environment"), averagely stable ("the cause is in the present tense, the probability of future re-occurrence is high, but the event is intermittent") and global in the limits of how much sport or participation to important events are determining for this athlete's achievements. The hypothetical CAVE scoring could therefore be similar to the one of athlete A.

We feel like hypothesizing that in cases like this it could be useful to integrate with other reading keys based on the dimensions of stability, internality and globality to define an explanatory style that has a predictive value about the attitude the athlete will have about future agonistic events.

We believe that the complexity level with which the athlete does his explanatory reasoning can have consequences on his future attitudes and behaviours, because the use of more complex explanations can coincide with a greater ability of the athlete to assume different perspectives and to consider in a less determining way the link between a cause and its effects.

Athlete A, besides referring to a wide number of causes, uses a series of verbs explicating the explanatory operation he is doing making the complexity level of this process emerge, which is the result of a self-questioning on the causes ("I questioned myself right away about the reason"), of a first interpretation ("I interpreted") that is afterwards questioned and enriched considering other possible causes ("I considered other possible causes") he starts to realize about ("I realize") making a change of perspective.

That is, the athlete uses mental verbs describing a reflective attitude aimed to the identification of the causes.

Always referring to the attributive complexity level it seems to us relevant to underline that the epistemic world in which A's attributive inferences can be put is the one of BELIEF: this is testified by the use of PaCLIs attenuating the level of certainty (the adjective "possible", the verb "believe" and the adverb "probably") the athlete gives to his own explanatory hypothesis.

Regarding athlete B, we notice that , besides the simplicity of the explanatory reasoning he makes, this, even if linking his reaction to an external and intermittent situation, attributes to the interaction of causal factors "important event" and "anxiety" or, more correctly, to the causal factor anxiety for the important events, a predictive power of inevitable failures. We understand this from the use of the past participle "assured" that also refers to a totally negative outcome (a flop) giving idea of what we called "force of the cause". In this case the Epistemic World of reference seems to be the one of Knowledge and this level of certainty seems not to live room for other possible interpretations.

We would expect from an athlete like B a greater probability to become victim of a self-prophecy that self-fulfills. Moreover the selective attention he puts towards this only causal factor could bring him to give up "a priori" and to practice with less conviction close to an important competition: the reasoning could be " if I already know (Knowledge) that I will do badly in great events, I have no reason to practice".

Let's give then the limit of not too complex attributive explanations (in the meaning of attributive complexity we are proposing) to the fact of being excessively rigid and deterministic (and therefore able to generate the conviction that a cause's consequences are inevitable) and to associate with a selective attention that risks to make alternative explanations, able to predispose the athlete to adaptive behaviours for future performances, cognitively non-accessible.

On the other hand the job of a psychotherapist or a sport psychologist working in the attributional re-training is also to make consider possible alternative causes in case those of the patient are not adaptive, therefore if the athlete , spontaneously, is able to consider a wide number of explanatory hypothesis, this should be an advantage.

We now look back at an example whose we presented the PaCLI analysis in paragraph 5, that seems to well represent the tendency of some athletes to focus the attention on one only explanation of the event proposed as strongly predictive of negative consequences. In this kind of explanatory attitude, that we very often noticed in athletes who make rigid readings of the counter-performance, the tendency is of listing a series of factors that could potentially have brought to a positive performance and exclude its causal role.

It is as if the athletes would negate the possibility that other factors, besides the one to which they attribute the cause of failure, contributed somehow to the occurring of the negative event.

Athlete Z

(…)Depending on how I run during practice I should make a wonderful timing, instead during competition I get stuck (…) I try to change, there comes another 3000, I try to have confidence in myself, I try not to think of anything negative and to convince myself that it would go well, because practice should be a perspective of competition…start, good sensations, anxiety still under control…we start I'm calm, and everything goes the way it has to go…until the other girls make a little spring and there is again the mental block..(…)

starting with a positive or negative thought the result of my competitions doesn't change. (...)
I already know that in spite of the hard work in practice the results don't come.

Athlete Z refers to a series of positive factors (practice, start, sensations, anxiety control) that occurred before or during competitions but from which no good performances came out. This way the athlete questions the possibility that the positive mental attitude or practice can be causal factors, and does this in an absolute way because she states with a declarative sentence expressed in present tense that the result of competition doesn't change and that she knows results do not arrive in spite of the hard work in practice. Z suggests then the conclusions of her reasoning as information of KNOWLEDGE, from which rigid and hardly changeable convictions derive. Such an attitude, through which the athlete excludes especially possible controllable causes (also concerning the same positive thought, the athlete states to make an attempt of control), can easily associate to a solid conviction of powerlessness as it clearly emerges in the following example concerning an athlete with similarly rigid "causal" thought:

> I throw the discus, I did my first Olympics 4 years after I started to do athletics and after 2 years from my first important results and the outcome at the Olympics was clear: 3 fouls. Can it happen, can it not happen? anyway from then my progress in general has developed to the point to reach today the world top, but when I face the event of the year it is an assured flop, apart from the Europeans of 1990 when I was finalist in every other competition it seemed that on platform there wasn't me, but the skeleton of many years before, up to 1993. Unforgettable year for me, the usual improvement of the National record that at the time was equivalent to the best world performance, 2 medals around the neck (international events) and at the world championships? just not to make a mistake I centred 3 fouls. This last experience was different from the previous ones, because the first qualification throw was perfect, long and regular, but a fall due to rain made me slip and I touched slightly the edge of the platform so my competition from there was over, the other two attempts was my other side of me who made them, who has fun to emerge only in the most important occasions so to create in me a strong belief of impossibility of success. I'm not telling you with how much pain I live this situation, because I have a very sensitive and altruist character...

Limiting our attention on the thought rigidity aspects, we can notice how in this example it is clear that the collocation of a causal link in the world of Knowledge ("when I face the event of the year it is an assured flop") can bring an athlete to develop strong convictions of impossibility of success, as in this case verbally explicated.
Following example to be considered:

> I didn't miss not even one practice and always put maximum effort. I didn't make particular tactic mistakes, but when I arrived on the final straight line I didn't have it any more. I'm not fast enough.

In this case the athlete comes to the conclusion that the only causal factor can be in relation with his scarce speed, because he excludes other more controllable and less stable factors as effort, practice and tactic organization of competition. The athlete proposes his interpretation as if it were a fact, an information of the world of Knowledge: the rigidity of his causal reasoning brings him to exclude other factors on which to work in order to do better in the future.

In other cases , as in the example we are going to report underneath, the reference to positive premises is followed by expressions with which the athlete put in the category of Knowledge also the expectations and therefore the future:

"...in the morning I had done the heat, I entered the final with the first timing, I was just a few tenths from the Italian Championship standard timing (...). So that was the time I had to win...I was fine because in the morning the heat went perfectly, quietly, I swam, I came close for two tenths to the timing of the Italian championships, therefore in the afternoon in the final it was enough only to repeat what I had done in the morning, stimulated by the fact that it was a final, so in final one always gives something more, and do this tempo for the Italians."

We only want to observe that the athlete identifies a causal relation between the positive factors he lists and the equally positive consequences that, from his point of view, should have occurred. In fact, the athlete uses the causal link "therefore" putting it exactly between these two positive premises and the expectations of success that logically follow, that is the fact of having to win. In this case we think that the verb "to have to", on one side, gives indications on the degree of certainty (Knowledge) the athlete attributes to expectations before competition and on the other side it represents an expression that indicates the athlete's sense of responsibility about the importance of taking advantage of the occasion. The expectation of success also derived by the underestimation of the task difficulty, in which "it was enough to repeat what I had done..." and by the conviction, expressed as an always valid rule (category of Knowledge) that "in final one always gives more".

It is the same athlete who realized that exactly expectations of certain success and the perception of having to win and not making mistakes brought him to failure:

"instead it happened that then surely the excitement, caring too much, knowing that you are there and can't make mistakes, made me lose".

The expectations, especially when deriving from very rigid causal reasoning in which to some factors it attributed a high predictive power, seem to often lead the athlete to focus the attention also in competition on the search of such factors (evaluation of everything to be right, self-evaluation), or bring them to perceive success not only as an (almost) known fact but also as due. This probably generates a little productive mental attitude during competition, that doesn't permit to act automatically as sometimes would be right. In fact, the athlete of the example reports a comparison between the beautiful sensations of the morning when everything came easy and the difficulties of the afternoon when, with the responsibility of having to win, he had the perception of having to control everything.

"The morning I didn't think of anything, I went to do the competition, I came out without problems, then in the afternoon you start to think how you need to swim, how you need to pass, you hope to make the timing, you hope not to make mistakes, (...). I arrived therefore to do the final in too high stress conditions".

6.2. Comparisons between Causal Explanations Differentiating by the Perception of Control

The extracts we are now going to compare are characterized by differences for what concerns the perception of control, element that, coherent with what stated in literature and reported in paragraph 1.2., we retain predictive of the performance's quality.

Athlete 1: pessimistic with high perception of control

"...the psychological aspect was determining, in fact if I had concentrated more surely I wouldn't have had such a dreadful start and from there I would have accelerated without contracting too much. To see the finish line at the horizon and to listen to the muscles charged and explosive, that's what I should have done. Instead I let emotionality take me and did a mess."

In spite of the attribution to causes configuring a pessimistic style (emotionality, internal, stable and global cause; poor concentration: internal and global cause), the athlete's perception of control seems however quite high, in fact especially concentration is a mostly controllable dimension and the same athlete refers about a behavioural strategy that helps him concentrate. It seems that this strategy can be used also not to be overwhelmed by emotions (the reasoning could be: "if I had concentrated more" through the look at the horizon and the listening to muscles "I would have accelerated without contracting too much"). We can hypothesize therefore that the athlete believes to have the resources to do better in future performances.

Between the relevant PaCLIs manifesting the perception of control we point out: the presence of hypothetical, because it opens the possible alternative "If I had concentrated more", looking at the possibility of exercise greater control; the past conditional with the expression "I should have done" that demonstrates that the athlete is afterwards conscious of the behaviours to have in order to obtain a different outcome.

Athlete 2: pessimistic with low perception of control

"I already started previously with the idea of not wanting to do it (...) also because(...)I earlier lived an unpleasant situation (...) that brought me perturbation (...) I have a very strong sensitivity and this madeit possible that all the energies (...) that I needed to have for competition didn't come out. And thenI saw myself in a situation of discomfort (...). So I did this competition without will(...) I stop running because I say "I don't feel like, I don't feel like because I have too much tension (...) conditioning me (...)" (...) If the athlete is conditioned by some conditions precluding also his will to do well, surely the competition will go badly".

Causal factors: 1) strong sensitivity; 2) non pleasant situation; 3) perturbation; 4) low motivation.

The athlete, of whom we reported the analysis of the entire texts in paragraph 3., mentions 4 factors (strong sensitivity; non pleasant situation; perturbation; low motivation) in causal relation between them, to which, more or less explicitly, he attributes the failure.

The strong sensitivity, in the athlete's reasoning, seems superior in hierarchy to the causal factors 3 and 4 that come out after the interaction between cause 1 and cause 2. If there had not been the strong sensitivity at first, the non pleasant situation would not have brought to the negative consequences reported by the athlete. If we would use the CAVE technique, following Peterson's guidelines (Peterson et al, 1992), factors 1 and 2, because interacting between them, would bring to an average score that considers high scores of internality, stability and globality of the "non pleasant situation" factor. Also considering the "perturbation" and "low motivation" factors, we would obtain a Cave score deriving from the average of the relative scores of 4 con-causes that defines a medium-high pessimism profile.

Looking at a comparison of explanatory styles of the two athletes on the base of the dimensions of internality, stability and globality, we would deduce that the first one is more pessimistic than the second one; however considerations on the perception of control bring to see the explanatory style of the first athlete probably as more adaptive.

Many linguistic indicators, in fact, demonstrate that the second athlete doesn't think he has the resources to resist to unpleasant situations stimulating his sensitivity. The unpleasant situation that "brought perturbation" , and the energies that "didn't come out" become the subjects of the athlete's sentences during com petition, who only notes to be in difficulty "I saw myself in a situation of discomfort". Still are the "tensions" to condition the athlete who becomes a passive object to whom any action and even will of action is "precluded", which means that the athlete believes not to have any possibility of control about this situation to the point that, when he finds himself in such conditions, the competition will "surely" go bad.

The adverb "surely", refers to another element differentiating the second athlete from the first one, that is the rigidity of his attributive process that, also for this reason, appears to be less adaptive.

We remind that athlete 2, who reports a total powerlessness in reacting to negative conditions, also in the report of the positive performance, in which he recognises in concentration one of the possible causes of success, describes this mental state as non controllable and as logical consequence of other factors such as the psychophysical sensations lived in that occasion.

In some cases the athletes describe the experience of competition as if they had not been the protagonists of their actions but had to undergo them passively and, from a grammatical point of view, structure the sentences putting as subjects parts of their body, cognitive functions, states of mind or external elements.

We find it interesting to report an example about this because we believe that these syntax choices that "de-centre" the speaker in comparison with the event he is telling about, give indications about the perception of control. It is as if the athlete had lived competition in a passive way and reports the sensation of not being able to oppose resistance to external forces that caused the failure. About this, it is interesting to underline the reference to the causal factor "concentration" that can be considered more or less controllable depending on how it is lived by the athlete. There are in fact surely some strategies to improve concentration, however not all athletes seem conscious of being able to do something and describe this mental state more as something that happens (as can be seen also in the example of paragraph 3.) and that is also conditioned by non controllable factors. In the following example, also concentration is reported as subject of the sentence ("my concentration was not tuned"). The picture of "depersonalization" is completed by the description of the athlete's passive observation ("I felt as if…" "I felt that…") that body and legs hindered him to take any kind of initiative.

The theme of concentration, to our opinion lived as a non controllable factor, comes back with the metaphorical reference to what was "happening" in the athlete's mind. The choice of the verb "to happen, to occur" gives the idea of a mental state developing in spite of the athlete's will who arrives to refer to himself as a "little himself", new subject of the sentence, powerless about thoughts and voices to which "he begged to be quiet and give him a break".

This example is interesting also concerning the temporal collocation, of which we will bring examples in the next paragraph, because the athlete realizes about the inadequacy of his psychophysical state based on evaluations he makes There and Then in competition.

> I lost the swimming competition…at the beginning I couldn't explain it to myself, I was favourite and I didn't even make in third place, but besides this, I was disappointed and bewildered by my performance. In the moment I had to get into water I felt as if something inside me broke in an instant, my concentration was not tuned with the competition times. Once into water I felt my body empty, light and motionless…the legs didn't oppose any strength to water and made me stay still…I was swimming, but I was moving in slow motion. But the strangest thing was what was happening in my mind, a whirl of thoughts, a twisted skein, a chorus of dissonant voices, they were telling me three thousand things at a second and a little myself was begging them to be quiet, to give him a break at least until the end of competition, after that they could even have devoured him…a hell!
>
> In a few instants I thought about the disappointed face my coach would have done, the very person who understands me more who with his eyes is able to give me confidence and strength…and maybe I could have started crying…

The choice to put as grammatical subject one or more parts of the body or other factors external to the speaker, which indicates what we have here intended as "Focus on the Object" has often resulted associated, in the analysed texts, to the presence of a sort of de-personification in which the reference to the emerging of another self associates to the syntax choice.

As this regards, we report two examples:

> "in every other competition it seemed that on platform there wasn't me, but the skeleton of many years before, (…) the other two attempts was the other side of me who made them, who has fun to emerge only in the most important occasions so to create in me a strong belief of impossibility of success".

> "(…) that time I didn't believe…I didn't really think I couldn't make it and at the fist game it was clear that it would continue like that, and instead…one after the other my best shots mocked by an unexpected, unusual answer.
>
> A flabby hand taking from me any hope game after game and leaving me to watch incredulous, as if I would get out of my body and stop on the terracing".

In the first example the subject becomes first the "skeleton of many years before" and the "the other side" of the athlete, lived as an antagonist and as able to bring the speaker to the perception of powerlessness. In this example results evident the relation between the metaphorical reference to these parts of the Self, on which the text is centred, and the perception of poor control the athlete lives in this situation. The first fragment's metaphor is expressed through the verb "it seemed" followed by the subjunctive "that there wasn't me", while in the second extract a metaphor is proposed through a declarative with which the athlete reports about a flabby hand hindered him to play well and continue to hope in a recover. Also in the second fragment then a part of the athlete's body becomes subject; he reports, in this case trough the formula "as if +subjunctive" the sensation of having "come out of the body" and stopped any initiative ("as if…I stopped on the terracing"). The Linguistic Focus on the Object is also present in the expression "my best shots mocked…".

We observe further that the experience of depersonalization ("a flabby hand"; "come out of my body") and powerlessness ("it took any hope from me") occurred following some very high and rigid expectations ("that time I didn't believe…I really didn't think I wouldn't make it and at the first game it was clear t would have continued that way") that probably brought the athlete to underestimate the agonistic effort, to think a negative outcome impossible ("it left me incredulous").

6.3. Comparisons between Causal Explanations Differentiating by Temporal Collocation

The following two transcripts are very similar from the explanatory styles point of view, both athletes considering the same causal factors (practice; start).

However, while athlete X realizes in the There and Then of competition that the conditions that according to him will determine failure are occurring, athlete Y only makes an analysis afterwards. From a linguistic point of view this is evident in the use: from X's side of a series of verbs that can be placed in the Mind category used in a descriptive way ("I thought right away"; "seeing myself behind"; "I understood"; " I realized"; again "I understood") indicating how the athlete activated an evaluation of inadequacy in the There and Then of competition ("I thought right away that I didn't practice enough"), deriving by a causal conviction (the fact that a good performance depends on the respect of a standard relative to the quantity of practice), and maintained a self-evaluative attitude also during competition ("seeing myself behind") that brought him to understand ("I understood; "I realized") that he wasn't going to make it.

We believe that, even if both athletes report counter-performances, X's tendency to activate attributive reasoning during competition can represent a mental attitude limiting the quality of performance.

Athlete X
(…) Before starting I thought right away that I didn't practice enough. At the shot I remained on the blocks and, seeing myself behind I understood that the competition was compromised. I stiffened a lot because for me it was spontaneous to run by force, in frequency, to try to catch up. In fact I realized that I was too far behind and it was a desperate try. Actually I perfectly know that to run by force is worse, but when you are so distant from the adversaries it is difficult to maintain the coolness to stay relaxed and run easy. After a few meters I understood that there was nothing left to do, now also the progression was compromised.

Athlete Y

(…) I believe that the difference between this competition and those when I did well was mainly in the start: I started really badly, I probably lost at least a tenth that in 100meters is a lot. It was a period in which I didn't have much time to practice and especially to take care of the details: this brought me to disregard the specific practice of the start, exit from the blocks and first steps.

6.3.1. Example of an Athlete Who Activates the Attributive Process Afterwards to Explain the Good Performance and During Performance in the Case of Negative Performance

We now present two reports referring, respectively, to the worst and best performance of the same athlete, noting that the mental attitude with which the athlete faced the two competitions is different especially about the fact that only in the occasion of the worst competition he activated an attributive process and self-evaluation thoughts.

"Let's start from the competition, this one, when I had negative sensations. It was last week's Velletri competition…eh…the sensation was negative exactly from the sensitive point of view…exactly the foot contact on the ground…I felt that…it wasn't the right day. At each step I understood that the push was not my usual and optimal , and therefore I was conscious step after step that I was going to do a negative performance. Moreover I started conditioned by the fact that the track didn't make a good impression on me for my characteristics because it's kind of a hard track,…. These are the sensations…seen the period of the year there was a little disappointment thinking that maybe the phase of seasonal decline had already started and therefore seeing that there were still some competitions to do …a little disappointed from this point of view. That's all.".

The nature of cognitive processes described by the mental verbs ("I felt"; "I understood"; "I was conscious") and the tense in which these verbs are expressed let us understand that the athlete made a evaluative process in the There and Then of competition, this leading him to understand that he was not going to make a good performance because he realized the presence of a series of factors (foot contact; non optimal push; very hard track) predictive of negative performances based on his criteria.

The hard track, the low efficient foot contact and the factors leading the athlete to frame the performance in a negative day (so non stable factors, external in some cases and certainly not pervasive) represent causes about which a positive change is predictable. It comes out therefore a picture of high optimism of the athlete (who, even if not explicitly attributing the causes of failure to these factors, puts them in relation with the awareness that he was going to fail).

However, if we consider that such attributive process occurred in the There and Then of competition, when the athlete couldn't oppose any adaptive behaviour to these obstacles, the reflection characterizing him have possibly played a negative role. It is therefore important to consider the moment when the attributive process happens: reasoning conducting to the same causes can be very adaptive or, on the contrary, non-adaptive, depending on the margin of action it opens (are there times and conditions to put into act behaviours that resolve such causes?).

"The best competition was...the one of my all times best performance since I compete, it was the one of Casal del Marmo...eh...they were the regional society championships. I did second place in Heat...absolute first of master with a timing of 52''4. I was very exciting because let's say I beat my rival of all times who always beat me and this time I beat him so that's why it was wonderful, well, other than the fact of having done a good timing. So in this case sensations were...eh...wonderful! Brilliant start; I managed to maintain well up to the 250 meters then I realized also in the last 150 meters that...I had the right push in my legs and the necessary strength to arrive well. From an emotional point of view I wanted to underline the fact that...my mood...I'm quite anxious right, so it made me very, it impressed me a lot the fact of not having noticed about an adversary in front of me. Who was a much younger boy than us, because I was so taken by trying to contrast my rival's action who was in the next lane that I didn't even notice to have another one in front of me who made a timing for me unthinkable, he was around the 51 then...But I was so taken by this, by this sensation, by the fact that I didn't have to be reached by the rival...that...well! Well ,it stroke me in a positive way. That was the maximum concentration ".

When he talks about the positive competition the athlete shows to have done in that competition an evaluation of his own possibilities of succeeding in it but more immediate (and not prolonged in time) as demonstrated by the expression "I noticed" and not any more "I understood" "I was conscious".

This indicates also the immersion in competition (during which something is realized, of which evidently one was not thinking about) and the absence of distraction from self-evaluative thoughts or relative to an explanatory reasoning.

This is demonstrated also by the use of the simple past tense instead of imperfect.

Moreover, the athlete goes back to using the verb "to realize" in negative form indicating the involvement in a competition with an adversary , as not even to realize that another athlete was in front. The description of this competition, where also an evaluation of the positive sensations is made ("the sensations were wonderful"; "the push was right") intensely involving the athlete("I was so taken"), makes it similar to an experience of flow in which athletes often report to have lived very positive sensations and not to have realized about some elements of the situation.

7. CONCLUSION

In this contribution we tried to put the accent on some cognitive and linguistic aspects regarding the way in which athletes make and verbally report their explanatory/attributive reasoning. Believing that these aspects can sometimes enrich the understanding of attributive processes, we proposed and presented a system of analysis that focuses the attention on PaCLIs, showing how an athlete's linguistic choices in reporting his experience can convey (besides internality, stability and globality of causal factors) information about the complexity of the causal reasoning, the rigidity of such reasoning, about the control he perceives on the performance and about his mental attitude at the time of competition and in the moment when he tells about it, both moments in which the athlete can activate his attributive process.

Even without having data confirming our predictions at disposal, we advanced the hypothesis that the differences the athletes show to have concerning the proposed dimensions of analysis can be significant also in terms of future performances and motivations.

To show these qualitative aspects, on one side we presented detailed examples, taken from the corpus of a research still in progress, where the athletes' attributive processes have been analysed through the PaCLI method and, on the other side, we compared the athletes' explanations that didn't differentiate in internality, stability and globality of the factors they identified as causes, but for other aspects emerging from their words and that would make us hypothesize more or less adaptive mental attitudes.

We tried to give examples showing how some attributive processes aspects can be interpreted referring to the degree of certainty (Epistemic Category of Knowledge, Unknown and Belief), to the cognitive-perceptual world (Semantic Categories of Body, Heart and Mind) and to the use, (world-constitutive or descriptive), the speaker makes of mental verbs referring to the attributive process thath can be put into act at the moment of the report or in the There and Then of competition, object of the same report.

The grid we obtained following the qualitative analysis of a corpus of 200 texts through this approach, is made of dimensions that can be studied on the base of these interpretative criteria: to frame the speaker's attitude basing on Epistemic Categories allows to get information about the degree of rigidity of his attributions.

In fact, the prevalence of Knowledge in the statements when the athlete explains the causal relations between specific factors and consequences of success and failure can indicate the rigidity of his thoughts implied in the attributive process. On the contrary, the category of Belief characterizes the statements of those athletes proposing more complex and less deterministic explanations (attributional complexity) and feel the need to specify that these explanations are hypothesis, suppositions that can be integrated with other possible interpretations of the event.

It is interesting to propose a reading of attributive processes on the base of Epistemic Categories also to describe a phenomenon we could observe quite often in the analyzed texts, that consists of some athlete's tendency to report episodes in which their expectations did not apply and, consequently, their system of convictions were questioned to the point of inducing them to ask themselves which could be the causes of unexpected failures. In these cases the athletes, not finding confirmation to their rigid expectations deriving from as much rigid convictions concerning the relation between a causal factor and a considered logic consequence (but that in this case doesn't happen), go from statements that can be framed in the category of Knowledge to more or less explicit questions in the surface structure of the conversation that collocate the cognitive attitude in the category of the Unknown. Let's make the hypothesis, for example, of an athlete who always thought that an improvement of the strength parameters was the determining factor for the improvement of speed, that is an athlete who identifies a strong causal relation between strength and speed and expects, following an increasing of load in practice, a sure improvement of his performance in the 100 meters in competition. When this athlete won't see this relation confirmed by facts, that is to say when he won't obtain the expected results even though he improved the strength, he will have to question his conviction and identify other possible factors able to condition his results.

If an athlete's convictions are very rigid and attached to a limited number of factors, it is probable that the passage from the world of Knowledge (rigid convictions) to the one of the Unknown (not knowing of alternative explanations) is quite abrupt and coincides with a tendency to think over and over characterized by a series of questions the athlete makes to himself trying to search for a possible cause that seems hardly identifiable in a situation where what happened is unexplainable for the athlete.

If the epistemic attitude at first were instead that of Belief, it's possible that the athlete, also in front of anexpected outcome, can integrate his attributive beliefs, not expressed as absolute truths, looking at a wider choice of possible explanations without coming to the conclusion that what happened is unexplainable.

In the chapter we say that could be relevant for the interpretation of attributive processes also to identify the moment when they develop, that is if the causal reasoning is made by the athlete at the moment of reporting, therefore a posteriori, or if instead it develops during the same competition about which he is talking. About this, we thought relevant two aspects that can be showed through Bongelli & Zuczkowski's model (2008b): 1) the distinction between the world-constitutive and the descriptive use of mental verbs referring to attributive processes; 2) the prevalence of the Semantic Category of Heart, Mind or Body.

When the athlete makes the attributive reasoning in the Here and Now he will tend to use mental verbs referring to such reasoning in a world-constitutive way (1), or not to use them (2):

1) I think/I retain that the cause of failure was X
   • mpp: (here and now I say that)
   • wcp: here and now I think, retain, that
   • dp: the cause of failure was X
2) The cause of failure was X
   • mpp: (here and now I say that)
   • wcp: (here and now I know, remember that)
   • the cause of failure was X

If instead the attributive reasoning of the There and Then of competition is reported, the mental verbs are necessarily explicated and proposed with descritptive use:

   • mpp: here and now I say that
   • dp: there and then I thought, retained, evaluated that
   • dp: I wouldn't make it (because X occurred)

Very often, as emerged from a previous experiment (Merola, 2008) in which comparisons between the athletes' reports of their best and worst performances were made, those concerning failures differentiate from the ones about the best performances exactly in reference to a different temporal collocation of the attributive processes.

The fact that an athlete reports a description of competition characterized mostly by sensations and without a self-evaluative mental attitude, or reasoning in terms of cause and effect accompanying the reading of the situation in the There and Then of competition, that is a prevalence of the semantic category of Heart in the There and Then of competition and an interpretation of the causes made only afterwards in the Here and Now of reporting, resulted often associated to optimal performances.

Works on the Flow indicate, between the factors that characterize this experience, a high involvement in the task that leads to a fusion between action and conscience, the absence of self-observation and a complete focusing of attention on the activity in progress (Jackson & Csikszentmihalyi, 1999): actually, when the world of Mind is reported also referring to the description of the There and Then of competition, it is important to distinguish between a cognitive activity of evaluation or causal reasoning and a mental programming activity on what needs to be done, that occurs when the athlete is concentrated.

About this, basing on theoretical contributions deriving from different scientific approaches, we think that experience a competition through Feeling (Heart Semantic Category) more than through Thinking (Mind Semantic Category) is more functional because, especially in the technical specialties the conscious thought , particularly that of self-monitoring, can block the automaticity of gestures and create self-occurring prophecies or vicious circles like that of anxiety, where the interpretation of a state of activation feeds the cognitive anxiety and this on its turn is negatively reflected on a physical level and on the performance. The Catastrophe Theory (Hardy, 1996) actually attributes to the cognitive component of anxiety, and therefore to thoughts of inadequacy of physiologic state, and not to the same physiologic state, that is the somatic anxiety, the cause of the negative relation between elevated state of activation and performance.

Some athletes describe concentration as a not totally controllable "event" deriving exactly from a state of grace characterized by very positive sensations; other athletes associate concentration to conscious attempts to focus the attention on key elements of performance. The greatest enemy of concentration and positive sensations, that are in some cases considered as the factors determining it and in other cases as consequences of this mental state, seems to be the thought of evaluation of the There and Then of competition that often derives from predetermined attributive convictions. That is, when an athlete is convinced of a causal relation between a factor and a negative outcome, at the moment when this factor occurs he is brought to negatively evaluate the situation, to "see himself in difficulty" and to think, always in the There and Then of competition, not to be able to make it (self-fulfilling prophecy).

Thoughts concerning factors that at the moment of competition are no more controllable, as for example the atmospheric conditions, rain, opposite wind or one's own athletic conditions ("there's too much wind"; "I'm not fit", "I've not trained enough", etc.) that become dangerous cause-effect reasoning, as "if there is favourable wind I won't be able to improve my personal", "I haven't trained enough to be able to hope for something good", etc. are harmful because they refer to non controllable aspects of the performance (one cannot make the rain stop nor recover the lost practices) and the risk is to consider too rigidly the cause-effect relation between negative situation and performance seen as necessarily negative.

The Feeling modality seems to be the best also in the moments previous to competition itself. We reported examples of athletes who, referring to thoughts and expectations pre-competition, list a series of factors that, based on their attributive convictions, would have previewed a success and that instead, in the case of the reported performance, lead to unpredictable failures. These athletes base their expectations, that as we said are not confirmed by the performance's outcome, on cause-effect reasoning that appear to make sense on a purely logical level but that evidently don't' have a particular predictive value.

Castelfranchi (2004), in the ambit of research on Artificial Intelligence, talks about the difference between the expressions "I believe I can do it" and "I feel I can do it" explaining that the second one refers to expectations deriving from somatic information besides from cognitive apparatus. The author underlines then the difference between an unconscious and automatic re-evocation of associated sensations as system of implicit and not arguable evaluation of events, typical of the "I feel I can do it " and the purely cognitive evaluations based on reasoning and facts.

Reasoning and cognitive evaluations supporting the athletes' expectations and that can be put in the semantic category of Mind, seem, also by observing our corpus's texts (where the athlete report previews that are not always confirmed), less predictive about the occurrence of successes than what the sensations of succeeding in it are (Heart Semantic Category).

One could hypothesize that the athlete can allow himself only afterwards (of competition) to assume a mental attitude that can be put in the category of Mind, putting in act a cognitive analysis of what worked out and what didn't in order to change and put into act adaptive behaviours for the future events. It seems instead important that the athlete's psychological state before competition, and therefore in the moment when expectations grow, and during its course, is characterized by experiences expressible through verbal terms that can be pictured in the semantic category of Heart. The logical reasoning risks to create thoughts and rigid expectations that bring the athlete's attention, also during competition, to verify the presence of other factors considered determining, to evaluate the inadequacy of the situation and of the own state compared to previously established criteria on the base of the own attributive convictions.

The "Feeling" doesn't request instead supplementary efforts of control of the own thought or the research of elements confirming that everything is all right: as in the flow experience the athlete is simply involved in a process in which everything comes to him automatically, in which he doesn't need to control his thought.

On the other hand, also the techniques of mental training proposed by sport psychologists and especially the cognitive strategies as the Five Step Strategy (Singer, 1986; 2000; Singer, et al., 1991), suggested to face the pre-competition in the self-paced competitions, aim at focusing the athletes' attention on principal elements of the task or situation (focusing of attention) and on the development of mental multi-sensorial images, so to start a virtuous concentration process that becomes automatic, that doesn't request, once learned, cognitive efforts and that doesn't allow the intrusion of disturbing thoughts of self-evaluation.

Once the athlete inserts in his pre-competition routine this mental habit, trying to revive sensations linked to previous situations of success, starting to have a series of behaviours as breathing control, listening to his own heartbeat and assuming a certain body posture, developing multi-sensorial mental images and concentrating on one detail of the situation, he will not have to make particular cognitive efforts to get rid of insidious thoughts concerning doubts about himself, or the evaluation of the situation.

Also Wegner (1994) Wenzlaff and Bates (2000), concerning the ironic processes of mental control, underline how the conscious attempts of sending away insidious thoughts are often not very effective and instead can produce opposite effects; some sport psychologists (Gardner & Moore, 2003) suggested that an alternative or supplemental approach to the enhancement of athletic performance may be achieved through strategies and techniques that target the development of mindful (non-judgmental) present-moment acceptance of internal experiences such as thoughts, feelings, and physical sensations, along with a clarification of valued goals and enhanced attention to external cues, responses, and contingencies that are required for optimal athletic performance.

The review of sport psychology literature about attributive styles, besides supporting the necessity to consider categories of analysis and dimensions allowing to understand the attributive processes in their complexity and about the peculiarities of the sportive situation, showed the opportunity to recover the dimension of "controllability" that is absent in the model of explanatory styles. This opportunity emerged also from the analysis of texts of our corpus that often seem to differentiate under this aspect more than about the dimensions defining optimism and pessimism.

We suggest in a purely observational way , because we don't have quantitative data supporting it, a final consideration concerning the tendency to a co-variation, in the athletes' reports, between some elements defining the dimensions of suggested analysis: in these we can observe how often the rigidity of the attributive process associates to a perception of poor control ("if it is sure that Y follows X, my space of action is limited") and to a temporal collocation in the There and Then of competition (because of a selective attention, if an athlete tends to think an effect strictly linked to a cause to the point of excluding other possible causes, it is probable that he will realize more easily about the presence of such cause in competition, or even he will behave in such a way as to make it more probable. Once he realizes the presence of a causal factor considered so powerful, it is reasonable that the athlete puts his mental effort in an attributive reasoning of the kind" because X then now Y will happen", and this preview will be much more felt the more rigid is the athlete's way of thinking.

The comparison between the athletes' reports of best or worse performances, together with the above mentioned considerations about the possible relation between rigidity of the attributive process, poor perception of control and collocation in the There and Then of competition, and to the fact that the predictions coming from reasoning often are not confirmed by results, suggest, coherent with scientific literature, that the distinction between the "Feeling" and the "Thinking" can constitute a possible reading key to interpret the expectations, mental attitude in competition and attributive processes.

REFERENCES

Abramson, L.Y., Seligman, M.E.P., & Teasdale, J. (1978). Learned helplessness in humans: critique and reformulation. Journal of Abnormal Psychology, 87, 49-74.

Adler, J.M., Kissel, E.C., and McAdams, D.P. (2006). Emerging from the CAVE: Attributional Style and the Narrative Study of Identity in Midlife Adults. Cognitive Therapy and Research, 30,1, 39-51.

Aijmer K. (1997). I think –an English modal particle, in Swan T., Westvik O. J. (eds.) Modality in Germanic languages. Historical and comparative perspectives, Mouton de Gruyter, Berlino-New York, 1-47.

Aikhenvald A. (2004). Evidentiality, Oxford University Press, Oxford.

Anderson, C.A. (1983). Motivational and performance deficits in interpersonal setting: The effect of attributional style. Journal of Personality and Social Psychology, 45, 1136-1147.

Austin J. L. (1962). How to do things with words, Oxford University Press, London.

Benson, M. J. (1989). Attributional measurement techniques: Classification and comparison of approaches for measuring causal dimensions. The Journal of Social Psychology, 129, 307–323.

Bertuccelli-Papi M. (1987). Probabily: a Pragmatic Account. Versus: quaderni di studi semiotici, 46, 59-68.

Bertuccelli-Papi M. (2001). Where Grice feared to thread: inferring attitudes and emotions, in G. Cosenza (ed.), Paul Grice's Paul Grice's Heritage, Brepols, Turnhout, 247-281.

Biddle, S. J. H., Hanrahao, S. J., & Sellars, C. N. (2001). Attributions: Past, present, and future. In R. N. Singer, H. A. Hausenblas, & C. M. Janellc (Eds.), Handbook of sport psychology, 2nd ed (pp. 444–471). New York: Wiley.

Biddle, S.J.H. (1993). Attribution research and sport psychology. In Singer, R.N., Murphey, M., & Tennant, L.K. (Eds.). Handbook of research on sport psychology (437-464). New York: Macmillan.

Biddle, S.J.H., Hanrahan, S.J., & Sellars, C.N. (2001). Attributions: Past, present, and future. In Singer, R.N., Hausenblas, H.A., & Janellc, C.M. (Eds.). Handbook of sport psychology, 2nd ed. (444-471). New York: Wiley.

Bongelli R., Zuczkowski A (2008a) Perceptual and Cognitive Linguistic Indicators, paper presented at XVI Symposium on perception and cognition, Kanizsa memorial lecture. Università degli studi di Trieste, october 2008.

Bongelli R., Zuczkowski A. (2008b) Indicatori Linguistici Percettivi E Cognitivi. Roma: Aracne.

Brawley, L.R., & Roberts, G.C. (1984). Attributions in sport: Research foundations, characteristics, and limitations. In Silva, J.M., & Weinberg, R.S. (Eds.), Psychological foundations of sport, 197-213. Champaign. IL: Human Kinetics.

Brosschot, J. F., & Thayer, J. F. (2004). Worry, perserverative thinking and health. In L. R. Temoshok (Ed.), Biobehavioral perspectives on health and disease (Vol. 6). New York: Harwood Academic.

Bukowski, W.M., & Moore, D. (1980). Winners' and Losers' Attributions for Success and Failure in a Series of Athletic Events. Journal of Sport Psychology, 2, 195-210.

Cacciari C., Levorato C. (1999), I cinque sensi e la loro traduzione linguistica: uno studio sui verbi dell'esperienza sensoriale, in A. Zuczkowski (ed.), Semantica percettiva. Rapporti tra percezione visiva e linguaggio, Istituti Editoriali e Poligrafici Internazionali, Pisa-Roma, pp. 39-68.

Cacciari C., Levorato C. (2003), "Res accendent lumina rebus". La descrizione dell'esperienza sensoriale, ovvero dei rapporti tra percezione e linguaggio, in U. Savardi, A. Mazzocco (eds.), Figura e sfondo. Temi e variazioni per Paolo Bozzi, Cluep, Padova, 179-200.

Cacciari C., Levorato C. (a cura di) (1992), Per una semantica ingenua dei verbi di percezione, Versus: quaderni di studi semiotici, 59/60, 121-139.

Cappelli G. (2007a). Translating English verbs of cognitive attitude into Italian: the difficulties of mapping two apparently equivalent complex systems, in M. Bertuccelli Papi, G. Cappelli, S. Masi (eds), Lexical complexity: theoretical assessment and translational perspectives, Plus Pisa University Press, Pisa, pp. 1-26.

Cappelli G. (2007b). Antinomy and verbs of cognitive attitude: When know is the opposite of think and believe, paper presented at IPRA conference, Goteborg, Sweden, 8-13 July 2007.

Cappelli G. (2007c). "I reckon I know how Leonardo da Vinci must have felt..." Epistemicity, evidentiality and English verbs of cognitive attitude, Pari Publishing, Pari (GR).

Cappelli G.(2005). Modulating Attitudes via Adverbs: a cognitivepragmatic approach to the lexicalisation of epistemological evaluation, in M. Bertuccelli, Papi (ed.), Studies in the semantics of Lexical combinatory patterns, Plus Pisa University Press, Pisa, 213-278.

Carston R. (2002). Thoughts and Utterances. The Pragmatics of Explicit Communication, Blackwell Publishing, Oxford.

Carver, C. S., & Scheier, M. F. (1982). Outcome expectancy, locus of attribution for expectancy, and self-directed attention as determinants of evaluations and performance. Journal of Experimental Social Psychology, 18, 184-200.

Castelfranchi (2004) Castelfranchi - "Provare per Credere". Per una teoria del sentire e delle valutazioni affettivo intuitive. Proceedings of the Italian Congress of Experimental Psychology, AIP, Sciacca, September 18-20 2004.

Castelfranchi, C. (1998). To Believe and to Feel: the case of «needs», in D. Canamero. Emotional and intelligent: the tangled knot of cognition. Papers from the 1998 AAAI Fall Symposium, 55-60. Menlo Park, Cal.: AAAI Press.

Chafe W. (1996). Evidentiality in English conversation and academic writing, in W. Chafe, J. Nichols (eds.), Evidentiality: the linguistic coding of epistemology, N. J. Ablex, Norwood, 261-72.

Chafe, W., Nichols, J. (1996). Evidentiality: the linguistic coding of epistemology, N. J., Ablex, Norwood.

Clifford, M. M. (1986). The effects of ability, strategy, and effort attributions for educational, business, and athletic failure. British Journal of Educational Psychology, 56, 169–179.

Conversazionali, 37, indirizzo web: www.tecnicheconversazionali.it

Corr, P.J., & Gray, J.A. (1995). Attributional style, socialization and cognitive ability as predictors of sales success. Personality and Individuals Differences, 18, 241-252.

Covington, M. V., & Omelich, C. L. (1979). Effort: The double-edged sword in school achievement. Journal of Educational Psychology, 71, 169–182.

Croft W., Cruse A. (2004). Cognitive Linguistics, Cambridge University Press, Cambridge.

Crossley, M. (2000). Introducing narrative psychology. Buckingham: Open University Press.

Csíkszentmihályi, M. (1990). Flow: The Psychology of Optimal Experience. New York: Harper and Row.

Csikszentmihalyi, M., Larson, R. (1984).Being Adolescent: Conflict and growth in the teenage years. Basic Books, New York.

Curtis, K. A. (1992). Altering beliefs about the importance of strategy. Journal of Applied Social Psychology, 22, 953–972

Den Boer, D.-J., Kok, G., Hospers, H. J., Gerards, F. M., & Strecher, V. J. (1991). Health education strategies for attributional retraining and self-efficacy improvement. Health Education Research, 6, 239–248

Faulkner, G., & Finlay, S.-J. (2002). It's not what you say, it's the way that you say it! Conversation analysis: A discursive methodology. Quest, 54, 49–66.

Fetzer A. (2002). Communicative intentions in context, in A. Fetzer, C. Meierkord (eds.), Rethinking sequentiality: Linguistics meets conversational interaction, Benjamins, Amsterdam, pp. 37-69.

Fetzer, A. (2004). Recontextualizing Context: Grammaticality meets Appropriateness, Amsterdam, Benjamins.

Fetzer, A. (2007). Cognitive verbs in political discourse, hand out, IADA Conference 2007, Munster.

Forsterling, F. (1988). Attribution theory in clinical psychology. Chichester: Wiley.

Fresco, D. M., Rytwinski, N. K., & Craighead, L. W. (2007). Explanatory flexibility and negative life events interact to predict depression symptoms. Journal of Social and Clinical Psychology, 26,5, 595-608.

Fresco, D. M., Rytwinski, N. K., & Craighead, L. W. (2007). Explanatory flexibility and negative life events interact to predict depression symptoms. Journal of Social and Clinical Psychology, 26, 595-608.   .

Fresco, D. M.,Williams, N. L., & Nugent, N. R. (2006). Flexibility and negative affect: Examining the associations of explanatory flexibility and coping flexibility to each other and to depression and anxiety. Cognitive Therapy and Research, 30, 201-210.

Gardner, F.L., & Moore. Z.E. (2003). Theoretical foundation for Mindfulness-Acceptance-Commitment (MAC) based performance enhancement. Paper presented at the Meeting of the Annual Conference of the American Psychological Association. Toronto.

Givon T. (1993), English Grammar: a Function-Based Introduction, Benjamins, Amsterdam.

Gordon, R.A. (2008) Attributional style and athletic performance: Strategic optimism and defensive pessimism. Psychology of Sport and Exercise 9:3, 336-350.

Gordon, R.A. (2008). Attributional style and athletic performance: Strategic optimism and defensive pessimism. Psychology of Sport and Exercise, 9, 336-350.

Grove, J.R., & Pargman, D. (1984). Behavioural consequences of effort versus ability orientations to Interpersonal competition. Australian Journal of Science and Medicine in Sport, 16, 16-20.

Grove, J.R., & Pargman, D. (1986). Attributions and performance during competition. Journal of Sport Psychology, 8, 129-134.

Hanrahan, S.J., Grove, J.R., & Hattie, J.A. (1989). Development of a questionnaire measure of sport-related attributional style. International Journal of Sport Psychology, 20, 114-134.

Hardy, L. (1996). A test of catastrophe models of anxiety and sports performance against multidimensional anxiety theory models using the method of dynamic differences. Anxiety, Stress & Coping, 9, 1, 69 - 86

Heider, F. (1944). Social perception and phenomenal causality. Psychological Review, 51, 358–374.

Heider, F. (1958). The psychology of interpersonal relations. New York: Wiley.

Helton, W. S., Dember, W. N., Warm, J. S., & Matthews, G. (2000). Optimism, pessimism, and false failure feedback effects on vigilance performance. Current Psychology, 18, 311–325.

Holschuh, J. P., Nist, S. L., & Olejnik, S. (2001). Attributions to failure: The effects of effort, ability, and learning strategy use on perceptions of future goals and emotional responses. Reading Psychology, 22, 153–173.

Huspek M. (1989). Linguistic variability and power: an analysis of you know/I think variation in working-class speech, Journal of Pragmatics, 13, 661-83.

Ifantidou E. (2001). Evidentials and Relevance, John Benjamins, Amsterdam.

Jackson, B., Sellers, R. M., & Peterson, C. (2002). Pessimistic explanatory style moderates the effect of stress on physical illness. Personality and Individual Differences, 32, 567–573.

Jackson, S., Csikszentmihalyi, M. (1999). Flow in sports: the keys to optimal experiences and performances. Champaign, IL: Human Kinetics.

Johnsen, B. H., Thayer, J. F., Laberg, J. C., Wormnes, B., Raadal, M., Skaret, E., Kvale, G., Berg, E. (2003). Attentional and physiological characteristics of patients with dental anxiety. Journal of Anxiety Disorders, 17, 75–87.

Jones, E. E., & Davis, K. E. (1965). From acts to dispositions: The attribution process in person perception. In L. Berkowitz, Advances in experimental social psychology, 2, 219–266). New York: Academic Press.

Karkkanen E. (1996), The marking of epistemic stance in American English conversational discourse. Paper presented at IPRA conference, 4-9 July 1996, Mexico City.

Kelley, H. H. (1967). Attribution theory in social psychology. In D. Levine, Nebraska symposium on motivation, 15, 192–240). Lincoln, NE: University of Nebraska Press

Kuhl, J. (1981). Motivational and functional helplessness: The moderating effect of state versus action orientation. Journal of Personality and Social Psychology, 40, 155-170.

Kukla, A. (1972). Foundations of an attributional theory of performance. Psychological Review, 79, 454-470.

Lazarus, R., & Folkman, S. (1984). Stress, appraisal, and coping. New York: Springer.

Lee, F., & Peterson, C. (1997) Content Analysis of Archival Data. Journal of Consulting and Clinical Psychology, 65, 6, 959-969.

Leith, L.M., & Prapavessis, H. (1989). Attributions of causality and dimensionality associated with sport outcomes in objectively evaluated and subjectively evaluated sports international. Journal of Sport Psychology, 20, 224-234.

Lieblich, A., Tuval-Mashiach, R., Zilber, T. (1998). Narrative research: Reading, Analysis and Interpretation. Newbury Park, CA: Sage.

Likert, R. (1932). A technique for the measurement of attitudes. Archives of Psychology, 140.

Linehan, M. M. (1993). Cognitive Behavioral Treatment of Borderline Personality Disorder. New York: Guilford Press.

Maier, S.F. and Seligman, M.E.P. (1976). Learned helplessness: Theory and evidence. Journal of Experimental Psychology: General, 105, 3-46.

Martin-Krumm, C.P., Philippe G. Sarrazin, P.G., Peterson, C., & Famose, J.P. (2003). Explanatory style and resilience after sports failure. Personality and Individual Differences, 35, 1685–1695.

McAuley, E. & Gross, J.B. (1983). Perceptions of causality in sport: An application of the causal dimension scale. Journal of Sport Psychology, 5, 72-76.

McAuley, E., Russell, D., & Gross, J.B. (1983). Affective Consequences of Winning and Losing: An Attributional Analysis. Journal of Sport and Exercise Psychology, 5,3, 278-287.

Merola, G. (2008). Individuare gli stili esplicativi con il metodo ILPEC. Poster presented at the Italian Congress of Experimental Psychology, AIP. Padava.

Moore, M. T. & Fresco, D. M. (2007). Depressive Realism and Attributional Style: Implications for individuals at risk for depression. Behavior Therapy, 38, 144-154.

Munton, A.G., Silvester, J., Stratton, P., & Hanks, H. (1999). Attributions in Action: A practical approach to coding qualitative data, Chichester: Wiley.

Mushin I. (2001). Evidentiality and Epistemological Stance, John Benjamins, Amsterdam.

Nicolini P. (2000). Mente e linguaggio: la proposizione costitutiva di mondo, Clueb, Bologna.

Nuyts J. (2001). Epistemic modality, Language and Conceptualization, John Benjamins, Amsterdam-Philadelphia.

Onishi, M. (1997). The grammar of mental predicates in Japanese. Language Sciences, 19,3, 219-233.

Orbach, I., Singer, R., & Murphey, M. (1997). Changing attributions with an attribution training technique related to basketball dribbling. The Sport Psychologist, 11, 294–304.

Orbach, I., Singer, R., & Price, S. (1999). An attribution training program and achievement in sport. The Sport Psychologist, 13, 69–82.

Papafragou, A., Li, P., Choi, Y., & Han, C. (2007). Evidentiality in language and cognition. Cognition, 103,2, 253-299.

Pennebaker J. W., Slatcher R. B, Cindy K. C. (2005). Linguistic markers of Psychological State through Media Interviews: John Kerry and John Edwards in 2004, Al Gore in 2000, Analysis of Social Issues and Public Policy, 5, 197-204.

Pennebaker, J.W. (2002). What our words can say about us: Toward a broader language psychology. Psychological Science Agenda, 15, 8-9. A brief and light summary of recent findings concerning the power of words in revealing personality and social situations.

Persson G. (1993). Think in a panchronic perspective, Studia Neophilologica, 63, 3-18.

Peterson, C. (1991). Further thoughts on explanatory style. Psychological Inquiry, 2, 50–57.

Peterson, C. (2000). The future of optimism. American Psychologist, 55, 44–54.

Peterson, C., & Seligman, M. E. P. (1984). Causal explanations as a risk factor for depression: Theory and evidence. Psychological Review, 91, 347–374.

Peterson, C., & Steen, T. A. (2002). Optimistic explanatory style. In C. R. Snyder & S. J. Lopez (Eds.), Handbook of positive psychology (pp. 244-256). New York: Oxford University Press.

Peterson, C., Luborsky, L., and Seligman, M.E.P. (1983). Attributions and depressive mood shifts: A case study using the symptom-context method. Journal of Abnormal Psychology, 92, 96-103.

Peterson, C., Schulman, P., Castellon, C., & Seligman, M. E. P. (1992). CAVE: Content analysis of verbatim explanations. In C.P. Smith (Ed.), Motivation and personality: Handbook of thematic content analysis (pp. 383-392). New York: Cambridge University Press

Peterson, C., Semmel, A., von Baeyer, C., Abramson, L.T., Metalsky, G.I., & Seligman, M.E.P. (1982). The Attributional Style Questionnaire. Cognitive Therapy and Research, 6, 287-300.

Petöfi J. S. (1973), Towards an Empirically Motivated Grammar Theory of Verbal Texts, Bielefelder Papiere zur Linguisik und Literaturwissenschaft, Universitat Bielefeld.

Petöfi J. S. (1980), Interpretazione e teoria del testo, in G. Galli (Ed.), Interpretazione e contesto, Marietti, Torino, pp. 21-43.

Petöfi J. S. (1981). La struttura della comunicazione in Atti 20, 17-38, in G. Galli (Ed.), Interpretazione e strutture, Marietti, Torino, pp. 101-157.

Petöfi J. S. (2004), Scrittura e interpretazione. Introduzione alla testologia semiotica dei testi verbali, Carocci, Roma.

Poligrafici Internazionali, Pisa – Roma, pp. 733, 748.

Polkinghorne, D. (1995). Narrative configuration in qualitative analysis. In J. A. Hatch, & R. Wisniewski (Eds.), Life history and narrative (pp. 5–24). London: Falmer Press.

Prapavessis, H., & Carron, A.V. (1988). Learned helplessness in sport. The Sport Psychologist, 2, 189-201.

Rees T, Ingledew, D. K., Hardy L. (2005) Attribution in sport psychology: seeking congruence between theory, research and practice. Psychology of Sport and Exercise 6, 189–204

Rees, T., Ingledew, D.K.,& Hardy, L. (2005). Attribution in sport psychology: Seeking congruence between theory, research and practice. Psychology of Sport and Exercise, 6, 189-204.

Rettew, D., & Reivich, K. (1995). Sports and explanatory style. In G. M. Buchanan, & M. E. P. Seligman (Eds.), Explanatory style (pp. 173–185). Hillsdale, NJ: Erlbaum.

Robinson, D. W. (1990). An attributional analysis of student demoralization in physical education settings. Quest, 42, 27–39.

Ross, A.J., Davies, J.B., Clarke, P. (2004). Attributing To Positive And Negative Sporting Outcomes: A Structural Analysis. Athletic Insight, 6,3.

Russell, D. (1982). The causal dimension scale: A measure of how individuals perceive causes. Journal of Personality and Social Psychology, 42, 1137–1145.

Schulman, P. (1995). Explanatpry style and achievement in school and work. In Buchanan, G.M., & Seligman, M.E.P. (Eds.), Explanatory style (pp. 159-171). Hillsdale, NJ: Lawrence Erlbaum Associates.

Scritti in onore di Anna Arfelli Galli, Eum, Macerata, pp. 217-238.

Seligman, M. E. P., Nolen-Hoeksema, S., Thornton, K. M., & Thornton, N. (1990). Explanatory style as a mechanism of disappointing athletic performance. Psychological Science, 1, 143–146.

Seligman, M.E.P. (1990). Learned optimism. New York: Knopf.

Seligman, M.E.P., & Schulman, P. (1986). Explanatory style as a predictor of productivity and quitting among life insurance salesmen. Journal of Personality and Social Psychology, 50, 832-838.

Seligman, M.E.P., Peterson, C., Schulman, P., and Castellon, C. (1992). The Explanatory Style Scoring Manual. In C.P. Smith (Ed.), Motivation and Personality: Handbook of Thematic Content Analysis. Cambridge University Press, 383.

Shinzato, R. (2004). Some observations concerning mental and speech act verbs. Journal of Pragmatics 36, 861-882.

Sholl B., Leslie A. (1999). Modularity, development, and 'theory of mind', Mind & Language, 14, 131–153.

Simon-Vandenbergen A. M. (1996). Image-building through modality: the case of political interviews, Discourse & Society, 7, 389-415.

Simon-Vandenbergen A. M. (1997). Modal (un)certainty in political discourse: a functional account", Language Sciences, 19, 341-356.

Simon-Vandenbergen A. M. (1998a). I think and its Dutch equivalents in parliamentary debates, in S. Johansson, S. Oksefjell, (eds.), Corpora and cross linguistic research. Theory, method and case studies, Rodopi, Amsterdam-Atlanta, 297-331.

Simon-Vandenbergen A. M. (1998b). The modal methaphor I don't think: system and text, in J. Van der Auwera, F. Durieux, L. (eds.), English as a human language. To honour Louis Goossens, Lincom Europa, München, 312-24.

Singer, R. N.; Cauraugh, J. H.; Murphey, M.; Chen, D.; Lidor, R. (1991). Attentional control, distractors, and motor performance. Human performance, 4, 55-69.

Singer, R. N.; Suwanthada, S.. (1986) The generalizability effectiveness of a learning strategy on achievement in related closed motor skills. Research Quarterly for Exercise and Sport, 57,3, 205-214.

Singer, R.N. (2000). Performance and human factors: Considerations about cognition and attention for self-paced and externally-paced events. Ergonomics, 43, 1661-1680.

Sinnott & Biddle, 1998) Sinnott, K., & Biddle, S. (1998). Changes in attributions, perceptions of success and intrinsic motivation after attribution retraining in children's sport. International Journal of Adolescence and Youth, 7, 137–144

Sparkes, A. C. (1999). Exploring body narratives. Sport, Education and Society, 4, 17–30.

Sperber D. (1997). Intuitive and reflective beliefs, Mind and Language, 12, 67-83.

Stein D., Wright S. (eds.) (1995), Subjectivity and subjectivisation, Cambridge University Press, Cambridge.

Stratton, P., Munton, A.G., Hanks, H., Heard, D.H., & Davidson, C. (1988). Leeds Attributional Coding System (LACS) Manual, Leeds: LFRTC.

Tennen, H., Affleck, G., Armeli, S., Carney, M.A. (2000). A daily process approach to coping: Linking theory, research, and practice. American Psychologist. 55,6, 626-636.

Thompson S., Mulac A. (1991). The Discourse conditions for the use of the complementizer 'that' in conversational English, Journal of Pragmatics, 15, 237-251.

Traugott E. (1995). The role of the development of discourse markers in a theory of grammaticalization , University of Manchester.

Tsui A. (1991), The pragmatic functions of I don't know, Text, 11, 607-622.

Vallerand, R.J. (1987). Antecedents of self-related affects in sport: Preliminary evidence on the intuitive-reflective appraisal model. Journal of Sport Psychology, 9, 161-182.

Venier F. (1991), La modalizzazione assertiva. Avverbi modali e verbi parentetici, Franco Angeli, Milano.

Wegner, D. M. (1994). Ironic processes of mental control. Psychological Review, 101, 34-52.

Weiner, B. (1974). Achievement Motivation and Attribution Theory, New Jersey: GL.

Weiner, B. (1979). A theory of motivation for some classroom experiences. Journal of Education Psychology, 71, 3-25.

Weiner, B., Frieze, I.H., Kukla, A., Reed, L., Rest, S., & Rosenbaum, R.M. (1971). Perceiving the causes of success and failure. Morristown, NJ: General learning Press.

Weizman E. (1999). Discourse Patterns in News Interviews on Israeli Television, in G. Toury, R. Ben Shachar (eds.) Hebrew: A Living Language, Haifa University, Haifa.

Wenzlaff, R. M. and Bates D. E. (2000), The relative efficacy of concentration and suppression strategies of mental control, Personality and Social Psychology Bulletin, vol. 26, pp. 1200-1212.

Wenzlaff, R., Bates D. (2000). The Relative Efficacy of Concentration and Suppression Strategies of Mental Control. Personality and Social Psychology Bulletin, 26, 10, 1200-1212.

White, R.W. (1959). Motivation reconsidered: The concept of competence. Psychological Review, 66, 297-333.

Yukelson, D., Weinberg, R.S., West, S. and Jackson,A.W. (1981), Attributions and Performance: An Empirical Test of Kukla's Theory. Journal of Sport & Exercise Psychology.

Ziegler, D. J., & Hawley, J. L. (2001). Relation of irrational thinking and the pessimistic explanatory style. Psychological Reports, 88, 483–488.

Zuczkowski A. (1995). Strutture dell'esperienza e strutture del linguaggio, Clueb, Bologna.

Zuczkowski A. (1999). Percezione della causalità e linguaggio, Clueb, Bologna.

Zuczkowski A. (2006). Il testo scritto: centramenti linguistici e organizzazioni cognitive, in P. Nicolini, B. Pojaghi (a cura di), Il rispetto dell'altro nella formazione e nell'insegnamento. Scritti in onore di Anna Arfelli Galli, Eum, Macerata, pp. 217-238.

Zullow, H. M., & Seligman, M. E. P. (1988). Pessimistic rumination predicts electoral defeat of presidential candidates: 1948-84. Manuscript submitted for publication

Zullow, H., Oettingen, G., Peterson, C., and Seligman, M.E.P. (1988). Pessimistic explanatory style in the historical record: Caving LBJ, Presidential candidates and East versus West Berlin. American Psychologist, 43, 673-682.

In: Handbook of Sports Psychology
Editor: Calvin H. Chang

ISBN: 978-1-60741-256-4
©2009 Nova Science Publishers, Inc.

Chapter 2

GENDER ROLE CONFLICT AMONG FEMALE RUGBY PLAYERS: GENDER ROLE EXPECTATIONS, OBSERVATIONS OF CONFLICT, AND COPING STRATEGIES

Melissa A. Fallon

College at Oneonta, State University of New York, USA

ABSTRACT

Gender role conflict theory proposes that female athletes experience role conflict because they are expected to enact both feminine and masculine gender roles, which reflect very discrepant expectations for a female athlete's behavior. Understanding these conflicting expectations for gender role behavior can lead to greater options for resolution and thereby remove some obstacles to sport participation for female athletes. This chapter presents findings from a qualitative study exploring how female rugby players negotiate gender role expectations and conflict, as women participating in a traditionally masculine sport. Eleven Caucasian female rugby players between the ages of 25 and 38 were interviewed regarding expectations for their behavior and gender expression, experiences of distress and conflict, and strategies for resolution. The results indicate that participants perceived numerous discrepant gender role expectations related to their appearance, physical activity and durability, sexual orientation, level of aggressiveness and assertiveness, and social behavior. Participants also described three different types of gender role conflict: conflict regarding being feminine enough, conflict about being too

This manuscript is based on Melissa A. Fallon's dissertation project, conducted under the direction of LaRae M. Jome, PhD. at the University at Albany. Interviews were conducted in fall 2002. This project was presented at the 2006 Annual Association for Women in Psychology conference in Ypsilanti, MI. an abbreviated form of this study was published in the Psychology of Women Quarterly, Vol 31(3), Sep 2007. pp. 311-321. The author would like to express her deepest appreciation to the coding team: Sarah Heimel, Heidi Park, Kristen Maul, Beckie Hanson and Tracy Wilcox. Additionally, I would like to acknowledge the contributions of the athletes who participated in this study for sharing their stories with openness, courage, humor and generosity. Correspondence regarding this manuscript can be addressed to Melissa A. Fallon, Ph.D., State University of New York, College at Oneonta, Counseling Center, 101 Counseling, Health and Wellness Center, Oneonta, NY 13820, email: fallonma@oneonta.edu.

feminine to play the sport, and concerns about how gender role behavior affects perceptions of their sexual orientation. In keeping with previous findings, participants perceived more conflicting expectations for their behavior than they reported to experience conflict problems. It also appears that the level of distress as the result of gender role conflict appears to be minimal. Participants displayed great resiliency and utilized numerous active coping strategies in the resolution and negotiation of discrepant expectations, which has not been documented in previous research. Coping strategies utilized include influencing the source of the expectations, resolving conflict internally and accommodating gender role expectations. Coping strategies will be discussed in detail so as to provide clinical resources for counseling and sport psychology practitioners in their work with female athletes. Additionally, the identification of different types of gender role conflict has implications for gender role conflict theory.

INTRODUCTION

A review of the literature on female athletes reveals benefits for women who participate in sports in terms of self-esteem (Hall, Durborow, & Progen, 1986), athletic competence (Miller & Levy, 1996), body image (Miller & Levy, 1996), indicators of mental health (International Society of Sports Psychology [ISSP], 2000), and academic achievement (Hanson & Kraus, 1998). However, the literature also indicated that women participate in sports with less frequency than men (Hanson & Kraus, 1998; Lopiano, 1993; Cheslock, 2007), and they participate in a limited range of sports (Matteo, 1986). While Title IX legislation (20 U.S.C. § 1681) acted to guarantee equal access for women to sports, there is no such mandate for equal prestige, economic or social rewards. Women's sports still struggle for financial support and social acceptance, as evidenced by the disparity in salary and media attention between professional male and female athletes (Disch & Kane, 2000). Despite recent advances in women's sports, there are also some persistent psychological obstacles to participation in athletics that have yet to be surmounted or adequately addressed. A comprehensive understanding of the relationship between sports participation and gender role behavior may provide direction in overcoming the obstacles that women face as athletes as many obstacles for female athletes may originate in the political and socio-cultural history of gender roles.

The historical oppression of women and narrow definition of acceptable gender role behavior creates a legacy of suspicion toward female athletes, as well as suspicion of all people who violate ascribed gender role behaviors (Bem, 1993). Women participating in traditionally masculine activities, like sports, violate the ascribed definitions of femininity. Gender role conflict theory (Allison, 1991; Rohrbaugh, 1979; Sage & Loudermilk, 1979; Wetzig, 1990) suggests that female athletes may experience conflict and distress as a result of perceiving contrasting or opposing expectations for their gender role behavior. Female athletes are assumed to experience role conflict as a result of trying to fulfill both the masculine and feminine gender roles (Rohrbaugh; Sage & Loudermilk; Wetzig).

The role of athlete has traditionally been associated with masculinity. Martin & Martin (1995) documented that both athletes and non-athletes identified that the cognitive schema or expectations for a female athlete and ideal female person are significantly different and that the role of athlete has significant overlap with masculine traits. Further they identified that the role of ideal athlete has no overlapping expectations with the role of ideal woman, whereas for male athletes the schema for ideal athlete and ideal man have significant overlap. Further, the masculine behaviors required for a sport vary according to sport. For instance, a good gymnast or skater is expected to be graceful and cheerful whereas a good basketball player or rugby player should be assertive, forceful and dominant in order to perform well at their sport.

Negative consequences often follow for people that refuse to fulfill gender role expectations. Those consequences can range from disappointment or criticism, as in the case of a parent or romantic partner, to ostracism or possibly even violence. In the case of the female athlete, rejection of the feminine gender role in one setting often takes the form of doubts about the overall adequacy of the athlete to fulfill the feminine gender role (Allison, 1991) as well as questions about the athlete's sexual orientation (Lenskyi, 1999). Bem (1993) discussed the stigma for people who act outside of their gender role and went on to discuss how people who violate their ascribed gender role norms are also assumed to violate the norms of heterosexuality.

The aim of this study was to present an in-depth understanding of female athletes with regard to gender role expectations and behavior. Research on gender role and female athletes has generally focused on the existence of gender role conflict in different populations, and the findings have been less than convincing for either side of the argument (Anthrop & Allison, 1983; Jambor & Weekes, 1996; Miller & Levy, 1996; Sage & Loudermilk; 1979). It is possible that findings have been inconsistent because the experience of gender role conflict is too complex to be measured quantitatively with current assessment tools.

Female rugby players were studied because rugby is the most nontraditional team sport for women (Matteo, 1986; Salisbury & Passer, 1982). Research suggested that athletes in nontraditionally feminine sports, as opposed to athletes in traditionally feminine sports, show greater differences in gender role attitudes in comparison with non-athletes (Sage & Loudermilk, 1979). Rugby has consistently been described as a masculine sport (Matteo, 1986; Salisbury & Passer, 1986). Theoretically, female athletes in nontraditional sports could be expected to perceive more conflicting gender role messages in comparison to female athletes in more feminine sports. It was reasoned that rugby players are an appropriate population for the study of gender role attitudes because of the masculine behaviors inherent in the sport, such as tackling and pushing other players away from the ball.

The questions addressed in this study were: What gender role expectations do female athletes perceive? What discrepant messages do they receive about their gender role behavior and participation in rugby? Do the discrepant messages they receive result in internal conflict or distress? How do they respond to the discrepant messages?

REVIEW OF LITERATURE

Present gender role theories fail to describe the experience of gender role expectations of female athletes adequately and have neither refuted nor confirmed assumptions about gender role conflict for female athletes. The premise of the gender role conflict theory is that female athletes are expected to fulfill both the feminine gender role and the role of athlete, which requires behavior associated with the masculine gender role (Allison, 1981; Desertrain &

Weiss, 1986; Rohrbaugh, 1979; Sage & Loudermilk, 1979). A review of gender role theory and research on gender role conflict provides further rationale and context for this study.

Gender role conflict has been proposed as a reason women avoid or quit sports (Sage & Loudermilk, 1979; Miller & Levy, 1996). It has been suggested that participation in athletics violates the ascribed gender role for women (Desertrain & Weiss, 1986; Martin & Martin, 1995; Sage & Loudermilk, 1979). Gender role conflict theorists proposed that female athletes are expected to fulfill both the masculine and feminine gender role, a potential cause of role conflict (Allison, 1991; Desertrain & Weiss, 1986; Rohrbaugh, 1979; Wetzig, 1990). A discussion of the bipolar construction of gender as well as the concept of androgyny provides the conceptual basis for the various gender role theories as applied to female athletes.

The presumed conflict in the gender role behavior of female athletes originates in the supposition that masculine and feminine gender roles require opposite and conflicting behaviors. This gender polarization can be illustrated through an examination of items from the Bem Sex Role inventory (1974), which assesses an individual's relative level of masculinity and femininity. Among the feminine items in Bem's Sex Role Inventory (1974) are yielding, cheerful, shy, affectionate, sympathetic, sensitive to the needs of others, compassionate, eager to sooth hurt feelings, soft-spoken, warm, tender, childlike, don't use harsh language and gentle. The masculinity scale has characteristics like self-reliant, independent, athletic, assertive, forceful, leadership abilities, willing to take risks, dominant, willing to take a stand, aggressive, competitive and ambitious. Traditional views of gender roles tend to see masculinity and femininity as opposites on the same spectrum (Bem, 1993). For instance, the feminine attribute yielding may be considered the opposite of the masculine quality aggressiveness.

Bem (1993) theorized that the tendency towards this kind of gender polarization acts to create rigid, mutually exclusive gender roles for men and women. Strict definitions for gender role behavior create an atmosphere such that anyone who deviates from the traditionally ascribed gender role is labeled deviant. This label of deviance is directly connected to historical and political stigmatization of feminists, homosexuals, and transgender people. Historically, the lack of understanding of people who transgressed traditionally ascribed gender roles led to a legacy of pathologizing female athletes (Bem, 1993). Women, particularly female athletes, who dressed or acted outside of the ascribed feminine gender role were assumed to have a gender identity disorder and suspected to be homosexual (Bem, 1993). Female athletes inherited this social legacy of abnormality in the form of suspicion about their gender role behavior and sexual orientation. Essentially, the origins of gender role theory lay in a social and political construction of gender that narrowly defined appropriate behavior for women.

In contrast, Bem (1974, 1993) described the concept androgyny as a feminist political response to the restrictive, traditional conceptualization of gender role behavior. This concept was an attempt to reconceptualize the healthy individual as having flexible gender role behaviors. She proposed that masculinity and femininity are independent constructs which do not necessarily oppose or conflict with each other. She proposed that people might be classified according to their gender role identification as either masculine (high in masculinity, low on femininity), feminine (high on femininity, low on masculinity), androgynous (high in masculinity and femininity), and undifferentiated (low in masculinity and femininity). She suggested that the new paradigm was an attempt to challenge the misnomer that a healthy individual identified with only her or his ascribed gender role.

Androgyny describes female athletes as enacting both the masculine and feminine gender roles in a positive and healthy expression of behavior. Female athletes are conceptualized as individuals who are not limited by their ascribed gender role.

More recently, Bem (1993) reviewed several criticisms of the androgyny model. First, she reported that androgyny continues to be a male centered conceptualization of mental health with aspects of femininity as an addendum. She suggested that this paradigm does nothing to increase the cultural value placed on the feminine experience. Androgyny as a concept also ignores the historical reality of gender inequity and fails to advance the cause of gender equity. In placing the locus of control for gender role behavior within the individual, androgyny ignores the political and social forces that continue to shape gender role behavior and makes no demands for change on the dominant, androcentric culture. Finally, Bem (1993) argued that the concept of androgyny endorses masculinity and femininity as real and complementary personality constructs and that the individual consciously integrates masculine and feminine behaviors because the behavior originates from their ascribed gender role. It is possible that many individuals are not concerned about whether their behavior is prescribed by the masculine or feminine gender role, a feminist ideal that is not adequately described by the term androgyny.

These polarized and androgynous conceptualizations of female athletes have significantly different implications for gender role conflict. The literature on gender role attitudes of female athletes suggests that many female athletes may identify with the masculine gender role (Burke, 1986; Hall, et al., 1986; Marsh & Jackson, 1986), and with the androgynous gender role (Hall et al., 1986) more than their non-athletic peers. However, there is still evidence that suggests female athletes experience gender role conflict at least to a small extent, which would suggest that androgyny may not be a complete conceptualization for the gender role identification of a female athlete.

The polarized conceptualization of gender role behavior is central to the theory of gender role conflict. Gender role conflict theory suggests that female athletes experience conflict because masculine behavior associated with athletics is in direct contrast to the socially ascribed feminine behavior expected of these athletes (Allison, 1991; Rohrbaugh, 1979; Wetzig, 1990). The theory suggests that the violation of ascribed gender role behavior inevitably leads to some pathology of identity. Bem (1993) described the premise of gender role conflict:

> Polarization of the human impulses exacerbates gender insecurity – as Freud himself would have understood – because no matter how well people manage to keep them under control, those gender inappropriate impulses not only produce a certain level of conflict and contradiction within the individual psyche; they also constitute an eternal internal threat to the male or female selves that people work so hard to construct and maintain. (p.149)

Bem proposed that the source of conflict lies in the socially constructed polarization of gender role behavior; however, the locus of pathology is generally situated in the individual's violation of normative behavior.

Desertrain and Weiss (1986) proposed that according to societal expectations, the roles of female and athlete are incompatible because the athlete role demands activities that are in direct conflict with the feminine gender role. The authors posited that in order to fulfill the requirements of the role of athlete, women need (at least temporarily) to relinquish the feminine gender role. Gender role conflict describes a woman's sense of struggle with her self-concept, which is caused by discrepant expectations of masculine (athlete) and feminine (gender role) behavior (Allison, 1991). Anthrop and Allison (1983) maintained that role conflict occurs when an individual cannot fulfill one or either role completely and is thus judged as inadequate by the dominant reference group.

Allison (1991) further theorized that gender role conflict theory reflects theorists' and practitioners' unconscious clinging to traditional gender stereotypes. Continuing to focus on gender role conflict for female athletes serves to propagate an unhealthy and erroneous stereotype of female athletes. Women's participation in sports is treated as a social "aberration" (Disch & Kane, 2000, p. 127). Further, Disch and Kane offered that female athletes are ignored by the media or accused of sexual deviance because of their violation of traditional gender role behavior. These authors argued that women who display athleticism characteristic of masculinity do not fit social schema for feminine behavior, thereby facing rejection in the form of criticism or invisibility.

Female athletes are also subject to cultural attempts to reinterpret their masculine behavior as a sign of homosexuality. Lenskyi (1999) suggested that female athletes are in jeopardy of being victims of homophobic harassment, because of a long held cultural belief that women who play men's sports are "sexually suspect" (p. 172). It appears that cultural conflict about the transgression of traditional gender roles has resulted in a projection of psychopathology onto the female athlete. Allison (1991) suggested that the gender role conflict theory represents an "intuitively comfortable and psychological way to deal with societal stereotyping" (p. 51). Given the potentially limiting power of the gender role conflict theory, it is important to examine the specific components and research derived from the theory.

Sage and Loudermilk (1979) studied gender role conflict among female athletes and operationalized gender role conflict as consisting of perceived and experienced conflict. Perceived gender role conflict refers to the "perception of conflicting expectations or orientations," and experienced role conflict concerns having "personally experienced role incompatibilities in enacting the roles of female/female athlete" (p. 91). In separating perceptions from experiences, the authors discriminated between the athlete's awareness of discrepant external gender role expectations and the internal experience of conflict resulting from the violation of ascribed gender role behavior. This construction allows for the possibility that an athlete may perceive that there are social repercussions from violating the ascribed gender role, but may not experience distress or internalize these repercussions. This conceptualization of gender roles and expectations also acknowledges that the conflict may be external to the athlete and be projected on the female athlete by others.

Research about gender role conflict suggests that female athletes appear to perceive more conflict than they actively experience and that a large percentage of athletes appear not to experience or perceive any conflict. Sage and Loudermilk (1979) studied 268 female varsity intercollegiate athletes from socially non-approved sports (i.e., softball, basketball, volleyball, field hockey, track and field) and from socially approved sports for women (i.e., tennis, golf, swimming and gymnastics). Level of social approval of sports was determined by the theoretically derived definition:

Sports in which strength, bodily contact, and endurance are emphasized have traditionally had low social approval and women participating in sports of these types have been socially stigmatized, while sports emphasizing skill, grace and beauty and not involving touching one's opponent have been more socially approved (P. 90).

Sage and Loudermilk studied the perception and the personal experience of gender role conflict among college athletes.

Regarding the perception of conflict, 19% of respondents reported that they perceived no role conflict, whereas 24% participants reported perceiving very little role conflict. Thirty percent of participants reported a moderate amount of perceived conflict, and 18% and 8% perceived a great, and a very great amount of conflict, respectively. Regarding the experience of conflict, 32% and 24% of respondents reported they experienced none or little conflict. Twenty-three percent of respondents reported experiencing a moderate amount of conflict, whereas 13% and 7% of participants reported experiencing a great or very great amount of conflict. Of note, the authors found that 44% of respondents reported perceiving role conflict "not at all" or "of little importance." Fifty-six percent of respondents reported that they experienced role conflict "not at all" or "of little importance." Essentially, Sage and Loudermilk (1979) found that although a significant number of female athletes reported perceiving gender role conflict, a smaller percent actually reported experiencing gender role conflict.

A chi-square test was used to determine if respondents differed significantly in the amount of role conflict they perceived in comparison to what they experienced. The participants in this study reported perceiving significantly more role conflict than they experienced ($\chi2(4) = 138.74$, $p < .01$), with the mean score for perceived role conflict of 2.7 and the mean score for experienced role conflict of 2.38 on a 5-point scale. Sage and Loudermilk (1979) reported that athletes in socially approved and non-socially approved sports did not significantly differ in their perceived role conflict, but they did differ significantly in their experienced role conflict. Players in nontraditional sports for women had a mean gender role conflict rating of 2.43, whereas women in traditional sports reported a mean of 2.17, ($\chi2(4) = 24.34$, $p < .01$). Sage and Loudermilk concluded that a significant percentage of female athletes perceive and experience role conflict; however, the perception of role conflict was greater than the personal experience of gender role conflict. This result suggests that although athletes may perceive conflicting messages, they do not tend to internalize all the conflict they perceive. The results also suggest no difference in the amount of role conflict perceived by athletes in traditional or nontraditional sports for women, but women in nontraditional sports may experience more conflict than women in traditionally feminine sports. There is a problem in extrapolating conclusions from this study because of the age of the study as the data were collected in 1976 and 1977. However, this was a pivotal study and many subsequent studies used Sage and Loudermilk's (1979) instrument or assessment techniques.

In a more recent study of the frequency of role conflict among female athletes, Miller and Levy (1996) investigated the relationship of gender role conflict, masculinity, femininity, physical appearance self-concept, athletic competence self-concept, body image, and athletic participation of parents of athletes and non-athletes in various collegiate level sports (i.e., basketball, volleyball, track & field, swimmers and golfers) and found that female athletes (n = 75) rated themselves as more masculine and less feminine than did the non-athletic college females (n = 69) as measured by the PAQ (Spence, Helmreich, & Stapp, 1975). The authors measured gender role conflict by combining selected items from the Sex Role Conflict Scale

(Chusmir & Koberg, 1986) and the Athletic Sex Role Conflict Scale (Sage & Loudermilk, 1979). The Sage and Loudermilk scale estimates perceived and experienced gender role conflict. The Chusmir and Koberg scale was created based on items from previous gender role conflict scales and was reported to measure the discrepancy between identification with a gender role and gender role behavior at work.

Miller and Levy (1996) found no significant differences between athletes and non-athletes in their level of sex role conflict. On a 5-point scale, female athletes reported a mean score of 2.81 (SD = .50), and non-athletes reported a mean score of 2.87 (SD = .50), with higher scores reflecting a greater amount of conflict. The authors did, however, find that female athletes reported significantly greater feelings of athletic competence and better body image than did non-athletes. Although no significant difference was found between the level of femininity reported by athletes and non-athletes, female athletes did report significantly higher scores for masculinity (M = 3.87, SD = .40) in comparison with non-athletes (M = 3.58, SD = .48). The authors reported that role conflict was inversely related to parent athletic participation and positively related to body image. It was suggested that parents who participate in athletic activities are role models for the resolution of role conflict for female athletes. This study suggested that both female athletes and non-athletes experience a moderate amount of gender role conflict, but that female athletes may not experience more conflict than non-athletes. A major concern about Miller and Levy's study is that very little information was provided about how physical appearance, athletic competence and body image self concept were measured. Results suggest that these three variables were inter-correlated and with the masculine scale of the PAQ, making the operational definitions of these constructs potentially even more important.

Anthrop and Allison (1983) conducted another study on perceived and experienced role conflict. They studied gender role conflict among high school female athletes (n = 133) following Sage and Loudermilk's (1979) instrumentation and operational definitions of perceived and expected gender role conflict. Although Anthrop and Allison theorized that adolescents have more identity development issues and should therefore have greater gender role conflict, they found that compared to Sage and Loudermilk's adult sample, their adolescent respondents reported less experienced gender role conflict (M = 2.18, on a 5-point likert scale with 5 representing high conflict) and similar amounts of perceived conflict (M = 2.37). Less than one percent of respondents reported they perceived no conflict, and 31% of respondents reported perceiving very little conflict. Fifty percent of respondents reported perceived conflict to be moderately problematic, whereas 14% and 2% of respondents, respectively reported perceiving conflict to be a great or very great problem. Three percent and 48% of respondents reported that experienced conflict was not problematic at all or just a little problematic. Thirty-nine percent of respondents reported that they experienced some problem with conflict, and 1.5% of respondents reported they experienced a great problem and 1.5% reported a very great problem with gender role conflict. In this sample, 32% and 50% of respondents reported that they perceived and experienced, respectively, no or little problem with gender role conflict. Anthrop concluded that respondents reported significantly more perceived role conflict (M = 2.37) than they experienced M = 2.18, $\chi 2(4) = 50.83$, p < .01.

In the same study, Anthrop and Allison (1983) also examined traditionality or social approval for women in selected sports. Like Sage and Loudermilk (1979), they defined socially approved sports as golf, tennis, swimming and gymnastics. Unlike Sage and

Loudermilk, however, their non-socially approved sports consisted of basketball, volleyball and track. There were no significant differences in the amount of role conflict perceived by athletes in either socially approved sports, non-socially approved sports, or by athletes participating in both socially and non-socially approved sports simultaneously. The authors did report that the differences in experienced role conflict approached significance, reporting means for socially approved (M = 2.03), non-socially approved (M = 2.22) and combined (M = 2.41). Again, Anthrop and Allison found evidence to suggest gender role conflict is perceived by athletes, but many athletes reported not internalizing the conflict to the extent it was perceived.

In a qualitative study of college female athletes from various sports, Krane, Choi, Baird, Aimar and Kauer (2004) studied how female athletes negotiate the expectations for feminine behavior and athleticism. They found three themes in how these athletes experience and negotiate these discrepant expectations. They described the influence of hegemonic femininity as their participants made comparisons of their bodies and behavior to the feminine ideal body image and expectations for decorum. Participants also identified the theme of athlete as "other" in discussing their experiences of marginalization and feeling different in their behavior, appearance and social contexts. Finally, participants identified positive aspects of these differences in terms of their physical abilities, pride in their athletic achievements and sense of personal power. The authors concluded that female athletes are required to perform different social roles that conflict at times but that the women in their study made active choices about negotiating these dual identities.

There appears to be some evidence that gender role conflict is experienced by some female athletes. Although a significant number of athletes perceive that they are being asked to fulfill discrepant gender roles, not all of these athletes actually experience conflict. Taken together, these studies raise questions about the phenomena of perceived and experienced conflict: What are the discrepant messages that female athletes receive about their gender role behavior? Why do some athletes perceive conflict and others do not? Why do some athletes who perceive conflict internalize it and others do not? How do athletes resolve internalized conflict? Why and how do athletes who experience conflict continue to participate in athletics? How do athletes avoid perceiving conflict in the first place?

There have been some attempts to describe the experience of conflict for female athletes. Anthrop and Allison (1983) reported that adolescent female athletes recognized they put forth as much effort and hard work as their male counterparts, but receive unequal recognition and reward for their work. Jambor and Weeks (1996) also reported that, although female athletes may experience conflict, the conflict is not necessarily about gender role behavior. In a qualitative case study, Jambor and Weekes (1996), studied a 36-year-old Caucasian college student who was also a female track athlete to investigate role conflict, social support, motivation, locus of control, imagery, anxiety, self-esteem and attentional focus. The authors reported that the athlete did not report experiencing conflict in relation to gender role behavior; rather for her, conflict may come from needing to balance the multiple social roles of mother, wife, student, athlete, etc.

Allison (1991) criticized the research on gender role conflict for the refusal to acknowledge findings of low levels of gender role conflict. She discussed Sage and Loudermilk's (1979) conclusion that the lack of statistical support for the gender role conflict theory was the result of the fact that women who experienced conflict had dropped out of sports. Miller and Levy (1996) also concluded that low levels of conflict were found because the women who experienced conflict were not playing sports anymore. The argument that sustains this persistent belief in gender role conflict appears to be faulty. The logic is that because little evidence for gender role conflict exists, women with conflict must have dropped out of sports, and because women drop out of sports because of gender role conflict, gender role conflict must therefore exist for female athletes. With no research about who drops out of sports, this argument has no merit, but it hampers efforts to dispel the gender role conflict theory.

It is clear that there is conflicting evidence supporting the existence of gender role conflict; however, the theory is particularly persistent and represents a limiting and potentially harmful conceptualization of the female athlete. The lack of other empirically supported models of gender role enactment may contribute to the tenacity of this theory. Allison (1991) suggested that persistent belief in the gender role conflict theory can negatively affect the provision of services to female athletes. Specifically, the assumption of stress or conflict resulting from the role of female athlete is erroneous and can contribute to the misidentification of actual sources of psychological distress. Additionally, to suggest that role conflict is the cause of distress limits the options for resolution of the client's problem (Allison).

Given the controversy over the existence of gender role conflict for female athletes, few definitive conclusions can be drawn. However, questioning the existence of gender role conflict for female athletes may be an exercise in futility. The presence or absence of conflict does little to explain the role of gender role behavior or identification as moderators of the benefits for female athletes. It has been suggested that gender role identification acts as a moderator for some of the benefits of sports participation for female athletes (Richman & Shaffer, 2000). Additionally, the existence of gender role conflict is based on a bipolar construction of gender. Given the support for the model of androgyny and Bem's (1993) contention that masculinity and femininity are independent constructs, there appear to be some theoretical inconsistencies in present gender role theory when applied to female athletes.

Given the disagreements about the existence of and theoretical basis for gender role conflict, it is possible that the negotiation of gender role expectations, identification and behavior may be a more complex issue than simply "Does gender role conflict exist?" Although it would be important to practitioners to know if gender role conflict is problematic for this population, it may be more valuable to know how gender role conflict manifests itself and how it is resolved in the lives of female athletes. Additionally, for female athletes who do experience gender role conflict, it would be important to know more specifically what that conflict feels like and how they resolve it. It would also be valuable to know how female athletes who perceive discrepant messages but do not experience gender role conflict manage the information or negotiate the discrepant expectations. Female athletes may lead the modern front in gender role reformation, and their experiences regarding gender role may lead to important educational and treatment advances. Therefore, it appears valuable to investigate the experiences of gender role of female athletes.

THE STUDY

The purpose of this study was to uncover female athletes' construction and negotiation of gender role expectations due to their participation in a nontraditionally feminine athletic activity. A qualitative method was chosen for the study because it provides the participants an opportunity to offer a more complex, specific and non-limiting method of describing their experiences than allowed by quantitative assessment procedure. The areas of investigation in this study reflect important determinants of participation in sport, self-perceptions in terms of gender and athlete identity, and the negotiation of multiple roles and expectations. Rugby players were sampled because they play the most nontraditional sport for women (Matteo, 1986; Salisbury & Passer, 1982) and, as such, may experience the largest discrepancy in gender role expectations.

Qualitative methods can provide an in-depth understanding of the context and gender role experiences of female athletes. Rather than the traditional focus on the existence of gender role conflict, this study used in-depth interviews to examine the complex gender role experience of female rugby players as it influences and is influenced by their participation in this sport. The questions under consideration for this study were: What expectations do these female athletes perceive for their gender role behavior? How do they negotiate discrepant expectations for behavior? What factors influence the perception and experience of conflict? How do discrepant expectations affect the female athlete's gender role behavior? How do these female athletes respond to discrepant expectations?

The areas of investigation in the interview protocol were selected because they were theorized to be important moderators of the experience of gender role or of the decision to participate in athletics. Social support (Eccles & Harold, 1991; Sarason, Sarason & Pierce, 1990; Weiss & Barber, 1995) for the individual and self-concept as an athlete (Hannover, 2000; Shamir, 1992; Stryker & Serpe, 1994) have been suggested to significantly influence a woman's participation in athletics and may influence how athletes negotiate gender role expectations. Given the questions guiding this investigation, further research and theory is reviewed in order to provide justification for these areas of investigation and the interview protocol.

Screening questions
1. How old are you?
2. Are you employed? Full- or Part-time?
3. How long have you been playing rugby?
4. For how long have you been playing rugby? Did you play last season? The season before that?
5. Are you currently playing on a non-college team? Do you currently have any injuries that prevent you from playing?

Interview Protocol
1. Have you played any other organized sports in the past calendar year? Any individual sports?
2. Did you play sports in high school? Which ones? In college? Which ones?
3. How did you come to play rugby?

4. Have you had any role models? Who are they? Do you have any role models for yourself as an athlete?
5. Would you say that rugby has influenced other parts of your life? How?
    (a) At work? At home? Socially? How does your family feel about your playing rugby? How do your friends feel about your playing rugby?
6. How does your partner or spouse (past or present) feel about your playing rugby?
    (a) Is your partner involved in rugby or other sports?
    (b) Has rugby influenced your relationship in any way? How?
    (c) Has your relationship influenced rugby in any way? How?
7. Childhood experiences

    (a) What kind of attitudes does your family have towards your playing sports? When you were a child? Now?
    (b) What kind of messages about sports did you receive growing up?
    (c) Did you feel the same or different about sports after puberty? Did your participation in sports or your feelings about sports change throughout your adolescence?
8. Athlete identity:
    (a) How athletic would you say you are? How athletic would you want to be? How important is it to you to be perceived as athletic?
    (b) Rugby is said to have a high risk of injury. What impact does this have on you? How have you dealt with that? Has it been a problem for you in any way? How?
    (c) What would you say is the stereotype of a female rugby player?
    (d) What do you think other people think of you when they find out you play rugby?
    (e) Has your body image (feelings about body shape or other physical characteristics) influenced your experience as an athlete? Has your experience as an athlete influenced your body image?
9. Femininity
    (a) Has your image of yourself as a woman changed since you started playing rugby? How?
    (b) Our society has stereotypes for how a woman is supposed to act. What are the stereotypes that you hear? How do you fit that stereotype?
    (c) What do you think it means to be feminine? What does feminine behavior look like? How do you know someone is feminine?
    (d) How important is it to you to be perceived as feminine?
    (e) What is it like to be a woman who plays rugby in terms of your femininity? What does it mean about your femininity?
    (f) How feminine would you say you are? How feminine would you want to be? How do you think other people perceive you in terms of femininity?
    (g) How has your body image (your feelings about your body shape and other physical characteristics) influenced your feelings as a woman?
10. Role Conflict
    (a) Overall, do you think rugby's been a good influence in your life? Why? In what ways?
    (b) Are there any ways or times that rugby has been bad for you? Please describe those ways or times.

(c) Has it caused any problems for you? In your relationships? In your career? In your friendships? In the way you feel about yourself?

(d) How did you deal with these problems (if there were any)?

(e) Have you ever considered quitting rugby? Why? Why did you decide to stay?

(f) How do you feel being a female rugby player affects other people's perceptions of you as a woman?

(g) There is a theory that female athletes should have conflict and distress because they are asked to meet society's expectations for a woman's behavior (i.e., stereotypes). These expectations for a woman's behavior are in conflict with the expectations of masculinity associated with being an athlete in rugby. Essentially the theory states that femininity and masculinity are opposites and that behaving in both of these ways can cause conflict or problems for a person.

    (i)   What do you think about this theory?

    (ii) Does this theory apply to you in any way? Have you had any experiences with conflict between being a woman and a rugby player?

    (iii) Have you seen this in your teammates?

    (iv) How do you deal with this conflict? How do you think other people deal with the conflict?

In this section, the influence of social support and role models will first be discussed, as they appear to be important determinants in the resolution of conflicts. Next, factors that influence identification with the role of athlete and with the feminine gender role will be discussed. The presence of gender role conflict requires identification with both the feminine and the athlete role in order for discrepant expectations for behavior to be perceived by the athlete. Finally, the sport of rugby will be described in order to provide a background and rationale for the selection of this population.

Social support for the participants was studied as it impacts their decision to participate as well as messages about expected gender role behavior. Eccles & Harold (1991) identified that important elements for understanding the female athlete's experience and choice to participate would necessarily include discussions about the athlete's current social support, childhood experiences of support for athletics, mentors, self-concept of ability, and gender role stereotypes. Social support is an important area of investigation in this study for two important reasons. First, social support significantly influences an athlete's decision to participate and persist in sports in the face of messages or disapproval of their gender role behavior (Eccles & Harold, 1991). Second, a player's social support network and access to role models are also major sources of messages about expectations for gender role behavior and possible strategies for the resolution of discrepant expectations.

Whereas social support is said to affect the athlete's decision to participate and her resolution of conflict (Bandura, 1977; Sarason et al., 1990; Weiss & Barber, 1995), self-concept as both an athlete and as a woman are important determinants in the perception of conflict between gender role expectations (Hannover, 2000). For gender role conflict to exist, two important sources of identity would need to present competing demands on the self-concept. Hence both the identity of athlete and of female gender role would need to be salient or important parts of the individual's self-concept (Stryker & Serpe, 1994). The more salient a role, the more it will motivate behavior, and the more likely the individual will be to seek out and perceive opportunities to enact that identity. Shamir (1992) suggested that in order for an individual's identity to be crystallized, the identity must first be socially recognized. Then the individual becomes attached to this identity and resists its relinquishment. If either role (feminine gender role or role of athlete) were not an important part of the athlete's self-concept, conflict would not exist. Self-concept or identity may be an essential moderator in negotiating discrepant gender roles and expectations.

Hannover (2000) discussed the cognitive construction of gender and identity. She suggested that a particular identity (e.g. as athlete, as woman) is shaped and activated by the individual's social context. Individuals learn the role and identity of athlete through sports. Hannover suggested that there is also a cognitive schema that teaches and prompts gender-congruent behavior. This cognitive schema needs to be activated by the environment; hence the feminine role and identity will be prescribed by environments where gender role information is communicated or emphasized. Further, it is suggested that information about gender incongruent behavior is integrated into other identities, such as that of athlete. Although female athletes may perform behaviors that are not consistent with the feminine gender role, they may not experience conflict because the gender identity schema is not activated during sports events. If an athlete attends to the environmental cues relevant only to the role at hand (athletics), the expectations for feminine behavior will not be acknowledged and no conflict will be perceived. This consideration is important because it represents one of the possible ways that an athlete can avoid perceiving conflict, a phenomenon that may be observed in this sample.

Given the impact of self-concept on the athlete's perception of gender role conflict and the possible implications for understanding the resolution of conflict, participants' sense of identity as an athlete and as a woman were investigated in this study. Specifically, questions were designed to tap the athlete's perception of success in each role, importance of the role and perception of social acceptance in the role. Various questions were designed to elicit information about the athlete's self-concept as a woman and as an athlete.

RUGBY

Rugby presents an optimal context in which gender role behavior may be observed in relation to sport. Rugby is a team sport in which players numbering 7, 10 or 15 attempt to score by moving the ball across the field by carrying, passing, kicking or grounding (Planet Rugby, 2001). An identifiable characteristic of rugby is the scrum, in which eight players of the same team bind together tightly and oppose the other team's scrum by trying to drive them back over the ball, which is placed in the middle of the opposing scrums. Planet Rugby, a commercial and educational organization, promotes rugby as a sport that involves physical contact among players and warns of the inherent physical risk to players. The Women's Sport Foundation website (2001) cites that there is a high risk of injury for this sport due to the tackling and various legal forms of physically fighting for the ball.

Rugby is a team sport, which also made it ideal for this study. Although studies have found that athletes in individual sports competition do identify with the role of athlete, Stryker and Serpe (1994) suggested that identification with a particular role is formed through interaction with one's social group. Shamir (1992) suggested that in order for an identity to become salient, it needs to be socially recognized. He found that social commitment to continue was positively correlated with leisure identity salience among college and non-college participants. While social recognition as an athlete is a difficult variable for which to control, the presence of teammates may ensure that there is social recognition and definition as an athlete, at the very least by her teammates.

In addition, the level of gender role conflict is predicted to be highest with a masculine sport such as rugby. Sage and Loudermilk (1979) suggested, "The degree of role conflict is likely to be related to the sport in which one participates, since acceptability of female participation varies according to type of sport" (p. 90). Rugby was chosen as the sport of investigation as it represents the most non-traditional team sport for women. Theoretically, female rugby players should have the most gender role conflict because they are performing an activity, i.e., physical fighting, that most violates the ascribed feminine gender role.

In several studies that ranked the relative femininity or masculinity of a sport, rugby has consistently been ranked as a masculine sport. Matteo (1986) surveyed the relative gender role associations of different sports as rated by 80 male and female undergraduate students. Sports were rated as stereotypically masculine, feminine or neutral on 9-point Likert scales, with 9 representing extremely feminine sports, 5 representing neutral sports, and 1 representing extremely masculine sports. Sports rated between 1.0 and 3.5 were considered to be masculine. Rugby was ranked 1.85 and placed into the category of masculine sports.

Salisbury and Passer (1982) surveyed female athletes in their estimation of how unfeminine certain sports were (i.e., tennis, volleyball, softball, track/long distance running, soccer, basketball, and rugby). Athletes from each sport ranked their own sport. Rugby was ranked as the least feminine sport. In a qualitative study of men's college rugby, Schacht (1996) described rugby as "femininity's antithesis," describing characteristic values such as "survival of the fittest," "no pain, no gain," and "relational rejection of the feminine" (p. 553). As such, rugby represents an excellent arena in which to study female athletes and their gender role attitudes.

Finally there are several aspects of the culture of rugby that also encourage the violation of feminine gender roles. Traditions like a penchant for public nudity, consumption of alcohol, and singing of rugby songs generally provide opportunity, encouragement and social pressure for the female rugby players to enact unfeminine behavior. Due to the lack of support and lack of popularity of the sport of rugby in the United States, few rugby clubs have access to locker rooms, so that players commonly change for matches in public view at the rugby pitch. It is also the tradition of some rugby clubs that players who score their first try (a scoring unit similar to a touchdown) may be required to "shoot the boot" (drink beer from a dirty cleat). After rugby matches, it is traditional that the home team hosts a social, commonly known as a "drink-up" where beer and food are served. Opposing teams will often participate in drinking games and sing rugby songs. The traditional content of rugby songs entails the glorification of one's team, explicit lyrics regarding sexual gratification for women, or drinking beer. While not all of these behaviors are specifically associated with the masculine gender role, many of them do transgress the expectations of the feminine gender role. As such, it appears that not only do the activities that constitute the sport of rugby call on participants to violate norms of femininity, but many of the social traditions associated with the sport also require players to enact nontraditionally feminine behaviors.

METHOD

Participants

Female athletes (n=11) from rugby clubs at the non-college club level of competition in the Eastern U. S. were recruited. Club teams were defined for the purpose of this study as teams that were not associated with an institution of higher learning and for which the members of the team were responsible for its management and financial support. Players were identified for recruitment for this study through rugby team e-mail and websites. Athletes were assessed during the athlete's season of play. Athletes on the current team roster who were between the ages of 25 and 45 were solicited for participation.

Athletes were recruited who had a minimum time commitment to the team of at least five hours per week during the competitive season. Five hours was chosen as the minimum time commitment because it allows two to three hours of actual competition and at least one practice session during the week. Shamir (1992) found that time commitment was positively correlated with the salience of a leisure activity identity for both college and non-college participants.

A sample size of 10-12 participants was identified as appropriate for this study given that Hill, Thompson and Williams's (1997) recommend between eight and 15 participants for a CQR study. Over 20 individuals responded to emails to solicit volunteers and twelve volunteers were invited to participate in the study. Twelve individuals were interviewed; however there was a malfunction with the recording equipment and one interview was not recorded. Participants ranged in age from 25 to 38, with a mean age of 28.5 years (SD=4.12) (see Table 1 for a description of the demographic characteristic of the sample). All possessed bachelor's degrees and five of the 11 participants had some form of graduate education. All were employed full-time, and no participants had children. All participants were Caucasian, which was not criteria for inclusion but representative of the population, in that rugby tends to be played by Caucasian women in the northeastern and mid-Atlantic United States.

Table 1. Participant Demographic Information

Participant	Age	Years playing rugby	Highest level of education	Gender of romantic partner
1	28	10	Graduate degree	Female
2	25	4	Bachelor's degree	Female
3	26	3	Bachelor's degree	Male
4	26	5.5	Bachelor's degree	Male
5	30	4	Graduate degree	Male & Female
6	25	5	Graduate degree in progress	Male
7	27	3.5	Graduate degree	Male
8	38	4	Bachelor's degree	Female
9	28	6	Bachelor's degree	Male
10	25	6	Bachelor's degree	Male
11	35	12	Graduate degree	Female

Although information about sexual orientation was not requested, all of the participants volunteered the gender of their past or present romantic partners. Six of the 11 participants described relationships with male partners. Four of the participants reported their romantic partners were women and one participant discussed her past relationships with both a man and a woman. Many participants identified their sexual orientation as heterosexual or lesbian, however not all participants identified their sexual orientation explicitly. The gender of participants' romantic partners was not originally identified as an important variable in this investigation, but is presented here because participants identified the importance of sexual orientation in understanding gender role conflict and voluntarily provided this information.

All participants were on the current roster of a non-college rugby team in the northeastern and mid-Atlantic United States. They also reported that they had been playing rugby for the previous two consecutive seasons. Players reported minor interruptions in play due to injury that prevented them from playing for a week or two but no participants reported any greater interruption in their season of play. The length of involvement in rugby ranged from three years to 12 years (M=5.73, SD=2.69). Although many participants reported they have exercise regiments outside of rugby practice, only three participants reported participating in organized sports other than rugby, i.e., softball, basketball, and ice hockey.

All but one participant reported playing sports in high school. Eight of the 11 participants reported that they participated in more than one sport in high school in the same academic year. These sports included basketball, softball, swimming, track and field, volleyball, soccer, squash and cheerleading. All but one participant reported participating in organized sports in college, i.e., crew, rugby, basketball, lacrosse, soccer, intramural flag football, softball, and track and field. Six participants reported having been introduced to rugby in college, and the others stated they joined rugby after college. Primarily, participants reported having been recruited or encouraged to play rugby through an acquaintance already connected with the sport. One participant joined her rugby team after she had read an article in the newspaper about the local team.

Instrumentation

The interview protocol was developed based on a review of the literature and in collaboration with the dissertation committee members. First the following demographic information was collected about each participant: racial or ethnic identification, age, number of children, highest level of education, other sports played and number of years playing rugby. The interview questions were designed to investigate areas identified in the literature as important determinants of the female athletes' participation in sports or gender role behavior. Specifically, these determinants include role models (Eccles & Harold, 1991; Miller & Levy, 1996; Sarason et al., 1990), social support during childhood and adulthood (Anthrop & Allison, 1983; Eccles & Harold; Jambor & Weekes, 1996; Miller & Levy; Sarason et al.; Weiss & Barber, 1995), current estimation of femininity and athletic ability (Burke, 1986; Salisbury & Passer, 1982; Eccles & Harold; Hall et al., 1986; Marsh & Jackson, 1986; Richman & Shaffer, 2000; Sarason et al.), desired level of femininity and athletic ability (Eccles & Harold), salience of feminine and athlete identities (Hannover, 2000; Shamir, 1992; Stryker & Serpe, 1994), and body image (Miller & Levy; Richman & Shaffer).

Finally, after the participant responded to all the interview questions, she was told about gender role conflict theory and asked her opinion about the negotiation of gender role expectations. Although this may be an unconventional research protocol, feminist psychologists view the client as the expert of her own life (Dutton-Douglas & Walker, 1988;

Hill & Ballou, 1998) and call on psychologists to act professionally in ways that "respect the woman and honors her perceptions of the world" (Dutton-Douglas & Walker, 1988 p. 14; Laidlaw & Malmo, 1990). Given these feminist principles and the implications of this research question, it seemed reasonable to include the athlete's informed view of the negotiation of discrepant messages for gender role behavior. This question was asked last so as not to bias answers about gender role conflict in the participant's life.

Procedures

Participants were recruited through e-mail and e-mail list services. Volunteers who met criteria for inclusion in the study were informed they were eligible to participate. Criteria for inclusion were: (a) the player was between the ages of 25 and 40 years old, (b) the player had been playing rugby for the two seasons immediately prior to the interview, (c) the player was on the current team roster, and this team was not associated with a college, (d) the player had no major injuries that prevent her from participating in team matches, and (e) the player was employed full-time. No incentives were offered to the volunteers for their participation in the study.

The investigator conducted all the interviews in order to ensure consistency (Hill, et al., 1997). Given travel constraints, one interview was conducted in-person and ten were conducted over the telephone. All interview questions were asked of each participant; however, follow up or clarification questions were added as necessary (Weiss, 1994). The interviews lasted between 45 minutes and 1½ hours.

Analysis

A qualitative method was used to obtain a descriptive understanding of the process by which female rugby players construct their understanding of gender. Consensual Qualitative Research (CQR; Hill et al., 1997; Hill, Knox, Thompson, Williams, Hess, & Ladany, 2005) methodology was chosen to guide the analyses of the interviews. Qualitative methodology allows for the description of phenomena through words rather than numbers. CQR allows for the intensive study and description of phenomena and places the meaning of the research question in the context of the participants' lives.

The process of CQR (Hill et al., 1997; 2005) calls for open-ended interview questions to obtain information about specific aspects of the phenomena under study. A group of judges reads the transcribed interviews, and raw data are coded into content domains. The domains are constructed by the coders to develop core ideas or themes, and a cross analysis is conducted to identify the consistency of these core ideas.

The coding team initially consisted of four women aged 23-32 who had familiarity with the topic, with one additional coder joining the team after coding had begun. Four of the 6 coders (including the first author) were current members of a non-college rugby team and participated in rugby events during the coding process. The fifth member did not play rugby but was a former track and field athlete in high school. The inclusion of female rugby players among the coders served to enhance the validity of the study by using members who could help avoid against misinterpretation of the data (Maxwell, 1996). All coders held at least a bachelor's degree, and had various levels of experience in the field of psychology, including graduate coursework in psychology, case management with people with disabilities, and teaching experience.

The coders and auditors were trained in CQR methods (Hill et al., 1997) by the investigator. Coders also read introductory texts on gender role behavior (Weiten & Lloyd, 2000, chap. 10) in order to provide a background on the theory. Additionally, in a preliminary meeting, coders and auditors were asked to explicate their feelings and biases in reference to the research question. Coders and auditors were encouraged to maintain a journal recording personal reactions to interviews and coding processes.

Using Hill et al.'s (1997) recommended steps, coders worked individually to develop a start list of categories or domains. Initially all four coders were given the same interview transcript to read and to evaluate the appropriateness of an initial list of domains. Subsequently, the coding team met to discuss the appropriateness of domain and construct a final list of domain categories. Preliminary descriptions of the kind of material belonging to each domain were also generated at this time, and the raw data were designated as belonging to one or more domains. The group discussed and came to consensus on the rationale and criteria for coding raw data into domains.

The four coders worked in rotating coding teams of two and transcripts were randomly assigned to coding teams. In the first phase of coding, the coders individually classify raw data into domains and then met with their partner to discuss and come to consensus on the classification of all the raw data in a transcript. In the case that consensus about a domain area could not be reached, coders were instructed to note both domains in their coding. Coders then individually re-read all transcripts with the data coded into domains and summarized the content within each domain. Coders came together in rotating teams of two to review their summaries and they submitted a final summary of coded domain material that was audited by another member of the coding team. Following the CQR (Hill et al., 1997; 2005) method, the coders rotated the role of auditor. The auditor's task was to review the coding for accuracy and provide feedback to the coders at each step of the coding process. Finally, the investigator summarized core ideas and domains across each case, and descriptions of clusters among core ideas and domains were developed in consultation with the project advisor.

RESULTS

The findings are presented around three main themes framed by the research questions: What discrepant messages do they receive about their gender role behavior and participation in rugby? Do the discrepant messages they receive result in internal conflict or distress? How do they respond to the discrepant messages?

Overall, participants perceived discrepant messages about many characteristics associated with gender role behavior. They recounted their own gender role conflict experiences and they depicted other women who they perceived to experience gender role conflict. They portrayed gender role conflict experiences in detail and differentiated between different types of conflict experiences regarding gender roles. Finally, the participants of this study offered many methods of negotiating discrepant messages, primarily focusing on efforts to influence the messages they receive, manage disapproval or internal conflict, and accommodate the gender role expectations.

The findings of this study are presented according to guidelines for consensual qualitative research methods laid out by Hill et al. (1997; 2005). Hill et al. advocated distinguishing between levels of themes in the data by using domains, categories and core constructs as the levels of organization of data. A core construct refers to the simplest or most basic theme describing the data. Groups of core constructs unite to illustrate larger themes called categories, which in turn can combine to depict even larger ideas called domains. Hill et al. suggested that core constructs that are endorsed by all participants are referred to as "general phenomena" and core constructs endorsed by greater than half of all participants be referred to as "typical" phenomena. Core constructs that are endorsed by less than half but more than two or three participants are referred to as "variant." Hill et al. suggested that core constructs endorsed by less than two or three participants be discarded. The results of this study were grouped according to the research questions into three domain areas: (a) discrepant messages about the gender role behavior they are expected to enact, (b) evidence of gender role conflict, and (c) responses to discrepant messages. Within each of these domains, a description of the main idea is presented followed by descriptions of the categories and core constructs.

Domain 1: Discrepant Messages for Gender Role Behavior

The first domain emerging from the data is a description of the discrepant messages participants received about their gender role behavior and their participation in rugby. They described receiving messages about their gender role behavior from their families, friends, peers, and coworkers via direct statements as well as through gender role stereotypes. Participants described the expectations associated with femininity and illustrated how these expectations are in direct opposition to the behavior expected of them as rugby players. They also explained that they receive both messages of approval and disapproval for their gender role behavior and their participation in rugby. Several core constructs of discrepant messages surfaced in the participants' interviews: appearance, body image, sexual orientation, passivity/ aggression, nurturance/competitive, fragility/durability, physicality, decorum and support for women's rugby (See table 2).

Table 2. Domains, Categories, and Core Constructs Emerging in the Study

Domain 1: Discrepant Gender Role Messages	Frequency of Core Constructs
Appearance	General
Fragility versus Durability	Typical
Sexual Orientation	Typical
Body Type	Typical
Passivity versus Aggression	Typical
Nurturance versus Competitiveness	Typical
Support versus Discouragement	Typical
Physicality	Typical
Decorum	Variant
Domain 2: Gender Role Conflict	
Perceived as Not Feminine Enough	Typical

Managing Both Masculinity and Femininity	Typical
Perceived as Too Feminine	Variant
Domain 3: Responses to Discrepant Gender Role Messages	
Influencing Messages	
Creating a Support Network	Typical
Creating Support for Rugby	Variant
Proving the Source Wrong	Variant
Avoiding Internal Conflict or Disapproval	
Direct Disagreement	General
Adaptive Gender Role Schema	Typical
Accepting Limitations	Typical
Accommodating Responses	
Bolstering Signs of Femininity	Typical

Note. General = applies to all or almost all cases; Typical = applies to at least half of the cases; Variant = applies to less than half of the cases

Appearance

The first core construct that was revealed described the discrepant messages that participants received about their appearance. Participants described receiving messages that they should have a feminine appearance and that their participation in rugby detracts from their feminine appearance. Participants revealed several external markers associated with a feminine appearance such as wearing make-up, doing their hair, wearing feminine clothing such as dresses or skirts, shaving their legs, and painting their toenails. They characterized a feminine appearance using terms such as "girly-girl," "dolled-up," and looking "fabulous." The participants described a vivid contrast in the appearance expected or associated with a feminine woman with that of a female rugby player. All 11 participants explained that these two roles are accompanied by some aspect of appearance, which indicates this is a general core construct.

Participants depicted the stereotypical appearance of a female rugby player as large, round, unattractive women who "don't shave their legs" and who wear their hair in a "crew-cut." They also explained that they get dirty and bruised playing rugby which does not fit with the expectations of a feminine appearance. One participant stated that female rugby players look like an "NFL player." Another participant shared how she understands that femininity is incompatible with the demands of rugby:

> Good women athletes develop these strong, muscular bodies and downplay some of the more feminine aspects like being a voluptuous woman, non-aggressor… Female athletes… perhaps because of the physical demands of sports are de-feminized… you're not gonna play sports in a dress. You're not gonna curl your hair and wear make-up on the field. It's just not practical. (Participant 4)

Participants also stated that they received more messages about the unacceptability of their masculine appearance in situations where feminine dress is expected. One participant recounted negotiating with her mother about when to stop playing rugby before her wedding in order not to mar her feminine appearance for the wedding photos. It appears that the messages participants received about their appearance are fairly discrepant messages between what women are expected to look like and what female rugby players look like.

Body Image

Another typical core construct that emerged depicted discrepant messages about the body image expectations associated with the feminine gender role and the stereotype of a female rugby player. Eight of the 11 participants reported receiving conflicting messages about expectations for body shape. Specifically, participants revealed that the body image associated with the feminine gender role is incompatible with the body image of female rugby players. Participants depicted the body image of a feminine woman as petite and thin. Models and actresses were identified as illustrations of the ideal feminine body shape. This body image is in direct contrast to the body image associated with the female rugby player, which is large, muscular and heavy. Participants portrayed the body shape of female rugby players as large, fat and "round." The physical contact necessary to be successful in rugby requires considerable fitness and strength. One participant captures the notion that larger and stronger women are valued in rugby: "In rugby… you want to be able to push your weight around, and the more weight you have to push, the stronger you are" (Participant 4). The nature of the sport results in the positive evaluation by rugby players of large and strong bodies. One player contrasted her reaction to her increase in muscle mass and fitness level as compared with the reaction of a non-athlete woman:

> I would just get such an amazing response from my team, from different people. "God, you're huge." Its funny, most women do not want to hear that phrase. But it's a big compliment on our team, and I can take it that way. (Participant 1)

It appears that participants recognize that their body shapes do not fit the commonly prescribed body shape for a feminine appearance. Another example of the body image contrast is illustrated by participants' accounts of having difficulty finding feminine clothing that fits an athletic body type. Participants described perceiving expectations that they need to be thin and petite in order to be feminine and that they have to be big, strong and athletic in order to succeed in rugby. This area of discrepant expectations suggests that participation in athletics requires and rewards non-traditional body types, which are expectations that conflict with the expectations of the feminine gender role.

Sexual Orientation

Sexual orientation surfaced as another core construct of discrepant messages related to gender role expectations. Specifically, participants explained that the stereotype of female rugby players as lesbian significantly influences the perception of their femininity because heterosexuality is required for identification as feminine. Of the 11 participants in this study, nine indicated that sexual orientation was connected with either the feminine gender role or their role as female rugby player, indicating that this is a typical core construct.

Participants described the stereotype of female rugby players as lesbian and suggested that outsiders to the rugby community readily apply this stereotype to them. One participant recounted being confronted with the stereotype by people outside of the rugby community, "A lot of people really assume that if you're a female rugby player… that you're gay. Unfortunately, I got that question a lot "oh are there are a lot of lesbians on your team?" (Participant 3) Participants offered that the lesbian stereotype of female rugby players is not a discrepant message for players who identified as lesbian. However, this assumption was offered as discrepant for players who identified as heterosexual and bisexual. Participants stated that heterosexual women occasionally have their sexual orientation questioned because of their involvement in rugby. The discrepant message here is that for heterosexual and bisexual athletes, there may be misinformation about their sexual orientation due to the lesbian stereotype of female rugby players.

Passivity Versus Aggression

Another core construct that emerged in the category of discrepant messages about gender role behavior involved contrasting expectations for the level of assertiveness by participants. Participants identified passivity or supporting roles as a typical characteristic of the feminine gender role and contrasted that with the assertiveness required by the sport of rugby. This core construct appears to be a typical category as eight participants depicted the contrast between the level of assertiveness expected of a feminine woman and a female rugby player.

Feminine behavior was portrayed as "passive," "prissy," "weak," and "unassertive." Participants described a feminine woman as a "cheerleader who supports other people's endeavors." They characterized a feminine woman as someone who downplays her competence, who needs help, and who acts "ignorant but cutesy." On the other hand they depicted the stereotype of a female rugby player as aggressive, independent, driven, competitive, powerful, confident, strong, brash and overwhelming. One participant reported that rugby players use "brute force" to accomplish the task of their sport. It appears that participants identify passivity as a core construct in the feminine gender role and acknowledge that as a female rugby player they participate in an activity that is in direct contrast to that characteristic of femininity.

Nurturance Versus Competitiveness

Another typical core construct that emerged from the data was the contrast between the nurturance associated with femininity and the competitiveness associated with athletic competition. This focus on the contrast between nurturance and competitiveness was endorsed by eight of the 11 participants. Specifically, it appeared that participants receive messages that they should be nurturing in order to be perceived as feminine, and that the competitiveness of rugby violates this expectation for nurturance.

Emotionality, nurturance, friendliness and approachability were offered as essential characteristics of the feminine gender role. They used adjectives like "tender," "kind," "healing," "open," "friendly," and "smiley" to depict this construct. It was common for participants to refer to the emotional or nurturing characteristic of femininity as "internal femininity." Many participants described these as internal qualities in contrast to "external femininity" or feminine appearance; however, these characteristics may be better characterized as qualities that are observed in the context of an interpersonal relationship.

On the other extreme of the spectrum for this construct is the characterization of a competitive or assertive woman as a "bitch" or someone who is "hard" and "icy." The quality "Bitch" was noted several times as the stereotype of a female rugby player. It appears that it is also connected to the core construct of assertiveness because the behaviors that get labeled as "bitchy" are assertive actions that display a lack of interpersonal sensitivity for the other person. Essentially, assertive actions receive the label of "bitch" as a result of the lack of interpersonal sensitivity required by competitive situations. One participant defined the term "bitch" as, "Someone who's basically gonna stand up for themselves and not let you walk all over them." (Participant 8) Another participant explained how she monitors the amount of assertive behavior she displays because it might lead to rejection, "I don't want to come off as a bitch... its weird. To people I don't even know, that I shouldn't care about but... I want people to like me and to do that, I feel like I need to be more feminine." (Participant 9) Thus it appears that interpersonal sensitivity is a quality expected of women, and women risk being labeled as a bitch for displaying the assertiveness which is required in competitive situations.

Fragility vs. Durability

The fragility of women also arose as a typical core construct of discrepant messages about gender role behavior. Ten of the 11 participants stated that their family, friends, romantic partners or coworkers expressed concern about the possibility of injury associated with rugby. Specifically, participants described messages that women are fragile and that the risk of physical injury in rugby is too great for women. Participants reported that people commonly expressed concern about physical injury in discovering that a woman plays rugby. Participants also identified the stereotype of female rugby players as risk-takers as identified through descriptors like "liberal," "tough," "open-minded," "willing to take risks," and "nonconformist."

Although fragility was not mentioned as a core construct of the feminine gender role, participants indicated that they do receive messages about women being more fragile than men.

> This guy... when he found out that I was playing... he didn't think that it was a positive thing. He said that I was gonna get hurt and [asked] if I thought about having kids--you know how would that impact me being able to have kids if I get hit all the time, and pretty... not ignorant statements but... not based on a lot of education or knowledge of the sport. (Participant 5)

Participants reported that many of their friends or family members were unsupportive until the participants proved that they were not fragile or susceptible to injury. This participant described her parent's reaction to her playing rugby:

> I don't think they're very excited about it. Deep down. But I think that over time as they've seen that I'm not a walking concussion... that they see the value in it and recognize... that I'm the type of person that I need to be physically active. And so I think they recognize that and they see it as a good outlet and... You know they've been supportive. (Participant 2)

Although participants do not identify fragility as part of the feminine gender role, they definitely receive messages about concern for their injury based on an idea that women are fragile. Participants explained that as they play rugby and do not get injured, it started to lessen the concern of their family and friends for their injury and allowed their family to support rugby more fully.

The possibility of injury appeared to give rise to other concerns about gender role behavior. One player expressed her concern about what people think of her injuries. She described fear that other people thought she was being abused by her boyfriend when she went to work with a black eye - a rugby injury. She suggests that her injuries might lead people to think that she is being abused by a man, which could have a negative effect on her career. Essentially, participants reported that their sport requires some physical risk and that they receive messages discouraging them from playing rugby because of the risk of injury.

Physicality

The extent of physicality associated with the different gender roles also emerged as a core construct of discrepant gender role expectations. The contrast in level of physicality associated with femininity and athleticism was offered by six participants suggesting this is a typical core construct of discrepant messages. The main idea in this area of discrepancy is that feminine women do not engage in physical activity, a message that is in contrast with the role of athlete.

Participants reported receiving messages that feminine women are afraid to get dirty or to get hurt, they avoid physical activity, they do not get sweaty or dirty, they do not work hard; they let men do the "yucky" work, and they are easily "grossed out". This image of women is in direct contrast to the athleticism associated with the stereotype of female rugby players. Participants identified the stereotype of a female rugby player as masculine tomboys who are athletic and like to "rough-house." Participants also depicted the stereotype of a female rugby player as athletic, describing qualities such as determined, fit, strong, tough, and competitive. Although the term athletic may apply to both men and women, it is traditionally associated more with the masculine gender role as evidenced by the fact that "athletic" is an item on the masculinity scale of the BSRI (Bem, 1974). Participants reported that it is this quality of physicality that leads their coworkers and friends to identify them as more masculine. Essentially, physical activity emerged as a construct by which femininity and masculinity are differentiated and participation in rugby requires an amount of physical activity that violates the feminine gender role.

Decorum

Another core construct that emerged for discrepant messages about gender role behavior concerns decorum. A picture of feminine women emerged as enacting a traditional set of guidelines concerning decorous social behavior. In contrast, participants characterized female rugby players as exhibiting behaviors antithetical to this propriety and characterized as "lewd." This core construct appears to be a variant construct, as five of the 11 participants described this in connection with either the femininity or the role of the female athlete.

Participants characterized the feminine gender role with descriptors such as "doesn't swear" and "acts ladylike," indicating there is some component related to manners for women. In contrast, the stereotype of female rugby players was characterized as "rude, crude, lewd," and brutish. Participants indicated that the traditional rugby songs about sexual gratification and drinking typify this construct. Sexual explicitness or forwardness appears to be an important quality associated with masculinity. The quality of politeness, modesty, and reservation in behavior emerges as discrepant messages about acceptable behavior for women.

Participants reported receiving messages about the decorum of their behavior not only through communicated expectations but also through their interactions. Several participants detailed how men often make sexually explicit comments about other women in an inclusive way.

> At work they'll talk about "ooh that girl's hot"... where they wouldn't do that with other female co-workers ... They definitely, I think, would talk more sexual around us or about other women or girls and definitely not think that we'd be offended by it. I think we're

perceived as one of the guys... and I think they're less afraid to say something sexual to us. (Participant 10)

It appears that the gender of their romantic partners does not impact this behavior, as participants who date men and women stated that men feel more comfortable making sexual comments about women to them. Hence participants received messages about their gender role behavior, but they were also treated differently because of their participation in the sport.

Support for Women's Rugby

Another area that surfaced as a typical core construct was conflicting messages about their participation in sports and in rugby. Eight of the 11 participants reported that they received messages that were both supporting and disapproving of their participation in rugby. Although the primary response to the athletes' participation in rugby was positive, there were enough negative responses to warrant classifying this as a typical core construct of discrepant messages.

Present and past support of family and friends was identified as essential to participants' athletic careers and the primary response to participation in rugby. Ten of the 11 participants stated that their family, romantic partners and acquaintances were supportive of their rugby careers. Seven and eight of the 11 participants stated that they received positive reactions from their friends and coworkers, respectively. Participants described that their participation in sports, but especially their participation in the sport of rugby, garners admiration from their peers because of the rigorous physical nature of the sport. Participants described that they also received many reactions of interest and support in rugby due to the novelty or relative lack of familiarity of the sport of rugby. It appears that participants do receive messages that they are supported in their athletic pursuits.

However, many participants also recounted emotionally laden experiences of disrespect or lack of support for female athletes. They described encounters with men, including male coaches, who directly expressed to them that women should not participate in masculine sports, communicating rejection or discouragement. Participants generally recounted these interactions with outrage and anger. One illustration of this type of rejection was offered by a participant who described what happened when her team accepted a trophy at a rugby tournament:

> We won a couple trophies and you know we're up there accepting our trophy and just saying thanks and the guys are chanting, "Show us your tits! Show us your tits!" And I'm like... that's ridiculous. Why would you do that? We just played our asses off to win these trophies. What the hell does that have to do with anything? (Participant 9)

Another negative message that emerged was that women were inferior athletes and women's sports were inferior versions of men's sports. Related to this idea, participants also described strong emotional reactions to the discrepancy in financial support and media attention for women's sports in comparison to men's. Another source of disapproving messages was the social traditions associated with rugby that encourage players to engage in public nudity, drinking and sexually explicit language. It appears that although the participants reported that they receive much support for their athletic endeavors, they also receive messages of disrespect and disapproval. While negative responses to rugby emerged as a variant occurrence, it appears that these experiences are particularly disturbing and prominent for some participants.

Domain 2: Gender Role Conflict

The second domain that emerged from the data was descriptions of gender role conflict and how it manifests itself in the athlete's life. Gender role conflict theory (Allison, 1991; Rohrbaugh, 1979; Sage & Loudermilk, 1979; Wetzig, 1990) suggests that individuals experience identity confusion and experience distress as a result of receiving discrepant expectations for behavior based on the feminine and masculine gender roles. Identity confusion was proposed because it is theorized that enactment of the masculine gender role associated with the role of athlete would compromise a woman's femininity or create confusion about her identity as a woman. This confusion is proposed to cause distress for the athlete.

In this section, descriptions of gender role conflict will be examined first. Three types of conflict about gender role behavior emerged from the accounts of witnessed or personally experienced conflict. Gender role conflict appeared to take one of three forms: (a) perceived as not feminine enough; (b) managing perceptions of masculinity and femininity; and (c) perceived as too feminine (see Table 2). Finally, observations of conflict and distress among the participants will be examined. Participants appeared to experience gender role conflict but few participants reported experiencing distress as a result.

Conflict about Being Perceived as Not Feminine Enough

The first type of conflict has to do with other people's perception of participants and their teammates as not feminine enough. Seven of the 11 participants gave accounts of this type of conflict indicating this is a typical core construct. Participants described a range of physical characteristics that determine a woman's ability to be perceived as feminine. Participants described factors like height, shoulder span, musculature, and facial traits as significant indicators of femininity that can act to limit a woman's ability to be perceived as feminine regardless of her gender role behavior. Three participants discussed the experience of being mistaken for a man because of a lack of feminine appearance. Participant 11 related her struggle to be perceived as feminine because of her natural body shape. She explained how her physical appearance limits her ability to be perceived as feminine.

> I mean I know I'm not perceived feminine. I'm often called "sir"... It's simply based on a physical perception. I recognize that. There's not a darn thing I'm gonna change about it. I've grown my hair long. It doesn't make a difference. Um I know there are a handful of things I can do. When I wear earrings and I don't wear a hat, it happens less. (Participant 11)

She went on to describe the discomfort caused when she gets approached because people think she is a man and should not be in a woman's bathroom. She also described that when she wore makeup to try to increase her feminine appearance, she was accused of being a transvestite. This participant reported that she would like to be athletic but have a more traditionally feminine appearance and body image. Other participants recounted similar experiences as uncomfortable and negative. Body shape or other genetic characteristics appeared to significantly influence whether a woman would be mistaken for a man.

This type of conflict did not only occur in participants who are naturally masculine in appearance. Another participant recounted a past experience of having her femininity questioned because of her athleticism. She described how her level of competitiveness and dedication to sports in high school led her peers to perceive her as masculine. She described that when she went to college she attempted to bolster her femininity so that her peers would perceive her as more feminine.

Another manifestation of this type of conflict is illustrated in the participants' distress about other people's reactions to their attempts to appear feminine. Some participants expressed enjoyment when they shocked people with very feminine dress, while others - women who are less likely to be identified as feminine - expressed displeasure about the shocked reactions of people.

> When I dress up… its not like someone else dressing up and someone saying "oh you look great!" its more like "wow you know I never thought I'd see you in a skirt!" or its always like comments that are more… almost derogatory…. 'Cause I don't wear them all the time but when I do… people just aren't used to it. (Participant 8)

She continued on to described that she feels feminine but does not get recognized for her femininity. Participants disclosed that the lack of recognition of their femininity causes distress because it contradicts and invalidates their own view of themselves as women.

Although it appears that the lack of external validation for a woman's femininity affects her self- concept, there are also external consequences for an unfeminine appearance. Another source of distress for unfeminine women is the risk of rejection or disapproval when they appear to act outside of the prescribed norms. One participant described the assumption that unfeminine women are not "normal:"

> I think that… there is a difference between males and females and that it might be disarming if there's a woman who comes off very, very masculine in the way she acts -- in the way she looks. And in the same way that I get turned off when there's a guy who's like extremely feminine in the way he acts and looks like. There's something in me that's "oh that's not really that normal." (Participant 6)

She declared that it is not socially acceptable for either men or women to express extreme forms of the opposite gender role. Participants also described that feminine women receive more social acceptance as rugby players than unfeminine women. Participants described that unfeminine women do not receive the same acceptance and support as feminine women.

The first type of gender role conflict refers to conflict and distress that results when a woman is not identified as feminine. Two sources of distress were identified as being associated with this type of conflict. First, unfeminine women were described as receiving messages invalidating or questioning their feminine identity and appearance. Second, there appears to be some negative social repercussions that result from the lack of a feminine appearance.

Conflict About Managing Perceptions of Masculinity and Femininity

The second type of gender role conflict that emerged from the data referred to the assumption of homosexuality that is associated with a woman's masculine behavior. Specifically, it appears that participation in masculine activities leads some observers to question a woman's sexual orientation. Participants declared that players with this type of conflict exert significant effort to ensure identification as heterosexual and to receive positive attention from men. The specific signs of this type of conflict were characterized as women who bolster their feminine appearance and display incongruence in the importance of rugby to their self-concept. Women who were described as experiencing this type of conflict generally displayed either or both of these behaviors. This type of conflict is classified as a typical construct because seven of the 11 participants endorsed this type of conflict.

The first sign of this type of conflict was identified in heterosexual women who need to bolster their feminine appearance or women who have inconsistent feminine gender roles on-and-off the field. One participant described that a teammate made special efforts to increase her feminine appearance in order to "ward off accusations" of homosexuality.

> I think of one teammate in particular who is really into the competitive aspect of rugby... there's people who have questioned her sexuality, and I think that's when she... cause she's straight - she is like having to bolster her own external image of femininity, even though that's not really who she is. But she's just kind of had to beef that up a little bit to... ward off the accusations... just changing her dress a little bit... putting on a little bit of jewelry ... getting more into hair products. (Participant 1)

She shared that her teammate needs to ensure that her femininity was visible to her teammates and others because people might question her sexual orientation. Another sign of this type of conflict that arose frequently is the player who needs to shower after the match and before the after-game party, commonly known as the drink-up. In certain rugby traditions it is a social infraction if players shower before the drink-up. Participant 8 explained that her teammate displayed this type of conflict because she needs to shower before the party in order to feel comfortable and be attractive to men. The need to shower before the party was perceived by many participants as discomfort with a woman's masculine appearance.

Participants reported that this type of conflict is also present when there is incongruence in the comfort level of a player's masculine appearance in different social situations or when a player downplays the importance of rugby or her competence on the rugby field. Participants assessed the importance of rugby to a woman's self concept based on the dedication, effort level, performance and time commitment they observed. Women who displayed any inconsistency in their actions or statements as to the value of rugby were identified as experiencing conflict about the importance of rugby and femininity. One participant described a player who displays both inconsistency in values and bolstering her feminine appearance.

> Generally we go straight from the pitch (rugby field) to the parties and... she'll make like a conscious effort to get cleaned up and that's fine! That's totally fine. But I often feel like she does that so that she's not perceived as being masculine. And when people ask her about her play she's like "oh you know, I'm just out there having a good time"... and that's true, but she definitely is into it a lot more than just having a good time... She even will tell you that she feels kind of torn you know about it so... When we go to a bar afterwards, there are obviously

guys there, and she feels the need to get approval from them, and she doesn't feel like she's getting that approval by being… by acting how she is on the field or by just being true to the person who she is on the field. You know, she comes off the field and she really changes. (Participant 5)

The notion of a discrepancy in the acted and stated importance of rugby emerges as an indicator a player has conflict about her level of masculinity.

Another area in which this conflict manifests itself is at the organizational level or at the level of social pressure. One participant described pressure for female athletes to be perceived as feminine in order to be socially accepted. One participant recounted that select-side or elite level coaches often required players to dress femininely after the match. In depicting the demands on female rugby players to bolster their femininity, participants described that there is pressure in professional women's sports for athletes to appear heterosexual and feminine in order to be perceived as attractive and receive attention and sponsorship.

Conflict About Being Perceived as too Feminine

The third type of gender role conflict that emerged from the data was a description of women who are identified as too feminine to play rugby. Participants described women who expressed interest in playing rugby but were unable to shed their feminine gender role in order to accomplish the tasks of the sport. One participant described that people question her ability to play rugby because of her feminine appearance. This type of conflict was described by five of the 11 participants, indicating it is a variant construct of gender role conflict. Several participants identified that occasionally highly feminine women attempted to join their team but could not play rugby because of the physicality of the sport.

This type of conflict appears to exist independent of messages about gender role expectations. The conflict appears to lie between the desire and ability of a woman to be flexible in her display of the feminine gender role. Participants described the fragility associated with the feminine gender role as incompatible with the physicality of the sport. One participant illustrated the problems a highly feminine woman would have playing rugby.

They would probably fall down the first time and cry. Because it is such a very aggressive sport… you've got to have some kind of strength behind you to play rugby, you know emotionally and physically. I think a lot of feminine women aren't strong… which maybe is a stereotypical response on my part but most women that I know that are very, very feminine are very weak also… and in rugby you can't be weak. You have to be a very strong - strong willed and strong physically. (Participant 8)

She stated that a very feminine woman would not be capable of playing rugby. Other participants discussed how certain characteristics of femininity (passivity, physical weakness, concern for appearance, unassertiveness) are not acceptable behavior during a match. Many participants stated that feminine women are teased by their teammates for their femininity, i.e. painting their nails, or feminine dress. Participants discussed that rugby requires behaviors that are antithetical to the feminine gender role. This type of conflict depicted women who have interest in playing rugby but are unable – or perceived to be unable - to be flexible in their femininity enough so as to complete the tasks of the sport.

Only one participant described a personal experience with this type of conflict. She reported that people often assume that she is too small to play rugby. She reported that this assumption does not cause her distress because it doesn't interfere with her ability to play rugby.

> I've been short my whole life (laughing) but it doesn't really affect me. I mean I've been hearing it my whole life. You can say "I'm too small" but I'm doing it so apparently I'm not too small. It doesn't really affect me at all. I just let them know I can handle my self. I've been playing for three years now and haven't had any problems. (Participant 3)

This participant describes that her small body size leads people to assume she is too feminine to play rugby, however she does not appear to internalize their negative opinions.

Observation of Conflict Among Participants

In this section, evidence of conflict and distress among the participants is presented. In the interview, participants were asked if they experienced any problems caused by rugby in several areas of their lives. They were then presented with the gender role conflict theory and asked to describe any conflict they experienced and any conflict they witnessed in their teammates. Finally the coding team also identified areas of gender role conflict in each participant's description of her gender role behavior.

Participants primarily reported that the discrepant expectations were not currently causing them distress. Typically, participants reported that rugby did not cause problems for them in the areas of self-esteem, romantic relationships, career, friendships, and relationships with family or romantic partners. Eight participants reported that rugby did not cause any problems in their self-esteem. Several participants reported that rugby was a positive influence on their self-esteem. Two participants did report that rugby caused them to feel bad about themselves when they performed poorly in a rugby match or in practice. Seven and six participants reported that rugby did not cause problems in their romantic relationships or friendships respectively. Of the seven participants who reported that their relationships were affected by rugby, all stated that the time commitment of rugby occasionally caused strain in their relationships. Another major problem that emerged was family or friends' disapproval of some of the social aspects of rugby, such as drinking and rugby songs. For all of these questions, the typical response was that rugby did not cause problems for them in their career, friendships, family/romantic relationships, or self-esteem.

The coders were also instructed to identify any evidence of conflict in the participants' narrative. Participants identified that nine of the 11 participants experienced some aspect of gender role conflict, suggesting this is a typical core construct. On Table 3, a listing of experiences of the types of conflict observed to be experienced by each participant is presented. The table also presents a summary of the evidence of conflict and the participants' stated level of distress and reaction to the conflict. Two participants were observed not to report any experiences of conflict.

Of the nine participants who were observed to experience conflict, only two participants were identified as experiencing distress indicating this is a variant core construct (see Table 4). Two participants were also identified to experience slight distress, another variant core construct. Finally, six participants were described as having no distress associated with the conflict experience, which is a typical core construct. One participant was identified as having experiences of two different types of conflict: not feminine enough and managing perceptions of femininity and masculinity. Six participants were observed to experience some conflict as a result of being perceived as not feminine enough. Only one participant was identified as experiencing conflict as a result of being perceived as too feminine. Three participants were observed to display conflict related to managing perceptions of masculinity and femininity.

Table 3. Observations of Conflict among Participants

Part	Conflict observed	Evidence of observed conflict	Response
1	Not feminine enough	Stated she would like to be slightly more feminine in appearance for formal dress occasions; stated she has trouble finding feminine clothing because of her muscular body shape	Slight distress related to problems shopping for clothing.
2	Not feminine enough	Stated in high school she was perceived as feminine by her peers and bolstered her feminine appearance in college	No current distress. Identified that she didn't like those people with whom she went to school.
3	Too feminine	Stated that people ask her if she's too small to play rugby.	No current distress. She replied, "Apparently I'm not too small."
4	Not feminine enough	She stated that she has been mistaken as a man.	Expressed slight distress about this. Stated she regards people who do this "with disdain."
	Managing perceptions	She also stated that she believes that people question her sexual orientation when they discover she plays rugby.	No distress experienced. Stated she doesn't "mind" if people do this.
5	Managing perceptions	She stated that a coworker stated her rugby injuries were "unattractive" and discouraged her from playing.	No distress evidenced. She stated her disagreement with his views.
6	None		
7	Not feminine enough	Stated that her coworkers rate her femininity lower because she plays rugby.	No distress evidenced. Stated that once a person gets to know her they have a more accurate perception of her femininity.
8	Not feminine enough	Stated people react negatively when she dresses femininely because she is not perceived as feminine.	Experienced distress and stated she wishes it were different.
9	Managing perceptions	Stated that she doesn't want people to see the lesbian stereotype of a female rugby player when they see her.	No distress evidenced. She wears make-up and dresses up to counteract the stereotype.
10	None		
11	Not feminine enough	Described being mistaken for a man and receiving rejection when she attempted to bolster her feminine appearance.	Described distress.

Next experiences of conflict were examined as to the amount of distress this conflict caused the participants. Six participants reported the conflict caused them no distress and they displayed responses of disagreement and disregard to the expectation that caused them conflict. For example, participant 5 describes her reaction to her coworker who tried to discourage her from playing rugby and told her that her rugby injuries make her unattractive:

> I laughed because… I think that its based on assumptions that are not… that are not backed with knowledge of the sport and of athletes and its just like ignorance… and I'm not gonna get angry at him. It's just that he doesn't know. So I just kind of laugh and say, "Ok, if that's how you feel, that's fine. But this is who I am and I enjoy it"… and we're still friends. (Participant 5)

Many participants described that negative reactions to rugby or discrepant messages about their gender role behavior does not cause them distress.

Table 4. Classification of Core Constructs of Experiences of Distress

Core construct	Generalized	Typical	Variant	Participants displaying construct
Observations of conflict		X		1, 2, 3, 4, 5, 7, 8, 9, 11
Experiences of conflict with no distress		X		2, 3, 4, 5, 7, 9
Experiences of conflict with slight distress			X	1, 4
Experiences of conflict with significant distress			X	8, 11

Participants who responded to conflict with irritation or annoyance were characterized as having slight distress. Two participants were characterized as having slight distress as a result of gender role conflict.

> I've got some set goals and I don't care if… my biceps are a little bit too big or you know quote/unquote too big. I don't care. I love it. But… I'm just thinking of, "What am I going to wear to my cousin's wedding?" and are my arms going to like bust out of like (laughing) and… Trying on clothes… I mean like this is the other part of like shopping that I hate is like… it's just finding things that fit and are flattering at the same time. It becomes a little bit of a chore because women's cuts… to get a size that fits my shoulders and my arms… and then the same thing for pants that have something that can accommodate my hamstrings but yet not drape over my waist is difficult. (Participant 1)

She reported that she hates shopping for formal events but she does not appear to internalize any negative messages about her body shape. The other participant who displayed slight distress described the experience of being mistaken for a man. She reported that she feels "disdain" and assumes the person is not really looking at her. She goes on to defend that she looks feminine and calls the other people "stupid" and "ignorant." (Participant 4) She does not appear to experience low self-esteem as a result of the incident.

There were also two participants who displayed some distress as a result of gender role conflict experiences. These were both in regard to conflict about not being feminine enough and these participants described that they experience rejection due to their large body size.

Participant 11 described her feelings that her "best efforts have always failed" with regard to appearing feminine:

> Even if this has been happening all my life, it's still embarrassing. It's still an uncomfortable feeling. It's still an uncomfortable feeling to come out of the stall and see women think that a man has just walked out of the stall. It's still an uncomfortable feeling. And as I've lost weight... it's happening more often than it ever was...'Cause even if I wore make-up... I've had people say I'm still a transvestite... I just can't soften it up enough. (Participant 11)

She goes on to describe that she would like to retain her athletic body but would also prefer to have a more feminine appearance than she has currently. The other participant who described experiencing distress stated that she isn't bothered that people perceive her as feminine except for when people appear to be shocked when she dresses femininely. She described their shocked reactions as "almost derogatory" and she wished it would not happen.

Domain 3: Coping Strategies

A large number of different strategies were offered for negotiating the discrepant expectations, addressing possible internal conflict, reacting to negative feedback from the environment, and accommodating expectations for gender role behavior. Because gender role conflict is essentially an internal quality, participants often cited the behaviors intended to resolve conflict as a sign that conflict exists. Hence, many of the resolutions may have already been mentioned in the discussion of indicators of conflict. Categories emerged to describe the possible options for responding to discrepant expectations. Specifically, it appears that participants use different strategies to describe attempts to (a) influence the messages that are received, (b) manage internal conflict or disapproval, and (c) accommodate the gender role expectations. Within each of these categories of responses, core constructs or coping strategies were identified (see Table 2).

Influencing Messages

The first group of coping strategies described the athletes' attempts to influence the expectation or the source of the expectation. These strategies involve active attempts to convince another person to change their opinion or to seek out people or contexts that provide validation. The coping strategies in the category of influencing messages are: proving the source wrong; creating support for rugby; and choosing or creating an alternate and supportive referent group.

Proving the Source Wrong

The first strategy describes attempts to prove the source or the message wrong. The athletes stated that when they experienced discrepant messages that indicated disapproval, they made efforts to disprove the opinion. Rather than agreeing-to-disagree with an opinion, participants who employ this strategy worked to change the opinion of the other. Four of the

11 participants offered this strategy as a possible resolution suggesting it is a variant core construct.

Participants reported that people who see female athletes as inferior act to inflame participants' desire to be a better athlete and prove others wrong. One participant reacted to the unequal support and regard for women's sports in comparison to men's sports.

> You'd hear things... such as "well, girls can't do that" or "girls aren't as good as guys"... and that definitely affects you to some extent... and I always took those things to heart because I've always been very competitive and so... a lot of time I would like try to prove people wrong... just so that I could hear them say that "you're right" or... get the satisfaction of saying "they can't say that anymore." (Participant 2)

She experienced satisfaction when she can disprove a negative opinion. Another participant shared how her parents' objections to her playing sports as a child actually encouraged her to be stronger in her intent to participate in athletics. Participants stated that negative opinions provoke them to fight for their opinion and even helped to cement their own opinions. Participants using this strategy reported that negative attitudes drive them to train harder, improve the level of play and become activists and proponents of women's sports. Essentially this strategy describes attempts to convince or prove the dissenting opinion wrong.

Creating Support for Rugby

The next strategy of influencing messages that emerged in the study described methods for creating support for rugby. Several participants described how they positively influence other people's reactions to rugby. They revealed that they can present information about rugby so that it leads others to support their endeavor and to withhold negative opinions. This strategy emerged as a variant construct, as it was endorsed by four of the 11 participants.

One participant reported that she puts a "spin" on rugby so others regard it positively. Another participant illustrated that her attitude and commitment to the sport dissuades people from sharing their negative reactions with her. She stated, "I don't come across too many people who speak negatively about the sport... I think that they also probably don't say too much because they realize... how much rugby is to me." (Participant 2) She went on to describe how she portrays rugby in a way that indicates how much it means to her, which discourages people from expressing disapproval of the sport. Another participant discussed how her positive attitude towards rugby helped to change her family and friends' negative opinions of rugby.

> I think it was my attitude towards it and I think that that's true in a lot of aspects of life... your attitude that you portray to other people... guides how they're going to react to you and I feel strongly that that was what had happened. You know both with my parents and with my friends that... because I was so positive about it and I spoke so highly of it and I really, really enjoyed it that they started to come around. (Participant 5)

She described that her attitude towards rugby influenced the attitudes of her family and friends in order to generate support for rugby. Essentially, the participants stated that presenting information in a positive way with confidence can help to shape the reactions of the people in their lives and create support for their endeavors.

Choosing or Creating an Alternate and Supportive Referent Group

Another strategy that emerged for influencing messages was to change the salient reference group or seek out contexts that valued them. This strategy emerged as a typical construct in the management of discrepant expectations, as it was endorsed by eight of the 11 participants. When messages of disapproval were perceived from a reference group, one strategy was to seek out other reference groups who would be more supportive. In the face of possible social rejection from a group of peers, participants described that they sought refuge in the rugby community.

Several participants reported that the rugby community is their primary social group as a result of the social atmosphere and the time commitment of rugby. Participants described that the rugby community is a tight-knit supportive community that is highly accepting of individual differences. Participants characterized the rugby culture as a "cult" or a "family" that shelters and insulates players from mainstream culture. The rugby community was depicted as a "sheltered" and accepting community that is especially accepting of gay and bisexual women. The rugby community appears to shelter participants from disapproval because they do not fit the ascribed feminine gender role.

One way the rugby community was said to provide recognition and positive evaluation was through access to non-traditional role models. Several participants described how role models from their rugby teams help them to feel accepted and helped improve their self-esteem, which they do not get from more mainstream role models.

> Unfortunately my body image has consumed a lot of my adult life and teenage life…a lot of low self-esteem about my body until recently and now you know I see so many women walking around in their sports bras and bathing suit tops and I think "well she looks like me! And that doesn't look that bad!" (Participant 9)

She explained that being around women who have body types more like herself helped her to evaluate her body more positively. Several participants gave accounts of a similar positive impact on their body image, self-esteem, and comfort with masculine behaviors. Participants conveyed that by choosing an alternate reference group or role model that values their interests and talents, they felt better about themselves and avoided disapproval.

Another method for seeking alternate reference groups was to seek out contexts that valued and rewarded participants' natural characteristics. Some participants described the context of rugby as a better fit for their body types and personalities. These participants characterized themselves as low on femininity and explained that they were valued by the rugby community for their natural physiques. They also shared that they experience rejection in other contexts because of those same masculine characteristics. They characterized the rugby community as the context that fit their identities.

> I was aware that I was different because of my athleticism … I was too big. I was too strong. … my size was at times a detriment… The coach would say, "Don't hurt your teammates and don't do this…" and I'd foul out of games a bit… I was very physical and I loved the physicality of it, but basketball at that time still wasn't into the contact you see now. So when I fell into rugby, it was like a natural fit. It brought me a sense that I'd found the right sport. (Participant 9)

This participant went on to chronicle her search for work and social contexts that better matched her identity. She reported currently working in an agricultural career and living on a farm, which suits her much more than her previous professional positions.

Another participant illustrated how her identity as a rugby player helped her to feel better about the rejection associated with being overweight. She explained that large people are considered "weak and lazy." She described that her association with a masculine sport and even her rugby position as a "prop" provides validation for her large size.

> Like all my life I've been a large person and this is the most accepted I've been... I can walk down the street and if I've got my rugby shorts on, I totally am comfortable in myself. Where if I'm dressed up... just kind of walking around town, I'm not as comfortable. I think for me, psychologically, when I have my rugby shorts on and I'm basically announcing "hey, I play rugby," it's like people look at me and give me more respect because they're like "ok, she is a strong mother fucker"...its more accepting for a man to be large than for a woman... So if I was more masculine, it was more accepted... it's ok that I'm big because I'm so strong... You know I'm as strong as a lot of men. (Participant 8)

She described that she is more comfortable in the role of an athlete and when she is wearing athletic clothing because of disapproval of her weight. It appears that these participants sought out contexts that matched and valued their natural characteristics.

Managing Internal Conflict or Distress

The second category of responses to discrepant messages described efforts to manage internal conflict or disapproval. Participants shared their reactions to their own internal conflict and to messages of disapproval from others. They described a variety of strategies for resolving distress due to either their own judgments or disapproval from other people. The core constructs that emerged in this category are developing an adaptive gender role schema, direct disagreement, exceptions to the rule, and acceptance of limits.

Adaptive Gender Role Schema

The first strategy for reacting to internal conflict or disapproval that emerged was a general schema for gender role behavior that attributed gender role behavior to context and valued flexibility and moderation in gender role behavior. When faced with disapproval or internal confusion about gender role behavior, participants offered what can be described as a schema for gender role behavior that included attributions and values that validated their behavior. Specifically, the context of a situation was identified as requiring different gender role behavior. The qualities of flexibility and moderation in gender role behavior were also identified as valuable because they assisted an individual to fulfill the gender role expectations required by the context of a situation. The components of context, flexibility and moderation were offered by nine of the 11 participants, suggesting this schema for gender role behavior is a core construct in the resolution of discrepant gender role expectations.

The context of a situation was characterized as presenting demands for gender role behavior. Participants suggested that different situations call for different gender role behaviors and the decision about how to enact gender behavior is based on the demands of the situation. Feminine behavior was expected in formal or professional situations, whereas aggressive and masculine behavior was expected and appropriate on the rugby pitch. Participants reported that they do not experience conflict in their gender role identity because they enact gender role behavior to match the demands of the social context in which the behavior occurs. One participant described that she matched her gender role behavior to the context, "I think there's a time and place for acting in a certain way in that I don't walk around my office environment acting the same way I would on the rugby field." (Participant 6)

When participants recognize social cues that indicate a certain type of behavior, they described the importance of flexibility of behavior in order to match the circumstances. One participant recounted the experience of being dubbed a tomboy by a stranger when she was on her way home from rugby practice wearing her rugby gear:

> He was like "So you're a real tomboy huh?" And I thought to myself "not if I put on a dress"... He made an assumption that I'm a tomboy but I'm not really. Growing up, I wasn't afraid to get dirty or to play around so... maybe some might call me a tomboy but... to me its about... context. You know in the context of rugby I might look like a tomboy. I might come off as rough or tough, athletic, strong... but if I'm gonna go out to a nice dinner to celebrate my birthday or a special occasion nobody would ever look at me and say you know "she's a tomboy," so I think it has a lot to do with the context. (Participant 4)

She illustrated how flexibility is important in order to match the context of the situation. She replied that the role of tomboy is not all of who she is and that she is flexible in the expression of different gender roles. Essentially she indicates that not only is her gender role behavior flexible, but her gender role identity is also flexible. She indicates that she can be a tomboy and a feminine woman and that these identities do not interfere with each other. Her tomboy side does not detract from her expression of femininity. They are seen as flexible roles, which are not conflictual to her.

Finally, participants stated personal values that moderation in gender role behavior is preferred. They described that extreme femininity or masculinity is not socially attractive, whether the person is enacting either the socially ascribed or the non-traditional gender role. Moderation in gender role enactment was identified as valuable in that it allows for flexibility in order to meet the requirement of the context. Thus a schema of context, flexibility and moderation emerged as an important coping strategy when faced with discrepant expectations for gender role behavior.

Direct Disagreement

Another core construct that emerged as a strategy to influence the message was disagreeing with and discrediting the source of the message. Ten of the 11 participants revealed this coping method for rectifying discrepant expectations. This strategy refers to outright disagreement with the message or source. Disagreement was generally based on a difference of opinion about the content of the message; however, attempts to discredit the source of information also arose as a component of this strategy. Essentially, distress was avoided because the message or the source of the message was declared to be incorrect or uninformed.

One example of this method is illustrated in the participants' descriptions of what part of the feminine gender role they do and do not assume or value. Participants frequently identified a part of the feminine gender role that they personally did not endorse or enact. One participant stated why the word feminine makes her "cringe" because it represents an unhealthy level of passivity:

> Just being completely passive or waiting for somebody to tell you what to do with your life…or to lead you around or show you the world instead of being proactive and doing it yourself. To me that's not…just being feminine… its just not living. So that makes me cringe because that's kind of what femininity is sometimes associated with. I just don't want to have anything to do with that part of it. (Participant 1)

She declared her outright rejection of the offending component of the feminine gender role expectation. Another participant recounted how she can hear a negative opinion of her participation in rugby and agree to disagree:

> I guess I'm the kind of person that - you have your own view about things and that's fine… and if they have any questions I will of course answer it and continue to be positive about the sport and about athletes… so I just kind of laugh and say "ok, if that's how you feel, that's fine" but this is who I am and I enjoy it. (Participant 5)

She indicated that the other person's opinion does not threaten her belief in her own opinion. She hears and acknowledges the dissenting opinion but she does not appear to internalize disapproval due to her disagreement with the information. Many participants explained that confidence in their opinion is an important part of being able to disagree with negative information and to be stalwart in their values. They also stated that women who lack confidence and need a lot of approval cannot employ this strategy because they are too susceptible to the opinions of other people.

Another strategy for disagreement with an expectation was to discredit the source of the information or their opinion. The source of the message or the information it is based upon was attacked. One participant described how she rejects negative information about her femininity by discrediting the source. In this case, she responds to someone who has mistaken her for a man, "I just think they're ignorant or stupid or something, like just careless - you know not paying attention… not taking the time… to really look at someone… I just have this reaction like 'what an idiot!'' (Participant 4) Many participants conveyed that their lack of concern about the opinions of their peers was based on dislike for the source, or the relative unimportance of the person expressing the opinion.

Another method of dismissing negative opinions was to attack the source based on level of knowledge or information about the sport. Many participants stated that some reactions to rugby are based on lack of knowledge about the sport. One participant described her reaction to a coworker who has just expressed disapproval for her participation in rugby, "I think that it's based on assumptions that he makes that are not… that are not backed with knowledge of the sport and of athletes. I guess it's just ignorance." (Participant 5) Most participants stated that generally people do not know a lot about rugby because it does not receive a lot of attention from the media. Participants described that education helps to dispel some negative information about the sport

I mean sometimes I'll explain it away if I have the patience you know "It's not really that big of a deal. It's not nearly as aggressive as you think. It's a much different sport..." and now it's to the point in the school at least in my community... [people] understand more and more about it and recognize that it's something that can be safe and ... you know isn't as physical as they might have originally had thought. (Participant 2)

Other participants revealed they use education about the sport to relieve discrepancies for other people about the different parts of their identity. In summary, some participants responded to negative opinions by disagreeing or discrediting the source and using education about the sport to alter the negative opinion.

Exceptions to the Rule

A variant core construct that emerged in this category was seeing oneself as an exception to the negative information. Participants portrayed themselves as complex or not fitting into simple categories for women. One participant used this method of coping as her primary method. She stated that she can express femininity and masculinity and it doesn't cause her conflict because she sees herself as "complex" and suggests that the stereotypes do not apply to her.

Um I guess I've always not fit... I think I'm kind of complex. I can do the rugby man... the guy thing and be out in my shorts and jersey all night and dirty socks and I don't care, but I also sometimes like to get dressed up you know... looking like a sexy girl and stuff... Probably my whole life... I think I was ahead of everybody. (Participant 10)

She continued with a demonstration of how she manages the negative aspects of the stereotype of the female rugby player by being the exception to the rule. She stated, "I'm known as the attractive, feminine rugby player 'cause they think it's such a contradiction. It's like this huge surprise." It appears that her method of coping with the possibility of negative stereotyping to her is to perceive herself as outside of those categories from which the negative opinion is derived. She does not disagree with the source or the viewpoint but she states that the stereotype doesn't apply to her.

Accepting Limitations

A final core construct in the category of responses to distress or disapproval referred to acceptance of limitations in terms of the feminine gender role. When participants accepted their limitations in terms of gender role expectations, they reported a reduction in distress due to failure to fulfill the expectation. It also appeared that this acceptance is also accompanied by a redefinition and reevaluation of self-expectations. This strategy emerged as a typical core construct, as it was offered by eight of the 11 participants in this study.

One major area in which this strategy was observed was in reference to body image and feminine physical appearance. Participants who viewed their appearances as low in femininity described feelings of failure that resulted from the lack of recognition for their femininity. In reference to why it is not important for her to appear feminine, one participant stated, "It's a sense that my best efforts have always failed." (Participant 11) She reported that she accepts that her appearance is not feminine and does not continue to make efforts to increase her femininity because she will not be successful. It appears that the distress caused by her lack of femininity occurs because of her sense of failure. When she accepted her limitations, she believed it decreased her distress because it released her from that sense of failure.

Another component in the acceptance strategy is the redefinition of femininity in order to retain a feminine identity. Many participants stated that they identified less with the external or appearance aspects of the feminine gender role. Instead, they identified more with the interpersonal aspects related to relationships and communication skills such as nurturance, healing, good listening skills, kindness, tenderness, emotionality, maternal feelings, empathy, openness, caring, compassion, and communication of feelings. They redefined femininity for themselves, emphasizing the parts of the feminine gender role that match their abilities or personalities.

Participants who rated themselves as low in feminine appearance explained that by recognizing that their external appearance was not feminine, they attended more to the internal qualities of femininity. One participant illustrated how she identifies with the interpersonal qualities of femininity and not the external appearance.

> Tenderness, kindness… I can be a big baby. I can cry very easily and can be very emotional in intense things… I can be extremely affectionate to those who I care about and love… and vulnerable and all those things but its more emotional. It's not a physical presentation to me. (Participant 11)

She suggested that people might not recognize her feminine qualities by her appearance but they would if they observed her in interpersonal relationships or in nurturing her animals. Participants also cited that their femininity is displayed through their caring and interaction for children and animals and through their enjoyment of entertaining and homemaking activities.

Accommodation Responses

The third category of responses to discrepant messages describes attempts to accommodate and conform to gender role expectations. There were some athletes who appeared to make personal changes in order to accommodate others' expectations so as to avoid the possibility of rejection. There were two core constructs in this category: bolstering external signs of femininity and devaluing the importance of rugby.

Bolstering External Signs of Femininity

The first strategy that emerged as a core construct of accommodation referred to efforts to increase their external feminine appearance. This emerged as a typical core construct, as six participants described this strategy. Participants explained that players attempt to increase feminine appearance by wearing feminine clothing, putting on make-up and wearing jewelry. One participant illustrated how she tailors her appearance in order to counteract the negative stereotype of female rugby players.

> Because I tried to get away from the rugby stereotype which, like I said is short, fat or round or unattractive or lesbian… I don't like to consider myself any of those things… And well I'm

not gay... I don't want them to - I don't want to be what they visualize so I... wear make-up and I do my hair. (Participant 9)

She characterized her efforts to restore her feminine appearance as a reaction to the stereotypical image of female rugby players. Several participants described players that bolster the perception of their femininity by drinking and flirting with men.

> They flirt with guys and make sure that they're getting that guy attention. I think some of them... goes and showers and cleans up and puts on their girly-girl clothes and you know they change their appearance so they can deal with it emotionally. (Participant 8)

She offered that flirting with men and having a "girly-girl" appearance helps women emotionally manage the disapproval of not appearing feminine. This strategy emerged as a typical construct of the reactions to discrepant messages.

Devaluation of the Importance of Rugby to Self-Image

The last strategy of accommodation that emerged refers to devaluing the importance of rugby to one's self-concept. Participants described teammates who appear to express discrepancy in the salience of their identity as an athlete. They gave accounts of players who display a high level of commitment to the sport on the field, but in certain social situations they may downplay or minimize the importance of rugby in order to appear more feminine.

> Because I see how they are on the field. You know they're very tough. They're very aggressive and then... like off the field when they're kind of asked about it ... They really downplay... how good they actually are or how strong they are and... You can kind of see the conflict because they are trying to be as good as they can on the field because they feel strongly about it but then off the field, its not... When people ask her about her play she's like "oh you know, I'm just out there having a good time" and that's true but she definitely is into it a lot more than just having a good time. (Participant 5)

She explained that her teammate downplays the importance of rugby and her level of commitment to the sport because she feels "torn" about the display of her lack of femininity. Two participants offered this strategy of managing possible disapproval occurring from discrepant expectations.

SUMMARY OF FINDINGS

Several themes emerged from the data describing different aspects of the phenomenon of gender role conflict. First, it appears that participants do perceive discrepant or conflicting expectations regarding gender role behavior. The women in this study acknowledged that their participation in rugby violates many aspects of the feminine gender role and this puts them at risk for disapproval or rejection. They described three different types of conflict associated with gender role: perceived as not feminine enough, managing perceptions of masculinity and femininity, and perceived as too feminine. Participants also described numerous strategies for responding to the discrepant expectations. Categories of strategies emerged from the data describing methods to influence the messages they receive, to manage internal conflict or distress, and to accommodate others' expectations for gender role behavior. A rich picture of the gender role behavior and expectations of these female rugby players emerged.

DISCUSSION

The purpose of this qualitative study was to uncover the messages about gender role received by female athletes, specifically female rugby players. Further the intent of this study was to understand the process by which these athletes may internalize, make decisions and experience conflict (or not) when they enact masculine traits by participating in this traditionally masculine sport. A variety of discrepant messages about expectations for gender role behavior emerged. Participants appeared to experience three distinct types of conflict regarding gender role expectations or behavior. Although participants were observed to experience some conflict, it was also observed that they appear to experience very little distress about this conflict. Finally, participants described numerous strategies for negotiating expectations and resolving distress from discrepant expectations.

The implications of the findings are discussed subsequently. First the implications for gender role conflict theory are discussed followed by a discussion about the implications for gender role theory in general. Next, the findings in each domain are examined. Finally, the limitations of the study are discussed followed by implications for further research.

Implications for Gender Role Conflict Theory

In examining the findings of this study, it appears that there were some aspects of the gender role conflict theory that were confirmed. Specifically, it appears that the present group of female athletes did receive discrepant expectations for their gender role behavior. As predicted by the theory (Desertrain & Weiss, 1986; Rohrbaugh, 1979; Sage & Loudermilk, 1979), the participants in this study did describe that the expectations of the feminine gender role contrast with the expectations of their role as athlete.

One surprising finding in this investigation is that gender role conflict is not one distinct experience but rather may manifest itself in various types. In this study, participants identified three different types of gender role conflict suggesting that the experience of conflict varies according to the relative gender role identification and sexual orientation of the individual. Specifically, it appears that participants who feel conflict because they are perceived as not feminine experience a different type of conflict than participants with conflict about being perceived as too feminine. Additionally, it appears that heterosexual and possibly bisexual women may experience a type of conflict that lesbian women do not.

This finding is significant because previously the experience of gender role conflict was treated as a one-dimensional construct and measured as such (Chusmir & Koberg, 1986; Sage & Loudermilk, 1979). Distinguishing the different types of conflict is important and may explain why the findings from previous studies about gender role conflict were inconclusive. Measuring these distinct conflict experiences as a one-dimensional construct may have resulted in inaccurate assessment. Existing instruments should be examined to determine which type of conflict was being assessed and instruments should be developed to provide for a comprehensive assessment of each type of conflict.

It also appears that the participants do encounter some experiences of conflict; however few participants appear to feel distressed as a result of these conflict experiences. This finding is a departure from previous theorists (Anthrop & Allison, 1983; Sage & Loudermilk, 1979; Wetzig, 1990) who proposed that the conflict causes strain and distress for female athletes. Although these investigations did not study distress related to gender role conflict, the authors stated distress for female athletes in the rationale for their studies. For example, Wetzig proposed that the distress associated with gender role conflict led to higher rates of substance abuse for female athletes.

The aim of this study was not to measure the distress of female athletes due to gender role conflict. Nevertheless, the lack of distress resulting from gender role conflict was striking. Participants primarily described that gender role conflict experiences were not a problem but merely an annoyance. Before further efforts and resources are dedicated to investigating these new findings about gender role conflict, it may be beneficial to confirm the findings about the level of distress female athletes experience as a result of gender role conflict. Participants in this study voiced more distress about the lack of support for women's sports than about their gender role conflict experiences. If the level of distress from gender role conflict is found to be low for female athletes, further investigations may be more beneficial if they were aimed at areas in which female athletes articulate distress or areas that further the understanding of gender role behavior in general, as opposed to specifically studying gender role conflict.

Finally, conflict theorists have suggested that participants with gender role conflict have to quit in order to resolve gender role conflict (Sage & Loudermilk, 1979; Miller & Levy, 1996). However, participants in this study appeared to be able to play with gender role conflict. Further, they described many different methods for resolving gender role conflict. The resolutions offered depicted participants as active and powerful in shaping their environment, as opposed to passive victims of social norms and expectations. The athletes in the present study did not appear to remain in conflict; rather they appeared to employ resolutions whenever possible. This observation is similar to findings in Krane, Choi, Baird, Aimar and Kauer's study (2004) of gender role expectations for college female athletes in various sports. Krane et al. found that female athletes were required to perform different social roles that conflict at times, but that the women in their study made active choices about negotiating these differing expectations. These participants displayed a resilience and active coping response rarely described in any of the current literature about gender role conflict. Gender role conflict theory should be expanded to describe their movement towards resolution. To end the discussion of gender role conflict at the assumption of psychopathology and not to investigate the result or resolution of conflict, presents an inaccurate picture of this population and gender role conflict experiences.

The current study provided a rich description of these female athletes and their gender role behavior. It does appear that these participants do experience some challenges in balancing the multiple roles of a female athlete. While a portrait of these participants emerged as active, resourceful and resilient in managing the challenges identified; it also appears that some athletes may use resolutions, such as bolstering feminine appearance or devaluing the importance or rugby, which are not necessarily healthy or constructive behaviors. Essentially, a complex portrait of these female athletes emerged.

Implications for Gender Role Theory

The findings of the present study also have implications for gender role theory. One important finding was the identification of different components of the feminine gender role as appearance, body image, sexual orientation, passivity/ aggression, nurturance/competitive, fragility/durability, physicality, and decorum. The identification of these different components is significant because the feminine gender role then becomes more of an umbrella term for a configuration of traits. These traits appear to be somewhat independent constructs, as illustrated in participants' discussions of women that are high in the nurturing qualities of femininity, but low in feminine appearance. Scales constructed on a one-dimensional model of gender role behavior may render poor assessments as a woman high on one component and low on another may render moderate scores, which may not be a true picture of her gender role behavior. While this study's aim was not to identify the components of the feminine gender role and it is probable that the list proposed by these participants is not complete, these results suggest that treating the feminine gender role as a one-dimensional construct is problematic. An investigation of the individual traits that comprise the feminine gender role may provide a richer and more accurate assessment of gender role behavior.

The finding of different components for the feminine gender role also has implications for the conceptualization of gender role behavior. Specifically, gender role behavior has been conceptualized as an unconstrained personality trait. However, the participants in the present study describe that there are physical limits to their ability to fulfill the feminine gender role. Some participants described that, due to certain natural physical traits, their attempts to increase their feminine appearance failed. It appears then that gender role is not necessarily a freely chosen behavior and some individuals experience limits in their ability to fulfill their ascribed gender role. Notably, the participants in this study who were observed to experience distress were women who were physically limited in their ability to be perceived as feminine. Ignoring the physical limits to fulfill a gender role may lead to misconceptions about the source of distress. Particularly, it is possible that the distress theorized to be associated with gender role conflict (Anthrop & Allison, 1983; Sage & Loudermilk, 1979; Wetzig, 1990) is actually distress about failure to fill a socially ascribed gender role because of physical limits over which the individual has no control. It is essential that the implications of physical limits on an individual's ability to fulfill an ascribed gender role be further researched and included in current conceptualizations of gender role behavior if researchers are to achieve an accurate picture of gender role behavior and any distress related to gender role conflict.

Domain 1: Discrepant Expectations for Gender Role Behavior

Participants received numerous conflicting messages about their participation in athletics. The documentation of conflicting messages is important because these messages may serve to confuse or discourage more vulnerable female athletes who are unable to withstand such criticism or disapproval. It would be important to understand how these conflicting messages affect the young athlete as she develops her identity as an athlete and experiences changes in her gender role identity due to puberty.

For the most part, participants appeared to define femininity in keeping with the traditional gender role definitions. They acknowledged that their participation in rugby violates many aspects of the feminine gender role. However, many also stated that they possess pre-existing physical traits or values that oppose aspects of the feminine gender role. Essentially, they appear to acknowledge that they defy or fail to fulfill the feminine gender role; however, it does not appear that they attribute all of the defiance to their involvement in rugby. Some participants offered that their participation in rugby is secondary to their already non-feminine appearance, values or behavior. Essentially, some participants believed that they were violating the feminine gender role norms long before they started playing rugby. Another corollary of this finding is that participation in sports did not appear to cause the conflict. Further, it is possible that non-athletic women may also experience difficulties with these discrepant gender role expectations.

Participants also gave interesting definitions of the feminine gender role. They described many aspects of behavior that comprise gender roles that are not generally included in indicators of gender role behavior. They specifically mentioned feminine appearance as pivotal in having other people recognize and validate their feminine identity. Stryker and Serpe (1994) stated that, in order for a particular identity to become salient, an individual needs to receive positive reinforcement for its enactment. The women in the present study who did not receive external validation for their feminine identity reported that this invalidation significantly affects their comfort with and perception of their own femininity. Additionally, these women appear to redefine femininity in a way that will garner them validation for the feminine traits they do display. Therefore, for these rugby players, feminine appearance seems to be not only a critical component of feminine identity but it also appears to critically influence how other feminine traits are enacted and socially recognized or reinforced.

Some of the core constructs identified in this domain have been identified in other research studies. The core construct of appearance has been found in other studies of female athletes. Krane et al.'s (2004) conducted a qualitative study of college female athletes from various sports and found that female athletes also described discrepant expectations for body shape in their qualitative study of gender role conflict. Likewise in Wesely's (2001) study of female body builders, female body builders were attracted to body building because they acknowledged they were not physically predisposed to fulfill the small, thin expectations for women and body building helped them to develop their natural physical characteristics or strengths. In an ethnographic study of female rugby player in the Midwestern U.S., Chase (2005) also documented evidence of the core constructs of appearance and discrepant expectations for body image. She also documented the physicality required by the sport of rugby and how this physicality clearly violates the requirements of the traditional feminine gender role. She also documented evidence of the core construct fragility vs. durability in her study as participants described concern by others for their physical safety and participants in her study showed pride in their physical injuries.

Disturbingly, it appears that female athletes experience some very potent experiences of disrespect or discouragement for their participation in women's sports, regardless of their relative level of femininity and masculinity. Participants reported that they encountered men and male coaches who expressed direct discouragement for women's sports and they displayed strong emotions of anger and outrage in recounting these experiences. Participants argued that women's rugby follows the same rules as men's rugby and is not a "watered-down version" of the sport. Participants in this study expressed that they had ways to influence that their family and friends provided support for women's rugby and that they primarily received messages of support for their participation in rugby. However in a study of female rugby players in New Zealand (Chu, Leiberman, Howe & Bachor, 2003), participants reported that their family and friends initially expressed shock and initial disapproval of their participation in Rugby. Given these stories of strong and outright disrespect and discouragement for the athletes in this study, support from family and friends might become more important for athletes to help them persist in the face of such negative messages.

It appears that despite the advances of Title IX legislation (20 U.S.C. § 1681), female athletes still face many negative attitudes in participating in sports. This finding also emphasizes the need for continued protection for female athletes under Title IX legislation. The discouragement and disrespect received by these participants highlights the need for continued education and measures to protect athletic opportunities for women. The participants' stories of discouragement and disrespect are particularly troubling given political efforts to limit Title IX benefits for female athletes in recent years. If anything, the stories these participants describe suggest that Title IX legislation has not yet completed the tasks or goals it was intended to achieve. Perhaps education and media attention for women's sports would provide more supportive messages and fewer discouraging messages about women's participation in sports.

On the other hand, there appears to be some unusual benefits for participants who were identified by peers as masculine. Participants described that when their male coworkers and friends identified them as athletic and masculine, they were sometimes treated inclusively as "one of the guys" and men would include them in conversations about sports and sexual commentary about other women, regardless of the participant's sexual orientation. Although these behaviors may not appear to be benefits on the surface, all participants who described these behaviors regarded them as a positive experience and evidence of respect and inclusion. The same behaviors enacted in an effort to dominate or exclude might be considered sexual harassment, but these women regarded it as a sign of greater respect. It is possible that when women emulate masculine behavior they receive some of the benefits of the position of power that men have historically held. It is possible their masculine pursuits allow them some access to the boys club, including greater respect and inclusion into men's confidences. So it appears that female athletes also receive some positive reinforcement for their masculine interests from their male peers and colleagues.

Domain 2: Gender Role Conflict

Description of Gender Role Conflict

The identification of different types of gender role conflict is especially noteworthy. Specifically, it suggests that assessment of gender role conflict should be broadened to include these distinct experiences. It also suggests that treatment of gender role conflict may require strategies tailored to the type of conflict.

Descriptions of conflict related to being perceived as not feminine enough highlighted the physical limits of a woman's ability to realize a feminine appearance. Interestingly, women who experienced this type of conflict appeared to increase the salience and importance of the nurturing or interpersonal qualities of femininity. They also appeared to seek out opportunities and environments that valued their body shape. When these participants sought out sports that value their body shape and provide them with a source of self-esteem, rugby may have become part of the solution for this type of conflict. This observation echoes the findings of Russell (2004) who documented that rugby values and rewards non-traditional body size for women. She also found that women with large body frames found rugby to be an avenue to achieving greater body satisfaction, which contradicted negative messages about their body shape received in other areas of their lives. The positive effects of rugby on athlete's body image were also found in Chase's ethnographic study of female rugby players (2005). Chase documented that female athletes changed the body shape they idealize from thin media-popularized images of women to athletic and strong body size and shape. Chase also identified that participants in her study appreciated the diversity and functionality of various nontraditional body shapes in rugby and suggested that in rugby women actively resisted normative constructions of the feminine gender role and body image expectations. Essentially, rugby may represent a coping strategy for conflict and rejection that is communicated from sources outside of the sports arena.

Conflict related to managing perceptions of femininity and masculinity describes conflict in a heterosexual woman whose sexual orientation is questioned because of her involvement in rugby. The source of this type of conflict lies specifically in the stereotype of female rugby players as lesbian and possibly also in the general notion of female athletes as "sexually suspect" (Bem, 1993; Lenskyj, 1999). Descriptions of the participants' experiences provide support for Bem's (1993) observation that women who act outside the prescribed gender role are assumed to be suspect in their sexual orientation.

The danger in misinformation about sexual orientation lies not only in the stigma of homosexuality, but also in reduced opportunities to find a heterosexual mate. It is not clear as to whether homophobia drives the need to appear feminine or whether the need to be seen as heterosexual is subservient to the appearance of femininity. What is clear is that their behavior is in direct response to external judgments or imagined punishments based on stereotypes. This type of conflict appears to be less an issue of conflict or confusion about identity but rather a fear of rejection or judgment. The source of distress appears to come from the lack of social acceptance for female athletes and for homosexuality.

Conflict related to being perceived as too feminine describes women who want to play rugby but are viewed as too feminine to perform the tasks of the sport. Only one participant was observed to experience this type of conflict so the conclusions about this type of conflict are necessarily limited. Further research should investigate this type of conflict more comprehensively. However, many participants described that feminine woman are teased for their feminine behaviors. Highly feminine women may be regarded as suspect by teammates and receive less support for their participation in a masculine sport. The suspicion of feminine women may be related to doubts as to whether the woman can fulfill the tasks assigned by the team. The success of a team depends on each player's ability to carry out her duties. Feminine women may be seen as less capable of fulfilling her duties.

This teasing and suspicion of feminine women may create obstacles for these women in entering a sport. If the athlete lacks confidence in her ability to perform her duties and receives messages of doubt from her teammates, she may be less likely to persist in the sport. It was proposed that women who experience gender role conflict have no option but to quit their sport (Sage & Loudermilk, 1979; Miller & Levy, 1996), which could be correct for some women with this type of conflict. Many participants stated that women who are too feminine have no resolutions available to them. While the participant in this study who was observed to experience this type of conflict did not appear to internalize the conflict and continued to play, it is possible that other women do quit as a result of this type of conflict. Because this participant did not appear to experience distress as a result of this type of conflict, does not mean that other women who experience this type of conflict do not experience distress. It would be important to interview other women who report experiencing this type of conflict in order to have a more accurate picture of this type of conflict.

Evidence of Conflict and Distress

One interesting finding regarding conflict was that behaviors the participants cited as evidence of conflict were also identified as resolutions for gender role conflict. One possible explanation for this is that conflict is essentially an internal feeling state, and internal feeling states in others can only be observed by external displays like expressions of distress or resolution behaviors. Another possible explanation why behaviors were discussed as signs of both conflict and resolutions is that people may not tend to stay in positions of conflict for long periods of time. When women experience distress, they may move immediately to relieve that stress by employing strategies for its resolution. Especially if there are available role models who demonstrate strategies of resolution, participants may not have to experience distress for any length of time because they have so many options for resolution. Regardless of why the same behaviors are identified as both a sign of conflict and resolution, it is problematic to conclude that female athletes experience conflict and distress solely because behaviors that might resolve the conflict are enacted. Fortunately, there were first-hand accounts of past experiences of conflict and resolutions, which details the behaviors that are both signs and resolutions.

Another interesting finding is that participants self-reported that they did not experience gender role conflict but the coders observed the participants to relate stories about a gender role conflict experience. Participants typically reported that rugby did not cause problems in their careers, relationships, self-esteem or friendships. The problems they reported regarding their relationships were generally related to the time commitment involved in rugby and how it interfered with their ability to develop relationships outside of the rugby community. These findings are in keeping with the findings of Jambor and Weekes (1996), who studied role conflict in a 36-year-old female track athlete. These authors found that her primary conflict was related to problems balancing the multiple roles of athlete, mother, wife, and student. Likewise, the participants in this study appear to regard the problems due to time commitments as minor and primarily report that rugby does not cause problems in the rest of their lives.

On the other hand, coders observed that many participants recounted stories of some incidents of conflict. One explanation for this discrepancy may be that since the participants were not observed to experience distress about their conflict experiences, they may not be aware of the conflict. This hypothesis is also supported by the fact that participants often described the same behaviors as signs of conflict and as resolutions. If the participants move quickly from conflict to resolution, they may not be aware of conflict feelings. Logically, it would seem that the participants should experience some feelings of conflict because the strategies for resolution are triggered or activated. It is possible that the resolutions alleviate any distress and that the resolutions are activated unconsciously so that the individual is not aware of feelings of conflict.

However, it is equally important to honor the self-report of participants' experiences of conflict. What the coders observed as conflict may be what Sage and Loudermilk (1979) termed perceived conflict as opposed to experienced conflict. Perceived gender role conflict was identified as the "perception of conflicting expectations or orientations," and experienced role conflict was defined as "personally experienced role incompatibilities in enacting the roles of female/female athlete" (p. 91). The participants in the present study reported that they perceive discrepant messages about the acceptability of their behavior based on traditional gender roles, however no participants reported they currently experienced conflict. The findings regarding perceived and experienced conflict in the present study is similar to previous findings. Sage and Loudermilk (1979) and Miller and Levy (1996) studied perceived and experienced gender role conflict among female college athletes. Both studies found that female athletes perceive gender role conflict but actually experience conflict to a much smaller degree. However, in both of these studies the authors found that some women did experience conflict. As such the findings in this study appear to support the findings in previous studies somewhat but not entirely. However, these observations of experienced conflict should be regarded with caution.

Domain 3: Responses to Discrepant Messages

The third domain that emerged from the qualitative findings was responses to the discrepant messages. It was previously hypothesized that the only resolution for gender role conflict was for a female athlete to quit her sport if she experienced gender role conflict (Sage & Loudermilk, 1979; Miller & Levy, 1996); however, participants in this study described many proactive roles for influencing the messages they receive, managing internal conflict or disapproval, and accommodating gender role expectations. The participants painted a portrait of the female athlete as active and powerful in her ability to manage messages of rejection, to influence her environment, and to create support for her endeavors. However, it does appear as if female athletes may also use some methods of resolution that may be detrimental to their self-esteem or mental health.

One important implication of the responses to discrepant messages offered by participants is that it provides the therapist with a start list of coping strategies for a client with gender role conflict problems. This start list of resolutions is important because previously there were no options offered for resolving gender role conflict and the only resolution for this conflict was assumed to be quitting the sport (Allison, 1991). This start list provides more options for clients and therapists working on gender role conflict issues.

Participants offered a number of strategies for influencing their environment. They described that they shape the response to rugby, choose the people they listen to and act to convince those around them of their point of view. These are active ways for shaping the gender role messages they receive. Previously, gender role theorists did not take into account a woman's ability to shape the gender role messages she receives.

The strategies for managing their own reactions describe efforts to respond when the individual perceives disapproval or experiences internal conflict. Notably, the strategies in this category appear to be primarily typical core constructs suggesting that these are the most useful strategies described by the participants. The high number of strategies used to manage disapproval may also be an indication of the extent of discouraging or disapproving messages these athletes receive about their participation in sports. Regardless of why these strategies are most frequently cited, the core construct of direct disagreement has been identified in other studies. Ross & Sinew (2007) studied Division I college softball players and gymnasts and found that the softball players acknowledged that their participation in sports do violate the traditional gender role for women but expressed direct rejection or displeasure with aspects of the traditional feminine gender role. Likewise, Chase (2005) found that female rugby players acknowledged and even enjoyed that they violate the feminine gender role for women.

The strategy of accepting limits on the ability to fill the feminine gender role is also a helpful coping strategy. The key to this coping mechanism may be the release from the sense of failure. It is possible that the sense of failure around the feminine gender role caused distress, which made the role more salient in the participants' identity. When the limitations were accepted, the distress from the sense of failure was relieved and the role was relegated to a place of lesser importance in the individual's identity. However, in contexts that activate this aspect of the feminine gender role, the distress and sense of failure may surface again as evidenced when less feminine participants in this study described their continued discomfort in formal dress occasions.

This domain also presents some important implications for the identification of the gender role schema that values context, flexibility and moderation in gender role behavior. Participants stated that they value and are rewarded for flexibility in their gender role behavior, which supports the concept of androgyny (Bem, 1993). They perceived the context of a situation as relevant to their enactment of gender role behavior, explaining why flexibility and moderation in gender role behavior is socially desirable.

The importance participants placed on context in activating gender role behavior captures almost exactly Hannover's (2000) description of the cognitive schema that activates gender-congruent behavior. The core construct of adaptive gender role schema also reflects what Royce, Gebelt & Duff (2003) labeled the "multiplicity of selves" in describing how female athletes can prioritize different identities based on matching it to the cultural context. Ross and Sinew (2007) described what they called "selective femininity" in describing that female college softball players and gymnasts were proficient at constructing a feminine appearance when the context required. Ross and Sinew's study documented that participants tended to enact a more feminine appearance for certain social situations and not as an apology for their participation in sports. In the current study, participants' description of the importance of context in determining their gender role behavior also suggests that there is a specific attribution style for gender role behavior, which significantly influences the relationship between gender role behavior and gender role identity. Further study of gender role attributions may contribute to the understanding of gender role identity and behavior.

Participants also offered strategies for accommodating gender role expectations that could have negative consequences for the athlete. It appears that some participants bolstered their feminine appearance in order to have their external appearance match their self-concept. Russell (2004) documented the bolstering of feminine appearance in her study of female rugby, cricket and netball athletes in England. Also Krane et al. (2004) described female athletes' attempts to bolster their feminine appearance through different methods, including wearing ribbons in their hair during competition. Bolstering feminine appearance could also be interpreted as a form of matching gender role behavior to a situation in which there is misinformation about gender role or sexual orientation. In the literature, bolstering feminine appearance is described as an attempt to compensate for violating the ascribed gender role norm (Rohrbaugh, 1979). Female athletes are assumed to enact this behavior as an apology for their masculine behavior.

While bolstering femininity does appear to be a reaction to issues of gender role conflict, it is not clear that it is an apology or that it is pathological. Participants revealed that women with gender role conflict experience some distress or low self-esteem, but the distress was not a result of the acknowledgment that they violate some norm which they believe to be correct. Participants described distress as the result of possible disapproval and rejection for their behavior or their appearance. Female athletes may feel bad because they receive punishment for their behavior and bolstering their femininity might be a way to avoid punishment or rejection. However this is not the same as apologizing for their behavior or appearance because they believe they are wrong in some way. Ross & Sinew (2007) reported that athletes in their study did not bolster their femininity to apologize for their participation in sports but rather matched their appearance to social situations, such as dating environments. There is no evidence to suggest that the behavior of bolstering one's femininity represents apologetic sentiments or acknowledgement of wrong-doing. Assuming this behavior represents an apology, pathologizes the female athlete without any evidence to support this assumption.

In response to the idea of transgressing traditional gender roles, participants described devaluing and disregarding the traditional gender role values as opposed to apologizing for their transgressions. They described the rules they transgressed as wrong and not their participation in non-traditionally feminine pursuits. It would also be important to understand if the behavior of bolstering femininity of female athletes is different from their non-athlete peers before any conclusions can be made. Many non-athletic women may engage in similar behaviors when opportunities for mate-seeking present itself. The question then stands as to whether this bolstering of feminine appearance is detrimental for women in general. As a coping strategy, encouraging the individual to alter their appearance to make them more attract to another may negatively affect their self-esteem and should probably not be the first strategy attempted. However this strategy could also be an attempt to match their gender role behavior to the context (responding to different contextual cues than their Lesbian or Bisexual teammates) and further research on this strategy is required before an assumption of pathology is associated with this strategy.

The second method for accommodating to societal messages about gender role behavior was devaluing the role of athlete. The act of devaluing the importance of an interest to which they exert substantial energy and time may eventually cause confusion about the individual's own evaluation of the importance of the activity. This confusion may cause cognitive dissonance for the individual, which can eventually lead the athlete to quit her sport. Thus although this strategy may help the individual avoid disapproval or rejection, it can increase the internal conflict and distress experienced. It would not be recommended that clinicians advocate for this accommodation response, but understanding this behavior when female clients enact it can also be helpful for the clinician.

Limitations

This study is subject to many of the limitations commonly associated with qualitative research. Core constructs identified in this study should be studied further both qualitatively and quantitatively to examine their reliability and validity. Furthermore, qualitative research is criticized for a greater possibility of bias. The attempt to eliminate bias is addressed through a diverse coding team and constant consultation with academic advisors. However, bias is an inevitable concern in all research and this study is no exception.

There are also significant problems in generalizing the findings of this study to other populations. First, female rugby players are a specific population with unique traits, which creates generalization problems for applying these findings to female athletes in other sports or even to rugby players from different geographical areas. Possibly one of the most important considerations affecting the generalizability of this study are the social traditions of women's rugby clubs that are specific to the sport and concern gender role behavior, such as rugby songs or "shooting the boot". Further, the average age of the women in this study was 28.5 years, and it is possible that their conflict about gender role behavior may have been resolved already. Younger women may have more conflict and may be more susceptible to gender role conflict because their gender role identity is still evolving.

There are also methodological concerns that could be addressed in further research studies. A larger sample size may also have improved the validity and reliability of these findings. This study would also have been improved if all interviews were conducted in the same manner, either on the phone or in-person. Additionally, the topic of gender role behavior as well the data collection method of interviews may be sensitive to the influence of social desirability on the part of participants. Further, all participants were volunteers who self-selected into the study possibly due to a particular interest in the subject of gender roles or psychology, which may represent some differences from other female rugby players.

Additionally, this particular pool of participants lives in a very specific historical context. They have witnessed the creation of the Women's National Basketball Association (WNBA), a professional women's football league, and the first professional soccer association, Women's United Soccer Association (WUSA), which were the first women's professional team sports to garner national attention and sponsorship. All interviews were completed before the financial collapse of the WUSA was announced.

Additionally, a few participants described witnessing the death of a female rugby player in a national tournament the year before this study was conducted. Several more mentioned they had knowledge of this player's death. Several players discussed this event and its impact on their feelings about injury. They also pointed to this event as the impetus for starting to wear headgear as a safety measure. These historical events create a generation of female athletes that have unique experiences that are not shared with the generations before or after them.

Additionally, these women have witnessed a tremendous shift in attitude toward female athletes since they were children. Some discussed the unique experience of being the only girls on co-ed teams because there were no single-sex opportunities for women. These were some of the first women to benefit from the increased opportunities provided by Title IX legislation (20 U.S.C. § 1681). Essentially, participants described many experiences of being local pioneers in the beginning of girls' mass entry into sports such as soccer and baseball. Participants also discussed the importance of media attention to female athletes in non-traditional sports that provided greater access to role models than previously available.

Implications for Future Research

Documentation of gender role behavior in a rapidly changing and diverse social context is difficult, but still a worthwhile challenge. The portraits of these women provide greater information and direction for future research and for improvement in psychological services for female athletes. First, it would be important to validate the findings of this study, including the description of types of gender role conflict, through further studies. It is important to understand how this phenomenon manifests itself in athletes in other sports of varying levels of femininity and in athletes of different age, race/ethnicity, and socioeconomic status. Additionally, while the subject of this study was women participating in sports, it is possible that some of these experiences may be shared by people participating in other non-traditional gender role arenas, such as women employed in occupations dominated by men or men participating in traditionally feminine activities.

Then, should the constructs identified in this study be found relevant to other female athletes, it would be beneficial to design education, prevention and treatment programs to allow women and girls increased access to athletics and to remove obstacles for women and girls in sports. Educational programs could be designed to garner more support for female athletes, to preempt conflict from discrepant messages about the value of women's sports, and to instruct athletes in coping strategies. Additionally, it is a hope that future research will expand the list of known coping methods for resolving discrepant messages of support. These strategies can be used to improve psychological services not only for female athletes but also to all clients struggling with the experience of disapproval or discrepant messages about their identities.

REFERENCES

Allison, M.T. (1991). *Role conflict and the female athlete: Preoccupations with little grounding.* Journal of Applied Sport Psychology, 3, 49-60.

Anthrop, J. & Allison, M. (1983). *Role conflict and the high school female athlete.* Research Quarterly, 54, 104-111.

Bandura, A. (1977). *Social learning theory.* Englewood Cliffs, NJ: Prentice-Hall, Inc.

Bem, S. L. (1993). *The lenses of gender*: Transforming the debate on sexual inequality. New Haven: Yale University Press.

Bem, S. L. (1981). *Bem sex role inventory professional manual.* Palo Alto, CA: Consulting Psychologists Press.

Bem, S.L. (1974). *The measurement of psychological androgyny.* Journal of Consulting and Clinical Psychology, 42, 155-162.

Burke, K.L. (1986). *Comparison of psychological androgyny within a sample of female college athletes who participate in sports traditionally appropriate and traditionally inappropriate for competition by females.* Perceptual and Motor Skills, 63, 779-782.

Chase, L.F. (2006) (Un)disciplined bodies: *A Foucauldian analysis of women's rugby.* Sociology of Sport Journal, 23(3), 229-247.

Cheslock, J. (2007). *Who's Playing College Sports?* Trends in Participation. East Meadow, NY: Women's Sports Foundation.

Chu, M. M. L.; Leberman, S.I.; Howe, B.L.; Bachor, D.G. (2003). *The Black Ferns: The experiences of New Zealand's elite women rugby players.* Journal of Sport Behavior, 26(2), 109-120.

Chusmir, L.H. & Koberg, C.S. (1986). *Development and validation of the sex role conflict scale.* Journal of Applied Behavioral Science, 22(4), 397-409.

Desertrain, G.S. & Weiss, M.R. (1988). *Being female and athletic: A cause for conflict?* Sex Roles, 18, 567-582.

Disch, L. & Kane M.J. (2000). *When a looker is really a bitch: Lisa Olson, sport and the heterosexual matrix.* In Birrell, S. & McDonald, M.G. (Eds.), Reading sport: Critical essays on power and representation (pp. 108-143). Boston, MA: Northeastern University Press.

Dutton-Douglas, M.A. & Walker, L.E.A. (1988). *Introduction to feminist therapies.* In Dutton-Douglas, M.A. & Walker, L.E.A. Feminist psychotherapies: Integration of therapeutic and feminist systems (pp. 3-11). Norwood, NJ: Ablex Publishing Corporation.

Eccles, J.S. & Harold, R.D. (1991). *Gender differences in sport involvement: Applying the Eccles' expectancy-value model.* Journal of Applied Sport Psychology, 3, 7-35.

Hall, E.G., Durborow, B. & Progen, J.L. (1986). *Self esteem of female athletes and nonathletes relative to sex role type and sport type.* Sex Roles, 15, 379-390.

Hannover, B. (2000). *Development of the self in gendered contexts.* In Eckes, T. and Trautner, H.M. (eds.), The developmental social psychology of gender (pp. 177-206). Mahwah, NJ: Lawrence Erlbaum Associates, Publishers.

Hanson, S.L. & Kraus, R.S. (1998). *Women, sports and science: Do female athletes have an advantage?* Sociology of Education, 71, 93-110.

Hill, C.E., Thompson, B.J. & Williams, E.N. (1997). *A guide to conducting consensual qualitative research.* The Counseling Psychologist, 25, 517-572.

Hill, C. E., Knox, S., Thompson, B. J., Williams, E. N., Hess, S. A., & Ladany, N. (2005). *Consensual qualitative research: An update.* Journal of Counseling Psychology, 52, 196-205.

Hill, M. & Ballou, M. (1998). *Making therapy feminist: A practice survey.* In Hill, M. (Ed.), Feminist therapy as a political act (pp. 1-16). Binghamton, NY: Harrington Park Press.

International Society of Sports Psychology (2000). *Physical activity and psychological benefits: A position statement.* Journal of Applied Sport Psychology, 4, 94-98.

Jambor, E.A. & Weekes, E. M. (1996). *The nontraditional female athlete: A case study.* Journal of Applied Sport Psychology, 8, 146-159.

Krane, V., Choi, Y.P.L., Baird, S.M., Aimar, C.M., & Kauer, K.J. (2004). *Living the paradox: female athletes negotiate femininity and masculinity.* Sex Roles 50(5/6), 315-329.

Laidlaw, T.A. & Malmo, C. (1990). *Introduction: Feminist therapy and psychological healing.* In Laidlaw, T.A., Malmo, C., and Associates Healing Voices: Feminist approaches to therapy with women (pp. 1-11). San Francisco, CA: Jossey-Bass Inc., Publishers.

Lenskyi, H.J. (1999) *Women, sport and sexualities: Breaking the silences.* In White, P. & Young, K. (Eds.), Sport and gender in Canada (pp. 170-181). Ontario, Canada: Oxford University Press.

Lopiano, D. (1993, April 9) *Gender equity and the Black female in sport*: Address presented at the 5th Annual Black Athletes in America Forum. [on-line] Available: http://www.womenssportsfoundation.org/templates/res_center/rclib/results_topics2.html?article=45&record=16

Marsh, H.W. & Jackson, S.A. (1986). *Multidimensional self-concepts, masculinity, and femininity as a function of women's involvement in Athletics.* Sex Roles, 15, 391-415.

Matteo, S. (1986). *The effect of sex and gender-schematic processing on sport participation.* Sex Roles, 15, 417-433.

Maxwell, J.A. (1996). *Qualitative research design*: An interactive approach. Thousand Oaks, CA: Sage Publications.

Martin, B.A. & Martin, J.H. (1995). *Compared perceived sex role orientations of the ideal male and female athlete to the ideal male and female person.* Journal of Sport Behavior, 18(4), 286-301.

Miller, J.L. & Levy G.D. (1996). *Gender role conflict, gender typed characteristics, self-concepts and sport socialization in female athletes and nonathletes.* Sex Roles, 35, 111-122.

Planet Rugby (2002). *Planet Rugby Official Website* [On-line]. Available: http://www.planet-rugby.com/laws/index.html/PR/ENG

Richman, E.L. & Shaffer, D.R. (2000). *"If you let me play sports": How might sport participation influence the self esteem of adolescent females?* Psychology of Women Quarterly, 24, 189-199.

Rohrbaugh, J.B. (1979). *Women: Psychology's Puzzle.* New York: Basic Books.

Ross, Sally R.; Shinew, Kimberly J. (2008). *Perspectives of women college athletes on sport and gender.* Sex Roles, 58(1-2), 40-57.

Royce, W.S., Gebelt, J.L., & Duff, R.W. (2003). *Female athletes: Being both athletic and feminine. Athletic Insight:* Online Journal of Sport Psychology, 5(1), 1-15.

Russell, Kate M.. (2004). *On versus off the pitch: The transiency of body satisfaction among female rugby players, cricketers, and netballers.* Sex Roles, 51(9-10), 561-574.

Sage, G.H. & Loudermilk, S. (1979). *The female athlete and role conflict.* Research Quarterly, 50, 88-96.

Salisbury, J. & Passer M.W. (1982). *Gender role attitudes and participation in competitive activities of varying stereotypic femininity.* Personality and Social Psychology Bulletin, 8, 486-493.

Sarason, I.G., Sarason, B.R. & Pierce, G.R. (1990). *Social support, personality and performance.* Applied Sport Psychology, 2, 117-127.

Schacht, S.P. (1996). *Mysogyny on and off the "pitch": The gendered world of male rugby players.* Gender & Society, 10, 550-565.

Shamir, B. (1992). *Some correlates of leisure identity salience: Three exploratory studies.* Journal of Leisure Research, 24, 301-323.

Spence, J.T., Helmreich, R. & Stapp, J. (1975*). Ratings of self and peers on sex role attributes and their relations to self-esteem and their conceptions of masculinity and femininity.* Journal of Personality and Social Psychology, 32, 29-39.

Stryker, S. & Serpe, R.T. (1994). *Identity salience and psychological centrality: Equivalent, overlapping or complementary concepts?* Social Psychology Quarterly, 57, 16-35.

Title IX of the Educational Amendments of 1972, 20 U.S.C.S. § 1681, 34 C.F.R. Part 106 (1972).

USA Rugby (2001). *Bylaws of USA rugby.* In USA Rugby Official Website [On-line]. Available: http://www.usarugby.org/about/bylaws.html

Weiss, M.R. & Barber, H. (1995). *Socialization influences of collegiate female athletes: A tale of two decades.* Sex Roles, 33, 129-140.

Weiten, W. & Lloyd, M.A. (2000). *Psychology Applied to Modern Life* (6th ed.). Stamford, CT: Wadsworth Thomson Learning.

Wesely, J.K. (2001). *Negotiating gender: Bodybuilding and the natural/unnatural continuum.* Sociology of Sport, 18, 162-180.

Wetzig, D.L. (1990). *Sex-role conflict in female athletes: A possible marker for alcoholism.* Journal of Alcohol and Drug Education, 35, 45-35.

Women's Sports Foundation (2002). *Women's Sports Foundation Official Website* [On-line]. Available: http://www.womenssportsfoundation.org/cgi-bin/iowa/sports/find/record.html

In: Handbook of Sports Psychology
Editor: Calvin H. Chang

ISBN: 978-1-60741-256-4
©2009 Nova Science Publishers, Inc.

Chapter 3

ADDICTION TO EXERCISE: A SYMPTOM OR A DISORDER?

Attila Szabo

Eötvös Loránd University, Faculty of Pedagogy and Psychology, Centre for Physical Education and Sport, Budapest, Hungary and National Institute for Sport Talent Care and Sports Services Division of Research and Foreign Relations, Budapest, Hungary

ABSTRACT

This chapter evaluates the psychological concept of exercise addiction from a scholastically multidisciplinary perspective. The most recent developments in the area of investigation are evaluated with reference to theory and critical analysis of extant research. The chapter summarizes the current knowledge about the psycho-physiological nature of exercise addiction. Further, it presents the conceptual hegemony in addressing the problem of exercise addiction within the scientific community. The characteristic and most prevalent symptoms of the disorder are discussed alongside the modes of risk-assessment. Subsequently, the underlying motives and several theoretical models of exercise addiction are reviewed. Finally, the research on exercise addiction is evaluated and directions for future research are suggested. Difference is made between primary exercise addiction in which the exercise behavior is the problem and secondary exercise addiction in which exercise is used as a means in achieving another objective, like weight loss. The chapter concludes with two brief sections summarizing plainly what we know today and what we still need to know about exercise addiction.

Keywords: compulsion, exercise dependence, obligatory exercise, obsession

1.0 FROM HEALTHY TO UNHEALTHY EXERCISE

1.1 Exercise is a Good Thing (In Moderation)

As consequence of technological development, machines are taking over man's work, which increases the likelihood of sedentary lifestyle in the contemporary societies. In most developed nations the amount of physical activity involved in the daily survival activities has been reduced to a minimum. However, the human body evolved to face and deal with physical challenges such as hunting, hiding, building shelters, and so on (Jones & Weinhouse, 1979; Péronnet & Szabo, 1993). Since the technological revolution takes place at an extremely fast pace in contrast to the biological evolution, the human organism cannot adapt evolutionarily to this very rapid shift from a physically active to physically passive or sedentary lifestyle. Therefore, it is unlikely that it can preserve its healthy or "natural" state of equilibrium, also known as homeostasis, in lack of physical challenges (Péronnet & Szabo, 1993). The only conceivable remedy for compensating for the lost physical activity that were part of humans' survival activities is to become increasingly more active in leisure activities. Indeed, in many industrialized nations substantial effort is invested in promoting physical activity, which is associated with healthy, positive, or even 'politically correct' forms of behaviours (Edwards, 2007). The mental and physiological benefits of physical activity are almost undisputed. There is a strong consensus within the scientific circles with regard to the value of integrating physical activity in one's regular lifestyle (Bouchard, Shephard, & Stephens, 1994; Warburton, Nicol, & Bredin, 2006).

According to the most recently published guidelines of the American Colleges of Sports Medicine (ACSM) and the American Heart Association, to promote and maintain health, healthy adults aged 18 to 65 years should engage in moderate-intensity aerobic or endurance exercises at least five times a week for at least 30 minutes on each occasion or high-intensity aerobic exercises three times a week for a minimum of 20 minutes each time (Haskell et al., 2007). Nevertheless, a combination of moderate- and high-intensity physical activities could also be adopted to meet the recommendations. For example, an individual can meet the recommendation by jogging or running 20 minutes twice a week and then walking briskly or cycling at a leisure rhythm for 30 minutes on two other days on the same week. Moderate-intensity aerobic exercise that is generally equivalent to a brisk walk, and noticeably increases the heart rate, could be accumulated to achieve the 30-minute minimum by performing separate bouts each lasting 10 to 15 minutes (Haskell et al., 2007). High-intensity exercises are represented by physical activities like jogging or running (depending on the person's physical condition), fast swimming, speed skating, or effortful cycling and to qualify as such they should cause rapid breathing and a substantial increase in heart rate. In addition to aerobic activities, every individual should perform physical exercises that maintain or increase muscular strength and resistance a minimum of twice every week. Finally, Haskell et al. state that since there is a dose-response relationship between physical activity and health, individuals may be better off exceeding the minimum recommended amounts of physical activity to further augment fitness, maintain or reduce weight, and to reduce the risk of various diseases.

Such a recommendation clearly mirrors to justifiability of large doses of physical activity. Nevertheless, Haskell et al. warn that increasing the dose of physical activity beyond the recommendations of the ACSM also increases the risks for injury and even cardiac complications. In spite of such warning, the positive correlation between the amount of exercise and health may be misinterpreted and in isolated cases (the term to remember throughout this monograph is: *isolated case* or *very rare case*) physical activity may be abused to lead to undesirable or harmful physical and psychological states. Indeed overdoing an adopted physical activity may not only result in severe physical injuries, but also in irreversible health effects or even fatal consequence (Cumella, 2005).

Overexercising to the point where one loses control over her or his exercise routine and walks a "path of self-destruction" (Morgan, 1979) is referred to as *exercise addiction* (Griffiths, 1997; Thaxton, 1982). The same concept is also often described as *exercise dependence* by a number of scholars (Cockerill & Riddington, 1996; Hausenblas & Symons Downs, 2002a). Further, some academics refer to the condition as *obligatory exercising* (Pasman & Thompson, 1988). In the public or mass media the condition is most frequently termed as *compulsive exercise* (Eberle, 2004) or as *exercise abuse* (Davis, 2000). It is important to note that all these synonymous words describe the same psychological condition. However, in light of some credible arguments, as elaborated below, alternating the terminology may be unproductive.

Whilst the term "dependence" is used as a synonym for addiction, the latter includes the former and also includes "compulsion" (Goodman, 1990). Accordingly, a general formula for addiction may be: *addiction = dependence + compulsion*. Goodman specifies that not all dependencies and compulsions may be classified as an addiction. Accordingly, in this monograph the term *exercise addiction* is considered to be the most appropriate because it incorporates both, dependence and compulsion. The rest of the text will explore this rare but intensively researched psychological condition.

1.2 From Commitment to Addiction

Glasser (1976) believed that too much of a good thing is better than too much of a bad thing. Therefore, he has introduced the term *positive addiction* in the scientific literature to describe the personally and socially beneficial aspects of a regular and persistent exercise behavior in contrast to some self-destructive behavior like tobacco, drug, or alcohol abuse. The "positive" prefix in conjunction with the term addiction led to the widespread and careless use of the term *exercise addiction* within both athletic and scientific populations. Indeed, a number of runners have claimed that they were *addicted* to running while they only referred to their high level of commitment and dedication to their chosen exercise. Morgan (1979) long ago has acknowledged that this is a semantic problem, because the "positive" prefix deters attention from incidences where a transition occurs from high levels of commitment to exercise to addiction to exercise. Therefore, to discuss the negative aspects of exaggerated exercise behavior, he has introduced the term *negative addiction* as an antonym to Glasser's positive addiction. The fact is, however, that all addictions represent a dysfunction and, therefore, they are *always* negative (Rozin & Stoess, 1993).

In fact, Glasser's (1976) "positive" notion referred to the benefits of *commitment* to physical exercise (a healthy behavior) in contrast to the negative effects of "unhealthy" addictions. Positive addiction in sport science and psychology literature may be perceived as a synonym for *commitment to exercise* (Carmack & Martens, 1979; Pierce, 1994). However, when commitment to exercise is used as a synonym to *exercise addiction* or to *exercise dependence* as termed by some scholars (Conboy, 1994; Sachs, 1981; Thornton & Scott, 1995) a major conceptual error is emerging. For example, Thornton and Scott (1995) reported that they could classify 77% of a small sample (n = 40) of runners as moderately or highly addicted to running. Such a figure is enormous if one thinks that among twenty thousand runners in a marathon race, for example, more than three quarters of the participants may be addicted! The figure is obviously exaggerated (Szabo, 2000). Therefore, some scholars have realized this problem and have attempted to draw a line between commitment and addiction to exercise (Chapman & De Castro, 1990; Summers & Hinton, 1986; Szabo, 2000; Szabo, Frenkl, & Caputo, 1997).

Commitment to exercise is a measure of how devoted an individual is to her/his activity. It is a measure of the strength of adherence to an adopted, healthy or beneficial activity that is a part of the daily life of the individual. For committed people, satisfaction, enjoyment, and achievement derived from their activity are the incentives that motivate them to stick to their sport or exercise (Chapman & De Castro, 1990). Sachs (1981) believed that commitment to exercise results from the intellectual analysis of the rewards, including social relationships, health, status, prestige, or even monetary advantages, gained from the activity. Committed exercisers, according to Sachs: 1) exercise for extrinsic rewards, 2) view their exercise as an important, but not the central part of their lives, and 3) may not experience major withdrawal symptoms when they cannot exercise for some reason (Summers & Hinton, 1986). Probably the key point is that committed exercisers *control* their activity (Johnson, 1995) rather than being controlled by the activity. In contrast to committed exercisers, addicted exercisers are: 1) more likely to exercises for intrinsic rewards, 2) aware that exercise is the central part of their lives and 3) experiencing severe deprivation feelings when they are prevented to exercise (Sachs, 1981; Summers & Hinton, 1986).

2.0 THE CONCEPT OF EXERCISE ADDICTION

2.1 Definition of Exercise Addiction

Before attempting to define exercise addiction, it should be noted that there is no simple or standard definition for addiction (Johnson, 1994). In Goodman's (1990) view, addiction is a behavioral process that could provide either pleasure or relief from internal discomfort (stress, anxiety, etc.) and it is characterized by repeated failure to control the behavior (state of powerlessness) and maintenance of the behavior in spite of major negative consequences. From Sachs' criteria mentioned in the previous section it is clear that exercise addiction includes: 1) salience, and 2) withdrawal symptoms. Salience, or high life priority and preoccupation with exercise, accompanied by increased bouts of exercise, are inherent in the term overexercising. The presence of withdrawal symptoms, on the other hand, is a separate manifestation of the problem.

It appears that the presence of withdrawal symptoms is a key feature in the description and definition of exercise addiction. Indeed, long ago Sachs and Pargman (1979) defined the exercise addicts as "persons who demonstrate psychological and/or physiological dependence upon a regularly experienced regimen of running. In these individuals the unfulfilled need or desire to run produces withdrawal symptoms" (p. 145). Later Sachs (1981) defined exercise addiction in reference to runners as "addiction of a psychological and/or physiological nature, upon a regular regimen of running, characterized by withdrawal symptoms after 24 to 36 hours without participation" (p. 118). Similarly, Morgan (1979) thought that exercise addiction is only present when "...two requirements are met. First, the individual must require daily exercise in order to exist or cope: the runner cannot live without running. Second, if deprived of exercise the individual must manifest various withdrawal symptoms (e.g. depression, anxiety, or irritability (p. 5). Others echo these definitions in the literature (Furst & Germone, 1993; Morris, 1989; Sachs & Pargman, 1984) and strengthen the assumption that withdrawal symptoms are a key aspect of exercise addiction. But could the mere experience of withdrawal symptoms imply or suggest the presence of exercise addiction in a diagnostic way? To answer this question a closer inspection of the literature examining withdrawal symptoms in habitual exercisers is necessary.

2.2 Withdrawal Symptoms

The literature reveals that withdrawal symptoms, although marking, are only one of the several symptoms of exercise addiction (Brown, 1993; Griffiths, 1997). Incorrectly, in the past many studies have simply assessed the mere presence, rather than the type, frequency, and the intensity of withdrawal symptoms (Szabo, 1995; Szabo et al., 1997). However, most habitual exercisers report negative psychological symptoms for times when they are prevented from exercise for an unexpected reason (Szabo, Frenkl, & Caputo, 1996; Szabo et al., 1997). Indeed, Szabo et al. (1996) conducted a survey research on the Internet and have shown that even participants in physically "light effort" types of exercises, like bowling, reported withdrawal symptoms when the activity (in this case bowling) was prevented. However, the intensity or severity of the withdrawal symptoms reported by the bowlers was less than that of aerobic dancers, weight-trainers, cross-trainers, and fencers (Szabo et al., 1996).

Consequently, it must be appreciated that the presence of withdrawal symptoms alone is insufficient for diagnosing exercise addiction. The intensity of these symptoms is a crucial factor in separating committed from addicted exercisers. Cockerill and Riddington (1996) do not even mention withdrawal symptoms in their list of symptoms associated with exercise addiction. In fact the presence of withdrawal symptoms, in many forms of physical activity, suggests that exercise has a positive effect on people's psychological and physical health. This positive effect is then, obviously, missed when an interruption in the habitual activity is necessary for an unwanted reason.

It is clear then symptom-based diagnosis of exercise addiction cannot be made simply on the presence or absence of withdrawal symptoms. The inspection of other symptoms, such as salience and tolerance that are common to other form of substance (e.g. alcohol) as well as behavioral addictions (e.g. gambling), and their co-occurrence needs to be evaluated. Indeed, most questionnaires aimed at the screening of exercise addiction are symptom-based. Six common symptoms of behavioral addiction were identified through the systematic observation of several behaviours such as exercise, sex, gambling, video games, and also the Internet. Based on Brown's (1993) general components of addictions, Griffiths (1996, 1997, and 2002) has reiterated them into the six common components of addiction. Later, Griffiths (2005) proposed a "components" model for addiction, going beyond exercise addiction whilst bringing the latter under a common umbrella with other addictions, based on the six most common symptoms (salience, mood modification, tolerance, withdrawal, conflict and relapse). Griffiths suggests that addictions are a part of a biopsychosocial process and evidence is growing that most if not all addictive behaviours seem to share these commonalities.

3.0 COMMON SYMPTOMS OF EXERCISE ADDICTION

3.1 Six Common Symptoms in Griffiths (2005) "Components" Model

3.1.1 Salience

This Symptom Is Present When The Physical Activity Or Exercises Becomes The Most Important Activity In The Persons' Life And Dominates Their Thinking (Preoccupation And Cognitive Distortions), Feelings (Cravings) And Behavior (Deterioration Of Social Behaviours). For Instance, Even If The Persons Are Not Actually Engaged In Exercise They Will Be Thinking About The Next Time They Will Be. The Mind Of The Addicted Individual Wanders Off To Exercise During Other Daily Activities Like Driving, Having Meals, Attending Meetings, And Even Between Conversations With Friends. The Closer Is The Planned Time For Exercise The Greater Is The Urge And Even Anxiety Or Fear From Not Starting On Time. The Addicted Exerciser Is Literally Obsessed With Exercise And Regardless Of The Time Of The Day, Place, Or Activity Performed Her Or His Mind Is Directed Towards Exercise During The Majority Of Waking Hours.

3.1.2 Mood Modification

This symptom refers to the subjective experiences that people report as a consequence of engaging in the particular activity and could be seen as a coping strategy (i.e., they experience an arousing "buzz" or a "high", or paradoxically tranquillizing feel of "escape" or "numbing"). Most exercisers report a positive feeling state and pleasant exhaustion after a session of exercise. However, the person addicted to exercise would seek mood modification not necessarily for the gain or the positive mental effect of exercise, but rather for the modification or avoidance of the negative psychological feeling states that she or he would experience if the exercise session were missed.

3.1.3 Tolerance

It is the process whereby increasing amounts of the particular activity are required to achieve the former effects. For instance, a gambler may have to gradually increase the size of the bet to experience the euphoric or satisfying effect that was initially obtained by a much smaller bet. The runner needs to run longer distances to experience the runner's high[1] (Stoll, 1997), a euphoric feeling state described later. Similarly, the addicted exercises needs larger and larger of doses of exercise to derive the effects experienced previously with lower

---

[1] A pleasant feeling associated with positive self image, sense of vitality, control, and a sense of fulfilment reported by runners as well as by other exercisers after a certain amount and intensity of exercise. The feeling has been associated with increased levels of endogenous opioids and catecholamines observed after exercise.

amounts of exercise. Tolerance is the main reason why individuals addicted to exercise progressively and continuously increase the frequency, duration and possibly intensity of the workouts.

3.1.4 Withdrawal Symptoms

These symptoms are the unpleasant psychological and physical feeling states, which occur when exercise is discontinued or it is significantly reduced. The most commonly reported symptoms are guilt, irritability, anxiety, sluggishness, feeling fat, lacking energy, and being in bad mood or depressed. The intensity of these states is severe in people affected by exercise addiction to the extent that they really feel miserable when the need of exercise is not fulfilled. The manifestation of these withdrawal symptoms in addicted individuals is clearly different from those experienced by committed exercisers who simply feel a void, or that something is missing, when exercising is not possible for a reason. Addicted exercisers have to exercises to overcome withdrawal symptoms even at the expense of other more important life obligations. In contrast, committed exercisers look forward to the next opportunity while prioritizing their obligations (Szabo, 1995).

3.1.5 Conflict

This symptom represents the conflicts between the exercise addicts and others around them (interpersonal conflict), conflicts with other daily activities (job, social life, hobbies and interests) or from within the individual themselves (intra-psychic conflict) which are concerned with the particular activity. Interpersonal conflict usually results from neglect of the relationship with friends or family because of the exaggerated time devoted to exercise. Conflict in daily activities arises because of the abnormally high priority given to exercise in contrast to even some of the survival activities like cleaning, taking care of bills, working, or studying for exams. Intra-psychic conflict occurs when the addicted person has realized that fulfilling the need to exercise takes a toll on other life endeavors, but she or he is unable to cut down or to control the exercise behavior.

3.1.6 Relapse

This is the tendency for repeated reversions to earlier patterns of exercise after a break whether that is voluntary or involuntary. The phenomenon is similar to that observed in alcoholics who stop drinking for a period of time and then starts over again and drink as much – if not more – than prior to the break from drinking. Relapse could be observed after injury (which is involuntary) or after a planned reduction in exercise volume as a consequence of personal decision to put a halt to the unhealthy pattern of exercise behavior or as a consequence of professional advice. Upon resumption of the activity, addicted individuals could soon end up exercising as much or even more as before the reduction of their volume of exercise.

3.2 Other Symptoms Observed in Exercise Addiction

3.2.1 Loss of Control Over Life-Activities (Griffiths, 1997)

The internal drive or urge for exercise becomes psychologically so intense that it preoccupies attention in the majority of waking hours by dominating the person's thoughts. Consequently, the affected individual is unable to pay attention or to properly concentrate on other daily activities. Until that urge is satisfied, other life-activities are deficiently performed or totally neglected. Upon fulfillment of the need to exercise, the affected person may function well and take care of some other mundane obligations but such a "normal" functioning is limited to the period encompassing the acute effects of the previous session of exercise or until the urge for another bout of exercise starts to rise again.

3.2.2 Loss of Control Over One's Exercise Behavior (Cockerill & Riddington, 1996; Johnson, 1995)

This is a phenomenon where self-set resolutions cannot be kept. The exerciser simply cannot resist the urge to exercise. While she or he may try to set limits in her/his exercise patterns, she/he is unable to respect those self-set limits. In short, lack of control denotes the inability to exercise with moderation. This is a phenomenon also observable in alcoholics (and in most addictions in general) who after several incidences of heavy drinking, and some severe consequences of such drinking pattern, make the resolution not to get drunk again. However, on the same day later, after making such a resolution, they get drunk again.

3.2.3 Negative, Non-Injury Related, Life Consequences (Griffiths, 1997)

Negative life events may occur as a result of overexercising. If life activities are ignored or superficially performed as a result of excessive exercise and too much preoccupation with exercise, on the long term, negative life consequences may emerge involving even loss of employment, poor academic performance, break-up in relationships and friendships, and other consequences generally considered to have undesirable effects on the person's life.

3.2.4 Risk of Self-Injury (De Coverley Veale, 1987; Wichmann & Martin, 1992)

At times of mild injuries the addicted exerciser cannot abstain from exercise and, thus, assumes the risk of self-injury by maintaining her/his physical activity. In more severe cases, the affected individual needs to see a medical professional who may advice the person to refrain from exercising until full recovery takes place. In spite of medical advice, the person addicted to exercise, will likely resume her or his exercise immediately upon experiencing minor alleviation in the discomfort associated with the injury – or in the early stages of recovery – thus exposing her- / himself to further and possibly more severe injuries triggering often irreversible health damages.

3.2.5 Social Selection and Withdrawal (Cockerill & Riddington, 1996

This is a behavior tendency by which the addicted person identifies with others who approve her or his exercise behavior and avoids the company of those who criticize her/his physical activity pattern. Such a social gravitation is generally observable in individuals suffering from others forms of behavioral (e.g. gambling) or substance (e.g. alcohol) addictions.

3.2.6 Lack of Compromise (Wichmann & Martin, 1992)

This symptom is closely related to the loss of control described above. Although there may be several warning signs related to the neglect of family or work responsibilities because of excessive exercise, the signs are insufficient to trigger a decision to compromise. Consequently, other life-commitments remain ignored even though the affected person is aware that the end result may be worst than undesirable.

3.2.7 Denial of a Problem or Self-Justification (Wichmann & Martin, 1992)

This represents a psychological defense mechanism known as rationalization. The person addicted to exercise explains or justifies the problem via conscious search for reasons why exercise, even in massive volume, is beneficial. The mass media and even scientific reports provide abundant reasons that could be used in the rationalization. The ACSM guidelines for exercise and the positive correlation between the dose of exercise and health (Haskell et al., 2007) are excellent anchors for justifying the exaggerated amounts of exercise.

3.2.8 Full Awareness of the Problem (De Coverley Veale, 1987)

The exercise addict person may know well that there are problems with her/his exercise behavior through feedback from other people or from some negative life-events directly resulting from overexercising. However, she/he feels powerless to take action against the problem.

3.3 A Newer Classification for Behavioral Addictions in General

More recently, two German scientists, Grüsser and Thalemann (2006) presented a newer classification for behavioral addictions based on some relatively common characteristics noticeable in several forms of addictions. These scholars conjecture that these characteristic symptoms may be signs for the possible diagnosis of a behavioral addiction, thus including exercise addiction. Nevertheless, the authors emphasize that cases need to be examined individually to determine whether the heavy involvement with the given behavior is indeed addictive or just an excessive one (non-pathological or related to another dysfunction). Indeed, symptoms alone may not be sufficient for the correct diagnosis, but a collection of *severe typical symptoms* in conjunction with *history of negative consequences,* due to the excessive indulgence in a given behavior, may pinpoint the presence of addiction. Grüsser's and Thalemann's characteristics are:

1) The behavior is exhibited over a long period of at least 12 months in an excessive, aberrant form, deviating from the norm in frequency and intensity
2) Loss of control over the excessive behavior (duration, frequency, intensity, risk) when the behavior started
3) Reward effect (e.g. excessive exercises is considered to be rewarding)
4) Development of tolerance (the behavior is conducted longer, more often and more intensively in order to achieve the desired effect; in unvaried form, intensity and frequency the desired effect fails to appear)

5) The behavior that was initially perceived as pleasant, positive and rewarding is increasingly considered to be unpleasant in the course of the addiction
6) Irresistible urge/craving to execute the behavior
7) Function (the behavior is chiefly performed to regulate emotions/mood)
8) Expectancy of effect (pleasant feelings are anticipated to result from the behavior)
9) Limited pattern of behavior (does not wish to try out new things)
10) Cognitive occupation with the build-up, execution and follow-up activities of the excessive behavior and possibly the anticipated effects of the excessively executed behavior
11) Irrational, perception of different aspects of the excessive behavior
12) Withdrawal symptoms (psychological and physical)
13) Continued execution of the excessive behavior despite negative consequences (health-related, occupational, social)
14) Conditioned/learned reactions (resulting from the confrontation with internal and external stimuli associated with the excessive behavior as well as from cognitive occupation with the excessive behavior)
15) Suffering (desire to alleviate perceived suffering)

Grüsser's and Thalemann's (2006) list of characteristics is clearly longer than the symptoms contained within the "components" model of addiction (Griffiths, 2005). However, the list incorporates most if not all, directly or implicitly, six components of addiction proposed by Griffiths. The question is whether fewer but typical symptoms of addiction are sufficient to help health professionals in the identification of the disorder or whether a longer list is needed? Albrecht, Kirschner, and Grüsser (2007) believe that clinical orientations, also reinforced by scientific evidence, highlight the commonalities between substance-related and non-substance related behavioral addictions. They believe that a standardized classification should describe all excessive or abused behaviours that meet the criteria of addictions as an addiction disorder and incorporate them into the diagnostic criteria. This will facilitate the accurate diagnosis (by using valid and reliable instruments) and also aid in the effective treatment of affected individuals. It is clear then that the proper assessment of exercise addiction is crucial in the identification the addiction as a dysfunction.

4.0 ASSESSMENT OF EXERCISE ADDICTION

Although symptoms are critical in the assessment of a health condition, as seen in the previous section, exercise addiction cannot be positively assessed simply on the basis of the presence or absence of withdrawal symptoms. A combination of symptoms co-occurring is a more precise index of maladaptive exercise. Currently, there are several exercise addiction questionnaires that are based on the most common symptoms of addictions. In general, the frequency and intensity of the symptoms reported by the respondents is computed to yield an exercise addiction score. However, these scores only measure the *degree of* or *the susceptibility to* exercise addiction, rather than positively diagnose the condition. In the following section the psychometrically validated most popular tools used for assessing exercise addiction will be briefly presented and evaluated.

4.1 The Exercise Addiction Inventory, (Eai - Terry, Szabo, & Griffiths, 2004)

This is the shortest psychometrically validated questionnaire to date (Appendix A). It consists of only six statements that correspond to the "components" model of addiction (Griffiths, 2005). Each statement is rated on a five-point Likert scale. The statements are coded so that the high scores reflect attributes of addictive exercise behavior: 1="strongly disagree", 2="disagree", 3="neither agree nor disagree", 4="agree", 5="strongly agree". The six statements that make up the inventory are: 1)

Appendix A. The Exercise Addiction Inventory, By Terry, A., Szabo, A., & Griffiths, M.

Directions: Listed below are six statements about people's exercise habits. Using the scale below, please circle the number that reflects the degree to which you agree or disagree that the given statement applies to you.

1 – strongly disagree 2 – disagree	3 – neither agree nor disagree				
4 – agree 5 – strongly agree					
1) Exercise is the most important thing in my life	1	2	3	4	5
2) Conflicts have arisen between me and my family and/or my partner about the amount of exercise I do	1	2	3	4	5
3) I use exercise as a way of changing my mood (e.g. to get a buzz, to escape etc.)	1	2	3	4	5
4) Over time I have increased the amount of exercise I do in a day.	1	2	3	4	5
5) If I have to miss an exercise session I feel moody and irritable	1	2	3	4	5
6) If I cut down the amount of exercise I do, and then start again, I always end up exercising as often as I did before	1	2	3	4	5

"Exercise is the most important thing in my life" (salience), 2) "Conflicts have arisen between me and my family and/or my partner about the amount of exercise I do" (conflict), 3) "I use exercise as a way of changing my mood" (mood modification), 4) "Over time I have increased the amount of exercise I do in a day" (tolerance), 5) "If I have to miss an exercise session I feel moody and irritable" (withdrawal symptoms), and 6) "If I cut down the amount of exercise I do, and then start again, I always end up exercising as often as I did before" (relapse).

The EAI cut-off score for individuals considered at-risk of exercise addiction is 24. This cut off represents those individuals with scores in the top 15% of the total scale score. High scores were considered to be the most problematic for the individual. A score of 13 to 23 was chosen to be indicative of a potentially symptomatic person and a score of 0 to 12 was deemed to indicate an asymptomatic individual. The EAI was developed on the basis of a sample of 200 habitual exercisers. The internal reliability of the original scale was excellent ($\alpha = .84$) and its concurrent validity was at least $r = .80$.

The EAI is the most recent and the shortest tool aimed at the assessment of risk of exercise addiction. It is also the easiest to interpret and the fastest to administer. The authors developed the scale to aid non-psychologist medical personnel, like orthopedic specialists (who often encounter individuals addicted to exercise in their practice due to injury) to easily and quickly gauge whether the person may be risk of exercise addiction.

4.2 The Obligatory Exercise Questionnaire (Oeq - Pasman & Thompson, 1988)

This questionnaire was a pioneering instrument aimed at the assessment of exercise addiction. It was modified from the Obligatory Running Questionnaire (ORQ - Blumenthal, O'Toole, & Chang, 1984). Later the OEQ has been modified to a version that is a more general measure of exercise activity (Thompson & Pasman, 1991). The new version of the questionnaire consists of 20 items pertaining to exercises habits, which are rated on a 4-point frequency scale: 1-never, 2-sometimes, 3-usually, 4-always. Two of the items are inversely rated during scoring. The psychometric properties of the questionnaire have been well established (Coen & Ogles, 1993). The internal reliability of the OEQ was reported to be $\alpha = .96$ and its concurrent validity was $r = .96$ (Thompson & Pasman, 1991).

Ackard, Brehm, and Steffen (2002) found that the OEQ (1991 version) has three subscales. These are exercise fixation (items associated with missed exercise and exercise to compensate for perceived overeating), exercise frequency (addressing frequency and type of exercise) and exercise commitment (indicating a sense of routine which cannot be missed). Ackard et al. believe that these subscales highlight the multifaceted nature of excessive exercise.

4.3 The Exercise Dependence Questionnaire (Edq - Ogden, Veale, & Summers, 1997)

The EDQ was developed with a sample of 449 participants who exercised for more than 4 hours a week. The EDQ consists of 29 items and it has 8 subscales: 1) interference with social/family/work life, 2) positive reward, 3) withdrawal symptoms, 4) exercise for weight control, 5) insight into problem, 6) exercise for social reasons, 7) exercise for health reasons, and 8) stereotyped behavior. The EDQ was found to have moderate to good internal reliability ranging from $\alpha = .52$ to $\alpha = .84$. Its concurrent validity with other instruments has not been reported. Further, certain items assess attitudes and social practices rather than addiction. Consequently the EDQ has been used only on relatively few occasions in researching exercise addiction.

4.4 Exercise Dependence Scale (EDS - Hausenblas & Symons Downs, 2002b)

Hausenblas and Symons Downs (2002a; 2002b) have developed the Exercise Dependence Scale (EDS). Exercise is described as a craving for exercise that results in uncontrollable excessive physical activity and manifests in physiological symptoms, psychological symptoms, or both (Hausenblas & Symons Downs, 2002a). The Exercise Dependence Scale is based on the Diagnostic and Statistical Manual of Mental Disorder-IV criteria for substance dependence (DSM IV - American Psychiatric Association, 1994). The Exercise Dependence Scale is able to differentiate between at-risk, non-dependent-symptomatic, and nondependent-asymptomatic individuals. It can also specify whether individuals may have a physiological dependence (evidence of withdrawal) or no physiological dependence (no evidence of withdrawal).

On the EDS 21-items questionnaire are rated on a 6-point Likert frequency scale ranging from 1 (*never*) to 6 (*always*). Evaluation is made in reference to the DSM-IV criteria (APA, 1994), screening for the presence of three or more of the following symptoms, most of them described in the previous section: 1) *tolerance*, 2) *withdrawal,* 3) *intention effects* (exercise is often taken in larger amounts or over longer period than was intended), 4) *loss of control,* 5) *time* (a great deal of time is spent in activities conducive to the obtainment of exercise), 6) *conflict,* and 7) *continuance* (exercise is continued despite knowledge of persistent or recurrent physical or psychological problems that are likely to have been caused or exacerbated by exercise).

A total score and subscale scores can be calculated for the EDI. The higher the score, the higher is the risk for addiction. The scale is rated with the aid of a scoring manual that comprises flowchart-format decision rules. The rules specify the items or the combinations of the items that that help in classifying the individual as being at risk, non-addicted-symptomatic or non-addicted asymptomatic on each criterion. Individuals who score in the addiction range, defined as 4 - 5 (out of 6) on the Likert scale on at least three of the seven criteria, are classified as 'at risk' for exercise addiction. Those who fulfil at least three criteria in the non-addicted symptomatic range, scoring around 3 on the Likert scale, or a combination of at least three criteria in the 'at risk' and non-addicted symptomatic range, but did not meet the criteria for exercise addiction, are classified as non-addicted symptomatic. Finally, individuals who endorse at least three of the criteria in the non-addicted asymptomatic range (1 - 2 on the on the Likert scale) are classified as non-addicted asymptomatic. It has been shown that the scale possesses good internal reliability ($\alpha =. 78$ to $\alpha =. 92$) and test–retest reliability ($r = 0.92$).

4.5 Less Widely Used Tools in the Assessment of Exercise Addiction

Prior to the development of psychometrically validated tools for gauging exercise addiction, the condition was investigated with interviews (Sachs & Pargman, 1979) and the

Commitment to Running Scale (CR – Carmack & Martens, 1979). However, using the CR has been criticized (Szabo et al., 1997), because addiction and commitment in exercise are two different constructs. While addiction is a dysfunction, commitment to exercise implies involvement in the activity for enjoyment and fun.

The *Negative Addiction Scale* (NAS – Hailey & Bailey, 1982) has been used primarily with runners. Its items measure the psychological rather than physiological aspects of compulsive running. Because of its mediocre psychometric characteristics, inference about scores that define a person as addicted to running is hard to be made.

The *Exercise Beliefs Questionnaire* (EBQ – Loumidis & Wells, 1998) assesses personal assumptions in exercise on the bases of four factors: 1) *social desirability*, 2) *physical appearance*, 3) *mental and emotional functioning*, and 4) *vulnerability to disease and aging*. The scale's internal reliability is relatively good, ranging between $\alpha = .67$ and $\alpha = .89$ and concurrent validity between $r = .67$ and $r = .77$).

Another instrument, the *Bodybuilding Dependency Scale* (BDS – Smith, Hale, & Collins, 1998), was developed specially to assess excessive exercise in bodybuilders. The questionnaire contains three subscales: 1) *social dependence* (individual's need to be in the weightlifting environment), 2) *training dependence* (individual's compulsion to lift weights) and 3) *mastery dependence* (individual's need to exert control over his/her training schedule). Because of its sports specificity the BDS has restricted range of employability in sport and exercise psychology.

4.6 Strengths and Limitations of Paper and Pencil Tools in Gauging Exercise Addiction

All exercise addiction questionnaires could only be used for surface screening or risk assessment but not for medical diagnosis. Therefore, the questionnaire method of assessment estimates the *likelihood of addiction* in the respondent. Even individuals scoring above average may not necessarily be addicted to exercise. Nevertheless, a score that is close to the maximum may suggest that there is a possibility or a high risk of addiction. For example, a score of 24 on the EAI needs to be considered as a potential warning sign. Still, the proper and unambiguous assessment of exercise addiction could only be established after a deep interview with a qualified health professional. Serving well for screening purposes, exercise addiction questionnaires direct the individual, or those who are concerned, in the right direction. In schools, sport and leisure facilities, they are quite useful for screening, but many addicted exercisers perform their activity in an informal setting, by simply going out for a run on their own. In fact, it is likely that most exercise addicts are loners in some sense because no structured physical activity classes or exercising friends could keep up with the massive amount and busy schedule of exercise in which they engage on a daily basis. Assuming that only about one to three percent of the exercising population may be affected by exercise addiction (Szabo, 2000, Terry et al., 2004) and that the majority of exercises addicts are "lone wolfs", the use of the questionnaires may have further limited value in assessment.

Although the assessment of exercise addiction is based on some general symptoms of addiction listed DSM IV (1994), the latter does not list exercise addiction as a separate category of dysfunction. There may be several reasons for the omission of exercises addiction from the DSM IV. First, the incidence of exercise addiction is very rare. The estimation is based on a few case-studies that are occasionally reported in the literature (Szabo, 2000). Ensuing, there is perhaps insufficient medical or scientific evidence on which the DSM IV could draw solid conclusions. Second, in contrast to the passive and *let go / let down* attitude common in addictive behaviours, exercise addiction requires substantial physical and mental effort, determination, and self-discipline. These characteristics are positive that are in conflict with the *quick fix* aspects of other addictions. A third reason, that may also be true in other addictions, is that exercise addiction identified on the basis of certain symptoms, may only be a *symptom in itself* of an underlying psychological or mental dysfunction in which exercise abuse is a means of escape from the problem rather than the route of the problem. Accordingly, if exercise addiction is indeed escape from one or more unpleasant or noxious life event(s), the motivational incentives beyond this escape or avoidance behavior need to be examined more closely.

5.0 MOTIVATIONAL INCENTIVES IN EXERCISE ADDICTION

At several places in this monograph it has been emphasized and re-emphasized that commitment to exercise is different from addiction to exercise, regardless of the amount of exercise. Motivation for exercise is another distinguishing characteristic between commitment and addiction. People exercise for specific reasons. The reason is often an intangible reward like being in shape, looking good, being with friends, staying healthy, building muscles, losing weight, etc. The personal experience of the anticipated reward strengthens the exercise behavior. Scholars known as behaviorists, adhering to one of the most influential schools of thought in the field of Psychology, postulate that behavior could be understood and explained through reinforcement and punishment. Accordingly, the *operant conditioning theory* suggests that there are three principles of behavior: *positive reinforcement*, *negative reinforcement*, and *punishment* (Bozarth, 1994). Positive reinforcement is a motivational incentive for doing something to *gain* a reward that is something pleasant or desirable (e.g., increased muscle tone). The reward then becomes a motivational incentive, which increases the likelihood of that behavior to reoccur. In contrast, negative reinforcement is a motivational incentive for doing something to *avoid* a noxious or unpleasant (e.g., gaining weight) event. The avoidance or reduction of the noxious stimulus is the reward, which then increases the probability of that behavior to reoccur. It should be noted that both positive and negative reinforcers increase the likelihood of the behavior (Bozarth, 1994), but their mechanism is different because in positive reinforcement there is a *gain following the action* (e.g. feeling revitalized), whereas in behaviours motivated by negative reinforcement one attempts to *avoid something bad or unpleasant before happening* that otherwise would occur (e.g. feeling guilty or fat if a planned exercise session is missed).

Punishment refers situations in which the imposition of some noxious or unpleasant stimulus or event or alternately the removal of a pleasant or desired stimulus or event reduces the probability of a given behavior to reoccur. In contrast to reinforcers, punishers suppress the behavior and, therefore, exercise or physical activity should never be used (by teachers, parents, or coaches) as punishment. Paradoxically, exercise addiction may be perceived as self-punishing behavior. It is a very rare form of addiction (compared to alcohol, tobacco or drug abuse) requiring substantial physical effort often to the point of exhaustion. Therefore, exercises addicts may be viewed as either masochistic or self-punishing individuals.

People addicted to exercise may be motivated by negative reinforcement (e.g., to avoid withdrawal symptoms) as well as positive reinforcement (e.g., *runner's high;* Pierce, 1994; Szabo, 1995). However, negative reinforcement, or avoidance behavior, is not a characteristic of the committed exercisers (Szabo, 1995). Indeed, committed exercisers maintain their exercise regimen for benefiting from the activity. On the other hand, addicted exercisers *have to do it* or else something will happen to them. Their exercise may be an "obligation" (also reflected by the popular term "obligatory exercise") that needs to be fulfilled or otherwise an unwanted life event could occur like the inability to cope with stress, or gaining weight, becoming moody, etc. Every time a person undertakes behavior to avoid something negative, bad, or unpleasant, the motive behind that behavior may be classified as negative reinforcement. In these situations the person involved *has to do it* in contrast to *wants to do it.*

There are many examples in other sport areas where a behavior initially driven by positive reinforcement may turn into negatively reinforced or motivated behavior. For example, an outstanding football player who starts playing the game for fun, after being discovered as a talent and being offered a service contract in a team, becomes a professional player who upon signing the contract *is expected* to perform. Although the player may still enjoy playing (especially when all goes well), the pressure or expectation to perform is the *"has to do"* new facet of football playing and the negatively reinforcing component of his (or her) sporting behavior. Table 1 illustrates the differences between the underlying motives in exercises behaviours driven by negative and positive reinforcement.

Table 5.1. Exercise behaviours driven by positive and reinforcement.

Positive reinforcement	Negative reinforcement
Origin: Behaviorist school of thought. Definition: Positive Reinforcement strengthens behavior because a tangible or intangible gain is secured as a result of the behavior.	Origin: Behaviorist school of thought. Definition: Negative Reinforcement strengthens behavior because a negative condition is stopped and/or avoided as a consequence of the behavior.
Examples: "I feel revitalized after exercise" (gains good feeling) "I like to decrease my running time on the same distance. (gains skill and confidence) "I lift weights to look good." (gains physical benefits, good looks)	Examples: "I run to avoid circulatory problems that my parents had." "I go to gym to avoid getting fat." "I have to run my 10 miles every day, or else I feel guilty and irritated." (avoids feeling of guilt and irritation)

Duncan (1974) in relation to drug addiction purports that addiction is almost identical with, and semantically is just another name for, avoidance or escape behavior when the unpleasant feeling is being negatively reinforced by drug taking. People addicted to exercise, in this view, reach for a means - with which they had past relief-inducing experience - that provides them with temporary escape from an ongoing state of emotional distress and struggle, which might be caused by mental dysfunction, or by psychosocial stress, or by an aversive social or physical environment. In Duncan's view, all addictions represent similar negatively reinforced behaviours.

Duncan states that negative reinforcement is a powerful mechanism in maintaining high-frequency and long-persistent behaviours. Animals that could have escaped a noxious stimulus or event by pressing a bar (negative reinforcement) will often do so to the point of ignoring other even instinctual activities like eating, sleeping, sexual activity, etc. Avoidance behaviours are highly resistant to extinction and even when they appear to have been finally eliminated, they tend to reoccur spontaneously. Consequently, the relapse rate in addictions, regardless of the form of addiction, is very high. In Duncan's view, the intensity, compulsiveness, and proneness to relapse, that are important characteristics in addictions, result from the fact that the behavior is maintained by negative reinforcement.

Although positive reinforcement like the runners' high and brain reward systems have been implicated in the explanation of exercise addiction, the motivational incentive in addiction may be more closely connected to prevention, escape, or avoidance of something unwanted as in some recent models of addiction (Baker et al., 2004). Accordingly, the process of addiction is more likely motivated by negative reinforcement in which the affected individual has to exercise to avoid an unwanted consequence.

6.0 MODELS EXPLAINING EXERCISE ADDICTION

6.1 The Sympathetic Arousal Hypothesis

A physiological model suggesting how adaptation of the organisms to habitual exercise may lead to addiction is based a Thompson's and Blanton's (1987) work. From most exercise physiology textbooks it is known that regular exercise, especially aerobic exercise like running, if performed for a sustained period, results in decreased heart rate at rest. While heart rate is only a crude measure of the body's sympathetic activity (which is directed by the autonomic nervous system), it is, nevertheless, a sensitive measure and it is often used to mirror sympathetic activity. A lower resting heart rate after training results from the adaptation of the organism to exercise. Figure 6.1 illustrates a hypothetical case in which the exerciser's initial basal heart rate (red line) on the average is about 62 beats per minute (bpm). Every single session of exercise (green line) raises the heart rate to well above 100 bpm (depending on exercise intensity of course) that upon recovery - following exercise - returns lo lower than the pre-exercise or basal heart rate. With repeated exercise challenge, resulting from aerobic training, and a concomitantly more efficient cardiovascular system, the basal heart rate, partially reflecting sympathetic activity, decreases. Lower sympathetic activity at rest means lower level of arousal. This new arousal state may be experienced as lethargic or energy-lacking state, which according to Thomson's and Blanton's hypothesis urges the exercises to do something about it, or to increase her or his level of arousal. The obvious means to do that is exercise. However, the effects of exercise in increasing arousal are only temporary and, therefore, more and more bouts of exercise may be needed to achieve an optimal state of arousal. Furthermore, not only the frequency but also the intensity of exercise sessions may need to increase due to training effect. Such an increase accounts for the tolerance in the addiction process.

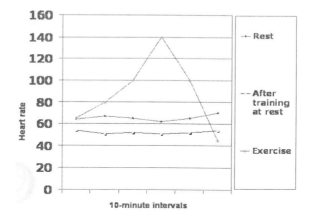

Figure 6.1. A hypothetical graph of how one's basal (resting) heart rate may decrease after prolonged aerobic training. Note that the green line illustrates the challenge in heart rate during one exercise session only. The adaptation, reflected by the difference between the red and the blue lines, may require several months and in some cases even longer.

Uncomfortable sensations of "non-optimal" level of arousal are a form of withdrawal feelings or symptoms that prompt the exerciser to get moving and engage in a workout. As the frequency of workouts and the reliance on exercise to regulate arousal increase, the behaviour progressively assumes a central part in the exerciser's life, which is known as salience. When the need to exercise is not fulfilled, the addicted person could feel lethargic, lacking energy, guilty, irritated, etc. (see Figure 6.2). He or she has to exercise, as mentioned above, to avoid a bunch of uncomfortable feelings. At this point the exerciser loses control over her/his exercise, which is no longer performed for fun or pleasure, but a negatively reinforced obligation.

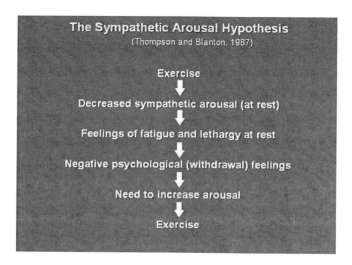

Figure 6.2. The Sympathetic Arousal Hypothesis

6.2 The Cognitive Appraisal Hypothesis

There is psychological explanation for exercise addiction as well. Some exercisers try to escape from their psychological problems (Morris, 1989). They are very few in numbers and use exercise as a means of coping with stress. Like others, who turn to drugs and alcohol in difficult life situations, exercisers may abuse their exercise so that behavioral addiction becomes evident (Griffiths, 1997). However, because exercise, in contrast to alcohol or drugs, involves significant physical effort (Cockerill & Riddington, 1996) it is an inconvenient coping method that requires strong self-determination, self-discipline, and possibly a bit of masochistic attitude. Therefore, the incidence of exercise addiction is very rare in contrast to other forms of escape behaviours.

Szabo (1995) proposed a cognitive appraisal hypothesis for the better understanding of the psychological path in exercise addiction, as summarized in Figure 6.3. Accordingly, once the exerciser uses exercise as a coping method with stress, the affected individual starts to depend on exercise to function well. She or he believes that exercise is a healthy means of coping with stress based on information from scholastic and public media sources. Therefore, she or he uses rationalization to explain the exaggerated amount of exercise that progressively takes a tool on other obligations and daily activities. However, when the interference of exercise with other duties and tasks obliges the exerciser to reduce the amount of daily exercise, a psychological hardship emerges, which is manifested through a set of negative feelings like irritability, guilt, anxiousness, sluggishness, etc. These feelings collectively represent the withdrawal symptoms experienced because of no or less exercise. When exercise is used to cope with stress, apart the collection of negative psychological feeling states there is also a loss in the coping mechanism (exercise). Concomitantly, the exerciser loses control over the stressful situations that she or he used to deal with by resorting to exercise.

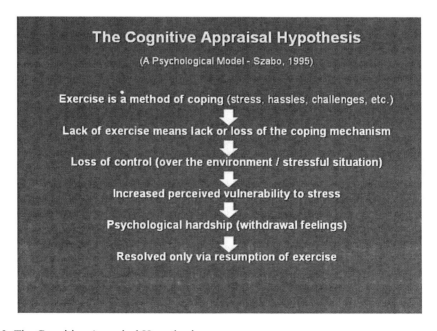

Figure 6.3. The Cognitive Appraisal Hypothesis

The loss of the coping mechanism, followed by the loss of control over stress, generates an increased perception of vulnerability to stress, therefore further amplifying the negative psychological feelings associated with the lack of exercise. This problem could be resolved only through resuming the previous pattern of exercise at the expense of the other obligations in the daily life. Obviously, while exercise provides an instant reduction in the negative psychological feelings, the ignorance or superficial treatment of other social and work obligations results in conflict with people, possibly losses at work or school, or even loss of job, altogether causing further stress. The addicted exerciser is then trapped in a vicious circle needing more exercise to deal with the consistently increasing life-stress, part of which is caused by exercise itself.

6.3 The Affect Regulation Hypothesis

The affect regulation hypothesis states that exercise has dual effect on mood. First it increases positive *affect* (defined as: momentary psychological feeling states of longer persistence than momentary emotions) and, therefore, contributes to an improved general *mood* state (defined as: prolonged psychological feeling states lasting for several hours or even days). Second, it decreases negative affect or the temporary state of guilt, irritability, sluggishness, anxiety, etc. and, therefore, further contributes to an improved general mood state (Hamer & Karageorghis, 2007). However, the affect-regulating effects of exercise are temporary and the longer is the interval between two exercise sessions the experience of negative affect becomes increasingly likely. In fact after prolonged periods of abstention from exercise (which are prolonged only in relation to the busy exercise-schedule of the addicted person, since otherwise they are as short as 24 to 36 hours; Sachs, 1981), these negative affective states become severe deprivation sensations or withdrawal symptoms, which are relieved only through exercise. Therefore, as the cycle continues more and more exercise is needed to experience improvement in affect and general mood, and in parallel the inter-exercise rest period needs to decrease to prevent the surfacing of withdrawal symptoms.

6.4 The Thermogenic Regulation Hypothesis

This model is based on physiological evidence that physical exercise increases body temperature. A warm body temperature induces a relaxing state with concomitant reduction in anxiety (similar to sun-tanning, Turkish or warm bath, and sauna effects). Consequently, physical exercise reduces anxiety (De Vries, 1981; Morgan & O'Connor, 1988) whilst inducing relaxation as a consequence of increased body temperature. Lower levels of anxiety and higher states of relaxation act as positive reinforcers for the exercise behavior. The pleasant psychological state emerging from the relaxing and anxiety relieving effects of exercise, conditions (teaches) the person to resort to exercise when they experience anxiety. Higher levels of anxiety may be associated with the need for more exercise. Consequently, the duration or the intensity – or even both modalities – may be increased to obtain a stronger antidote to anxiety. The expectation of such dose-response relationship between exercise and anxiety eventually leads to tolerance that is another common characteristic in exercise addiction.

6.5 The Catecholamine Hypothesis

This hypothesis is based on the empirical observation that increased levels of catecholamines in the body may be observed after exercise (Cousineau et al., 1977). Catecholamines, among other functions, are heavily involved in the stress response and sympathetic responses response to exercise. In light of the catecholamine hypothesis, it is speculated that central catecholaminergic activity is altered by exercise. Because central catecholamine levels are involved in regulating mood and affect and play an important role in mental dysfunctions like depression, the alteration of catecholamines by exercise is an attractive speculation. To date, however, there is inconclusive evidence to this surmise. Indeed, it is unclear whether the peripheral changes in catecholamines have an effect on brain catecholamine levels or vice versa. Furthermore, the changes in brain catecholamine levels during exercise in humans are unknown, because direct measurement in the human brain is not possible.

6.6 The Endorphin Hypothesis

This model is a very popular one in the literature because it is connected to the phenomenon of "runner's high" (defined again as: the pleasant feeling associated with positive self image, sense of vitality, control, and a sense of fulfillment reported by runners as well as by other exercisers after a certain amount and intensity of exercise. The feeling has been associated with increased levels of endogenous opioids and catecholamines observed after exercise). The surmise behind this model is that exercise leads to increased levels of endorphins in the brain, which act as internal psychoactive drugs yielding a sense of euphoria. In fact this hypothesis is analogous to substance or drug addiction (e.g. heroin, morphine, etc.) with the notable exception that the psychoactive agent (beta endorphin) is generated internally during exercise instead of being administered from the outside. This is an elegant model and if there were evidence for this hypothesis it would explain why exercise addicts would resort to exaggerated or even masochistic amounts of exercise to internally-generate the "drugs" that other addicts buy from dealers. Indeed, both the catecholamine hypothesis and the endorphin hypothesis have been implicated in the euphoric feeling of runners high. If exercise addiction could also be driven by positive reinforcement, then the most plausible explanation is the runner's high phenomenon. Consequently, this highly disputed but anecdotally repeatedly reported psychological feeling states needs to be evaluated.

7.0 THE RUNNER'S HIGH PHENOMENON

"I believe in the runner's high, and I believe that those who are passionate about running are the ones who experience it to the fullest degree possible. To me, the runner's high is a sensational reaction to a great run! It's an exhilarating feeling of satisfaction and achievement. It's like being on top of the world, and truthfully... there's nothing else quite like it!" Sasha Azevedo (http://www.runtheplanet.com/resources/historical/runquotes.asp)

For many decades, marathon runners, long distance joggers, and even average runners have reported a feeling of euphoria replacing the fatigue and pain of physical exertion caused by long sessions of exercise. Such euphoria triggers a sensation of "flying", effortless movement, and has become a legendary goal referred to as "the zone" (Goldberg, 1988). The runner's high phenomenon has been closely linked to exercises addiction. The existence of runner's high is subject of heated debate in the scientific and scholastic circles. The question is whether a biochemical explanation for the runner's high exists, or it is a purely psychologically conceptualized and popularized terminology. Exercise addiction, if driven by positive reinforcement, would require an explanation that has physiological and biochemical foundations. Runners (and most habitual exercisers) experience withdrawal symptoms when their exercise is prevented. The symptoms include guilt, irritability, anxiety, and other unpleasant feelings (Szabo, 1995). Research shows that the human body produces its own opiate-like peptides, called endorphins, and like morphine, these peptides could cause dependence (Farrell, Gates, Maksud, & Morgan, 1982) and, consequently, may be the route of withdrawal symptoms. In general, endorphins are known to be responsible for pain and pleasure responses in the central nervous system. Morphine and other exogenous opiates *bind to the same receptors* that the body intended for endogenous opioids or endorphins, and since morphine's analgesic and euphoric effects are well documented, comparable effects for endorphins could be anticipated (Sforzo, 1988).

Research has been conducted to examine the effects of fitness levels, gender, and exercise intensity on endogenous opioid – mainly beta-endorphin – production during cycling, running on a treadmill, participating in aerobic dance, and running marathons. Biddle and Mutrie (1991) reported research that has shown that aerobic exercise could cause beta-endorphin levels to increase fivefold in contrast to baseline levels. Fitness levels of the research participants appears to be irrelevant as both trained and untrained individuals experience an increase in beta-endorphin levels, although the metabolism of beta-endorphins appears to be more efficient in trained athletes (Goldfarb & Jamurtas, 1997).

A decade ago, Goldfarb et al. (1998) researched gender differences in beta-endorphin production during exercise. Their results could not reveal gender-differences in beta-endorphin response to exercise. Other studies have demonstrated that both exercise intensity and duration are factors in increasing beta-endorphin concentrations. For example, the exercise needs to be performed at above 60% of the individual's maximal oxygen uptake (VO_2 max; Goldfarb & Jamurtas 1997) and for at least 3 minutes (Kjaer & Dela, 1996) to detect changes in endogenous opioids.

Researchers have further examined these findings by examining the correlation between exercise-induced increase in beta-endorphin levels and mood changes using the Profile of Mood States (POMS) inventory (Farrell et al., 1982). The POMS was administered to all participants before and after their exercise session. Respondents give numerical ratings to five negative categories of mood (tension, depression, anger, fatigue and confusion) and one positive category (vigor). Adding the five negative affect scores and then subtracting from the total the vigor score yields a "total mood disturbance" (TMD) score. In Farrell's study the TMD scores improved by 15 and 16 raw score units from the baseline, after subjects exercised at 60% and 80% VO_2 max. Quantitatively, mood improved about 50%, which corresponds to clinical observations that people's moods are elevated after vigorous exercise workouts. Farrell et al. (1982) using radioimmunoassay also observed two- to fivefold increase in plasma beta-endorphin concentrations as measured before and after exercise.

However, Farrell et al.'s research is inconclusive. First, only six well-trained endurance athletes were studied and the six showed large individual variations in beta-endorphin response to submaximal treadmill exercise. Second, the exercise-induced changes in mood scores were not statistically significantly different between pre- and post-exercises scores. Third, no significant relationship between mood measures obtained with the POMS inventory and plasma beta-endorphin levels were found. Therefore, the obtained results cannot prove conclusively that beta-endorphins cause mood elevations. A more questionable issue, however, also recognized by Farrell et al. is that the beta-endorphin measures in the experiment comes from plasma - which means that this type of beta-endorphin is located in the periphery. Because of its chemical makeup, beta-endorphin cannot cross the blood brain barrier (BBB). Hence, plasma beta-endorphin fluctuations do not reflect beta-endorphin fluctuations in the brain. Some researchers have speculated that endogenous opiates in the plasma may act centrally and therefore can be used to trace CNS activity (Biddle & Mutrie, 1991). At this time, such a surmise concerning beta-endorphins could only rely on circumstantial evidence that met-enkephalin and dynorphin two opioids, which show a modification mechanism that could possibly transport them across the BBB (Sforzo, 1988). Unfortunately, direct measurement of changes in brain beta-endorphins involves cutting open the brain and doing radioimmunoassay on brain slices. Animal studies, using rats, have been performed and they have shown an increase in opioid receptor binding after exercise (Sforzo, Seeger, Pert, Pert, & Dotsen, 1986).

In humans, to work around this problem, researchers proposed that naloxone could be a useful in testing whether beta-endorphins played a role in CNS-mediated responses like euphoria and analgesia. Since it is a potent opioid receptor antagonist, it competes with beta-endorphin to bind the same receptor. Thus, injection of naloxone into humans should negate the euphoric and analgesic effects produced by exercise, if beta-endorphin perpetrates such effects indeed. It was found that naloxone decreased the analgesic effect reportedly caused by runner's high, but other researchers who conducted similar experiments remain divided about these results. As for naloxone's effects on mood elevation, Markoff, Ryan and Young (1982) observed that naloxone did not reverse the positive mood changes induced by exercise.

Mounting evidence demonstrates that beta-endorphins are not necessary for the euphoria experienced by exercisers. Harte, Eifert, and Smith (1995) noted that although exercise produces both positive emotions and a rise in beta-endorphin levels, the two are not necessarily connected. Indeed, physically undemanding activities like watching humor or listening to music produce identical elevations in mood to exercise (Szabo, 2006; Szabo, Aisnsworth, & Danks 2005) although accompanying elevations in beta-endorphins could not be observed after humor (Berk et al., 1989) or music (McKinney, Tims, Kumar & Kumar, 1997). Similarly, Harte et al. (1995) found that both running and meditation resulted in significant positive changes in mood. In addition to taking mood measures, Harte et al. have also measured plasma beta-endorphin levels of the participants. As expected, those in the meditation group did not show a rise in beta-endorphin levels in spite of reported elevations in mood. Such results seem to further question the link between mood improvement and changes in beta-endorphin levels after exercise.

Answering the improved mood and increased beta-endorphin levels connection question inversely, experiments were carried out in which beta-endorphin was directly injected into the bloodstream of healthy participants. The results failed to show any changes in mood (Biddle & Mutrie, 1991). On the other hand, beta-endorphin injections had a positive effect on clinically depressed patients (Biddle & Mutrie, 1991). Further, electroconvulsive therapy, used to treat patients with depression, also increased plasma b-endorphin levels.

The lack of beta-endorphin release during meditation and the lack of mood alteration after beta-endorphin injection, call for attention on factors that influence beta-endorphin levels. In an effort to consolidate peripheral beta-endorphin data with the central nervous effects, researchers have realized that the peripheral opioid system requires further investigation. Taylor et al. (1994) proposed that during exercise acidosis is the trigger of beta-endorphin secretion in the bloodstream. Their results showed that blood pH level strongly correlated with the beta-endorphin levels (acidic conditions raise the concentration of b-endorphin, buffering the blood attenuates this response). The explanation behind such observations is that acidosis increases respiration and stimulates a feedback inhibition mechanism in the form of beta-endorphin. The latter interacts with neurons responsible for respiratory control, and beta-endorphin, therefore, serves the purpose of preventing hyperventilation (Taylor et al., 1994). How is then this physiological mechanism connected to CNS-mediated emotional responses? Sforzo (1988) noted that since opioids have inhibitory functions in the CNS, if a system is to be activated through opioids at least one other neural pathway must be involved. Thus, instead of trying to establish how peripheral amounts of beta-endorphin act on the CNS, researchers could develop an alternate physiological model demonstrating how the emotional effects of opioids may be activated through the inhibition of the peripheral sympathetic activity (Sforzo, 1988).

While the "runner's high" phenomenon may never be empirically established as a fact and beta-endorphins' importance in this event is questionable, other studies have shown how peripheral beta-endorphins affect centrally-mediated behavior. Electro-acupuncture used to treat morphine addiction by diminishing cravings and relieving withdrawal symptoms, caused b-endorphin levels to rise (McLachlan, Hay, & Coleman, 1994). Since exercise also increases beta-endorphin levels in the plasma, McLachlan et al. (1994) investigated whether exercise could lower exogenous opiate intake. Rats were fed morphine and methadone for several days and then randomly divided into two groups of exercisers and non-exercisers. At that time, voluntary exogenous opiate intake was recorded to see if the exercise would affect the consumption of opiate in exercising rats. The results showed that while opiate consumption has increased in both groups, exercising rats did not consume as much as non-exercising animals and the difference was statistically significant (McLachlan et al., 1994). These findings suggest that exercise does decrease craving.

In conclusion, the connection between beta-endorphins, runner's high, and exercise addiction remains an elegant explanation without sufficient empirical support. It is likely that the intense positive emotional experience, to which athletes, runners, and scientist refer as runner's high, is evoked by several mechanisms acting jointly. Szabo (2006) has shown that while exercises and humor are equally effective in decreasing negative mood and increasing positive mood, the effects of exercise last longer than that of humor. These results are evidence for the involvement of more than one mechanism in mood alterations after physically active and relatively passive interventions. With reference to exercise addiction, although intensive positive feelings may be motivational factors to indulge in more and more exercise, when the exerciser loses control over her/his exercise (that happens in addiction by definition) the activity becomes an obligation. It has to be performed or else craving or withdrawal symptoms interfere with the normal functioning of the individual. Consequently, while the runner's high may be a factor at the onset of exercise addiction, the maintenance of this compulsive behavior occurs via negative, rather than positive reinforcement. It is reasonable to conclude then, that the runner's high phenomenon is only weakly or distantly associated with exercise addiction.

8.0 CORRELATES OF EXERCISE ADDICTION

Researchers have looked at the correlates of exercise addiction but have been unable to identify when or why a transition takes place from "healthy" to "unhealthy" exercise behavior (Johnson, 1995). Exercise addiction appears to be positively related to anxiety (Morgan, 1979; Rudy & Estok, 1989) and negatively related to self-esteem (Estok & Rudy, 1986; Rudy & Estok, 1989). Further, the length of experience with a particular physical activity appears to be positively associated with exercise addiction (Furst & Germone, 1993; Hailey & Bailey, 1982; Thaxton, 1982). If experience is associated with exercise addiction, it is reasonable to speculate that a major life event change (or stress) may trigger addiction that is evinced through "revolutionary" rather than evolutionary changes in the habitual physical activity pattern of the individual. The affected individual may see this form of coping as healthy on the basis of popular knowledge and the media-spread information about the positive aspects of exercise.

Indeed, the media plays an important role in what people believe about and expect from their exercise. The media-propagated positive image of the exercising individual provides a mask behind which some exercisers with severe emotional distress may hide. Thus the media-projected positive information about physical activity could be used to deny the existence of the problem (a characteristic of addictive behaviours) and to delay its detection to the advanced stages when all symptoms of addiction are vividly present. Because of such a possible delay, it is likely that only case studies, presented in the literature, reflect genuine cases of exercise addiction. Indeed, a random sample of habitual exercisers may contain very few cases, if any (!), of exercise addicts (Morris, 1989).

9.0 RESEARCH ON EXERCISE ADDICTION

"I moved to a new town and decided to join a health club as a way of meeting people. Soon, exercise began to become a focal part of my life and I became more determined to keep fit and improve my physique. Gradually the three hours a day I was doing increased to six hours and I started to become totally obsessive about exercise. I wouldn't miss a day at the gym. I just lost sight of my body really - I just had to do my workout, come what may, and get my fix." (Source: Evening Standard, 01/08/2000).

9.1 Personality-Oriented Research

Personality-oriented research or the trait approach is based on the assumption that aberrant or pathological personality characteristics, like obsessive-compulsiveness and narcissism, are instrumental in the etiology of exercise addiction. Researchers are trying to identify those personality characteristics that predispose an individual to exercise addiction.

Investigators in this area are faced with several difficulties around the definition and assessment of exercise addiction as well as around the general difficulty in personality research in disentangling stable from changeable characteristics.

In an early widely cited but relatively controversial study, Yates, Leehay and Shisslak (1983) suggested that addicted male runners resembled patients suffering of anorexia nervosa on certain personality dispositions (introversion, inhibition of anger, high expectations, depression, and excessive use of denial) and labeled this resemblance as the anorexia-analogue hypothesis. To test their hypothesis Yates et al. examined the personality characteristics of 60 male heavy exercisers and contrasted their responses to those commonly reported by patients diagnosed with anorexia nervosa. While supporting data were not provided, Yates et al. claimed that running and extreme dieting were both dangerous attempts to establish an identity, as either addicted to exercise or as anorexic. This research has been severely criticized for a number of shortcomings including the lack of supporting data, poor methodology, lack of relevance to the average runner, over-reliance on extreme cases or individuals, and exaggerating the similarities between the groups (Blumenthal, O'Toole, & Chang, 1984). Indeed, subsequent research has failed to show undisputable commonalities between the personality characteristics of people affected by exercise addiction and those suffering of eating disorders (e.g., Blumenthal et al., 1984; Coen & Ogles, 1993). Consequently, the anorexia analogue hypothesis for a substantial period was seen as only speculative and has failed to gather empirical support.

In another early study Estok and Rudy (1986) examined 57 marathon and 38 non-marathon female runners on physical (e.g., shin splints and knee or hip pain) and psychosocial symptoms (e.g., anxiety and self-esteem), as well as addictive behaviours using a 14-item questionnaire developed by the authors themselves. The results revealed that marathon runners scored significantly higher on addictive behaviours in comparison to the non-marathon runners. The frequency of injuries among marathon runners was also significantly higher than in non-marathon runners. However, the authors attributed the differences in the incidence of injuries to the actual differences in running distance between the two groups and not to the level of addiction to running. Although no differences, between the marathon and non-marathon running groups, for psychological symptoms were found, there was a negative correlation between addiction scores and self-esteem, suggesting proneness to addiction in people with low self-esteem.

Yates et al. (1992) investigated the personality characteristics of male and female runners who ran a minimum of 15 miles (24 km) per week. According to participants' responses on an 18-item exercise addiction questionnaire developed by the authors, and on the basis of a semi-structured interview, runners could be classified as either obligatory (addicted) or non-obligatory (not addicted) exercisers. Ten male and 17 female participants were classified as obligatory runners, while the non-obligatory group comprised 20 males and 19 females. Participants completed the Profile of Mood States (POMS) inventory (McNair, Lorr, & Droppleman, 1981), the Eysenck Personality Questionnaire (Eysenck & Eysenck, 1991), the Minnesota Multiphasic Personality Inventory (Dahlstrom & Welch, 1960), the Bem Sex Role Inventory (Bem, 1981), the Internal-External Locus of Control Scale (Rotter, 1966), the Eating Attitudes Test (Garner & Garfinkel, 1979), and the Beck Depression Inventory (Beck, Ward, Mendelson, Mock, Erbaugh, 1961). Yates et al. found that obligatory runners were more likely to follow a strict diet, be preoccupied with their body, run alone, and report more positive changes in self-concept and control over their lives since taking up running than the non-obligatory runners. Further, the obligatory male runners were twice as likely to obtain elevated scores on the Minnesota Multiphasic Personality Inventory (MMPI) compared to the non-obligatory male runners. Therefore, Yates et al. have found some limited evidence for differences in personality measures of addicted and non-addicted runners.

Davis, Brewer, and Ratusny (1993) investigated the relationships between personality characteristics of addiction, obsessive-compulsiveness, and exercise addiction with exercise behavior. They tested 185 physically active male and female participants who completed the Commitment to Exercise Scale (Davis et al., 1993), the Addiction Scale (Eysenck & Eysenck, 1991), the Obsessive-Compulsive Personality Scale (Lazare, Klerman, & Armour, 1966), and the Drive for Thinness, Body Dissatisfaction, and Bulimia Subscales of the Eating Disorder Inventory (Garner, Olmsted, & Polivy, 1983). Participants were also interviewed about their exercise history over the past year. Davis et al. found that obsessive-compulsive personality characteristics in males were positively related to exercise frequency. In contrast to their hypothesis, exercise frequency was inversely related to addictiveness. Therefore, the hypothesized positive relationships between obsessive-compulsiveness, addictiveness, exercise addiction, and exercise behavior could not be demonstrated.

Coen and Ogles (1993) further examined the anorexia analogue hypothesis and tested the personality characteristics believed to be common to anorexics and runners (e.g., anxiety, perfectionism, and ego identity). A sample of 142 male marathon runners completed the Obligatory Exercise Questionnaire (Thompson & Pasman, 1991), the Multidimensional Perfectionism Scale (Frost, Marten, Lahart, & Rosenblate, 1990), the Trait Subscale of the State-Trait Anxiety Inventory (Speilberger, Gorsuch, Lushene, Vagg, & Jacobs, 1983), the Ego Identity Scale (Tan, Kendis, Fine, & Porac, 1977), and a short demographic questionnaire on running characteristics. A median split on the Obligatory Exercise Questionnaire was used to classify runners as either obligatory or non-obligatory using Yates et al.'s terminology for addiction to running. The authors have found that the obligatory (addicted) runners have reported more perfectionist characteristics compared to the non-obligatory runners. Specifically, obligatory runners were more concerned about making mistakes, have set higher personal standards for themselves, had more doubts about their actions, and had a higher need for organization than their non-obligatory runners. Obligatory runners also reported greater trait anxiety compared to the non-obligatory group. On the basis of these findings it was concluded that the anorexia analogue hypothesis was partially supported because only some of the personality characteristics proposed by Yates et al. (1983) were associated indeed with addictive running.

Later, in contrast to the study by Coen and Ogles (1993), Iannos and Tiggemann (1997) failed to disclose personality differences between addicted to exercise and non-addicted individuals. They examined 205 male and female participants who were divided into three groups according to the number of hours they exercised per week: light (0 to 5 hours), medium or moderate (5 to 11 hours), and excessive (more than 11 hours). The participants completed an author-developed questionnaire, which assessed their level of exercise addiction, the Rosenberg Self-esteem Scale (Rosenberg, 1965), the Internality Subscale of the Locus of Control Inventory (Levenson, 1981), the Obsessive-Compulsive Scale (Gibb, Bailey, Best, & Lambrinth, 1983), and the Drive for Thinness and Bulimia Subscales of the Eating Disorder Inventory. The results showed that excessive exercisers reported more disordered eating behaviours than the light and moderate exercisers. Further, women scored higher than men. In spite of the relationship between the amount of exercise and disordered eating, statistically no significant differences were found between the amount of exercise and the personality characteristics of self-esteem, locus of control, and obsessive-compulsiveness. These authors concluded that high volumes of exercise alone could not be connected with a pathological personality.

Hagan and Hausenblas (2003) examined the relationship between exercise addiction scores and perfectionism. They tested 79 university students who completed self-report measures of their exercise behavior, perfectionism, and exercise dependence symptoms. The authors have found that participants with high exercise addiction scores reported more perfectionism and larger volumes of exercise than participants with low scores of exercise addiction. The connection between perfectionism and exercises addiction warrants further investigation, because it may yields at least a partial answer to why exercise addicts, investing tremendous energy in their addiction, differ from other addicts who resort to "easy to reach" means to satisfy their cravings.

In a later study, Hausenblas and Giacobbi (2004) focused on the proposed link between a number of specific dimensions of personality (neuroticism, extraversion, agreeableness, openness, conscientiousness) and exercise addiction. They hypothesized that there would be a positive correlation between exercise addiction and neuroticism. Hausenblas and Giacobbi tested 390 university students. The participants completed several inventories including the NEO Five Factor Inventory (Costa & McCrae, 1992) used to measure the levels of five personality dimensions (neuroticism, extraversion, openness, agreeableness, and conscientiousness), the Exercise Dependence Scale (EDS - Hausenblas & Symons Downs, 2002b) to assess symptoms of exercise addiction, the Leisure Time Exercise Questionnaire (Godin & Shephard, 1985) to gauge leisure activities, and the Drive for Thinness Scale (Garner, 1991) that was actually a subscale of the Eating Disorder Inventory-2 (Garner, 1991). The results of this study showed that proneness to exercise addiction, as based on the EDS scores, were positively correlated with neuroticism and extraversion while being negatively correlated with agreeableness. Openness and conscientiousness were unrelated failed to exercise addiction scores.

Summing up the research effort on the connection between exercise addiction and personality, it is clear that causal relationship has not been demonstrated. Any linkages between the two variables are correlational rather than causal in nature. The observed group differences (high versus low addiction scores) are inconsistent and they could be traced to many factors associated with exercise history and experience as well as beliefs and expectations associated with exercise. The popularity of investigations into personality and exercise addiction could be explained by the convenience of research in this area, relying on questionnaire data, and scholars' eagerness to pinpoint a consistent and common characteristic among exercise addicts that could be conceived as a warning sign in the etiology of exercise addiction.

9.2 Beta-Endorphin and Exercise Addiction Research

Only one study, published 15 years ago, has examined the link between beta-endorphins and exercise addiction. The study was based on previously published evidence (e.g. Farrell et al., 1982) that there is a considerable increase beta-endorphin levels after exercise, especially aerobic activities. Then, Pierce et al. (1993) studied the connection between plasma beta-endorphin levels and proneness to exercise addiction in eight women who trained in aerobic dance. The participants completed an exercise addiction assessment prior to taking part in a 45-minute session of continuous aerobic dance. Plasma beta-endorphin concentrations were measured both before and after the exercise session. The results revealed that mean plasma beta-endorphin levels were statistically significantly higher after the exercise in comparison to pre-exercise levels. The percent change scores (difference scores) between pre- and post-exercise beta-endorphin levels were then correlated with the exercise addiction scores. The result of the correlation was statistically not significant. Consequently, the research concludes that exercise addiction is not related to changes in plasma beta-endorphin levels after aerobic exercise.

9.3 Preponderance of Exercise Addiction

A common question posed by scientist and media reporters pertains to the prevalence of exercise addiction. The question is valid given that substantial research attention has been dedicated to the issue. Empirical research on the preponderance of exercise addiction is limited. The author is only aware of a few studies that could possibly provide an answer. The first account by Thornton and Scott (1995) projects an inflated figure. These authors examined a group pf 40 runners who were, on average, running over 40 miles per week. Using the Commitment to Running Scales (Carmack & Martens, 1979) the results revealed that 77% of the sample of runners studied could be classified as moderately or highly addicted to running. The authors have found that the predominant personal motives for the studied runners were related to mastery, competition, and weight regulation, although health concerns and fitness were also important incentives. The commitment to running scores, that were interpreted as addiction indices by the authors, were related to the frequency of running and distances run, but not to the number of years of running. A regression analyses showed that mastery and social recognition were key predictors of the levels of running commitment. The authors suggested those runners who start running for health promotion or maintenance, there is a potential risk of developing an obsessive commitment to running, and this may be more likely for those who are prone to stress. A major problem with this study is that the authors equated high levels of commitment to running with exercise addiction, which in fact was proven to represent two unrelated concepts (Szabo et al., 1996).

Two studies looked at the incidence of classifiable cases during the development and validation of two different exercise addiction questionnaires. Using the Exercise Dependence Scale (EDS) Hausenblas and Symons Downs (2002) identified that 2.5% of the studied sample could be classified as being addicted to exercise. Similarly, Terry, Griffiths and Szabo (2004), in the course of development of the Exercise Addiction Inventory (EAI), reported that 3.0% of the sample could be identified as at risk of exercise addiction. The two questionnaires, the EDS and the EAI, are highly correlated ($r = 0.81$; $p < 0.001$) with each other. The rates of exercise addiction reported in conjunction with the development of the EDS and EAI are low, supporting the argument that exercise addiction is rare (Szabo, 2000; De Coverley Veale, 1995). Indeed, a later study substantiated the validity of such estimates about the preponderance of exercise addiction.

Szabo and Griffiths (2007) examined the prevalence of self-reported symptoms of exercise addiction in sport sciences students at a British university and in a sample drawn from the general exercising population. A total of 455 participants (261 sports science students and 194 controls) completed the Exercise Addiction Inventory (EAI – Terry, Szabo, & Griffiths, 2004). The sport science students had significantly higher mean scores on the EAI than exercisers from the general population. It was also found that 6.9% (18 out of 261) sport science students were possibly addicted to exercise, since they scored 24 or more on the EAI, compared to only 3.6% (7 out of 194) of the general exercising population, a result that approached ($p < 0.09$) but it did not reach the conservative level ($p < .05$) statistical significance. The findings of Szabo and Griffiths raise the possibility that sports science students may be more susceptible to exercise addiction than exercisers in the general population. At the same time, their findings confirm, that the preponderance of exercise addiction in the general exercising population is about 3% to 4%.

It should be noted that exercise addiction questionnaire only assess the risk or likelihood of exercise addiction. Consequently, questionnaires alone cannot be considered as diagnostic tools. The genuine cases of exercise addiction cannot be identified through scientific research. They surface occasionally in medical practices when the psychological burden or physical injury forces the affected person to seek help. Therefore, the 3% or near estimates of exercise addiction in the exercising population may be a very crude index and only represent high risk cases rather than actually diagnosed cases.

9.4 Case Studies of Exercise Addiction

Griffiths (1997) presents the only case study published in a scholastic paper. Joanne, aged 25, did not see herself as addicted to exercise, though her habit took up several hours of each day, occupied her thoughts continuously, and the craving for exercise had even forced her to walk out of university exams. She was obsessed with exercise, mostly a type of martial arts, but any form of exercise would do. Joanne described the buzz resulting from exercise as a feeling like being on amphetamines. With time she had developed a tolerance for exercise, and therefore she had to increase the volume of her exercise continuously to feel all right and to function normally. If she could not fulfil her need to exercise, she would get anxious and irritable, and suffered of headaches and nausea. She has spent money beyond her means to fund her habit, and has lost friends and even her partner to it. Joanne's case illustrates how the exercise addict loses control over her exercise and the extreme negative life events that may have permanent consequences, like abandoning an exam or losing a partner.

Another exercise addiction case, voluntarily shared with the public by the affected person, was published in the London *Evening Standard*, (August 01, 2000): Jackie Pugsley enjoyed her job as a schoolteacher. She had never been particularly sporty at school but in her twenties she started making up for lost time, taking up sports including tennis, squash, aerobics, badminton and circuit training, to help kick-start her social life. What started as a hobby became an obsession, until she became so addicted to exercise that she was forced to give up her work. The 36-year-old was the first person to complete the treatment programme at The Priory Hospital Bristol in 1996. Jackie described her obsession with exercise:

"I moved to a new town and decided to join a health club as a way of meeting people. Soon, exercise began to become a focal part of my life and I became more determined to keep fit and improve my physique. Gradually the three hours a day I was doing increased to six hours and I started to become totally obsessive about exercise. I wouldn't miss a day at the gym. I just lost sight of my body really - I just had to do my workout, come what may, and get my fix."

At the height of her addiction Jackie was exercising for up to eight hours a day, starting with two hours on her exercise bike before work. She would walk for an hour at lunchtime, and then head off for a two-hour run after work, followed by a three-hour workout at the gym. Holidays would be spent at health farms and she would even get out the exercise bike on Christmas Day. Her dress size dropped from 14 to eight, and her weight slipped down to seven stone (and she is more than 5 ft 8in).

"I stopped doing the sports I actually enjoyed and was fixated about high-impact aerobic exercise. Instead of using sport to enhance my social life, I was becoming more and more isolated and was not enjoying the exercise at all"

By the time Jackie was admitted to hospital the regime had taken a physical toll. A combination of severe cramps and low blood pressure meant she was unable to walk for 10 days.

"Even though I was in agony I had to be sedated because I couldn't cope without the exercise. I had grown so acclimatized to pain that I didn't even question it. I had my amount of workout that I had to do. I might have spent the evening in the gym and been so exhausted that I would just about be able to climb the stairs - it didn't matter. Once I was inside I made myself spend another hour on my exercise bike."

After several relapses Jackie was able to manage her addiction, although she was still seeing a psychiatrist for a while.

Joanne and Jackie's cases illustrate vividly the potentially irreversible negative consequences of exercise addiction. Cases like theirs do not surface in a randomly studied research sample; instead they may appear in medical practices. The affected individuals may seek medical help only when the negative consequences, resulting from excessive exercise, already took a toll on their lives and any further lengthening of the cycle could result in severe or even deadly consequences. Such diagnosed cases cannot be studied with questionnaires on which the bulk of exercise addiction literature is based. Nonetheless, paper and pencil tools, yielding knowledge about personality characteristics, needs and desires of people, could assess the potential risk for exercise addiction. As such research into exercise addiction is of paramount importance for prevention. From, the previous section it is known that only a small fraction of the exercising population may be affected by exercise addiction (3-4%), then one may question the effort invested in this area of research. However, considering that the consequences of exercise addiction may be life threatening, all effort invested in knowledge to be used for timely prevention is justified. Indeed, the 3-4% figure may seem to be small. However, the 3% figure is large if one considers that the exercising population is growing consistently as illustrated by data that in 2003 one third (33%) of the adult population in the United States (U.S.) engaged regularly in moderate physical activity (more than 30 minutes at least 5 times a week). It is noteworthy to mention that the U.S. target for 2010 is 50% (U.S. Department of Health & Human Services, 2004). Therefore, the number of those who statistically may be affected by exercise addiction (around the whole world) could be counted in millions. Should then there be a stronger justification for continued research effort in this area?

9.5 Exercise Addiction and Withdrawal Symptoms

Szabo (1995, 2000) claimed that all exercisers experience withdrawal symptoms at times when exercise is not possible for interfering reasons. He stressed, however, that those who are addicted to exercise would experience stronger deprivation sensations than those who are simply highly committed to exercise. Aidman and Woollard (2003) reported results that seem to provide support for Szabo's contention. They tested the connection of exercise addiction to mood and resting heart rate response to a 24-hour exercise deprivation from scheduled training in competitive runners. Sixty competitive runners, who had been training at least five times a week, were randomly assigned into an experimental (exercise-deprived) and a control group. Participants completed the Profile of Mood States (POMS) inventory, the Running Addiction Scale (RAS), and provided resting heart rate (RHR) measurements. Half of the participants missed the next scheduled training (exercise-deprived group), while the other half continued to train uninterruptedly (controls). Both groups completed again the POMS and provided RHR within 24 hours after the experiment. The results showed that the exercise-deprived group reported substantial withdrawal symptoms of depressed mood, reduced vigor and increased tension, anger, fatigue and confusion (measured by POMS), as well as significantly elevated RHR, within 24 hours after the missed training session. The control group showed no changes in mood or RHR. More importantly, the observed negative changes in mood and RHR response in the exercise-deprived group were associated with exercise addiction scores. Those who scored under the median experienced significantly less mood change and RHR shifts than hose with addiction scores above the median. Further, correlations between addiction scores and magnitude of increases in tension, anger, confusion, depression and RHR ranged from $r = 0.46$ to $r = 0.58$. The authors concluded that exercise addiction scores in habitual exercisers are associated with emotional and heart rate responses to exercise deprivation, indicating that the magnitude of these responses may, in turn, serve as early markers of exercise addiction. In accord with Szabo (1995, 2000) the severity of withdrawal symptoms is an important index for differentiating committed exercisers from those who re addicted.

10. 0 EXERCISE ADDICTION AND EATING DISORDERS

De Coverley Veale (1987) differentiated between primary and secondary exercise dependence. In the previous sections primary dependence was examined. Secondary exercise dependence is a common characteristic of eating disorders such as Anorexia Nervosa and Bulimia Nervosa (De Coverley Veale, 1987). In these disorders, excessive exercise is considered to be an auxiliary feature used in caloric control and weight loss. Secondary exercise dependence occurs in different "doses" in people affected by eating disorders. It was estimated that one third of anorectics may be affected (Crisp, Hsu, Harding, & Hartshorn, 1980).

10.1 The Relationship between Exercise Addiction and Eating Disorders

A team of long-distance runners published the founding work in this area. This work has been briefly mentioned in the personality and exercise addiction section, but because it marks the foundation of research into exercise addiction and eating disorders it needs to be briefly re-introduced in this section as well. Yates et al. (1983) were themselves runners and at the same time scholars specialized in eating disorders. They observed a striking resemblance between the psychology of anorectic patients and the very committed runners with whom they run. They labeled this group of runners as *obligatory runners*. In the course of their research they interviewed sixty marathoners and closely examined the traits of a subgroup of male athletes who corresponded to the "obligatory" category. They reported that male obligatory runners resembled anorexic women in some personality traits, such as expression of anger, high self-expectation, tolerance of pain, and depression as well as in some demographic details. Yates et al. (1983) related these observations to a unique and hazardous way of establishment of self-identity. This work has marked the foundation of research into the relationship between exercise and eating disorders.

10.2 The Analogy between Anorexia and Excessive Exercising

Since Yates et al. (1983) published their article, a large number of studies have examined the relationship between exercise and eating disorders. A close examination of these studies (Table 10.1) reveals some opposing findings to the original report. For example, three studies comparing anorectic patients with high level, or obligatory, exercisers (Blumenthal, O'Toole & Chang, 1984; Davis et al., 1995; Knight, Schocken, Powers, Feld, & Smith, 1987) failed to demonstrate an analogy between anorexia and excessive exercising. The differences in methodology between these inquiries are, however, significant. They all looked for an analogy between excessive exercise and anorexia, but from a different perspective. Blumenthal et al. (1984) and Knight et al. (1987) examined a mixed gender sample's scores on a popular personality test (the Minnesota Multiphasic Personality Inventory - MMPI). Davis et al. (1995) tested an all female sample using specific questionnaires aimed at assessing compulsiveness, commitment to exercise, and eating disorders. Finally, Yates et al. (1983) looked to some demographic and personality parallels between obligatory runners and anorectic patients. Further, the classification of the exercise behavior may have differed in these studies. Therefore, these studies are not easily comparable.

The controversy between the above studies may be partly solved by considering the results of a study by Wolf and Akamatsu (1994) who studied female athletes who showed tendencies for eating disorders. These females, however, did not manifest the personality characteristics associated with eating disorders. Thus, in agreement with Blumenthal et al.'s (1984) and Knight et al.'s (1987) explanation, differences between obligatory exercisers and anorectic patients may outweigh substantially the similarities reported by Yates et al. (1983). In another theoretical article, Yates, Shisslak, Crago, and Allender (1994) also admit that the comparison of excessive exercisers with eating disordered patients is erroneous because the two populations are significantly different.

Table 10.1. A summary table on research into exercise addiction and eating disorders.

Author(s)	Participants	Objectives	Measurements	Conclusion about the relationship between exercise and eating disorders
Ackard, Brehm, & Steffen (2002)	586 female university students	to examine the connection between excessive exercise, disordered eating and a number of psychological measures	Obligatory Exercise Questionnaire, Eating Disorders Inventory, The Center for Epidemiological Studies-Depression scale, Trait Meta-Mood Scale Bulimia Test, The Family Environment Scale, Rosenberg Self-Esteem Scale, and Body Image Assessment	One group clearly manifested eating disorder traits and behaviors, as well as signs of psychological disturbance. Another group who exercised with equal intensity but less emotional fixation showed the fewest signs of eating disorders and psychological distress.
Adkins & Keel (2005)	162 male and 103 female university students	to test whether the compulsive or excessive aspects of exercise are more closely related to eating disorders	Eating Disorder Inventory, Reasons for Exercise Inventory, and the Obligatory Exercise Questionnaire	Compulsive exercise may be a better definition than excessive exercise in connection with bulimia
Blumenthal, O'Toole, & Chang (1984)	compared 24 anorectics to 43 obligatory runners	to assess the similarity between Anorexia Nervosa and obligatory running	Minnesota Multiphasic Personality Inventory (MMPI); Clinical diagnosis based on the DSM II and the DSM III (Diagnostic and Statistical Manual of Mental Disorders)	Runners and anorectics are different. The relationship is superficial on the basis of the ten subscales of the MMPI.
Brewerton, Stellefson, Hibbs, Hodges, & Cochrane (1995)	110 anorexic, bulimic or both females grouped into compulsive and non-compulsive groups	to compare compulsively exercising and non-exercising patients suffering from eating disorders	Diagnostic Survey of the Eating Disorders; Clinical diagnosis based on the DSM III for Anorexia Nervosa and Bulimia Nervosa	Related compulsive exercise to elevated body dissatisfaction in patients with eating disorders and it was more prevalent (39%) in anorectics than in bulimics (23%).
Davis (1990a)	86 exercising and 72 non-exercising women	to compare body image and weight preoccupation between exercising and non-exercising women	Eysenck Personality Inventory; Body Image Questionnaire; and Subjective Body Shape; Eating Disorder Inventory (EDI)	Body-dissatisfaction was related to poorer emotional well-being in the exercise group only. EDI scores did not differ between the groups.
Davis (1990b)	53 exercising and 43 non-exercising women	to study addictiveness, weight preoccupation, and exercise patterns in a non-clinical population	Addictiveness with the Eysenck Personality Questionnaire (EPQ); Body Focus; Eating Disorder Inventory (EDI)	Addictiveness was related to weight and dieting variables in both groups and to perfectionism in the exercise group. EDI scores did not differ between the groups.

Table 10.1. (Continued).

Author(s)	Participants	Objectives	Measurements	Conclusion about the relationship between exercise and eating disorders
Davis, Brewer, & Ratusny (1993)	88 men and 97 women	to present a new "Commitment to Exercise" questionnaire and to study the relationship between exercising and obsessive compulsiveness, weight preoccupation and addictiveness	Addictiveness; Commitment to exercise; Obsessive compulsiveness; Eating Disorder Inventory (EDI), "Drive for Thinness" subscale	Presents validity and reliability data for the two factor (obligatory exercising and pathological exercising) "Commitment to Exercise Questionnaire. Excessive exercising was found to be distinct from eating disorders.
Davis et al. (1995)	46 anorexic patients, 76 high-level exercisers, 55 moderate exercisers, all females	to test the relationship between obsessive compulsiveness and exercise in anorectics in contrast moderate and high-level exercising controls	Commitment to exercise, Obsessive compulsiveness; Eating Disorder Inventory (EDI), "Drive for Thinness" subscale	Weight preoccupation and excessive exercising were related in both high-level exercisers and anorectics.
French, Perry, Leon, & Fulkerson (1995)	852 female students	to observe changes, over a three-year period, in psychological and health variables in dieting and non-dieting women	Negative emotionality; Self-concept; Eating Disorders Symptom Scores (based on DSM III), Restrained Eating Scale, Eating Disorder Inventory	Dieting habits were not related to physical activity levels over three years, but dieters reported greater decreases in physical activity than non-dieters.
French, Perry, Leon, & Fulkerson (1994)	1494 adolescents	to examine correlates of symptoms of eating disorders, including food preferences, eating patterns, and physical activity	Food preference and eating patterns questionnaires and Eating Disorders Symptoms	High-performance sport participation was found to be a predictor of eating disorders symptoms.
Levine, Marcus, & Moulton (1996)	77 females (44 assigned to regular walking & 33 controls) suffering from binge eating disorder	to examine the effects of an exercise intervention in the treatment of obese women with binge eating disorder	Beck Depression Inventory; Eating Disorder examination (a semi-structured clinical interview)	Binge eating disorder was successfully managed through a 24-week (aimed to burn 1000 calories per week) walking program
Mond, Hay, Rodgers, & Owen (2006)	3472 women who engaged in regular exercise	to better conceptualize the meaning of "excessive exercise"	A composite questionnaire measuring eating disorders, psychopathology, quality of life (health-related) psychological distress, and exercise behavior	Excessive is excessive when its postponement triggers guilt or when it is performed solely to influence weight or physical shape

Table 10.1. (Continued).

Author(s)	Participants	Objectives	Measurements	Conclusion about the relationship between exercise and eating disorders
Pasman & Thompson (1988)	90 participants (45 males and -45 females) equal in three groups: obligatory runners, obligatory weight lifters and sedentary controls	to examine body image and eating disturbance in obligatory runners and weight-lifters and in sedentary controls	Obligatory Exercise Questionnaire; Eating Disorders Inventory (EDI); Body Self relations Questionnaire (BSRQ)	Runners and weightlifters reported greater eating disturbance than controls. Females also reported greater eating disturbance than males.
Richert & Hummers (1986)	345 students	to examine the relationship between exercise pattern risk for eating disorders	Eating Attitude Test (EAT)	Exercise was positively correlated with EAT scores and participants with high EAT scores showed a preference for jogging.
Szymanski & Chrisler (1990)	66 female athletes and 20 non-athletes	to test the link between eating disorders, gender roles, and training	Bem Sex-Role Inventory; Eating Disorders Inventory (EDI)	Athletes scored higher on most subscales of the EDI than non-athletes.
Thiel, Gottfried, & Hesse (1993)	84 low-weight male athletes (25 wrestlers & 59 rowers)	to study the prevalence of eating disorders in male athletes who, by the nature of their sport, are pressured to maintain low weight	Eating Disorder Inventory (EDI)	52% of the athletes reported binging and 11% of the respondents evinced sub-clinical eating disorders. Concludes that low-weight wrestles and rowers should be considered at risk for eating disorders.
Williamson et al. (1995)	98 female college athletes	to study the risk factors involved in the development of eating disorders in female college athletes	Social Influence; Sports Competition Anxiety Test (SCAT); Athletic self-appraisal; Interview for Diagnosis of Eating Disorders	Validated a psychosocial model of risk factors for the development of eating disorders in female college athletes. the model suggests that social influence, performance anxiety and self-appraisal together influence body-size concern which in turn is a strong determinant of eating disorder symptoms

Table 10.1. (Continued).

Author(s)	Participants	Objectives	Measurements	Conclusion about the relationship between exercise and eating disorders
Wolf & Akamatsu (1994)	120 male and 168 female students classified as 159 exercisers and 129 non-exercisers	to study the relationship between exercise and eating disorders in college students	Eating Disorder Inventory (EDI); Eating Attitude Test (EAT)	Women involved in athletics demonstrated more anorectic/bulimic attitudes and greater weight preoccupation than non-exercising women but they did not manifest the same personality characteristics as female non-exercisers with the same level of eating disorder
Yates, Leehey, & Shisslak (1983)	60 male long-distance or trail runners	to study the similarity between obligatory running and Anorexia Nervosa	Interview	Found resemblance between obligatory running and Anorexia and, thus, marked the interest in further exploration of the relationship

10.3 Prevalence of Eating Disorder Symptoms in Exercisers and Non-Exercisers

Davis (1990a; 1990b) and Davis, Brewer and Ratusny (1993) conducted a series of studies (Table 10.1) in which they examined exercising and non-exercising individuals and their tendency for eating disorders. In none of these studies was exercise behavior clearly related to eating disorders. Opposing these conclusions are the results reported by French, Perry, Leon, and Fulkerson (1994), Pasman and Thompson (1988), Richert and Hummers (1986), Szymanski and Chrisler (1990), and Wolf and Akamatsu (1994). Because similar measurements were used in general, the discrepancy between the two sets of studies may be most closely related to the definition of exercise. In the latter set of studies either excessive exercisers or athletes were tested in contrast to those tested in the first set. However, the definition of "excessive exercise" needs to be standardized in research. Four factors including mode, frequency, intensity, and duration, must be reported. Otherwise it is unclear what is meant by "excessive exercise" or "athlete". Reporting only one or two exercise parameter(s) is often insufficient, especially in studies dealing with eating disorders because the latter is suspected to occur only in a very limited segment of the physically active population.

The majority of the reviewed studies (10.1) suggest that a high level of exercise or athleticism is associated with symptoms of eating disorders. The determinants of this relationship are not well known. Williamson et al. (1995) proposed a psychosocial model for the development of eating disorder symptoms in female athletes (Figure 10.1). The authors revealed that overconcern with body size that was mediated by social influence for thinness, anxiety about athletic performance, and negative appraisal of athletic achievement, was a primary and strong determinant of the etiology of eating disorder symptoms. This model should be given serious consideration in the future and tested in several segments of the exercising population.

Although women are at higher risk for developing eating disorders (Yates et al., 1994), male athletes may be at risk too. For example, Thiel, Gottfried, and Hesse (1993) reported a high frequency of eating disorder symptoms and even sub-clinical incidences of eating disorders in low weight male wrestlers and rowers (Table 10.1). This report attracts attention to the fact that in some sports (i.e., gymnastics, boxing, wrestling), in which weight maintenance is critical, athletes may be at high risk for developing eating disorders. Athletes in these sports may turn to often "unhealthy", weight control methods (Enns, Drewnowski, & Grinker, 1987). This high-risk population, however, has received little attention in the literature. In the future more research should be aimed at this athletic population.

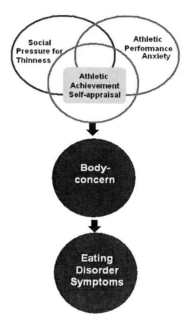

Figure 10.1. A psychosocial model for the development of eating disorder symptoms in female athletes proposed by Williamson et al. (1995).

The relationship between physical activity and eating disorders is not always negative. It is wrong to assume that exercise is directly related to eating disorders. Only a very small segment of the physically active population is affected negatively. One study, purposefully included in Table 10.1, has used physical activity successfully as a means of treatment for eating disorders. Levine, Marcus, and Moulton (1996) have shown that a simple walking regimen, performed three to five times a week and aimed to the burn 1000 calories, was efficient in managing binge eating disorders in a clinically diagnosed sample of obese women. In fact, about 71% of the experimental group was abstinent from binge eating by the end of the six-month study.

10.4 Is Excessive Physical Activity the Cause or the Consequence of Eating Disorders?

In view of De Coverley Veale's (1987) classification of "secondary exercise dependence" excessive exercise is a consequence of eating disorders. In these conditions exercise is used as a means for decreasing body weight (Blumenthal, Rose, & Chang, 1985; De Coverley Veale, 1987). However, Davis (1990a) argues that exercise may foster a higher degree of body narcissism and a distorted perception of one's body size which, in turn, may trigger eating disturbances. She suggests that it may be inappropriate to perceive exercise simply as the consequence of eating disorders. Indeed some exercisers may resort to dieting for the sake of better performance (De Coverley Veale, 1987). However, to date there is insufficient evidence to claim that exercise may be a contributing factor to eating disorders. Therefore, the hypothesis proposed by Davis (1990a) needs further scrutiny. The model proposed by Williamson et al. (1995) may be a valuable starting point in future studies.

10.5 Recommendations for Future Research on Exercise Addiction and Eating Disorders

The majority of studies on the relationship between exercise and eating disorders have no conceptual foundation. Therefore, future studies need to use psychosocial models, such as that proposed by Williamson et al. (1995), to test the relationship and causality between physical activity and eating disorders. A clear definition of what is meant by *excessive exercise* or *high-level exercise* or *athlete* must be presented in future studies to allow for comparability with other studies. Currently some research is adding more confounding notions to this area of research. The conclusion of Mond et al. (2006) and their call for a new operational definition for excessive exercise as reference to quality rather than quantity (i.e. "exercise is excessive when its postponement is accompanied by intense guilt or when it is undertaken solely to influence weight or shape.") does certainly not help. By definition *excessive* refers to the *amount* or volume of exercise and if this characteristic is not as influential in eating disorders as some psychological constructs, like the nature and intensity of deprivation feelings when exercise is not possible or the motives for why exercise is undertaken, the correct operational definition should be adopted and standardized. Terms like d*ysfunctional* exercise or *misused* exercise would surely be more adequate terms then *excessive* exercise. This is more than a problem with semantics. It is a shortage of operational definition without which no quality research could be carried out reliably. After resolving such basic problems, longitudinal studies that monitor both exercise behavior and eating habits, along with psychological factors such as anxiety, self-concept, body-image or body-concern, may be the most promising in the quest for a clearer understanding of the relationship between exercise and eating disorders.

11.0 WHAT WE KNOW

- Exercise addiction should not be equated with commitment to exercise.
- Exercise addiction is best understood in runners since other exercisers have seldom been examined.
- Exercise addiction is rare (approximately 3% of the exercising population is affected) but its consequences may be extremely severe.
- A significant proportion of people suffering from eating disorders resort to high levels of physical activity to lose weight. The condition is known as secondary exercise addiction or dependence.
- The personality characteristics of anorectics and highly committed exercisers are significantly different.
- A relationship between exercise and eating disorders is evident in athletic populations, particularly high-level exercisers and professional athletes.
- Female athletes, and those in sports participated in within weight categories, are at greater risk than other athletes of developing eating disorders.

12.0 WHAT WE NEED TO KNOW

- What igniting events or factors trigger exercise addiction?
- What is the role of exercise history, anxiety, and self-esteem in the etiology of exercise addiction?
- To what extent is excessive exercising a consequence of eating disorders?
- Could moderate exercise have a positive effect on some eating disorders?
- What are the relationships between aspects of athleticism, body image/concern, exercise and eating disorders?
- What is the risk of competitive athletes developing eating disorders?

13.0 GENERAL CONCLUSIONS

Physical exercise in moderation seldom carries negative consequences. In most cases of psychological dysfunction associated with exercise behavior, physical activity is a means of coping with emotional problems. The coping mechanism could be abused, whether exercise, alcohol, or medication. The abuse of the former is rare because there is physical effort involved, in contrast to the latter two (Cockerill & Riddington, 1996). Thus genuine exercise addiction is relatively rare in the exercising population (Morris, 1989; Terry et al., 2004). People affected by eating disorders often use exercise as a means of weight control. Some correlates of excessive exercise are anxiety, low self-esteem, and long-term fidelity to the activity, as well as distorted body-image in some cases of eating disorders. Generally, excessive physical activity is unlikely to be a cause of psychological dysfunction, but rather a symptom of the latter.

REFERENCES

Ackard, D. M., Brehm, B. J., & Steffen, J. J. (2002). *Exercise and eating disorders in college-aged women: profiling excessive exercisers.* Eating Disorders, 10, 31-47.

Adkins, C.E., & Keel, P.K. (2005). *Does "excessive" or "compulsive" best describe exercise as a symptom of bulimia nervosa?* International journal of Eating Disorder, 38, 24-29.

Aidman, E. & Woollard, S. (2003). *The influence of self-reported exercise addiction on acute emotional and physiological responses to brief exercise deprivation.* Psychology of Sport & Exercise, 4(3), 225-236.

Albrecht, U., Kirschner, N.E., & Grüsser, S.M. (2007). *Diagnostic instruments for behavioural addictions: an overview.* GMS Psycho-Social Medicine, 4:Doc11, Retrieved February 21, 2008 from: http://www.egms.de/pdf/journals/psm/2007-4/psm000043.pdf

American Psychiatric Association. (1995). *Diagnostic and Statistical Manual of Mental Disorders.* (4th ed.). Washington, DC: American Psychiatric Association.

Baker, T.B., Piper, M.E., McCarthy, D.E., Majeskie, M.R., & Fiore, M.C. (2004). *Addiction motivation reformulated: an affective processing model of negative reinforcement.* Psychological Review, 111, 33-51.

Beck, A. T., Ward, C. H., Mendelson, M., Mock, J., & Erbaugh, J. (1961). *An inventory of measuring depression.* Archives of General Psychiatry, 4, 561-571.

Berk, L.S., Tan, S.A., Fry, W.F., Napier, B.J., Lee, J.W., Hubbard, R.W., Lewis, J.E., & Eby, W.C. (1989). *Neuroendocrine and stress hormone changes during mirthful laughter.* American Journal of Medicine and Science, 298(6), 390-396.

Biddle, S. & Mutrie, N. (1991). *Psychology of Physical Activity and Exercise:* A Health-Related Perspective. Springer Verlag London Ltd.

Blumenthal, J.A., O'Toole, L.C., & Chang, J.L. (1984). *Is running an analogue of anorexia nervosa?* Journal of the American Medical Association (JAMA), 252, 520-523.

Blumenthal, J.A., Rose, S., & Chang, J.L. (1985). *Anorexia nervosa and exercise: Implications from recent findings.* Sports Medicine, 2, 237-247.

Bouchard, C., Shephard, R.J., & Stephens, T. (Eds.) (1994). *Physical activity, fitness, and health.* Champaign, IL: Human Kinetics.

Bozarth, M.A. (1994) *Physical dependence produced by central morphine infusions: an anatomical mapping study.* Neuroscience & Biobehavioral Reviews, 18, 373-383

Brewerton, T.D., Stellefson, E.J., Hibbs, N., Hodges, E.L., & Cochrane, C.E. (1995). *Comparison of eating disorder patients with and without compulsive exercisisng.* International Journal of Eating Disorders, 17, 413-416.

Brown, R.I.F. (1993). *Some contributions of the study of gambling to the study of other addictions.* In W.R. Eadington & J.A. Cornelius (Eds.), Gambling behavior and problem gambling (pp. 241-272). Reno: University of Nevada Press.

Carmack, M.A., & Martens, R. (1979). *Measuring commitment to running: A survey of runners' attitudes and mental states.* Journal of Sport Psychology, 1, 25-42.

Chapman, C.L., & De Castro, J.M. (1990*). Running addiction: Measurement and associated psychological characteristics.* The Journal of Sports Medicine and Physical Fitness, 30, 283-290.

Cockerill, I.M., & Riddington, M.E. (1996). *Exercise dependence and associated disorders: a review*. Counselling Psychology Quarterly, 9, 119-129.

Coen, S. P., & Ogles, B. M. (1993). *Psychological characteristics of the obligatory runner: A critical examination of the anorexia analogue hypothesis*. Journal of Sport & Exercise Psychology, 15, 338-354.

Conboy, J.K. (1994). *The effects of exercise withdrawal on mood states of runners*. Journal of Sport Behavior, 17, 188-203.

Costa, P.T., Jr., & McCrae, R.R. (1992). Revised NEO *Personality Inventory and five-Factor Inventory Professional Manual*. Odessa, Fl: PsychologicalAssessment Resources.

Cousineau, D., Ferguson, R.J., De Champlain, J., Gauthier, P., Cote, P., & Bourassa M. (1977). *Catecholamines in coronary sinus during exercise in man before and after training*. Journal of Applied Physiology, 43, 801-806.

Crisp, A.H., Hsu, L.K.G., Harding, B., & Hartshorn, J. (1980). *Clinical features of anorexia nervosa: A study of a consecutive series of 102 female patients*. Journal of Psychosomatic Research, 24, 179-191.

Cumella, E.J. (2005). *The heavy weight of exercise addiction*. Behavioral Health Management, 25(5), 26-31.

Dahlstrom, W. G., & Welch, G. S. (1960). *An MMPI Handbook*. Minneapolis, University of Minnesota Press.

Davis, C. (2000). *Exercise abuse*. International Journal of Sport Psychology, 31, 278-289.

Davis, C. (1990a). *Body image and weight preoccupation: A comparison between exercising and non-exercising women*. Appetite, 15, 13-21.

Davis, C. (1990b). *Weight and diet preoccupation and addictiveness: The role of exercise*. Personality and Individual Differences, 11, 823-827.

Davis, C., Brewer, H., & Ratusny, D. (1993). *Behavioral frequencey and psychological commitment: Necessary concepts in the study of excessive exercising*. Journal of Behavioral Medicine, 16, 611-628.

Davis, C., Kennedy, S.H., Ralevski, E., Dionne, M., Brewer, H., Neitzert, C., & Ratusny, D. (1995). *Obsessive compulsiveness and physical activity in anorexia nervosa and high-level exercising*. Journal of Psychosomatic Research, 39, 967-976.

De Coverley Veale, D.M.W. (1987). *Exercise Dependence*. British Journal of Addiction, 82, 735-740.

De Vries, H.A. (1981). *Tranquilizer effect of exercise: A critical review*. The Physician and SportsMedicine, 9(11), 47-53.

Duncan, D.F. (1974). *Drug abuse as a coping mechanism*. American Journal of Psychiatry, 131, 724.

Eberle, S.G. (2004). *Compulsive exercise: Too much of a good thing?* National Eating Disorders Association. Retrieved October 23, 2007 from: http://www.uhs.berkeley.edu/edaw/CmpvExc.pdf

Edwards, P. (2007). *Promoting physical activity and active living in urban environments*. Active Living, 16(5), 27-30.

Enns, M.P., Drewnowski, A., & Grinker, J.A. (1987). *Body composition, body-size estimation and attitudes toward eating in male college athletes*. Psychosomatic Medicine, 49, 56-64.

Estok, P.J., & Rudy, E.B. (1986). *Physical, psychosocial, menstrual changes/risks and addiction in female marathon and nonmarathon runner*. Health Care for Women International, 7, 187-202.

Evening Standard (2000). *Case history: Jackie's tale.* August 01, 2000. Retrieved February 21, 2008 from: http://www.thisislondon.co.uk/newsarticle-953584-details/Case+history%3A+Jackie%27s+tale/article.do

Eysenck, H. J., & Eysenck, S. B. G. (1991). *Manual of the Eysenck Personality* Scale. London: Hodder & Stoughton.

Farrell, P., Gates, W.K., Maksud, M.G., & Morgan, W.P. (1982). *Increases in plasma b-endorphin/b-lipotropin immunoreactivity after treadmill running in humans.* Journal of Applied Physiology 52(5), 1245-1249.

French, S.A., Perry, C.L., Leon, G.R., & Fulkerson, J.A. (1994). *Food preferences, eating patterns, and physical activity among adolescents: Correlates of eating disorders symptoms.* Journal of Adolescent Health, 15, 286-294.

French, S.A., Perry, C.L., Leon, G.R., & Fulkerson, J.A. (1995). *Changes in psychological variables and health behaviors by dieting status over a three-year period in a cohort of adolescent females.* Journal of Adolescent Health, 16, 438-447.

Frost, R. O., Marten, P., Lahart, C., & Rosenblate, R. (1990). *The dimensions of perfectionism.* Cognitive Therapy and Research, 14, 449-468

Furst, D.M., & Germone, K. (1993). *Negative addiction in male and female runners and exercisers.* Perceptual and Motor Skills, 77, 192-194.

Garner, D.M. (1991). *Eating Disorder inventory-2 manual.* Psychological Assessment Resources, Odessa, FL.

Garner, D. M., & Garfinkel, P. E. (1979). *The eating attitudes test: An index of the symptoms of anorexia nervosa.* Psychological Medicine, 9, 273-279.

Garner, D. M., Olmsted, M. P., & Polivy, J. (1983). *Development and validation of a multidimensional Eating Disorder Inventory for anorexia and bulimia.* International Journal of Eating Disorders, 2 (2), 15-34.

Gibb, G. D., Bailey, J. R., Best, R. H., & Lambrinth, T. T. (1983). *The measurement of obsessive-compulsive personality.* Educational and Psychological Measurement, 43, 1233-1238.

Glasser, W. (1976). *Positive Addiction.* New York, NY: Harper & Row.

Godin, G. & Shephard, R.J. (1985). *A simple method to assess exercise behavior in the community.* Canadian Journal of Applied Sport Science. 10, 141-146.

Goldfarb, A.H. & Jamurtas, A.Z. (1997*). b-Endorphin response to exercise: an update.* Sports Medicine 24(1), 8-16.

Goodman, A. (1990). *Addiction: definition and implications.* British Journal of Addiction, 85, 1403-1408.

Griffiths, M.D. (1996). *Behavioural addiction: an issue for everybody?* Journal of Workplace Learning, 8 (3), 19-25.

Griffiths, M. (1997). *Exercise addiction: A case study.* Addiction Research, 5, 161-168.

Griffiths, M.D. (2002). *Gambling and gaming addictions in adolescence. Leicester:* British Psychological Society/Blackwells.

Griffiths, M.D. (2005). *A 'components' model of addiction within a biopsychosocial framework.* Journal of Substance Use, 10(4), 191-197.

Grüsser, S.M., & Thalemann, C.N. (2006). *Verhaltenssucht-Diagnostik*, Therapie, Forschung. Bern: Huber.

Hagan, A. L., & Hausenblas, H. A. (2003). *The relationship between exercise dependence symptoms and perfectionism.* American Journal of Health Studies, 18, 133- 137.

Hailey, B.J., & Bailey, L.A. (1982). *Negative addiction in runners: A quantitative approach.* Journal of Sport Behavior, 5, 150-153.

Hamer, M., & Karageorghis, C.I. (2007). P*sychobiological mechanisms of exercise dependence.* Sports Medicine, 37(6), 477-484.

Harte, J.L., Eifert, G.H., & Smith, R. (1995). *The effects of running and meditation on beta-endorphin, corticotropin-releasing hormone and cortisol in plasma, and on mood.* Biological Psychology 40, 251-265.

Haskell, W.L., Lee, I.M., Pate, R.R., Powell, K.E., Blair, S.N., Franklin, B.A., Macera, C.A., Heath, G.W., Thompson, P.D., & Bauman, A. (2007). *Physical activity and public health: updated recommendation for adults from the American College of Sports Medicine and the American Heart Association.* Medicine & Science in Sports & Exercise, 39(8), 1423-1434.

Hausenblas, H.A., & Giacobbi, P.R. Jr. (2004). *Relationship between exercise dependence symptoms and personality.* Personality and Individual Differences. 36, 1265-1273.

Hausenblas H.A., & Symons Downs, D. (2002) *Exercise dependence: a systematic review.* Psychology of Sport Exercise, 3, 89-123.

Hausenblas, H.A., & Symons Downs, D. (2002). *How much is too much? The development and validation of the exercise dependence scale.* Psychology and Health, 17, 387-404.

Iannos, M., & Tiggemann, M. (1997). *Personality of the excessive exerciser.* Personality and Individual Differences, 22, 775-778.

Johnson, M.D. (1994). *Disordered eating in active and athletic women.* Clinics in Sports Medicine, 13, 355-369.

Johnson, R. (1995). *Exercise dependence: When runners don't know when to quit.* Sports Medicine and Arthroscopy Review, 3, 267-273.

Jones, R.D., & Weinhouse, S. (1979). *Running as self-therapy.* Journal of Sports Medicine, 19, 397-404.

Kjaer, M. & Dela, F. (1996). *Endocrine Response to Exercise* (pp. 6-8) In L. Hoffman-Goetz, (Ed.). Exercise and Immune Function. Boca Raton. CRC, 1.20, 1996.

Knight, P.O., Schocken, D.D., Powers, P.S., Feld, J., & Smith, J.T. (1987). *Gender comparison in anorexia nervosa and obligate running.* Medicine and Science in Sports and Exercise, 19(suppl.), 396, S66.

Lazare, A., Klerman, G. L., & Armour, D. J. (1966*). Oral, obsessive and hysterical personalities patterns: An investigation of psychoanalytic concepts by means of factor analysis.* Archives of General Psychiatry, 14, 624.

Levenson, H. (1981). *Differentiating among internality, powerful others and chance.* In H. Lefcourt (Ed.), Research with the locus of control construct volume I: Assessment methods. New York: Academic Press.

Levine, M.D., Marcus, M.D., & Moulton, P. (1996). *Exercise in the treatment of binge eating disorder. International* Journal of Eating Disorders, 19, 171-177.

Loumidis, K.S., & Wells, A. (1998). *Assessment of beliefs in exercise dependence: the development and preliminary validation of the exercise beliefs questionnaire.* Personality of Individual Differences, 25, 553-567.

Markoff, R.A., Ryan, P., &Young, T. (1982). *Endorphins and mood changes in long-distance running.* Medicine & Science in Sports and Exercise, 14, 11-15.

McKinney, C.H., Tims, F.C., Kumar, A.M., & Kumar, M. (1997). *The effect of selected classical music and spontaneous imagery on plasma β-endorphin.* Journal of Behavioral Medicine, 20(1), 85-99.

McLachlan, C.D., Hay, M., & Coleman, G.J. (1994). *The effects of exercise on the oral consumption of morphine and methadone in rats.* Pharmacology, Biochemistry and Behavior 48(2), 63-568.

McNair, D. M., Lorr, M., & Droppelman, L. F. (1981). *Profile of Mood States* Manual. San Diego, CA: Educational and Industrial Testing Services.

Mond, J.M., Hay, P.J., Rodgers, B., & Owen, C. (2006). *An update on the definition of "excessive exercise" in eating disorders research.* International Journal of Eating Disorders, 39, 1047-153

Morgan, W.P. (1979). *Negative addiction in runners.* The Physician and Sportmedicine 7, 57-71.

Morgan, W.P. & O'Connor, P.J. (1988). *Exercise and mental health.* In R.K. Dishman (Ed.), Exercise Adherence: Its Impact on Public Health, (pp. 91-121). Champaign, IL. Human Kinetics.

Morris, M. (1989). Running round the clock. Running, 104, (Dec.) 44-45.

Pasman, L., & Thompson, J.K. (1988). *Body image and eating disturbance in obligatory runners, obligatory weightlifters, and sedentary individuals. International* Journal of Eating Disorders, 7, 759-777.

Péronnet, F., & Szabo, A. (1993). *Sympathetic response to psychosocial stressors in humans: Linkage to physical exercise and training.* In P. Seraganian (Ed.), Exercise Psychology: The Influence of Physical Exercise On Psychological Processes (pp. 172-217). New York: John Wiley & Sons.

Pierce, E.,, Eastman, N., Tripathi, H., Olson, K., Dewey, W. (1993). B- *Endorphin response to endurance exercise: Relationship to exercise dependence.* Perceptual and Motor Skills. 77, 767-770.

Pierce, E.F. (1994). *Exercise dependence syndrome in runners.* Sports Medicine, 18, 149-155.

Richert, A.J., & Hummers, J.A. (1986). *Patterns of physical activity in college students at possible risk for eating disorder. International* Journal of Eating Disorders, 5, 775-763.

Rosenberg, M. (1965). *Society and the adolescent self-image.* Princeton, NJ: Princeton University Press.

Rozin, P., & Stoess, C. (1993). *Is there a general tendency to become addicted?* Addictive Behaviors, 18, 81-87.

Rudy, E.B., & Estok, P.J. (1989). *Measurement and significance of negative addiction in runners.* Western Journal of Nursing Research, 11, 548-558.

Sachs. M.L. (1981) *Running addiction.* In M. Sacks & M. Sachs (Eds.), Psychology of Running (pp. 116-126), Champaign, ILL: Human Kinetics.

Sachs, M.L., & Pargman, D. (1979). *Running addiction: A depth interview examination.* Journal of Sport Behaviour, 2, 143-155.

Sachs, M.L., & Pargman, D. (1984). *Running addiction.* In M.L. Sachs & G.W. Buffone (Eds.), Running as therapy: An integrated approach (pp. 231-252), Lincoln, NE: University of Nebraska Press.

Sforzo, G.A. (1988). *Opioids and exercise: an update.* Sports Medicine 7, 109-124.

Sforzo, G.A., Seeger, T.F., Pert, C.B., Pert, A., & Dotsen, C.O. (1986*). In vivo opioid receptor occupation in the rat brain following exercise.* Medicine and Science in. Sports and Exercise, 18, 380-384.

Smith, D., Hale, B., & Collins, D. (1998). *Measurement of Exercise Dependence in Body Builders. **Journal of Sports Medicine and Physical Fitness**, 38, 1-9.*

Speilberger, C. D., Gorsuch, R. L., Lushene, R., Vagg, P. R., & Jacobs, G. A. (1983). *Manual for the State-Trait Anxiety Inventory* (STAI). Palo Alto, CA: Consulting Psychologist Press.

Stoll, O. (1997). *Endorphine, Laufsucht und Runner's High*. Aufstieg und Niedergang eines Mythos. Leipziger Sportwissenschaftliche Beiträge, 38, 102-121.

Summers, J.J. & Hinton, E.R. (1986). *Development of scales to measure participation in running*. In Unestahl, L.E. (Ed.). Contemporary Sport Psychology, (pp. 73-84), Veje: Sweden.

Szabo, A. (1995). *The impact of exercise deprivation on well-being of habitual exercisers*. The Australian Journal of Science and Medicine in Sport, 27, 68-75.

Szabo, A. (2000). *Physical activity as a source of psychological dysfunction*. In Biddle S.J.H., Fox, K.R.,& Boutcher, S.H. (Eds.). Physical activity and psychological well-being (pp. 130-153). London: Routledge.

Szabo, A. (2006). *Comparison of the psychological effects of exercise and humour*. In Andrew M. Lane (Ed.). Mood and Human Performance: Conceptual, Measurement, and Applied Issues (Chapter 10, pp.201-216). Hauppauge, NY: Nova Science Publishers, Inc.

Szabo, A., Frenkl, R., & Caputo, A. (1996). *Deprivation feelings, anxiety, and commitment to various forms of physical activity: A cross-sectional study on the Internet*. Psychologia, 39, 223-230.

Szabo, A., Frenkl, R., & Caputo, A. (1997). *Relationships between addiction to running, commitment to running, and deprivation from running*. European Yearbook of Sport Psychology, 1, 130-147.

Szabo, A., Ainsworth, S.E., & Danks, P.K. (2005). *Experimental comparison of the psychological benefits of aerobic exercise, humour, and music*. HUMOR: International Journal of Humor Research, 18(3), 235-246.

Szabo, A., & Griffiths, M.D. (2007). *Exercise addiction in British sport science students*. International Journal of Mental Health and Addiction, 5(1), 25-28.

Szymanski, L.A., & Chrisler, J.C. (1990*). Eating disorders, gender role, and athletic activity. Psychology* A Journal of Human Behavior, 27, 20-29.

Tan, A. L., Kendis, R. J., Fine, J. T., & Porac, J. (1977*). A short measure of eriksonian ego identity*. Journal of Personality Assessment, 41, 279-284.

Taylor, D., Boyajian, J.G., James, N., Woods, D., Chicz-Demet, A., Wilson, A.F., & Sandman, C.A. (1994). *Acidosis stimulates b-endorphin release during exercise*. Journal of Applied Physiology, 77(4), 1913-1918.

Terry, A., Szabo, A., & Griffiths, M.D. (2004). *The exercise addiction inventory*: A new brief screening tool. Addiction Research and Theory, 12, 489–499.

Thiel, A., Gottfried, H., & Hesse, F.W. (1993). *Subclinical eating disorders in male athletes*. Acta Psychiatrica Scandinavica, 88, 259-265.

Thaxton, L. (1982). *Physiological and psychological effects of short-term exercise addiction on habitual runners*. Journal of Sport Psychology, 4, 73-80.

Thompson, J.K., & Blanton, P. (1987). *Energy conservation and exercise dependence: A sympathetic arousal hypothesis*. Medicine and Science in Sports and Exercise, 19, 91-97.

Thompson, J.K., & Pasman, L. (1991). *The obligatory exercise questionnaire*. Behavioural Assessment Review, May, 116-118.

Thornton, E.W., & Scott, S.E. (1995). *Motivation in the committed runner: Correlations between self-report scales and behaviour*. Health Promotion International, 10, 177-184.

U.S. Department of Health and Human Services – Public Health Service (2004). *Progress Review; Physical Activity and Fitness.* Retrieved 02 February 2008 from: http://www.healthypeople.gov/Data/2010prog/focus22/

Warburton, D.E.R., Nicol, C.W., & Bredin, S.S.D. (2006*). Health benefits of physical activity: the evidence.* Canadian Medical Association Journal, 174(6), 801.809.

Wichmann, S., & Martin, D.R. (1992*). Exercise excess.* The Physician and Sportsmedicine, 20, 193-200.

Williamson, D.A., Netemeyer, R.G., Jackman, L.P., Anderson, D.A., Funsch, C.L., & Rabalais, J.Y. (1995). *Structural equation modeling of risk factors for the development of eating disorder symptoms in female athletes.* International journal of eating Disorders, 17, 387-393.

Wolf, E.M., & Akamatsu, T.J. (1994). *Exercise involvement and eating disordered characteristics in college students.* Eating Disorders, 2, 308-318.

Yates, A., Leehey, K., & Shisslak, C.M. (1983). *Running-An analogue of anorexia ?* New England Journal of Medicine, 308, 251-255.

Yates, A., Shisslak, C. M., Allender, J., Crago, M., & Leehey, K. (1992). *Comparing obligatory to nonobligatory runners.* Psychosomatics, 33, 180-189.

Yates, A., Shisslak, C.M., Crago, M., & Allender, J. (1994). *Overcommitment to sport: Is there a relationship to the eating disorders?* Clinical Journal of Sport Medicine, 4, 39-46.

PEER REVIEWED PUBLISHED WORKS FROM THE AUTHOR ON WHICH THIS CHAPTER IS BASED

Szabo, A. (1995). *The impact of exercise deprivation on well-being of habitual exercisers.* The Australian Journal of Science and Medicine in Sport, 27, 68-75.

Szabo, A., Frenkl, R., & Caputo, A. (1996). *Deprivation feelings, anxiety, and commitment to various forms of physical activity:* A cross-sectional study on the Internet. Psychologia, 39, 223-230.

Szabo, A., Frenkl, R., & Caputo, A. (1997). *Relationships between addiction to running, commitment to running, and deprivation from running.* European Yearbook of Sport Psychology, 1, 130-147.

Szabo, A. (1998). *Studying the psychological impact of exercise deprivation: are experimental studies hopeless?* Journal of Sport Behavior, 21, 139-147.

Szabo, A. (2000). *Physical activity and psychological dysfunction.* In Biddle, S., Fox, K., & Boutcher, S. (Eds.). *Physical Activity and Psychological Well-Being* (Chapter 7, pp. 130-153). Routledge, London

Szabo, A. (2001). *The dark side of sports and exercise: Research Dilemmas.* Paper presented at the 10th World Congress of Sport Psychology, May 30, 2001, Skiathos, Greece.

Terry, A., Szabo, A., & Griffiths, M. D. (2004). *The exercise addiction inventory: A new brief screening tool.* Addiction Research and Theory, 12, 489–499.

Griffiths, M.D., Szabo, A., & Terry, A. (2005). *The exercise addiction inventory: a quick and easy screening tool for health practitioners.* British Journal of Sports Medicine, 39, e30 (http://bjsportmed.com/cgi/content/full/39/6/e30)

Szabo, A., Ainsworth, S.E., & Danks, P.K. (2005). *Experimental comparison of the psychological benefits of aerobic exercise, humor, and music.* HUMOR: International Journal of Humor Research, 18(3), 235-246.

Szabo, A. (2006). *Comparison of the psychological effects of exercise and humor.* In Andrew M. Lane (Ed.). Mood and Human Performance: Conceptual, Measurement, and Applied Issues (Chapter 10, pp.201-216). Hauppauge, NY: Nova Science Publishers, Inc.

Rendi, M., Szabo, A., & Szabó, T. (2007). *Exercise and Internet addiction: commonalities and differences between two problematic behaviours.* International Journal of Mental Health and Addiction. 5, 219-232.

Szabo, A., & Griffiths, M.D. (2007). *Exercise addiction in British sport science students.* International Journal of Mental Health and Addiction, 5(1), 25-28.

Szabo, A., Velenczei, A., Szabó, T., & Kovács, A. *(2007).* Exercise addiction. Magyar Sporttudományi Szemle (Hungarian Review of Sport Sciences), 8(31), 43(Abs.).

In: Handbook of Sports Psychology
Editor: Calvin H. Chang

ISBN: 978-1-60741-256-4
©2009 Nova Science Publishers, Inc.

Chapter 4

STRESS IN YOUNG ATHLETES: TIME FOR A DEVELOPMENTAL ANALYSIS?

Paul J. McCarthy[1] and Jamie B. Barker[2]

Department of Psychology, Glasgow Caledonian University,
Glasgow, G4 0BE, UK[1]
Centre for Sport and Exercise Research, Faculty of Health, Staffordshire University,
Stoke-on-Trent, ST4 2DF, UK[2]

ABSTRACT

It is difficult to think of a subject of greater bearing to our understanding of sport than the effect of emotions on sport performance. Researchers interested in exploring emotions among youth athletes have a unique opportunity to examine their thoughts, feelings, and behaviors in a rich and dynamic natural laboratory. Despite this opportunity, our understanding of emotional experience among young athletes is relatively uncharted territory in pediatric sport psychology. Stress and enjoyment have well developed and integrated literatures and provide a solid base for further emotion research among youths in sport (Scanlan, Babkes, & Scanlan, 2005). Current research, however, is beginning to address other issues in different contexts with emotion as a central element such as coping (Holt & Mandigo, 2004; Nicholls, 2007; Raedeke & Smith, 2004), burnout (Hill, Hall, Appleton, & Kozub, 2008) and perfectionism (Appleton, Hall, & Hill, 2009) illustrating that many intrapersonal, situational and significant other sources of positive and negative emotion exist. This chapter reviews the literature on stress and anxiety among young athletes with an emphasis on burnout, perfectionism and coping.

INTRODUCTION

Sport embodies a rich tapestry of emotion framing a unique natural setting to explore emotional experience. Because emotions influence how well the athlete performs, researchers strive to understand, explain and predict which emotions influence athletes and their performances (Jones, 2003). Although researchers generally understand how pleasant and unpleasant emotions affect athletes and their performances, the scales of emotion research tip strongly in favor of unpleasant emotions, especially stress and anxiety (Jackson, 2000).

While much ink flows from psychologists' pens to explain how stress and anxiety influence sport performers, we know less about these emotional experiences in young athletes. Yet, millions of children and adolescents participate in sport at recreational and elite levels (De Knop, Engström, Skirstad, & Weiss, 1996). And how they perceive their sport experience sows emotional responses which affect their motives to engage and remain in sport (Scanlan et al., 2005). For example, stress often precedes burnout (Gould, Greenleaf, & Krane, 2002) and dropout (Gould & Diffenbach, 1999; Smith, 1986), whereas, enjoyment prompts athletes to take part (Weiss & Petlichkoff, 1989) and commit to sport (Carpenter & Scanlan, 1998). When youths stay in sport, they strengthen their talent and likelihood of fulfilling their potential as elite athletes (Côté, 1999; Côté, Baker, & Abernethy, 2007). By understanding the relations between emotions and performance in competitive sport, we can begin to create a climate where youths profit socially, emotionally, physically and psychologically from sport.

A first step to understand young athletes' emotional experiences is to appreciate sport from their perspective and evaluate how participating in sport shapes psychosocial change (Brustad & Weiss, 1987). Few sport psychologists incorporate a developmental perspective to interpret how intrapersonal and social factors contribute to affective experiences and motivational patterns of the young athlete (Brustad & Weiss, 1987; Scanlan et al., 2005; Weiss & Bredemeier, 1983), though the shoots of developmentally based emotion research in youth sport are sprouting (Harwood & Knight, 2009; McCarthy, Jones, & Clark-Carter, 2008; Weiss & Weiss, 2006). We argue in this chapter that understanding stress in youth sport accrues psychological, social, emotional and physical benefits for young athletes. In particular, we explain the methods used to measure stress and outline a perspective involving cognitive and social development to understand emotional experience in youth sport. Finally, we briefly tackle three key research themes relating to stress in youth sport: burnout, perfectionism and coping.

WHY SHOULD WE STUDY STRESS AMONG YOUNG ATHLETES?

Stress represents an individual's appraisal of a situation as too taxing or exceeding one's resources, risking one's sense of well-being (Lazarus, 1966). For example, stress generates numerous discrete emotions such as anger, anxiety, fear, happiness and pride (Crocker, Hoar, McDonough, Kowalski, & Niefer, 2004; Lazarus, 2000). Although sport psychologists swap the terms stress and anxiety in their research, (e.g., Passer, 1988, Scanlan, 1986), anxiety is defined differently representing an emotional response to perceived threat comprising cognitive concerns and physiological arousal (Naylor, Burton, & Crocker, 2002). An athlete feels threatened when the costs of failure count, but the demands for performance exceed the athlete's resources (Martens, 1977) and it is this perceived imbalance and anticipated harmful consequences, rather than the reality, that produces the negative emotional response (Scanlan et al., 2005).

A criticism of research on stress and anxiety in youth sport is that it is mainly descriptive and often atheoretical, lacking a perspective to unpick the complex relations among young athletes' motivation for sport and their emotional reactions to sport (Smith, Jones, & Roach, 2001). Despite this shortcoming, more researchers are adopting a social cognitive perspective to understand emotional experience in sport by including the social context, the athlete's motivation and understanding of success and failure in sport (Duda & Ntoumanis, 2005). In addition, the sport setting permits us to explore and understand emotional experience among youth in a rich and dynamic natural laboratory that might be ethically unacceptable in experimental procedures. Competitive youth sport also offers a rich developmental context that encompasses social, cognitive, motor and physical components. Because of the motivational consequences of stress, understanding the relation among this emotional response, cognitive and social development, we could improve our guidance for parents, coaches and sport psychologists in youth sport. In other words, knowing the relevant sources of stress as a function of developmental progression should allow us to organize sport programs to reduce stress and optimize the experience for all participants (Scanlan et al., 2005). First, however, we need to measure stress accurately and we shall discuss measurement in the next section.

HOW DO WE MEASURE STRESS IN YOUTH SPORT?

Sport psychologists apply both qualitative and quantitative research methods to study stress among young athletes. Depending on the cognitive maturity of the athlete, some methods (e.g., focus groups) might be more suitable than other methods (e.g., psychometric inventory; Hennessy & Heary, 2005). Researchers typically examine stress among young athletes by their emotional reactions to competitive sport and the performance consequences that result (Scanlan & Lewthwaite, 1984). Also, coping behaviors and their influence on emotions, though such research is limited, illuminate the study of stress in youth athletes (Smith et al., 2001).

Sport researchers have primarily measured stress responses in competitive youth sport in the form of state anxiety. State anxiety represents ". . . subjective, consciously perceived feelings of tension and apprehension associated with . . . arousal of the autonomic nervous system" (Spielberger, 1966; p. 17), and is measured by changes in behavioral, physiological and psychological responses. Behavioral indicators of state anxiety include insomnia, losing one's appetite, nervous laughter and being jittery. Physiological changes include increased heart rate, respiration, galvanic skin responses, and palmar sweating. Psychological measures include state anxiety and other in-depth measurements of negative thoughts and feelings (Scanlan et al., 2005). Because public performances are divided into phases (i.e., pre-, mid-, and post-situation) placing distinct normative demands on the individual (Lazarus & Folkman, 1984), state anxiety is often measured before, during and sometimes after sport competition. State anxiety is usually measured using one of a few validated measures such as the State Anxiety Inventory for Children (STAIC; Spielberger, 1973), the Competitive State Anxiety Inventory (CSAI; Martens, Burton, Rivkin, & Simon, 1980), and the Competitive State Anxiety Inventory-2 (CSAI-2; Martens, Burton, Vealey, Bump, & Smith, 1990).

Because sport takes place in a public arena, it invites young athletes to display their competencies and compare themselves to others. These comparisons become the yardstick by which these young athletes evaluate themselves. Regrettably, many coaches, parents, peers and fans determine a young athlete's success in competition by the outcome, which is typically uncertain. For these reasons, young athletes are primed to worry about their performance. A young athlete's cognitive anxiety centers on at least three antecedents: beliefs about the quality of preparation, perceived competence and control of the challenge and the performer's appraisal of an opponent's ability. The antecedents of somatic anxiety differ from those of cognitive anxiety and are similar to conditional responses to the actual or imagined performance setting (Smith et al., 2001).

Competitive settings evoke greater anxiety for some young athletes more than for others, revealing competitive trait anxiety, a personality disposition that reflects individual differences in the tendency to perceive threat and experience stress in sport competition (Lewthwaite, 1990; Martens, 1977). Higher levels of competitive trait anxiety relate to more frequent and/or intense competitive state anxiety (Scanlan & Lewthwaite, 1984; Scanlan & Passer, 1978, 1979), less effective attentional focus (Albrecht & Feltz, 1987), less successful performance (Taylor, 1987) and stronger preferences to avoid competition (Lewthwaite & Scanlan, 1989). Psychologists usually measure trait anxiety using one of three instruments, the Sport Competition Anxiety Test for children (SCAT-C; Martens, 1977), the Sport Anxiety Scale (SAS; Smith, Smoll, & Schutz, 1990) or the Sport Anxiety Scale-2 (SAS-2; Smith, Smoll, Cumming, & Grossbard, 2006). The SCAT reflects a unidimensonal measure that cannot distinguish between or measure differences in somatic and cognitive anxiety. The SAS and SAS-2 yield a multidimensional measure of cognitive and trait anxiety in sport performance settings. Smith et al. (2006) developed the SAS-2 because the 3-factor structure of the original SAS could not be reproduced in child samples. In addition, several items on the scale produced conflicting factor loading in adult samples. Whether young athletes actually understand what they are completing, is questionable because young athletes in the concrete operations stage of development (Piaget, 1954) often struggle to understand such instruments. During this stage, they develop their ability to use language and communicate, helping themselves to be understood as well as understand others. The emergence of metalinguisitic awareness – the ability to think and talk about language and its properties (Bialystock, 1993) – helps children to read and write (Tunmer & Chapman, 2002). Despite these developing capacities to understand language, we still need to check that children understand what a questionnaire is asking them to do. One useful strategy to assess children's ability to read and understand questionnaires is to use a Flesch-Kincaid readability assessment (Harrison, 1980). This scale allows the researcher to establish the reading levels of the sample and the appropriateness of the scale for those children. Indeed, asking children to express their emotional self-perception ability is challenging and such distinction may not be possible at a young age (Harris, 2000). Smith et al. (2006) established that the 3-factor SAS structure broke down because children's emotional self-perception capabilities did not allow them to differentiate between the three aspects of subjectively experienced anxiety indexed by its terms. Only a few studies address the cognitive affective discrimination because most studies focused on children's ability to distinguish between discrete emotions rather than their ability to make cognitive affective distinctions (Smith et al., 2006; Turner & Barrett, 2003).

Sport psychologists use qualitative research methods (e.g., interviews and focus groups) to overcome these difficulties with children (Hennessy & Heary, 2005) and to gain a broader and deeper knowledge of sources of stress. Interviews with various young athletes including golfers, wrestlers, and figures skaters formed an understanding of competitive stress as well as stress associated with interactions during practices and off the field of play (Cohn, 1990;

Gould, Eklund, & Jackson, 1993; Gould, Finch, & Jackson, 1993; Gould, Jackson, & Finch, 1993; Scanlan, Stein, & Ravizza, 1991). More recently, researchers have begun to examine stress in youth sport using a developmental perspective (Harwood & Knight, 2009). Together, these methods sketch a sound understanding of sources of stress among young athletes.

STRESS IN YOUTH SPORT PERFORMERS

Many factors contribute to young athletes stress such as personality, performance expectations, competition outcomes, general hassles of the sport and others' expectations, evaluations and feedback (Scanlan et al., 2005). Although we have a credible descriptive understanding of what young athletes worry about before, during and after competitive sport, we know much less about the relation between young athletes' motivation to take part in sport, and their emotional reactions to sport. In addition, we hardly know about the developmental sources of stress among young athletes (Harwood & Knight, 2009; Scanlan et al., 2005). In this section, we explore cognitive and social development in youth sport within a lifespan model and introduce a social cognitive perspective to explore the relation among the social context of sport, the athletes' achievement goal orientation, subjective understanding of success and failure and the emotions experienced before, during and after competition (Smith et al., 2001).

Understanding the Cognitive and Social Development of the Young Athlete

Young athletes' emotional development is multifaceted and shaped uniquely by cognitive and social development, affecting how they generate, regulate and report emotions. Children typically enter adult organized youth sport during the concrete operational stage of cognitive development (age 7-12); a stage of cognitive development characterized by logical thinking and tangible events (Piaget, 1954). This stage represents concrete operations because one can perform operations only on images of tangible objects and actual events (Weiten, 2004). During this stage of development, children master reversibility and decentration (Foster & Weigand, 2008). Reversibility allows the child to mentally undo an action (e.g., figure out how a skill works) and decentration allows the child to focus on more than one feature of a problem simultaneously (e.g., control the ball and discover who is in the best position to receive the ball). Children with these new skills can appreciate many ways to examine things and solve problems. As children mature into adolescents, they display a greater ability to think abstractly, idealistically and logically; their objective view of world recedes and their subjective and idealistic image advances (Santrock, 1998). This stage is recognized as the formal operational stage of cognitive development (Piaget, 1954). From a cognitive perspective, many changes during the formal operational stage of cognitive development help young athletes to adapt to sports by selectively attending to relevant stimuli while disregarding irrelevant information (Ross, 1976). Long-term memory improves helping them to acquire and retain knowledge, make decisions, solve problems and think critically. Adolescents can also generate opinions, take different perspectives, anticipate consequences and assess the credibility of information sources better than children (Crocker et al., 2004). In other words, adolescents emerge much more able to cope with the demands of competitive sport.

The family remains the principal environment of social relations for most children during the concrete operational stage of development. Children begin to learn more about themselves in increasingly complex social networks. At this stage of development, children figure out who they are and what makes them unique (Hewstone, Fincham, & Foster, 2005). They begin to understand their capacities and limitations and deal with the emotions that these assessments cause. Many of these assessments involve comparing oneself with others. The friends children make depend upon personality compatibility and mutual expectation (Damon, 1983). Children refer to shared activities and cooperation to describe their friends. For example, 'we play football together' and 'take turns in goal'. Adolescents spend increasing amounts of time in the company of their peers (Brown & Klute, 2003). Peer relations form a crucial influence on their sense of identity. As children mature during adolescence, they can develop mature perspective taking. Perspective taking is the ability to assume another person's point of view and understand his or her thoughts and feelings. It is necessary to understand interpersonal relationships, intimate response and the connection between social encounters such as reciprocal sharing of emotions and being socially sensitive to the emotional displays and communication of others (Crocker et al., 2004)

Cognitive and Social Development within Sport

Within youth sport, we understand development best as a set of stages. Three stages of participating in sport emerge between early childhood and late adolescence, influencing the stages of those that dropout, remain for recreational motives or become elite performers. Côté and his colleagues (Abernethy, Côté, & Baker, 1999; Beamer, Côté, & Ericsson, 1999; Côté, 1999) identified these stages while examining the careers of elite Canadian and Australian athletes in rowing, gymnastics, basketball, netball and field hockey. These stages represent the sampling (age 7-12), specializing (age 13-16), and investment or recreational (age 17+) years. Parents usually launch a child's sporting career during the sampling years. During these years, children develop basic identities, motives, values and beliefs about sport, which are critical for staying involved in sports long-term (Côté & Hay, 2002). Next, children enter the specializing years where they begin specializing in one or two sports. Although enjoyment and excitement remain strong motives for these children, sport-specific skill development dominates. Children chose one activity over another because of critical incidents such as positive experiences with a coach, encouragement from an older sibling, success and/or simple enjoyment of the activity. Finally, the child moves into the investment years or the recreational years. In the investment years, the child commits to achieving excellence in one activity. Now, strategy, skill development and competition are the most important elements. Children that do not invest in a specific activity but do remain in sport enter the recreational years for enjoyment and health benefits (Côté & Hay, 2002).

Wylleman and Lavallee (2004) proposed a holistic life-span approach of the sport and post sport career of elite athletes based on data from active and former talented athletes, professional and elite athletes, and Olympians. Within this model, four levels run concurrently: athletic, psychological, psychosocial and academic/vocational. On an athletic level, athletes can pass through four possible stages tentatively linked to approximate ages.

First, the initiation stage (6 – 7 years) is when the young athlete begins organized sport. Second, the development stage (12 – 13 years) is when the athlete's talent is recognized; more intense training and participation in competitions follows. Third, the mastery stage (18 – 19 years) occurs when the athlete begins participating at the highest competitive level. Finally, the discontinuation stage reflects the elite athlete's transition out of competitive sport (28 – 30 years). Although these stages are normative, differences across sports are clear. For instance, at age 18 – 19, the mastery stage for female gymnasts may be ending (Kerr & Dacyshyn, 2000) whereas it may be just beginning for male rowers (Wylleman, De Knop, Menkehorst, Theeboom, & Annerel, 1993; Wylleman & Lavallee, 2004).

The second layer of the model represents the psychological level and consists of three stages based on different conceptual frameworks for psychological development. For example, Erikson's (1963) developmental stages, Piaget's (1963) stages of cognitive development and Havighurst's (1973) developmental tasks over the lifespan. These stages are childhood, adolescence, and adulthood. The third layer represents the psychosocial development of athletes based on their athletic involvement. An athlete perceives various contributions from others during an athletic career. For example, parents play a key role in socializing their child into sport; however, as the child gets older, although parents are still involved, peers play a more significant role in the psychosocial relationship. Finally, the fourth layer represents the academic transitions into primary education, secondary education, higher education and vocational training or a professional occupation of the athlete. Briefly, the life-span model provides a developmental perspective on transitions athletes face at athletic, psychological, psychosocial and academic or vocational levels.

Measuring Emotional Responses Developmentally

Over 25 years ago, Weiss and Bredemeier (1983, p. 217) insisted that sport psychologists investigate children's sport experiences within a developmental framework, "In essence, we must stop objectifying children as subjects for research and instead focus on the changes in cognitive structures and abilities that will help us understand maturational differences in psychological behaviors". Scanlan et al. (2005) suggested integrating established developmental lines of research with the sources of stress to strengthen the broad base of existing knowledge. At least two study directions are possible. First, integrate the findings on children's development of the concept of ability with sources of stress to understand emotional responses in the cognitive component. As children develop cognitively, they make clearer distinctions between effort and ability (Fry & Duda, 1997; Nicholls, 1978). Younger children equate outcome with effort leading to high perceptions of competence and experience high enjoyment. As children mature cognitively, however, they can differentiate ability and effort requiring one to play well and try hard to maintain perceptions of high competence and a continuing experience of positive affect. By combining these two research areas, perhaps we can understand how the development of children's conceptions of ability and effort influence their stress in sport.

The second direction combines research on developmental changes in sources of competence information with sources of stress. Research on the saliency of significant others as sources of competence information suggest a shift from adult-centered to peer-centered social evaluation as children develop into adolescence (Horn & Hasbrook, 1986; 1987; Horn

& Weiss, 1991). This research indicated that parents, coaches and peers contribute significantly to athletes' emotional responses. Although the overall emotional responses may remain the same, the relative importance of coaches, parents and peers as specific sources may change as the child matures. By combining the two areas, we can take an important first step to understand how emotional responses vary with developmental progression in the social component.

Competitive Stress and Goal Orientation in Youth Sport

To understand stress in youth sport within a social cognitive perspective we turn to the theoretical approach proposed by Nicholls (1989) and colleagues (Ames, 1992; Dweck, 1999). According to achievement goal theory (Dweck, 1986, 1999; Nicholls, 1984, 1989), individuals strive to demonstrate success through competence. Briefly, goal orientation theory states that there are two basic dispositions individuals can have to varying degrees in achievement situations: task and ego goal orientation. Task orientation defines success by getting better and trying hard whereas, ego orientation defines success by winning and outperforming others. Young athletes aspire to demonstrate success through competence (Nicholls, 1984, 1989, 1992); however, their age can affect how they judge their competence. Children under 11 or 12 years cannot distinguish the concepts of luck, effort, and task difficulty from ability. They believe that they improve through greater effort, which shows more ability, and increased learning reflects increased competence. Children over 11 or 12 years can distinguish effort from ability and appreciate that more effort might not always lead to a better performance because they are limited by their ability. That is why younger children show an undifferentiated concept of ability whereas older children have a differentiated concept of ability and can adopt either perspective (Nicholls, 1984, 1989, 1992).

The view children assume of their ability affects how they judge their competence. Children with a less differentiated view of ability are predicted to use self-referenced judgements of competence and define success by learning, improving and mastering tasks. These children are task-involved and focus on mastering tasks rather than comparing their ability to others. Children with a more differentiated view of ability feel successful by demonstrating superior ability compared to others. These children are ego-involved and in competitive settings, if they do not win, and thereby do not demonstrate superior ability, their perceived competence is undermined (Nicholls, 1984, 1989, 1992).

According to achievement theory (Dweck, 1986, 1999; Nicholls, 1984, 1989), high task-involved children, regardless of their perceived ability, will show adaptive learning strategies and behaviors in competitive sport. These children trace success by self-referent criteria such as personal mastery, improving skills and effectively solving problems. Because high task-involved children view achievement as a means in itself, rather than a means to an end, competence is construed by attaining these forms of self-referent goals (Weiss & Ferrer-Caja, 2002). High ego-involved children that possess high perceived ability should show a similar pattern of behaviors. Although success and competence are determined in normative terms, their perceived high ability influences their prospect of success. These individuals embrace challenging tasks and engage in adaptive behaviors to ensure their skill superiority. In contrast, high ego-involved children with low perceptions of competence are suggested to avoid achievement settings and experience tension and anxiety because normative goals are salient but they lack confidence in achieving a better performance than others (Brustad, Babkes, & Smith, 2001; Duda & Ntoumanis, 2005). These individuals could develop maladaptive behaviors including dropping out of sport (Duda, 1987).

Hall and Kerr (1997) examined the conceptual links between goal orientations and achievement anxiety among junior fencers (ages 10-18). Ego orientation related positively to cognitive anxiety 2 days, 1 day, and 30 minutes before a fencing tournament. Task orientation negatively related to cognitive anxiety 1 day and 30 minutes before the tournament. Dweck and Leggett (1988) argued that ego orientation could foster vulnerability towards helplessness because the shortage of ability emerges which threatens self-esteem as the child contemplates the weight of failure. The resulting anxiety disrupts attention and induces both ineffective strategy selection and possible wishes to escape. The task-oriented focus, however, does not threaten self-esteem and there is less chance of feeling anxious over negative ability judgment.

The interplay between the person, the environment and the task strongly influences the stress youths experience in sport. For example, young athletes worry about making mistakes and performing poorly (Gould & Weinberg, 1985; Scanlan & Lewthwaite, 1984). Those with low self-esteem suffer greater precompetitive stress than those with high self-esteem (Scanlan & Passer, 1978, 1979). They stress when they expect themselves and the team to perform poorly. Scanlan and Passer (1978, 1979) uncovered that male and female youth soccer players who reported lower team expectancies experienced higher precompetition stress than peers who maintained higher performance expectations (Scanlan & Passer, 1978, 1979). This was also true for young male wrestlers (Scanlan & Lewthwaite, 1984) and high school golfers (Cohn, 1990).

Young athletes also experience situational sources of stress. These comprise contextual elements of the sport such as the type of sport, importance of competition, motivational climate, and events that occur during competition or hassles within the larger sport context (Scanlan et al., 2005). For instance, young athletes in individual sports experienced higher stress than team sport athletes with individual contact sports showing higher stress than non-contact individual sports. Playing difficult shots in golf triggered stress (Cohn, 1990). Losing a soccer game by a close margin elicited greater stress than losing games by a larger margin (Passer & Scanlan, 1980). Scanlan and colleagues (Scanlan & Lewthwaite, 1984; Scanlan & Passer, 1978, 1979) recorded that the fun experienced by children during a game was inversely related to postcompetition stress, whether they won or lost. In other words, regardless of game outcome, players who experienced less fun during the game experienced greater stress after the game than players who experienced more fun (Scanlan & Passer, 1979). It is difficult, however, to determine the causal nature of this relationship, that is, did higher stress experienced during the game result in less fun or that less fun experienced during the game resulted in higher stress. Young athletes, especially elite young athletes, also endure hassles within the larger sport context such as political bureaucracy, financial and travel demands that cause stress (Gould, Finch, et al., 1993; Scanlan et al., 1991). Young athletes who dropped out of sport explained that early success positively affected their focus, commitment and investment in swimming, however, these young athletes may not have been capable of handling pressure associated with success. Dropouts also felt pressured to move up to higher levels of competition before they felt they were ready (Fraser-Thomas, Côté, & Deakin, 2008). Research among junior tennis players showed that playing up to a higher age division was associated with burnout (Gould, Udry, Tuffey, & Loehr, 1996).

Finally, young athletes compete publicly and interact with their coach, peers and parents, all of whom hold potential to evaluate them. Young athletes experience stress when they strive to meet what parents and coaches expect of them. They also stress about receiving negative feedback and performance evaluations (Bray, Martin, & Widemeyer, 2000; Cohn, 1990; Gould, Jackson et al., 1993; Scanlan et al., 1991). Young competitive skiers reporting greater concern about what their competitors and friends thought of their general skiing ability, rather than evaluation of specific performances, had higher levels of stress (Bray et al., 2000). Leff and Hoyle (1995) examined perceptions of parental support (i.e., encouragement, involvement, positive affect) and pressure (i.e., expectations, pressure to play well) among high-level competitive tennis players (ages 6-18 years). Greater perceived support and lower perceived pressure from mothers and fathers positively related to greater enjoyment, perceived tennis competence and global self-esteem. Fraser-Thomas et al. (2008) explained that dropout athletes experienced two opposing sources of parental pressure: to stay involved because their parents had not had similar opportunities in their youth and swim well because their parents had been high-level athletes.

BURNOUT AND PERFECTIONISM IN YOUTH SPORT

The proliferation of investment in centers of excellence for youth sport across the world to develop champions has important psychological implications for young athletes. In essence, the primary focus of such centers is to develop excellence and/or professional status in a particular sport. Although some young athletes achieve this goal, many do not and are systematically withdrawn from the center. Indeed, throughout such centers young athletes are under substantial pressure to achieve (Hill et al., 2008). Paradoxically, rather than creating an environment for athletes to develop, it is likely that achievement striving in such pressurized conditions contributes to burnout in some athletes (Hill et al., 2008).

Building on Maslach and Jackson's (1981) work, Raedeke (1997) conceptualized burnout as a syndrome of physical and emotional exhaustion, reduced sense of athletic accomplishment and sport devaluation. Using a valid and reliable measure of these symptoms, and informed by contemporary theory (e.g., Coakley, 1992; Cresswell & Eklund, 2006a, 2006b; Gustafsson, Kentta, Hassmen, & Lundqvist, 2007; Raedeke, 1997; Raedeke & Smith, 2004; Smith, 1986) research has identified some of the critical antecedents of the burnout syndrome, largely based upon Smith's (1986) cognitive-affective model. According to Smith (1986), burnout develops because of chronic stress caused by regularly appraising ones physical and mental resources as insufficient to meet achievement demands. In sport, the process of striving to achieve at rising demands may contribute to the development of burnout when athletes perceive performance in training and competition is consistently substandard (Cresswell & Eklund, 2006a, 2006b). Moreover, in such circumstances it is possible the demands of the particular sport pose more than a challenge for the individual, and thus, some may begin to appraise achievement striving as threatening to their self-worth (Jones, Meijen, McCarthy, & Sheffield, in press). This process could lead to considerable disaffection as investment in training and competition becomes psychologically aversive (Smith, 1986). If this process continues, it advances a gradual shift from an intense desire to succeed and a behavioral commitment to sporting excellence, to a pattern of physical, cognitive and emotional disengagement reflective of burnout (Cresswell & Eklund, 2006a, b; Hill et al., 2008).

Perfectionism as an Antecedent of Athlete Burnout

Previous research on Smith's (1986) model has highlighted the importance of personality factors that affect central appraisal processes and therefore make athletes vulnerable to experience threat and anxiety (Kelley, 1994; Kelley, Ecklund, & Ritter-Taylor, 1999; Kelley & Gill, 1993). In particular, one personality factor that affects the appraisal process (Hall, Kerr, & Mathews, 1998) and the development of burnout is perfectionism (Flett & Hewitt, 2005; Hall, 2006; Lemyre, Hall, & Roberts, 2007). Although no agreed definition of perfectionism exists, many researchers see it as a multidimensional personality disposition. It is (Frost, Marten, Lahart, & Rosenblate, 1990; Hewitt & Flett, 1991) characterized by striving for flawlessness performances and setting excessively high standards accompanied by tendencies for overly critical evaluations of one's behavior and an over-sensitivity to mistakes (Flett & Hewitt, 2002; Frost et al., 1990; Rice & Preusser, 2002). How perfectionism affects performance is a contentious issue because some researchers argued that perfectionism represents a psychological characteristic that makes Olympic champions (Gould, Dieffenbach, & Moffet, 2002), and helps performers when learning new sports tasks (Stoll, Lau, & Stoeber, 2008), while others see perfectionism as a maladaptive characteristic that undermines, rather than helps, athletic performance (Anshel & Mansouri, 2005; Flett & Hewitt, 2005). Although some researchers argue that perfectionism is ultimately a debilitating characteristic (Flett & Hewitt, 2002), others contend that in the absence of negative criticism, perfectionism has useful motivational properties that yield adaptive achievement striving and a healthy pursuit of sporting excellence (Haase & Prapavessis, 2004; Stoeber & Otto, 2006; Terry-Short, Owens, Slade, & Dewey, 1995). To illustrate, Stoeber and colleagues (Stoeber & Kersting, 2007; Stoeber, Otto, Pescheck, Becker, & Stoll, 2007; Stoeber, Stoll, Pescheck, & Otto, 2008) reported that striving for perfectionism in the absence of negative performance appraisal, leads to adaptive patterns of achievement cognition, affect, and behavior. The dominant view from the sport psychology research is that striving for perfectionism does not lead to debilitation (Flett & Hewitt, 2002; Hall, 2006; Stoeber & Otto, 2006). Rather it is when perfectionism evokes harsh self-criticism, a ruminative response style and a focus upon personal and interpersonal inadequacies that motivational debilitation is likely (Hill et al., 2008; Flett & Hewitt, 2006; Thompson & Zuroff, 2004). Typically, when athletes use these processes consistently to evaluate achievement outcomes during training and competition, they may become vulnerable to burnout (Hill et al., 2008). Although few researchers have examined the relationship between perfectionism and athlete burnout, current findings do suggest certain specific maladaptive dimensions of perfectionism to be critical antecedents of the burnout syndrome. For example, comparing a group of junior elite tennis players with high levels of burnout with a control group on dimensions of perfectionism, Gould et al. (1996) determined that burned-out players reported higher levels of concern over mistakes, but lower personal standards. Because concern over mistakes is seen as a core aspect of the self-critical dimension of perfectionism and personal standards a core aspect of the positive striving dimension (Stoeber & Otto, 2006), the results suggested that only self-critical perfectionism is related to athlete burnout, whereas positive striving perfectionism is not

(Stoll et al., 2008). Using a sample of 151 male youth soccer players from centers of excellence in the UK, Hill et al. (2008) examined the degree of association between self-orientated and socially prescribed perfectionism and symptoms of athlete burnout. They also examined whether unconditional self-acceptance mediated such relationships. Data supported the contention that a contingent sense of self-worth is central to both socially prescribed and self-oriented perfectionism and that this association may underpin maladaptive achievement striving and increase vulnerability to athlete burnout. In particular this study supports suggestions that negative dimensions of perfectionism may be critical antecedents of athlete burnout (Gould et al., 1996), and that both self-orientated and socially prescribed forms of perfectionism can render young athletes vulnerable to its development (Flett & Hewitt, 2005; Hill et al., 2008).

HOW DO YOUNG ATHLETES COPE?

Although research on coping among young athletes is underdeveloped, the existing coverage helps us understand the general strategies young athletes use to cope in competitive sport. We understand young athletes' emotional, physiological and behavioral responses to competition as the consequence of a process of cognitive appraisal (Smith et al., 2001). Cognitive appraisal represents the process where people assess the situation's significance and evaluate their capacity to cope with the demands (Folkman, Lazarus, Dunkel-Schetter, DeLongis, & Gruen, 1986). According to Lazarus' (1991) cognitive-motivational-relational theory, cognitive appraisal and coping are processes to generate and regulate emotions. The appraisal of a situation determines the quality and intensity of an emotional response rather than the situation itself. Situations involve primary and secondary appraisals. Primary appraisals determine the relevance of the event or situation for the individual and comprise goal relevance, goal congruence, and type of ego involvement. In secondary appraisal, a person evaluates (a) coping options, (b) individual responsibility, and (c) future expectations. And a person evaluates what action might prevent harm, moderate it, or produce additional harm or benefit. Coping behaviors form two categories: problem-focused coping and emotion-focused coping (Folkman & Lazarus, 1988; Lazarus, 1991, 2000). In problem-focused coping, a person acts to change part of the person-environment relationship, either by altering an aspect of the environment, or by changing one's situation within it. In contrast, emotion-focused coping influences only what is in the mind of the person (Lazarus, 2000). Lazarus' theory reveals a valuable framework to study emotion because the value placed on individual differences in motivation, and the personal resources and environment combine to produce personal meaning and emotion.

To cope, a person consciously attempts to manage the demands and intensity of events perceived as stressful or improves one's personal resources in an attempt to reduce or manage one's perceived stress intensity (Lazarus, 1999). The critical mediator of an athlete's selection of coping strategies is his or her cognitive appraisal of the event or situation (Anshel & Delaney, 2001). Folkman (1984) predicted that task-oriented coping strategies should correlate positively with positive affect whereas emotion- and avoidance-oriented coping strategies should correlate positively with negative affect. Research with children (Crook,

Beaver, & Bell, 1998) and athletes (Crocker & Graham, 1995; Ntoumanis & Biddle, 1998) has supported this assumption.

Athletes cope more effectively with the demands of the athletic environment either by attempts to change their cognitions, emotional responses, or behaviors or influence the environment. Athlete-based interventions develop and enhance psychological skills that influence performance such as systematic goal setting (Danish, Nellen, & Owens, 1996), concentration (Moran, 2009), mental rehearsal (Cumming & Ramsey, 2009) and stress management (Thomas, Mellalieu, & Hanton, 2009). Situationally based interventions include coach-and parent-based interventions (Smith & Smoll, 1997) and team building (Hardy & Crace, 1997).

Only two studies have examined age-related differences in coping responses. First, Goyen and Anshel (1998) reported that adults cope by responding more frequently with concentration and focusing on what they had to do next in comparison to adolescents. Bebetsos and Anoniou (2003) reported that older badminton players coped better with adversity and reported higher emotional self-control than younger athletes report.

Some studies have examined coping among young athletes to establish which strategies help them cope with situational, situational and significant other sources of stress. For example, Holt and Mandigo (2004) examined how 33 male youth cricket players (Mean age = 11.9 years) coped with performance-related worries. They completed two concept maps detailing (a) recent performance worries they had experienced playing cricket, and (b) their associated coping responses. Results revealed that the majority of performance worries involved making mistakes. Most cricketers used both emotion-focused coping and problem-focused coping with some cricketers reporting no coping strategy. Eubank and Collins (2000) collected pre-event state anxiety intensity and direction data from 22 youth sport participants in two training and two competition environments with in-event anxiety and coping data being obtained from the 'high stress' competition condition. Coping strategies were measured using the trait version of the COPE scale (Carver, Scheier, & Weintraub, 1989). Facilitators appeared to use problem- and emotion-focused coping in response to stress whereas debilitators were limited in their use of coping constructs. Lohaus and Klein-Heßling (2000) evaluated different relaxation training types to help children (aged 7-14) to cope with stress. Over five training sessions, children received different relaxation techniques. They used a sensoric approach (progressive muscular relaxation), an imaginative approach and a combined approach (imaginative and sensoric). They also had two control conditions. One control condition had non-tension producing stories instead of systematic relaxation training. The other control condition had no intervention. The results showed clear short-term effects on physiological parameters (blood pressure, heart rate and body temperature) as well as subjective ratings of mood and somatic condition. The differences between the training conditions were small and the long-term effects after two month were small in relation to the short-term effects. Nicholls (2007) examined coping effectiveness among Scottish international adolescent golfers (mean age = 16.6 years) over 28 days during their competitive season using daily coping effectiveness diaries. They participants reported 56 effective coping strategies and 23 ineffective coping strategies; however, the same coping strategies were often rated as being both effective and ineffective when they were used to manage the same stressor. Ntoumanis, Biddle, and Haddock (1999) reported that task orientation was associated with problem solving coping strategies such as trying hard, seeking social approval and restricting competing activities. High ego-oriented athletes were more likely to use an emotion-focused strategy venting emotions.

SUMMARY

Only a few pediatric sport psychology researchers have accepted Weiss and Bredemeier's (1983) appeal to focus on cognitive structures and abilities to understand psychological behaviors among young athletes. Although we have a descriptive understanding of stress, burnout, perfectionism and coping, the greater challenge is to understand these constructs from a developmental perspective contributing to a better understanding of young athletes' cognitive, social, emotional and physical development through sport. Having marshaled the evidence it is clear that our understanding of stress and associated constructs among young athletes is acceptable; however, we have much more developmental work to do. We can begin by integrating Scanlan et al.'s (2005) suggestion and combine the findings on children's development of the concept of ability with sources of stress to understand emotional responses in the cognitive component. We can also combine research on developmental changes in sources of competence information with sources of stress to understand how emotional responses vary with developmental progression in the social component.

Another fruitful but under researched topic in youth sport is fear of failure. The basis for fear of failure is when someone perceives the consequences of failure aversively and the anticipation of a threatening outcome elicits fear (Sagar, Lavallee, & Spray, 2007). Fear of failure is associated with burnout (Rainey, 1995), youth dropout (Orlick, 1974), and athletic stress (Gould, Horn, & Spreeman, 1983). Sagar et al. (2007) recommended that researchers should explore how coaches and parents contribute to the development of fear of failure among youth athletes. Coaches and parents should recognize the physical, psychological and time demands on children during the sampling and specializing years of sport participation and remember that children are not mini-adults (Gould, Wilson, Tuffey, & Lochbaum, 1993). Physical training, instruction and social support aligned with the child's physical, social and psychological development are key objectives within youth sport (Smith, Smoll, & Passer, 2002; Weiss, 1991). We need more interventions to help coaches recognize and respond to the needs of young athletes such as Smith, Smoll, and Cumming's (2007) motivational climate intervention for coaches on young athletes' sport performance anxiety. They reported that those athletes who played for the trained coaches showed decreases on all subscales of the SAS-2 and on the total anxiety score from preseason to late season. The intervention was equally useful for boys and girls' teams. The control group athletes reported increases in anxiety over the season. From a developmental perspective, Vealey (1988) suggested that children are developing physically and psychologically and may benefit more from PST than older athletes who have already internalized dysfunctional responses to competition. In addition, youth athletes performing in stressful environments and may benefit from developing psychological skills to cope with demands of competition, safeguard against the adverse effects of competitive anxiety and enjoy the challenge of practice and competition (Hanton & Jones, 1999; Kim & Duda, 2003).

REFERENCES

Abernethy, B., Côté, J., & Baker, J. (1999). *Expert decision-making in sport.* Canberra: Australian Institute of Sport Publication.

Albrecht, R. R., & Feltz, D. L. (1987). *Generality and specificity of attention related to competitive anxiety and sport performance.* Journal of Sport Psychology, 9, 231-248.

Ames, C. (1992). *Achievement goals, motivational climate, and motivational processes.* In G. C. Roberts (Ed.), Motivation in sport and exercise (pp. 161-176). Champaign, IL: Human Kinetics.

Anshel, M. H., & Delany, J. (2001). *Sources of stress, cognitive appraisals, and coping strategies of male and female child athletes.* Journal of Sport Behavior, 24, 239-353.

Anshel, M. H., & Mansouri, H. (2005). *Influences of perfectionism on motor performance, affect, and causal attributions in response to critical information feedback.* Journal of Sport Behavior, 28, 99–124.

Appleton P. R., Hall, H. K., & Hill, A. P. (2009). *Relations between multidimensional perfectionism and burnout in junior-elite male athletes,* Psychology of Sport and Exercise, 10, 457-465.

Beamer, M., Côté, J., & Ericsson, K. A. *"A comparison between international and provincial level gymnasts in their pursuit of expertise".* Proceedings of the Tenth European Congress of Sport Psychology, Prague, Czech Republic, 1999.

Bebetsos, E., & Antoniou, P. (2003). *Psychological skills of Greek badminton athletes.* Perceptual and Motor Skills, 97, 1289 – 1296.

Bialystok, E. (1993). Metalinguistic awareness: *The development of children's representations of language.* In C. Pratt & A. F. Garton (Eds.), Systems of representation in children: Development and use. Chichester: John Wiley & Sons.

Bray, S. R., Martin, K. A., & Widemeyer, W. N. (2000). *The relationship between evaluative concerns and sport competition state anxiety among youth skiers.* Journal of Sports Sciences, 18, 353-361.

Brown, B. B., & Klute, C. (2003). *Friendships, cliques, and crowds.* In G. R. Adams, & M. D. Berzonsky (Eds.), Blackwell handbook of adolescence. Oxford: Blackwell.

Brustad, R., & Weiss, M. R. (1987). *Competence perceptions and sources of worry in high, medium, and low competitive trait-anxious young athletes.* Journal of Sport Psychology, 9, 97-105.

Brustad, R. J., Babkes, M. L., & Smith, A. L. (2001). *Youth in sport: Psychological considerations.* In R. N. Singer, H. A. Hausenblas & C. M. Janelle (Eds.), Handbook of research in sport psychology (2nd ed., pp. 604-635). New York: John Wiley & Sons Inc.

Carpenter, P. J., & Scanlan, T. K. (1998). *Changes over time in the determinants of sport commitment.* Pediatric Exercise Science, 10, 356-365.

Carver, C. S., Scheier, M. F., & Weintraub, J. K. (1989). *Assessing coping strategies: A theoretically based approach.* Journal of Personality and Social Psychology, 56, 267-283.

Coakley, D. (1992). *Burnout among adolescent athletes*: A personal failure or social problem. Sociology, 9, 271–285.

Cohn, P. J. (1990). *An exploratory study of sources of stress and athlete burnout in youth golf.* The Sport Psychologist, 4, 95-106.

Côté, J. (1999). *The influence of the family in the development of talent in sport.* The Sport Psychologist, 13, 395-417.

Côté, J., Baker, J., & Abernethy, B. (2007). *Practice and play in the development of sport expertise.* In R. Eklund & G. Tennenbaum (Eds.). Handbook of sport psychology (3rd Ed.). Hoboken, NJ: Wiley.

Côté, J., & Hay, J. (2002). *Family influences on youth sport performance and participation.* In J. M. Silva III & D. E. Stevens (Eds.), Psychological foundations of sport, (pp. 503-519). Boston, MA: Allyn & Bacon.

Cresswell, S. L., & Eklund, R. C. (2006a). *The nature of player burnout in rugby: Key characteristics and attributions.* Journal of Applied Sport Psychology, 18, 219–239.

Cresswell, S. L., & Eklund, R. C. (2006b). *Changes in athlete burnout over a thirty-week "rugby year".* Journal of Science and Medicine in Sport, 9, 125–134.

Crocker, P. R. E., & Graham, T. R. (1995). *Coping by competitive athletes with performance stress*: Gender differences and relationships with affect. The Sport Psychologist, 9, 325-338.

Crocker, P. R. E., Hoar, S. D., McDonough, M. H., Kowalski, K. C., & Niefer, C. B. (2004). *Emotional experience in youth sport.* In M. R. Weiss (Ed.), Developmental sport and exercise psychology: A lifespan perspective (pp. 197-221). Morgantown, WV: Fitness Information Technology.

Crook, K., Beaver, B., & Bell, M. (1998). A*nxiety and depression in children: A preliminary examination of the utility of the PANAS-C.* Journal of Psychopathology and Behavioral Assessment 20, 333–350.

Cumming, J., & Ramsey, R. (2009). *Imagery interventions in sport.* In S. Mellalieu & S. Hanton, Advances in applied sport psychology: A review (pp. 5-36). London: Routledge.

Damon, W. (1983). *Social and personality development: Infancy through adolescence.* New York: Norton.

Danish, S. J., Nellen, V. C., & Owen, S. S. (1996). *Teaching life skills through sport: Community-based programs for adolescents.* In J. L. Van Raalte & B. W. Brewer (Eds.). Exploring sport and exercise psychology (pp. 205-227). Washington, DC: American Psychological Association.

De Knop, P., Engström, L-M., Skirstad, B. & Weiss, M.R. (1996). *Worldwide Trends in Youth Sport.* Champaign, IL: Human Kinetics.

Duda, J. L. (1987). *Toward a developmental theory of motivation in sport.* Journal of Sport Psychology, 9, 130-145.

Duda, J. L., & Ntoumanis, N. (2005). *After-school sport for children: Implications of a task-involving motivational climate.* In Mahoney, J. L., Larson, R. W., & Eccles, J. S. (Eds.), *Organized activities as contexts of development*: Extracurricular activities, after-school and community programs (pp. 311-330). Mahwah, NJ: Erlbaum.

Dweck, C. S. (1986). *Motivational processes affecting learning.* American Psychologist, 41, 1040-1048

Dweck, C. S. (1999). *Self-theories:* Their role in motivation, personality, and development. Philadelphia: Psychology Press.

Dweck, C. S., & Leggett, E. L. (1988*). A social-cognitive approach to motivation and personality.* Psychological Review, 95, 256-273.

Erikson, E. H. (1963). *Childhood and society.* New York: Stonton.

Eubank, M., & Collins, D. (2000). *Coping with pre- and in-event fluctuations in competitive state anxiety:* A longitudinal approach. Journal of Sports Sciences, 18, 121-131.

Flett, G. L., & Hewitt, P. L. (2002). *Perfectionism and maladjustment: An overview of theoretical, definitional, and treatment issues.* In G. L. Flett, & P. L. Hewitt (Eds.), Perfectionism: Theory, research, and treatment (pp. 5–31). Washington, DC: American Psychological Association.

Flett, G. L., & Hewitt, P. L. (2005). *The perils of perfectionism in sports and exercise.* Current Directions in Psychological Science, 14, 14–18.

Flett, G. L., & Hewitt, P. L. (2006). *Positive versus negative perfectionism in psychopathology.* Behaviour Modification, 30, 472–495.

Folkman, S. (1984). *Personal control and stress and coping processes: A theoretical analysis.* Journal of Personality and Social Psychology, 46, 839-852

Folkman, S., & Lazarus, R. S. (1988). *Coping as a mediator of emotion.* Journal of Personality and Social Psychology, 54, 466-475.

Folkman, S., Lazarus, R. S., Dunkel-Schetter, C., DeLongis, A., & Gruen, R. J. (1986). *Dynamics of a stressful encounter: Cognitive appraisal, coping and encounter outcomes.* Journal of Personality and Social Psychology, 50, 992-1003.

Foster, D. J., & Weigand, D. A. (2008). *The role of cognitive and metacognitive development in mental skills training.* Sport and Exercise Psychology Review, 4, 21-29.

Fraser-Thomas, J., Côté, J., & Deakin, J. (2008). *Understanding dropout and prolonged engagement in adolescent competitive sport.* Psychology of Sport and Exercise, 9, 645-662.

Frost, R. O., Marten, P., Lahart, C., & Rosenblate, R. (1990). *The dimensions of perfectionism.* Cognitive Therapy and Research, 5, 449–468.

Fry, M. D., & Duda, J. L. (1997*). A developmental examination of children's understanding of effort and ability in the physical and academic domains.* Research Quarterly for Exercise and Sport, 68, 331-344.

Gould, D., & Diffenbach, K. (1999). *Psychological issues in youth sports: Competition anxiety, overtraining, and burnout.* In R. M. Malina (Ed.), *Organized sport in the lives of children and adolescents.* Michigan Youth Sport Institute Conference Proceedings, May 23-26.

Gould, D. R., Dieffenbach, K., & Moffett, A. (2002). *Psychological characteristics and their development in Olympic champions.* Journal of Applied Sport Psychology, 14, 172–204.

Gould, D., Eklund, R. C., & Jackson, S. A. (1993). *Coping strategies used by U. S. Olympic wrestlers.* Research Quarterly for Exercise and Sport, 64, 83-93.

Gould, D., Finch, L. M., & Jackson, S. A. (1993). *Coping strategies used by national champion figure skaters.* Research Quarterly for Exercise and Sport, 64, 453-468.

Gould, D., Greenleaf, C., & Krane, V. (2002). *Arousal-anxiety and sport behavior.* In T. S. Horn (Ed.), Advances in sport psychology (2nd ed., pp. 207-241). Champaign, IL: Human Kinetics.

Gould, D., Horn, T., & Spreeman, J. (1983). *Sources of stress in junior elite wrestlers.* Journal of Sport Psychology, 5, 159 – 171.

Gould, D., Jackson, S. A., & Finch, L. M. (1993). *Sources of stress in national champion figure skaters.* Journal of Sport & Exercise Psychology, 15, 134-159.

Gould, D., Udry, E., Tuffey, S., & Loehr, J. (1996). *Burnout in competitive junior tennis players: I. A quantitative psychological assessment.* The Sport Psychologist, 10, 322–340.

Gould, D., & Weinberg, R. (1985). *Sources of worry in successful and less successful intercollegiate wrestlers.* Journal of Sport Behavior, 8, 115-127.

Gould, D., Wilson, C. G., Tuffey, S., & Lochbaum, M. (1993). *Stress and the young athlete: The child's perspective.* Pediatric Exercise Science, 5, 286-297.

Goyen, M. J., & Anshel, M. H. (1998). *Sources of acute competitive stress and use of coping strategies as a function of age and gender.* Journal of Applied Developmental Psychology, 19, 469 – 486.

Gustafsson, H., Kentta, G., Hassmen, P., & Lunqvist, C. (2007). *Prevalence of burnout in competitive adolescent athletes.* The Sport Psychologist, 21, 21-37.

Haase, A. M., & Prapavessis, H. (2004). *Assessing the factor structure and composition of the Positive and Negative Perfectionism Scale in sport.* Personality and Individual Differences, 36, 1725–1740.

Hall, H. K. (2006). *Perfectionism: A hallmark quality of world class performers, or a psychological impediment to athletic development?* In: D. Hackfort, G. Tenenbaum (Eds.), Perspectives in sport and exercise psychology; Essential processes for attaining peak performance (Vol. 1, pp. 178–211), Oxford UK: Meyer & Meyer Publishers.

Hall, H. K., & Kerr, A. W. (1997). *Motivational antecedents of precompetitive anxiety in youth sport.* The Sport Psychologist, 11, 24-42.

Hall, H. K., Kerr, A. W., & Matthews, J. (1998). *Precompetitive anxiety in sport: The contribution of achievement goals and perfectionism.* Journal of Sport & Exercise Psychology, 20, 194–217.

Hanton, S., & Jones, J. G. (1999). *The acquisition and development of cognitive skills and strategies:* I. Making the butterflies fly in formation. The Sport Psychologist, 13, 1–21.

Hardy, C. J., & Crace, R. K. (1997). *Foundations of team building: Introduction to the team building primer.* Journal of Applied Sport Psychology, 9, 1-10.

Harrison, C. (1980). *Readability in the classroom.* Cambridge, UK: Cambridge Educational.

Harris, P. L. (2000). *Understanding emotions.* In M. Lewis & J. M. Haviland-Jones (Eds.), Handbook of emotions, (2nd ed., pp. 281 – 292). New York: The Guilford Press.

Harwood, C., & Knight, C. (2009). *Stress in youth sport: A developmental investigation of tennis parents.* Psychology of Sport and Exercise, 10, 447-456.

Havighurst, R. J. (1973). *History of developmental psychology: Socialization and personality development through the lifespan.* In P. B. Baltes & K. W. Schaie (Eds.), Lifespan developmental psychology: Personality and socialisation (pp. 3-24). New York: Academic Press.

Hennessy, E., & Heary, C. (2005). *Valuing the group context: The use of focus groups with children and adolescents.* In S. M. Greene & D. M. Hogan (Eds.), Researching children's experiences: Approaches and methods (pp. 236 – 252). London: Sage.

Hewitt, P. L., & Flett, G. L. (1991). *Perfectionism in the self and social contexts: Conceptualization, assessment, and association with psychopathology.* Journal of Personality and Social Psychology, 60, 456–470.

Hewstone, M., Fincham, F. D., & Foster, J. (2005). *Psychology.* Oxford: Blackwell Publishers.

Hill, A. P., Hall, H. K., Appleton, P. R., & Kozub, S. A. (2008). *Perfectionism and burnout in junior elite players: The mediating influence of unconditional self-acceptance.* Psychology of Sport and Exercise, 9, 630-644.

Holt, N., & Mandigo, J. L. (2004). *Coping with performance worries among youth male cricket players.* Journal of Sport Behavior, 27, 39-57.

Horn, T. S., & Hasbrook, C. (1986). *Informational components influencing children's perceptions of their physical competence.* In M. Weiss & D. Gould, (Eds.), Sport for children and youths: Proceedings of the 1984 Olympic Scientific Congress (pp. 81-88). Champaign, IL: Human Kinetics.

Horn, T. S., & Hasbrook, C. (1987). *Psychological characteristics and the criteria children use for self-evaluation.* Journal of Sport Psychology, 9, 208–221.

Horn, T. S., & Weiss, M. R. (1991). *A developmental analysis of children's self-ability judgments in the physical domain.* Pediatric Exercise Science, 3, 310-326.

Jackson, S. A. (2000). *Joy, fun and flow state in sport.* In Y. L. Hanin (Ed.), Emotions in sport (pp. 135-155). Champaign, IL: Human Kinetics.

Jones, M. V. (2003). *Controlling emotions in sport.* The Sport Psychologist, 17, 471-486.

Jones, M. V., Meijen, C., McCarthy, P. J., & Sheffield, D. (in press). *A theory of challenge and threat states in athletes.* International Review of Sport & Exercise Psychology.

Kelley, B. C. (1994). *A model of stress and burnout in collegiate coaches: Effects of gender and time of season.* Research Quarterly for Sport and Exercise, 65, 48–58.

Kelley, B. C., Ecklund, R. C., & Ritter-Taylor, M. (1999). *Stress and burnout among collegiate tennis coaches.* Journal of Sport & Exercise Psychology, 21, 113–130.

Kelley, B. C., & Gill, D. L. (1993). *An examination of personal/situational variables, stress appraisal, and burnout in collegiate teacher coaches.* Research Quarterly for Exercise and Sport, 64, 94–102.

Kerr, G., & Dacyshyn, A. (2000). *The retirement experiences of elite female gymnasts.* Journal of Applied Sport Psychology, 12, 115-133.

Kim, M. S., & Duda, J. L. (2003). *The coping process: Cognitive appraisals of stress, coping strategies, and coping effectiveness.* The Sport Psychologist, 17, 406-425.

Lazarus, R. S. (1966). *Psychological stress and the coping process.* New York: McGraw-Hill.

Lazarus, R. S. (1991). *Emotion and adaptation.* Oxford: Oxford University Press.

Lazarus, R. S. (1999). *The cognition-emotion debate: A bit of history.* In T. Dalgleish & M. J. Power (Eds.) *Handbook of cognition and emotion* (pp. 3-19). Chichester: Wiley.

Lazarus, R. S. (2000). *How emotions influence performance in competitive sports.* The Sport Psychologist, 14, 229-252.

Lazarus, R. S., & Folkman, S. (1984*). Stress, appraisal, and coping.* New York: Springer.

Leff, S. S., & Hoyle, R. H. (1995). *Young athletes' perceptions of parental support and pressure.* Journal of Youth and Adolescence, 24, 187-203.

Lemyre, P. N., Hall, H. K., & Roberts, G. C. (2007). *A social cognitive approach to burnout in athletes. Scandinavian* Journal of Medicine & Science, 18, 221-234.

Lewthwaite, R. (1990). *Threat perception in competitive trait anxiety: The endangerment of important goals.* Journal of Sport & Exercise Psychology, 12, 280-300.

Lewthwaite, R.& Scalan, T. K. (1989). *Predictors of competitive trait anxiety in male youth sport participants.* Medicine and Science in Sports and Exercise, 21, 221-229.

Lohaus, A., & Klein-Heßling, J. (2000). *Coping in childhood: A comparative evaluation of different relaxation techniques.* Anxiety, Stress, and Coping, 13, 187-211.

McCarthy, P. J., Jones, M. V., & Clark-Carter, D. (2008). *Understanding enjoyment in youth sport: A developmental perspective.* Psychology of Sport and Exercise, 9, 142-156.

Martens, R. (1977). *Sport Competition Anxiety Test.* Champaign, IL: Human Kinetics.

Martens, R. Burton, D., Rivkin, F., & Simon, J. (1980*). Reliability and validity of the Competitive State Anxiety Inventory* (CSAI). In C. H. Nadeau, W. R. Haliwell, K. M. Newell, & G. C. Roberts (Eds.). Psychology of motor behavior and sport – 1979 (pp. 91-99). Champaign, IL: Human Kinetics.

Martens, R., Burton, D., Vealey, R. S., Bump, L. A., & Smith, D. E. (1990). *Development and validation of the Competitive State Anxiety Inventory-2.* In R. Martens, R. S. Vealey, & D. Burton (Eds.), Competitive anxiety in sport (pp. 117-190). Champaign, IL: Human Kinetics.

Maslach, C., & Jackson, S. E. (1981). *The measurement of experienced burnout.* Journal of Occupational Behaviour, 2, 99–113.

Moran, A. P. (2009). *Attention in sport. In S. Mellalieu & S. Hanton, Advances in applied sport psychology:* A review (pp. 195-220). London: Routledge.

Naylor, S., Burton, D., & Crocker, P. R. E. (2002). *Competitive anxiety and sport performance.* In J. Silva & D. Stevens (Eds.), Psychological foundations of sport (pp. 132-154). Boston: Allyn & Bacon.

Nicholls, A. R. (2007). *A longitudinal phenomenological analysis of coping effectiveness among Scottish international adolescent golfers.* European Journal of Sport Science, 7, 169-178.

Nicholls, J. G. (1978). *The development of the concepts of effort and ability, perceptions of academic attainment, and the understanding that difficult tasks require more ability.* Child Development, 49, 800-814.

Nicholls, J. G. (1984). *Achievement motivation: Conceptions of ability, subjective experience, task choice, and performance.* Psychological Review, 91, 328-346.

Nicholls, J. G. (1989). *The competitive ethos and democratic education.* Cambridge, MA: Harvard University Press.

Nicholls, J. G. (1992). *The general and the specific in the development and expression of achievement motivation.* In G. C. Roberts (Ed.), Motivation in sport and exercise (pp. 31-56). Champaign, IL: Human Kinetics.

Ntoumanis, N., & Biddle, S. J. H. (1998). *The relationship of coping and its perceived effectiveness to positive and negative affect in sport.* Personality and Individual Differences. 24, 773-788.

Ntoumanis, N., Biddle, S. J. H., & Haddock, G. (1999). *The mediating role of coping strategies on the relationship between achievement motivation and affect in sport.* Anxiety, Stress, and Coping, 12, 299–327.

Orlick, T. D. (1974). *The athletic dropout: A high price of inefficiency.* Canadian Association for Health, Physical Education and Recreation Journal, November/December, pp. 21–27.

Passer, M. W. (1988). *Determinants and consequcnes of children's competitive stress.* In F. L. Smoll, R. A. Magill, & M. J. Ash (Eds.), Children's sport (3rd ed., pp. 203-227). Champaign. IL: Human Kinetics.

Passer, M. W., & Scanlan, T. K. (1980). *The impact of game outcome on the postcompetition affect and performance evaluations of youth athletes.* In C. H. Nadeau, W. R. Halliwell, K. M. Newell, & G. C. Roberts (Eds.), Psychology of motor behaviour and sport – 1979 (pp. 100-111). Champaign, IL: Human Kinetics.

Piaget, J. (1954). *The construction of reality in the child*. New York: Basic Books.

Piaget, J. (1963). *The origins of intelligence in children*. New York: Norton.

Raedeke, T. D. (1997). *Is athlete burnout more than just stress? A sport commitment perspective*. Journal of Sport & Exercise Psychology, 19, 396–418.

Raedeke, T. D., & Smith, A. L. (2004). *Coping resources and athlete burnout: An examination of stress mediated and moderation hypotheses*. Journal of Sport & Exercise Psychology, 26, 525–541.

Rainey, D. (1995). *Stress, burnout and intention to terminate among umpires*. Journal of Sport Behaviour, 18, 312–323.

Rice, K. G., & Preusser, K. J. (2002). T*he Adaptive/Maladaptive Perfectionism Scale*. Measurement and Evaluation in Counseling & Development, 34, 210–222.

Ross, A. (1976). *Psychological aspects of learning disabilities and reading disorders*. New York: McGraw-Hill.

Sagar, S. S., Lavallee, D., & Spray, C. M. (2007). *Why young elite athletes fear failure: Consequences of failure*. Journal of Sports Science, 25, 1171-1184.

Santrock, J. W. (1998). *Adolescence* (5th ed.). Boston: McGraw-Hill.

Scanlan, T. K. (1986). *Competitive stress in children*. In M. R. Weiss & D. Gould (Eds.), Sport for children and youths (pp. 113-118). Champaign, IL: Human Kinetics.

Scanlan, T. K., & Lewthwaite, R. (1984). *Social psychological aspects of competition for male youth sport participants:* I. Predictors of competitive stress. Journal of Sport Psychology, 8, 25-35.

Scanlan, T. K., Babkes, M. L., & Scanlan, L. A. (2005*). Participation in sport: A developmental glimpse at emotion*. In J. L. Mahoney, R. W. Larson, & J. S. Eccles, Organized activities as contexts of development: Extracurricular activities, after-school and community programs (pp. 275-309). Mahwah, New Jersey: Lawrence Erlbaum Associates, Publishers.

Scanlan, T. K., & Passer, M. W. (1978). *Factors related to competitive stress among male sport participants*. Medicine and Science in Sports, 10, 103-108.

Scanlan, T. K., & Passer, M. W. (1979). *Sources of competitive stress in young female athletes*. Journal of Sport Psychology, 1, 151-159.

Scanlan, T. K., Stein, G. L., & Ravizza, K. (1991). *An in-depth study of former elite figure skaters:* III. Sources of stress. Journal of Sport & Exercise Psychology, 13, 103-120.

Smith, N. C., Jones, B. & Roach, N. K. (2001). *Competitive stress and coping in young sport performers*. In Maffulli, N., Chan, K. M., Macdonald, R., Malina, R. M. and Parker, A. W. (Eds.). Sports medicine for specific ages and abilities. London; Churchill-Livingstone.

Smith, R. E. (1986). *Toward a cognitive-affective model of burnout*. Journal of Sport Psychology, 8, 36-50.

Smith, R. E., & Smoll, F. L. (1997). *Coaching the coaches: Youth sports as a scientific and applied behavioral setting.* Current Directions in Psychological Science, 6, 16-21.

Smith, R. E., Smoll, F. L., & Cumming, S. P. (2007). *Effects of a motivational climate intervention for coaches on young athletes' sport performance anxiety*. Journal of Sport & Exercise Psychology, 29, 39-59.

Smith, R. E., Smoll, F. L., Cumming, S. P., & Grossbard, J. R. (2006). *Measurement of multidimensional sport performance anxiety in children and adults:* The Sport Anxiety Scale-2. Journal of Sport & Exercise Psychology, 28, 479-501.

Smith, R. E., Smoll, F. L., & Passer, M. W. (2002). *Sport performance anxiety in young athletes.* In F. L. Smoll & R. E. Smith (Eds.), Children and youth in sport: A biopsychosocial perspective, (pp. 501 – 536). Madison, WI: Brown & Benchmark.

Smith, R. E., Smoll, F. L., & Schutz, R. W. (1990). *Measurement and correlates of sport-specific cognitive and somatic trait anxiety:* The Sport Anxiety Scale. Anxiety Research, 2, 263-280.

Spielberger, C. D. (1966). *Theory and research on anxiety.* In C. S. Spielberger (Ed.), Anxiety and behavior (pp. 3-20). New York: Academic Press.

Spielberger, C. D. (1973). *Preliminary test manual for the State-Trait Anxiety Inventory for Children ("How I feel questionnaire").* Palo Alto, CA: Consulting Psychologists Press.

Stoeber, J., & Kersting, M. (2007). *Perfectionism and aptitude test performance: Testees who strive for perfection achieve better test results.* Personality and Individual Differences, 42, 1093–1103.

Stoeber, J., & Otto, K. (2006). *Positive conceptions of perfectionism: Approaches, evidence, challenges.* Personality and Social Psychology Review, 10, 295–319.

Stoeber, J., Otto, K., Pescheck, E., Becker, C., & Stoll, O. (2007). *Perfectionism and competitive anxiety in athletes: Differentiating striving for perfection and negative reactions to imperfection.* Personality and Individual Differences, 42, 959–969.

Stoeber, J., Stoll, O., Pescheck, E., & Otto, K. (2008). *Perfectionism and achievement goals in athletes: Relations with approach and avoidance orientations in mastery and performance goals.* Psychology of Sport and Exercise, 9, 102-121

Stoll, O., Lau, A., & Stoeber, J. (2008). *Perfectionism and performance in a new basketball training task: Does striving for perfection enhance or undermine performance?* Psychology of Sport and Exercise, 9, 620-629.

Taylor, J. (1987). *Predicting athletic performance with self-confidence and somatic and cognitive anxiety as a function of motor and physiological requirements in six sports.* Journal of Personality, 55, 139-153.

Terry-Short, L. A., Owens, R. G., Slade, P. D., & Dewey, M. E. (1995). *Positive and negative perfectionism.* Personality and Individual Differences, 18, 663–668.

Thomas, O., Mellalieu, S. & Hanton, S. (2009). *Stress management in applied sport psychology.* In S. Mellalieu & S. Hanton, Advances in applied sport psychology: A review (pp. 124-164). London: Routledge.

Thompson, R., & Zuroff, D. C. (2004). *The level of self-criticism scale: Comparative self-criticism and internalised self-criticism.* Personality and Individual Differences, 36, 419–430.

Tunmer, W. E., & Chapman, J. W. (2002). *The relation of beginning readers' reported word identification strategies to reading achievement, reading-related skills and academic self-perceptions.* Reading and Writing, 15, 341-358

Turner, C. M., & Barrett, P. M. (2003). *Does age play a role in the structure of anxiety and depression in children and youths? An investigation of the tripartite model in three age cohorts.* Journal of Consulting and Clinical Psychology, 71, 826-833

Vealey, R. S. (1988). *Future directions in psychological skills training.* The Sport Psychologist, 2, 318-336.

Weiss, M. R. (1991). *Psychological skill development in children and adolescents.* The Sport Psychologist, 5, 335-354.

Weiss, M. R., & Bredemeier, B. J. (1983). *Developmental sport psychology: A theoretical perspective for studying children in sport.* Journal of Sport Psychology, 5, 216-230.

Weiss, M. R., & Ferrer-Caja, E. (2002). *Motivational orientations and sport behavior.* In T. S. Horn (Ed.), Advances in sport psychology (2nd ed., pp. 101-183). Champaign, IL: Human Kinetics.

Weiss, M. R., & Petlichkoff, L. M. (1989). *Children's motivation for participation in and withdrawal from sport: Identifying the missing links.* Pediatric Exercise Science, 1, 195-211.

Weiss, W. M., & Weiss, M. R. (2006). *A longitudinal analysis of commitment among competitive female gymnasts.* Psychology of Sport and Exercise, 7, 309-323

Weiten, W. (2004). *Psychology: Themes and variations* (6th ed.). United Kingdom: Wandsworth/Thompson.

Wylleman, P., De Knop, P., Menkehorst, H., Theebom, M., & Annerel, J. (1993). *Career termination and social integration among elite athletes.* In S. Serpa, J. Alves, V. Ferreira, & A. Paula-Brito (Eds.). Proceedings of the VIII World Congress on Sport Psychology (pp. 902-906). Lisbon: International Society of Sport Psychology.

Wylleman, P., & Lavallee, D. (2004). *A developmental perspective on transitions faced by athletes.* In. M. Weiss (Ed.), Developmental sport and exercise psychology: A lifespan perspective (pp. 507-527). Morgantown, WY: Fitness Information Technology.

In: Handbook of Sports Psychology
Editor: Calvin H. Chang

Chapter 5

SPORT AND SPIRITUALITY: A REVIEW OF THE LITERATURE

Quinten K. Lynn[1] Kenneth I. Pargament and and Vikki Krane[2]
Kansas State University[1]
Bowling Green State University[2], USA

ABSTRACT

Recently, sport psychology has given increasing attention to the role of religion and spirituality in sport. Much of this research examines the prominence and similarities between sport and religion as well as disparate religious beliefs and practices athletes incorporate in their sport participation. However, this research lacks an overarching conceptual framework grounding sport and religion in sound theory amenable to empirical observation. This chapter provides a critique of the literature on sport and religion from various fields of study. It begins by examining research comparing sport and religion as social institutions. It then turns to research from sport psychology, which examines the role of religion and spirituality in the lives of athletes, including their athletic performance. Next, borrowing from the psychology of religion, the constructs of spirituality and sanctification are presented as a framework for understanding the convergence between sport and religion. These theoretically driven and empirically supported constructs address the limitations of previous research and provide an original perspective for understanding how athletes integrate their sport and spirituality. Finally, future directions addressing the inherent vicissitudes of sport are suggested.

INTRODUCTION

Until recently, the fields of the psychology of religion and sports psychology were strangers to each other. However, in the past few years, an interest in the intersection of these two disciplines has begun to bloom. Sport psychology researchers and practitioners are becoming more aware of the central role religion plays for many athletes. This new awareness is engendering a serious look at where and how these two fields intersect; that is, what role religion might have in sport. More specifically, this awareness is raising questions about how religion might influence individual sport performance. Unfortunately, as this is new terrain, not much is known about the possible positive or negative impact of religion on sport performance. Consequently, not much is known about how to harness the potential benefits and how to minimize the potential dangers of religion as they relate to sport performance.

This paper examines the current literature with respect to the intersection of religion and sport. First, literature from the fields of sociology and cultural studies will be reviewed. Second, relevant literature from sports psychology will be considered. Third, research from the psychology of religion germane to the topic will be discussed, with a particular focus on the topic of spirituality. Finally, we will offer suggestions for future research as it relates to the intersection between spirituality and sport performance.

SPORT AND RELIGION: SOCIOLOGICAL STUDIES

The convergence of sport and religion in North America, and many other parts of the world, is apparent. Religious symbols are visible at nearly all collegiate and professional sporting events, including signs of the cross, "What Would Jesus Do" logos drawn on athletes' wrist bands and shoes, signs advertising the biblical verse (John 3:16), and athletes praying after scoring touchdowns or before batting. Similarly, theology has been quick to use sports terminology and metaphors in its teachings, e.g., equating Christ to "our" quarterback, following God's game plan, etc. This relationship between sport and religion is not a recent union; signs of this link can be found in Greek and Roman traditions. For example, the ancient Olympic Games were played to honor the gods as well as the state (Novak, 1992). However, not until the past 20-30 years have scholars begun to examine this relationship and how it plays out in the lives of athletes. In the following section, we take a brief look at the sociological literature examining the relationship between sport and religion, its potential implications for sport performance, and critiques of this literature.

Similarities between Sport and Religion

Much of the scholarly work on the topic of the relationship between sport and religion has focused on the similarities between the two. Hoffman (1992) argues that for many people, sport takes on religious quality and significance. For example, often, avid sports fans are labeled as zealots or described as religiously devoted to their favorite sports teams. This intense attraction people have toward sports is often compared with that seen within religious faiths.

Theorists (e.g., Hoffman, 1992; Nesti, 2007; Robinson, 2007) also stress that sport functions in similar ways to religion. Religion and sport both serve social functions, such as affording an atmosphere wherein similar beliefs are discussed (e.g., religions provide followers an atmosphere, as well as locations, to discuss theological doctrine, while sport provides fans an atmosphere, as well as location, to discuss the merits of sports doctrine, such as the value of a strong defense), and they both shape and reinforce critical values of American society (e.g., hard work, teamwork, character development). Furthermore, sport and religion both have rituals that reinforce a community's commitment to society's core values (e.g., Mass, the Olympics) (Hoffman).

Hoffman (1992) and others (e.g., Coakley, 2001) note other similarities between sport and religion. For example, both have special places and buildings for gatherings and special events. Sport has its stadiums and arenas, while religion has its churches and synagogues. Both have scripts and stories aimed at personal betterment. Sport has playbooks, practices, and time-outs, while religion has scriptures, rituals, and retreats. Both are often controlled by specific, structured hierarchies. Sport has coaches, commissioners, and owners, while religion has pastors, priests, dioceses, and prophets. Both have events celebrating their core values during certain times that are set aside as special, which are often held on the Sabbath. Sport has Super Bowl Sunday, the World Cup, and March Madness, while religion has Sunday services, Ramadan, Lent, and Passover. Both incorporate important rituals before, during, and after major events. Sport has initiations, band parades, halftime pep talks, and hand shaking after the game; religion has baptisms, opening and closing hymns, and processions. Both contain legends and heroes. The deeds of heroes in sport are told by fans, coaches and journalists; and these heroes are enshrined in halls of fame. In religion, heroes are elevated to sainthood and their stories are told repeatedly by members of congregations and clergy, and memorialized in the sacred literature. Hoffman (1992) also points out that both evoke intense emotions, can give deep personal meaning to people's lives, provide a social network and sense of belonging, and provide a distraction from daily stressors (e.g., work, political, social, and economic issues).

Because of the functional and structural similarities between sport and religion, some athletes and fans might find in sport what others find in religion (e.g., community, guiding values, strong emotional experiences). These similarities might also allow individuals to bring their religious beliefs and practices to sport more easily than if there were no similarities. This in turn might impact athletic performance indirectly. For example, athletes might make meaning of their athletic experience through a religious filter and be more apt to use religious forms of coping while participating in sport.

Perhaps because of their functional and structural similarities, the institutions of sport and religion have appealed to each other over the past few centuries to champion their own purposes. Since the 19th century in the United States, for example, Christian religions have used sport to promote spiritual growth by affirming that the body ought to be an instrument for good works. This movement, known as "Muscular Christianity," evolved into using sport as a way to retain parishioners, especially young men, and to proselyte and convert others through developing church based sports activities and leagues (Prebish, 1993; Coakley, 2001; Watson, 2007). More recently, many religious groups have associated themselves with high-profile sports and athletes as a way of marketing themselves to potential followers (Prebish, 1993). For example, organizations such as the Fellowship of Christian Athletes (FCA) and Athletes in Action (AIA) enlist popular sports personalities to reach audiences that would not normally be interested in their message. Similarly, church-affiliated colleges and universities have used sports to promote themselves and recruit students. Institutions of higher learning such as Notre Dame, Boston College, Brigham Young University, and Liberty University have been quick to point to their sport heritage as a way to market themselves (Prebish).

In sum, by appealing to the public's interest, many religious organizations and institutions have recruited and retained members through sport.

Prebish (1992) points out that sport has been equally quick to align itself with religion as a means to promote itself. For example, many university and professional teams hold Sunday services, offer pre-game prayers, and have clergy members travel with them. If for no other reason, by involving religion, sport provides its athletes with another way of coping with its exigencies.

The increased melding of sport and religion has likely allowed athletes to bring their religious beliefs to their sport and for religions to be present in locker rooms. Doing so creates climates in teams and athletic departments that foster expression of religious beliefs and practices by some, and, quite likely, the hiding of religious attitudes by others. It is possible that these religiously-oriented climates are indirectly related to sport performance. For example, in a highly religious climate some athletes might feel comfortable allaying their anxiety by praying. While this blending of sport and religion might foster positive experiences and performances for some athletes, it could have the opposite effect on others.

Sport as a Religion

Many authors suggest that, even though sport and religion have a number of similarities, they are essentially distinct entities and institutions. Others, however, go further and suggest that sport is a religion in itself. One such author, Novak (1992), argues that sport is the natural religion. He maintains that, like religion, sport is an expression of a deep impulse, a longing for freedom, symbolic meaning, and perfection. Athletes express this impulse through various means: asceticism, respect for the body, respect for factors and powers beyond their control, a reverence for the place and time of competition, and a sense of shared fate and comradeship.

Novak (1992) enumerates several key components of religions and notes that sport contains these same elements. First, religions and sport are highly organized and structured. Religious services and sport begin with ceremonies (e.g., parades), contain rituals (e.g., coin toss, pre-game speech), customs are followed (e.g., rules of the game), designated people stand to officiate and ensure that rituals are performed correctly (e.g., officials and referees), and often those engaged in the rituals wear sacred vestments (e.g., uniforms). What's more, the believers (e.g., the crowd) attending the liturgies (e.g., soccer game) are expected to be immersed in the ceremonies, to be engaged in the process, to unite with those performing, be it through prayer, chanting, and/or singing.

Second, religion and sport require and are based on asceticism. That is, devout followers as well as athletes are to strive for perfection through self-discipline. Through this discipline the mind can will the body to perform properly and character is developed. Third, often in life what individuals plan and what actually occurs are strikingly different from each other. Religion and sport allow people to understand and cope with these discrepancies by attributing them to chance and fate (e.g., God's will, catching a good break). Fourth, individuals are regularly faced with aging, dying, uncertainty, lack of control, cowardice, guilt, failure, and other challenges that are made explicit by both religion and sport. Fifth, time is sacred in both religion and sport. Sacred time, Novak argues, is time separated from normal routines. Participation in sacred time allows one to forget about ordinary time. Sacred time is saturated with exuberance, joy, and peace. In religion this can be seen during religious holidays, in sport this can be seen in the final minutes of a close game. Finally, religions and sport provide heroes, symbols, and myths that individuals can look to for wisdom and reassurance.

For Novak (1992), sport, though not a traditional religion or a religion of the highest form, remains nevertheless a real religion. The religion of sport can be subtle and its followers might not be religious in the traditional sense, but their devotion is real and they benefit from their devotion nonetheless.

Like Novak (1992), Prebish (1992, 1993) considers sport to be a religion. However, Prebish takes the argument somewhat further. Whereas others see parallels between sport and religion (e.g., Hoffman, 1992) or see sport as religion-like or as a lesser form of religion (e.g., Novak), Prebish contends that sport is every bit as much a religion as any traditional religion.

> *Sport is religion* for growing numbers of Americans, and this is no product of simply facile reasoning or wishful thinking. Further, for many, sport religion has become a more appropriate expression of personal religiosity than Christianity, Judaism, or any of the traditional religions. (p.48)

Prebish defines religion as "a means of ultimate transformation." For him, sport is a religion insofar as its followers experience "ultimate reality," their lives change because of their encounter with the ultimate, and they reinvest what they have gained through their encounter with the ultimate into society in a productive manner.

Prebish (1993) is quick to admit that the task of ultimate transformation is not easy for sport to accomplish. He notes, however, that not all sport is religion, nor that every sport experience is an encounter with the ultimate, and that the same can be seen in traditional religions. That is, not everybody who seeks the ultimate (i.e., God) has an experience with the ultimate, nor does every parishioner experience the ultimate during every sacred ritual, act, or meeting. Notwithstanding the difficulty in experiencing the ultimate, Prebish argues that athletes and fans alike do have moments wherein their experiences transcend the mundane and leave them awe-inspired.

To assist its participants in connecting with the ultimate, sport provides different rituals, both public and private, as well as holidays, legends, heroes, and shrines. Some of these rituals include chants, hymns, songs (e.g., "Take Me Out To The Ballgame"), parades, and seasonal festivals (e.g., Super Bowl). Central to most Christian services is the ritual of communion, a ritual symbolizing the connection between people and God. In sport the central ritual is the game itself, an act of communion in which athletes and fans connect, become interdependent, and establish a sense of solidarity (Prebish, 1992). By immersing themselves in these rituals, which are held in sacred stadiums during sacred times, athletes and fans are said to experience something that extends beyond themselves, something different from reality, something ultimate.

Prebish (1992) maintains that much of traditional religion is private by nature, as is the case with sport religion. Personal and private training, practice, and prayer all allow the athlete to prepare for the future, to help him/her cope with the demands of life, both in and out of sport, and to help him/her prepare for his/her fate (Prebish).

It is clear that Prebish (1992, 1993) draws many of the same comparisons between sport and religion as those made by other authors. However, for him, these similarities are not superficial parallels. Prebish sees no difference in the meaning or significance of these terms (e.g., sacred, dedication, sacrifice, commitment, prayer, ritual, festival, suffering, worship) when applied to sport or religion.

> What it boils down to is this: if sport can bring its advocates to an experience of the ultimate, and this (pursuit and) experience is expressed through a formal series of public and private rituals requiring a symbolic language and space deemed sacred by its worshiper, then it is both proper and necessary to call sport itself a religion. It is also reasonable to consider sport the newest and fastest-growing religion, far outdistancing whatever is in second place. (Prebish, 1992, p. 53)

Viewing sport as a religion might afford insight into how sport and religion are related and impact performance. For example, if athletes follow their sport religion with fervor and zeal, this might foster skill development and improvement in performance. If sport religion is able to help athletes face existential issues as Prebish (1992) argues, its followers would appear to be at an advantage for coping with the inherent bumps and potholes encountered in sport.

Dissimilarities between Sport and Religion

Notwithstanding these evident similarities, this approach to understanding the relationship between sport and religion often minimizes and/or ignores the many differences between these institutions. Coakley (2001) points to several essential differences between sport and religion. First, religious practices, rituals, beliefs and meaning are cemented in the sacred and transcendent realm, whereas sport is grounded in the mundane. Second, the purpose of sport is to focus on the material such as winning, while religion's purpose is to focus on the transcendent and to pursue spiritual goals. Third, religion is built upon the foundation of faith while sport is rooted in concrete rules. Fourth, religion encourages and emphasizes cooperation among believers while sports emphasize competition. Finally, while religion engenders a spirit of compassion and service, sport engenders a commitment to personal achievement and dominance over others.

Chandler (1992) echoes this critique contending that it is easy to see how sport has been confused with religion, and/or compared with religion, as many who study the relationship assume that what they observe allows them to understand complex phenomena. Instead, she argues that what is observed does not completely capture the depth and intricacies of religion and spirituality.

Higgs (1992) is one of many who argue that sport is not a religion. For Higgs, though sport is often compared to religion and war, it would be a mistake to equate them. Sport belongs "in the realm of the beautiful" (p. 91), religion to the divine, and, thus, they do not easily mix, if at all. Additionally, encounters with beauty (i.e., sport) and the divine result in vastly different experiences. While contact with beauty often "pleases, reassures, [and] composes" (p.95), contact with the sacred often "disrupts, unsettles, strikes down, lifts up, and transforms" (p. 95). An athlete may experience pleasure while competing, but rarely, if ever, does an athlete experience "seizures of holy fear on the playing field" (p. 97).

Higgs (1992) continues by examining the prize sought by sport and religion. While sport seeks dominance, winning, trophies, fame, personal glory, money, the prize sought by religion is quite different, one that precipitates wonder, humility, stillness, and hope.

Similarly, while sport may foster pleasure, religion fosters joy. For Higgs (1992), pleasure and joy are not synonyms:

> Pleasure derives from an expansion or indulgence of the self in sports, play, sex, eating, drinking, etc.; joy, by contrast, comes from worship of the Other, from giving due homage and praise, and on rare occasion from encounter with the Holy. (p. 96)

Moreover, the joy that comes from religion is often unpredictable, all-consuming, and the product of much spiritual effort, while the pleasure derived from sport is often predictable, transient, limited, and easily produced.

Finally, not only does Higgs (1992) argue that the similarity between sport and religion is superficial, he contends that by equating the two, sport takes on inappropriate power and position and the sacred component of religion is sullied and cheapened. "The most that play can do is to make the world bearable; the most that sports can do is to make it beautiful. When claims are made for them beyond these roles, they too become part of the problem." (p. 101)

Critique of Sociological Research

This literature provides a unique analysis of the relationship between sport and religion in much of Western society. By focusing on the many similarities between the two, it points to ways in which religion might influence athletic performance and athletes might cope with the problems they encounter. The literature also has several critical limitations.

One limitation of the literature is that the relationship between sport and religion is generally viewed distally; that is, the focus is on superficial similarities between sport and religion, such as hierarchical and organizational similarities, the use of pageantry in both sport and religion, and how participants and onlookers interact. This distal approach fails to consider more proximal relationships between sport and religion, such as the perceived spiritual nature of sport for some athletes and the role of sport within athletes' spiritual frameworks.

To better understand these proximal relationships, analyses will need to occur at the individual level and address how individuals meld sport and religion and how this melding is experienced. This highlights another limitation of the sociological literature: a lack of empirical support. Though conclusions about the links between religion and sport may appear self-evident, they are not grounded in systematic observation and measurement. Future research in this field should systematically observe and measure the relationship between sport and religion and its impact on the lives of athletes (including performance issues), coaches, fans, and church-goers alike.

Another limitation to this literature is its failure to consider the substantive content of religion and spirituality. For example, it does not address images of God, how the sacred is understood and experienced, how an individual might draw on spiritual resources to conserve their relationship with the sacred, or how an individual might integrate religious beliefs, values, and practices within the context of sport. To illuminate the relationship between sport and religion a more substantive approach is needed.

Research from the field of sport psychology has begun to address these limitations by taking an empirical approach to examining the religious beliefs and practices of athletes.

SPORT AND RELIGION: SPORTS PSYCHOLOGY

Not until recently have sport psychologists begun to seriously examine the role of religion and spirituality in sport. In the past eight to nine years, however, the role of religion in sport, especially in the lives of athletes, has begun to receive increased attention in the sport psychology community. The following will discuss the theoretical work in the field of sport psychology, which examines how religion or spirituality might influence athletes' performances and how sport and spirituality might be integrated into sport psychology consulting. Research that has been conducted on this topic will also be examined.

Theoretical Bases for Considering the Role of Religion in Sport

Recently, sport psychologists have been calling for greater attention to religious and spiritual issues in athletes (e.g., Balague, 1999; Ravizza, 2002; Watson & Nesti, 2005). Emphasizing a more holistic athlete-centered approach, they argue that it is insufficient and even inappropriate to focus solely on the physical, emotional, and mental strengths and weaknesses of athletes. These researchers note the centrality of religion in the lives of many athletes, especially those at the elite level (see Balague, 1999), and suggest that religious beliefs and rituals ought to be discussed, understood, and, when appropriate, incorporated into mental skills training programs.

More specifically, Watson and Nesti (2005) make several specific suggestions about how spiritual issues might be incorporated into applied work with athletes. First, current mental skills training programs might benefit from broadening their scope to include spiritual issues. For example, in their work with athletes, consultants could discuss how specific religious and spiritual practices (e.g., prayer) might be used to help with performance issues, such as coping with anxiety, focusing, and dealing with injury. Second, consultants could include spiritual issues in their discussions of the meaning of athletic performance. Similarly, religious beliefs could be relevant to discussions of secondary issues with athletes, such as the athlete's well-being and the quality of their experience with sport. Finally, integrating spirituality into the consultancy process might allow for new discussions and perspectives on self-understanding and personal growth.

Also advocating the inclusion of spiritual issues in sport psychology, Wiese-Bjornstal (2000) suggests that an athlete's spirituality is a resource often untapped by consultants. She asserts that spirituality can serve as a protective factor against stress and as a useful coping strategy when athletes are faced with challenges affecting their spirit, mind, and/or body. Wiese-Bjornstal suggests a model of how athletes' spirituality can be of use before and after an injury. Before an injury healthy athletes can draw upon their religious beliefs and practices and spirituality to alleviate and/or buffer against stress, use their membership in religious communities to gain social support, and use their beliefs and practices to reduce their stress levels and espouse healthy practices (e.g., eating healthy foods as a way to honor the body). After an injury, athletes can draw upon their beliefs and practices to reduce stress and anxiety, gain social support, shape their perception of control, and directly cope with the injury.

Speaking directly to the use of prayer, Watson and Czech (2005) suggest three ways that sport psychology consultants and athletes might use this religious practice in their work together. First, prayer might be used as a way of coping with anxiety. Second, prayer might assist athletes in finding meaning to their abilities and performance. Finally, prayer might help athletes put their sport experiences in perspective. In the end, Watson and Czech argue that avoiding and/or ignoring an athletes' spirituality is unethical as it is the consultant's responsibility to work from within the athlete's worldview, and for many athletes their religions and spirituality greatly shapes their worldview. Watson and Czech also suggest that ignoring such beliefs might hurt the collaborative relationship. Failing to address these often central issues might make the rapport building process more difficult (Storch & Farber, 2002), and result in interventions that are incongruent with an athlete's religious and spiritual beliefs. For example, for some religious athletes, the practice of hypnosis would not be appropriate as it might suggest that the athlete is giving up control of her body. Similarly, positive self-talk could be inappropriate to some athletes who view it as antithetical to the virtue of humility.

In sum, a number of theorists have called for greater mindfulness of the religious and spiritual beliefs of athletes. They maintain that this awareness is especially important when working with athletes directly as many athletes might have religious beliefs that influence their sport participation. Furthermore, these beliefs and practices could be helpful resources for athletes to draw upon before, during, and after performances, and they could also provide athletes a way of making meaning of their athletic abilities and pursuits.

Though these suggestions are based on observations and personal experience, they are theoretical rather than empirical in nature. Unfortunately, research examining the interface between sport and religion is sparse. Relatively few studies have been conducted that address the issue through qualitative methodologies, and though more quantitative research has been published, it is very much in its embryonic stage.

Empirical Evidence

Very few qualitative studies examining religious and spiritual characteristics of elite athletes have been published. In their interviews with 15 Olympic track and field athletes from the United States, Vernacchia, McGuire, Reardon, and Templin (2000) found that religious beliefs impacted athletes in several important ways. First, several athletes stated that their religious and/or spiritual beliefs helped them develop their athletic ability. For example, one athlete stated that his/her relationship with the Lord helped guide, protect, motivate and heal him/her during his/her career. Second, athletes noted that they drew upon their religious beliefs to cope with the many challenges they faced (e.g., injury, training, performance, demanding schedule) and to persevere through difficult times. Finally, religious beliefs appeared to provide athletes with deeper meaning to their experiences, be they positive (e.g., winning events) or negative (e.g., losing, injury).

In Park's (2000) interviews with 180 members of the Korean National team, raw data themes indicated that prayer was often used as a coping strategy. In fact, 40 of the athletes interviewed stated that they used prayer as a way to manage stress. One athlete stated:

> I always prepared my game with prayer from the major games to the minor games. The content of my prayer to God is to help me do my best in practice time. I committed all things to God, without worry. ...These prayers make me calmer and more secure and I forget the fear of losing. It resulted in good play. (p. 3)

Explicitly examining the role of prayer in the lives of athletes, Czech, Wrisberg, Fisher, Thompson, and Hayes (2004) reported four emergent themes in their interviews with nine NCAA Division I Christian athletes. First, these athletes often used prayer as a technique to enhance performance. For example, prayers were offered as a way to deal with stress. As one athlete stated:

> I would use a kind of praying relaxation breathing technique. I would breathe in real deep and out real deep and just kind of let go of all the anxiety by putting it on God's shoulders. I would say to myself, let go and let God take over. (p.7)

Other prayers asked for safety for the participant, teammates, and opponents during competition. Athletes also reported offering prayers to help them perform to the best of their abilities. None of the athletes stated that they prayed to win.

The second theme that emerged from these interviews was that prayer was very much a part of the athletes' routines, both during practice and competition. Third, athletes gave thanks in their prayers for the opportunity to perform, for their talent, and to be able to participate in sport. For some, this gratitude served as a source of motivation. One athlete commented:

> You kind of thank God for providing the opportunity. You realize He did provide this opportunity. I incorporated a "thank you performance." I know there are a lot of athletes out who do this. When I would step onto the field, I would basically say, okay, God, I am thankful for my family. And through my intensity on the field today, I am going to show you how thankful I am. I would use this as a form of motivation. (p.8)

The final theme was related to what athletes perceived as God's will. That is, most athletes believed that the outcome of their performance and their ability to perform was under the control of God's will. For these athletes, this perspective helped them cope with the inevitable highs and lows they experienced in sports.

This research provides unique and compelling evidence supporting the interface between sport and religion. Indeed, it appears religion's place in the lives of athletes, and consequently sports, is multi-faceted, common, and quite powerful. Religious beliefs and practices appear to serve several functions which help athletes perform, cope with the highs and lows of sport, and provide deeper meaning to their experiences.

Though this research is encouraging, it is limited in several respects. First, these studies are marked by small sample sizes and a lack of diversity among participants with respect to ethnicity, age, skill level, sport, and religious affiliation. Second, for the most part, the scope of these studies was rather broad and lacked depth. Vernacchia, McGuire, Reardon, and

Templin (2000) and Park (2000) were more interested in general characteristics and experiences of elite athletes rather than religious themes in particular. Consequently, their studies focused exclusively on the question of whether religious beliefs were involved in sports rather than the ways specific religious beliefs were used. Though Czech et al. (2004) investigated a more focused topic; prayer represents only one of many religious and spiritual beliefs and practices that might be used by athletes. Finally, this research focused solely on positive aspects of religion and spirituality. Future research will need to take a more even-handed approach to the topic.

As a result of these limitations, caution should be used in generalizing the findings and making claims about the extent to which and how religious beliefs are used by athletes. Notwithstanding these limitations, the research provides unique insight into the religious and spiritual domain of athletes and provides fertile ground for future research.

Other researchers in sport psychology have sought to better understand the relationship between sport and religion using quantitative methodologies. However, like their qualitative counterparts, their numbers are few. In fact, most quantitative research appears to come from only a few samples. One of the goals of this research is to establish religion and spirituality as important variables that may influence athletic performance, participation, and enjoyment. As such, simple designs have been used to address basic questions such as athletes' level of religiousness, how religious orientation might influence athletes' behavior and/or psychological makeup and whether religious athletes differ from non-religious athletes.

An important question to be answered when examining sport and religion is the relative level of religiousness between athletes and non-athletes. In their pilot investigation, Storch, Kolsky, Silvestri, and Storch (2001) examined the role of organizational religiousness (e.g., church attendance), non-organizational religiousness (e.g,. prayer and meditation), and intrinsic religiousness (e.g., degree to which individual integrates their religious beliefs into their life endeavors) in the lives of student-athletes (members of an intercollegiate varsity sport team) and non-athlete students. The authors hypothesized that athletes would have higher levels of all three forms of religiousness than non-athletes. Data were obtained from 248 students (84 athletes) who filled out questionnaires about their religiousness, gender, ethnicity, and athlete/non-athlete status. Findings indicated that athletes reported higher levels of organizational and intrinsic religiousness than non-athletes. The results were moderated by gender; male non-athletes reported lower degrees of organizational, non-organizational, and intrinsic religiousness than male and female athletes and female non-athletes.

Storch, Roberti, Bravata, and Storch (2004) sought to replicate these findings using a similar sample but a different measure of religiousness. Unlike the Duke Religion Index (DRI), which was used in the previous study, the Santa Clara Strength of Religious Faith-Short Form was selected to measure strength of religious faith, defined as an intrinsic motivation to personal religious beliefs. This measure is based on the assumption that religious institutions are not necessarily a part of religious faith. Again, athletes were hypothesized to report higher strength of religious faith than non-athletes. Two-hundred twenty six participants (57 athletes; i.e., members of an intercollegiate varsity sports team) were involved in the study with 74% of the sample being female. As hypothesized, athletes reported greater strength of religious faith than non-athletes. Furthermore, neither a main effect for gender nor an interaction of athletic status and gender was found.

As in the previous study, this investigation was limited in several respects: restricted sample characteristics, the possibility of demand characteristics and socially desirable responses, a unidimensional assessment of religiousness, and no distinction regarding the nature of the sport involvement of the athlete (team vs. individual). Notwithstanding these limitations, this study provides confirmatory evidence that religion is an important aspect of many athletes' lives. They suggest that religion is not an insignificant variable in the lives of athletes.

While religion appears to be important to many athletes, these studies do not speak to how religion may manifest itself in the lives of athletes. Citing the observations made by applied sport psychology practitioners (e.g., Balague, 1999) about the different roles religion has in the lives of some athletes, Storch and his colleagues (e.g., Storch, Kolsky, Silverstry, & Storch, 2001; Storch & Storch, 2002a; Storch, Storch, Kovacs, Okun, & Welsh, 2003; Storch, Storch, Welsh, & Okun, 2002) examined the relationship between religiousness and psycho-social well-being in athletes.

Storch, Storch, Welsh, and Okun (2002) examined the relationship between religiousness and depression in athletes. The authors hypothesized that religiousness would protect against the effects of depression. Participants were 105 (51 female) intercollegiate varsity sports team members from various sports teams with various religious affiliations. Participants completed the DRI and the Depression subscale of the Personality Assessment Inventory (PAI), which assesses cognitive, affective, and physiological symptoms of depression. The only statistically significant finding was a negative relationship between intrinsic religiousness and affective symptoms of depression ($r = -.21$, $p<.05$). Although not robust, these results indicate that, for intercollegiate athletes, intrinsic religiousness may act as a buffer against affective symptoms of depression. This study also provides additional preliminary evidence suggesting that religious is related to athletes' well-being.

As aggression among athletes has received increasing attention recently, Storch and Storch (2002b) examined the possibility that intrinsic religiousness acts as a protective factor against aggression in athletes. One hundred and five (51 women) Division I intercollegiate athletes with a mean age of 19.9 years participated in the study. Intrinsic religiousness was measured by a subscale of the DRI, and aggression was measured by the Aggression scale of the PAI which consists of three subscales: aggressive attitude (e.g., "My anger never gets out of control," reversed scored), verbal aggression (e.g., "People would be surprised if I yelled at someone," reversed scored), and physical aggression (e.g., "Sometimes I'm very violent"). Results indicated that intrinsic religiousness was negatively associated with aggressive attitudes and verbal aggression ($rs = -.20$ and $-.22$, respectively, $p<.05$), but not physical aggression. That is, higher levels of intrinsic religiousness were related to lower levels of aggressive attitudes and verbal aggression. These findings offer preliminary evidence for the role religiousness might play in reducing the likelihood of aggression in athletes. By way of conjecture, lower levels of aggressive attitudes and verbal aggression might help facilitate positive athlete-coach relationships as well as team cohesion.

Storch, Storch, Kovacs, Okun, & Welsh (2003) examined the relationship between religiousness and substance use in intercollegiate athletes. They hypothesized that higher levels of intrinsic religiousness would be negatively related to substance use. Participants included 105 (51 female) Division I intercollegiate athletes from a variety of individual and team sports. Athletes were of diverse ethnicity and religious affiliation. The Intrinsic Religiosity subscale of the DRI was used to assess intrinsic religiousness, the Alcohol Problems subscale of the PAI was used to assess frequency and quantity of consumption, and two questions were developed by the researchers to assess the use of marijuana and other recreational drugs. Intrinsic religiousness was negatively associated with alcohol use ($r= -.37$, $p<.001$), marijuana use ($r= -.27$, $p<.01$), and other recreational drug use ($r= -.21$, $p<.05$). This study gives support to the recurring theme that religiousness in athletes may protect against deleterious behaviors and symptoms.

Storch et al.'s research has important implications for athletes' well-being and suggests that higher levels of religiousness in athletes are related to empirically based mental health variables. However, the authors' publications can be criticized for their restricted sample (i.e., data appear to come from only a few samples from the southeastern portion of the U.S.) and lack of consistent results. For example, in their study of the relationship between religiousness and depression in college athletes, Storch, Storch, Welsh, and Okun (2002) found that religiousness in athletes was inversely related to affective symptoms of depression; however, Storch, Kovacs, Roberti, Bailey, Bravata, and Storch (2004) reported that religiousness was not significantly related to psychological adjustment which included a measure of depression. Similarly, in two separate publications (Storch & Storch, 2002a; Storch, Storch, & Adams, 2002) examining the relationships between athletes' level of religiousness and social support and levels of social anxiety, results failed to reach significant levels.

Another limitation of these studies by Storch et al. is their focus on the relationship between global measures of religiousness and mental health variables. This approach does little to elucidate the role of religion in athletes' participation in sport and fails to clarify the degree to which athletes perceive their participation in sport as religious and/or spiritual in nature. The use of more proximal variables to measure the relationship between sport and religion in athletes would assist researchers in better understanding the link between sport and religion for athletes and its potential impact on athletes' involvement in sport. A more proximal approach could assess the degree to which athletes perceive their participation in sport as sacred, the degree to which athletes' participation in sport is integrated into their religious/spiritual beliefs, and/or the extent to which athletes use religious rituals while participating in sport, and the outcomes of these perceptions, beliefs, and behaviors.

In sum, these studies lend initial empirical support to the notion that religiousness is an important construct for some athletes. Furthermore, higher intrinsic religiousness appears to be related to better psychological outcomes (e.g., lower levels of aggressive attitudes, verbal aggression, affective symptoms of depression) and less substance use. However, these studies also showed non-significant links between religiousness in athletes and several psychological variables (e.g., social support, social anxiety, trait anxiety, loneliness, and cognitive and physiological symptoms of depression). Given the correlational design of these studies, it is unclear to what extent religious beliefs and practices may or may not influence athletes and by what processes religiousness might influence athletes.

Future research needs to address these issues by using more sophisticated statistical techniques (e.g., path analysis), more diverse samples (e.g., professional and high school athletes, team and individual sports athletes), and more proximal measures of religiousness. For example, examining religious coping styles of athletes might better illuminate the relationship between religion and anxiety in athletes. Additionally, research to date provides little insight into how religiousness might be related to issues of performance. It could be argued that athletes with greater well-being might be more likely to work hard, get along with teammates and coaches, and be positive and optimistic in their approach. Unfortunately, these possibilities have not been assessed.

Also missing from this research is an overarching theoretical framework amenable to observation and measurement. Such a theory would need to provide insight into the religious and spiritual domain of athletes by addressing more proximal and substantive components of spirituality. It would also need to offer explanations about the degree to which athletes perceive sport as a spiritual experience and/or an integral component to their spirituality and how those perceptions translate into behaviors within the context of sport and religion.

By examining the degree to which athletes perceive their involvement in sport as sacred and how such perceptions are associated with specific sport and spiritual beliefs, attitudes and practices, researchers could assess the role of sport in athletes' spirituality at a more proximal level. One way this could be accomplished is by approaching the subject through the lens of sanctification, a construct from the field of the psychology of religion.

SPORT AND RELIGION: PSYCHOLOGY OF RELIGION

One line of research that might provide a conceptual framework for understanding the connection between sport and religion focuses on the power of perceptions of the sacred; that is, sanctification. This research suggests that seemingly ordinary things, such as sport, can be perceived as having spiritual significance and, thus, play an integral part in individuals' spirituality. This perspective also points to several important implications for athletes who sanctify their participation in sport, including performance and coping issues.

Sanctification, as defined by Pargament and Mahoney (2005), refers to a "process through which aspects of life are perceived as having divine character and significance" (p. 183). This process allows for the mundane to take on transcendent qualities and the ordinary to become extraordinary. For example, through the process of sanctification, people (e.g., the Pope, a rabbi, the Buddha), places (e.g., temples, synagogues, Holy Land), time (e.g., the Sabbath), and cultural artifacts (e.g., hymns, books) can take on sacred qualities. Just as some people perceive mundane objects as having divine character and significance, some athletes may perceive their bodies, participation in sport, and the manner in which they compete as having divine character and significance; that is, they may see these things as sacred.

In studying sanctification, researchers have pointed to two ways in which objects are perceived to be sacred. The first is through perceiving objects as "manifestation[s] of one's images, beliefs, or experience of God" (i.e., theistic sanctification) (Pargament & Mahoney, 2005, p. 183). In many religious traditions followers are taught that many aspects of life and the world are a manifestation of God and God's power. For example, some individuals view the earth as a manifestation of God's creative power and thus as a sacred object. Additionally, many traditions hold that certain ways of living reflect the presence of God (e.g., following God's law, following the "golden rule") and that good deeds are a manifestation of God. As it might apply to sport, some athletes might believe that their bodies are a divine creation and the use of their bodies in sport is a manifestation of God's creative power and benevolence. Others might view their athletic abilities as talents and/or gifts from a benevolent God.

Another, and less direct, way in which objects become sanctified (i.e., non-theistic sanctification) is by "investing objects with qualities that are associated with the divine" (Pargament & Mahoney, 2005, p. 185). Included in these sacred qualities are attributes of transcendence (e.g., holy, saintly), ultimate truth and purpose (e.g., blessed, consecrated), and boundlessness (e.g., eternal, wondrous) (Pargament & Mahoney). Thus, it is possible for individuals who do not believe in God or a higher power to perceive certain aspects of life as sacred. Again, many examples of this form of sanctification exist in our culture. Cemeteries are often referred to as hallowed ground, wars are described as holy, and individuals are described as saintly. Similarly, in sport, objects such as the playing field are described as holy, athletic events are described as epic, and standout athletes are said to be worshipped. Also, it is possible that athletes view their bodies, performance, and experiences as heavenly, inspiring, or soul stirring.

The construct of sanctification, as described in the psychology of religion literature, provides a framework for understanding and measuring the extent to which athletes perceive their participation in sport as sacred. The same literature suggests several important implications of sanctification, all of which can be applied to athletes' perception of their sport participation.

First, because sacred objects are of great import to individuals, "people are likely to invest more of themselves in the pursuit and care of those things that are sanctified than in the search for other ends" (Pargament & Mahoney, 2005, p.188). For example, Mahoney et al. (2005b) examined personal strivings (i.e., typical goals and objectives that individuals try to attain in their daily behavior) in a community sample and the extent to which these individuals sanctified their strivings; that is, the extent to which they believed their strivings were a manifestation of God and/or possessed sacred qualities. Higher levels of sanctification of strivings were associated with greater commitment to the strivings, attributions that their strivings were more important, and greater belief that their ten most important strivings dominated their lives. Furthermore, participants reported spending more "time thinking, reading, studying, and doing things or talking with others about their most sanctified strivings" (p. 258). In addition, participants had greater confidence in their ability to achieve their strivings when their strivings were thought to be a manifestation of God or imbued with sacred qualities. It is possible that athletes who perceive their participation in sport as sacred will be more likely to invest more of themselves in their sport and have more confidence in their ability to achieve their athletic goals, as suggested by this and other (Mahoney et al., 2005a) research.

Second, "people are more likely to try harder to preserve and protect sanctified aspects of life that have been threatened than other aspects" (Pargament & Mahoney, 2005, p.189). For example, many people view the presence of Americans on their nations' soil as a desecration of something sacred and will go to extreme measures to preserve and protect the sanctity of their land. Individuals may also draw upon their spiritual resources as a way to preserve and protect their sense of the sacred (e.g., prayer, forgiveness, sacred rituals, spiritual support) (Pargament, 1997). Empirical research indicates that individuals make attempts to preserve and protect the sacred aspects of their lives. For example, in a study by Mahoney et al. (2005a) with 289 college students, the sanctification of the body (e.g., perceiving the body as a gift from God, describing body as holy) was related to higher levels of health protective behaviors (e.g., wearing a seat belt, avoiding overworking, eating sensibly) and to lower levels of smoking and alcohol use. As it relates to athletes and sport, this research on sanctification suggests that athletes who sanctify their participation in sport may be more likely to preserve and protect their athletic participation. These efforts may take several forms, including, maintaining healthy habits, preparing for and competing in athletic competitions within the parameters of the rules, and taking a strong stance against those who cheat and/or tarnish the sports' reputation.

Third, perceiving certain aspects of life as sacred is likely to elicit spiritual emotions (Pargament & Mahoney, 2005). Higgs (1992) and others (cf. James, 1902, Otto, 1928) have noted that experiences of the sacred are often accompanied by feelings of joy, adoration, gratitude as well as feelings of awe, reverence, and humility. Unfortunately, as Pargament and Mahoney (2005) point out, very little empirical research has examined the relationship between sanctification and the eliciting of spiritual emotions.

One study that might be indirectly related to this topic is by Dillon and Tait (2000) who examined the relationship between spirituality and being "in the zone." The authors argued that the phenomenological experiences of being in the zone and having a "spiritual high" are similar in that both are often described as states of euphoria, effortlessness, and self-transcendence. Because of their phenomenological similarities, Dillon and Tait hypothesized that higher levels of spirituality would be related to higher rates of experiencing being in the zone. To assess spirituality and being in the zone, the authors developed two measures, the Spirituality in Sports Test (SIST) and the Zone Test (ZT), respectively. The SIST is a 10-item scale which asks respondents to indicate how frequently they "use or look to [their spirituality] in different situations they might encounter as a member of a sports team" (p. 193). For example, "I use spirituality or religiosity as a way to help me with the emotional roller coaster of winning and losing" (p. 195). The ZT is a 10-item scale which asks respondents to indicate how often they have been in the zone based on descriptions athletes have given of being in the zone. A sample item includes, "I have had the feeling of being able to move around, between, or through my opponents" (p.195).

Participants included 62 students, 42 of whom were members of an intercollegiate team, while the rest were involved with other sports teams (e.g., intramural teams). Results indicated a significant relationship between spirituality and being in the zone ($r= .49$, $p< .001$). This study suggests that by using spiritual techniques to cope with their sport experiences athletes are more often in the "zone," a phenomenological state that has often been described by language laden with spiritual emotions, such as the "feeling of being outside 'oneself'" (p. 97). Thus, the theory and research of sanctification suggest that athletes who sanctify their participation in sport may be more likely to experience a wide range of emotions, including those associated with the divine and sacred.

A final implication of sanctification according to Pargament and Mahoney (2005) is that sacred objects serve as resources individuals can draw upon. Thus, individuals are likely to gain greater satisfaction and well-being from pursuing and experiencing objects they perceive as sacred.

Several empirical studies appear to support this proposal. For example, in a study by Emmons (1999) with three samples of college-aged and older community adults, strivings were coded into several categories. One category was spiritual strivings, those strivings with spiritual and/or religious content. Spiritual strivings were related to higher levels of well-being, greater purpose of life, and marital and overall life satisfaction when compared to personal strivings (i.e., those without spiritual/religious content). Furthermore, spiritual strivings were more highly valued, perceived as less difficult, pursued for more intrinsic reasons, and associated with lower levels of goal conflict when compared to personal strivings. Similarly, in a study of community members, Mahoney et al. (2005b) found that higher levels of sanctification of strivings were related to higher self-reported levels of meaning obtained from the strivings, more joy and happiness derived from the strivings, and more perceived support from family, friends, and God in their pursuit of these strivings. Additionally, in examining the sanctification of sexual intercourse, Murray-Swank, Pargament, and Mahoney (2005) found that both men and women who sanctified the act of sexual intercourse reported greater pleasure and satisfaction from the sexual act. One might expect, then, that athletes who sanctify their participation in sport may be more likely to report higher levels of satisfaction and well-being from their involvement in sport and pursuit of their sports related goals.

Elsewhere, Pargament (1997, 2007) has argued that individuals who sanctify an aspect of life will be more likely to draw on sacred resources as a way to cope with significant problems. For example, couples who sanctify their relationships might be more likely to pray together to help create peace and harmony in their relationships, or individuals who sanctify their lives generally might tend to seek guidance from God when faced with difficult decisions. Within sport, athletes who sanctify sport might turn to sacred resources such as religious coping to help navigate the inherent turbulence of athletics.

In sum, theoretical and empirical work on sanctification offers an interesting and useful psycho-spiritual framework for understanding the relationship between sport and religion. More specifically, this framework can be used to examine the degree to which athletes perceive sport to be a manifestation of God and imbue sport with divine qualities. This framework offers understanding about the role of sport in the lives of athletes and proposes implications about the relationship between sport, religion, performance and coping.

CONCLUSION

Practical Implications

As mentioned above, theoretically, sanctification has several important implications for sport participation, including coping with anxiety. As athletes perceive their involvement in sport as sacred they might be more likely to invest more of themselves in their sport. This might lead to greater commitment, a stronger work ethic and greater subsequent levels of confidence. In efforts to preserve and protect the sacred, athletes might engage in healthier habits, including better nutrition, not over training, avoiding harmful and elicit substances, and adhering to workout plans. Additionally, these athletes might be more apt to obey the rules of their sport and look more critically against those who defame their sport through poor sportspersonship. Experiencing spiritual emotions might help athletes stay motivated and encouraged during difficult training or performance periods, and seeking those sacred emotions might provide motivation similar to chasing a "runner's high."

Sanctifying sport involvement might also lead athletes to draw on sacred resources. One such resource is religious coping. Throughout their participation in sport athletes are faced with challenges, trials, and demands that cause them significant stress and anxiety. During these times, they are likely to attempt to bring balance, control, and predictability back into their lives. Religious coping is one such technique. Religious coping, defined as "a search for significance in times of stress in ways related to the sacred" (Pargament, 1999), is a process wherein the individual's relationship with the sacred can be called upon to offer strength and support during difficult times. Two common forms of religious coping that might be especially salient for athletes are benevolent reappraisals and collaborative coping. Benevolent reappraisals consist of redefining stressors as spiritually benevolent events. For example, athletes might view losing a game, going through a slump or being injured as an opportunity to grow closer to God. Collaborative religious coping is the process of gaining control of a situation through a partnership with God. For example, an athlete faced with a daunting task such as competing against a talented opponent, performing at a large venue or beginning a new workout regimen might ask God for the strength to cope with the difficulty.

While religious coping may take many forms, research indicates that prayer is the most common form. Furthermore, research suggests that religious coping is a unique process in predicting positive outcomes such as reduction of anxiety and depressive symptoms, greater sense of control, life satisfaction, and, in one study, lower rates of mortality (Pargament, Magyar-Russell, Murray-Swank, 2005; Pargament, 2007). As noted above, research also suggests that athletes experience similar benefits when using prayer as a way to cope with the exigencies of sport (Park, 2000; Vernacchia et al., 2000; & Czech et al., 2004).

Understanding that some athletes might integrate draw on their spirituality to cope with the pressure of their sport has important implications for coaches and sport psychology consultants. First, coaches and consultants need to be mindful and sensitive to this reality and create environments that are respectful of athletes' religious and spiritual beliefs, or lack thereof. For example, coaches and consultants should avoid speaking from the point of reference of a specific religious tradition. Not only might this alienate those who do not belong to that or any faith tradition, but it also assumes that those from the same faith tradition share identical beliefs and/or that they are equally satisfied with their faith tradition. Speaking from a religious or spiritual perspective also assumes those athletes with spiritual beliefs would find such talk useful, beneficial, or desirable. Similarly, not all athletes draw upon sacred resources to navigate the tumult of sport and, thus, they might become uncomfortable, frustrated, or alienated when coaches or consultants speak to them from a religious or spiritual perspective.

Coaches and sport psychology consultants can also create environments that are sensitive to and respectful of athletes' integration of spirituality and sport by giving them space to draw upon their spirituality. For example, coaches might give their teams several minutes before competitions to meditate, pray, and/or reflect on important issues. Similarly, consultants could ask athletes if and how they integrate their spirituality and their involvement in sport; such a question conveys a respect for athletes' spirituality without assuming athletes perceive their participation in sport as sacred. A willingness to explore these perceptions and beliefs allows consultants to better understand how athletes cope with anxiety as they prepare for and perform during competition and to better understand what interventions will likely be of most benefit to athletes. Discussing spirituality within the context of sport also allows the consultant to be aware of potential interventions that might be inappropriate (e.g., encouraging an athlete to reflect upon their many abilities and strengths might be perceived by an athlete as vanity).

By being sensitive to athletes' spirituality, coaches and consultants are more likely to gain athletes' trust and create a supportive and affirming environment. It also allows for better understanding of the whole person and what resources might, or might not be, available to work with.

In sum, research from various disciplines indicate that spirituality is vital topic within sport psychology. This research suggests that for many athletes, spirituality is a salient topic they carry with them to the playing field. The theory of sanctification suggests new ways of understanding the manner in which athletes fuse their spirituality with their sport participation. Sanctification also provides ways of understanding how and why athletes might choose to cope with anxiety in spiritual ways. This understanding can help coaches and sport psychology consultants to work effectively and creatively with athletes to help them manage their anxiety and perform to their potential.

REFERENCES

Balague, G. (1997). *Understanding identity, value, and meaning when working with elite athletes.* The Sport Psychologist, 13, 89-98.

Chandler, J. M. (1992). *Sport is not a religion.* In S.J. Hoffman (Ed.), Sport and religion (pp. 55-61). Champaign, IL: Human Kinetics.

Coakley, J. (2001). *Sport in society: Issues & controversies.* New York: McGraw-Hill.

Czech, D. R., Wrisberg, C., Fisher, L., Thompson, C., & Hayes, G. (2004). *The experience of Christian prayer in sport- an existential phenomenological investigation.* Journal of Psychology and Christianity, 2, 1-19.

Dillon, K. M., & Tait, J. L. (2000). *Spirituality and being in the zone in team sports: A relationship?* Journal of Sport Behavior, 23, 91-100.

Emmons, R. A. (1999). *The psychology of ultimate concerns: motivation and spirituality in personality.* New York: Guilford Press.

Hoffman, S. J. (1992). *Sport and religion.* Champaign, IL: Human Kinetics.

James, W. (1961). *The varieties of religious experience.* New York: Simon and Schuster.

Mahoney, A. et al. (2005). *The sanctification of the body and behavioral health patterns of college students. International* Journal for the Psychology of Religion, 15, 221-238.

Mahoney, A., Pargament, K. I., Cole, B., Jewell, T., Magyar, G., Tarakeshwar, N., Murray-Swank, N. A., & Phillips, R. (2005). *A higher purpose: The sanctification of strivings in a community sample.* The International Journal for the Psychology of Religion, 15(3), 239-262.

Murray-Swank, N., A., Pargament, K., I., Mahoney, A. (2005). *At the crossroads of sexuality and spirituality: The sanctification of sex by college students.* The International Journal for the Psychology of Religion, 15, 199-219.

Nesti, M. (2007). *The spirit of sport.* In J. Parry, S. Robinson, N. J. Watson, & M. Nesti (Eds.), Sport and Spirituality: An introduction (pp. 119-134). London: Routledge.

Novak, M. (1992). *The natural religion.* In S.J. Hoffman (Ed.), Sport and religion (pp. 35-42). Champaign, IL: Human Kinetics.

Otto, R. (1928). *The idea of the holy: An inquiry into the non-rational factor in the idea of the divine and its relation to the rational.* London: Oxford University Press.

Pargament, K. I. (1997). *The psychology of religion and coping*: Theory, research, practice. New York: Guilford Press.

Pargament, K. I. (1999). *The psychology of religion and coping?* Yes and no. The International Journal for the Psychology of Religion, 9, 3-16.

Pargament, K. I. (2007*). Spiritually integrated psychotherapy:* Understanding and addressing the sacred. New York: Guilford Press.

Pargament K. I., Magyar-Russell, G., & Murray-Swank, M. A. (2005). *The sacred and the search for significance: Religion as a unique process.* Journal of Social Issues, 61(4), 665-687.

Pargament, K. I., & Mahoney, A. (2005). *Sacred Matters: Sanctification as a vital topic for the psychology of religion.* The International Journal for the Psychology of Religion, 15, 179-198.

Park, J. (2000). *Coping strategies used by Korean national athletes.* The Sport Psychologist, 14, 63-80.

Prebish, C. S. (1992). *"Heavenly father, divine goalie": Sport and religion.* In S.J. Hoffman (Ed.), Sport and religion (pp.43-54). Champaign, IL: Human Kinetics.

Prebish, C. S. (1993). *Religion and sport:* The meeting of the sacred and the profane. Westport, CT: Greenwood Press.

Ravizza, K. (2002). *A philosophical construct: A framework for performance enhancement.* International Journal of Sport Psychology, 33, 4-18.

Robinson, S. (2007). *Spirituality: A story so far.* In J. Parry, S. Robinson, N. J. Watson, & M. Nesti (Eds.), Sport and Spirituality: An introduction (pp. 7-21). London: Routledge.

Storch, E. A., & Farber, B. A. (2002). *Psychotherapy with the religious athlete.* Annals of the American Psychotherapy Association, 3, 15-17.

Storch, E. A., Kolsky, A. R., Silvestri, S. M., & Storch, J. B. (2001). *Religiosity of Elite College Athletes.* The Sport Psychologist, 15, 346-351.

Storch, E. A., Kovacks, A. H., Roberti, J. W., Bailey, L. M., Bravata, E. A., & Storch, J. B. (2004). *Strength of religious faith and psychological adjustment in intercollegiate athletes.* Psychological Reports, 94, 48-50.

Storch, E. A., Roberti, J. W., Bravata, & Storch, J. B. (2004). *Strength of religious faith: A comparison of intercollegiate athletes and non-athletes.* Pastoral Psychology, 52, 479-483.

Storch, E. A., & Storch, J. B. (2002a). *Correlations for organizational, nonorganizational, and intrinsic religiosity with social support among intercollegiate athletes.* Psychological Reports, 91, 333-334.

Storch, E. A., & Storch, J. B. (2002b). *Intrinsic religiosity and aggression in a sample of intercollegiate athletes.* Psychological Reports, 91, 1041-1042.

Storch, E. A., Storch, J. B., & Adams, B. G. (2002). *Intrinsic religiosity and social anxiety of intercollegiate athletes.* Psychological Reports, 91, 186.

Storch, E. A., Storch, J. B., Kovacs, A. H., Okun, A., & Welsh, E. (2003). *Intrinsic religiosity and substance abuse in intercollegiate athletes.* Journal of Sport & Exercise Psychology, 25, 248-252.

Storch, E. A., Storch, J. B., Welsh, E., & Okun, A. (2002). *Religiosity and depression in intercollegiate athletes.* College Student Journal, 36, 526-531.

Vernacchia, R. A., McGuire, R. T., Reardon, J. P., & Templin, D. P. (2000). *Psychosocial characteristics of Olympic track and field athletes.* International Journal of Sport Psychology, 31, 5-23.

Watson, N. J., & Nesti, M. (2005). *The role of spirituality in sport psychology consulting: as analysis and integrative review of literature.* Journal of Applied Sport   Psychology,   17, 228-239.

Watson, N. J. (2007). *Muscular Christianity in the modern age.* In J. Parry, S. Robinson, N. J. Watson, & M. Nesti (Eds.), Sport and Spirituality: An introduction (pp. 80-94). London: Routledge.

Watson, N. J., & Czech, D. R. (2005). *The use of prayer in sport: implications for sport psychology consulting.* Athletic Insight, 7(4).

Wiese-Bjornstal, D. (2000). *Spirit, Mind, and Body.* Athletic Therapy Today, 5, 41-42.

In: Handbook of Sports Psychology
Editor: Calvin H. Chang

ISBN: 978-1-60741-256-4
©2009 Nova Science Publishers, Inc.

Chapter 6

COPING IN COMPETITIVE SPORT SETTINGS

Olga Molinero, Alfonso Salguero and Sara Márquez[*]
School of Physical Activity and Sport Sciences, University of León, Spain

ABSTRACT

To manage the stressors they face in competitive settings athletes must develop a range of cognitive and behavioural coping skills. Athletes who use maladaptative coping strategies or fail to interpret sport-related events accurately and to react in a rational manner, will experience chronic stress that frequently leads to reduced performance quality and, eventually, to burnout and sport dropout. Therefore, athletes who participate in competitive sports need to employ effective psychological skills and coping strategies in order to satisfy their expectatives and to improve their performance. Although different questionnaries aimed to identify coping strategies used by athletes have been developed in the last few years, establishment of the most adequate instruments to determine under which situations cognitive and behavioral coping strategies reach its optimal efficacy is still required.

INTRODUCTION

In general, researchers looking at coping agree that its study essential in order to understand the effects of stress on people. The way in which individuals face up to stress may reduce or increase the effects of adverse events and conditions in life, not only in their emotional and short-term aspects, but also over the longer term, leading to changes in physical and mental health [128].

As early as the start of the twentieth century, the work of Sigmund Freud traced a route for exploring the mechanisms involved in self-regulation of human emotions and behaviours. Scientific study of coping lies within a long tradition of research investigating emotional adaptation and self-regulation of behaviour [10, 26, 82], based primarily on clinical studies. Over the last twenty years, researchers associated with socio-cognitivism and interactionism

---

[*] Contact: sara.marquez@unileon.es

have proposed explanations of the processes through which individuals administer and regulate their emotions and behaviours [16, 23, 36, 43, 82, 84, 102]. This proliferation of great conceptual overviews reflects the complexity and multi-dimensional nature of human adaptation. This, in turn, significantly complicates any operational use of the concept of behavioural self-regulation [45].

Recent work [26, 95, 45] conceptualizes *self-regulation* or *self-control* as a second-order construct, sub-divisible into mutually exclusive adaptation mechanisms (coping, defence, control of feelings, basic psychological skills or BPSs). These are mechanisms that may play a complementary part in psychological adaptation [26]. This gives rise to a fresh conceptual and terminological problem to which various authors have pointed [26, 27, 48, 102, 114, 135]. Table 1 is intended to clarify differences and similarities, at both functional and conceptual levels.

At a functional level, *coping* is just an adaptation mechanism playing a part in managing situations, emotions and avoidance of situations. Unconscious use of *defences* is an attempt to protect the people involved from unpleasant emotions, allowing them to avoid exposure to situations they find threatening. In this way, the *adaptation mechanism* permits no more than a modification of the objective demands of a situation. Moreover, use of *basic psychological skills* is aimed at maximizing human performance. Finally, affective regulation is directed towards direct and indirect management (for instance, avoidance) of the emotional state and of mood [45].

The relationships that are normally established between the various different adaptation mechanisms may be seen in Figure 1, where coping has a broad functional field. This is because it includes conduct intended to face up to objective requirements and to manage the emotions accompanying a stressful situation. Furthermore, a substantial part of the basic psychological skills and strategies for affective regulation are covered, respectively, by task-centred coping strategies and emotion-centred coping strategies (coping based on adapting) [45].

To concentrate on *coping*, the proliferation of definitions that have emerged once again reflects the complexity and multi-dimensional nature of human adaptation [45]. Lazarus and Folkman [82] defined *coping* as the *set of cognitive and behavioural efforts, constantly changing, that are used or developed to manage the specific demands or requirements, whether external or internal, of a given situation, assessed as going beyond the individual's resources*, or, in other words, the *process of managing internal or external demands that people see as exceeding or going beyond their capacities* [81, 82], a definition which still remains valid. This definition explicitly supposes that individuals can use a large range of coping behaviours to try to administer the demands of a stressful situation. On the one hand, the multi-dimensional nature of this concept has forced researchers to group coping behaviours together into a limited number of meaningful sets or *clusters*. On the other, this has encouraged those who have striven to render coping operational and study it through valid measurement tools [45].

Table 1. Definition and conceptual analysis of coping, defenses, affect regulation strategies and fundamental psychological skills [45]

Concept	Definition	Adaptative processes	Behavior types			Functions			Intention		Theoretical source			
			Behaviors	Cognitions	Intra-psychological	Manage situation	Manage emotions	Avoid situation and emotions	Intentional and voluntary	Unconscious and involuntary	Stress Theories	Psycho-dinamic Model	Emotion regulation	Sport Performance Theories
Coping	Constantly changing cognitive and behavioral actions used by individuals to manage the internal and external demands encountered during a specific stressful situation [82]	X	X	X		X	X	X	X		X			
Defences	Unconscious mechanisms used to protect the person from negative emotional consequences of a threatening event [26]	X			X		X	X		X		X		
Affect Regulation Strategies	Intentional processes to modify or maintain mood state and emotions [114]	X	X	X			X	X	X				X	
FPS	Behavioral and cognitive actions for action regulation to facilitate human performance [102]	X	X	X		X	X		X					X

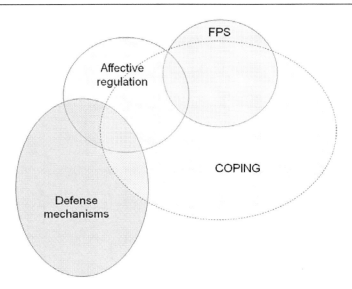

Figure 1. Coping conceptual frontiers [45].

COPING DIMENSIONS

As a response to the need to bring together methods for coping into meaningful groupings (*clusters*), a considerable range of typologies for coping have been developed [112, 140, 128]. According to these, as is shown in Table 2, a total of up to 400 coping strategies and more than seventeen hierarchical models for coping may be identified.

A number of researchers have taken as a basis the distinction made by Lazarus and Folkman [81] between the two main functional dimensions of coping. The first dimension, *task-oriented coping* or TOC, refers to actions that have as their object to change or control some aspect of a situation perceived as stressful. This dimension includes specific strategies such as increasing efforts, planning and logical analysis. The second dimension, *emotion-oriented coping*, or EOC, represents actions used with the aim of changing the significance of a stressful situation so as to regulate its negative outcome on emotions. In this second case, the basic premise is that it is possible to facilitate adjustment or adaptation by means of regulation of the emotions. This can be achieved by avoiding the stressing agent, setting it in a new cognitive framework, or concentrating selectively on the positive aspects of the situation [21]. This dimension includes specific strategies such as distancing oneself, self-control, seeking social support, accepting responsibility or re-assessing the situation positively. Despite the heuristic value of this consensus typology, various authors have proposed the existence of a third functional dimension [17, 37], supported by the results of second-order factor analysis [67, 139]. This third dimension, *avoidance coping*, or *distraction-oriented coping*, represents actions taken to ignore the task and to redirect attention to stimuli not relevant for it, and includes strategies such as denial or the use of alcohol and drugs.

Table 2. Higher order distinctions among coping categories [128].

Distinction /Author	Definition
Emotion-focused coping vs. Problems-focused coping [82]	"Coping that is aimed at managing or altering the problem causing the distress" vs. "coping that is directed at regulating emotional responses to the problem"
Problem-focused coping vs. Emotion-focused coping vs. appraisal-focused coping [100]	"Dealing with the reality of the situation…seeks to modify or eliminate the source of the stress" vs. "handling emotions aroused by a situation…responses whose primary function is to manage the emotions aroused by stressors and thereby maintain affective equilibrium" vs. "primary focus on appraising and reappraising a situation…involves attempts to define the meaning of a situation"
Responses that modify the situation vs. responses that function to control the meaning of the problem vs. responses that function for the management of stress [115]	"Responses that change the situation out of which the strainful experience arises" vs. "responses that control the meaning of the strainful experience after it occurs but before the emergence of stress" vs. "responses that function more for the control of the stress itself after it has emerged"
Approach vs. avoidance [124]	"Cognitive and emotional activity that is oriented either toward or away from threat"
Engagement vs. disengagement [23]	"Responses that are oriented toward either the source of stress, or toward one's emotions and thoughts" vs. "responses that are oriented away from the stressor or one's emotions/thoughts"
Control vs. escape [79]	"Proactive take-charge approach" vs. "staying clear of the person or situation or trying not to get concerned about it"
Primary vs. secondary vs. relinquishment of control Coping [125]	Efforts to influence objective events or conditions vs. efforts to maximize one's fit with the current situation vs. relinquishment of control
Assimilation (vs. helplessness) Accommodation (vs. rigid perseverance) [13]	"Transforming developmental circumstances in accordance with personal preferences" and "Adjusting personal preferences to situational constraints"
Alloplastic vs. autoplastic coping [118]	Coping directed toward changing the environment vs. directed toward changing the self
Volitional, effortful, controlled vs. involuntary, automatic coping [22]	Responses to stress that involve volition and conscious effort by the individual vs. responses that are automatized and not under conscious control
Behavioral vs. cognitive coping [79]	"Taking action or doing something" vs. "mental strategies and self-talk"
Social vs. solitary [79]	"Utilize methods that involve other people or . . . be done alone"
Proactive coping [6]	"Efforts undertaken in advance of a potentially stressful event to prevent it or modify its form before it occurs"
Direct vs. indirect coping [7]	Coping in which an individual emits an overt motor behavior to deal with a stressful event vs. coping in which "the organism responds to the stressful event by enlisting the aid of a conspecific"

Another theoretical aspect of interest is a definition the response as a *feature* or *state*. In accordance with a paradigm of coping as a feature, it would represent actions that people normally carry out in stressful situations [3, 12, 16]. According to this approach, coping responses should be stable. However, this point of view is in contrast to the process-oriented approach, which defines coping as responses dependent upon the context [81] and explicitly assumes that responses should change as a function of the stressful situation and of its various phases [24].

COPING AND SPORTS PERFORMANCE

A great deal of effort has been put into learning more about the psychological characteristics separating the most successful athletes from those not so successful. However, very little work has been done on the relationship between specific coping strategies and performance [41]. When people are competing, they may be affected by a number of potential stressors, including pain, fear, lack of confidence, psychological demands, pressure from trainers, and the needs of the sport in question [32, 55, 66, 103]. An inability to face up to tension is a significant factor in the failures of participants in many sorts of sport [80].

The occurrence of stressful situations during sports competitions often brings with it changes in psychological functioning, such as a lessened capacity to concentrate, loss of focus of attention, increased anxiety, or from the point of view of the body, greater muscular tension [93]. *Acute stress* occurs when an athlete interprets a situation as stressful, such as criticism from the trainer, comments made by opponents or spectators, the occurrence of an injury, or making a mistake. When a situation interpreted as stressful is prolonged over time, what is called *chronic stress* makes an appearance. This distinction is of importance, because acute stress and chronic stress require different kinds of coping strategies to achieve the greatest effectiveness in reducing their intensity [54]. In any case, a failure to deploy an appropriate response to acute stress often leads to a decline in performance capacity and even to giving up the sport involved. This makes it plain that athletes who participate in competitive sports need to make use of psychological skills and effective coping strategies so as to meet their expectations and improve their performance.

Over recent years a certain number of researchers have studied the strategies used by athletes to face up to the stressful situations characteristic of a competitive environment [93]. One approach, the first, concentrated on identifying the coping strategies in different sports [34, 55, 56]. Together with an in-depth description of the ploys employed by athletes, these studies permitted the identification of various groupings of types of strategy.

On the basis of systematic models of coping [41, 63, 82], a second line of research was aimed at an examination of what specific strategies turn out most useful for dealing with internal and external demands in competitive environments. The coping strategies of athletes have been associated with variables such as *perceived control* [3, 61], *self-efficacy* [61], *anxiety feature* [41, 53], *self-confidence* [58], *anxiety state* [109], *target orientation* [73, 110], *motivational climate* [110], *positive and negative affections* [29] or *performance measures* [41, 61], among others. Nevertheless, although significant advances have been achieved in both qualitative and quantitative research, little effort has been devoted to developing quantitative measurements for coping in sport.

FACTORS THAT SHAPE COPING

As previously indicated, the definition of coping provided by Lazarus and Folkman [82] assumes that individuals use coping behaviours in an attempt to adapt to the challenges, threats and requirements of a stressful situation. In this way, the use of coping behaviours might aid individuals to tame such demands. Nonetheless, employing these behaviours does not guarantee success or the psychological adaptation of the person concerned. The factors or strategies that may be able to play differing complementary parts in managing stressful situations are varied [128] and a combination of them may bring about different effects on the emotional experience and psychological adjustment of individuals [133]. Similarly, a given particular strategy may have varying repercussions according to the situation in which it is used. All of these topics require to be subjected to empirical study. Lazarus and Folkman [83] presented an integrating model bringing together the triggers and outcomes of coping. In this model, coping is seen as a constantly changing process that mediates relationships between triggers and outcomes over the short and the long term. Hence, the transactional model of Lazarus and Folkman [83] proposes a variable that can be brought into the model either as a trigger or as a consequence of coping in the context of a longitudinal study, as shown schematically in Figure 2.

Numerous pieces of research have looked into the triggers and outcomes of the various different strategies for coping. However, because sportsmen constitute a very specific population, the following table shows those pieces of work in which the phenomenon of athletes has been considered, together with details of the factors on which the research concentrated (Table 3).

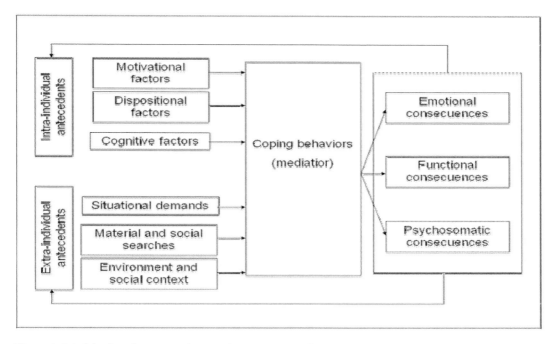

Figure 2. Model of coping antecedents and consequences [83].

Table 3. Coping influencing factors in sport settings (adapted from [45]).

Factors	Authors
ANTECEDENTS	
Intra-individual factors	
Personal characteristics	
Age	[87]

Table 3. (Continued)

Gender	[29][47][75][76][87][138][65][5]
Experience level	[47][87][138][65][62][107]
Cognitive factors	
Control perception	[3][47] [45] [61][70][71]
Self-efficacy feeling	[61]
Perceived importance	[47]
Stress perception	[3][70][71][5]
Stresing events (self-reported)	[89]
Competence perception	[71]
Success concept	[71]
Motivational factors	
Self-determined motivation	[1][46]
Goal achievement	[71][110][117][77]
Dispositional factors	
Optimism	[8][58][105]
Self-confidence state	[58]
Anxiety state	[38][41][53][64]
Resilience state	[8][69]
Self-handicaping tendence	[119]
Sport identity	[78]
Cognitive style	[3][70]
Attributional style	[127]
Dispositional coping style	[53]
Extra-individuales factors	
Situational-related factors	
Situational stability	[30][85]
Inter-situacional constancy	[53][70]
Inter-contextual constancy	[126]
Intra- situacional constancy	[51]
Contextual factors	
Perceived Motivational Climate	[71][110][77]
Perceived Social Support	[8][101]
CONSEQUENCES	
Emotional consequences	
Somatic and Cognitive State Anxiety	[47][60][109][5][97]
Positive and Negative Affect	[1][29][50][47][108][110][97]
Subjective well-being	[8][46]
Flow State	[68][20]
Functional consequences	
Objetive Performance Index	[41][61][129][116]
Subjetive Goal-related Index	[1][47][116]
Objetive Goal-related Index	[50]
Coping Perceived Efficacy	[71][108]
Survival (Sport perseverance)	[129]
Psychosomatic consequences	
Sport injuries	[87][40]
Burnout	[57][120]

ASSESSMENT TOOLS

Empirical evidence from Sports Psychology tends to support the view that coping actions change with the situation [44, 127], in the same situation as a function of time [131,30], and with the various phases of a situation [15, 51]. In consequence of these discoveries, many researchers prefer a process-oriented approach to coping [18, 31]. Indeed, it is from this angle that questionnaires on coping, such as the *Ways of Coping Questionnaire* (WOCQ; [42]) or the *COPE Inventory* [17], have been adapted for the environment of competitive sports.

The WOCQ [42] measures strategies for coping that are supposed to be applicable to numerous stressful situations. Despite the extent to which it has been used, in the last few years criticisms have been voiced of the clarity, conceptual specificity and applicability of the items in this questionnaire [9, 132]. Moreover, it has been demonstrated that the questionnaire shows a certain lack of internal consistency and some factor instability [19, 113].

Despite these limitations, in the field of sport modifications of the items in the WOCQ has led to *Ways of Coping for Sport* (WOCS, [88]) and the *Modified Ways of Coping Questionnaire* (MWOCQ, [28]). These versions, as might be expected, present the same conceptual and methodological weaknessses as the original questionnaire. In the first place, the structure of factors reveals inconsistencies between different versions, which might be explained by the lack of conceptual specificity of the sub-scales [47]. In addition, various items have greater weight in certain factors for some versions than in others. Furthermore, in the case of the WOCS there are inconsistencies between different samples. For example, it was shown that in a sample of 130 Australian basketball players the best fit in factor analysis was found with a model using eight factors, while in a sample of 630 Australian athletes the most appropriate model included just four factors [59].

As a reaction to the lack of theoretical relevance of the WOCQ, the *COPE Inventory* [17] was developed. This is a questionnaire that looks at fifteen coping strategies in various stressful situations. Factor analysis of the questionnaire with a sample of 978 American university students showed the validity of the model. Sports psychologists soon recognized the usefulness of this questionnaire [55, 38]. A confirmatory factor analysis with 870 Australian athletes demonstrated the factor validity of the COPE and the superiority of a fourteen-factor model (fusing the two social support scales) over the original with fourteen factors [35].

Crocker and Graham [29] developed a version of the COPE specifically for sport. This *Modified-COPE* (MCOPE) has nine scales from the original COPE and three scales from the sports version of the WOCQ. The results of factor analyses, both exploratory and confirmatory [35], gave acceptable support for the factor structure of this questionnaire.

The need to have available a questionnaire that was valid, reliable and as specific as possible for the field of sport led to the development of the *Athletic Coping Skill Inventory-28* (ACSI-28, [130]). The results principal component analysis based on the responses of 637 athletes to an assessment tool with 87 items gave rise to an eight-factor model. Nevertheless, confirmatory analysis showed the superiority of a model with seven factors [130]. The test-retest reliability of the tool was confirmed, as was its convergent validity [129]. Nonetheless, the heterogeneity amongst the items makes it difficult to see whether they represent any concrete training skill [102]. Moreover, some items measure coping efficiency more than coping strategies. This might cause distortions in its application [25, 111] or lead to errors when undertaking interventions to improve performance. This is a questionnaire oriented towards features, which does not consider changes in coping strategies in different situations or different phases of the same situation.

In a context broader than that specific to coping with stressful situations, Rost and Schermer [121,122], taking as a basis the integration of two different diagnostic strategies (traditional questionnaires and behaviour analysis based on interviews), proposed a new framework for assessing anxiety and stress that took into consideration their sequential nature, that is, the succession of precursors, forms of appearance, reinforcement and coping strategies. On the foundation of this model, the University of Leuven built up a battery of three *Questionnaires on the Causes, Manifestations and Coping Strategies for Anxiety in Competitive Sport* [33, 137]. Authors of the present paper some years ago prepared a Spanish version of these questionnaires, whose construct validity was shown by means of factor analysis [90] and the study of their internal consistency and simultaneous validity [91]. Factor analysis indicated the existence of four triggers for anxiety in a competitive situation: cognitive anxiety, lack of control over external factors, social anxiety and feelings of inadequacy. Four factors also emerged in respect to manifestations of anxiety: physiological manifestations, emotional manifestations, mental distortions or loss of concentration, and worry. As for coping strategies, two were identified, *active coping* and *passive coping*.

Use of the Spanish version of the *Questionnaires on Causes, Manifestations and Coping Strategies for Anxiety in Competitive Sport* permitted identification of sex and age differences in the components of competitive anxiety. The results obtained from a sample of 331 subjects of both sexes suggested that sportswomen attribute their anxiety to self-doubt and fear of receiving negative comments more than do sportsmen [94]. Moreover, as age increases, less attention is paid to whether or not comments are positive, while there are greater differences noted in the demands arising from the action and the chances individuals think they have [134]. An analysis of the components of anxiety in people practising individual versus team sports showed that athletes involved in individual sports develop physiological and emotional manifestations more frequently, as also mental distortions and loss of concentration less frequently than those participating in team sports. In this case, they also used avoidance strategies to a greater degree [92].

Independently of their respective psychometric strengths and weaknesses, questionnaires on coping in a sports context share the limitation of having been developed from questionnaires created to solve problems posed in the field of general psychology. As coping strategies change with the situation [44, 126], the relevance of the content of a questionnaire designed for use in a clinical or community environment is, at the very least, subject to question. There is the risk it will leave out features of importance for coping in sport or include irrelevant aspects causing psychometric problems [9].

To overcome this limitation an *Approach to Coping in Sport Questionnaire* (ACSQ) [72, 74] was developed. This questionnaire, whose first version contained 78 items, was applied to a sample of 275 Korean university athletes. This showed that there was a structure of factors in which six types of coping could be identified. A study with 311 American athletes confirmed the existence of these categories [73]. The revised version with 32 items offers acceptable construct validity, while very recently the psychometric properties of its Spanish version have been studied [74].

A further step forward was that taken by the authors [47] who drew up the *Inventaire des Stratégies de Coping en Compétition Sportive* (ISCCS), or Inventory of Coping Strategies in

Competitive Sport, which permits identification of the strategies used by athletes both before and after competitions. The conceptual model of this ISCCS is grounded in the hierarchical organization of the construct coping, and includes ten coping strategies often used by athletes. Each item in its turn: a) is an indicator for a single way of coping; b) can be used in a wide range of individual and team sports; c) can be used before and during competitions; and d) is conceptually different from the cognitive (self-starter status, perceived control), affective (self-esteem, confidence), or contextual (climate, cohesion) aspects related to coping [47].

Each of the ten strategies in the ISCCS can be organized into second-order dimensions which represent *task-oriented coping, distraction-oriented coping* and *avoidance-oriented coping*. Task-oriented coping corresponds to strategies that can be used to manage the internal and external requirements of the competition. Distraction-oriented coping represents strategies that may be employed to divert attention momentarily away to matters not related to the competition. Avoidance-oriented coping includes strategies to avoid the process which might lead to fulfilling objectives [47]. A study with 316 French Canadian athletes allowed confirmation of the validity of the questionnaire, as also fit to a ten-factor structural model, and its convergent validity was shown by an analysis of association with various sub-scales of the MCOPE and WOCQ [47, 48].

A table is included below by way of a summary of the various tools that have been developed to assess coping, with the applications and special characteristics of each of them (Table 4).

Table 4. Coping assessment instruments.

Questionnaire	Abbreviated	Author	Year	Utility	Observations
Ways of Coping Questionnaire	WOCQ	Folkman & Lazarus	1985	Measures coping strategies in stressful situations	Lack of clarity, conceptual specificity and applicability. Factorial inestability
Ways of Coping for Sport	WOCS	Madden et al.	1989	Specifically applied to sport contexts	Inconsistency in certain samples
COPE Inventory	COPE	Carver et al.	1989	Measures 15 coping strategies in different stressful situations	Non sport specific
Cuestionarios de Causas, Manifestaciones y Estrategias de Afrontamiento	CCMEA	Márquez & Tabernero	1993	Measures stress antecedents, manifestations and coping strategies	From General Psychology
Modified-COPE	MCOPE	Crocker & Graham	1995	Specifically adapted to sport	COPE and 3 WOCS sacles

Table 4. (Continued)

Questionnaire	Abbreviated	Author	Year	Utility	Observations
Athletic Coping Skill Inventory-28	ACSI- 28	Smith et al.	1995	Sport-specific	Items heterogeneity
Approach to Coping in Sport Questionnaire	ACSQ	Kim & Duda Kim et al.	1997 2003	Sport- specific	Sport specific outside the clinical or community environment
Inventaire des Strategies de Coping en Competition Sportive	ISCCS CICS	Gaudreau & Blondin	2002a	Athletes strategies before and during competition	Allows organizing in second order dimensions

RECENT RESEARCH

Nicholls and Polman [104] undertook and over-view of the literature available on coping in the field of sport. They found that from 1988 until 2004 the number of pieces of work that had been completed in this area was not very large. Only 64 studies dealt with the topic of coping among athletes and any potential differences between sexes and age-groups or the effectiveness of the various strategies this specific population used. In an attempt to bring that work up to date, a search was conducted covering from 2004 to the present day. It proved possible to find nearly 40 pieces of work continuing the lines of earlier research. Studies on the properties of coping, related factors, practical applications and differences by variables were all well represented (for example, to quote the most recent [11, 121, 2, 136, 4, 107]) but for the greater part they were all based on the same assessment tools.

A noteworthy number of these pieces of research were carried out by the creators of the ISCCS, Gaudreau and colleagues [46, 52, 85, 86]. The current paper's authors' work is on these same lines and has the intention of adapting this new tool to a larger range of populations of athletes. In the case of the Spanish population, the absence of tools in Spanish specifically developed for the field of sport that would permit identification of second-order dimensions and measure strategies for coping taking into consideration possible changes in different situations or in different phases of the same situation fully justifies the development and use of a Spanish adaptation of the ISCCS [96, 97]. The process of validating the Spanish version was carried out by performing an extensive study that demonstrated a five-factor structure (Table 5), with good reliability (Table 6) and good correlation with the factors of other questionnaires measuring the same or similar constructs (COPE, CSAI-2 and PANAS) (Tables 7 and 8).

Table 5. Factorial composition of the CICS Spanish version.

Factors	Coping strategies per factor	Items
Factor 1 (F1)	Mental imagery/ Effort	10
Factor 2 (F2)	Mental disengagement/ Resignation	7
Factor 3 (F3)	Seeking social support/ Logical analysis	9
Factor 4 (F4)	Social withdrawal/Venting of unpleasant emotion	7
Factor 5 (F5)	Relaxation	5

Table 6. Mean inter-item correlation and Cronbach alphas for factors of the CICS Spanish version.

Factors	Inter-item correlation mean	Cronbach's Alpha
F1	.601	.863
F2	.686	.851
F3	.574	.814
F4	.663	.844
F5	.523	.767
Mean	.609	.828

Table 7. Pearson correlation between CICS and COPE subscales. *: p<0.05. **: p<0.01.

	CICS Scales									
COPE Scales	CICS F1 Imagery/Effort		CICS F2 Mental distraction/Resignation		CICS F3 Support/ Logical analysis		CICS F4 Social withdrawal/ Venting of emotion		CICS F5 Relaxation	
	Pearson	p	Pearson	p	Pearson	p	Pearson	p	Pearson	p
Self-distraction	.320	.032*	.340	.022*	.184	.226	.433	.003**	.406	.006**
Active Coping	.668	.00**	.024	.876	.434	.003**	.269	.074	.220	.146
Denial	.439	.003**	.426	.003**	.401	.006**	.423	.004**	.366	.013*
Use of substances	-.091	.553	.215	.157	-.177	.246	-.038	.805	.124	.18
Seeking sociall support emotional	.510	.00**	-.031	.842	.638	.00**	.216	.154	.316	.034*
Seeking social support instrumental	.561	.00**	.130	.394	.591	.00**	156	.306	.376	.011*
Behavioral disengagement	.107	.486	.73	.00**	.120	.433	.336	.024*	.277	0.065
Venting of emotions	.281	.061	.379	.010*	.148	.332	.565	.00**	.199	.191
Positive reappraisal	.515	.00**	.198	.193	.476	.001**	.226	.135	.431	.003**
Planing	.648	.00**	.117	.45	.486	.001**	.244	.106	.358	.016*
Humor	.205	.177	.510	.00**	.336	.024*	.257	.088	.267	.076
Aceptance	.322	.031*	.152	.318	.225	.138	.193	.205	.045	.771
Religion	.410	.005**	.162	.287	.285	.058	.363	.014*	.392	.008**
Self-blaming	.234	.121	.207	.172	.150	.324	.245	.105	-.146	.338

Table 8. Pearson correlation between CICS , CSAI- 2 and PANAS subscales. *: p<0.05. **: p<0.01.

CICS Scales	CSAI-2 Scale						PANAS Scale			
	Cognitive Anxiety		Somatic Anxiety		Self-confidence		Positive Affect		Negative Affect	
	Pearson	p	Pearson	p	Pearson	p	Pearson	p	Pearson	p
CICS F1 Imagery/Effort	202	.183	.016	.918	.486	.001**	.657	.00**	.106	.488
CICS F2 Mental distraction/ Resignation	.258	.088	207	.171	-.233	.124	-.282	.061	.662	.00**
CICS F3 Support/Logical Analysis	.043	.781	.235	.120	.093	.541	.465	.001**	.109	.474
CICS F4 Social withdrawall/ Venting of emotion	.180	.236	.371	.012*	.015	.924	-.05	.746	.479	.001**
CICS F5 Relaxation	.061	.691	.099	.517	.220	.147	.266	.078	.141	.355

With regard to the profile of Spanish athletes, Table 9 shows preliminary data relating to second-order dimensions: strategies for task-oriented coping (TOC), emotion-oriented coping emotions (EOC) and coping based on avoidance or distraction-oriented coping (DOC). The scores attained by the subjects were higher in TOC and DOC than EOC (Table 9), with significant correlations being found between TOC/DOC and EOC/DOC.

Table 9. Mean and standard desviations of Task oriented, Emotion oriented and Disengagement oriented coping (n=129).

Dimensions	Min.	Max.	Mean	Sd
Task oriented coping	1.07	4,.23	2.59	.59
Emotion/distraction oriented coping	1.00	4.14	1.72	.73
Disengagement oriented coping	1.00	4.86	2.03	.77

Both these results and those noted previously demonstrate that strategies centred on the problem are those most frequently used in confronting stressful situations that occur during competitions. A number of researchers have studied the sort of confrontation strategies used by athletes. All of them have reached the conclusion that the fact that a strategy is used more frequently does not mean that it is effective, but rather that the effectiveness of coping is related to the choosing of the strategy to be employed [106]. Hence, Nicholls, Holt and Polman [103], when working with golfers, discovered that certain strategies such as persevering, routines, increasing concentration and putting in more effort gave good results. In contrast, forcing the game and speeding it up were ineffective for such players and their performance. This is a pointer to future lines of research that may well be of great interest within Sports Psychology, with an eye to achieving better performances from athletes.

REFERENCES

[1]   Amiot, C.E., Gaudreau, P., & Blanchard, C.M. (2004). *Self-determination, coping and goal attainment in sport.* Journal of Sport and Exercise Psychology, 26, 396-411.

[2]   Anderson, R., & Hanrahan, S.J. (2008). *Dancing in pain: pain appraisal and coping in dancers.* Journal of Dance Medicine and Sciences, 12(1), 9-17.

[3]   Anshel, M. H., & Kaissidis, A. N. (1997). *Coping style and situational appraisals as predictors of coping strategies following stressful events in sport as a function of gender and skill level.* British Journal of Psychology, 88, pp.263-276.

[4]   Anshel, M.H., & Si, G. (2008). *Coping styles following acute stress in sport among elite Chinese athletes: a test of trait and transactional coping theories.* Journal of Sport Behavior, 31(1), 3-19.

[5]   Anshel, M.H., & Sutarso, T. (2007). *Relationship between sources of acute stress and athletes' coping style in competitive sport as a function of gender.* Psychology of Sport and Exercise, 8(1), 1-24.

[6]   Aspinwall, L.G., & Taylor, S.E. (1997). *A stich in time: self-regulation and proactive coping.* Psychological Bulletin, 121, 417-436.

[7]   Barrett, K.C., & Campos, J.J. (1991). *A diacritical function approach to emotions and coping.* In M. Cummings, A.L. Greene & K.H. Karraker (Eds.), Life-span developmental psychology: Perspectives on stress and coping. (pp. 21-41). Hillsdale, NJ: Erlbaum.

[8]   Baltzell, A. (1999). *Psychological factors and resources related to rowers' coping in elite competition.* Non-published Doctoral Thesis, Boston University, Boston, MA.

[9]   Ben-Porath, Y. S., Waller, N. G., & Butcher, I. N. (1991*). Assessment of coping: an empirical illustration of the problem of inapplicable items.* Journal of Personality Assessment, 57, 162-176.

[10] Boekaerts, M., Pintrich, P.R., & Zeidner, M. (2000). *Handbook of self-regulation.* San Diego, Ca: Academic Press.

[11] Bolgar, M.R., Janelle, C. & Giacobbi, P.R. (2008). *Trait anger, appraisal and coping differences among adolescent tennis players.* Journal of Applied Sport Psychology, 20(1), 73-87.

[12] Bolger, N. (1990). *Coping a as personality process: a prospective study.* Journal of Personality and Social Psychology, 59, 525-537

[13] Brandstädter, J., & Renner, G. (1990). *Tenacious goal pursuit and flexible goal adjustment: Explication and age-related analysis of assimilative and accommodative strategies of coping.* Psychology and aging, 5, 58-67.

[14] Carver, C.S., Scheier, M.F., & Weintraub, J.K. (1989). *Assessing coping strategies: a theoretically based approach.* Journal of Personality and Social Psychology, 56(2), 267-283.

[15] Carver, C. S., & Scheier, M. F. (1994). *Situational coping and coping dispositions in a stressful transaction.* Journal of Personality and Social Psychology, 66(1), 184-195.

[16] Carver, C.S., & Scheier, M.F. (1998). *On the self-regulation of behavior.* New York: Cambridge University Press.

[17] Carver, C. S., Scheier, M. F., & Weintraub, I. K. (1989). *Assessing coping strategies: a theoretically based approach.* Journal of Personality and Social Psychology, 56, 267-283.

[18] Cerin, E., Szabo, A., Hunt, N., & Williams, C. (2000). *Temporal patterning of competitive emotions: a critical review.* Journal of Sport Sciences, 18, 605-626.

[19] Clark, K. K., Bormann, C. A., Cropanzano, R. S., & James, K. (1995). *Validation evidence for three coping measures.* Journal of Personality Assessment, 65, 434-455.

[20] Colgan, D.B. (2007). *Psychological, physiological and situational factors affecting performance in adolescent figure skaters.* Dissertation Abstract International: Section B: The Sciences and Engineering, 67(7B), 3746.

[21] Compas, B. E. (1987). *Coping with stress during childhood and adolescence.* Psychological Bulletin, 101, 393-403.

[22] Compas, B.E., Connor-Smith, J.K., Osowiecki, D., & Welch, A. (1997) *Effortful and involuntary responses to stress: implications for coping with chronic stress.* In B.J. Gottleib (Ed.). Coping with chronic stress. (pp. 105-130). New York: Plenum Press.

[23] Compas, B. E., Connor-Smith, J. K., Saltzman, H., Harding Thomsen, A., & Wadsworth, M. E. (2001). *Coping with stress during childhood and adolescence:*

Problems, progress, and potential in theory and research. Psychological Bulletin, 127, 87-127.

[24] Compas, B. E., & Epping, I. E. (1993). *Stress and coping in children and families.* In C. F. Saylor (Ed.), Children and disasters (pp. 11-28). New York: Plenum Press

[25] Coyne, I. C., & Gottlieb, B. H. (1996). *The mismeasure of coping by checklist.* Journal of Personality, 64, 959-991.

[26] Cramer, P. (1998). *Coping and defense mechanism: what's the difference?* Journal of Personality, 66, 919-946.

[27] Cramer, P. (2000). *Defense mechanism in psychology today.* American Psychologist, 55, 637-646.

[28] Crocker, P. R. E. (1992). *Managing stress by competitive athletes: ways of coping.* International Journal of Sport Psychology, 23, 161-175.

[29] Crocker, P. R. E., & Graham, T. R. (1995). *Coping by competitive athletes with performance stress: gender differences and relationships with affect.* The Sport Psychologist, 9, 325-338.

[30] Crocker, P.R., & Isaak, K. (1997). *Coping during competitions and training sessions: are youth swimmers consistent? International* Journal of Sport Psychology, 28(4), 355-369.

[31] Crocker, P. R. E., Kowalski, K. C., & Graham, T. R. (1998). *Measurement of coping strategies in sport.* In J. L. Duda (Ed.). *Advances in sport and exercise psychology measurement.* (pp. 149-161). Morgantown, WV: Fitness Information Technology.

[32] Dale, G. A. (2000). *Distractions and coping strategies of elite decathletes during their most memorable performances.* The Sport Psychologist, 14,17-41.

[33] Du Bois, G. (1989*). Oorzaken, verschijngsvormen en versterking van falangaast in de copetitiosport: constructie van een meetinstrument.* Leuven: Instituut voor Lichamelijke Opleiding.

[34] Eklund, R. C. (1996). *Preparing to compete: a season-long investigation with collegiate wrestlers.* The Sport Psychologist, 10, 111-131.

[35] Eklund, R. C., Grove, R. J. & Heard, P. N. (1998). *The measurement of slump-related coping: factorial validity of the COPE and the Modified-COPE inventories.* Journal of Sport and Exercise Psychology, 20, 157-175.

[36] Elliot, A.J., & McGregor, H.A: (2001). *A 2x2 achievement goal framework.* Journal of Personality and Social Psychology, 80, 501-519.

[37] Endler, N.S., & Parker, J.D. (1994). *Assessment of multidimensional coping: Task, Emotion and Avoidance Strategies.* Psychological Assessment, 6(1), 50-60.

[38] Eubank, M., & Collins, D. (2000). *Coping with pre- and in-event fluctuations in competitive state anxiety: A longitudinal approach.* Journal of Sport Sciences, 18, 121-131.

[39] Feinstein, J. (1986). *A season on the brink.* New York: MacMillan.

[40] Falkstein, D.L. (2000). *Prediction of athletic injury and post-injury emotional response in collegiate athletes: a prospective study of an NCAA Division I football team. Dissertation Abstract International: Section B*: The Sciences and Engineering, 60(9), 4885.

[41] Finch, L.M. (1994). *The relationships among coping strategies, trait anxiety and performance in collegiate softball players.* Eugene, Or: Microform Publications.

[42] Folkman, S., & Lazarus, R.S. (1985). *If it changes it must be a process: study of emotion and coping during three stages of a college examination.* Journal of Personality and Social Psychology, 48(4), 150-170.

[43] Freund, A.M., & Baltes, P.B. (2002). *Life-management strategies of selection, optimization and compensation: Measurement by self-report and construct validity.* Journal of Personality and Social Psychology, 82, 642-662.

[44] Frydenberg, E., & Lewis, R. (1994). *Coping with different concerns: consistency and variation in coping used by adolescents.* Australian Psychologist, 29, 45-48.

[45] Gaudreau, P. (2004). *Les stratégies de coping utilisées par les athlètes en situation de compétition sportive: Développement d'un modèle multidimensionnel du coping, de ses antécédents et de ses conséquences.* Tesis Doctoral. Montréal: Université du Montréal.

[46] Gaudreau, P., & Antl, S. (2008). *Athletes' broad dimensions of dispositional perfectionism: examining changes in life satisfaction and the mediating role of sport-related motivation and coping.* Journal of Sport and Exercise Psychology, 30(3), 356-382.

[47] Gaudreau, P., & Blondin, J.P. (2002a). *Development of a questionnaire for the assessment of coping strategies employed by athletes in competitive sport settings.* Psychology of Sport and Exercise, 3, 1-34.

[48] Gaudreau, P., & Blondin, J.P. (2002b). *A hierarquical model of coping in competitive sports: Integrating coping strategies and coping functions.* In K.C. Kowalski (Ed.). *Assessing coping in sport and physical activity symposium: Conceptual, measurement and theoretical issues. Assessing coping in sport and physical activity symposium: conceptual, measurement, and theoretical issues.* Symposium conducted at the annual meeting of the Canadian Society for Psychomotor Learning and Sport Psychology, Vancouver, BC.

[49] Gaudreau, P., & Blondin, J.P. (2004). *Different athletes cope differently during a sport competition: a cluster analysis of coping.* Personality and Individual Differences, 36(8), 1865-1878.

[50] Gaudreau, P., Blondin, J.P., & Lapierre, A.M. (2002). *Athletes' coping during a competition: Relationship of coping strategies with positive affect, negative affect and performance-goal discrepancy.* Psychology of Sport and Exercise, 3, 125-150.

[51] Gaudreau, P., Lapierre, A.M., & Blondin, J.P. (2001). *Coping at three phases of a competition: Comparison between pre-competitive, competitive and post-competitive utilization of the same strategy.* International Journal of Sport Psychology, 32, 369-385.

[52] Gaudreau, P., Ali, M.E., Marivain, T. (2005). *Factor structure of the Coping Inventory for Competitive Sport with a sample of participants at the 2001 New York marathon.* Psychology of Sport and Exercise, 6, 271-288.

[53] Giacobbi, P. R., & Weinberg, R. S. (2000). *An examination of coping in sport: individual trait anxiety differences and situational consistency.* The Sport Psychologist, 14, 42-62.

[54] Gottlieb, B. H. (1997). *Conceptual and measurement issues in the study of coping with chronic stress.* In B. H. Gottlieb (Ed.), Coping with chronic stress. (pp 3-42). NewYork: Plenum Press.

[55] Gould, D., Eklund, R. C., & Jackson, S. A. (1993). *Coping strategies used by US Olympic wrestlers.* Research Quarterly for Exercise and Sport, 64, 83-93.

[56] Gould, D., Finch, L. M.. & Jackson, S. A. (1993). *Coping strategies used by national champion figure skaters.* Research Quarterly for Exercise and Sport, 64, 453-468.

[57] Gould, D., Udry, E., Tuffey, S., & Loehr, J. (1996). *Burnout in competitive junior tennis players: I. A quantitative psychological assessment.* The Sport Psychologist, 10, 322-340.

[58] Grove, R. J. & Heard, P. N. (1997). *Optimism and sport confidence as correlates of slump-related coping amongathletes.* The Sport Psychologist, 11, 400-410.

[59] Grove, R.J., Lavallee, D., & Gordon, S. (1997). *Coping with retirement from sport: The influence of athletic identity.* Journal of Applied Sport Psychology, 9, 191-203.

[60] Hammermeister, J., & Burton, D. (2001). *Stress, appraisal and coping revisited: Examining the antecedents of competitive state anxiety with endurance athletes.* The Sport Psychologist, 15, 66-90.

[61] Haney, C. J., & Long, B. C. (1995). *Coping effectiveness: a path analysis ofself-efficacy, control, coping, and performance in sport competitions.* Journal of Applied Social Psychology, 25, 1726-1746.

[62] Hanton, S., Neil, R., Mellalieu, S.D., & Fletcher, D. (2008). *Competitive experience and performance states: an investigation into multidimensional anxiety and coping.* European Journal of Sport Science, 8(3), 143-152.

[63] Hardy, L., Jones, G., & Gould, D. (1996). *Understanding psychological preparation for sport*: Theory and practice of elite performers. Chichester, GB: Willey.

[64] Hatzigeorgiadis, A., & Chroni, S. (2007). *Pre-competition anxiety and in-competition coping in experienced male swimmers.* International Journal of Sport Science and Coaching, 2(2), 181-189.

[65] Holt, N.L., Hoar, S., & Fraser, S.N. (2005). *How does coping change with development? A review of childhood and adolescence sport coping research.* European Journal of Sport Science, 5(1), 25-39.

[66] Holt, N. L., & Hogg, J. M. (2002). *Perceptions of stress and coping during preparations for the 1999 women's soccer world cup finals.* The Sport Psychologist, 16, pp.251-271.

[67] Hudek-Knezevic, J., Kardum, I., & Vukmirovic, Z. (1999). *The structure of coping styles: a comparative study of Croatian sample.* European Journal of Personality, 13, 149-161.

[68] Jackson, S.A., Thomas, P.R., Marsh, H.W., & Smethurst, C.J. (2001). *Relationships between flow, self-concept, psychological skills and performance.* Journal of Applied Sport Psychology, 13. 129-153.

[69] Joyce, y., Smith, R., & Vitaliano, P. (2005). *Stress-resilience, illness and coping: a person-focused investigation of young women athletes.* Journal of Behavioral Medicine, 28(3), 257-265.

[70] Kaissidis-Rodafmos, A., Anshel, M. H., & Porter, A. (1997). *Personal and situational factors that predict coping strategies for acute stress among basketball referees.* Journal of Sports Sciences, 15, 427-436.

[71] Kim, M.S. (1999). *Relationship of achievement-related dispositions, cognitions, and the motivational climate to cognitive appraissals, coping strategies and their effectiveness in sport.* Non-published Doctoral Thesis, Purdue University, NC.

[72] Kim, M. S., & Duda, J. L. (1997). *Development of a questionnaire to measure approaches to coping in sport.* Journal of Applied Sport Psychology, Supp 9, S115.

[73] Kim, M. S., & Duda, J. L. (1999). *Predicting coping responses: An integration of Lazarus' transactional theory of psychological stress and coping and goal perspective theory.* Proceedings of the Annual Meeting of the Association for the Advancement of Applied Sport Psychology, 41.

[74] Kim, M. S., Duda, J. L., Tomás, I., & Balaguer, I. (2003*). Examination of the psychometric properties of the Spanish version of the Approach to Coping in Sport Questionnaire.* Revista de Psicología del Deporte, 12, 197-212.

[75] Kolt, G.S., Kirkby, R.J., & Lindner, H. (1995). *Coping processes in competitive gymnasts: Gender differences.* Perceptual and Motor Skills, 81, 1139-1145.

[76] Kowalski, K.C., & Crocker, P.R. (2001). *Development and validation of the Coping Function Questionnaire for adolescents in sport.* Journal of Sport and Exercise Psychology, 23, 136-155.

[77] Kristiansen, E., Roberts, G.C., & Abrahamsen, F.E. (2008). *Achievement involvement and stress coping in elite wrestling.* Scandinavian Journal of Medicine and Science in Sports, 18(4), 526-538.

[78] Lally, P. (2007). *Identity and athletic retirement: a prospective study.* Psychology of Sport and Exercise, 8(1), 85-99.

[79] Latack, J.C., & Havlovic, S.J. (1992). *Coping with job stress: a conceptual evaluation framework for coping measures.* Journal of Organizational Behavior, 13, 479-508.

[80] Lazarus, R. S. (2000). *How emotions influence performance in competitive sports.* The Sport Psychologist, 14, 229-252.

[81] Lazarus, R.S., & Folkman, S. (1984a). *Coping and adaptation.* In W.D. Gentry (Ed.). The handbook of Behavioral Medicine. (pp.282-325). New York: Guilford.

[82] Lazarus, R. S., & Folkman, S. (1984b). *Stress, appraisal, and coping.* New York: Springer.

[83] Lazarus, R.S., & Folkman, S. (1987). *Transactional theory and research on emotions and coping.* European Journal of Personality, 1, 141-169.

[84] Locke, E.A., & Latham, G.P. (2002). *Building a practically useful theory of goal setting and task motivation.* American Psychologist, 57, 705-717.

[85] Louvet, B., Gaudreau, P., Menaut, A., Genty, J., & Deneuve, P. (2007*). Longitudinal patterns of stability and change across three competitions: a latent class growth analysis.* Journal of Sport and Exercise Psychology, 29(1), 100-117.

[86] Louvet, B., Gaudreau, P., Menaut, A., Genty, J., & Deneuve, P. (2009). *Revisiting the changing and stable properties of coping utilization using latent class growth analysis: a longitudinal investigation with soccer referees.* Psychology of Sport and Exercise, 10(1), 124-136.

[87] Madden, C., & Kirkby, R.J. (1989). *Coping styles of competitive middle distance runners.* International Journal of Sport Psychology, 20, 208-216.

[88] Madden, C., Kirkby, R. J., & McDonald, D. (1989). *Coping styles of competitive middle distance runners. International* Journal of Sport Psychology, 20, 287-296.

[89] Madden, C., Summers, J.J., & Brown, D.F. (1990). *The influence of perceived stress on coping with competitive basketball.* International Journal of Sport Psychology, 21(1), 21-35.

[90] Márquez, S. (1992). *Adaptación española de los cuestionarios de antecedentes, manifestaciones y consecuencias de la ansiedad ante la competición deportiva.* I. Estructura factorial. Revista de Psicología del Deporte, 2, 25-38.

[91] Márquez, S. (1993). *Adaptación española de los cuestionarios de antecedentes, manifestaciones y consecuencias de la ansiedad ante la competición deportiva. II. Consistencia interna y validez simultánea.* Revista de Psicología del Deporte, 3, 31-40.

[92] Márquez, S. (1994). Diferencias en los componentes de la ansiedad competitiva entre practicantes de deportes individuales y colectivos. Revista de Entrenamiento Deportivo, VIII, 11-14.

[93] Márquez, S. (2004). *Ansiedad,* estrés y deporte. Madrid: EOS.

[94] Márquez, S., & Tabernero, B. (1993). *Diferencias de sexo y edad en los componentes de la ansiedad competitiva.* Apunts: Educación Física y Deportes, 34, 68-72.

[95] Mathews, G., Schwean, V.L., Campbell, S.E., Saklofske, D.H., & Mohamed, A.A. (2000). *Personality, self-regulation and adaptation.* In M. Boekaerts, P.R. Pintrich y M. Zeidner (Eds.). *Handbook of self-regulation.* San Diego, Ca: Academic Press. 171-207.

[96] Molinero, O.; González Boto, R.; Salguero, A.; Márquez, S. (2006). *Adaptación del Cuestionario de Estrategias de Afrontamiento en la Competición Deportiva (ISCCS) a una población española: estudio preliminar.* IV Congreso de la Asociación Española de Ciencias del Deporte, Coruña. Universidade da Coruña.

[97] Molinero, O.; Salguero, A.; Márquez, S. (2008). *Coping Inventory for Competitive Sport: convergent and concurrent validity of the Spanish Version.* Archivos de Medicina del Deporte, 25 (6), 510.

[98] Molinero, O.; Salguero, A.; Máquez, S. (Non- published). *Structural model of the Coping Inventory for Competitive Sport Spanish Version.*

[99] Molinero, O.; Salguero, A.; Márquez, S. (Non- published*). Perfil de afrontamiento del deportista español mediante el uso del ISCCS.*

[100] Moos, R.H., & Billings, A.G. (1982*). Conceptualizing and measuring coping resources and coping processes.* In L. Goldberger & S. Breznitz (Eds.).Handbook of stress: Theoretical and clinical aspects. (pp. 212-230). New York: Free Press.

[101] Mummery, W.K., Schofield, G., & Perry, G. (2004). *Bouncing back: the role of coping style, social support and self-concept in resilience of sport performance.* Athletic Insight, 6(3). Available on the World Wide Web: http://www.athleticinsight.com/ Vol6Iss3/BouncingBack.htm

[102] Murphy, S., & Tammen, V. (1998). *In search of psychological skills.* In J.L. Duda (Ed.). Advances in sport and exercise psychology measurement. (pp. 195-209). Morgantown, Wv: Fitness Information Technology.

[103] Nicholls, A. R., Holt, N. L., & Polman, R. C. J. (2005). *A phenomenological analysis of coping effectiveness in golf.* The Sport Psychologist, 19, 111 – 130.

[104] Nicholls, A.R., & Polman, R.C.J. (2007). *Coping in sport: a systematic review.* Journal of Sports Sciences, 25(1), 11-31.

[105] Nicholls, A., Polman, R., Levy, A.R., & Backhouse, S.H. (2008). *Mental toughness, optimism, pessimism and coping among athletes.* Personality and Individual Differences, 44(5), 1182-1192.

[106] Nicholls, A., Polman, R., Levy, A., Taylor, J., & Cobley, S. (2007). *Stressors, coping and coping effectiveness: gender, type of sport and skill differences.* Journal of Sport Sciences, 25(13), 1521-1530.

[107] Nieuwenhuys, A., Hanin, Y.L., & Bakker, F.C. (2008). *Performance-related experiences and coping during rçaces: a case of an elite sailor.* Psychology of Sport and Exercise, 9(1), 61-76.

[108] Ntoumanis, N., & Biddle, S.J.H. (1998). *The relationship of coping and its perceived effectiveness to positive and negative affect in sport.* Personality and Individual Differences, 24, 773-788.

[109] Ntoumanis, N., & Biddle, S.J.H. (2000). *Relationship of intensity and direction of competitive anxiety with coping strategies.* The Sport Psychologist 14, 360-371.

[110] Ntoumanis, N., Biddle, S. J. H., & Haddock, G. (1999). *The mediating role of coping strategies on the relationship between achievement motivation and affect in sport.* Anxiety, Stress and Coping, 12, 299-327.

[111] Oakland, S., & Ostell, A. (1996). *Measuring coping: a review and critique.* Human Relations, 49, 133-155.

[112] Parker, J. D., & Endler, N. (1992). *Coping with coping assessment: a critical review.* European Journal of Personality, 6, 321-344.

[113] Parker, J. D. A., Endler, N. S., & Bagby, M. R. (1993). *If it changes, it might be unstable: examining the factor structure of the ways of coping questionnaire.* Psychological Assessment, 5, 361-368.

[114] Parkinson, B., & Totterdell, P. (1999). *Classifying affect-regulation strategies.* Cognition and Emotion, 13, 277-303.

[115] Pearlin, L. I., & Schooler, C. (1978). *The structure of coping.* Journal of Health and Social Behavior, 19, 2-21.

[116] Pensgaard, A.M., & Duda, J.L. (2003). *Sydney 2000: the interplay between emotions, coping and the performance of Olympic-level athletes.* The Sport Psychologist, 17(3), 253-267.

[117] Pensgaard, A.M., & Roberts, G.V. (2003). *Achievement goal orientations and the use of coping strategies among Winter Olympians.* Psychology of Sport and Exercise, 4, 101-116.

[118] Perrez, M., & Reicherts, M. (1992). *Stress, coping and health.* Seattle, Wa: Hogrefe & Huber.

[119] Prapavessis, H., Maddison, R., & Grove, R.J. (2003). *Self-handicapping tendencies, coping and anxiety responses among athletes.* Psychology of Sport and Exercise, 4, 357-375.

[120] Raedeke. T.D., & Smith, A.L. (2004). *Coping resources and athlete burnout: an examination of stress mediates and moderation hypotheses.* Journal of Sport and Exercise Psychology, 26(4), 525-541.

[121] Ridnour, H., & Hammermeister, J. (2008). *Spiritual well-being and its influence on the athletic coping profiles.* Journal of Sport Behavior, 31(1), 81-93.

[122] Rost, D. H., & Schermer, F. J. (1989a). *The various facets of test anxiety: a subcomponent model of test anxiety measurement.* In R. Schwarzer, H. M. Vander Ploeg, & C. D. Spielberger (Eds.), Advances in test anxiety research. Vol. 6. (pp 37-52). Hillsdale: Lawrence Erlbaum Associates.

[123] Rost, D. H., & Schermer, F. J. (1989b). *The assessment of coping with test anxiety.* In R. Schwarzer, H. M. Vander Ploeg & C. D. Spielberger (eds.), Advances in test anxiety research. Vol. 6. (pp 179-191). Hillsdale: Lawrence Erlbaum Associates.

[124] Roth, S., & Cohen, L. J. (1986). *Approach, avoidance, and coping with stress.* American Psychologist, 41, 813-819.

[125] Rudolph, K.D., Denning, M.D., & Weisz, J.R. (1995). *Determinants and consequences of children's coping in the medical setting: Conceptualization, review and critique.* Psychological Bulletin, 118, 328-357.

[126] Sellers, R.M. (1995). *Situational differences in the coping processes of student-athletes.* Anxiety, Stress and Coping, 8, 325-336.

[127] Sellers, R.M., & Peterson, C. (1993). *Explanatory style and coping with controllable events by student-athletes.* Cognition and Emotion, 7(5), 431-441.

[128] Skinner, E. A., Edge, K., Altman, J., & Sherwood, H. (2003). *Searching for the structure of coping: A review and critique of category systems for classifying ways of coping.* Psychological Bulletin, 129, 216-269.

[129] Smith, R.E., & Christensen, D.S. (1995). *Psychological skills as predictors of performance and survival in professional baseball.* Journal of Sport and Exercise Psychology, 17, 399-415.

[130] Smith, R. E., Schutz, R. Smoll, F. L., & Ptacek, J. T. (1995). *Development and validation of a multidimensional measure of sport-specific psychological skills. The Athletic Coping Skills Inventory-28.* Journal of Sport and Exercise Psychology, 17, 379-387.

[131] Stewart, S. M., & Schwarzer, R. (1996*). Stability of coping in Hong Kong medical students: a longitudinal study.* Personality and Individual Differences, 20, 245-255.

[132] Stone, A. A., Greenberg, M. A., Kennedy-Moore, E., & Newman, M. G. (1991). *Self-reported, situation-specific coping questionnaires: what are they measuring?* Journal of Personality and Social Psychology, 61, 648-658.

[133] Suls, J., & David, J.P. (1996). *Coping and personality*: Third time's the charm? Journal of Personality, 64, 468-477.

[134] Tabernero, B., & Márquez, S. (1994). *Interrelación y cambios temporales en los componentes de la ansiedad-estado competitiva.* Revista de Psicología del Deporte, 5, 53-67.

[135] Thomas, P.R., Murphy, S.M., & Hardy, L. (1999).*Test of performance strategies. Development and preliminary validation of a comprehensive measure of athletes' psychological skills.* Journal of Sport Sciences 17, 697-711.

[136] Vernacchia, R.A.; & Henschen, K.P. (2008). *The challenge of consulting with track and field athletes at the Olympic Games. International* Journal of Sport and Exercise Psychology, 6(3), 254-267.

[137] Verwilt, M. (1989). *Faalangast in de competitiesport: verwerkingsstrategien. Constructie van een meetinstrument.* Leuven: Instituut voor Lichamelijke Opleiding.

[138] Yoo, J. (2000). *Coping profile of Korean competitive athletes.* International Journal of Sport Psychology, 32, 290-303.

[139] Zautra, A. J., Sheets, V. L., & Sandler, I. N. (1997). *An examination of the construct validity of coping dispositions for a sample of recently divorced mothers.* Journal of Personality and Social Psychology, 74, 256-264.

[140] Zeidner, M., & Endler, N. S. (1996). *Handbook of coping: theory, research, and applications.* New York: Wiley.

In: Handbook of Sports Psychology
Editor: Calvin H. Chang

ISBN: 978-1-60741-256-4
©2009 Nova Science Publishers, Inc.

Chapter 7

SUPPLEMENTATION IN BODYBUILDING: PSEUDOSCIENCE, MARKETING AND MUSCLE DYSMORPHIA

Philip E Mosley[*]
Royal Brisbane and Women's Hospital, Brisbane, Australia

ABSTRACT

Bodybuilders pursue a muscular physique through a specific programme of weightlifting and nutrition. The sport is growing rapidly in popularity, especially amongst young males in the Western world.

Ever since the development of bodybuilding as an athletic pursuit there has been a market for nutritional supplements. These purport to increase the participant's ability to attain a hitherto unobtainable physique through such means as increasing strength or decreasing body fat. The promotional strategies for such supplements tap directly into men's insecurities about their bodies and most assertions about efficacy are not supported by scientific evidence.

For most individuals bodybuilding remains a healthy pastime that forms a balanced part of an active lifestyle. However, evidence is growing that for a number of men bodybuilding has facilitated the emergence of a unique disturbance of eating, exercise behaviour and body image termed muscle dysmorphia.

In this chapter I provide an overview of the bodybuilding subculture and discuss the development of the supplement industry. Existing literature on the prevalence of supplementation amongst bodybuilders is reviewed, together with data on the type of products marketed to consumers. The physiological validity of the claims made by purveyors of such preparations is assessed in light of existing evidence. I highlight the use of cynical marketing strategies that target vulnerable individuals and link such behaviour to the rise of muscle dysmorphia amongst male bodybuilders. Existing regulatory frameworks in the United States and the European Union are outlined and these are considered in the context of concerns about potential physical and mental ill effects. Future directions for research in this field are discussed, including an urgent need

[*] Correspondence: Department of Mental Health, Royal Brisbane and Women's Hospital, Herston, Queensland, 4029, Australia, E-mail: philmosley@doctors.net.uk, Telephone: +61 (0)451 469634

to obtain an up to date assessment of current trends in nutritional supplements and a pressing requirement to assess the physical and mental consequences of long-term supplementation.

INTRODUCTION

Bodybuilding is a visual discipline. Devotees of the sport pursue a lean muscular physique through a regime of anaerobic resistance training and a tailored programme of nutrition. Although female bodybuilders exist, it is primarily a male-dominated activity. In the sport of competitive bodybuilding individuals display their physiques to a panel of judges, who score each entrant on the basis of the size, symmetry and definition of his musculature.

The aesthetic qualities of bodybuilding differentiate it from the activity of powerlifting, where the goal is purely to lift the heaviest weight possible for just one repetition. In fact, powerlifters often carry excess fat in order to increase the quantity of muscle they can pack onto their oversized frames.

Perhaps the first ever bodybuilder was Eugen Sandow (1867-1925), a Prussian who began his career as a sideshow strongman but soon began displaying his physique as a work of art. The sport grew slowly throughout the twentieth century; by the late 1970s the bodybuilding subculture remained small and largely overlooked, based primarily in its adopted home in southern California.

The world was exposed to bodybuilding in 1977 with the release of Arnold Schwarzenegger's cult film "Pumping Iron", a documentary showcasing the bodybuilding lifestyle as the "Austrian Oak" prepared to take his 6th Mr Olympia title, the highest accolade in competitive bodybuilding. As the ebullient Schwarzenegger rose to stardom as a Hollywood actor, bodybuilding became accepted into mainstream Western fitness culture.

Today, the muscled bodybuilding physique is a ubiquitous presence throughout the entertainment and advertisement industries. Bodybuilding competitions are held in many cities, especially in the United States. Many men now lift weights as part of their workout regime and although few may aspire to the overblown bodies of modern Mr Olympia competitors, the fitness trade is booming. In a quest for toned biceps and "six-pack" abdominals, more men than ever are joining gyms, reading fitness magazines and experimenting with performance-enhancing dietary supplements.

THE TRAINING, DIET AND LIFESTYLE OF A BODYBUILDER

The desire for a sculpted rather than a brawny or functional figure influences the bodybuilder's pattern of weight training as compared to the routine followed by the powerlifter or the sportsman. A powerlifter's aim is to be as strong as possible in only a few planes of motion, whereas a sprinter will concentrate on those lifts that transfer to an increase in straight-line speed. A bodybuilder, however, wishes to develop all muscle groups equally, regardless of their functional significance. Most bodybuilders therefore split their workouts into clusters of exercises that focus on the muscles in only one or two specific groups. Different muscles are targeted in consecutive sessions in a predetermined cycle until all body parts have been trained. In this way a bodybuilder can train to maximal intensity each session without risking injury or burnout. Furthermore, during a given session each muscle group is developed from different angles and in different planes of motion using a selection of various exercises to ensure maximal stress on the muscle tissue. The number of repetitions performed during each set of exercises is that which is believed to produce the greatest level of muscle hypertrophy in the working fibres – usually in the range of eight to ten.

Prolonged high-intensity aerobic cardiovascular activity, such as distance running, is avoided by the bodybuilder on account of its perceived detrimental effect on muscle growth. Low-intensity cardiovascular exercise or short bursts of high-intensity training are used sparingly, primarily as a tool to aid fat loss and increase muscular definition.

In order for the bodybuilder to gain muscle he must consume more calories than he expends during exercise. For the bodybuilder to appear lean and toned, however, he must reduce his body fat, which requires a calorific deficit. As a means to reconcile these conflicting demands bodybuilders tend to alter their diet and workout routines according to the calendar: training for size in the off-season ("bulking") and slowly reducing body fat several months before a competition ("cutting"), in order to retain the majority of any added muscle mass. Many bodybuilders employ nutritional supplements as a means of augmenting or accelerating their bulking or cutting cycles.

The quest for the idealised physique of the bodybuilder demands the wholehearted adoption of all that promotes muscle gain with the exclusion of all that impedes productive training. Tiring workouts and bland high-protein, low-carbohydrate, low-fat foods are in; late nights, parties, drinking and fast food are out. Even modest developments in physical prowess require months of toil at the parsimonious coalface of the weights room. Therefore it is scarcely surprising that bodybuilders are always searching for agents, natural or synthetic, illegal or legal, that can increase mental or physical performance in the gym, speed fat loss, suppress appetite, improve recovery or enhance muscle gain.

THE HISTORY OF NUTRITIONAL SUPPLEMENTATION IN BODYBUILDING

In the early days of bodybuilding athletes relied on protein-rich foods such as milk, eggs and meats with added vegetables, fruits and whole grains. It is noteworthy that bodybuilders were aware of the ketogenic principles of the Atkins diet long before its widespread dissemination into the public arena. Nutritional gurus of the era also advocated the muscle-building properties of such entities as beef extract, desiccated liver, brewers' yeast and wheat germ oil.

The expansion in the supplement industry was chiefly promoted by the skilful merchandising of the man who led the commercialisation of bodybuilding in the sixties and seventies: Joe Weider. Owner of the most popular fitness magazines of the age, Weider signed up the top bodybuilding stars to lucrative contracts that permitted him to use their image to promote any product he saw fit. A growing number of men began to experiment with bodybuilding in an attempt to emulate the success of Weider's protégé: Arnold Schwarzenegger, and nutritional supplements became heavily marketed within these magazines. The most widely promoted product at this time was dehydrated protein powder, either sourced from soy or from a mixture of milk and eggs and reconstituted with either water, milk or cream.

Anabolic steroids proved to be a major challenge to the dominance of the supplement industry. Initially synthesised by the pharmaceutical trade as an alternative to purified gonadal hormones, their legitimate therapeutic application has now been largely superseded by more sophisticated drugs. Their first use as a successful ergogenic supplement was by the medal-winning post-war Russian Olympic weightlifting team. In response to the chemical enhancement of the Eastern-Bloc nations the United States Olympic team physician Dr John Ziegler worked with CIBA pharmaceuticals to develop the most widely-used anabolic steroid of the 20th century: Dianabol (methandrostenolone), licensed by the US Food and Drug Administration in 1958 and administered to US athletes. The bodybuilding community were quick to become off-label users of this and other derivative drugs.

Fuelled by anabolic steroids bodybuilders were now able to make gains in muscle mass far superior to those previously possible with the traditional dietary supplements of Weider and his contemporaries. In an attempt to preserve their prolific source of income the bodybuilding media sought to discredit the efficacy and safety profile of steroids whilst continuing the deception that the expanding physiques of the top bodybuilders were founded upon revolutionary breakthroughs in the science behind protein powders and other "natural" products.

In the United States anabolic steroids were belatedly criminalised under the Anabolic Steroid Control Act of 1990. Those caught in possession of steroids for the purposes of personal athletic or cosmetic enhancement now faced arrest and prosecution. By this time the prevalence and dosage regimes of steroid use amongst men lifting weights had grown enormously and prior to their ruling US Congressional hearings considered reports of an "epidemic" of abuse of such drugs by high-school students (Buckley, Yesalis, Friedl *et al*, 1988).

This important legislative move left many bodybuilders craving the anabolism of their previous steroid habit but now unable or unwilling to acquire their fix. This was a prime marketing opportunity for the supplement companies who stepped in with an enormous range of "natural" products that promised steroid-like gains. Popular "anabolic enhancers" of this period included dibencozide, derived from the B12 family of vitamins, gamma oryzanol, an ester extracted during the processing of rice bran oil, and chromium picolinate, a trace element linked to the regulation of glucose tolerance (Barron & Vanscoy, 1993).

In an attempt to circumvent the prohibition of anabolic steroids the supplement industry developed and marketed "prohormones". Precursors of anabolic hormones, once ingested these compounds are converted from an inactive substrate to an active anabolic agent by normal metabolic pathways. In this way, it was claimed, bodybuilders could gain access to the mass-building power of anabolic steroids, but without the negative legal implications. Androstenedione was the first prohormone to be marketed; it achieved widespread notoriety in the late nineties after being used by several leading American sporting stars. As time progressed manufacturers discovered that they could create more powerful products by bypassing the process of metabolic conversion altogether and releasing supplements that already contained active forms of testosterone. This was tantamount to creating new oral anabolic steroids; consequentially all existing prohormones were added to the updated United States Anabolic Steroid Control Act of 2004.

The professional bodybuilders of today continue to use intramuscular anabolic steroids in prolific quantities as part of a sophisticated doping regime that has expanded to include other mass-inducing injectables such as insulin and recombinant growth hormone. Other illicitly procured drugs such as ephedrine, clenbuterol and thyroxine are employed to stimulate fat-loss during the "cutting" phase. The muscularity of the contestants in the Mr Olympia contest has progressed year on year to reach a previously unprecedented current zenith of size and definition.

The pharmaceutically engineered physiques of these contemporary bodybuilders are still pictured on the pages of bodybuilding magazines cheerfully promoting the modern non-pharmaceutical wares of the supplement industry. The endorsement of the professional bodybuilder is clearly designed to furnish the unwitting reader with the impression that a particular supplement's proprietary mixture of exotic herbs or unusual minerals is the key to unlocking the secret of enormous growth.

The analysis and commentary that follows will primarily focus on those nutritional adjuncts that can be legally purchased through bodybuilding magazines, health-food stores, gymnasia and Internet retailers. The spectrum of ergogenic products available to the modern bodybuilder will be quantified and assertions of potency assessed against existing evidence. The unrealistic steroid-based bodybuilding physique deceptively promoted by the supplement industry will be linked to the development of an emerging body image disorder in men known as muscle dysmorphia.

THE PREVALENCE OF SUPPLEMENTATION AMONGST BODYBUILDERS

Very little published material formally assesses the use of dietary supplements by bodybuilders. The pattern of supplementation amongst a small sample of competitive bodybuilders was analysed in a detailed survey (Brill & Keane, 1994). Almost 60 percent of bodybuilders spent a considerable sum of money on supplements every month ($25-$100) with a small number (5 percent) spending over $150. The type of supplement used was dependent on the sex of the bodybuilder and the phase of the training cycle. Male bodybuilders in a bulking phase were most likely to use protein powders whilst female bodybuilders in a cutting phase were most likely to use fat burners. Another more recent study (Morrison, Gizis & Shorter, 2004) sampled regular users of a New York gym in an attempt to determine the extent of and rationale for supplement use. A majority of gym users took supplements (84.7%). The authors found that younger men were most likely to take supplements such as protein powder, ephedra and creatine in an attempt to build muscle.

Several pieces of circumstantial evidence also point to the widespread use of supplements by those seeking to augment their sporting performance or physical development. There has always been a wealth of supplements on offer to the fitness enthusiast from a cornucopia of producers and suppliers, which can be easily obtained through magazines, the Internet, at gyms or at one of many high-street health stores. Even supermarkets and convenience stores are beginning to stock a range of sports supplements. The burgeoning market in sports supplements is necessarily dependent upon an appropriately sized demand from consumers, although the proportion of true bodybuilders amongst this population is uncertain.

AN EDUCATION IN SUPPLEMENTATION

Experienced bodybuilders in the gym have traditionally been a reliable resource for the young man seeking to develop his musculature. This may take the form of demonstrating a lifting technique, or providing nutritional advice. Supplementation may also be discussed in this context, which most often takes the form of an anecdotal account where n equals the bodybuilder in question. Many experienced bodybuilders will have used anabolic steroids in addition to basic food supplements and may use such discussion to encourage participation in steroid use.

In the pre-Internet age, direct marketing of supplements was confined to bodybuilding or fitness magazines. Today, many supplements are sold directly through Internet retailers rather than through mail order or health stores. The online bodybuilding community has grown in accordance with the rise in popularity of the sport; on the message boards of Internet chat rooms its devotees can discuss any aspect of the lifestyle, from training plans to steroid use. In this online environment, users can evaluate supplements directly alongside advertisements placed by retailers.

LEGALLY AVAILABLE NUTRITIONAL SUPPLEMENTS

Very little scientific attention has been devoted to the range of supplements that are legally available to the contemporary bodybuilder. Over 15 years ago a survey of 12 popular American health and fitness magazines identified advertisements for 311 individual products (Philen, Ortiz, Auerbach & Falk, 1992). The purported health benefits of each preparation were classified according to the claims made in the promotional copy. No effect whatsoever was listed for 90 (28.9%) of the 311 products, with the most frequently marketed outcome being muscle growth in 59 (19.0%) of the advertisements. From each of these advertisements data was also collected on each supplement's specific constituent ingredients. Amongst 311 products, 914 ingredients were listed, of which the most frequently mentioned were unspecified amino acids. Over a fifth (22.2%) of the products listed no ingredients whatsoever, one product claimed to contain the prescription medicine levodopa (with no information on dosage or side-effects) and several products declared the presence of glandular material (such as neonatal pituitary hypothalamus concentrate) without indicating the origin of such matter. Where dosage information was given, it mostly pertained to items that had no established recommended daily allowance (RDA). However, one folic acid product suggested a dose twenty-five times that of the United States RDA.

Grunewald and Bailey (1993) contacted 37 companies that had placed advertisements in issues of 5 popular bodybuilding magazines. The companies responded with literature describing the products that each produced and marketed. A list of 624 supplements was compiled. The authors found that many products were accompanied by more than one performance-related claim – collectively over 800 were generated amongst the 624 products. In a similar fashion to the study of Philen *et al*, the most frequently asserted benefit of supplement use was muscle gain. One third of all supplements were represented by only 3 categories: amino acids, vitamin preparations and protein powders.

SUPPLEMENTATION AND SCIENTIFIC EVIDENCE

The supplement industry is eager to convince consumers that its products have been developed by means of breakthroughs in scientific research. Some magazine advertisements even feature distinguished-looking physicians in white coats posing next to microscopes in the laboratory. The text of promotional literature is littered with pseudoscientific jargon such as "nanomolecular dispersion", "dynamic nutrient transport", "anti-catabolic technology", and "musclebuilding matrix".

At the same time as Philen et al's analysis of supplement advertisements, an evaluation of 19 popular natural products marketed for enhanced athletic prowess contrasted manufacturers' claims about potency with existing scientific evidence (Barron & Vanscoy, 1993). The results of this study were insightful. In 8 of these 19 products the alleged benefits were completely unsubstantiated by the biomedical literature. In a further 6 cases, animal or human data was used in a misleading or inappropriate fashion to support disingenuous conclusions. In 1 case the theoretical advantage of the supplement was founded on data from animal studies with no direct link to human use for ergogenic purposes. Only 4 of the 19 products could boast any scientific support from human trials. In their survey of commercially marketed supplements for bodybuilders, Grunewald & Bailey also evaluated the purported performance claims for 20 different categories of supplement. In a similar fashion to Barron & Vanscoy, the authors found that many of these claims were questionable when existing scientific evidence was examined.

Yet supplement companies earnestly press their scientific credentials upon unwitting consumers. There are several means by which scientific data can be misrepresented to produce an illusion of evidence.

- Inappropriately link the normal biological functions of compounds to the sphere of athletic performance.
- Inappropriately connect the benefits of rectifying deficiency to improving performance with supplementation.
- Inappropriately extrapolate data from animal studies directly to human bodybuilders.

Several examples of such erroneous marketing are detailed below.

Desiccated Liver

Extracting erroneous conclusions from scientific date is not a novel phenomenon; the archetypal example of such a process occurred over 50 years ago. In one experiment laboratory rats were placed into a drum of cold water from which they could not escape. Those rats fed with a supplementary diet of desiccated liver swam for longer than those fed on a normal laboratory diet alone or fed with a supplementary diet of B vitamins (Ershoff, 1951). These results were used to promote desiccated liver tablets as an endurance-boosting supplement and they became one of the most popular ergogenic aids of the era. Although they are no longer ubiquitous in the pages of bodybuilding magazines, having been overtaken by more fashionable (and expensive) products, their muscle building and energising properties are still publicised through health stores and Internet websites.

Chromium

Advertisements in the bodybuilding media sell market chromium as an anabolic activator for strength athletes, encouraging growth hormone release and increasing muscle uptake of amino acids via promotion of insulin activity. In reality, chromium is an essential trace element found in foods. It plays a critical role in carbohydrate metabolism through its function as a component of glucose tolerance factor. Rats with induced non-insulin dependent diabetes have been reported to exhibit improved glucose tolerance after ingestion of chromium (Govindaraju, Ramasami & Ramaswamy, 1989). Evidence also suggests that chromium administration decreases serum cholesterol and lipoprotein levels in human subjects (Press, Geller & Evans, 1990). Some athletes that restrict their weight may suffer from dietary-related chromium deficiency, but this is highly unlikely in the bodybuilder who is encouraged to maintain a high calorific intake to support muscle synthesis. Clearly, such data clearly do not directly substantiate the claims of the supplement industry that chromium supplementation translates to an increase in muscle mass. In fact, well-controlled studies evaluating the effect of chromium supplementation in strength training athletes have shown no benefit in terms of increased lean body mass, with excess chromium merely being excreted in the urine (Clancy, Clarkson, DeCheke *et al*, 1994).

Protein Powders

One of the most well-established nutritional supplements, protein powders are re-constituted with water or milk and provide the bodybuilder with up to 40 grams of protein per serving. Different powders contain different blends of amino acids, are broken down at differing rates and some are mixed with carbohydrates to provide extra calories. They are marketed as a convenient means to increase total intake of protein, thereby providing fatigued muscles with the essential building blocks for growth. Bodybuilders are encouraged to take several servings of protein per day, especially before and after exercise, to ensure that their bodies remain persistently primed for anabolism.

Weightlifters and bodybuilders do require more protein than their sedentary counterparts to maintain a positive nitrogen balance – an increase from 0.8 g of protein per kg per day to 1.4 – 1.8 g is recommended by some authorities, with novice strength athletes needing a higher protein intake than experienced weightlifters (Lemon, 1995). Such a moderate increase in daily protein requirements can be met from typical dietary sources, with most athletes already increasing their calorific intake to support the demands of exercise. Interestingly, increasing protein intake above these levels, despite the claims of the supplement industry, does not increase whole body protein synthesis but merely increases amino acid oxidation – i.e. intake exceeds that necessary for growth (Tarnopolsky, Atkinson, MacDougall *et al*, 1992).

BODYBUILDERS AND SCIENTIFIC EVIDENCE

Why do bodybuilders continue to use nutritional supplements despite poor evidence of efficacy? A bodybuilder desperately seeking gains in size, strength or leanness is unlikely to apply the rigorous methodology of the scientist to the analysis of the evidence base for ergogenic supplementation. In truth, the scanty data on supplementation seems to foster a culture of self-experimentation amongst bodybuilders: naturalistic case-reports of self-administered dosage regimes abound on the forums of bodybuilding websites and in the changing rooms of gymnasia. Unravelling disingenuous marketing strategies is complex, requiring an appreciation of scientific methodology and a critical mindset. The bodybuilder therefore places less emphasis on dry scientific literature and more on the anecdotal reports of trusted gym users and the seductive messages of supplement companies.

However much bodybuilders may enjoy experimentation, they do not think like scientists. The randomised-controlled trials of the clinician are designed to identify substances that increase the performance of a majority of athletes most of the time. The physician therefore counsels against supplement use because of a lack of firm evidence of benefit. The bodybuilder, however, is of a different mindset: as long as there is no firm evidence of a *lack of benefit* he is prepared to trial supplements in the hope of eventually discovering a product that produces tangible results.

Supplement use is expensive; bodybuilders may expend a sizeable portion of their income solely on "basic" products such as protein powders. But such is the price of getting big: fundamentally, as any committed athlete, a determined bodybuilder wishes to succeed in his sport. Nutritional supplements may be taken as insurance against possible deficiency; it is better to ingest an excess of protein than to risk losing muscle because of a negative nitrogen balance.

MARKETING STRATEGIES OF THE SUPPLEMENT INDUSTRY – A SUMMARY

In conclusion, the marketing strategies of the nutritional supplement industry are founded upon the fallacy that the average bodybuilder can also share the lean muscular physique of the superstars that grace the pages of its magazines. In reality, developing such an enormous physique necessitates the use of prodigious quantities of anabolic steroids, yet relatively ineffectual nutritional supplements are promoted as an essential tool in the arsenal of the growing bodybuilder. Pseudoscientific jargon and distorted clinical data create an illusion of technical credibility, whereas a measured analysis of the evidence quickly refutes many of these disingenuous claims. The range of products available to the unwitting consumer is vast and many a gullible customer will be left out of pocket with little demonstrable benefit. More importantly, a growing body of evidence suggests that there exists a subset of young men who may be particularly vulnerable to these misleading promotional tactics. The connection between bodybuilding and the rise of muscle dysmorphia is discussed in the next section.

BODYBUILDING AND MUSCLE DYSMORPHIA

Bodybuilding itself is not an unwholesome endeavour. Most bodybuilders develop a healthy body through an enjoyable exercise routine and a nutritionally balanced diet. A rise in physicality often parallels a rise in self-esteem and may improve the body image of participants (Pickett, Lewis & Cash, 2005).

However, just as women have long-been recognised to suffer with body image-related anxieties, evidence suggests that increasing numbers of young men are also becoming dissatisfied with their appearance. The nature of this dissatisfaction is not a desire for smaller and slimmer bodies, as is most often the case in women, but rather larger and more muscular ones (Pope, Gruber, Mangweth *et al*, 2000).

Clinical Features

Muscle dysmorphia is an emerging body image disturbance that primarily affects men and entails a pathological preoccupation with overall muscularity and leanness. It was first described in a population of American male bodybuilders (Pope, Katz & Hudson, 1993). These men were dissatisfied with their appearance despite being highly muscular. They declined social invitations in favour of working out and refused to be seen at the beach in anything but baggy clothes. Pope and his colleagues subsequently coined the term muscle dysmorphia and proposed a set of operational diagnostic criteria, categorising the phenomenon as a subtype of body dysmorphic disorder (Pope, Gruber, Choi, Olivardia & Phillips, 1997). Afflicted individuals erroneously believe themselves to be inadequately small and weak, expressing a desire to gain muscle without gaining fat. Characteristic associated behaviours include long hours of lifting weights and excessive attention to diet at the expense of social and occupational activities. Concern about physical inadequacy produces significant distress, functional impairment and may drive the bodybuilder to train through injury or experiment with harmful performance-enhancing drugs.

Prevalence

The prevalence of muscle dysmorphia is difficult to estimate. Pope claims that up to 10 percent of the bodybuilders he has studied exhibit prominent symptoms of muscle dysmorphia and that the total number of males of all ages in the USA who have used anabolic steroids may exceed 2 million (Pope, Phillips & Olivardia, 2000). Amongst a population of bodybuilders, some may not meet the formal criteria for muscle dysmorphia but may still be affected by body image concerns that cause them significant levels of distress. Conversely, many bodybuilders displaying severely pathological behaviour, even those abusing anabolic steroids, may feel that their activities are simply part of a healthy lifestyle and will not present to health services.

Classification as an Eating Disorder

Although now provisionally grouped with body dysmorphic disorder, Pope and his colleagues originally labelled muscle dysmorphia "reverse anorexia". This was based upon the prevalence of past anorexia nervosa and the similarity in body-related concerns and behaviours amongst the original population of bodybuilders to men that suffered from eating disorders. Individuals with anorexia nervosa and with muscle dysmorphia both demonstrate a specific maladaptive pattern of behaviour, namely an obsessive drive to exercise and to restrict their diet. Both disorders value leanness and demonise adiposity. In this way the distinctive cognitions and rigorous lifestyle of the obsessive bodybuilder in his pursuit of bigness parallel the phenomenology of the man with an eating disorder in his pursuit of thinness. If the core psychopathology in anorexia nervosa is over-evaluation of eating, shape and weight, a similar over-evaluation occurs in muscle dysmorphia, but in a different direction. This author contends, therefore, that muscle dysmorphia is a novel expression of an eating disorder in males (Mosley, 2009). This is consistent with a trans-diagnostic view of the eating disorders that considers individual manifestations such as anorexia or bulimia nervosa as one single entity, with substantial migration of patients between diagnoses over time but overall stability of the concept of disordered eating (Milos, Spindler, Schnyder & Fairburn, 2005).

SEPARATING BODYBUILDING FROM MUSCLE DYSMORPHIA

Case studies suggest that muscle dysmorphia is almost always found in individuals heavily involved in bodybuilding rather than simple weightlifting. (Lantz, Rhea & Cornelius, 2002). As the prime motivation of bodybuilding is to become bigger and leaner, one must wonder if it is possible to distinguish between a healthy enthusiasm for bodybuilding and muscle dysmorphia given that the underlying rationale for both is the same. It is difficult to separate the two populations in a formal study without introducing a tautological selection bias, but one study claims that individuals with muscle dysmorphia differ from normal bodybuilders on the basis of measures such as body dissatisfaction, eating attitudes, prevalence of anabolic steroid use and lifetime prevalence of DSM-IV mood, anxiety and eating disorders (Olivardia, Pope & Hudson, 2000). In other words, bodybuilders who display an ordinary level of dedication to their sport do not experience the profound body image disturbance, subjective distress and impaired functioning reported by individuals with frank muscle dysmorphia. It is crucial to distinguish those men for whom bodybuilding represents a tool for self-improvement from men for whom it has become a manifestation of a pathological obsession with body shape.

LINKING BODYBUILDING TO MUSCLE DYSMORPHIA

Increasing numbers of men are emulating the bodybuilding lifestyle in an attempt to change their body shape. If this sport does not itself produce a disturbance of body image, eating and exercise, it seems to at least facilitate the emergence of muscle dysmorphia as a new clinical manifestation of an underlying pathology shared with the traditional eating disorders.

Men are now confronted with social pressures to conform to a superficial stereotype of the ideal male, a tension that has traditionally been associated with femininity. The contemporary media suggests that the steroid-enhanced, lean, muscular physique embodies not only the healthy lifestyle to which males should aspire, but also the minimum physical standard that men are expected to attain. The modern child plays with action figurines that portray heroes whose bodies have become implausibly muscled over the years (Pope, Olivardia, Gruber & Borowiecki, 1999). Just as semi-naked females have long been used to sell everyday products, the stripped male torso is now a ubiquitous advertising tool (Pope, Olivardia, Borowiecki & Cohane, 2001). This unfeasible external manifestation of masculinity is likely to leave many young men feeling inadequate about the muscularity of their own bodies; some turn to bodybuilding in an attempt to put on size. A minority of men are constitutionally predisposed to developing an eating disorder and are at risk of a frank disturbance of body image such as that seen in muscle dysmorphia.

LINKING THE SUPPLEMENT INDUSTRY TO MUSCLE DYSMORPHIA

The aggressive advertising of the supplement industry may also be a factor in the rise of muscle dysmorphia amongst young men. The supplement industry employs the outlandish figure of the professional bodybuilder to target insecurities in the body image of the modern male. As these men persist in their struggle to develop a hypermasculine body they turn to nutritional supplements for anticipated steroid-like gains in size and strength. Ultimately, these products are over-hyped and ineffective. The futility of this endeavour is likely to worsen the pathological behaviour of the male at risk of muscle dysmorphia, who may now experiment with anabolic steroids as a means to obtain his desired physique.

Supplement manufacturers recommend that their products be consumed in precise and complicated dosage regimes. Some supplements should be taken 30 minutes prior to exercise, others immediately after a workout and others before sleep. Some compounds should be ingested throughout the day. Sticking to these intricate schedules generates behavioural rigidity and may worsen pathological behaviour in the obsessive bodybuilder.

MEDICAL COMPLICATIONS

The discussion thus far has centred upon the psychological risks posed by nutritional supplementation in bodybuilding. What remains unmentioned, however, is that all supplement users are potentially exposing themselves to physical and psychiatric ill health: a hazard that remains at present poorly defined. Two examples are detailed below.

Ephedrine

Ephedrine is a sympathomimetic amine derived from the Ephedra genus of plants. The purified alkaloid or its herbal precursor is often mixed with caffeine and used by bodybuilders as a weight loss aid, by virtue of its stimulant and appetite suppressant properties. It is also a component of decongestant remedies and is used in traditional Chinese medicine for the treatment of asthma and bronchitis. After a series of adverse events associated with the administration of either ephedrine or herbal ephedra for ergogenic purposes the United States Department of Health and Human Services commissioned a meta-analysis investigating the efficacy and safety profile of this supplement (Shekelle, Hardy, Morton *et al*, 2003).

As regards efficacy, the authors concluded that there was evidence to support ephedrine / ephedra as a promoter of weight loss. However, only a modest amount of weight was lost in the short term: approximately 0.9 kg per month above that lost with placebo over a duration of approximately 4 months. There was insufficient data to draw any conclusions about whether this weight loss was maintained beyond 6 months, which is one of the standard criteria for the evaluation of weight loss products. By contrast, approved pharmacotherapeutic weight loss agents such as orlistat or silbutramine show losses of up to 4.5 kg per month over placebo in controlled trials. These losses continue for up to 12 months.

As regards safety, the authors analysed safety data from clinical trials and discovered that consumption of ephedrine / ephedra was associated with a 2 - 3 fold increase in the risk of developing signs of autonomic hyperactivity, upper gastrointestinal pain, palpitations and psychiatric symptoms. An additional evaluation of case reports identified 5 deaths, 5 myocardial infarctions, 11 cerebrovascular events, 4 seizures and 8 psychiatric cases as sentinel events associated with prior ephedrine / ephedra consumption. Half of these events occurred in patients 30 years old or younger, raising the possibility of a causal link between ephedrine / ephedra consumption and serious adverse effects.

The fallout from this meta-analysis led the United States Food and Drug Administration to prohibit any marketing of ephedrine alkaloids for reasons other than for asthma, colds, allergies, other disease, or use in traditional Asian medicine. In the United Kingdom, ephedrine has always been and remains a prescription only medicine. Bodybuilders are now therefore unable to legally obtain ephedrine as a component of over the counter "fat burners" but its illicit administration remains commonplace amongst bodybuilders who still "stack" the drug with caffeine and often aspirin. It is unclear whether bodybuilders are unaware of the risks associated with this drug or whether they still continue to use ephedrine in spite of these risks because they value short term weight loss over long term health.

Creatine

Creatine is a nitrogenous organic acid found abundantly in vertebrate skeletal muscle. It functions as a carrier and donor of phosphate groups, which are essential to the generation of energy at the cellular level. Natural creatine functions as a short-term energy store for working muscles and creatine levels are considered the limiting factor in short, high-intensity activities. Strenuous bursts of exercise such as sprinting can exhaust creatine supplies in several seconds. Aerobic recovery time regenerates phosphorylated creatine to allow further bursts of activity.

Approximately half of the total body creatine store is synthesised endogenously by the liver, pancreas and kidney from the amino acids arginine, glycine and methionine. The remainder is acquired from dietary sources, principally meat and fish. Supplementation with oral creatine can increase total body creatine levels.

Many athletes ingest creatine in powder or capsule form in an attempt to saturate skeletal muscle stores and thereby increase power, speed or strength during high-intensity brief bursts of exercise. Bodybuilders also document a rapid increase in total body mass and muscle size after supplementation with creatine. Although various *in vitro* (Ingwall, Weiner, Morales, Davis & Stockdale, 1974) and histochemical (Olsen, Aagaard, Kadi *et* al, 2006) work has suggested that creatine can stimulate increased muscle synthesis, a large proportion of these gains in weight and size are thought to be due to an increase in intramuscular water retention due to an increased osmotic creatine load.

Common side effects of creatine ingestion include gastrointestinal bloating and muscle cramping but such occurrences are anecdotal and transient. Case reports have described cholestatic hepatitis (Whitt, Ward, Deniz *et al*, 2008) and acute renal failure (Thorsteinsdottir, Grande & Garovic, 2006) in bodybuilders supplementing with creatine. Of course such evidence is only suggestive and cannot definitively establish any causal relationship between creatine ingestion and deleterious sequelae. Although short-term studies of renal and liver function in small groups of athletes have been reassuring (Poortmans & Francaux, 2000), well controlled studies investigating the adverse effects of long-term creatine supplementation are sparse and none have followed subjects for over 5 years. Controlled scientific studies do not take account of the propensity of bodybuilders to exceed recommended dosages in an attempt to maximise ergogenic benefit – in one case report a bodybuilder precipitated acute renal failure after continuing to self-administer the "loading dose" of creatine for four weeks (Yoshizumi & Tsourounis, 2004).

Summary

From a medical perspective, very little data is available on the long-term sequelae of supplement ingestion or on the recommended safe daily dosages of many of the ingredients championed in supplement preparations. Scant attention is given towards warnings of potential side effects and little mention is made of potential contraindications such as pregnancy or heart disease. Paradoxically, although fitness enthusiasts often employ supplements for their perceived pharmaceutical properties, they are less likely to declare these supplements to a physician eliciting a drug history. The reasons for this are unclear. Perhaps consumers do not consider supplements to be drugs in the medical sense, or perhaps users fear disapproval from the medical profession.

Health professionals should routinely enquire about supplement use during a medical history and should consider the potential mental and physical ill effects posed by supplement use. Adverse reactions to supplements should be reported to public health authorities in an attempt to quantify the level of risk. Bodybuilders are essentially unwitting participants in long-term, uncontrolled toxicity studies.

CURRENT REGULATION

In a consensus statement, the American Dietetic Association, Dieticians of Canada and the American College of Sports Medicine (2000) concluded that "supplements may be required by athletes who restrict energy intake, use severe weight-loss practices, eliminate one or more food groups from their diet, or consume high-carbohydrate diets with low micronutrient density. Nutritional ergogenic aids should be used with caution, and only after careful evaluation of the product for safety, efficacy, potency, and whether or not it is a banned or illegal substance."

In the United States, the existing regulatory framework mitigates against such a careful evaluation. The Dietary Supplement Health and Education Act (DSHEA) of 1994 established that nutritional supplements should be classified as foods rather than drugs. Food supplements are thus subject to some regulation by the Food and Drug Administration (FDA) but escape the level of scrutiny applied to prescription medications and over the counter drugs. At the time this was hailed as a victory for consumer freedom but may instead reflect a successful lobbying campaign on the part of the supplement industry (Gupta, 2004).

Under the provisions of DSHEA, manufacturers of dietary supplements are not required to provide evidence of efficacy or safety prior to marketing the product – any outlandish claim can be put forward as long as an accompanying disclaimer is included. In order to initiate regulatory action against a nutritional supplement, the FDA must demonstrate that the product is unsafe. Fontanarosa, Rennie & DeAngelis (2003) discuss the hazards of this "postmarketing" regulatory framework in relation to the safety data on ephedra and ephedrine.

The European Union (EU) directive 2002/46/EC harmonised EU legislation on nutritional supplements with the aim of protecting consumer safety. This regulatory framework introduced a "positive list" of specific vitamins and minerals that may be included in food supplements together with a list of their chemical equivalents. In the United Kingdom, the directive survived a legal challenge in the European Court of Justice brought by the supplement industry, who argued that a move to outlaw many of their longstanding products was neither proportionate nor justified.

Supplements that do not meet with these compositional requirements were to have been prohibited from sale in the EU from 1st August 2005. However, in order to grant supplement manufacturers the opportunity to make a case for inclusion of their preparations on the positive list, this date was extended until 31st December 2009, provided an appropriate scientific dossier supporting the safety and bioavailability of each individual substance had been submitted to the European Commission by 12th June 2005.

In a response to a parliamentary question in July 2006, the United Kingdom Minister for Health stated that 421 dossiers had been submitted to the European Food Safety Authority, the agency tasked with determining the safety of food supplements under the directive. Clearly this agency faces an immense bureaucratic, scientific and ethical burden. It must set limits for the safe levels of vitamins, balancing the need to protect the public with the desire to preserve consumer freedom. The long-term effects of this regulatory framework are unclear. The supplement industry in many EU member states is still marketing food supplements that have not undergone an appropriate safety evaluation.

Conclusions

In this chapter I have provided an overview of the sport of bodybuilding and charted the rise of the nutritional supplement industry as increasing numbers of young men seek to change their body shape by adding muscle and decreasing fat. An enormous range of different products can be legally purchased by the aspiring bodybuilder, but most are similar both in their marketed claims to maximise muscle growth and their objective fallibility when reliable scientific evidence is examined. Supplement manufacturers not only distort existing scientific data to support the potency of their preparations but also use the images of steroid-laden bodybuilders to promote their wares, giving the impression that such physiques can be realistically achieved by the average male. These tactics contribute to the pressure on men to conform to a hypermasculine ideal and may worsen the pathological behaviour of a subset of vulnerable bodybuilders. Such men may go on to develop muscle dysmorphia, a new expression of eating disorders in males, which is facilitated by the sport of bodybuilding. Some supplements can also be detrimental to physical health and current regulations are still inadequate to control for these risks.

Future work and updates of previous scientific enquiry are therefore required:

- What range of nutritional supplements is available to the contemporary bodybuilder? Are there any new products in vogue? Are the products of fifteen years previous still marketed? Does muscle growth remain the most heavily advertised benefit?
- What is the current prevalence and pattern of supplement use amongst bodybuilders? What are the characteristics of men that supplement? Are these men more likely to go on to develop muscle dysmorphia?
- Are there any long-term physical or mental consequences of heavy supplementation?
- Is there a role for more intrusive regulation of nutritional supplements and their promotion? Should this be at the expense of consumer freedom?

There is a paucity of up to date literature on these topics. As bodybuilding continues to grow in popularity and as muscle dysmorphia emerges as a clinical entity, it is likely that these questions will become more pertinent.

References

The American Dietetic Association, Dieticians of Canada & the American College of Sports Medicine. (2000*). Position of the American Dietetic Association, Dieticians of Canada, and the American College of Sports Medicine: Nutrition and Athletic Performance.* Journal of the American Dietetic Association, 100: 1543-1556.

Barron, R.L., & Vanscoy, G.J. (1993). *Natural Products and the Athlete: Facts and Folklore.* The Annals of Pharmacotherapy, 27: 607-615.

Brill, J.B., & Keane, M.W. (1994). *Supplementation patterns of competitive male and female bodybuilders.* International Journal of Sports Nutrition, 4: 398–412.

Buckley, W.E., Yesalis, C.E. III, Friedl, K.E., Anderson, W.A., Streit, A.L. & Wright, J.E. (1988). *Estimated prevalence of anabolic steroid use among male high school seniors.* Journal of the American Medical Association, 260: 3441-3445.

Clancy, S.P., Clarkson, P.M., DeCheke, M.E., Nosaka, K., Freedson, P.S., Cunningham, J.J. & Valentine, B. (1994). *Effects of chromium picolinate supplementation on body composition, strength and urinary chromium loss in football players.* International Journal of Sports Nutrition, 4: 142-153.

Ershoff, B.H. (1951). *Beneficial Effect of Liver Feeding on Swimming Capacity of Rats in Cold Water.* Proceedings of the Society for Experimental Biology and Medicine, 77: 488-491.

Fontanarosa, P.B., Rennie, D. & DeAngelis, C.D. (2003). *The Need for Regulation of Dietary Supplements – Lessons From Ephedra.* Journal of the American Medical Association, 289: 1568-1570.

Govindaraju, K., Ramasami, T. & Ramaswamy, D. (1989). *Chromium(III)-Insulin Derivatives and Their Implication in Glucose Metabolism.* Journal of Inorganic Biochemistry, 35: 137-147.

Grunewald, K.K. & Bailey, R.S. (1993). *Commercially Marketed Supplements for Bodybuilding Athletes.* Sports Medicine, 15: 90-103.

Gupta, S. (2004). *Beyond Ephedra.* TIME Magazine. January 12th 2004. Time Inc.

Ingwall, J.S., Weiner, C.D., Morales, M.F., Davis, E. & Stockdale, F.E. (1974). *Specificity of creatine in the control of muscle protein synthesis.* Journal of Cell Biology, 62: 145-151.

Lantz, C.D., Rhea, D.J. & Cornelius, A.E. (2002). *Muscle dysmorphia in elite-level power lifters and bodybuilders: a test of differences within a conceptual model.* Journal of Strength and Conditioning Research, 16: 649-655.

Lemon, P.W. (1995*). Do athletes need more dietary protein and amino acids?* International Journal of Sports Nutrition, 5: S39-61.

Milos, G., Spindler, A., Schnyder, U. & Fairburn, C.G. (2005). *Instability of eating disorder diagnoses: prospective study.* British Journal of Psychiatry, 187: 573-578.

Morrison, L.J., Grizis, F. & Shorter, B. (2004). *Prevalent use of dietary supplements among people who exercise at a commercial gym.* International Journal of Sports Nutrition and Exercise Metabolism, 14: 481–492.

Mosley, P.E. (2009). *Bigorexia: Bodybuilding and Muscle Dysmorphia.* European Eating Disorders Review, 17: 191-198.

Olivardia, R., Pope, H.G. Jr. & Hudson, J.I. (2000). *Muscle dysmorphia in male weightlifters: a case-control study.* American Journal of Psychiatry, 157: 1291-1296.

Olsen, S., Aagaard, P., Kadi, F., Tufekovic, G., Verney, J., Olesen, J.L., Suetta, C. & Kjaer, M. (2006). *Creatine supplementation augments the increase in satellite cell and myonuclei number in human skeletal muscle induced by strength training.* Journal of Physiology, 573: 525-534.

Pickett, T.C., Lewis, R.J. & Cash, T.F. (2005). *Men, muscles, and body image: comparisons of competitive bodybuilders, weight trainers, and athletically active controls.* British Journal of Sports Medicine, 39: 217-222.

Philen, R.M., Ortiz, D.I., Auerbach, S.B. & Falk, H. (1992). *Survey of Advertising for Nutritional Supplements in Health and Bodybuilding Magazines.* Journal of the American Medical Association, 268: 1008-1011.

Pope, H.G. Jr., Gruber, A.J., Choi, P., Olivardia, R. & Phillips, K.A. (1997). *Muscle dysmorphia. An under-recognised form of body dysmorphic disorder.* Psychosomatics, 38: 548-557.

Pope, H.G. Jr., Gruber, A.J., Mangweth, B., Bureau, B., deCol, C., Jouvent, R. & Hudson, J.I. (2000). *Body image perception among men in three countries.* American Journal of Psychiatry, 157: 1297-1301.

Pope, H.G. Jr., Katz, D.L. & Hudson, J.I. (1993). *Anorexia nervosa and "reverse anorexia" among 108 male bodybuilders.* Comprehensive Psychiatry, 34: 406-409.

Pope, H.G. Jr., Olivardia, R., Borowiecki, J.J. III & Cohane, G.H. (2001). *The growing commercial value of the male body: a longitudinal survey of advertising in women's magazines.* Psychotherapy and Psychosomatics, 70: 189-192.

Pope, H.G. Jr., Olivardia, R., Gruber, A. & Borowiecki, J. (1999). *Evolving ideals of male body image as seen through action toys.* International Journal of Eating Disorders, 26: 65-72.

Pope, H.G. Jr., Phillips, K.A. & Olivardia, R. (2000). *The Adonis Complex*: The Secret Crisis of Male Body Obsession. New York: Free Press.

Poortmans, J.R. & Francaux, M. (2000). *Adverse effects of creatine supplementation: fact or fiction?* Sports Medicine, 30: 155-170.

Press, R.I., Geller, J. & Evans, G.W. (1990). *The effect of chromium picolinate on serum cholesterol and apolipoprotein fractions in human subjects.* Western Journal of Medicine, 152: 41-45.

Shekelle, P.G., Hardy, M.L., Morton, S.C., Maglione, M., Mojica, W.A., Suttorp, M.J., Rhodes, S.L., Jungvig, L. & Gagné, J. (2003). *Efficacy and safety of ephedra and ephedrine for weight loss and athletic performance: a meta-analysis.* Journal of the American Medical Association, 289: 1537-1545.

Tarnopolsky, M.A., Atkinson, S.A., MacDougall, J.D., Chesley, A., Phillips, S. & Schwarcz, H.P. (1992). *Evaluation of protein requirements for trained strength athletes.* Journal of Applied Physiology, 73: 1986-1995.

Thorsteinsdottir, B., Grande, J.P. & Garovic, V.D. (2006). *Acute renal failure in a young weight lifter taking multiple food supplements, including creatine monohydrate.* Journal of Renal Nutrition, 16: 341-345.

United Kingdom Parliament. (2006). *House of Commons Hansard Written Answers for 3rd July 2006* (pt 1405).

Whitt, K.N., Ward, S.C., Deniz, K., Liu, L., Odin, J.A. & Qin, L. (2008). *Cholestatic liver injury associated with whey protein and creatine supplements.* Seminars in Liver Disease, 28: 226-231.

Yoshizumi, W.M. & Tsourounis, C. (2004). *Effects of creatine supplementation on renal function.* Journal of Herbal Pharmacotherapy, 4: 1-7.

In: Handbook of Sports Psychology   ISBN: 978-1-60741-256-4
Editor: Calvin H. Chang   ©2009 Nova Science Publishers, Inc.

Chapter 8

THE IMPORTANCE OF INTERPERSONAL STYLE IN COMPETITIVE SPORT: A SELF-DETERMINATION THEORY APPROACH

Philip M. Wilson, J. Paige Gregson and Diane E. Mack*

Behavioural Health Sciences Research Lab, Department of Physical Education & Kinesiology, Faculty of Applied Health Sciences, Brock University, St Catharines, Ontario, L2S 3A1 Canada

ABSTRACT

Background: Research suggests that coach-athlete interactions with can be a stressful aspect of competitive sport (Horn, 2008). Perceptions of autonomy support, structure, and involvement have been advocated by Deci and Ryan (2002) within the framework of Self-Determination Theory (SDT) as key elements of interpersonal support during most interactions that can invoke adaptive (or debilitative) responses.

Purpose: The purpose of this study was (a) to review the evidence concerning the role of interpersonal support provided by coaches to athletes using SDT as a framework, and (b) test the psychometric properties of an instrument (Interpersonal Supportiveness Scale-Coach; ISS-C) designed to assess perceived autonomy support, structure, and involvement experienced by athletes from coaches.

Summary: The wealth of evidence suggests that interactions between competitive athletes and coaches have been examined mainly with reference to perceived autonomy support experienced by competitive athletes from their coaches. In comparison, substantially less evidence is available concerning the role of perceived structure and involvement as they relate to athlete-coach interactions within sport. Results of the psychometric analyses provide initial albeit limited support for the structural validity and internal consistency reliability of ISS-C responses although concerns regarding discriminant validity were evident. Overall, the results of this study suggest perceived

---

* Correspondence concerning this manuscript can be sent to: Philip M. Wilson, PhD, Department of Physical Education & Kinesiology, Faculty of Applied Health Sciences, Brock University, 500 Glenridge Avenue, St Catharines, Ontario, L2S 3A1, Canada. Tel: (905) 688-5550 Ext. 4997. Fax: (905) 688-8364. Email: phwilson@brocku.ca

structure and involvement could be assessed with the ISS-C in athletes and warrant consideration in future sport research embracing SDT as a conceptual approach.

Keywords: Instrumentation, Interpersonal Style, Construct Validity, Self-Determination Theory

INTRODUCTION

> "He is a very good communicator and can speak to the players in their own language. He is also very well organized. His team allies structure with individual talent." (Andy Roxborough [Union of European Football Associations (UEFA) Technical Director] describing the importance of José Mourihno to the playing staff at Chelsea Football Club)

Coaches represent a powerful socializing agent in the context of sport (Amorose, 2007). Anecdotal evidence supports the integral role played by coaches at a variety of levels ranging from youth sport to professional contexts. Empirical research has verified the impact that coaches can have on a range of factors linked with sport performance including motivation, training habits, and well-being (Horn, 2008). For example, research in youth sport has revealed that coaches who display an autocratic interpersonal style characterized by minimal feedback provided in a contingent fashion often stifle athlete development, increase propensity for burnout, and promote dropout across time (Gould, Udry, Tuffey, & Loehr, 1996; Pelletier, Fortier, Vallerand, & Brière, 2001). Complimentary evidence in high performance sport contexts implicates coaching style as a critical variable that can facilitate performance in Olympic caliber athletes and yield benefits to the coach in the context of optimizing athlete development (Mallett, 2005).

One theory that illustrates the importance of interactional styles from social agents such as coaches in sport contexts is Self-Determination Theory (SDT; Deci & Ryan, 2002; Mageau & Vallerand, 2003). SDT's guiding principles are organized around an organismic-dialectical framework whereby human organisms are naturally endowed with the capacity for personal growth, assimilation with the social world, and internalization of ambient norms and values into a coherent sense of self (Ryan & Deci, 2007). These innate capacities do not occur in a social vacuum and require appropriate 'inputs' (or supports) from the social context to nourish (or forestall) the development of human endeavors across contexts such as sport (Ryan & Deci, 2007).

Recent conceptual work has illustrated the importance of examining socio-contextual issues pertaining to coach's interactional style that may impact athlete development and sport performance (Mageau & Vallerand, 2003). Within the framework of SDT, Deci and Ryan (2002) advocate for the importance of understanding the role of autonomy support, structure, and involvement that characterize the interactional style of social agents (e.g., coaches) in the context of competitive sport settings. Autonomy support refers to the process of minimizing pressure to conform and offering a perception of choice and a sense of personal initiation regarding the behaviors undertaken (Deci & Ryan, 2002). The second element of interpersonal styles demarcated within SDT is structure which concerns the provision of suitable feedback towards goal progress and clarifying the outcomes to be expected from investment in the target behavior (Deci & Ryan, 2002). Finally, involvement concerns the ability to display a true interest in a person's well-being and acknowledge the difficult challenges they may be facing in contexts such as sport (Deci & Ryan, 2002).

The inherent appeal of distinguishing between different elements that comprise a particular coaching style for understanding motivational and developmental issues in athletes cannot be discounted. Horn (2008) notes, however, that relatively little is known about the role of perceived structure and involvement in comparison to autonomy support in sport contexts. Recent narrative reviews implicate the synergy between various dimensions of the coaches' interpersonal style as an important area warranting empirical attention to understand motivational processes in sport (Amorose, 2007; Mageau & Vallerand, 2003). Building upon previous conceptual work (Amorose, 2007; Horn, 2008; Mageau & Vallerand, 2003), the overall purpose of this investigation was two-fold. First, the status of research concerning the coaches' interpersonal style displayed in sport was examined using concepts drawn from SDT. In particular, this phase of the investigation conducted a review of existing research to determine the extent to which studies have examined the concepts of perceived autonomy support, structure, and involvement proposed by Deci and Ryan (2002) within sport. Second, a new instrument (Interpersonal Supportiveness Scale-Coach; ISS-C) modified from previous studies (Tobin, 2003; Williams, 2002) was tested to determine the degree to which perceptions of autonomy support, structure, and involvement from coaches can be assessed in competitive athletes.

STUDY 1

The purpose of study 1 was to review the literature examining coach-athlete interactions using SDT as a guiding framework to determine the evidence available regarding perceived autonomy support, structure, and involvement in sport contexts.

Method

Data Selection

Literature searches of available electronic databases (e.g., PsychInfo, SportDiscus, etc.) were completed using search terms (e.g., autonomy support, sport, coach, etc.) to identify studies for initial examination. Each key word was selected on the basis of theoretical considerations (Deci & Ryan, 2002) in an attempt to represent the focal constructs of interest to this study. Studies were retained for analysis on the basis of the following inclusion criteria: (a) Sampling frame was exclusive to athletes competing in sport; (b) Autonomy support, involvement, or structure were assessed in the study; (c) Data were reported in English; and (d) Items focused on perceptions of interpersonal support from the coach as opposed to other social agents (e.g., parents, athletes, etc.).

Data Coding

A detailed coding sheet was developed based on Cooper's (1982) recommendations to reduce ambiguity in the coding process. Two coders assessed all studies retained from the data selection process and coded each study independently before examining discrepant codes and reaching final consensus. As a final check on the coded data, one member of the research team who was not involved in the initial data selection or coding process reviewed fifty-percent of the studies coded to ensure consistency of data reported from each coder.

Results

Study Characteristics: Sixteen investigations were located resulting in 17 studies that met the inclusion criteria for further consideration (see Table 1). Most of the retained studies were published investigations (70.6%) with conference presentations (17.6%) and graduate dissertations (11.8%) comprising the remainder of the sample. One study used a quasi-experimental design while the remaining investigations (94.1%) were classified as non-experimental designs given that no variable manipulation was evident in the study protocol with reference to autonomy support, structure, or involvement per se. Four (23.5%) studies reported changes in interpersonal support constructs across time. All studies coded used a non-probability, purposive approach to sampling.

Participant Characteristics: Participants ranged in age across studies from 11.10 to 23.77 years (M_{age} = 17.61; SD_{age} = 3.88). Most of the studies used samples drawn from team-based (47.1%) rather than individual-based sports (17.6%) with less than a third of the studies using samples comprised of both team and individual sport athletes (29.4%). Athlete gender was reported in 88.2% of the investigations with the corpus of studies using samples comprised of both male and female athletes (70.9%). A small number of investigations (5.9%) used only male athletes. Ethnic origin was seldom reported (82.4%) with those investigations that did report ethnicity (17.6%) noting that the samples were of "mixed" ethnic origin

Instrumentation: Six different instruments in total were identified across the studies coded for this investigation. All instruments coded reported using context-specific item content (see Table 1). No single item instruments were identified in the studies coded for this investigation. Only 23.5% of the coded studies used instrumentation developed exclusively for use in sport contexts. The majority of studies coded (52.9%) restricted their focus to perceived autonomy support alone while 23.5 percent examined structure and involvement in conjunction with autonomy support. Two studies (c.f., Blanchard, Amiot, Perrault, Vallerand, & Provencher, in press; Pelletier et al., 2001) examined the degree to which athletes felt the coach emitted a controlling interpersonal style.[1] The focus of items was almost exclusively concerned with perceptions of supportiveness from coaches (88.2%) while two investigations (11.8%) included additional items addressing support from parents and fellow athletes as well as coaching staff. Items addressing sources of support in athletes beyond the coach were not considered within the analysis for this study.

Score psychometrics: Structural validity was tested in less than half of the coded studies (47.1%). Most of the coded studies (88.2%) tested score reliability using internal consistency estimates (Cronbach's α; Cronbach, 1951) and one study reporting stability coefficients across time using the intraclass correlation. Estimates of internal consistency reliability (see

---

[1] A controlling interpersonal style is a manner of interacting with people that stands in contrast to an autonomy-supportive approach (Deci & Ryan, 2002). For the purposes of this review, a controlling interpersonal style refers to the extent to which athletes' perceived their coach(s) to behave in a "coercive, pressurizing, authoritarian way" (Pelletier et al., 2001) such that they direct athletes to "behave in a way they think is right" (Blanchard et al., in press).

Table 1. Characteristics of studies measuring perceived autonomy support, structure, and/or involvement in competitive athletes.

Author(s)	N	M_{age}	Sample	Sport	Instrument	Reliability
Pelletier et al.	296	19.20	Mixed	Mixed	IBS	0.75-0.79
Pelletier et al.	369	15.60	Mixed	Individual	IBS	0.81-0.83
Guillett et al.	253	15.00	Female	Team	IBS	0.88
Gagné et al.	33	13.00	Female	Individual	CPPS	0.79-0.83
Reinboth et al.	265	16.44	-	Team	HCCQ	0.84
Whitehead et al.	135	20.17	Male	Team	SCQ	0.96
Cumming et al.	113	11.10	Mixed	Team	IBS	0.84
Whitehead et al.	240	-	Mixed	Mixed	SCQ	0.93
Smith et al.	213	21.02	Mixed	Mixed	HCCQ	0.93
Amorose & Anderson-Butcher	581	17.50	Mixed	Mixed	SCQ	*
Kabusch (study 2)	11	21.45	Mixed	Individual	IBS	-
Kabusch (study 3)	133	23.77	Mixed	Mixed	IBS	-
Conroy & Coatsworth	165	11.20	Mixed	Team	ASCQ	0.84
Adie et al.	539	22.75	Mixed	Team	HCCQ	0.85
Gregson & Wilson	104	19.92	Mixed	Team	ISS-C	0.74-0.90
Mouratidis et al.	202	15.62	-	-	-	0.83
Blanchard et al.	207	18.00	Mixed	Team	CPPS[†]	0.66

Note. N = Sample size reported for analysis. M_{age} = Mean age of sample reported within the study in years. Sample = Gender composition of the sample reported in the study (Male = male only sample; Female = female only sample; Mixed = male and female athletes sampled). Sport = Nature of the sport comprising the sample (Individual = athletes drawn from sports characterized as individual only; Team = athletes sampled from sports characterized as team-based sports only; Mixed = athletes sampled from sports characterized as either team-based or individual-based within the sample). Instrument = Name of the instrument used to assess coaching support factors in the study (HCCQ = Health Care Climate Questionnaire. SCQ = Sport Climate Questionnaire. CPPS = Children's Perceptions of Parents Scale. IBS = Interpersonal Behavior Scale. ASCQ = Autonomy Supportive Coaching Questionnaire. ISS-C = Interpersonal Supportiveness Scale-Coach). Reliability = Assessments of internal consistency reliability reported in study across all interpersonal support constructs drawn from SDT using Cronbach's (1951) coefficient alpha. - = Information was either (a) not presented or (b) not clear from the data presented within the manuscript. † Three items were adapted from the CPPS to quantify perceived controlling interpersonal coaching styles. * The reliability coefficients for particular subscales are not reported but a range of 0.70 to 0.96 is offered across responses from multiple constructs.

Table 1 for values and ranges) recorded in coded studies ranged across constructs from a lower bound of 0.66 to an upper bound of 0.96 respectively. On average, the estimates of internal consistency reliability for perceived autonomy support ($M_\alpha = 0.85$; $SD_\alpha = 0.08$; Range $= 0.69$-0.96; $n_{studies} = 11$) were slightly higher than structure ($M_\alpha = 0.83$; $SD_\alpha = 0.08$; Range $= 0.75$-0.90; $n_{studies} = 3$) which was in turn marginally higher than involvement ($M_\alpha = 0.81$; $SD_\alpha = 0.05$; Range $= 0.76$-0.88; $n_{studies} = 4$) and considerably higher than controlling interpersonal coaching styles ($M_\alpha = 0.75$; $SD_\alpha = 0.12$; Range $= 0.66$-0.83; $n_{studies} = 2$).

Summary of Study 1

The purpose of study 1 was to review evidence concerning perceived interpersonal coaching style using research embracing SDT as a guiding framework. On the basis of this review it appears that the bulk of the literature concerning coaches' interpersonal style has focused on perceived autonomy support more so than perceptions of structure, involvement, or feelings of coercive power emanating from the coaching staff. The emphasis on perceived autonomy support in the existing literature limits to a certain degree conclusions that can be drawn about the impact of coaches' interpersonal style in sport contexts and to a lesser extent limits understanding of SDT-based principles that could be of practical importance in sport contexts. Few studies have used sport-specific instruments and limited psychometric work appears to be evident in terms of structural validity issues integral to the process of construct validation (Messick, 1995).

STUDY 2

The purpose of study 2 was to evaluate the structural validity of responses to a new instrument (ISS-C) designed to measure perceptions of autonomy support, structure, and involvement experienced by athletes from the head coach in sport contexts.

Method

Participants

Participants were 64 male ($M_{age} = 20.52$ years; $SD = 1.74$ years) and 91 female ($M_{age} = 19.52$ years; $SD = 2.35$ years) athletes competing in 9 different sports within either the Canadian Interuniversity Sport (CIS) or the Ontario University Athletics (OUA) systems. On average, athletes indicated competing in CIS/OUA sport for between 1 and 6 years ($M = 2.08$ years; $SD = 1.19$ years). Self-reported training history varied across in-season ($M = 15.92$ hours/week; $SD = 5.59$ hours/week), off-season ($M = 8.78$ hours/week; $SD = 5.79$ hours/week), and pre-season ($M = 11.00$ hours/week; $SD = 6.34$ hours/week) time periods but did not differ as a function of athlete's gender (Wilk's $\Lambda = 0.97$, $F_{3,147} = 1.39$, partial $\eta^2 = 0.03$). Most of the athletes listed their status on their team as either a starter (40.4%) or non-starter (41.1%) with the remaining athletes (15.2%) reporting that their role as a starter varied and lacked stability.

Instruments

Demographics. Each athlete provided data concerning age, starting status, number of years spent playing their primary sport, ethnicity, gender, highest level of sport competition, and amount of time spent training across pre-season, in-season, and off-season periods.

Interpersonal Supportiveness Scale-Coach (ISS-C). Athletes completed 18 items that were adapted from two existing instruments for the present study. The items were designed to measure perceived autonomy support, structure, and involvement experienced in relation to the head coach of their sport. Six items were initially designed to assess each ISS-C dimension. Following a stem that contextualized each item (see Table 2), athletes provided responses using a 7-point Likert scale with verbal anchors at 1 (Not at all true), 4 (Somewhat true), and 7 (Very true). The autonomy support items were modified from the short-form of the Health Care Climate Questionnaire (HCCQ; Williams, Freedman, & Deci, 1998). The structure and involvement items were modified from Tobin's (2003) work on social-contextual influences on exercise motivation and behavior. The full complement of ISS-C items used in this study is presented in Table 2.

Table 2. Items used to measure interpersonal support from the head coach in the ISS-C.

Autonomy Support
I feel that my coach provides me with choices and options
I feel understood by my coach
My coach encourages me to ask questions
My coach listens to how I would like to do things
My coach tries to understand how I see things before suggesting a new way to do things
My coach conveys confidence in my ability to do well in sport
Structure
My coach makes it clear to me what I need to do to learn the skills and strategies of my sport
My coach gives me activities to perform that are suitable to my level
My coach makes it clear to me what to expect from engaging in training
My coach helps me feel confident about learning the skills and strategies of my sport
My coach makes sure I understand the best way to learn skills and strategies of my sport
My coach provides clear feedback about my progress
Involvement
My coach finds time to talk with me
My coach doesn't seem to think of me often (R)
My coach spends a lot of time with me
My coach is often disapproving and unaccepting of me (R)
My coach puts time and energy into helping me
My coach is not very involved with my concerns (R)

Note. These are the modified items included in the initial version of the ISS-C administered to all
athletes in phase 2 of this study. (R) = item weas reverse coded prior to subsequent data analyses.
The following stem preceeded the ISS-C items: "These questions are related to your expereinces
interacting with your head coach. Coaches have different styles in dealing with athletes, and we
would like to know more about how you have felt about your encounters with your head coach."

Procedures and Data Analyses

Athlete data was gathered via paper-and-pencil techniques in small-group settings (n = 102) and using a secure internet-based interface (n = 53). The same researchers were responsible for all data collection procedures which utilized standardized instructions in all test administrations to reduce potential biases inherent in data collection.

Data analyses proceeded in iterative stages. First, data were screened for conformity with distributional assumptions and presence of missing values. Second, the structural validity of ISS-C scores was tested using a 3-phase application of confirmatory factor analysis (CFA) advocated by Jöreskog (1993) and Hoffman (1995). Phase 1 tested 3 unidimensional models representing each subscale of the ISS-C to identify and eliminate problematic items. Phase 2 of the analysis examined all-possible 2-factor subsets of ISS-C subscales to identify conceptually ambiguous items and test discriminant validity by examining the 95% confidence interval around the point estimate of the correlation between the latent factors. All 2-factor latent measurement models were free to correlate in the analysis. Three models each comprised of two latent factors were tested in phase 2 of the analysis. Phase 3 tested the full 3-factor latent measurement model using the trimmed pool if ISS-C items retained from phases 1 and 2 respectively. Problematic ISS-C items were identified at each stage if they (a) exhibited low ($< |0.40|$) standardized loadings on their target latent factor, (b) displayed large ($> |2.00|$) residuals in the standardized matrix for each measurement model tested, or (c) contributed to modification indices suggestive of item ambiguity whereby improvements in model fit could be obtained if manifest items were loaded onto non-target latent factors of the ISS-C measurement model. Finally, descriptive statistics and reliability estimates (Cronbach's α; Cronbach, 1951) were estimated for the ISS-C responses.

Maximum Likelihood (ML) estimation was used in all CFA analyses given the utility of this estimator in small samples where the data typically deviate from normality (West, Finch, & Curran, 1995). Multiple indices of global model fit were used (Comparative Fit Index [CFI], Incremental Fit Index [IFI], Root Mean Square Error of Approximation [RMSEA], Standardized Root Mean Square Residual [SMRSR]) in combination with modification indices and individual parameter estimates to make evaluative decisions concerning the structural validity of ISS-C response. While the value of global model fit indices indicative of an acceptable fit between the sample data and a measurement model is debatable (c.f., Markland, 2007), values greater than 0.90 and 0.95 for the CFI and IFI are typically considered indicative of a tenable fit between the underlying measurement model and the observed data. Values not exceeding 0.08 for the RMSEA and 0.05 for the SRMSR were also used as markers of fit between the implied model and the observed ISS-C responses.

Results

Preliminary Data Screening

No more than 5.16 % of the data were missing on any manifest item with no out of range responses evident in the sample data and univariate distributions approximating normality (see Table 3). No discernible pattern was evident in the missing responses which on the basis of Little's (1988) test was deemed missing completely at random ($\chi^2 = 15.91$, $df = 17$, $p = 0.53$). All missing values were replaced using the expectation maximization algorithm. Mardia's coefficient (27.27) suggested considerable multivariate kurtosis was evident in the sample data.

Phase One: Single Scale CFA Measurement Models

Joint consideration of the pattern of standardized factor loadings, distribution of standardized residuals (z), and the global model fit indices (see Table 4) suggested no particular concerns with reference to the 6-item perceived autonomy support measurement model. Examination of the modification indices in conjunction with the pattern and magnitude of standardized residuals resulted in the removal of 1 structure and 2 involvement items. Following the removal of these ISS-C items, the pattern of global model fit indices and the moderate-to-strong standardized factor loadings per latent factor ($p < .05$ in all instances) in each measurement model supported the retention of 15 ISS-C items although it is noteworthy that the RMSEA point estimate and upper boundary of the 95% confidence interval are beyond the common threshold for each measurement model.

Table 3. Descriptive statistics for manifest items used in CFA analyses

Latent Subscales and item abbreviations	M	SD	Skew.	Kurt.
Perceived Autonomy Support				
Coach provides choices/options	4.86	1.49	-0.50	-0.14
Coach understands me	4.50	1.60	-0.17	-0.78
Coach is confident in my ability	5.10	1.42	-0.65	-0.11
Coach encourages questions	5.06	1.46	-0.52	-0.37
Coach listens to how I do things	4.21	1.68	-0.15	-0.74
Coach tries to understand my views	4.30	1.66	-0.06	-0.83
Perceived Structure				
Coach clarifies skills/strategies	5.24	1.47	-0.85	0.24
Coach gives me suitable activities	5.45	1.37	-0.79	0.20
Coach clarifies training expectations	5.53	1.36	-1.13	1.16
Coach instills confidence in me	5.07	1.39	-0.40	-0.51
Coach ensures skills/strategies clear	4.97	1.41	-0.29	-0.62
Coach provides clear feedback	4.41	1.76	-0.28	-0.82
Perceived Involvement				
Coach finds time to talk with me	4.75	1.87	-0.49	-0.96
Coach doesn't think of me often	4.62	1.58	-0.27	-0.74
Coach spends lots of time with me	3.46	1.49	0.40	-0.40
Coach disapproving/unaccepting	5.61	1.49	-1.04	0.12
Coach not involved with me	5.07	1.50	-0.33	-0.91
Coach puts in time/energy to help	4.90	1.42	-0.44	-0.54

Note. M = Mean. SD = Standard Deviation. Skew. = Univariate Skewness. Kurt. = Univariate Kurtosis.

Phase 2: Subscale Pair CFA Measurement Models

Examination of all possible 2-factor latent measurement models (see Table 4) resulted in the removal of 1 additional structure item from the pool of ISS-C items. This item was discarded on the basis of the large modification indices displayed which indicated a substantial improvement in model fit could be obtained if this item was allowed to load on the involvement factor. This item also exhibited a pattern of large standardized residuals ($z > |2.0|$) in comparison to the other elements in the matrix of standardized residuals. The pattern of global model fit indices and distribution of standardized residuals along with the moderate-to-strong factor loadings (see Table 4) for each pair of 2-factor latent measurement models suggested no additional items as candidates for elimination at this stage of the analysis.

Table 4. Global Model Fit Indices for CFA of ICC-S scores

Measurement Models	χ^2	df	p	CFI	IFI	RMSEA (90% CI)	SRMSR	M_λ
Single Factor Models								
Autonomy Support	19.22	9	< .05	0.98	0.98	0.09 (0.03-0.14)	0.03	0.74
Structure	29.17	9	< .01	0.97	0.97	0.12 (0.07-0.17)	0.04	0.81
Structure (Trimmed 5 item model)	22.85	5	<.01	0.97	0.97	0.15 (0.09-0.22)	0.03	0.83
Involvement	57.31	9	< .01	0.85	0.85	0.19 (0.14-0.23)	0.10	0.65
Involvement (Trimmed 4-item model)	1.49	2	>.05	1.00	1.00	0.00 (0.00-0.15)	0.02	0.72
Two-Factor Models								
Autonomy Support-Involvement	57.20	34	<.01	0.97	0.97	0.07 (0.03-0.10)	0.04	0.73
Autonomy Support-Structure	145.26	53	<.01	0.92	0.93	0.11 (0.09-0.13)	0.06	0.77
Structure-Involvement	77.22	26	<.01	0.94	0.94	0.11 (0.08-0.14)	0.05	0.77
Autonomy Support-Structure (Trimmed)	114.95	43	<.01	0.93	0.93	0.10 (0.08-0.13)	0.05	0.77
Structure-Involvement (Trimmed)	38.74	19	<.01	0.97	0.97	0.08 (0.04-0.12)	0.04	0.77
Full Measurement Model								
3 Factor, correlated model	146.46	74	<.01	0.95	0.95	0.08 (0.06-0.10)	0.05	0.76

Note: χ^2 = Chi-square test statistic. *df* = Degrees of freedom. *p* = Probability-value. *CFI* = Comparative Fit Index. *IFI* = Incremental Fit Index; *RMSEA* = Root Mean Square Error of Approximation. *90% CI* = 90 percent confidence interval around *RMSEA* point estimate. *SRMSR* = Standardized Root Mean Square Residual. λ = Standardized parameter loading of a manifest item on a latent factor (loadings ranged from 0.55 to 0.91 across measurement models). Trimmed refers to a reduced item model per CFA test run in sequential fashion starting with the single-factor models and encompassing all models tested through to the CFA of the full measurement model.

Phase 3: CFA of Trimmed Item, Full ISS-C Measurement Model

The global model fit indices observed in the CFA of the full 3-factor, correlated measurement model (see Table 4) suggested no grave areas of concern regarding the structural validity of the trimmed pool of ISS-C items in this sample. Inspection of the distribution of standardized residuals (0.0% $z > |2.00|$) in conjunction with the moderate-to-strong standardized factor loadings (see Table 4) provide evidence for the tenability of this measurement model in the sample data. Phi-coefficients (ϕ) revealed a pattern of strong inter-factor relationships (see Table 4). Bias-corrected 95% confidence intervals computed using bootstrapping procedures (n = 1000 samples with replacement) around each ϕ point estimate were as follows: (a) ϕ autonomy support-structure = 0.54-0.83; (b) ϕ autonomy support-involvement = 0.83-1.02; and (c) ϕ structure-involvement = 0.52-0.83 respectively.

Internal consistency reliability estimates (Cronbach, 1951) ranged from 0.81 to 0.90 across item-level responses within each ISS-C subscale (see Table 5). Athletes indicated they experienced greater perceptions of structure in comparison to autonomy support and involvement and less involvement compared with autonomy support from the head coach (Cohen's (1992) d values ranged from 0.40 to 1.37 respectively). Bivariate correlations (see Table 5) between ISS-C subscale scores were strong (i.e., Pearson $r_{12} \geq |0.50|$; Cohen, 1992).

Table 5. Descriptive Statistics, Internal Consistency Reliability, and Bivariate Correlations in Study 2

Variables	M	SD	Skew.	Kurt.	α	1	2	3
ISS-C Autonomy Support	4.67	1.22	-0.22	-0.37	0.88	-	0.71	0.94
ISS-C Structure	5.26	1.21	-0.66	0.06	0.90	0.65	-	0.69
ISS-C Involvement	4.43	1.27	-0.06	-0.53	0.81	0.79	0.57	-

Note. ISS-C = Interpersonal Supportiveness Scale-Coach. M = Mean. SD = Standard Deviation. Skew. = Univariate Skewness. Kurt. = Univariate Kurtosis. α = Cronbach's Coefficient alpha (Cronbach, 1951). Correlations in the lower diagonal of the matrix (Pearson r's) are based on pairwise comparisons with equivalent sample sizes across each element in the matrix. Phi-coefficients are presented in the upper diagonal of the matrix from the CFA of the full measurement model detailed in Table 4.

Summary of Study 2

The purpose of study 2 was to test the structural validity and reliability of scores derived from the ISS-C in a sample of competitive athletes. Overall, the results of this study provide mixed support for the psychometric integrity of the final ISS-C measurement model. Estimates of reliability suggest minimal evidence of measurement error in the ISS-C item scores retained from the iterative CFA model testing approach embraced in this study. The resultant ISS-C measurement model is largely consistent with interpretations derived from SDT given the pattern of relationships evident between perceived autonomy support, structure, and involvement. Notwithstanding these positive observations, it is hard to provide omnibus support for the ISS-C given (a) the loss of four of the original 18 items in the iterative CFA model testing, and (b) the considerable degree of statistical overlap evident between perceived autonomy support and involvement in the full, 3-factor ISS-C measurement model.

DISCUSSION

The overall purpose of this study was to (a) review the SDT-based evidence concerning the assessment of perceived autonomy, structure, and involvement with specific reference to coaches, and (b) examine the psychometric properties of scores derived from an instrument adapted from the work of Tobin (2003) in exercise settings and Williams et al. (1998) in health care contexts to capture the degree to which athletes feel that their coaches provide support for their own decision making (i.e., autonomy support), feedback regarding their progress (i.e., structure), and interact with them in a manner that conveys a genuine sense for their worth and well-being (i.e., involvement). Overall, the results of study 1 suggest that perceived autonomy support appears to be the dominant interpersonal style concept assessed with reference to the coach in applications of SDT in sport. The results of study 2 imply that the assessment of both perceived structure and involvement alongside autonomy support seems plausible although additional work pertaining to issues of construct validation concerning the ISS-C appears justified at this juncture.

WHAT DO WE KNOW ABOUT PERCEIVED AUTONOMY SUPPORT, STRUCTURE, AND INVOLVEMENT FROM COACHES IN SPORT?

The observations derived from study 1 provide a synopsis of the current state of research concerning the perceived interpersonal style attributed to coaches in sport contexts from the standpoint of Deci and Ryan's (2002) SDT framework. A number of interesting points from study 1 seem worthy of note and offer a platform for the development of additional lines of research on coaching using SDT. First, it seems clear that the focal point of previous SDT-based research in sport examining coaches' interpersonal styles has centered largely on the concept of perceived autonomy support. This focus mirrors the development of research concerning interpersonal support using SDT in other physical activity contexts (c.f., Edmunds, Ntouamnis, & Duda, 2008) and the broader SDT literature outside of sport and exercise settings (c.f., Deci & Ryan, 2008). One plausible reason for this focus on perceived autonomy support concerns the availability of instrumentation (i.e., the long and short form of the Climate Questionnaires) that appears both versatile and useful in terms of capturing the degree to which social agents such as sport coaches provide support for personal autonomy. In line with previous reviews of the coaching literature in sport (Amorose, 2007; Mageau & Vallerand, 2003) and the SDT framework (Deci & Ryan, 2002), it seems reasonable to suggest that a broader array of dimensions including perceptions of both structure and involvement combined with autonomy support comprise the nature of effective interpersonal styles displayed by coaches in sport contexts. The extent to which these components of a coaches' interpersonal style interact with one another in a synergistic fashion to facilitate the development of motivation and ultimately effect performance in sport contexts remains an area ripe for additional inquiry (Amorose, 2007; Mageau & Vallerand, 2003).

A second noteworthy observation derived from study 1 concerns the nature of instrument development research within the framework of SDT concerned with coaches' interpersonal style in sport contexts. Less than twenty-five percent of the instrumentation used in the research studies comprising the sample for study 1 employed a sport-specific tool to measure interpersonal style dimensions. Such observations are not entirely inconsistent with the development of literature in related areas of self-perception research (c.f., Fox & Wilson, 2008; Wilson, Mack, Gunnell, Oster, & Gregson, 2008) whereby initial lines of evidence develop using instrumentation that is adapted from other contexts. It also seems evident that limited attention has been afforded the assessment of structural validity in previous investigations concerning coaches' interpersonal style in competitive sport. The lack of a rigorous and systematic approach to construct validation and instrument development in this area is surprising and worthy of additional inquiry (c.f. Amorose, 2007; Messick, 1995).

One final noteworthy issue evident from the results of study 1 concerns the scope of the available evidence concerning interpersonal styles perceived by athletes in relation to coaches in sport contexts. The results of study 1 suggest that research examining coaches' interpersonal style in sport has been limited in terms of the sampling frames utilized and the assessment of variability in perceived interpersonal styles exhibited by coaches across time. Inspection of the data presented in Table 1 implies that the focus of previous investigations appears to be largely concerned with either youth sport contexts (43.8% of the coded studies included athletes aged ≤ 16.0 years) or young adults at the time of data collection. The extent to which dimensions of interpersonal style characterized by perceived autonomy support, structure, and involvement are relevant to, and representative of, effective coaching behaviors in other athletic cohorts (e.g., master-level athletes) remains open to speculation and future research. It is also interesting to note that relatively few studies examined variation over time in perceived interpersonal styles exhibited by the coaching staff in the context of sport. Coaches' interpersonal styles are not likely to remain stagnant across the competitive season and likely respond to performance (e.g., win:loss records) and contextual variation (e.g., stage of competitive season, nature of the opponent, athletes' characteristics, etc.). The extent to which variability (or stability) in dimensions of perceived interpersonal styles exhibited by coaches impacts athletes' indices of psychological need satisfaction, motivation, and well-being would appear to be a logical step for additional research in this area.

The results of study 2 provide mixed support for the ISS-C as an instrument to measure perceived autonomy support, structure, and involvement experienced by athletes from their head coaches. Reliability estimates from this sample of Canadian athletes indicate that the ISS-C items retained in the final model produce scores containing minimal error variance which is helpful in establishing patterns of relationships with important consequences of coach-athlete interactions (Amorose, 2007; Horn, 2008; Mageau & Vallerand, 2003). Combined with the omnibus indices of model fit displayed in Table 4 that support the tenability of the 3 factor ISS-C measurement model, it seems reasonable to suggest that the instrument holds promise as a starting point to advance the assessment of interpersonal style dimensions attributable to coaches with specific reference to the concepts of structure and involvement in line with SDT.

Consideration of the final measurement model retained for the ISS-C presents at least two areas of concern with reference to the instrument. The iterative approach to model testing utilized in study 2 resulted in the elimination of two ISS-C items each designed originally to measure perceived structure ('My coach makes it clear to me what I need to do to learn the skills and strategies of my sport'; 'My coach provides clear feedback about my progress') or perceived involvement ('My coach is often disapproving and unaccepting of me'; 'My coach is not very involved in my concerns'). While the removal of these ISS-C items resulted in a better fitting model in study 2, it raises questions concerning the degree to which the remaining ISS-C items represent the full conceptual bandwidth of perceived structure and involvement from coaches in line with the conceptual boundaries for each concept outlined by Deci and Ryan (2002). Two of the original ISS-C items could have been problematic based issues of technical quality pertaining to item length or the double-barreled nature of each item that can affect comprehension due to lack of focus within the item (c.f., Crocker & Algina, 1986; Streiner & Norman, 2008). The other ISS-C items may have been interpreted as overly vague with reference to issues of 'progress' and 'concerns' from the athletes that could extend beyond the confines of competitive sport (e.g., progress in university or concerns over grades that impact eligibility). Future research would do well to examine the relevance and representation inherent in all ISS-C items using the procedures advocated by Dunn and colleagues (Dunn, Bouffard, & Rogers, 1999).

An additional concern with reference to the final ISS-C measurement model concerns the degree of statistical overlap evident between dimensions of coaches' interpersonal style particularly in terms of the relationship between perceptions of autonomy support and involvement. Inspection of the matrix of correlations presented in Table 5 suggests that these dimensions of coaches' interpersonal style share considerable overlap with one another (i.e., at least 62.41% common variance). The magnitude of this statistical overlap combined with the evidence indicating that the 95% bias-corrected confidence interval encompasses unity in this sample of Canadian-based athletes suggests it is difficult to conclude that the dimensions of perceived autonomy support and involvement measured by the ISS-C are sufficiently divergent from one another to claim they are a congeneric in nature. Given that comparable observations have been reported elsewhere (Kabush, 2007), it seems reasonable to suggest in line with Tobin (2003) that the assessment of perceived autonomy support and involvement with the ISS-C items lacks distinction in terms of domain clarity that is an important component of the instrument development process (Crocker & Algina, 1986; Streiner & Norman, 2008). Previous research supports the importance of testing item content relevance and representation empirically in the context of instrument development (Crocker & Algina, 1986; Dunn et al., 1999) and such an approach seems like a logical step for research concerning the ISS-C and the assessment of perceived interpersonal style dimensions in physical activity settings outside of sport where motivation is an important issue (c.f., Wilson, Mack, & Grattan, 2008).

LIMITATIONS AND SUMMARY REFLECTIONS

While the results of this multi-part study are insightful and theoretically informative, a number of limitations should be acknowledged and future directions conferred to advance coaching research using SDT. First, the focus of study 1 concerned the context of sport and the target of coaching staff whilst excluding other physical activity contexts and potential socializing agents that warrant attention. Second, no empirical analyses were undertaken with the evidence reviewed in study 1. Sufficient studies appear available in terms of the evidence-base concerning perceived autonomy support to consider more empirically-driven methods such as meta-analysis to understand the effects of socio-contextual supports on motivational issues in competitive athletes. Third, the data collected in study 2 relied on intact groups from a restricted range of CIS-based sports that were assessed on a single occasion. This approach limits the external validity attributable to the interpretations made with reference to the ISS-C as an instrument for assessing SDT-based constructs in sport and restricted the range of psychometric issues that were tested in study 2. Future studies would do well to collect data from more diverse samples of athletes representing multiple levels (e.g., recreational, professional) and sport types (e.g., team vs. individual) on multiple occasions to address issues of stability and change evident in scores derived from the ISS-C. Finally, a restricted range of psychometric issues were examined in study 2 with reference to ISS-C scores. Future research may wish to examine relationships between concepts measured by the ISS-C and other variables drawn from SDT's nomological network (Cronbach & Meehl, 1955) to identify the extent to which the scores from the ISS-C can be interpreted with confidence in the context of competitive sport.

In summary, the overall purpose of this study was to (a) examine the status of the literature concerning applications of SDT to study perceived interpersonal styles exhibited by coaches in sport contexts, and (b) explore the feasibility of a new instrument designed on the basis of previous research by Tobin (2003) and Williams et al. (1998) to assess perceptions of interpersonal style attributable to coaches in sport. It seems apparent from the results of study 1 that the focal point of previous sport research concerning interpersonal styles has centered on autonomy support with limited attention focused on the process of instrument development and evaluation. The results of study 2 indicate that the ISS-C may be a useful instrument for the assessment of dimensions of perceived interpersonal style from the coach in competitive athletes. Such an observation should be tempered with caution prior to additional research examining a broader range of construct validation issues with reference to the ISS-C and additional studies investigating the congeneric nature of the perceived autonomy support and involvement factors. The ISS-C represents an initial attempt to measure perceptions of structure and involvement alongside perceived autonomy support experienced by competitive athletes in sport setting with reference to coaches. Given the importance of coach-athlete interactions to player development and sport performance additional studies using SDT to guide concept and instrument development appear justified.

References[*]

Adie, J. W., Duda, J. L., & Ntouamnis, N. (2008). *Autonomy support, basic need satisfaction, and the optimal functioning of adult male and female sport participants*: A test of basic needs theory. Motivation & Emotion, 32, 189-199.[†]

Amorose, A. J. (2007). *Coaching effectiveness: Exploring the relationship between coaching behavior and self-determined motivation.* In M. S. Hagger & N. L. D. Chatzisarantis (Eds.), Intrinsic motivation and self-determination in exercise and sport (pp. 209-228). Champaign, IL: Human Kinetics.

Amorose, A. J., & Anderson-Butcher, D. (2007). *Autonomy-supportive coaching and self-determined motivation in high school and college athletes*: A test of self-determination theory. Psychology of Sport & Exercise, 8, 654-670.[†]

Blanchard, C. M., Amiot, C. A., Perrault, S., Vallerand, R. J., & Provencher, P. (in press). *Cohesiveness, coach's interpersonal style, and psychological needs: Their effects on self-determination and athletes' subjective well-being.* Psychology of Sport & Exercise. [†]

Cohen, J. (1992). *A power primer.* Psychological Bulletin, 112, 155-159.

Conroy, D. E., & Coatsworth, J. D. (2007). *Assessing autonomy-supportive coaching strategies in youth sport.* Psychology of Sport & Exercise, 8, 671-684.[†]

Cooper, H. (1982). *Scientific guidelines for conducting integrative research reviews.* Review of Educational Research, 52, 291-302.

Crocker, L., & Algina, J. (1986). *Introduction to classical and modern test theory*. Fort Worth, TX: Harcourt Brace Jovanovich College Publishers.

Cronbach, L. J. (1951). *Coefficient alpha and the internal structure of tests*. Psychometrika, 16, 297-234.

Cronbach, L. J., & Meehl, P. E. (1955). *Construct validity in psychological tests*. Psychological Bulletin, 52, 281-303.

Cumming, S. P., Battista, R. A., Standage, M., Ewing, M. E., & Malina, R. M. (2006). *Estimated maturity status and perceptions of adult autonomy support in youth soccer players*. Journal of Sport Sciences, 24, 1039-1046.[†]

Deci, E. L., & Ryan, R. M. (2008). *Facilitating optimal motivation and psychological well-being across life's domains*. Canadian Psychology, 49, 14-23.

Deci, E. L., & Ryan, R. M. (2002). *Handbook of self-determination research*. Rochester, NY: University of Rochester Press.

Dunn, J. G. H., Bouffard, M., & Rogers, W. T. (1999). *Assessing item content-relevance in sport psychology scale-construction research: Issues and recommendations*. Measurement in Physical Education & Exercise Science, 3, 15-36.

Edmunds, J., Ntouamnis, N., & Duda, J. L. (2008). *Testing a self-determination theory-based teaching style intervention in the exercise domain*. European Journal of Social Psychology, 38, 375-388.

Fox, K. R., & Wilson, P. M. (2008). *Self-perceptual systems and physical activity*. In T. S. Horn (Ed.), Advances in sport psychology (3rd Edition) (pp. 49-64). Champaign, IL: Human Kinetics.

Gagné, M., Ryan, R. M., & Bargmann, K. (2003). *Autonomy support and need satisfaction in the motivation and well-being of gymnasts*. Journal of Applied Sport Psychology, 15, 372-390.[†]

Gould, D., Udry, E., Tuffey, S., & Loehr, J. (1996). *Burnout in competitive tennis players I: A quantitative assessment*. The Sport Psychologist, 10, 322-340.

Gregson, J. P., & Wilson, P. M. (2008*). Dimensions of perceived coaching style and athlete motivation: A self-determination theory perspective*. Journal of Sport & Exercise Psychology, 30, S173.[†]

Guillett, E., Sarrazin, P., Carpenter, P. J., Trouilloud, D., & Cury, F. (2002). *Predicting persistence or withdrawal in female handballers with social exchange theory*. International Journal of Psychology, 37, 92-104.[†]

Hoffman, R. (1995). *Establishing factor validity using variable reduction in confirmatory factor analysis*. Education & Psychological Measurement, 55, 572-582.

Horn, T. S. (2008). *Coaching effectiveness in the sport domain*. In T. S. Horn (Ed), Advances in sport psychology (3rd edition) (p. 239-268). Champaign, IL: Human Kinetics.

Jöreskog, K. G. (1993). *Testing structural equation models*. In K. A. Bollen & J. S. Logn (Eds.), Testing structural equation models (pp. 294-316). Newbury Park, CA: Sage.

Kabusch, D. (2007*). Investigating the impact of coach communication of training plans on athlete's motivation, perceptions of coach, training preparation, and daily planning*. Unpublished doctoral dissertation, University of Ottawa, Ottawa.[†]

Little, R. J. (1988). *A test of missing completely at random for multivariate data with missing values*. Journal of the American Statistical Association, 83, 1198-1202.

---

[*][†]Denotes research examined in study 1 of this investigation.

Mageau, G. A. & Vallerand, R. J. (2003). *The coach-athlete relationship: A motivational model.* ***Journal of Sports Science, 21,*** 883-904.

Mallett, C. (2005). *Self-determination theory: A case study of evidence-based coaching.* The Sport Psychologist, 19, 417-429.

Markland, D. (2007). *The golden rule is there are no golden rules: A comment on Paul Barrett's recommendations for reporting model fit indices in structural equation modeling.* Personality & Individual Differences, 42, 851-858.

Messick, S. (1995). *Validity of psychological assessment: Validation of inferences from persons' responses and performances as scientific inquiry into score meaning.* American Psychologist, 50, 741-749.

Mouratadis, M., Vansteenkiste, M., Lens, W., & Sideridis, G. (2008*). The motivating role of positive feedback in sport and physical education: Evidence for a motivational model.* Journal of Sport & Exercise Psychology, 30, 240-268.†

Pelletier, L. G., Fortier, M., S., Vallerand, R. J., & Brière, N. M. (2001*). Associations among perceived autonomy support, forms of self-regulation, and persistence: A prospective study.* Motivation & Emotion, 25, 279-306.[†]

Pelletier, L. G., Fortier, M. S., Vallerand, R. J., & Tuson, K. M. (1995). *Toward a new measure of intrinsic motivation, extrinsic motivation, and amotivation in sports: The Sport Motivation Scale (SMS).* Journal of Sport & Exercise Psychology, 17, 35-53.†

Reinboth, M., Duda, J. L., & Ntouamnis, N. (2004). *Dimensions of coaching behavior, need satisfaction, and the psychological and physical welfare of young athletes.* Motivation & Emotion, 28, 297-313.[†]

Ryan, R. M., & Deci, E. L. (2007). *Active human nature: Self-determination theory and the promotion and maintenance of sport, exercise, and health.* In M. S. Hagger & N. L. D. Chatzisarantis (Eds.), Intrinsic motivation and self-determination in exercise and sport (pp. 1-19). Champaign, IL: Human Kinetics.

Smith, A., Ntouamnis, N., & Duda, J. (2007). *Goal striving, goal attainment, and well-being: Adapting and testing the self-concordance model in sport.* Journal of Sport & Exercise Psychology, 29, 763-782.[†]

Streiner, D. L., & Norman, G. R. (2008). *Health measurement scales: A practical guide to their development and use* (4th Edition). Toronto, ON: Oxford University Press.

Tobin, V. J. (2003). *Facilitating exercise behavior change: A self-determination theory and motivational interviewing perspective.* Unpublished doctoral dissertation, University of Wales, Bangor.

West, S. G., Finch, J. F., & Curran, P. J. (1995). *Structural equation models with nonnormal variables: Problems and remedies.* In R. H. Hoyle (Ed.), Structural equation modeling: Concepts, issues, and applications (pp. 56-75). Thousand Oaks, CA: Sage.

Whitehead, J. R., Young, J., P., Brinkert, R. H., & Short, S. E. (2006). *Effects of scholarship status and coaching style on the motivation of Division II football players.* Medicine & Science in Sports & Exercise, 38, S226.[†]

Whitehead, J. R., Dornik, M., Wilson, P. M., Short, S. E., & Short, M. W. (2007). *The effects of social support on pain or injury treatment help-seeking in collegiate athletes.* Medicine & Sciences in Sports & Exercise, 39, S412.[†]

Williams, G. C. (2002). *Improving patients' health through supporting the autonomy of patients and providers.* In E. L. Deci & R. M. Ryan (Eds.), **Handbook of self-determination research** (pp. 233-254). Rochester, NY: University of Rochester Press.

Williams, G. C., Freedman, Z. R., & Deci, E. L. (1998). *Supporting autonomy to motivate glucose control in patients with diabetes.* Diabetes Care, 21, 1644-1651.

Wilson, P. M., Mack, D. E., & Grattan, K. P. (2008*). Understanding motivation for exercise: A self-determination theory perspective.* Canadian Psychology. 49, 250-256.

Wilson, P. M., Mack, D. E., Gunnell, K., Oster, K., & Gregson, J. P. (2008*). Analyzing the measurement of psychological need satisfaction in exercise contexts: Evidence, issues, and future directions.* In M. P. Simmons (Ed.), Sport and exercise psychology research advances (pp.361-391). Hauppauge, NY: Novapublishing.

AUTHOR'S NOTE

This study was supported in part by two grants from the Social Sciences and Humanities Research Council of Canada (SSHRC) awarded to the first and third authors. The data comprising study 2 were collected as a portion of an undergraduate honor's thesis completed by the second author under the supervision of the first author. The second author was supported by a Joseph M. Bombardier scholarship from SSHRC at the time of writing this manuscript.

In: Handbook of Sports Psychology
Editor: Calvin H. Chang

ISBN: 978-1-60741-256-4
©2009 Nova Science Publishers, Inc.

Chapter 9

PERFORMING UNDER PRESSURE: ATTENTIONAL CONTROL AND THE SUPPRESSION OF VISION IN BASKETBALL FREE-THROW SHOOTING

Mark R. Wilson[*1] *and Samuel J. Vine*[1]

University of Exeter, St. Luke's Campus, Exeter, UK[1]

ABSTRACT

The aim of this study was to test the predictions of attentional control theory (Eysenck et al., 2007) in a sporting environment. We adopted a basketball free-throw task and examined the gaze behavior of participants during the occlusion period (when the ball and arms block the target as the ball is raised). Previous research (Vickers, 1996) has shown that skilled performers fixate on the target early in the aiming phase (the quiet eye) but do not look towards the target when their hands and the ball enter their field of view. This attentional control strategy was termed the location suppression hypothesis by Vickers (1996) and it is suggested that such suppression of visual processing prevents interference from the moving hands and ball in the visual field, preserving the aiming commands derived from the quiet eye. Skilled players suppress their vision during the occlusion period by blinking or directing their gaze to other locations, rather than try to maintain a fixation on the occluded target. We propose that anxiety may alter this optimal strategy, as attentional control theory suggests that anxious individuals have less efficient *negative* attentional control and are less able to inhibit attentional capture from distracting stimuli.

Ten basketball players took free-throws in two counterbalanced experimental conditions designed to manipulate the anxiety they experienced. Point of gaze was measured using an ASL Mobile Eye tracker and gaze behavior during the occlusion period (including blinks, fixations to other locations and fixations to the ball) was determined using frame-by-frame analysis. The manipulation of anxiety resulted in significant reductions in suppressed vision and free-throw success rate, thus supporting the predictions of attentional control theory. Anxiety impaired goal directed attentional

---

[*]Person to whom all correspondence should be sent: Dr Mark Wilson, School of Sport and Health Sciences, University of Exeter, St. Luke's Campus, Exeter EX1 2LU, UK, Tel: +44 1392 262891, Fax: +44 1392 264726, Email: Mark.Wilson@ex.ac.uk

control (suppressed vision) at the expense of stimulus-driven control (longer duration of fixations to the ball and hands). The findings suggest that attentional control theory may be a useful theoretical framework for examining the relationship between anxiety and performance in visuomotor sport skills.

Keywords: Anxiety, quiet eye, location suppression, inhibition, visuomotor performance

INTRODUCTION

The ability to control attention and remain focused has frequently been discussed as a key component of successful sporting performance (e.g., Janelle, 2002; Moran, 1996; Orlick, 1990). Attention can be thought of as the cognitive system that facilitates the selection of some information for further processing while inhibiting other information from receiving further processing (Smith & Kosslyn, 2007). One aspect of this system is concentration, or the ability to focus effectively on the task at hand while ignoring distractions. However, what exactly should performers focus on in order to produce their best performances? Why might performers become distracted and 'lose' concentration in high-pressured environments? These questions have received considerable research interest over recent years, and this chapter aims to integrate research findings and theoretical developments from both fields. First, we will review research adopting 'point of gaze' recording as an objective measure of 'what' performers focus on in far aiming tasks, before reviewing contemporary theories pertaining to the influence of anxiety on attention.

AIMING, ATTENTION AND PERFORMANCE: THE QUIET EYE

Our understanding of what individuals attend to while performing sport skills has been greatly advanced by the development of light-weight and mobile gaze-tracking technology. Not only are we able to determine the specific cues which performers use to help them make decisions and prepare motor responses, but we can also assess the timing of when these cues are used in relation to the motor action being performed (Vickers, 2007). Many sports involve some form of aiming, whether it be throwing, kicking or striking an object to a player, target or goal. Unlike when aiming to a near target, the performer only has control over the object until the point of release when aiming to a far target (Vickers, 1996). Research examining far aiming tasks has identified the role of higher-order cognitive processing, whereby the visuomotor strategy is attuned to obtaining visual information to enable the pre-programming of the ensuing motor response (Williams, Singer & Frehlich, 2002). The findings from such research have shown that in order to be successful at aiming to a far target the final fixation made by the performer must not only be on the target, but also for long enough duration to ensure accuracy (Vickers & Williams, 2007).

This particular fixation has been termed the 'quiet eye' (QE; Vickers, 1996), and has been defined as the final fixation to a target before the initiation of the motor response. A number of studies have demonstrated that longer QE periods are indicative of superior performance in aiming tasks such as billiards (Williams et al., 2002); rifle shooting (Janelle et al., 2000); simulated archery (Behan & Wilson, 2008); golf putting (Vickers, 1992); and basketball free-throw shooting (Vickers, 1996). Vickers proposed that the QE is a period of time when task relevant environmental cues are processed and motor plans are coordinated for the successful completion of the upcoming task. Theoretically, longer QE periods therefore allow performers an extended duration of programming, while minimizing distraction from other environmental cues (Vickers, 1996; 2007).

Research investigating the QE has indicated that while the location and duration of the final fixation is an important indicator of performance in aiming tasks, the timing of the QE with relation to the movement phases of the skill may be equally as important (Behan & Wilson, 2008; Vickers, 2007). Vickers (2007) suggests that while it is important to know where to look and for how long, it may also be important to know *when* to look: Target information gained too early or too late may not lead to the same levels of accuracy. Indeed, research has demonstrated that early, as well as long QE periods, are related to better performance (see Vickers, 2007 for a review).

Vickers' (1996) original work in developing the concept of the QE period examined basketball free-throw shooting as a particularly interesting far-aiming task; one where the target is occluded for a period during the completion of the skill. Vickers found that skilled performers fixated on the target early in the aiming phase (early onset of QE) but did not look towards the target when their hands and the ball entered their field of view; despite the fact that this is the key propulsion phase of the shooting action (Vickers, 1996). These findings indicate that although the free throw was of long enough duration for visual feedback to impact the movement outcome, skilled performers had learned to suppress their vision, by blinking or moving their gaze freely during the shooting action. Vickers (1996) referred to this finding as the location suppression hypothesis (LSH) and suggested that such suppression of visual processing prevented interference from the moving hands and ball in the visual field, preserving the aiming commands derived from the QE.

Figure 1 presents exemplar eye-tracker data demonstrating the location suppression hypothesis in basketball free-throw shooting. The point of gaze is indicated in each frame by the small, red circular cursor, representing 1° visual angle. The other larger, magenta cursor visible in the scene is the 'background' presentation of the pupil and corneal reflection relative positions, used to calculate point of gaze.

Vickers' research has furthered our understanding of the attentional and visuomotor control structures underlying successful performance in the basketball free-throw. It is now possible to determine where and when attention should be directed in order to be most effective. Furthermore, Vickers has demonstrated that effective visual attention can be learned using a specially designed pre-shot routine. Indeed, Harle and Vickers (2001) developed such a QE training programme, focusing on an early QE onset and subsequent location suppression, which was taught to a group of female university basketball players. The authors found that QE training significantly improved the free-throw performance of the players in both a laboratory environment and during game-play over the subsequent two seasons.

The work of Vickers and colleagues has provided a useful objective measure of visual attentional control in far aiming tasks. However, as many sports performances occur under conditions of high levels of ego threat, sport psychologists need to understand how anxiety may influence attentional control and subsequent performance. As Janelle (2002) highlights; "Given the heavy reliance on visual input for decision making and response planning in sport tasks, logical questions concern whether and how visual attention is modified under increased anxiety" (p. 237). The following section introduces some attentional theories which provide mechanistic accounts of how anxiety may impact upon performance.

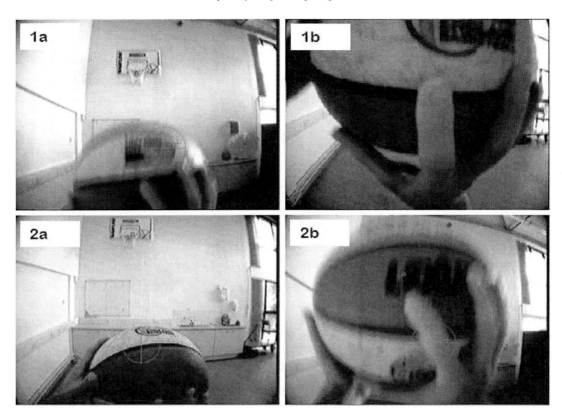

Figure 1. Four frames from the eye-tracker video file showing the point of gaze of a participant during the lift phase of two free-throws; one in the control and one in the high threat condition. In the control condition (top), a fixation on the net can be seen early in the lift phase as the ball starts to enter the visuomotor workspace (1a), followed by a blink (loss of 'magenta' pupil) during the occlusion period (1b). In the high threat condition (bottom), a similar early fixation on the hoop is evident (2a), followed by a fixation towards the target (at the ball) during the occlusion period (2b).

ANXIETY, ATTENTION AND PERFORMANCE

While Boutcher (2002) may have bemoaned the absence of frameworks by which to study the influence of attention on sport skills, recent advances in mainstream cognitive psychology have provided sport psychologists with a number of attentional theories related to the influence of *anxiety* on performance. Over the last 15 years or so, a number of these theoretical developments have been tested in sport environments, as summarized briefly below.

The conscious processing (reinvestment) hypothesis (CPH: Masters, 1992). The CPH argues that perceived pressure may cause the performer to focus disproportionally on the *process* of performance. The proposed mechanism of disruption is therefore the effortful allocation of attention to previously automated processes: Under pressure, "the individual begins thinking about how he or she is executing the skill, and endeavors to operate it with his or her explicit knowledge of its mechanics" (Masters, 1992, p.345). By 'reinvesting' in the knowledge base that supports performance, the fluency associated with expert performance is disrupted, causing performance to break down. The CPH is a form of self awareness theory (see Baumeister, 1984) which was developed specifically for sport and has received considerable support in the sport anxiety literature (see Masters & Maxwell, 2008 for a review on reinvestment in sport).

The theory of ironic mental processes (Wegner, 1994). Wegner's theory of ironic processing concerns the proposition that the instruction to avoid a thought or action may ironically increase the tendency to engage in this thought or action (Janelle, 1999). Wegner (1994) proposes that consciousness comprises of an intentional operating process and an ironic monitoring process. The ironic monitoring process is automatic and scans the contents of consciousness for any unwanted thoughts. The role of the controlled intentional process is to replace any unwanted thought with a more appropriate task-related one. When attentional resources are taxed, the controlled intentional process can be compromised resulting in the manifestation of unwanted thoughts. As a particular drain on attentional resources, the effects of anxiety on ironic processing effects have recently received support in aiming skills including football penalties (Bakker, Oudejans, Binsch, & Van der Kamp, 2006) and golf putting (Woodman & Davis, 2008).

Attentional narrowing (Cue utilization hypothesis; Easterbrook, 1959). One of the earliest and most influential models of attentional narrowing was developed by Easterbrook (1959). He postulated that arousal narrows attention, restricting the range of incidental cues that are used (i.e. the attentional field narrows). As a result, performance on central tasks will be facilitated at the expense of performance on peripheral tasks. Janelle, Singer and Williams (1999) found support for attentional narrowing effects due to heightened anxiety in an auto racing simulation, as participants were less successful at detecting peripherally presented targets when anxious, although central task performance was maintained.

Processing efficiency theory (PET; Eysenck & Calvo, 1992). PET predicts that cognitive anxiety, in the form of worry, has two main effects. Firstly a reduction in the processing and storage ability of the central executive of the working memory causes a reduction in the attentional resources available for the task at hand. Second, worry acts to motivate the performer, stimulating increases in on-task effort and auxiliary processing resources and strategies. This compensatory effort is aimed at maintaining performance at a desired level and serves to reduce, or eliminate, apprehension associated with worrisome thoughts related to the aversive consequences of poor performance (Eysenck & Calvo, 1992). The efficiency with which a performer processes information when anxious is therefore reduced, potentially leading to poorer performance (see Wilson, 2008 for a review of research testing PET in sport environments).

Attentional control theory (ACT; Eysenck, Derakshan, Santos & Calvo, 2007). ACT is an extension and development of PET which is more explicit about the influence of anxiety on attentional control than its predecessor. The authors relate the predicted impairment of attentional control to a disruption in the balance of two attentional systems first outlined by Corbetta and Schulman (2002); a goal-directed (top-down) attentional system and a stimulus-driven (bottom-up) attentional system. Generally, anxiety is associated with an increased influence of the stimulus-driven attentional system and a decreased influence of the goal-directed attentional system (Eysenck et al., 2007). One of ACT's primary predictions is that anxiety impairs the *inhibition* function of the central executive, which involves using attentional control to resist disruption or interference from task-irrelevant stimuli (Eysenck et al., 2007) This impairment in *negative* attentional control thereby hampers a performer's ability to resist intrusive internal (e.g. worrying cognitive intrusions), or external (visual), distractions (Wilson, 2008).

While all five theories have received support in the sport psychology literature and share a number of mechanisms, the current study aims to utilise ACT's explicit predictions regarding the way in which anxiety may impact upon *distractibility*. Vickers' conceptualization of QE and location suppression provides objective measures of effective attentional control with which to test ACT's predictions. Goal-directed control in the free-throw requires an early QE onset followed by suppressed vision as the ball and hands enter the performer's visual field and occlude the hoop. When anxious, this specific attentional control strategy may be impaired due to a greater influence of stimulus-driven attentional control processes.

INTEGRATING RESEARCH AREAS: IS THE QUIET EYE AFFECTED BY ANXIETY?

To date, there have only been three studies which have examined the influence of anxiety on the quiet eye period (Behan & Wilson, 2008; Vickers & Williams, 2007; Wilson, Vine & Wood, 2009). Vickers and Williams (2007) found that elite biathletes who maintained or increased their QE duration during high pressure competition, compared to low pressure practice, were less susceptible to sudden performance disruption or 'choking'. Of the ten participants tested, only 3 maintained their QE durations when anxious and these were the only participants to perform better in competition than practice. Behan and Wilson (2008), in a simulated archery task found that under conditions of elevated cognitive anxiety, QE durations were reduced, and performance impaired compared to a low pressure condition. Recently, Wilson, Vine et al. (2009) found that under high levels of cognitive anxiety, QE periods and subsequent performance were also significantly reduced in a basketball free throw task.

Wilson, Vine et al.'s (2009) study provides the back-drop to the current investigation, as the authors discussed their results in relation to Eysenck et al.'s (2007) ACT. When anxious, participants were unable to maintain their long QE durations despite the onset of the QE period being similar to when they were less anxious. Wilson et al. postulated that participants were less able to inhibit distracting thoughts, thus causing subsequent impairment of attentional control (as measured by QE duration). Instead of maintaining one aiming fixation to one location (QE), as they did under control conditions, anxious participants used significantly more fixations to a number of targets around the hoop. The authors were not able to clarify *how* worrisome thoughts might explicitly have impacted upon QE, except to reiterate Eysenck et al.'s (2007) postulation that internal distractions (worrying thoughts) become more salient when anxious. These threat-related stimuli are predicted to be preferentially processed at the expense of goal-directed processing, normally derived from the extended QE.

The objective of the current investigation is to re-examine the attentional control strategy of these performers, but with an emphasis on the occlusion period; when the ball and hands occlude the hoop. To date no research has examined if performers' ability to suppress their vision is impaired when anxious. The optimal (goal-directed) strategy of first directing an early fixation to one point on the front of the hoop, allowing for a long QE and, second, suppressing vision for the period when the ball and arms occlude the hoop (the location suppression hypothesis [LSH]; Vickers, 1996) may therefore be impaired. ACT (Eysenck et al, 2007) predicts that when anxious, individuals are less able to inhibit attentional capture from distracting stimuli, therefore, we propose that the greatest disruption to attentional control should occur during the occlusion period as opposed to disrupting the early onset of QE. Specifically, anxious participants are predicted to spend more time fixating on the ball and arms and use less suppression techniques (blinking and looking elsewhere) than they did in the control condition.

METHODS

Participants

Ten male basketball players from university teams (Mean age, 20.3 years, $SD = 0.9$) with 7.1 years of experience ($SD = 1.9$) volunteered to take part in the study. All players took free-throws for their teams during the current season (mean percentage accuracy, 64.6%, $SD = 9.91$). Participants attended individually and had the general nature of the study explained to them. Written information was provided and written consent was gained from all participants. Local ethics committee approval was obtained prior to the start of testing.

Apparatus

The free throws were taken from standard distance (i.e., 4.60 m) and to a hoop set at standard height (3.04m) from the ground. Gaze was measured using an Applied Science Laboratories (ASL; Bedford, MA) Mobile Eye tracker. This lightweight system measures eye-line of gaze at 25Hz, with respect to eye and scene cameras, mounted on a pair of glasses. The system works by detecting two features, the pupil and corneal reflection (determined by the reflection of an infrared light source from the surface of the cornea), in a video image of the eye. The relative position of these features is used to compute visual gaze with respect to the head-mounted optics.

The system incorporates a recording device (a modified DVCR) worn in a pouch around the waist and a laptop (Dell inspiron6400) installed with 'Eyevision' (ASL) recording software. A circular cursor, representing 1° of visual angle with a 4.5-mm lens, indicating the location of gaze in a video image of the scene (spatial accuracy of ± 0.5° visual angle; 0.1° precision) is viewed in real time on the laptop and recorded for offline analysis. The DVCR was linked to the laptop via a 10-meter fire wire cable, permitting near normal mobility for the participant. The experimenter and the laptop were located behind and to the right of the participant, to minimize distraction.

An externally positioned digital video camera (Canon, MDl01) was located 3 metres to the right of the participants, perpendicular to the direction in which they were shooting (i.e. sagittal plane). The view allowed the entire free-throw action of each participant to be captured for subsequent offline analyses.

Measures

State anxiety. State anxiety levels were measured prior to each block of 10 free throws using the Mental Readiness Form-Likert (MRF-L; Krane, 1994). The MRF-L was developed to be a shorter and more expedient alternative to the CSAI-2 (Martens, Burton, Vealey, Bump, & Smith, 1990), allowing anxiety to be reported during, as well as prior to performance. The MRF-L has three bipolar 11-point Likert scales that are anchored between *worried–not worried* for the cognitive anxiety scale, *tense–not tense* for the somatic anxiety scale, and *confident–not confident* for the self-confidence scale. Participants are asked to record how they feel 'right now' when completing the scales. Krane's validation work on the MRF-L revealed correlations between the MRF-L and the CSAI-2 subscales of .76 for cognitive anxiety, .69 for somatic anxiety and .68 for self-confidence. Mean values were computed for each scale from the participants' self-reports made prior to and during each testing condition (see Procedure). As with previous research investigating the effect of worry on sporting performance (e.g., Wilson, Smith et al., 2007; Wilson, Chattington et al., 2007), the cognitive anxiety scale provided the main focus for the research.

Movement phases. Three movement phases were highlighted based on a set of strict rules derived from existing research (Vickers, 2007), in order that gaze behavior could be determined in relation to the motor actions. The preparation phase was coded as a consistent 1000 ms prior to the first upward movement of the ball for all participants. The lift phase was coded from the first upward movement of the ball until extension of the elbow occurred. The extension phase was coded from the first extension at the elbow until the ball left the fingertips.

Occlusion period. The occlusion period was defined as the period of time during shot execution when the hoop was not visible, due to the upward movement of the ball and arms The onset of the occlusion period was defined in relation to the onset of the preparation phase (in milliseconds) and its duration was also measured in milliseconds.

Quiet eye period onset. The quiet eye period was operationally defined as the final fixation to a single location or object in the visuomotor workspace within 1° of visual angle for a minimum of 120 ms (3 frames). Six key gaze locations were categorized for determining QE onset; the left rim, right rim, front rim, back rim, backboard and 'other', based on previous literature (Harle & Vickers, 2001; Vickers, 1996). In the basketball free-throw, the QE has an onset that occurs before the final extension of the arms; the first video frame where the angle between upper and lower arm starts to increase (Vickers, 2007). QE onset is reported relative to how long it occurred after the initiation of the preparation phase (in ms).

Suppressed vision. Vickers (1996) identified two visual strategies indicative of suppressed vision; brief eye closures (i.e. blinking) and moving gaze freely (i.e. not looking towards occluded target). The total duration of the time when the eyes were momentarily closed (i.e. no point of gaze registered) was calculated in milliseconds. Fixations to locations other than the ball, hands or arms during the occlusion period (i.e. not towards the target) were classed as 'other' and the total fixation duration to these locations was calculated in milliseconds. Fixations towards the target (on the ball, hands, or arms) were classed as 'ball' and again the total fixation duration to these locations was calculated in milliseconds. Fixations were defined as a gaze which remained on a location (within $1°$ visual angle), for a minimum of 120 ms, or 3 frames (as Wilson, Vine, et al., 2009). A single measure of suppressed visual control was calculated to represent the total amount of time (in milliseconds) during the occlusion period in which vision was suppressed, as opposed to being target focused. This measure was defined mathematically as: (total blink duration + total 'other' fixation duration – 'ball' fixation duration).

Performance. The performance measure consisted of the number of shots required to achieve the criterion level of 10 successful and 10 unsuccessful free-throws. Specifically, free-throw percentage success in each condition was adopted as the measure of performance effectiveness in the current study (number of successful throws x 100 / total number of throws).

PROCEDURE

After reading the written information introducing the study and providing informed consent, participants were allowed to take practice free throws with and without the eye-tracker being fitted in order to become familiar with the testing surroundings and the equipment being used. Calibration of the eye-tracker consisted of participants looking at a grid presented at the same distance as the hoop, displaying 9 individually numbered crosses arranged in a 3x3 format. Participants were then provided with instructions related to the condition in which they were going to perform under and were asked to give a reading from the 3 scales on the MRF-L.

Before every block of ten shots participants were asked to face the external camera and clap their hands in front of their face, in order that a clear event could be used to time-lock the footage from the external camera and the eye-tracker scene camera for subsequent offline analyses. Each block of ten free-throws was split into five sets of two consecutive throws, with an experimenter returning the ball to the participant after each throw. This was to ostensibly follow the typical game situation whereby free-throws occur in pairs. After every pair of free throws a quick calibration check was performed using the calibration grid and several distinguished points on the backboard. If necessary, the line of gaze was re-calibrated quickly before proceeding with the testing protocol.

After every 10 free throws the video data was saved and the participants were then asked to report their current anxiety levels using the MRF-L. This procedure was repeated until the participants had performed 10 successful free throws and 10 unsuccessful free throws (as Vickers, 1996), although they were unaware of this requirement. The participants were then allowed a five minute rest before the second condition was explained and the same testing procedure followed. At the end of the testing period, participants were debriefed about the true purpose of the study.

Experimental Conditions

Participants were asked to take free throws in 2 counter balanced conditions, designed to manipulate the level of anxiety experienced. In the control condition, non-evaluative instructions were provided to participants, asking them to do their best but stressing that their success rate would not to be used for comparison with other participants. In the high threat condition several manipulations were used to attempt to ensure that high levels of pressure were created (see also Behan & Wilson, 2008). Participants were informed that their success rate and performance levels were to be compared among their teammates and that their team's average success rate was going to be compared to other teams within the same competitive league.

Financial rewards were offered to the 3 participants with the best free-throw accuracy (£30 for first place, £20 for second and £10 for third). Non-contingent feedback was also used (see Williams & Elliott, 1999) whereby participants were informed that their previous 20 free throws put them in the bottom 30% when compared to other participants that had already taken part. The previous 20 free throws were either from their warm up or the control condition depending upon whether they were completing the high threat condition first or second. The participants were informed that being in the bottom 30% meant that the data was of no use for the study and that they should try and be more accurate.

Data Analysis

Fixation and movement phase data were calculated via frame-by-frame analysis of the eye-tracker and external video camera video files, using Quiet Eye Solutions software (www.QuietEyeSolutions.com). The software time-locks the two video files and allows coding of the movement phases from the external video, in relation to the coding of the gaze behavior (gaze location and duration) from the eye-tracker. Figure 2 shows the split screen view of the Vision-in-Action (Vickers, 1996) video data, with the left side showing the external video of the participant performing the free throw. The right side shows the view from the scene camera of the eye tracker, with the point of gaze indicated by the red circular cursor, representing a 1° visual angle. The software time-locks the two video files and allows coding of the movement phases from the external video, in relation to the coding of the gaze behavior (gaze location and duration) from the eye tracker.

As with previous studies examining the quiet eye period (e.g., Behan & Wilson, 2008; Harle & Vickers, 2001; Vickers, 1996; Williams et al., 2002; Wilson, Vine et al., 2009) a subset of shots were selected for frame-by-frame analyses. If ten successful shots were made before ten misses, then all misses were included and a randomly selected group of ten successful shots. This procedure was reversed if ten misses occurred first. A random number generator (www.random.org) was used to select the ten random shots to be analyzed by inputting the total number of successful shots or misses into the generator and selecting the first ten numbers generated. Values for gaze behavior and movement phase dependent variables were calculated for the10 successful shots and 10 misses for each condition and used in subsequent statistical analyses.

Figure 2. A screen grab of the Quiet Eye Solutions software analysis environment; showing the external video of the participant (left), the view from the scene camera of the eye-tracker (right) and the coding entry fields (centre).

RESULTS

Anxiety and performance accuracy data were subjected to paired samples t-test analyses (control vs high threat conditions). Quiet eye onset, occlusion onset, occlusion duration, and the measure of suppressed vision were all subjected to a fully repeated measures 2x2 ANOVA: condition (control, threat) x accuracy (hit, miss). Effect sizes (ω^2) were calculated as outlined in Howell (2002).

Cognitive State Anxiety: Mrf-L

Participants reported significantly higher cognitive anxiety scores in the high threat (mean rating of 5.05, $SD = .90$) than the control (mean rating of 3.29, $SD = 1.24$) condition, $t(9) = 5.17, p < .005, \omega^2 = 1.30$.

Performance

Performance, as measured by free-throw percentage accuracy, was lower in the high threat (50.50%, SD = 5.07) than the control (68.60%, SD = 11.02) condition, $t(9)$ = 5.52, $p <$ .001, ω^2 = 1.50.

Quiet Eye Onset

A significant main effect was found for accuracy, $F(1,9)$ = 9.98, $p < .05$, ω^2 = .30, with earlier quiet eye onsets occurring for successful shots (hits) as opposed to misses. There was no significant main effect for threat, $F(1,9)$ = 2.43, p = .15, ω^2 = .18, and no significant interaction effect. The quiet eye onset data is presented in Figure 3.

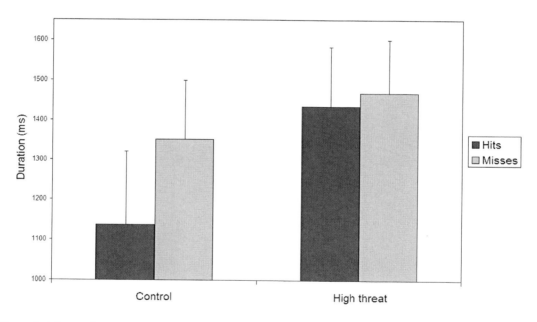

Figure 3. Mean quiet eye onset (ms after initiation of preparation phase) for successful (hits) and unsuccessful (misses) shots, during control and high threat conditions (with standard error bars).

Suppressed Vision

A significant main effect was found for threat, $F(1,9)$ =7.30, $p < .05$, ω^2 = .70, with longer suppressed vision occurring in the control as opposed to high threat condition. There was no significant main effect for accuracy, $F(1,9)$ = 0.55, p = .48, ω^2 = .08, and no significant interaction effect, $F(1,9)$ = 0.05, p = .83. The suppressed vision data is presented in Figure 4, and the separate durations for each gaze strategy making up the suppressed vision measure (i.e., blink, fixations on ball / hands, fixations to other targets) are presented in Table 1.

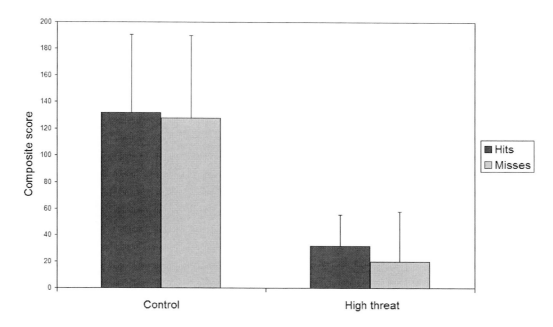

Figure 4. Mean composite measure of suppressed vision (blink duration + fixation duration to other locations – fixation duration to ball in ms) for successful (hits) and unsuccessful (misses) shots, during control and high threat conditions (with standard error bars).

Table 1. Mean (standard deviation) gaze behavior durations (ms) during the occlusion period for successful (hits) and unsuccessful (misses) shots, during control and high threat conditions.

Variable (ms)	Control		High Threat	
	Hit	Miss	Hit	Miss
Blink	180 (130.97)	168 (143.35)	100 (78.31)	96 (84.74)
Ball	80 (49.88)	72 (41.31)	108 (26.99)	108 (26.99)
Other	32 (31.55)	32 (41.31)	40 (26.66)	32 (31.55)

Occlusion Duration

Although there was no significant main effect for threat, $F(1,9) = 4.73$, $p = .058$, $\omega^2 = 0.51$, the effect size was moderate, with shorter occlusion durations occurring in the high threat compared to control condition. There was no significant main effect for accuracy $F(1,9) = .935$, $p = .359$, $\omega^2 = 0.13$ and no significant interaction effect, $F(1,9) = .091.$, $p = .770$. The occlusion duration data is presented in Figure 5.

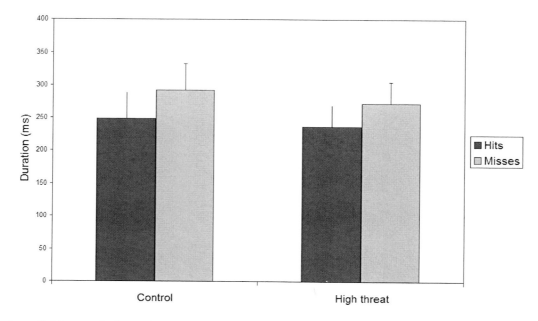

Figure 5. Mean occlusion period duration (ms) for successful (hits) and unsuccessful (misses) shots, during control and high threat conditions (with standard error bars).

Occlusion Onset

No significant main effects were found for threat, $F(1,9) = 3.26$, $p = .104$, $\omega^2 = 0.12$, or accuracy, $F(1,9) = 1.64$, $p = 2.32$, $\omega^2 = 0.10$, and there was no significant interaction effect, $F(1,9) = 4.02$, $p = .076$. The occlusion onset data is presented in Figure 6.

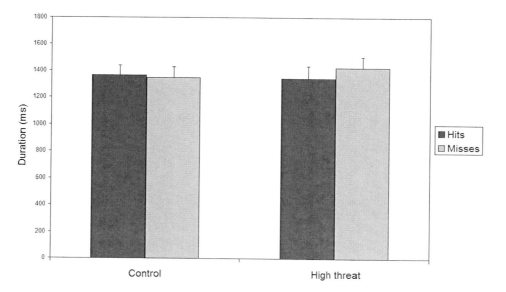

Figure 6. Mean occlusion period onset (ms after initiation of preparation phase) for successful (hits) and unsuccessful (misses) shots, during control and high threat conditions (with standard error bars).

DISCUSSION

This study aimed to test the predictions of attentional control theory (ACT; Eysenck et al., 2007) in a sports environment using a basketball free throw task. The free-throw is an interesting aiming task in terms of visuomotor control, as the target is occluded by the object being thrown just prior to the propulsion phase of the action. Given these constraints on the timing and location of attention in this task, it is interesting to examine how optimal attentional control (early quiet eye onset and suppression of vision during occlusion period) might be impaired when performers are anxious. We have previously shown that anxiety significantly reduced the *duration* of the quiet eye period of free throw shooters and discussed these results in relation to an impairment of attentional control (Wilson, Vine et al., 2009). However, with this re-analysis we are explicitly testing ACT's fourth hypothesis, which predicts that anxious individuals are less able to inhibit the allocation of their attention to (external) distracting stimuli (Eysenck et al, 2007, p. 344-346). We proposed that during the execution of the free throw, anxious performers may be more distracted by the ball and arms, thus disrupting 'normal' (goal-directed) attentional control, as outlined in Vickers' (1996) location suppression hypothesis (LSH).

Anxiety and Performance

Participants reported significantly higher levels of cognitive anxiety in the high threat as opposed to control condition, supporting the effectiveness of the experimental manipulation in elevating worry. While anxiety levels may not have been as high as in '*real*' high-pressure competition, the reported values were similar to those outlined in previous studies using the MRF (e.g., Wilson, Smith et al., 2007; Wilson, Chattington et al., 2007). Performance was significantly worse in the high threat compared to control condition (a 26% reduction in free-throw success rate), suggesting that participants choked under pressure. We proposed that increased anxiety may have impaired attentional control, thus explaining the significant drop in performance in the high threat condition (as Behan & Wilson, 2008; Vickers & Williams, 2007; Wilson, Vine et al., 2009).

Attentional Control

As ACT predicts that anxiety impacts upon the distractibility of individuals, attentional control should be most impaired during the occlusion period, when the rising ball enters the visual field and occludes the target. However, this impairment in the inhibition function (negative attentional control) should not prevent the performer from initiating an efficient early QE onset; the initial component of Vickers' (1996) LSH attentional strategy. As predicted, the manipulation of threat had no impact on the timing of the QE onset (Figure 3); with participants initiating their QE onset approximately 1300ms after the preparation phase in both conditions. Attentional control does not appear to have been impaired *early* in the shot preparation as would have been evidenced by later, and hence less efficient, QE onsets. However, the significant difference in QE onset between shots which were successful (hits) compared to unsuccessful (misses), demonstrates the importance of this attentional strategy in gaining critical aiming information early enough to successfully perform the motor action.

The primary measure of attentional control during the occlusion period (suppressed vision) *was* however significantly impaired in the high threat condition (Figure 4). Table 1 reveals that participants fixated much more on the ball and used less blinks when anxious, compared to in the control condition. This increase in duration of fixations to the ball during the occlusion period is particularly marked because the duration of the occlusion period was 14% shorter in the high threat as opposed to control condition; an almost significant reduction ($p = .058$; see Figure 5). Instead of adopting the optimal LSH attentional strategy used during the control condition, anxious participants' attention appears to have been 'captured' by the ball as it occluded the target. ACT proposes that an anxiety-induced impairment of negative attentional control makes an individual more distractible, and hence may have caused the attention-grabbing movement of the ball into the visual field to become more salient.

However, there is an alternative explanation for a ball-focused strategy which has less to do with the distracting nature of the ball itself, but rather is more reflective of a desire to 're-check' the location of the target just prior to the final extension phase of the movement. Because of the perceived negative consequences of poor performance in the high threat condition, performers may have tried to maintain a target-focused gaze strategy, rather than trust the aiming information gained from their early quiet eye. As the ball was in line with the hoop location during the occlusion period (see Figure 1, 2b) this might also explain why gaze was directed at the ball during this period. Previous research examining aiming performance in sport tasks has also shown that anxious participants do attempt to re-check target locations in a less efficient way. For example, Wilson, Smith et al. (2007) in a golf putting task found that participants directed significantly more 're-checking' glances to the target hole location in a high as opposed to low threat condition. These authors suggested that this less efficient attentional strategy was due to decay of distance cues in working memory caused by the pre-emption of attentional resources by worry. A similar effect may be occurring in the current study, with performers trying to re-fixate on the approximate location of the occluded target in order to attempt to ensure accurate aiming. Ironically, this strategy is likely to have detrimental effects on performance, as the original aiming commands derived from the quiet eye period will be disrupted by the later, less accurate commands.

While tests of ACT's predictions related to impairment of inhibition and negative attentional control are still limited (see Derakshan, Ansari, Hansard, Shoker, & Eysenck, 2009), the current results suggest that Vickers' conceptualization of location suppression is a valid measure of negative attentional control in free-throw shooting. Future research therefore needs to continue to examine the LSH in basketball and other far aiming sport tasks, in order to further our understanding of how and why attentional control is disrupted and performance degraded. However, as the LSH may be a very specific attentional strategy, relevant only to skills like the free-throw where the target is fully occluded during the completion of the motor act (see Williams et al., 2002), it is important that researchers also attempt to determine objective measures of effective attentional control for other skills.

For example, our general finding that anxious sports performers' gaze may be drawn towards inappropriate visual targets, disrupting subsequent performance, has also recently been demonstrated in a soccer penalty task (Wilson, Wood & Vine, 2009). Rather than the target being fully occluded during the shot, in soccer a goalkeeper stands on the goal line and aims to prevent the shot from going past him/her into the goal. Penalty takers directed significantly more fixations of longer duration to the centrally located goalkeeper in a high threat compared to control condition. This disruption in negative attentional control had an effect on subsequent performance, with participants hitting their shots to more central locations (closer to the goal keeper) in the high threat condition. Instead of fixating on the corners of the goal (the optimal target area), as they did in the control condition, anxious participants' gaze was directed towards the goal keeper, disrupting aiming commands and shot direction. These gaze results from soccer support those presented in this chapter and suggest that it may be important to actively inhibit visual distractions in order to be successful in performing target-related sport skills under pressure.

Implications

As already mentioned, although the current results are supportive of the predictions of ACT, more research is required to further our understanding of how and why anxiety disrupts the inhibition of distracting stimuli in far aiming tasks. The results gathered so far do tentatively suggest that attentional control training regimes may be a useful strategy to protect performers from the negative influence of anxiety. One way in which attention could be directed to a series of cues to maintain appropriate attention is through a suitably designed pre-performance routine (e.g., Boutcher, 2002; Moran, 1996). For example, Singer's (2002) five step approach includes an explicit attentional component directing performers' focus to one external relevant feature of the task (e.g., the hoop in basketball). Such an external focus of attention should not only prevent reinvestment (Masters & Maxwell, 2008) but also help to block disruptive thoughts and emotions.

However, as the results of the current study have demonstrated, it may not be sufficient to simply direct individuals' gaze to a target, as they might attempt to maintain this gaze inappropriately (e.g., try to maintain a fixation on the hoop when it is occluded). More explicit gaze control instructions may be required to ensure that aiming information gained is timely, and negative attentional control applied, if required. Harle and Vickers (2001) have previously demonstrated that it is possible to train an explicit gaze control strategy in basketball free-throw shooting. Players were taught to focus on the front of the hoop and say the phrase "sight…focus" to maintain the fixation for an optimal quiet eye period (about 1500ms for the free-throw task). They were then informed to either blink or allow their gaze to wander freely as the ball came into their visual field (suppressed vision). While Harle and Vickers did not include an anxiety manipulation in their study, other researchers (e.g., Wilson & Richards, in press) have highlighted how an effective pre-shot routine might allow a performer to 'focus with a quiet eye and execute with a quiet mind' to protect against performance disruption due to increased pressure.

CONCLUSION

This chapter has sought to test the predictions of ACT (Eysenck et al., 2007) using a previously validated measure of attentional control, conceptualized for the free-throw task (i.e., location suppression hypothesis, Vickers, 1996). As predicted, negative attentional control and performance were significantly impaired in the high threat condition, suggesting that attentional mechanisms may underlie 'choking' under pressure. We were particularly interested in the effect of visual distractions on performers' attentional control and demonstrated that such distractions may become more salient when performers are anxious. These findings add strong support for the predictions of ACT in motor task performance under pressure and may offer a mechanistic explanation as to why free-throws are missed in pressure environments.

REFERENCES

Bakker, F.C., Oudejans, R.D., Binsch, O., & Van der Kamp, J. (2006). *Penalty shooting and gaze behavior: Unwanted effects of the wish not to miss.* International Journal of Sport Psychology, 37, 265-280.

Baumeister, R.F. (1984). *Choking under pressure: Self-consciousness and paradoxical effects of incentives on skillful performance.* Journal of Personality and Social Psychology, 46, 610-620.

Behan, M. & Wilson, M. (2008). State anxiety and visual attention: The role of the quiet eye period in aiming to a far target. Journal of Sports Sciences, 26, 207-215.

Boutcher, S.H. (2002). *Attention and sport performance.* In T. Horn (Ed.), Advances in sport psychology, 2nd Edition (pp. 441-457). Champaign, IL: Human Kinetics.

Corbetta, M. & Shulman, G.L. (2002). *Control of goal-directed and stimulus-driven attention in the brain.* Nature Reviews Neuroscience, 3, 201–215.

Derakshan, N., Ansari, T.L., Hansard, M., Shoker, L., & Eysenck, M.W. (2009). *Anxiety, inhibition, efficiency and effectiveness: An investigation using the antisaccade task.* Experimental Psychology, 56, 48-55.

Easterbrook, J. A. (1959). *The effect of emotion on cue utilization and the organization of behavior.* Psychological Review, 66, 183 – 201.

Eysenck, M.W. & Calvo, M.G. (1992). *Anxiety and performance: The processing efficiency theory.* Cognition and Emotion, 6, 409-434.

Eysenck, M.W., Derakshan, N., Santos, R. & Calvo, M.G. (2007). *Anxiety and cognitive performance:* Attentional control theory. Emotion, 7, 336-353.

Harle, S. & Vickers, J.N. (2001). *Training quiet eye improves accuracy in the basketball free-throw.* The Sport Psychologist, 15, 289-305.

Howell, D.C. (2002). *Statistical methods for psychology* (5th ed.). Boston MA: PWS-Kent.

Janelle, C.M. (1999). *Ironic mental processes in sport: Implications for sport psychologists.* The Sport Psychologist, 13, 201-220.

Janelle, C. M. (2002). *Anxiety, arousal and visual attention: A mechanistic account of performance variability.* Journal of Sports Sciences, 20, 237 – 251.

Janelle, C.M., Singer, R.N., & Williams, A.M. (1999). *External distraction and attentional narrowing: Visual search evidence.* Journal of Sport & Exercise Psychology, 21, 70-91.

Janelle, C.M., Hillman, C.H., Apparies, R., Murray, N.P., Meili, L., Fallon, E.A., & Hatfield, B.D. (2000). *Expertise differences in cortical activation and gaze behavior during rifle shooting.* Journal of Sport & Exercise Psychology, 22, 167-182.

Krane, V. (1994). *The mental readiness form as a measure of competitive state anxiety*. The Sport Psychologist, 8, 189-202.

Martens, R., Burton, D., Vealey, R., Bump, L., & Smith, D. (1990). *Development of the CSAI-2*. In R. Martens, R. Vealey & D. Burton (Eds.), Competitive anxiety in sport (pp. 127-140). Champaign IL: Human Kinetics.

Masters, R.S.W. (1992). *Knowledge, knerves and know-how: The role of explicit versus implicit knowledge in the breakdown of a complex motor skill under pressure*. British Journal of Psychology, 83, 343-358.

Masters, R.S.W. & Maxwell, J.P. (2008). *The theory of reinvestment*. International Review of Sport and Exercise Psychology, 1, 160-183.

Moran, A. P. (1996). *The psychology of concentration in sport performers*: A cognitive analysis. Hove, East Sussex: Psychology Press.

Orlick, T. (1990). *In pursuit of excellence*. Champaign, Illinois: Leisure Press.

Smith, E. E., & Kosslyn, S. M. (2007). *Cognitive psychology*: Mind and brain. Upper Saddle River, NJ: Pearson/Prentice-Hall.

Vickers, J.N. (1992). *Gaze control in putting*. Perception, 21, 117-132.

Vickers, J.N. (1996). *Visual control when aiming at a far target*. Journal of Experimental Psychology: Human Perception and Performance, 2, 324–354.

Vickers, J.N. (2007). *Perception, cognition and decision training:* The quiet eye in action. Champaign IL: Human Kinetics.

Vickers, J.N., & Williams, A.M. (2007). *Performing under pressure: The effects of physiological arousal, cognitive anxiety, and gaze control in biathlon*. Journal of Motor Behavior, 39, 381-394.

Wegner, D. M. (1994). *Ironic processes of mental control*. Psychological Review, 101, 34-52.

Williams, A. M., & Elliott, D. (1999). *Anxiety, expertise, and visual search strategy in karate*. Journal of Sport and Exercise Psychology, 21, 362 – 375.

Williams, A. M., Singer, R. N., & Frehlich, S. G. (2002). *Quiet eye duration, expertise, and task complexity in near and far aiming tasks*. Journal of Motor Behavior, 34, 197 – 207.

Wilson, M. (2008). *From processing efficiency to attentional control: A mechanistic account of the anxiety-performance relationship*. International Review of Sport and Exercise Psychology, 1, 184-201.

Wilson, M. & Richards, H. (in press). *Putting it together: Skill packages for pressure performance*. In D. Collins, A. Abbott & H. Richards (Eds) Psychology for physical performance. Oxford, England: Elsevier Science.

Wilson, M., Smith, N.C., & Holmes, P. S. (2007a). *The role of effort in influencing the anxiety – performance relationship: Testing the conflicting predictions of processing efficiency theory and the conscious processing hypothesis*. British Journal of Psychology, 98, 411–428.

Wilson, M.R., Vine, S.J., & Wood, G. (2009). *The influence of anxiety on visual attentional control in basketball free-throw shooting*. Journal of Sport and Exercise Psychology, 31, 152-168.

Wilson, M.R., Wood, G. & Vine, S.J. (2009). *Anxiety, attentional control and performance impairment in penalty kicks*. Manuscript submitted for publication.

Wilson, M., Chattington, M., Marple-Horvat, D. E., & Smith, N. C. (2007b). *A comparison of self-focus versus attentional explanations of choking*. Journal of Sport and Exercise Psychology, 29, 439–456.

Woodman, T. & Davis, P.A. (2008). *The role of repression in the incidence of ironic errors.* The Sport Psychologist, 22, 183-196.

In: Handbook of Sports Psychology
Editor: Calvin H. Chang

ISBN: 978-1-60741-256-4
©2009 Nova Science Publishers, Inc.

Chapter 10

SELF-REGULATION, TRAINING AND PERFORMANCE

Gilles Kermarrec and Denis Pasco

Faculty of Sport and Physical Education, LISyC – EA 3889, European University of
Brittany, University of Brest, France

ABSTRACT

The purpose of this study was to investigate the self-regulation strategies employed by elite kitesurfers during self-paced training. It was hypothesized that declared self-regulation strategies could predict athletes' involvement in training and performance in future competitions. The participants were seventy-five male kitesurfers, chosen based on their performances in previous, European, French and international kitesurfing competitions. In order to enhance content validity, researchers used interviews with kitesurfers. A discriminant analysis tested construct validity, and Cronbach's Alpha coefficients were calculated to test the reliability of each sub-scale. Multiple regressions showed that self-regulation strategies could predict training involvement ($R^2=.26$). Training involvement is quite a good predictor of performance ($R^2=.11$). These results should be attested external validity for the SRSPTQ (Self-Regulation Strategies in Self-Paced Training Questionnaire). The procedure allowed us to propose 13 sub-scales with satisfactory psychometric properties. Self-regulation strategies in kitesurfing were identified using the SRSPTQ.

Keywords: Involvement, Training, Self-regulation Strategies, Performance

INTRODUCTION

For many years, researchers in sports psychology have paid increased attention to the role of self-regulation strategies in the performing-learning process (Crews, Lochbaum, & Karoly, 2001). Moreover, supporters of this perspective suggest that the effectiveness of sports training programs partly depends on what athletes know, think, and do while controlling, enhancing and modifying their involvement. Indeed, if the athletes' participation is important to the learning or performing process, understanding the factors that influence how they engage in training is even more important to researchers and coaches. Additionally, research in sports psychology has indicated that motor learning may be positively influenced by self-regulation and learning strategies (Singer, Lidor, & Cauraugh, 1993). Generally speaking, athletes can be described as self-regulated learners if they are metacognitively, motivationally, and behaviorally active participants during learning situations (Zimmerman & Kitsantkas, 1998).

Assessing Self-Regulation Strategies Kite Surfers use in Training Settings

Development and validation of a self-regulation strategy scale with experts in kite surfing pre-competitive training settings.

The Self-Regulation Model

From a cybernetics point of view (Carver & Scheier, 1998), the concept of self-regulation is a complex, multilevel process that enables living systems to remain balanced. The essence of regulation in all fields is to inform an active system of the results of its actions and to correct them according to those results. A system is considered as self-regulating if it collects and processes information itself and goes on to modify certain settings in order to maintain homeostasis, or a balance, in the way it functions.

The way in which systems take charge of their cognitive functioning in this manner may be automatic or voluntary (Lefebvre-Pinard & Pinard, 1985). However, in sports, self-regulation is most likely to be part of the conscious control of one's own activity and/or actions (Kirschenbaum, 1984; Hardy & Nelson, 1988; Chen & Singer, 1992).

This behavior is understood to be the result of a process comparing the perception of the desired state (goal) and the perception of a present state (metacognition). If subjects perceive a discrepancy between these two states, a retroactive loop (feedback) leads them to mobilize available resources in order to reduce this divergence. This mobilization occurs in the form of strategies. However, if the discrepancy is too great, subjects can also modify their goals (give up, pull out of a competition, etc.). Sometimes, by modifying the goal in order to reduce the discrepancy, subjects are in fact trying to protect themselves (self-perceptions, self-esteem, self-efficacy). They therefore trigger a regulatory loop leading to the use of self-handicapping strategies (Thill, 2001). Effective self-regulation therefore enables individuals to maintain their involvement in goal-driven activities over time and in various contexts (Thill, 2001, p.193).

Goals, metacognitive knowledge or knowledge about context, and strategies are considered as interactive components utilized by the participants during the self-regulation process (Kermarrec, Todorovitch, Fleming, 2004).

SELF REGULATION IN SPORT AND EXERCISE

Self-regulation (SR) strategies are usually defined as a set of processes or behaviors used to control thought, information processing, emotion or action. Research indicates that it is important to conceptualize SR in the field of sports and exercise (Chen & Singer, 1992; Kirschenbaum, 1984), and that it is important to study the mechanisms influencing self-regulation and performance relationships. Research reviewing self-regulation in sport and exercise Crews, Lochbaum, & Karoly (2001) and Kermarrec (2004) identified descriptive, predictive and training studies.

In predictive studies, SR variables are manipulated to correlate with performance or task involvement. Most of the time, researchers have reduced SR processes to a relatively small number of components, ignoring elements such as the role of time or context effects.

In training studies, SR strategies (biofeedback, imagery instruction, etc.) are tested, and researchers focus on improving performance or task involvement. Most training studies have demonstrated the effectiveness of self-regulation training and teaching strategies on athletes' behavior and performance (Singer & Cauraugh, 1985). Therefore, these instructional approaches had to overcome problems relating to strategy transfer. Athletes could develop SR and acquire strategies when instructed, but failed to use these strategies systematically in competitive contexts, without instruction (Singer, DeFrancesco & Randall, 1989).

Descriptive studies have also aimed to identify and measure SR variables, that is to say, the strategies used by the athletes. These studies required a battery of questionnaires that gauge various aspects of SR. Most of these questionnaires are general SR strategy questionnaires used by researchers in sport settings (Thill & Brunel, 1995; Ommundsen, 2003; Barkoff, Heiby & Pagano, 2007). Very few of them were adapted or designed for sports (Anshel, 1995) or physical education contexts (Shen & Chen, 2003; Kermarrec & Michot, 2008). Moreover, researchers have also completed descriptive studies through observations and interviews in motor learning contexts for experts (Ille & Cadopi, 1999) and novices (Weiss & Klint, 1987). Despite the fact that many typologies have been proposed, at least two types of strategy have been frequently described: learning strategies and management strategies.

Learning strategies or primary strategies (Dansereau et al., 1979; Singer & Cauraugh, 1985) are specific and facilitate the acquisition of knowledge or skills in a particular domain (e.g., motor learning). Support strategies, secondary strategies (Dansereau et al., 1979; Singer & Cauraugh, 1985), or management strategies (Kermarrec, 2004) help to organize and optimize "internal context" (e.g., emotion, motivation, attention) or "external context" (e.g., social relations, materials, time allocation).

Descriptive studies serve to investigate the alleged differences in the way SR functions (Anshel, 1995). Research into self-regulated processes in various fields suggests that learning and performing are highly contextualized (Crews & al., 2001). Most of these studies have focused on learning strategies and have been conducted in educational contexts (Pintrich, 2004). In previous studies we have demonstrated how learning strategies can be described through three approaches to learning in physical education settings (Kermarrec, Todorovitch and Fleming, 2004). The first learning approach consists of *training* and/or *repeating*. This low-level information processing (Craick & Lockhart, 1972; Thill & Brunel, 1995; Thill, 2001) can be associated with the self-regulation components of managing motivation, time and tasks. A second learning approach consists of *thinking and understanding*. In order to plan their actions, athletes listen to verbal instructions and seek help from peers or their coach. These learners use high-level information processing (Craick & Lockhart, 1972) and favor declarative and explicative action monitoring (Thill & Brunel, 1995; Thill, 2001). A third learning approach in sport consists of *associating non-verbal information*. Learning strategies such as using imagination, watching demonstrations, or imitation should be used. These aspects of extended information processing (Craick & Tulving, 1975) are associated with management strategies such as managing and focusing attention. Reducing peer interactions should favor the transformation from declarative action components (e.g., image, instructions, etc.) to procedural components. As this empirical approach to learning was linked to physical education settings, it should be well adapted to competitive sports contexts.

Table 1. Self-Regulation Strategies in Sport (adapted from Kermarrec, 2004)

Self-Regulation Strategies in Sport	
Learning Strategies	Means used to best process information relating to disciplinary content
LOW LEVEL strategies Practice and training strategies	Organize one's own training method; force oneself to repeat the same exercise, etc.
DEEP LEVEL strategies Development strategies and Monitoring strategies controlling activities	Systematically looking for knowledge of the result compared to the action: relating cause to the desired effect; planning one's actions through a series of sub-goals Organizing different action possibilities in the form of action rules
EXTENDED strategies	Using visualization to associate intentions and sensations; goals and mental images. Focus attention on priority information
Support or management strategies	Strategies designed to facilitate and to organize learning or training: when, where, with whom, in what conditions, at what rhythm, one should train in order to improve
External context management	Adapting the difficulty of a task Consulting resources in order to gain information (video, internet, etc). Appropriate time management strategies. Strategies asking for help from teachers or peers. Managing attention; increasing or maintaining attention, Strategies for diverting attention, managing stress, emotions, facing difficulties
Internal context management	Motivational or emotional strategies: fixing objectives, self-encouragement strategies, self-handicapping strategies, strategies for preserving confidence in one's abilities.

PURPOSE OF THE STUDY

The aim of this study was to describe the self-regulation strategies used by kitesurfers in a pre-competitive training setting. Although extensive research has been conducted on the use of self-regulatory processes in laboratory situations, few efforts have been made to measure the role of self-regulated components in naturalistic settings. In order to describe self-regulation strategies, three different measures were used: behavior analysis (Ille & Cadopi, 1999), clarification interviews (Weiss & Klint, 1987) and self-regulation strategy questionnaires (Thill & Brunel, 1995; Anshel, 1995). In order to describe spontaneous strategies, questionnaires should be situated according to context (Kermarrec & Michot, 2008). This paper aims to develop and test a self-regulation strategies scale in a pre-competitive kitesurfing training setting.

DEVELOPING THE PRELIMINARY VERSION OF THE QUESTIONNAIRE AND VALIDATING THE CONTENT OF A SCALE FOR KITESURFING SELF-REGULATION STRATEGIES

Kitesurfing is a new sport which consists of, firstly, being pulled along by a kite attached to a board similar to a surfboard, snowboard or wakeboard, and secondly to recreate set maneuvers, or to invent new moves. Kitesurfing training settings are essential for investigating self-regulation because such a recent sport has not yet developed teams or training structures. Training programs for acquiring new skills therefore depend on each individual, with athletes planning and designing their own training processes. Kitesurfing should be a particularly interesting field in which to study self-regulation.

The development and validation of the questionnaire for self-regulation strategies in kitesurfing training was devised using the recommendations from Vallerand & Hess (2000). Validating a questionnaire depends on three main features: content validity, construct validity and reliability.

Content validity indicates whether or not the study measures that which it is designed to measure. It refers to the meaning that can be attributed to the different items on the scale and relates to subjective, rather than quantitative assessment (Vallerand & Hess, 2000). The questionnaire's content validity is here linked to the development of the initial version, and the way in which the items on the questionnaire were formulated.

Participants

The questionnaire had to be in English because the participants were international. French, English, Australian, South African, and American kitesurfers are used to speaking in English across the world while training or preparing for competitions. Three bilingual kitesurfing experts (two kitesurfers and one coach) were invited to assist us in developing the questionnaire.

Procedure

Self-regulation strategy items were developed in according to the categories outlined in Kermarrec, Todorovitch & Fleming (2004). Learning-strategy and management-strategy questionnaires were developed and tested in a physical education setting (Kermarrec &

Michot, 2008; Michot & Kermarrec, 2005). In order to adapt these questionnaires, researchers used previous interviews with the three bilingual kitesurfing experts.

Discussion about self-regulation for these interviews was based on 6 learning strategies (with 4 items per strategy) and 7 management strategies (with 3 items per strategy) issued from physical education contexts. The six learning strategies that were used included: (1) *to look at and to imitate*, (2) *to think about and seek understanding,* (3) *to visualize and imagine,* (4) to *focus attention on,* (5) *to follow advice* and (6) *to repeat and to practice.*

The seven management strategies that were used during the interviews included: (1) *to manage attention*, (2) *to seek help*, (3) *to manage the task and to adjust its difficulty*, (4) *to manage time*, (5), *to reduce peer interactions*, (6) *to manage motivation*, and (7) *to self-evaluate*.

Results

Following the interviews, the learning strategy "to imitate and to look at" was completed with a specific item for kitesurfing: kitesurfers have confirmed that the use of videos can be helpful for training. So, in the scale, five items were connected to the first learning strategy (to imitate). Because training contexts are so different from school contexts, some of the management strategies were not relevant. The "attention" management strategy seems to be very similar to, if not the same as, the attention-focusing learning strategy. This category was considered useless by experts in the field. The strategy "to seek help" was also removed as it seems to be specific to educational contexts (students looking to the teacher for help). In kitesurfing, there are very few coaches, and advice is therefore much more likely to come from peers. For many athletes, however, exchanging information, advice and instructions can prove to be essential for improvement. The "task management" sub-scale proved problematic in terms of meaning. The notion of tasks is not a concept used by kitesurfers. Rather, the term maneuver or move seems more appropriate, and better adapted to the interests of the athletes. Finally, the term "exercise" was chosen in order to reformulate the three items initially proposed from the PE contexts. In addition, the kitesurfers themselves identified another method that they often use to improve, that relates to the subscale "task management". They start with a well-known move and progressively attempt to make that move more and more difficult by modifying it a little at a time. In order to represent this self-regulatory behavior, we added the item "I tried to modify the exercise little by little to improve my skills". Finally 7 management strategies were selected and their corresponding items adapted.

The initial version of the self-regulation questionnaire should assess athletes' involvement using 13 self-regulation strategies. The preliminary questionnaire was composed of 46 items. It was approved by the committee (the two researchers and the three experts).

It was agreed that the questionnaire would be presented along with the following instruction: "You have just completed a training session to learn a new kitesurfing exercise. Read the following sentences carefully. Do these suggestions accurately describe what you did or thought during this session? Please answer as honestly as possibly, bearing in mind what you have just done." Self-regulation engagement was recorded on a likert scale for each strategy with response option ranging from 1 (*never used*) to 4 (*very often used*).

Internal and External Validation of the Scale for Kitesurfing Self-Regulation Strategies

Using the initial version of the questionnaire, we conducted tests of internal and external validity during a pre-competition training period.

Construct validity consists of verifying that the scale does indeed measure the different structures as suggested by the theoretical research. The tool is evaluated in three stages. (1) In order to analyze factorial structure, we did not conduct a prior exploratory study. Indeed, when scale items are taken from an existing model or previous study, it is possible to use a confirmatory analysis (Vallerand & Hess, 2000). (2) In order to define the various construct dimensions, we tried to evaluate whether or not the sub-scales can be used to significantly identify the subjects' (kitesurfers) behavior. (3) Finally, the external validity of the scale is tested using the constructs' correlation. We can compare the measures defined here with psychological measurements using other psychological scales. These scales would evaluate the factors which, in theory, are linked to self-regulation involvement: motivation scales, causal attribution, self-perception, etc. Here, we wanted to study the relationships between use of self-regulation strategies and "objective" measurements such as the number of training sessions per week, or performance in competitions following a certain training period. We looked for a way to ensure the scale had "predictive validity".

Finally, we tested the reliability of the scale. A scale's *reliability* refers to the precision of the measurements taken, independently of the phenomena being studied (Vallerand & Hess, 2000). Temporal reliability is not a particularly relevant criterion when evaluating cognitive involvement within a specific context at a specific time. The reliability of a scale such as this, measuring psychological involvement in training contexts depends on internal coherence and internal consistency reliability. We studied internal consistency by calculating Cronbach's alpha coefficient (Cronbach, 1951) for each of our tool's subscales.

The study was organized during a pre-competitive period so that kite surfers were in the process of planning and conducting their own training programs. Prior to each competition, the athletes had at least four days to familiarize themselves with the water and to train. They were presented with our questionnaire during this preparation period.

Participants

The participants were seventy-five male kite surfers. Participants were chosen based on their performances in previous kitesurfing competitions. They represented participants at national and international levels of competition in kitesurfing.

In order to collect data from international-level kitesurfers, we went to the kitesurfing world championships in New Caledonia and to an international competition in Istanbul. The national-level participants were all present at the final of the French kitesurfing championships. We also collected data in France at semi-final level.

Fifty-four men and twenty-one women (n=75) were selected for the present study. All subjects were identified as either international elite achievers (n=35), national elite achievers (n=28), or national junior achievers (n=12) in kitesurfing.

Procedure

Kitesurfers were administered the questionnaire during one of the training periods. The researchers explained what they would be asked, and why we were interested in understanding their strategies. Participants felt comfortable talking to the experimenters as we were only able to work within the context of these competitions thanks to our collaboration with internationally renowned kitesurfers. Participants' were, of course, reassured as to the confidential nature of the data collected. They were advised that the questionnaire was not a test and that there were no right or wrong answers. After each kitesurfer had completed their questionnaire, they were thanked and encouraged for the upcoming competition.

Results

Internal Validity

In order to further confirm the self-regulation model in a pre-competitive kite surfing setting, a multivariate analysis with discrimination function was used to measure to what extent each item belongs to a category. According to statistical analysis, the independent variables (items) were clearly separated into six groups for learning strategies and seven groups for management strategies (dependent variables).

Firstly, a multivariate inference test (Statistica, 08) was conducted in order to verify that the collected responses do indeed enable us to predict which items belong to which sub-scales. In order to ensure the validity of the questionnaire, it is important that participants to not simply always answer "I agree entirely", no matter what training technique they actually use. Wilks' lambda test (Lambda = .00; p < .01) proves the model's ability to discriminate (the 13 sub-scales are here considered to be the dependent variables).

The discriminatory analysis was also used to evaluate the internal validity of the prior classification of items. The discriminatory analysis automatically calculates classification functions in order to determine which group (sub-scale) each observation (item) is most likely to belong to. The probability of an observation belonging to a particular group was calculated using Mahalanobis distances. For each group (sub-scale) on our questionnaire, we identified the position of a point or centroid, representing the means of all the observed variables and the predetermined classes within that group. For each sub-scale, the Mahalanobis distances were calculated for each of these centroids. Each observation is classified into the group to which it is closest, that is to say, the group with the lowest Mahalanobis distance. The probability of an observation belonging to a particular group is inversely proportional to its Mahalanobis distance from that group's centroid. Here, all observations, all items, were correctly classed following the analysis, thus confirming their place in the subscales as determined *a priori*.

Thirdly, working from the squares of the Mahalanobis distances (D^2) between the centroids of each group, we were able to test the significance of the distances between groups and therefore to determine how each sub-scale discriminates between participants. In other words, what are the relationships between the construct's different dimensions? Does the use of one or more self-regulation strategies really represent a difference between the participants?

None of the sub-scales were significantly far from the other sub-scales. The results show, on the one hand, that it was difficult to differentiate between participants using only one of the categories of self-regulation strategy and, on the other hand, that they tended to use a number of categories of strategy at the same time, rather than using them exclusively. In accordance with the procedure used and the results obtained in previous studies (Kermarrec & Michot, 2008), we considered that grouping the strategies together might make it easier to distinguish between the participants' behavior more accurately. We therefore tried to identify self-regulation profiles for kitesurfers based on their use of multiple learning and management strategies, and then tested this hypothetical hierarchical factorial structure.

In addition, the identification of a hierarchical structure of the construct is based on a discriminant function analysis. A canonical analysis of the data revealed that the first three factors (or discriminant functions) were significant: F1 (330) = 445; p < .01; F2 (290) = 70; p <.01; F3 (252) = 19; p <.01]. Table 1 showed how, for each of the two factors, these items are distributed according to their standardized coefficients (β). The higher the coefficient, the stronger the item's contribution to the discrimination between groups.

Factor 1 is essential and its effect can be interpreted to suggest a way of regrouping the strategies (of the sub-scales) according to three self-regulation profiles.

The strategies relating to motivation; to be the best or to improve on the last competition, seem to be associated with a reduction of relationships with others and of attention focusing. This self-regulation profile ($45 < \beta < 150$) characterizes the athletes motivated by managing their potential and optimizing their performance during the upcoming competition, rather than learning new moves. A large number of items and strategies contribute to the discriminatory function between $-10 < \beta < 20$; there are many learning strategies (imitation, understanding, practice), and management strategies in which the athletes are greatly involved in modifying their abilities: managing, modifying the task or the exercise, self-evaluation. This self-regulation profile points to personal involvement in the individual learning processes for acquiring new skills.

A third self-regulation profile could be characterized by collaborative learning or group training sessions ($-25 < \beta < -170$). Looking for help from others is associated with attention paid to instructions or advice as well as time management. In order to learn by following advice from peers, it seems that kitesurfers use mental imagery processes.

We then went on to conduct another confirmatory analysis. We calculated the squares of Mahalanobis distances (D^2) between the centroid of each group (3 profiles) and tested the significance of these inter-group distances. The results of this second classification function analysis are particularly interesting as the three new categories are well spaced: profile 1 (performance optimization) vs. profile 2 (individual learning) [$D^2 = 158 \times 10^4$; $F(41,1) = 67063$, p<. 01]; profile 1 (performance optimization) vs. profile 3 (collaborative learning) [$D^2 = 476 \times 10^4$; $F(41,1) = 168925$, p<. 01]: profile 3 (collaborative learning) vs. profile 2 (individual learning) [$D^2 = 85 \times 10^4$; $F(41,1) = 39913$, p<. 01].

This study of construct validity therefore reveals a 3-level hierarchical factorial structure with 46 items (behaviors) grouped into 13 categories of self-regulation strategy which can also be grouped into three categories: three self-regulation involvement profiles for kitesurfing training.

Internal Consistency

Cronbach's Alpha Coefficient (Cronbach, 1951) is a technique designed to estimate the internal consistency of a test in order to establish the "degree of reliability" of the different items within each of the sub-scales. In other words, do the items designed to measure each category of strategy actually measure the same thing?

This index, which varies from 0 to 1, measures consistency which, as the value of the index increases, becomes more and more satisfactory. Generally speaking, an acceptable alpha coefficient falls between .61 and .92 (Nunnally, 1978).

The software *Statistica* offers a standardized calculation of Cronbach's Alpha coefficient. For this study, the 13 sub-scales had an index value of between .55 and .85.

Four of the sub-scales had a rather low index. The reliability of these sub-scales can be improved by deleting certain items. The reliability of the sub-scale relating to the learning strategy "to think about and to seek understanding" can be improved by deleting the item "I tested a number of different solutions in order to find the most effective". In this way, the Cronbach's alpha for this subscale can be increased to .67. For the sub-scale evaluating task management strategies, the alpha coefficient was improved from .59 to .63 by deleting the item "I decided by myself which exercises to do in order to improve my skills". Nevertheless, two of the management strategies were evaluated using sub-scales with rather unacceptable reliability: managing motivation through progress (.59), and especially self-evaluation (.55). In future studies the items relating to these sub-scales should be revised in order to improve the uniformity of the items. The number of items in each sub-scale could also be increased so as to represent the diversity of self-evaluation and motivation management methods.

External Validity

The components from the self-regulation model included the learning and management strategies employed by the participants. The learning and management strategies used by the participants indicate the processes that the participants use when they engage in learning by training. More specifically, learning strategies represent the means or behaviors that individuals use to select or to process information concerning the acquisition of the information presented in the training sequences, while management strategies represent the means or behaviors that are used to mentally organize the learning context or to facilitate information processing (Kermarrec, Todorovitch & Fleming, 2004).

Reliability was tested between four measures. The use of learning strategies (LS) and management strategies (MS) in kitesurfing were identified using the Self-Regulation Strategies in Self-Paced Training Questionnaire (SRSPTQ). Training involvement was reported to the number of training sessions per week (TI). The kitesurfers' performance (P) measure refers to the level of competition that they would be able to attain following this training period. The performances were reported with a range of 1 (French national championship), 2 (European championship) or 3 (World championship).

The results (see figure 1) suggest many relationships between the declared self-regulation strategies, training frequencies, and (performance) achievement in kitesurfing.

Firstly, regressions showed that self-regulation strategies could predict training involvement (R^2=.26; $p < .01$). Training involvement is quite a good predictor of performance (R^2=.11; $p < .01$). The use of management strategies is related to the use of learning strategies (β = .64; $p < .01$). However, the use of learning strategies alone does not account for involvement in frequent training sessions. These results should be attested external validity for the SRSPTQ.

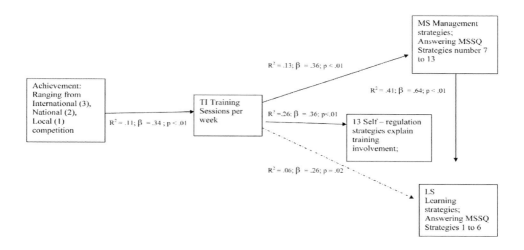

Figure 1: Links between stated self-regulation strategies, training frequencies and (performance) achievement in kitesurfing.

DISCUSSION

The major purpose of this study was to develop an inventory designed to measure the use of self regulation strategies in pre-competitive kitesurfing training settings.

Using a confirmatory factor analysis technique, we determined a hierarchical structure. The sub-scales defined by previous studies and the theoretical framework were represented by 46 items and 13 sub-scales. A factorial analysis enabled us to identify three approaches to self-regulation in pre-competitive kitesurfing training settings. The reliability of many of the sub-scales led us to distinguish SR processing when athletes (1) aimed to perform by managing attention and motivational and social resources; (2) aimed to optimize their own learning processes by imitating, understanding, practicing, self-evaluating and managing tasks; and (3) aimed to organize collaborative learning processes by seeking help, listening to instructions or advice, visualizing or using imagery, and managing time.

Internal consistency analysis indicated that intrinsic motivation and self-evaluation subscales should be improved for future studies. However, two of our items should be deleted, leaving a scale with only 44 items.

This article proposes an evaluative tool for self-regulatory strategies and raises two theoretical issues: self-regulation is a complex process which we have tried to approach from a broad point of view, and it is also a contextualized process, depending greatly on the resources available in specific training or practice contexts.

If we compare the strategies used in kitesurfing with those detailed in the literature, the one evaluation scale suggested here can be used to measure processes and strategies which are often studied using a number of separate tools. The findings correspond to literature from other fields such as educational psychology and sports psychology where the components we identified for the kitesurfing setting were found in other learning and performance contexts. Specifically, learning or primary strategies such as *listening to instructions* (Dansereau, 1985; Zimmerman & Martinez-Pons, 1986), *to think and seek understanding* (Singer& Gerson, 1979; Weinstein & Mayer, 1986), *to watch and to imitate* (Kitsankas, Zimmerman, Clearly, 2000), *to visualize and to imagine* (Singer & Gerson, 1979; Singer 1988), to focus attention (Singer & Gerson, 1979; Singer 1988), and *to repeat and to practice* (Weinstein & Mayer, 1986; Zimmerman & Martinez-Pons, 1986) are usually identified as the components of self-regulation. In the context or sport, these self-regulation components are used in order "to select and to govern attentiveness in a learning situation, the management of information and retrieval skills, and the construction of a solution to a problem" (Singer & Cauraugh, 1985). The use of video or photos (e.g., to imitate) seems to be more specific to learning in pre-competitive sport settings.

However, it is important that self-regulated learners establish and maintain the right attitudes toward learning through effective management strategies. Management strategies identified by researchers as support or secondary management strategies associated with the self-regulation process were found to concur with our findings. Among these management strategies were (1 & 2) *to manage social resources* (Gernigon & al., 1999), (3 & 4) *to manage intrinsic or extrinsic motivation* (Dansereau, 1985; Singer & Gerson, 1979), (5) *to manage time* (Judd, McCombs, & Dobrovolny., 1979; Singer & Gerson, 1979; Weinstein & Mayer, 1986; Son & Metcalf, 2000), (6) *to manage the task and to adjust its difficulty* (Zimmerman & Martinez-Pons, 1986), and (7) *to self-evaluate* (Dansereau, 1985; Singer & Gerson, 1979; Zimmerman & Martinez-Pons, 1986.)

Although the strategies identified here seem to concur with those detailed in the literature, the self-regulation profiles used to characterize the athletes' involvement are specific to the context of kitesurfing. During this pre-competitive period, athletes make a number of deliberate choices: either they try to improve on their current performance or they try to learn new moves. Similarly, they either work alone, or they collaborate with other athletes in order to improve. In future studies, it would be interesting to see whether or not these types of involvement or self-regulation affect, or are correlated with, personality or motivational factors (self-confidence, self-esteem, self-efficacy), or with performance.

Table 2.

	Content of scale	Internal Validity				Reliability
	Items	F1	F2	F3		Cronbach's alpha
1	I studied photos or videos (before attempting this move)	22,1	-6,93	2,07	LS 1 To watch and to imitate	.70
6	I made the effort to carefully watch one element of this move	23,4	-6,11	1,41		
13	I watched other kitesurfers	21,5	-6,91	1,88		
18	I watched specific movements as other kitesurfers accomplished the moves	21,5	-9,84	3,01		
24	I attempted to imitate those who completed the moves successfully	22,1	-7,07	1,59		
2	I tried to go through the move in my head	-27,2	7,07	-3,86	LS2 To imagine and to simulate	.76
9	I tried to go through the exact movements in my head	-26,1	8,78	-1,88		
16	I imagined myself doing the right move or accomplishing the exercise	-26,9	7,42	-1,55		
21	I practiced in my head before actually attempting the move	-26,0	7,46	0,11		
3	I thought about my mistakes	18,1	-13,5	1,06	LS3 To understand and to think about	.55 .67 if item 15 is deleted
8	I looked for different ways of completing the move and observed the consequences of each technique	16,16	-14,82	-1,35		
12	I analyzed the technical move and thought about how I could improve my performance	18,5	-14,7	-1,35		
15	I tested a number of different possibilities in order to find the most effective	16,9	-14,2	-0,99		
10	I concentrated on something in particular. Example: the trajectory of the fin	42,5	-0,13	-10,6	LS4 Focussing attention	.62
20	I thought to myself "only think about the right position or movement"	43,7	-2,19	-11,6		
23	I specifically concentrated on one particular aspect: the movement, the wind, the kite, etc	43,2	0,27	-12,2		
4	I tried to follow advice	-80,9	-3,17	0,15	LS5 Following advice	.60 0.63 if item 19 is deleted
7	I remembered advice I had been given previously while I was attempting the move	-82,9	-0,65	1,31		
11	I tried to follow written or verbal explanations to the best of my ability	-81,9	0,56	3,04		
19	I discussed the movements that had to be done to achieve a specific exercise with other kitesurfers	-79,1	0,45	2,23		
5	I thought that I should practice the exercise regularly	-6,39	15,2	-3,82	LS6 To repeat and to practice	.65
14	I practiced many times in order to succeed	-9,85	14,5	-4,21		
17	I forced myself to practice the move as often as possible	-6,72	15,4	-4,48		
22	I often practiced the same move over and over again	-6,00	14,9	-4,51		

Table 2. (Continued)

Item	Statement				Factor	Loading
25	I worked with other kitesurfers who also wanted to improve	-42,2	30,0	-9,48	MS 1 Working with a group	.73
39	I chose to spend time with specific kitesurfers so that I could learn faster	-43,1	30,7	-8,64		
46	I chose to work with specific kitesurfers so that I could improve	-41,0	30,1	-10,1		
34	I worked alone in order to be able to think about the move and to concentrate	45,3	-28,5	7,93	MS2 Working alone	.77
37	I set myself apart from the others so as to work quietly	45,1	-30,6	4,81		
44	I worked alone voluntarily in order to improve	44,5	-29,5	6,16		
26	I tried to do my best	64,6	3,61	7,10	MS3 Self-motivation through improvement	.59
36	I told myself that I needed to improve	65,9	4,55	4,88		
43	I told myself that I could succeed	67,9	3,37	6,57		
28	I told myself that I needed to be the best	151	31,3	11,4	MS4 Motivation through competition	.85
30	I tried to perform better than the others	152	31,0	12,2		
45	I tried to be even better than the other kitesurfers	151	29,4	14,1		
27	I rested for a moment in order to improve the move afterwards	-175	8,98	12,8	MS5 Time Management	.83
33	I took the time to recuperate between two attempts	-176	8,58	13,5		
42	I took the time to get my breath back between two attempts	-178	8,98	12,2		
29	I decided by myself which exercises I should do in order to improve	-9,47	-28,7	-0,21	MS6 Task Management	.59 0.62 if item 29 is deleted
41	I tried to find the exercise which best suited me in order to improve	-10,3	-26,7	-1,48		
35	I tried to alter the exercise little by little in order to improve my skills	-8,83	-27,3	-1,86		
31	I tried to decrease or to increase the difficulty of the exercise	-9,3	-28,1	0,15		
32	I evaluated myself	12,7	-2,10	-9,00	MS7 Self-evaluation	.54
38	I identified my level	13,5	-3,22	-8,87		
40	I tried to see whether or not I had improved	14,2	-3,43	-8,29		

Finally, from a theoretical standpoint, the hierarchical structure of the construct leads us to question the concept of "strategy". Learning strategies could be considered an intermediary cognitive structure. It is these strategies that create a link between the conscious goals, worries, and priorities in athletes' involvement, and the contextualized behaviors that the subject can implement and control. The strategies therefore provide a link between the goal (to learn or to perform) and the means of achieving that goal (watching a peer accomplish a move). The strategies are a certain kind of procedural knowledge; "how to learn or to perform" (Kermarrec, 2004). This knowledge is stored in the form of rules for managing cognitive activity; they guide the subject's actions through successive or step-by-step behavior in order to mobilize certain elementary means of information processing. Strategies can be both explicitly and implicitly activated (Masters, 1992; Singer, 2001). They can be directly triggered by the context through habit, in a relatively automatic manner, or can be activated voluntarily in new or unplanned contexts. This characteristic of strategies could prove interesting for both researchers and coaches alike. Indeed, considering that self-regulatory strategies used by athletes are consciously accessible, it would be possible to design tools for strategy evaluation that rely on verbal data (questionnaires). Evaluating the strategies stated by the athletes helps the coach to adapt his/her training methods, modifying the procedures to fit the athlete's profile and information processing techniques. The coach could also help the athlete to change his/her involvement in self-regulation.

In conclusion, we would like to examine the problems faced by research into self-regulation in sport. In sports psychology literature, there is often a distinction between descriptive and predictive approaches, and "training studies" (Crews, & al., 2001). These approaches all refer to one major concern in sports science research: the analysis of performance factors and conditions in order to design improved and innovative training techniques. However, the development of self-regulation capacities for athletes has often faced difficulties when transferring strategies acquired during training to real performance or competition situations (Singer, Lidor & Cauraugh, 1993; Kermarrec, 2004). Skills transfer relies greatly on the similarities between training and performance conditions. Using simulations and virtual reality technology seems to be a promising way of researching sports self-regulation and mental capacity training. This innovative practice will be developed in a following chapter.

REFERENCES

Barkhoff, H., Heiby, E.M. & Pagano, I.S. (2007). *Self-Regulation Skills of a Competitor Type vs. a Training Champion Athlete in Artistic Roller Skating: A Season Long Case Study in Elite Sport Competitions.* Athletics Insight, 9, 2, 43-55.

Anshel, M.H. (1995). *An examination of self-regulation cognitive-behavioural strategies of Australian elite and non-elite competitive male swimmers.* Australian Psychologist, 30, 78-83.

Crews, D.J., Lochbaum, M.R., & Karoly, P. (2001). *Self-regulation: concepts, methods and strategies in sport and exercise.* In R.N. Singer, H.A. Hausenblas, & C.M. Janelle (Eds), Handbook of Sport Psychology (pp. 566-581). New York, NY: Wiley & Sons.

Chen, D., & Singer, R. N. (1992). *Self-regulation and cognitive strategies in sport participation.* Journal of Sport Psychology, 23, 277-300.

Craick F.I.M., Lockhart R.S. (1972). *Levels of processing. A framework of memory research.* Journal of Verbal Learning and Verbal Behavior, 11 : 671-684.

Craick F.I.M., Tulving E. (1975). *Depth of processing and the retention of words in episode memory.* Journal of Experimental Psychology, 104 (3) : 268-294.

Cronbach, L. J. (1951). *Coefficient alpha and the internal structure of tests.* Psychometrica, 16, 297-334.

Dansereau, D. F. (1985). *Learning strategy research.* In J. W. Segal (Ed.), Thinking and Learning Skills (pp. 209-239). Hillsdale, NJ: Lawrence Erlbaum associates.

Dansereau, D. F., et al. (1979). *Evaluation of learning strategy system.* In J.R. O'Neil, & C. D. Spielberger (Eds.), Cognitive and Affective Learning Strategies (pp. 3-43). London: Academic Press.

Gernigon, C., D'Arripe-Longuevilli, F., & Debove, V. (1999*). Effects of learning context and gender on help-seeking, situational indexes of achievement and motor skill acquisition.* Journal of Sport and Exercise Psychology, 21, S48

Ille, A., & Cadopi, M. (1999). *Memory for movement sequences in gymnastics : effects of age and skill level.* Journal of Motor Behavior, 31 (3), 290-300.

Judd, W. A., McCombs, B. L., Dobrovolny, J L. (1979). *Time management as a learning strategy for individualized instruction.* In J. R. O'Neil, & C. D. Spielberger (Eds.), Cognitive and affective learning strategies (pp. 133-173). London: Academic Press.

Karoly, P. (1993). *Mechanisms of self-regulation: A systems view.* Annual Review of Psychology, 44, 23-52.

Kermarrec, G., Todorovich, J. R., & Fleming, J., (2004). *Investigation of the self-regulation components students used in a physical education setting.* Journal of Teaching in Physical Education, 2, 23, 123-142.

Kermarrec, G. (2004). *Autorégulation et stratégies* [self-regulation and strategies]. Sciences & Motricité, 3, 56, 9-38.

Kermarrec, G. & Michot, T. (2008*). Développement et validation d'une échelle de mesure situationnelle des stratégies d'apprentissage en contexte scolaire.* [Development and validation of a learning strategies' scale in school context]. Canadian Behavioural Science Review,

Kirschenbaum, D. S. (1984). *Self-regulation and sport psychology: Nurturing an emerging symbiosis.* Journal of Sport Psychology, 6, 159-183.

Kitsantkas, A., Zimmerman, B. J. (1998). *Self-regulation of motoric learning: a strategic cycle view.* Journal of Applied Sport Psychology, 10 (2), 220 – 239.

Kitsantkas, A., Zimmerman, B. J., Cleary, T. (2000). *The role of observation and emulation in the development of athletic self-regulation.* Journal of Educational Psychology, 92(4), 811-817.

Lefebvre-Pinard, M., & Pinard, A. (1985). *Taking charge of one's cognitive activity: A moderator of competence.* In E. D. Neimark, R. De Lisi, J. L. Newman (Eds.), Moderators of Competence (pp. 191-209). Hillsdale, NJ: Erlbaum.

Masters, R. S. W. (1992). *Knowledge, nerves and know-how: The role of explicit versus implicit knowledge in the breakdown of a complex motor skill under pressure.* British Journal of Psychology, 83, 343-358.

Michot, T. & Kermarrec, G. (2005). *Développement et validation d'une échelle de mesure situationnelle des stratégies de gestion en contexte scolaire. [Development and validation of a management strategies' scale in school context].* Cahiers de l'URAFF, 36.

Nunnaly, J.C. (1978). *Psychometric Theory.* New – York : Mc Graw – Hill.

Ommundsen, Y. (2003). *Implicit Theories of Ability and Self-regulation Strategies in Physical Education Classe,* Educational Psychology, 23, 2, 142-157

Pintrich, P. R. (2004). *A conceptual framework for assessing motivation and self-regulated learning in college students.* Educational Psychology Review, 16 (4), 385-407.

Shen, B. & Chen, A. (2006). *Examining the interrelations among knowledge, interests, and learning strategies,* Journal of Teaching in Physical Education, 25, 182-199.

Singer, R. N. (1988). *Strategies and metastrategies in learning and performing self-paced athletics skills.* The Sport Psychologist, 2, 49-68.

Singer, R. N. (2001). *Pre-performance state, routines, and automaticity: What does it take to realize expertise in self-paced events?* Journal of Sport and Exercise.

Singer, R. N., & Gerson, R. F. (1979). *Learning strategy, cognitive processes, and motor learning.* In J. R. O'neil, & C. D. Speilberger (Eds.) Cognitive and Affective Learning Strategies (pp. 215-247). London: Academic Press.

Singer, R. N., & Cauraugh, J. H. (1985). *The generalizability effect of learning strategies for categories of psychomotor skills.* Quest, 37, 103-119.

Singer, R. N., DeFrancesco, C., & Randall, L. E. (1989). *Effectiveness of a global learning strategy practiced in different contexts on primary and transfer self-paced motor tasks.* Journal of Sport and Exercise Psychology, 11, 290-303.

Singer, R. N., Lidor, R., & Cauraugh, J. H. (1993). *To be aware or not aware? What to think about while learning and performing a motor skill.* The Sport Psychologist, 7, 19-30.

Son. L. K., & Metcalf, J. (2000). *Metacognitive and control strategies in study-time allocation.* Journal of Experimental Psychology, Learning, Memory, and Cognition, 26(1), 204-221.

Thill, E. (2001). *La régulation en ligne des conduites* [On line self - regulation]. In F. Cury et P. Sarrazin (Eds.) Théories de la motivation et pratiques sportives (pp. 194-219). Paris: Presses Universitaires de France.

Thill, E., & Brunel, P. (1995). *Ego Involvement and task-involvement: Related conceptions of ability, effort, and learning strategies among football players.* International Journal of Sport Psychology, 26(1), 81-97.

Vallerand, R. J. & Hess U. (Eds). (2000) *Méthodes de recherche en psychologie.* Paris : Gaëtan Morin Editeur.

Weinstein, C. E. & Mayer, R. E. (1986). *The teaching of learning strategies.* In M. C. Wittrock (Ed.) Handbook of Research on Teaching (p. 315-327). New York: MacMillan.

Weiss, M. R., & Klint, K. A., (1987). *Show and tell in the gymnasium : an investigation of developmental differences in modeling and verbal rehearsal of motor skills. research* Quarterly for Exercise and Sport, 58, 234-241.

Zimmerman, B. J., Martinez-Pons, M. (1986). *Development of a structured interview for assessing student use of self-regulated learning strategies.* American Educational Research Journal, 23(4), 614-628.

In: Handbook of Sports Psychology
Editor: Calvin H. Chang

ISBN: 978-1-60741-256-4
©2009 Nova Science Publishers, Inc.

Chapter 11

ATHLETE PERFORMANCE, COPING AND ANXIETY: CLINICAL ISSUES FOR THE CONSULTANT

Thomas W. Miller

University of Connecticut, Storrs, Connecticut, USA

Keywords: Sports consultation, anxiety, performance issues

INTRODUCTION

Performance, coping and anxiety are critical ingredients for the consultant in working with athletes at all levels. Consultation in sport requires competency and specificity. The greater the specificity of the service in terms of offering information and training that will assure athletes can adapt to both the known and unknown factors that will operate to pose threats to their career should be the primary goal (Miller, Ogilvie,. Branch, 2008). In consultation with agents or coaches, appealing to individual athletes who could benefit from any aspect of sports consultation requires each having an empirical basis to the consultation services. New recruits whether to a college or pro team will confront a number of issues within the purview of the sports consultant when signing a contract. As a consultant, it is essential to emphasize to agents and others within college or professional organizations why it is imperative that an extensive psychometric study be utilized for the benefit of both athlete and coaching staff. Individual assessment helps to diagnose potential problems and will be instructive for the organization in understanding enhancing the individual's probability of making and completing effectively in the athletic arena.

COMPETITIVE STATE ANXIETY

Anxiety is a fundamental experience of life and in competitive sport it provides a significant role for the athlete, the coach and the sports psychologist (Miller, Kraus, Adams, Bilyeu,. Ogilvie 1999; Miller, Ogilvie, Branch 2008). State anxiety was widely believed to be correlated with performance and arousal and was viewed as an uncomplicated Inverted-U

(Yerkes and Dodson, 1908). This suggested that an athlete's performance, that is the athletes best performance could be achieved with an average level of arousal. Furthermore, if the level of arousal were too low (or too high) poor performance would ensue. The Multidimensional Theory of Anxiety (Martens et al., 1990), and the Catastrophe Model (Hardy & Fazey, 1987), are the two prominent theories that have emerged in the study of this phenomenon. Competitive state-anxiety usually follows a pattern of subjective feelings of tension and inadequacy, combined with heightened arousal of the autonomic nervous system, (Hackfort & Schwenkmezger, 1989). The intensity and duration of the anxiety alternates according to; the amount of stressful stimuli the athlete encounters, and the period of subjective threat created by the stimuli (Hackfort & Schwenkmezger, 1989).

In the last decade of the twentieth century, Hardy & Parfitt, (1991) argued that when individuals are cognitively anxious, they continue in their attempts to deal with the demands of the task. Noteworthy is the fact that the amount of physiological arousal the athlete experiences could interfere with their performance, either by distraction, reducing their capacity to process cognitive information, or by causing them to consciously divert cognitive resources to maintaining effort, rather than to their performance in competitive sport. In the first decade of the twenty-first century, our understanding of this phenomenon is still best explained by Hardy & Fazey's (1988) "catastrophe model." Furthermore, it should also be noted that the majority of the research has been conducted by the same small number of sport scientists, thus limiting the evidence base of the research required to strengthen the model's position as a solution to the competitive anxiety phenomenon.

CAREER DEVELOPMENT AS A DEVELOPMENTAL PROCESS

Preparing an athlete for an athletic career must be viewed as a "developmental process" (Ogilvie &Tutko 1996; Miller, 1996; Miller, Vaughn & Miller, 1990). This process requires at least three areas of concentration: First, an extensive examination of the personality the athlete brings to sport and competition. Second, the learning style of the athlete and how unique characteristic plays out in every aspect of their sport relevant behavior. Third a need for a summary report offering a practical program that transmits how best the coaching staff can enable the individual athlete to realize athletic ability and maximize skill and competitive potential, this their competitive style. Figure 1 summarizes the critical ingredients in preparing the4 athlete for effective performance, adequate coping with competitive sports and the anxiety often experienced in the game.

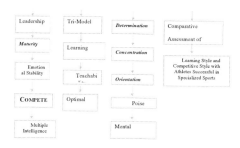

Figure 1. Developmental Process and Clinical Assessment Factors for Athletes

COMPONENTS OF PERFORMANCE

In the sport environment, those who have invested in the talent will have little patience with moderate or mediocre practices or game performance. This will carry over to fan and community expectations. How then should athletes be trained to adapt to the expectations in the sport environment? The Learning Styles Profile (LSP) (Ogilvie, 1997) is composed of four separate factors grouped into the following configuration (TriModal Learning, Learning Preferences, Teachability, and Optimal Learning), with three independent categories (Cognitive Learning, Feedback Preference and Outcome/Process). These four factors are defined as follows:

Tri-Model Learning

This factor is composed of three categories: Visual Learning, Kinesthetic Learning and Trial and Experience, three modes or ways of learning athletic skills, from Limited Use (low scores) to Seeing, Feeling and Trying different ways of experiencing a skill while learning how to do it or do it better (high scores).

Learning Preferences

This factor is composed of the categories of Amount of Information, Rate of Change and Caution/Risking, which reflect the athlete's preference for either less information, slower changes or a more conservative approach (low scores) to liking more information, faster changes and taking risks necessary to learn (high scores).

Teachability

This factor is composed of Willingness to Change, Interpersonal Control, Facilitation for Change and Ability to Trust, from needing proof, wanting control, with an independent, guarded and reluctant approach (low scores) to a more open-minded, easy-going style, able to seek help and invest trust in a coach/teacher and hence being ready to learn (high scores).

Optimal Learning

This factor is composed of Skill Rating, Learning Comfort, Ability to Change, Efforting Level, Frustration Tolerance, Commitment to Change and Compliance, from being dissatisfied with one's skills, nervous while learning, have difficulty making changes, trying too hard, frustrated, uncommitted or not having good practice habits and needing guidance to change otherwise restricted learning (low scores) to being interested in improving, able to be relaxed while learning, adept at making necessary changes with a casual and patient approach, able to stick with skill changes and practice them well until effective (high scores).

Determination

This factor is composed of four categories: Intrinsic Motivation, Sport Commitment, Competitive Orientation, Ability to Activate and Will to Win. These attributes reflect individuals' athletic motivation and investment in sport one's ability to raise activation/energy to get up for competition and profiles how driven and competitive they perceive themselves to be, from Uninvested (low scores) to Commited (high scores).

Concentration

This factor is composed of External Distractibility, Internal Distractibility, Ability to Focus, Presence of Focus and Duration of Focus. These attributes are concerned with athlete's attentional skills. Concentration is indicated from Distracted (low scores) to Focused (high scores).

Orientation

This factor is composed of Situational Focus, Extrinsic Motivation and Optimal Activation. These categories are less concerned with prescribed skills for athletes (such as concentration) and have to do more with individual and stylistic approaches to competition. Orientation is reflected from External (low scores) to Centered (high scores).

Poise

This factor is composed of Pre-Performance Activation, Ability to Deactivate, Fear of Failure, Fear of Success and Performance Under Pressure. These categories are concerned with an athlete's response to competitive stress, fears associated with performing in competition and the mental skills and qualities necessary for optimal performance. It is measured from Affected (low scores) to Calm (high scores).

Mental Toughness

This factor is composed of Outlook, Self-Talk, Self-Confidence, Self-Concept, Victim/Fighter and Ability to Recover. These attributes measure and athlete's approach towards competition, the personal characteristics supporting their performance and their tendencies during and after adverse circumstances, from Sensitive (low scores) to Tough (high scores).

COMPETITIVE STYLES PROFILE CATEGORY DESCRIPTIONS

Determination

Intrinsic Motivation – An athlete's level of internal motivation, from unmotivated from within (low scores) to having a strong inner drive (high scores).

Sport Commitment – The importance and athlete places on their sport in relation to other life interests, from relatively unimportant (low) to invested (high scores).

Ability to Activate – The ability to raise one's activation or energy levels for competition, from being difficult (low scores) to being able to get up for it (high scores).

Will to Win – The athlete's attitude towards the results of competition, from being relatively unconcerned (low scores) to having a "killer instinct" (high scores).

Concentration

External Distractibility – The athlete's tendency to be distracted before or during competition by sights or sounds (low scores) to being unaffected by outside sources (high scores).

Internal Destructibility – The tendency to be distracted by the inner noise of one's own thoughts (low scores) to being able to achieve mental quiet while competing (high scores).

Ability to Focus – The ability to direct one's attention and concentrate, from being difficult and unfocused (low scores) to being able to achieve an intense focus (high scores).

Presence of focus – The ability to focus on the task at hand, from drifting into the past or future (low scores) to concentrating well in the here and now (high scores).

Duration of Focus – The ability to sustain one's concentration, from having a short span of attention (low scores) to being able to stay focused for an extended period of time (high scores).

Orientation

Situational Focus – The athlete's tendency to focus only when it's critical (low scores) to always concentrating, regardless of the situation (high scores).

Extrinsic Motivation – The athlete's level of motivation from outside sources, from being driven by recognition, status or rewards (low scores) to external factors being unimportant (low scores).

Optimal Activation – The energy or activation level where athletes tend to compete or perform optimally, from being best when up (low scores) to being at their best when relaxed (high scores).

Poise

Pre-Performance Activation – The athlete's energy or activation level experienced immediately before competing or performing, from being very nervous up (low scores) to performing best when relaxed (high scores).

Ability to Deactivate – The athlete's ability to lower activation or energy levels when needed, from being difficult (low scores) to being able to relax (high scores).

Fear of Failure – The anxiety level associated with the possibility of competing/performing below one's abilities, from being fearful (low scores) to being able to risk defeat (high scores).

Fear of Success – The anxiety level associated with the possibility of competing/performing at or above one's abilities, from being burdened (low scores) to unaffected (high scores).

Performance Under Pressure – The effect of competitive pressure on one's athletic abilities, from being sabotaged (low scores) to having the ability to perform optimally under stress (high scores).

Mental Toughness

Outlook – An athlete's attitude going into a competition or performance, from being pessimistic (low scores) to being optimistic (high scores).

Self-Talk – The quality and emotional tone of one's self-talk during competition, from being negative or critical (low scores) to being encouraging and positive (high scores).

Self-Confidence – The level of belief in one's athletic abilities, from being doubting (low scores) to being confident (high scores).

Self0Concept – The level of one's self-esteem, from being conflicted (low scores) to being secure (high scores).

Victim/fighter – The athlete's tendency under adverse conditions to respond more as a passive victim (low scores) to being a pro-active fighter (high scores).

Ability to recover - -The athlete's response after negative circumstances, from being difficult to bounce back (low scores) to being resilient (high scores).

ADAPTATION ISSUES IN ROOKIE CAMP

There will be adaptation issues beginning in rookie training camps that the athletes may not anticipate. This will involve the reaction to them of the team veterans on the team. To some veterans, the new athlete will be seen as a threat to their career. If the rookie makes the team, one of the veterans is likely to be dropped or traded. The clinical issue is that the rookie may not be embraced by the team members and this may result in isolation with possible clinical implications.

The Influence of Coaching Style on Performance

The coaching staff will be composed of individuals, each with their own perception as how to develop new talent. They are extremely quick to develop their own particular stereotype, or characterize the recruit in personal terms. Each may have a different approach to refining their motor skills. These coaches may have rather large egos and expect immediate conformity. Their goals for individual athletes are often extreme with regard to motor and kinesthetic challenges.

Coping with Loneliness and Isolation in Sport

A subtle threat for many athletes will have been the loss of supporting relationships once out of their high school or university programs. The loss of "superstar" status and the recipient of special attention and provisions may result in performance anxiety and functional depression. For the consulting sport psychologist, the question is: "How do we strengthen independence and reduce false expectations on the part of the rookie athlete?"

Prevention intervention training must address developing an awareness on the part of athletes to recognize and seek assistance for clinically related problems and teaching strategies for dealing with the media and how to conduct interviews that will be self protecting without causing resentment or misperceptions?

Teaching/Coaching

Assessment measures that can define in precise terms how the rookie learns most efficiently and how the rookie prefers to be taught and the quality of relationship that best fits the personal needs of the athlete while learning new material available. The ideal protocol involves completing a psychological evaluation. The clinician outlines essential differences and defines how each learning environment may be structured to meet such individual differences in the athlete. Coaches must realize that the diagnostic value of testing is designed to aid them achieving their goal if better understanding their attitude not trying to tell them how to coach. The consultant's primary responsibility will be translating the coach's goals by applying insights derived from the study of their athletes. In order to survive, the consultant must maintain a wholesome balance between being an agent for the coach while never sacrificing the ethical responsibility to the athlete.

The Service Area Covered Under Performance Enhancement

Assessment of sport specific attributes can enhance the direction of an athlete's future. It is rare to find an athlete that could not benefit from working on less well developed personal attributes or learning and competitive skills that need improvement. This aspect of the consultation could require considerable special attention by the consultant. It would require attention to every aspect of performance such as the cognitive factors that supports or interferes with performance. Determining the mental or emotional factors that contribute to "personal best performances" is essential. The need for insight into all factors associated with arousal control and goal setting is essential for coaching staff to understand the needs of athletes for which they have coaching responsibilities (Miller, Vaughn, Miller 1990).

Once again the model of a detailed enhancement program for athletes exposing the insights generated, and how such are applied in modification program. Particular reference to how a member of the coaching staff should be trained to maintain the modification program. Ideally with the athlete's approval, a detailed developmental program would be shared with the coach of the team. Every elite athlete has accepted the merit of this proposal. Obviously specific personal attributes have been excluded, those that would make no positive contribution to the athletes performance future.

LIFE ENHANCEMENT ASSESSMENT PROGRAM (LEAP)

Clinical research has shown that many athletes are poorly prepared for their careers or the subsequent retirement from competition and may face considerable difficulties in coping with the significant life changes that accompany their sport careers and sport identities (Miller, Adams, Kraus, Clayton,. Miller, Anderson, Ogilvie 2001; Miller, 1996). Athletes will likely encounter many of the following situations, frustrations, and realities during and/or following their professional career: problems with the cycles and career transitions and emotional and financial factors associated with the career developmental process. There will also be the need to work after they stop playing retirement at a relatively young age, no idea how to logically approach the end and no real control over the eventual outcome of their careers.

The causes for termination of an athlete's career are most frequently a function of one or more of three factors: age, deselection, or injury. The factors influence a variety of psychological, social, and physical issues that contribute to the likelihood of post-career distress and concern. Age: physical deterioration causes ability and performance to decrease; deselection: "survival of the fittest" disregards players who do not meet the necessary performance criteria; injury: whether severe or minor, may force a premature end to an athletes career and free choice: athletes chose to end their careers voluntarily, recognizing they are ready for change. The LEAP program provides consultation and services to identify post-career transition needs; to determine feelings of athletes regarding career transition and to devise simple workable solutions to meet the athletes' needs. In order to achieve these goals, several procedures are designed and implemented. These include: preparation of player profiles; development of career portfolios; establishing relationships with educational institutions and arranging flexible distance learning through wed based technology. Each athlete, no matter what level of education or career aspiration engages in a series of interest and aptitude evaluations, personality assessment and career placement opportunities. In establishing a successful plan for the athlete will have to accept and support the reality of "life during and after sport." The best type of preparation for career transition involves education geared toward this transitional phase in their life. The term education is used in a broad sense and far exceeds the bounds of the classroom and the traditional teacher/student situation. It includes individual analysis through interest and aptitude inventories, counseling and advisement, and placement services.

Critical Issues Regarding Athletes Emotional Welfare

This will be the most sensitive area of consultation. Should the athlete show clinical signs of anxiety, depression or personality defects, signs of pathology, areas where (s)he is experiencing serious emotional liabilities, it is essential to consult with psychiatric and medically related specialists. Hopefully your professional contract with agents or teams will stipulate your ethical, moral and professional responsibilities with regard to areas of privileged communication. In team situations, the consulting clinical specialist must establish rapport and commitment from the athlete as to how one is obligated to refer for treatment when confronting situations where clinical issues arise.

Professional issues related to "powers of referral" should be confirmed with the athlete. It is sometimes difficult to protect athletes from public exposure when they act out conflicts in the public's eye. The art of salvaging the character at these times require inordinate skill by the consultant.. Once again the contracting party must be made aware as to how professionals will be expected to react while protecting the organization from community outrage, but still maintaining professional obligations to the athletes need for sheltering from the public eye.

TRANSITIONING A CAREER IN SPORTS

Transitional issues in an athlete's life are also a critical area and often a difficult one. There is always a question of agents and coaches feelings in preparing for the future needs of athletes. Some teams already bring in specialists for post-sport career planning. Several professional sport organizations have service but it is not well used by the athletes. There is little written about the effects, utility or practicality of such programs. Ogilvie (1961) initiated a career planning program for a professional football team. This was a time when most players had to work in the off season. The program generated great enthusiasm on the athletes part, but coaches did not accept the program. Most coaches did not want the players to think about anything else but the present during the season. Some coaches refused to let the players attend.

Consulting sport specialists should be cognizant of two cultural factors in this work (1) independence and (2) collaborative involvement. These seem to be very critical issues that consultants consider in the interference between coach, athletes and the organization. At what point do they become the coach's or athletes private or personal consultant. Lowman (1998) explored relevant paradigms for creating an intellectually viable consulting role applicable to athletes and coaches. It is argued that consulting psychology (as applied to organizations) needs its own models and training paradigms that address organizational, group, and, above all, individual perspectives. Consulting psychologists providing services to sport programs in organizational consulting psychology need to be housed in their own academic homes, not as too-often-welcome guests in others'.

Sport consultants must deliver sound advice in career adjustment, transitions and in counseling.. The great strength is the ability to deliver objectivity and a willingness to call it as it is. Together with objectivity there must possess good problem-solving ability, identified in an occupational analysis of consulting psychology as the single most important component of professional identity among consulting sport specialists (Robinson-Kurpius, Fuqua, Gibson, Kurpius, & Froehle, 1995).

A viable "theory of change" has been advocated by Lowman (1998) and Miller, TW, Kraus, RF, Adams, J, Bilyeu, J. Ogilvie, B. (1999). Miller (2008) argues consulting needs a viable theory of change and of changing with application to the sport and athletic arena. Such a theory must be based on and consistent with an understanding of the component parts of organizations-individual, group, and organizational. Argyris's (1971) model, for example, advocated that the organizational interventionists' goal was not the generation of change per se but rather the creation of the conditions of self-awareness and recognition from which decisions about change can be made. Process theories (e.g., Schein, 1987) additionally have their role and value in a vigorous consulting sport psychology to teams and to athletic organizations.

Transitions in Sport Consulting

Sport consultants are moving through a series of transitions. The transitions include culture, vulnerability, and willfulness, which are three prominent components of any organizational change effort. Even robustly healthy teams and athletic organizations are fragile, vulnerable systems, highly dependent on their environment and, with a few wrong or unintentional moves, fast on their way to their inevitable demise. Sport cares not one bit about the survival of a particular team, much less of a single athlete. Against this reality, defenses are critical. Denial, for example, is a markedly efficient tool that creates a necessary illusion of invulnerability often used by athletes. Individual and organizations whose existence has been threatened grow thicker defenses or die.

From traditional models, sport consultants and others will become part of a network of healthcare professionals contracting with multiskilled specialists in a network of athletic services. These shifts will be driven by cost containment, captivation and contracts for services that focus on efficiency and use financial incentives to replace what has come to be known as fees for services by consultants.

As we approach the challenges of the next decade, physicians in sports consultants providing clinical care and treatment must begin to consider a number of the issues raised by Covey et al., which encourage us to understand our unique endowments as human beings. These endowments reside in the space between stimulus and response, as well as in the art and science of good consulting. They capture what Covey called the four endowments. .

The Four Endowments Covey discusses are *self-awareness*, which is our capacity to stand apart form our winds and losses and examine our thinking, our understanding of the whole person and our motives in sports medicine. The second human endowment is well recognized in the clinician's personal development and addresses the Jungian concept that is known as *conscience*. Covey et al. Argue that conscience connects us with the wisdom of the ages and the understanding of human potential. It adds a character component to the development of our players and coaching staff. The third endowment is that of *independent wealth*, which is seen as our ability as sports medicine specialists to recognize all that we are capable of being and to act in our best interest as well as in the best interest of our players. The fourth endowment is *imagination*, which is the power to envision creative innovation and the direction for which we are responsible for the personal and professional development of our athletes.

Consulting sport specialists which vision for the future must engage fellow professionals and consumers through: (i) effective interpersonal skill development; (ii) new models of conflict management; (iii) quality tools for athletic management; and (iv) research on mastering cognitive and kinesthetic skills as well as communication skills. All of these tools are within the repertoire of the sports medicine profession, which has a rich history of development and use of a 'multiple intelligence' perspective. As changes in the profession employ the use of multiple intelligence pathways, we must begin to recognize that athlete expectations coaching outcomes must be the result of mutually discussed and agreed dimensions of clinical services.

Sports scientists must possess a good understanding of the use of multiple intelligence and a medium of educating and coaching athletes. Throughout his theory of multiple intelligences, Gardner identified several intelligence models that enrich our understanding of how athletes and other learn new material. Linguistic intelligence reflects the ability to see and develop patterns in language and to shape words and phrases that embody concepts and convey meaning, an essential factor in good coaching. Logical-mathematical intelligence includes the ability to visualize relationships between objects and the environment, and how actions would alter the relationships, an essential skill for athletes to master. Spatial intelligence is characterized by the spatial aptitude which encompasses the ability to imagine, sense environmental changes, solve mazes and interpret locations using maps. The spatial intelligence, which relates directly to visual acuity, allows one to visualize how an object would look or feel from a different perspective (Miller, Kraus, Adams, Bilyeu, Ogilvie 1999).

Of critical importance to athletes and their coaches is bodily kinesthetic intelligence, which is characterized by the ability to use the body to accomplish complex and intricate activities or manipulate objects with well-controlled finesse. Overt actions are not the sole reflections of the bodily kinesthetic intelligence. Detailed movement, including manual dexterity, is the core of bodily kinesthetic aptitude. Interpersonal intelligence is characterized by Gardner as the 'teacher' or coach. This model encompasses the ability to understand people's motivations, as well as skills in leadership, organization and communication. The ability to comprehend aspects of character in players is a primary feature of this intelligence model.

The interpersonal model of intelligence is what Gardner calls 'one's self-understanding.' This intelligence allows individuals to recognize their strengths and weaknesses, motivations, and aptitudes. Interpersonal intelligence allows an individual to assess situational in light of personal strengths and weaknesses and to determine the best approach to ensure successful resolutions in both sport and in life.

Consultants in sports, no matter what their location or specific job titles or duties, are the Yankees in the tradition-dominant South. They are the interlopers whose ideas are often prima facie wrong simply because they are different and because they address not just the prospect of change but also the necessarily painful self-awareness that usually must precede all long-lasting change. As organizations and as individuals within organizational settings, we are programmed to put the best face on situations we may know to be wrong or bed. Organizational consultants who would deal with more than the superficial, who would create more than well-paying but ephemeral organizational "change lite," need strong medicine, but first they need strong skills in assessment to know what medicine goes with what dysfunction.

As Harry Levinson (1972) has so often and persistently reminded us, intervention without diagnosis is doomed to futility or superficiality.

Sports medicine, and sport psychology a science-based practice of organizational consulting psychology, remain elusive. Micro-theories and techniques are no substitute for an integrated theory of organizational health and of organizational dysfunction that recognizes and accounts for all relevant levels: individual, group, organizational, and systemic. Consulting sport psychologists who would be effective need to understand and integrate viable theories of individuals, groups, and organizations, and need robust and tested "theories of change" and the subsequent stresses related to change in order to help the athletes that they serve.

Clinical models that tap social psychological models of life stress and how it is processed is of critical value. Miller and Veltkamp (1994) have introduced a model that helps us understand how athletes and other process such things as "fear of success" and "fear of failure." Miller (1996) summarizes several theories and models that suggest stressful life events cause psychopathology. This is based on empirical studies of extreme situations that are often life threatening, and it is referred to as the victimization model. A second model argues a predisposition approach, wherein social conditions mediate the causal relation between stressful life events and resulting psychopathology. Such a model argues that one has a vulnerability to stressful life experiences.

The "additive burden model" contrasts with the vulnerability model in that it argues that personal dispositions and social conditions make independent causal contributions make independent causal contributions to the occurrence of psychopathology rather than mediate a stressful life experience. The "chronic burden model" (Miller 1989) forgoes the issue of any recent life event but argues in favor of stable personal dispositions and social conditions, which alone can cause the adverse changes in psychological and physical condition.

The "proneness model" (Miller 1989; Miller, & Veltkamp, 1996) suggests the presence of disorder leads to stressful life events that, in turn, exacerbate the disorder. This adds a new dimension to the directionality of the causal relationship between stressful life events and psychopathology. Of considerable concern to the clinical research area is the interaction between personal predisposition and social circumstances, which is an estimate of the way in which any person adjusts to a stressful experience. Miller and Veltkamp (1994) suggest an anxiety based processing model that indicates stages in which the athlete moves. The process of moving through a transition does not always proceed in order, in predictable stages. Athletes may move through the process in different ways, often cycling back and forth among the stages and revisiting the implications of the stressful life transition. This figure depicts the process of accommodating change as part of stressful transitions. Miller & Veltkamp (1994), suggest that in processing of anxiety related to the sport activity, they proceed through a cognitive processing of the anxiety or fear. In the case of fear of failure, they experience thoughts related to such fear that results in denial, avoidance, detachment, irritability, agitated behavior, hypervigilance, cognitive disorganization, sleep difficulty recurrent distress, and re-experiencing of the perceived failure through flashbacks. It is in this period that feel entrapped within this cycle and feel numbing which results in failure to produce. Through some triggering event, the athlete is realized and the person can go through a cognitive re-evaluation of the anxious feelings and thoughts and fear of failure. Sport professionals can be of most help at this stage. . In this process, they re-visit their anxiety provoking experiences and the psychological fear and helplessness that they have experienced. Based on the adaptation, support, and response of those who are involved in their lives and in their treatment, they work towards a resolution that may enhance their p[performance in sport. Figure 2 and summarizes the five stages in which the person transitions in dealing with the trauma.

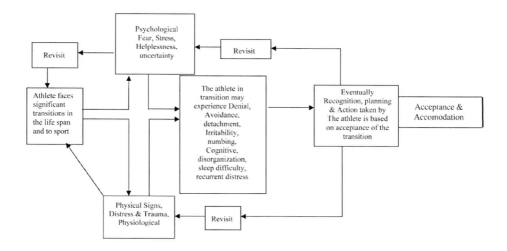

Figure 2. Cognitive Processing of Anxiety with sport transitions.

Sports medicine will require a cutting edge understanding of the genetic interface with learning styles and systems of cognitive processing of athletes. Diagnostic evaluation as we have known it will be replaced by a more complex analysis system of networks which will analyze how genetic factors that influence motivation and behavior in athletes is affected by intellectual and personality markers that result in more complex thinking and reasoning in athletes. Physicians in sports medicine will, by necessity, be multiskilled specialists providing clinical services to athletes and coaches. Breakthroughs in technology, including new diagnostic models and intervention techniques, will impact athletic competition. Training programs and formal education in sports medicine will be offered through new technology, and through mediums employing distance learning technologies featuring the world's best recognized physicians, educators, scientists, researchers and professional consultants in sport and athletic competition.

Sports scientists, clinicians and educators will realize new paradigms of service provision that will include clinical algorithms and pathways of care modified by genetic breakthroughs, technology and new interventions for sports clinicians. Virtual reality technology will generate new models in the kinesiology of sport. Athletic 'supercenters' will feature medical health care, dietetics, exercise, medical screening and sport and behavioral counseling for athletes and coaches. New alliances in medicine, education, athletics and science will emerge with physicians as significant partners in treating the health care needs of athletes. Databases will hold key information in addressing patterns of play that can be expected of players influenced by physical, psychological, genetic and biochemical characteristics. The role of sports medicine in the domains of academics, athletics and sports science represents an enormous wealth of talent and energy. Consultation issues in sports psychology whether with a division one, college basketball team or a professional team presents unique situations for the consultant? Considerations in the spectrum of training programs present a variety of areas in which the sport psychologist must prepare adequately. Adaptation issues in rookie camp, variable treatment by coaching staff members and the service area covered under performance enhancement are addressed. The sports medicine specialist with 2020 vision must be competent and capable of understanding, adapting and making the necessary changes in practice, science, research and delivery of services to meet the growing changes in the world of sport over the next decade.

ACKNOWLEDGMENTS[*]

The author wish to acknowledge the support and assistance of Bruce Ogilvie Ph.D., Charles Lowe, Ph.D., Orlando Tubby Smith, Randy Edsell, Jill Livingston, MLS, Tag Heister, MLS Deborah Kessler, MLS, Miranda Rogers, Amber Alexander, Tina Lane, and Brenda Frommer for their contributions to the completion of this manuscript.

REFERENCES

Covey, S Stephen Covey, Roger Merrill, Rebecca R. Merrill (1994) *First Things First:* To Live, to Love, to Learn, to Leave a Legacy. New York: Simon and Schuster Publishers

Hackfort, D. & Schwenkmezger, P. (1989). *Measuring Anxiety in Sports: Perspectives and Problems.* In D. Hackfort & C. D. Speilberger (Eds.), Anxiety in Sports: An International Perspective (pp. 55-74). Washington, DC: Hemisphere.

Hardy, L. (1990). *A Catastrophe Model of Performance in Sport.* In J. G. Jones & L. Hardy (Eds.), Stress and Performance in Sport (pp. 81-106). Chichester, England: Wiley.

Hardy, L. & Parfitt, G. (1991). *A Catastrophe Model of Anxiety and Performance.* British Journal of Psychology, 82, 163-178.

Hardy, L. & Fazey, J. (1987). *The Inverted-U Hypothesis: A Catastrophe For Sport Psychology?* Paper Presented at the Annual Conference of the North American Society For the Psychology of Sport and Physical Activity. Vancouver. June.

Hardy, L., Maiden, D. S. & Sherry, K. (1986). *Goal-setting and Performance: The Effects of Performance Anxiety.* Journal of Sports Sciences, 4, 233-234.

Hardy, L., Parfitt, G. & Pates, J. (1992). *Performance Catastrophes in Sport: A Test of the Hysteresis Hypothesis.* Journal of Sports Sciences, 12, 327-334.

Levinson, H. (1992). *Fads, fantasies and psychological management. Consulting Psychology* Journal: Practice and Research, 44, 1-12.

Lowman, R. L. (1996). *Dysfunctional work role behavior.* In K. Murphy (Ed.), Individual differences and behavior in organizations (pp. 371-415). San Francisco: Jossey-Bates.

---

*Requests for reprints are sent to: Thomas Miller, Ph.D., ABPP, Professor & Senior Research Scientist, Department of Psychology & Center for Health Intervention and Prevention, University of Connecticut, Storrs Connecticut 06268

Martens, R., Burton, D., Vealey, R. Bump, L. & Smith, D. (1990*). The Development of the Competitive State Anxiety Inventory-2 (CSAI-2).* In R. Martens, R. S. Vealey & D. Burton (Eds.). Competitive Anxiety in Sport (pp. 117-190). Champaign, IL: Human Kinetics.

Miller, TW. , Vaughn, M. & Miller, J.M. (1990). *Clinical Issues in Therapy with Stress Oriented Athletes.* Sports Medicine 9(4) 320-379.

Miller, T. W. (1996) *Theory and Assessment of Stressful Life Events.* Madison CT: International Universities Press Incorporated.

Miller, T.W. & Veltkamp, L. J. (1996) *Trauma Accommodation Syndrome.* In: Miller, T.W. (Ed) Theory and Assessment of Stressful Life Events, Madison, Connecticut: International Universities Press, Inc. 95-98.

Miller, T.W., Ogilvie, B. C., Branch, J (2008) *Sports Psychology Consultation: Influence of Gender on Learning Style in Athletes.* Consulting Psychology Journal: Practice and Research. 60(30-279-285.

Miller, T.W., Adams, J.M., Kraus, R.F., Clayton, R. Miller, J.M., Anderson, J. and Ogilvie, B. (2001) *Gambling as an Addictive Disorder Among Athletes: Clinical Issues in Sports Medicine.* Journal of Sports Medicine. 31(3) 1-12.

Miller, TW, Kraus, RF, Adams, J, Bilyeu, J. Ogilvie, B. (1999) *Sports Medicine in the New Millennium: A Vision for 2020.* Sports Medicine 28 (3) 145-9.

Ogilvie, B.C. (1976) *Psychological consistencies with the personality of high-level competitors.* In A.C. Fisher (Ed.) Psychology of sport (pp. 335-358). Palo Alto, CA: Mayfield, Publishers

Ogilvie, B.C. (1979) *The sport psychologist and his professional credibility.* In P. Klavora & J.V. Daniels (Eds.) Coach, Athlete and the sport psychologist (pp. 44-55). Champaign, IL: Human Kinetics, Incorporated.

Ogilvie, B.C., & Tutko, T. A. (1996) *Problem Athletes and how to handle them.* London: Pellham, Publishers.

Ogilvie, B.C., Greene, D. and Baillie, P. (1997) *Interpretive Statistical Manual for Competitve and Learning Styles Profile for Athletes,* Coaches, and Sports Psychologists. New York: author.

Peters, T. (1997, October). *Lessons in leadership (workshop).* (Available from the Tom Peters Group, Palo Alto, CA; E-mail Tjpet@aol.com.

Robinson-Kurpius, S.E., Fuqua, D., Gibson, G., Kurpius, D.J., & Froehle, T. (1995). *An occupational analysis of consulting psychology: Results of a national survey.* Consulting Psychology Journal: Practice and Research, 47, 75-88.

Rohrer, Hibler and Replogle, Inc. (1981). *The managerial challenge: A psychological approach to the changing world of management.* New York: New American Library.

Weigel, R. G. (1995, August). *One size does not fit all. In Product and process consultation from a university counseling center perspective.* Symposium presented at the Annual Convention of the American Psychological Association, New York.

Yerkes, R. M. & Dodson, J. D. (1908). *The Relation of Strength of Stimulus to Rapidity of Habit Formation.* Journal of Comparative and Neurological Psychology, 18, 459-482.

In: Handbook of Sports Psychology
Editor: Calvin H. Chang

ISBN: 978-1-60741-256-4
©2009 Nova Science Publishers, Inc.

Chapter 12

THERAPEUTIC VALUE OF SPORT FOR CHILDREN WITH DISABILITIES

Thomas W. Miller*, Rebecca S. Timme,
Lindsay Burns and John Ragsdale
University of Kentucky, Lexington, Kentucky

INTRODUCTION

Developmentally disabled children and their families face numerous challenges throughout their lives. The focus of this chapter is to provide health care professionals with models that may be beneficial in the care and treatment of children with a spectrum of disabilities. Attention to both physical and psychological aspects of their involvement in sport activities will be explored as well as their ability to perform, coping mechanisms, and anxiety that may be experienced. Decreasing maladaptive behaviors with these children will be explored, including necessity for redirection to task and inappropriate communication. The clinical assessment of disabled children prior to their participation will be discussed in detail, as well as how to match a sport with a child. Existing contemporary models of sport involvement such as the "Miracle League" model will be examined (Miracle League 2008). This program is specifically designed for children with developmental disabilities and may include programs in baseball, basketball, swimming, martial arts and other sport activities. The importance of future clinical research will be discussed.

The opportunity for sports participation among individuals with disabilities has grown dramatically in recent decades. A thorough understanding of the issues involved as well as the how to address the concerns is paramount for anyone who works with disabled individuals. The benefits of sports participation for the disabled are numerous. Nationally, rates of obesity in the general population are increasing, and the disabled tend to have lower levels of fitness and higher rates of obesity than their nondisabled peers. There is a growing body of literature

Thomas W. Miller, Ph.D., ABPP, Professor Department of Psychiatry & Rebecca S. Timme, D.O., Department of Psychiatry & Department of Pediatrics; Lindsay Burns M.D. & John Ragsdale M.D. Department of Pediatrics, College of Medicine, University of Kentucky, Lexington Kentucky 40509-1810

demonstrating improved outcomes in multiple health measures with fitness programs and sports participation. In addition, sports participation helps develop a healthy self-concept, builds confidence, and improves overall quality of life. Sports also provide children with special needs with valuable social interactions, both with other disabled individuals, as well as their nondisabled peers.

Keywords: Sport, Children, Disabilities, special needs

RISKS AND BENEFITS OF SPORT PARTICIPATION

Participation in sports, recreational and physical activities, is essential to maintain a physically handicapped child's normal muscular strength, flexibility and joint function, not to mention control weight in individuals with syndromes, such as Prader-Willi or other physical and mental disabilities in which obesity is a common complication. (Murphy & Carbone 2008) What is not commonly discussed are the psychological issues, risks and benefits surrounding sport participation in the child with disabilities. On one hand, athletic activity and participation, both integrated with typically developing children or with other handicapped children provide enhancement of the child's self-esteem, a decrease in the discrepancy between the child's ideal and actual self-concept, and a decrease in restriction with peers. On the other hand, when children are involved in sports at levels their mental development is unprepared for, the psychological strain can be difficult and felt by all involved, including the child, coach, team, and parents. Pre-participation anxiety, for example, is an often seen problem in the typically developing child that can have further reaching consequences if experienced in a child with disabilities. Promoting sports or athletic involvement in children with disabilities is something all persons involved with the child's care should encourage. However, understanding the various aspects, both physical and psychological, of this involvement can help us guide the child into the areas best suited for him or her.

The benefits of participation in organized physical activity are many and research on the benefits of sports and physical activity in the typical child is extensive. Regular physical exercise is associated with an increase in self-esteem and self-concept and decrease in anxiety and depression (Health 2006). Over the years, studies have also given credence to the obvious - that children with disabilities benefit in similar ways as non-disabled children, but with arguably further reaching benefits on the child's psyche. A review by Gabler-Halle and colleagues in 1993 discussed the positive relationship between exercise and behavior management. Their work showed the positive effects of regular physical activity on stereotypic behaviors, maladaptive behaviors and work performance for persons with cognitive impairment (Gabler-Halle, Halle et al. 1993). Just the addition of routinized exercise during the day can help a disabled child's "acting-out" behaviors and allow them to participate more fully in learning the skills that might help them succeed later in life. This is also a good point for the caretakers of these children to learn that regular exercise can go a long way. Other small but significant studies have also shown the positive effect of even moderate exercise in decreasing maladaptive behaviors, such as self-stimulating behaviors in autistic boys. In addition the positive effect of exercise in decreasing the maladaptive behaviors was not related to an increased level of tiredness in the child as shown by the improvement of post-exercise tasks of behavior and academic performance over the children who were not involved in exercise.(Dykens, Rosner et al. 1998) What are needed now are more large-scale, double-blinded studies that confirm these small but significant findings. Little is also known regarding the long-term effects of exercise for this spectrum of children with special needs.

SELF ESTEEM AS CRITICAL FOR CHILDREN WITH DEVELOPMENTAL DISABILITIES

Self-esteem is important for all children. Another way in which sports has a positive effect on children with disabilities is seen in the improvement of a child's self-esteem or self-concept. For a long time, it has been known that sports and competition increases subjective ratings of self-esteem for both non-disabled and disabled children, regardless of the disability. In the development of an individual's concept of self there are different constructs, one of which states that the early development of the self is global and undifferentiated. (Werner 1957) With increasing age our self-concept changes, becoming increasingly differentiated and hierarchically. Some believe are we grow we divide our esteem into various domains including social, physical, interpersonal, academic, familial, and other types (Dykens, Rosner et al. 1998). Children with mental disabilities may demonstrate less differentiation of their self-concept, especially in their physical and academic domains, than age-matched peers. Zigler, Balla et al (1972) found in their study of self-image, in groups of institutionalized and non-institutionalized typical and mentally handicapped children, that in general the disparity between a child's real self-image and imagined self-imagine decreases with increasing mental age. As the children grew older, their view of their idealized selves came closer to their ratings for their real selves. Therefore a younger child will have a more difficult time reconciling who he wants to be to his actually capabilities than a child at an older mental age equivalent. This study showed further that children with cognitive handicaps actually had a smaller disparity between ideal and real self concepts compared to age-matched peers. This result, however, occurred because mentally challenged children tended to rate their ideal self-images significantly lower than that of typical developing children of the same mental age. This was believed to demonstrate that mentally handicapped children tended to lower their goals and aspirations and have overall lower self-images than did typical children of the same age. This study also showed that, independent of developmental level, institutionalized children had significantly lower idealized self image scores than non-institutionalized. (Zigler, Balla et al. 1972)

In this study, Zigler, Balla et al.(1972) refuted a previously held theory that mentally retarded children had inflated and unrealistic self-concepts. Instead, his study found that, whether institutionalized or not, mentally retarded children had overall lower self-images than did typical children of the same age.(Zigler, Balla et al. 1972) The importance of this study is that parents and coaches must be aware of the needs of a child with mental handicaps and help prepare the child for what is appropriate to expect of him or herself for a given activity. The adults caring for children with mental handicaps need to be further aware that this special group begins with lower self-esteem than their typically developed colleagues. So while helping to bridge a child's idealized self-concept with their true level of skills, one must also be aware of their already lowered sense of self and help to raise it. Helping to bridge this gap between the idealized self and current self-concept, will hopefully make the sport a more enjoyable experience for the child. Also, the knowledge that children with mental handicaps often begin with a lowered self-image should encourage the parents and coaches to focus on positive aspects of the game, such as the participation in the competition instead of the winning, will enhance the child's experience.

INTERNATIONAL SPECTRUM OF SPORT PARTICIPATION

Several small international studies have shown how involvement in sports enhances not only a child's sense of mastery and self-esteem, but also self-identity and self-perception. A small study by Simpson and Meaney divided mild MR children into 2 groups. One group learned to ski for during a half-day each week, while the control group did not. The group participating at the ski school showed significant changes in their self-concept that corresponded to the magnitude of gains in learning to ski, demonstrating that participation in a physical activity in which success and positive outcomes are achieved can mean equally significant and meaningful changes in the child's self-concept. (Simpson & Meaney 1979)

Self-concept for the cognitively impaired adolescent differs still from that of the younger child or his typically developing peer due to the lack of skills, both physically and emotionally. Teens with mental retardation progress through adolescence with the same preoccupations as non-MR teens – emancipation, identity development and sexuality, although many persons in society tend to forget this. The deficient competency and limited skill set (poorer communication, comprehension, coordination, time conceptualization and orientation) inadequately equips the adolescent with mental retardation to deal with this developmental task of assuming an independent role that society expects of other adolescents. Pressures from both society, to develop at a pace faster than the adolescent's skills are able to accomplish, and from family, who often inadvertently restrict the child's burgeoning independence, keep the adolescent from successfully adjusting to the demands of puberty. When these adolescent begin to be unable to complete such core developmental tasks, self esteem then begins to suffer. (Levy-Shiff, Kedem et al. 1990) This is where sports participation is able to help. Ninot, Bilard et al (2005) discussed competence in its role within an individual's self-concept. Competence in a young adolescent is composed of five domains; scholastics and intellectual performance, social acceptance, athletic and leisure activities, physical appearance, and conduct. As stated previously, cognitive maturational level determines the accuracy of self-evaluation between the idealized versus the real self. When expectations of competencies do not match with reality, it greatly affects a child or adolescent's self esteem, especially an adolescent with intellectual impairment. (Ninot, Bilard et al. 2005) Involvement in social and physical activities has been shown to lessen the gap between expectation and the reality thus enhancing an adolescent's overall self-concept. (Johnson, Fretz et al. 1968).

However given the same cognitive level of functioning, individuals with physical disabilities have the same developmental level of self-concept as that of typically developing peers. As a child develops and begins to understand oneself, he/she eventually compares herself to other children. In those children with a physical disability but normal intelligence, there is recognition that they differ from other children. A parent, teacher or coach might then hear a child announce his or her physical disability "I have a wheelchair" or "I need to wear braces" *as a characteristic of Erikson's classic phase of autonomy vs. shame and doubt.* Encouragement of this form of self-expression is recommended in that it promotes the continued development of a child's self-concept and self-esteem (Molnar & Alexander 1999; Erikson 1980).

ANXIETY AND COPING IN SPORT FOR CHILDREN WITH SPECIAL NEEDS

As many persons know who have ever participated in some type of competition, anxiety is a typical emotion, especially among children and adolescent playing a sport. Studies looking at the level of anxiety in physically disabled athletes are few and far between. Studies in the able-bodied literature focused on competition anxiety using the Competitive State Anxiety Inventory-2 (CSAI-2) which measures the intensity of anxiety by looking at 3 aspects of anxiety: cognitive, somatic and perceived confidence. (Ferreria, Chatzisarantis et al, 2007) Some youth have excessive amounts of worry prior to game time which can be seen as counterproductive to the positive effects of sports. Ferreira et al looked at anxiety in national and international level athletes with disabilities in four different sports (swimming, wheelchair marathon, track and field athletics and indoor soccer), between the ages of 15-49 years old at 3 time periods prior to their sport competition. They showed, as other had before them, that the intensity of somatic anxiety increases as the competition approaches. Unlike previous authors, however, their data showed cognitive anxiety remained stable prior to the competition. Self-confidence also remains stable but decrease just prior to the competition, supporting previous studies. (Ferreira, Chatzisarantis et al. 2007) There is discussion of a "competitive trait anxiety" (CTA), a personality disposition that reflects a person's tendency to experience stress and/or anxiety in situations involving sport competition. Persons with this trait tend to experience apprehension more frequently and possibly to a greater degree than someone with lower CTA levels. In non-disabled male youth athletes, global feelings of low self-esteem and a lack of self-confidence in performance capabilities were found to be related to higher levels of somatic CTA. There is little reason to believe this same function does not exist in our physically disabled athletes. Studies with non-disabled youth also have shown that when emphasis is placed on winning, there is enhanced worrying about failure. (Ferreira, Chatzisarantis et al. 2007) This is why sports programs geared toward the mentally and physically disabled, such as the "Special Olympics" and "The Miracle League," focus on the success of the individual in participation and acquisition of skills, not just in winning.

In such organizations, the focus in on the enhancement of the individual's self-worth and replacing past failures with future successes is what the sport and team experience is all about. Weiss, Diamond et al (2003) collected data from participants in the Ontario Special Olympics program and found that the number of medals won, the length of time of participation in Special Olympics and the total number of competitions were all components in an individual's feelings of self-worth, however only the latter was a significant predictor of this enhanced self-worth (Weiss, Diamond et al. 2003). One cannot forget the other variables that are a major component of programs such as The Special Olympics including peer acceptance, parental support and a positive coaching style which has an effect on studies with these programs. Balla and Zigler showed that children with mental retardation, if given experiences of past successes, were more likely to expect success in the future. Whereas, those children in the study that were preconditioned for failure exhibited strategies during the actual trial that emphasized their assumption of future failures, those children that had previous known success used strategies that emphasized expected future success. (Balla & Zigler 1971) These organizations that help to establish experiential success in these children's' lives are crucial to their development as productive individuals later in life.

ENJOYMENT OF THE SPORT ACTIVITY VS WINNING

There have, in fact, been several studies showing enjoyment, not winning, as the strongest predictor of commitment, or desire to continue in a sport. (Scanlan 1993) Upon closer examination through questionnaire and interview of 5th grade students in England participating in sports education, MacPahil, Gorely et al.(2008) discovered multiple reasons to why children continue with the sports they do. First was the aspect of fun and enjoyment, second was the affiliation with a team and the sense of belonging and building of friendships. Third, the promotion of autonomy of the child through increased responsibilities and development of a particular skill and fourth, a certain amount of enjoyment seems to be derived from factors such as competition and the excitement of a competitive field. Even in this study, in which the children were encouraged to simply "try their best rather than focus on….winning" the fact that competition was involved was reflected in the children's interviews as a component of what made game time enjoyable. (MacPhail,Gorely et al.2008).

THE BENEFITS OF PHYSICAL ACTIVITY

Participation in physical activity provides multiple health benefits to children worldwide. The rate of obesity in our youth, both with and without disabilities, is on the rise. According to the American Academy of Pediatrics policy paper on "Active Healthy Living: Prevention of Childhood Obesity through Increased Physical Activity" revised as of May 2006, 15% of America's youth were either overweight or obese; a number that has tripled since the 1960's (Health 2006). The nationally-conducted NHANES survey found a similar rate among children of 16% overweight, with an additional 31% being at-risk of overweight. Among children with physical limitations, this same study found rates of 30% overweight and 51% at-risk of overweight (Bandini 2005). This can be explained in part by risk factors for obesity that are commonly seen among disabled children (Minihan, Fitch et al 2007). They may have limited mobility, decreased coordination, reduced vision or hearing, and can tire easily, limiting their energy expenditures. Some are on medications such as antidepressants or mood stabilizers which promote weight gain. Because of medical problems, there also may be less time or income within the family to devote to physical activity. There may be a lack of opportunities in the community or a societal or parental reluctance to their participation. Given these issues, it is not surprising that physically disabled children are more than two times as likely to be overweight compared to non-disabled children (Bandini, Fitch et al 2005). For the disabled, obesity brings numerous health sequelae, including pressure sores, musculoskeletal pain, fatigue, and depression (Rimmer, Rowland et al 2007). Long-term consequences of obesity include increased rates of diabetes mellitus, cardiovascular disease, hypertension, sleep apnea, and osteoarthritis.

Clearly, obesity has become a major public health issues, especially among the disabled. This creates an environment where physical activity plays an even greater role. In addition to combating obesity, participation in sports brings other physical benefits to the disabled person. Sports participation improves strength, flexibility, joint function, and balance. It improves cardiovascular fitness and endurance, improves deconditioning, and decreases rates of osteoporosis (Murphy & Carbone 2008). For the child, sports participation translates into improved mobility and function with day-to-day tasks and thus improvement in his or her overall quality of life.

For many children, motives for participating in physical activity include fun and social interaction, and this is true for disabled children as well (Crocker, Hoar et al 2004, Mharada &Sipwestein 2009). There have, in fact, been several studies showing enjoyment is the strongest predictor of commitment, or desire to continue in a sport (Scanlan, Carpenter et al 1993). Via questionnaire and interview of 5th grade students in England participating in sports education, MacPahil, Gorley et al (2008) found multiple reasons why children continue with sports. First was fun and enjoyment. Second was the affiliation with a team, the sense of belonging, and the building of friendships. Third, was the promotion of autonomy of the child through increased responsibilities and development of a particular skill? And fourth were the enjoyment of competition and the excitement of a competitive field. Even in this study, in which the children were encouraged to simply "try their best rather than focus on….winning" the fact that competition was involved was reflected in the children's post-study interviews as a component of what made game time enjoyable. In addition to the health benefits, sports promote socialization, improve self-image, and increase enjoyment of life.

PEDIATRIC MARKERS IN ASSESSING READINESS

In assessing readiness for a child with special needs becoming involved in a sport activity, a pre-participation physical should be performed in addition to regularly scheduled comprehensive exams. Most experts suggest scheduling the pre-participation physical four to six weeks in advance of the commencement of the sport to allow for time to pursue any concerning findings from the history or exam (Hergenroeder 1997). The sports physical can be a valuable tool for continuing anticipatory guidance, addressing stress during competition, encouraging injury prevention and evaluating the patient for conditions that could affect sports participation (Greydanus 2004). Patients with disabilities are specifically at risk for co-morbidities that could affect their ability to tolerate strenuous activity or could exclude them from participation in certain sports. The history and physical exam are crucial for discovering orthopedic and medical conditions that could disqualify a patient from sports (Greydanus 2004). This section will review the elements of the pre-participation physical and how to adapt this visit for a patient with a disability.

A thorough review of a patient's past medical history helps identify their degree of disability and pinpoint areas of possible injury during sports. The spectrum of disability is broad and includes conditions ranging from hearing impairment to cerebral palsy, so the history needs to be broad and in-depth (Patel 2002). Because most appointment times are limited, a review-of-systems method of history taking can be helpful if the child is not well known to the practitioner. The history should include medical conditions, surgeries, medications, recent illnesses, complaints of chest pain or palpitations, complaints of shortness of breath, coughing episodes with exercise, hearing or vision problems, musculoskeletal complaints or injuries, nutrition, weight history, and immunization status (Greydanus 2004) A practitioner may have to adapt a standard history for the patient's disability, for example if a patient has Down's syndrome then the history should include neck pain or previous evaluation for atlanto-axial subluxation. Aside from the child's personal history, a family history should also be explored for any history of sudden death with exertion, Marfan syndrome, cardiomyopathy or lipid disorders.

The American Academy of Pediatrics (AAP) Committee on Sports Medicine and Fitness released a statement in May of 2001 outlining medical conditions that affect sports participation (Committee on Sport Medicine, 2001). This statement includes medical conditions that are typically cleared for participation, conditions that need evaluation prior to sports clearance, and the few conditions that are excluded from play. The two conditions that should be excluded are carditis (due to the risk of sudden death with exercise) and fever (which can increase cardiovascular effort and lead to overheating) (Committee on Sport Medicine 2001). Diarrhea should also be a relative contraindication due to the risk of dehydration. This statement is a useful reference to identify the conditions that should be further investigated before sports participation. If a practitioner is unsure if a specific condition is safe for sports participation, then the corresponding specialist should be consulted before clearance is granted.

The physical examination can be helpful in evaluating the patient's disabilities and conditions but also in identifying new abnormalities. Height, weight and BMI should be measured to evaluate nutritional status and growth. Although there is limited data on eating disorders in patients with disabilities, every patient should be evaluated to ensure proper nutritional intake to sustain strenuous activity and to assess for body image distortion. A skinfold test on the posterior triceps is one simple way to assess nutritional status. (Hergenroeder 1997) A full set of vitals should be obtained including blood pressure, heart rate, respiratory rate, and body temperature. The patient's vital signs can be a clue to underlying pathology which could potentially exclude them from participation. Blood pressure should be compared to standard values adjusted for height percentile, age, and gender. If hypertension exists, good control needs to be established before the athlete is permitted to play. If the blood pressure is 5 mm Hg above the standardized 99th percentile, the athlete should be excluded from play (AAP Committee 1997). If fever is discovered during the pre-participation physical, it should be evaluated and treated before the child is cleared for participation.

The head and neck exam should include a visual acuity test; an athlete with acuity worse than 20/40 in one or both eyes should be referred to a specialist for evaluation before participation. An child with acuity worse than 20/200 is legally blind and should wear protective eyewear during sports but should not be excluded from participation (Hergenroeder 1997).

A thorough cardiovascular exam should be performed to evaluate heart rate and rhythm, and the presence of any murmurs or additional heart sounds should be noted. If the child has a known cardiac diagnosis and there is any uncertainty by the primary practitioner, a cardiac specialist should be consulted to clear the patient for participation. If the athlete has any complaints of shortness of breath, syncopal episodes, chest pains, or palpitations, the cardiovascular exam assumes an even greater role in the pre-participation physical. It should be remembered that hypertrophic cardiomyopathy still remains the most common cause of sudden cardiac death in young athletes. Other diagnoses that could contribute to sudden cardiac death are Marfan syndrome, Brugada syndrome, arrhythmias, and myocarditis (Greydanus 2004).

The pulmonary exam should assess for comorbid conditions such as asthma or thoracic restriction from scoliosis or obesity. Special attention should be paid to any concerning signs such as clubbing or cyanosis.

A thorough neurologic and musculoskeletal exam should be performed to evaluate function and responsiveness. The practitioner should refrain from focusing on the area of disability, but rather look globally to assess abilities and identify any possible risk factors for injury. Any previously-sustained injuries should be evaluated along with the major muscle groups and joints. If repetitive motions are performed during participation, the affected muscles and joints should be inspected and manipulated to evaluate for overuse injuries (Hergenroeder 1997). Muscle strength, muscle mass, and stamina should also be assessed (Patel 2002). Some patients will need to choose a sport based on their musculoskeletal abilities and this topic will be discussed in more detail in the following section.

Lastly, the pre-participation physical is an opportunity for inspection of any prosthetics, orthotics, or assistive devices. These adjuncts should be evaluated for function and the adjacent skin for breakdown (Patel 2002).

MATCHING ATHLETIC ACTIVITY AND THE CHILD

Matching a child with special needs with a sport begins with a physician assessment and involves an ongoing partnership among the patient, parent, and physician. The goals of participation should be clearly understood and the child's best interest kept in mind throughout the process (Murphy 2008). Careful attention should first be paid to the intensity level the child can tolerate and level of contact that is appropriate. Some sports, such as basketball, running, and soccer, make high aerobic demands on athletes and may not be appropriate for children with cardiovascular or pulmonary conditions. Other sports, such as bowling and golf, make low demands and are typically well-tolerated by most children. The potential for contact in the sport must also be considered since contact may not appropriate for children with certain musculoskeletal conditions or bleeding disorders. Thus, high contact sports such as football, lacrosse, and wrestling should be avoided in these children. A noncontact sport such as badminton, swimming, or tennis may be a better option (Committee on Sport Medicine 2001). Other specific limitations should be addressed such as amputations or children who are wheelchair bound (Patel 2002).

Consideration should be given to programs which are integrated with nondisabled peers versus segregated programs. Some children may benefit from socialization with nondisabled peers whereas others may feel added pressure to perform. Additionally, certain necessary modifications to the sport may be difficult to achieve in some integrated settings. At times, choices among integrated and segregated programs may be limited by local availability.

Lastly, but of great importance, one should consider the child's psychological maturity and preferences in an attempt to find a sport which he or she will enjoy. For the endeavor to be successful, it is crucial that the child willingly, and hopefully excitedly, participates. Only then, will all the mental, social, and physical benefits of the activity be achieved. Matching athletic activity with disabled children is a complex process. It involves a thorough understanding of the child's limitations and abilities and clinical judgment about an appropriate sport. It also involves an assessment of the appropriateness of integration with nondisabled peers, as well as partnering with the child to find a mutually acceptable choice. Despite the complexity, when done correctly, this process will ultimately benefit the child with fewer injuries and a more-rewarding experience.

Once a sport is chosen, attention should be paid to equipment, field, and rules modification, if necessary, to ensure a safe and enjoyable experience. Assistive technology, especially for amputees, can be very beneficial. Additional protective equipment, beyond what is required of nondisabled participants, may be required. The rules of the game may also need to be modified depending on the child's physical abilities and psychological maturity (Patel 2002).

Many barriers exist to sport participation that must be addressed. In particular, coaches and parents often express concerns with regards to safety. However, research has shown rates of injury are similar among disabled and nondisabled athletes (Patel 2002). Common injuries include sprains, strains, contusions, and abrasions (Patel 2002). With proper preparation, injuries can be minimized and the common ones can be anticipated and managed easily. Other concerns include whether the individual will experience frustration or anxiety at his or her limitations, especially in integrated play. Health care providers, in particular, have a responsibility to address these concerns and promote sport activities among the disabled because of the clear physical, psychological, and social benefits.

Among the many choices for sport involvement, disabled individuals participate in most of them, with baseball and basketball being very common. Many good models exist for including the disabled in sports, including physical education programs in schools for the disabled, the Miracle League, the Cerebral Palsy Athletic Association, the Paralympics, and the National Wheelchair Basketball Association.

THE MIRACLE LEAGUE MODEL AND CHILDREN WITH SPECIAL NEEDS

The Miracle League offers opportunities for children with mental and/or physical challenges to engage in sport activities that include baseball. The organization designs and constructs custom baseball fields that have a rubberized turf to prevent injuries, wheelchair-accessible dugouts and a completely flat surface to eliminate barriers to wheelchair-bound or visually-impaired children (Miracle League 2008).

The Miracle League website (Miracle League 2008) notes that there are 180 Miracle League organizations across the country including Puerto Rico--80 completed fields and 100 under construction. The Miracle League is proud to serve more than 25,000 children and young adults with disabilities. In 1997 Rockdale Youth Baseball Association's coach Eddie Bagwell invited the first child with special needs Michael to play baseball on his team; Michael a 7 year old child in a wheel chair attended every game and practice, while cheering on his 5 year old brother play America's favorite pass-time. And in 1998, the Rockdale Youth Baseball Association (RYBA) formed the Miracle League to further its mission of providing opportunities for all children to play baseball regardless of their ability. The disabled children in the community had expressed the desire to dress in uniforms, make plays in the field, and round the bases just like their healthy peers. The league began with 35 players on four teams (Miracle League 2008).

At the time there were no programs for the Miracle League to replicate. It was decided that Every player bats once each inning All players are safe on the bases Every player scores a run before the inning is over (last one up gets a home run) Community children and volunteers serve as 'buddies' to assist the players Each team and each player wins every game The main concern was the playing surface, presenting potential safety hazards for players in wheelchairs or walkers. In its spring 1999 season, the Miracle League gained support and became a source of pride for all involved as participation grew to over 50 players. During that season, the magnitude of the need for such a program was recognized. It was learned that there are over 50,000 plus children in Metro Atlanta who are disabled to some degree that keeps them from participating in team sports. That is when the dream of building a unique baseball complex for these special children was conceived.

The Rotary Clubs of Rockdale County and Conyers stepped forward to form the Rotary Miracle League Fund, Inc., a 501 (c) 3 organization. The new organization had two objectives: (1) raise the funds necessary to build a special complex with facilities that meet the unique needs of the Miracle League players, and (2) assist in the outreach efforts for Miracle Leagues across the country. With the help of community volunteers and companies, the design and construction of the first Miracle League complex was underway. The complex would include a custom-designed field with a cushioned rubberized surface to help prevent injuries, wheelchair accessible dugouts, and a completely flat surface to eliminate any barriers to wheelchair-bound or visually impaired players. The design also included three grass fields, which could be converted to the synthetic rubber surface as the league grew. In addition, accessible restrooms, a concession stand, and picnic pavilion were included in the design (Miracle League 2008). Other community efforts have seen collaborative efforts generate the a twenty-first century opportunity for children with special needs to enjoy the sport experienece as witnessed by the founding sponsorship model involving Toyota Motor Manufacturing, BB&T and Rotary Club of Lexington to form the "Bluegrass Miracle League" in Lexington, Kentucky.

THE ROLE OF BUDDIES

"Buddies" assist "Miracle League" players in all aspects of the game. Buddies are adolescents and adults who play baseball, youth church groups, high school and college team members, residents in child psychiatry and pediatrics, boys and girls scouts and to mention a few. As a result, the parents, children and volunteers are all brought together – special needs and mainstream alike-in a program, which serves them all through service to children with special needs. The website notes that the Miracle League (2008) has received local and national media attention. The league has been chronicled in the local newspaper, televised locally on NBC, ABC, Connecting with Kids and FOX, Atlanta affiliates and nationally on CNN, MSNBC and Fox Sports. In July 2001, the league was profiled on a segment of HBO's Real Sports. Articles profiling the league appeared in People, Family Circle and Rotary International magazines, and Paula Deen. In January 2002 two men from the Miracle League were awarded the Martin Luther King Humanitarian Award and on January 24th PAX TV's "It A Miracle" told the story of Conyers Miracle League Player Lauren Gunder. February 2002 the Miracle League Players were featured in Rotary Internationals' PSA, chosen out of 500 applicants. Winter of 2002 the Miracle League again was profiled in the Georgia Tech Alumni Magazine. January of 2002 won the 11ALIVE TV Community Service Award and June of 2002 took the Jefferson Award, The American Institute for Public Services, founded by Jacqueline Kennedy Onassis and Senator Robert Taft, Jr. One of the greatest achievements for the Miracle League Model was being inducted to The Baseball Hall of Fame in 2006. The publicity from these media events, coupled with positive word of mouth, raises awareness among the families of children with special needs and allows the Miracle League Association to take the program across the country (Miracle League 2008).

The Miracle League received the 2008 National Consortium for Academics and Sports Award. Presently there are 200 Miracle League Organizations across the country including Puerto Rico, 100 completed rubberized fields, and 100 fields under construction. The Miracle League is proud to serve over 80,000 children and young adults with disabilities. The goal of every Miracle League is to serve approximately 1.3 million children. This goal is being realized with the help of communities, volunteers, parents, donators, individual sponsors, and corporate sponsors. The Miracle League believes that "Every Child Deserves a Chance to Play Baseball. (Miracle League 2008)"

TAKE HOME LESSONS IN SPORT FOR SPECIAL NEEDS CHILDREN

Pediatricians, child psychiatrists, child psychologists and other health care professionals, as experts in child development, can help parents and coaches determine readiness of a child to participate in organized sports. Readiness is often defined relative to the demands of the sport. Because different sports and even the same sport may vary widely with respect to demands and expectations, pediatricians must understand these demands to help determine if they are appropriate for the physical and cognitive maturation of participants. Prior to participation, children with special needs need evaluations by health care professionals. Annual examinations for children with special needs afford opportunities to promote physical activity and address issues of readiness as they enter into organized sports.

Educators, health care professionals and medical staff can further advocate safe sports participation by promoting better education and training of youth sports coaches. Standards for coaching competency are available, and certification for youth sports coaches should address these competencies

In an effort to optimize the benefits and reduce risks involved in organized sports for children and to preserve this valuable opportunity for young people to increase their physical activity levels, the American Academy of Pediatrics recommends the following:

1. Sport activity programs for children with special needs should complement, not replace, the regular physical activity that is a part of free play, child-organized games, recreational sports, and physical education programs in the schools. Regular physical activity should be encouraged for all children regardless of their level of participation in organized sports activities.
2. A spectrum of health care professionals including nurses, pediatricians, child psychiatrists, child psychologists, occupational therapists, medical residents and interns, speech pathologist and audiologists, special educators, counselors and other health care professionals can bring special expertise to such programs for children with special needs. Such professionals can provide valuable insight and assess developmental readiness and medical suitability for children and preadolescents to participate in organized sports and assist in matching a child's physical, social, and cognitive maturity with appropriate sports activities.
3. Health care professionals can take an active role in programs of sport for children with special needs by educating coaches about developmental and safety issues, monitoring the health and safety of children involved in organized sports, and advising committees on rules and safety.
4. Educational and health care professionals are encouraged to take an active role in identifying and preserving goals of sports that best serve young athletes.

DIRECTIONS FOR FUTURE CLINICAL AND APPLIED RESEARCH

There is a dearth of research on clinical aspects of sport activity for developmentally disabled children and limited evidence-based research that addresses children with special needs. Educators have addressed this focus area but often through case study methods and limited evidence-based efforts. More rigorous integrated multidisciplinary efforts holds promise for a better research agenda. Clinical research addressing sport readiness within the population of developmentally disabled children and their counterparts into adulthood would be especially beneficial. Additional research and resources are needed to determine the optimal time for children to begin participating in organized sports; to identify safe and effective training strategies for growing and developmentally disabled adults who may benefit from continued sport activity; to develop programs in youth sports for healthcare professionals in relevant disciplines; and to educate coaches and sport staff about unique needs and characteristics of persons with disability; and to develop effective injury prevention strategies and programs to safeguard those who participate in these programs.

ACKNOWLEDGMENTS

The authors wish to acknowledge the support and assistance of Diane Alford, National Executive Director, The Miracle League, Robert F. Kraus M.D., Lon Hays M.D., Charles Lowe Ph.D. Jeffrey Fisher Ph.D. Kevin Haury, Lexington Rotarians and other colleagues for their inspiration in the preparation of this manuscript. In addition, the assistance of Jill Livingston MLS, Tag Heister MLS, Lesli Broyles and Betty Downing are appreciated. Dr. Miller is now a Professor Emeritus, and Senior Research Scientist with the Center for Health, Intervention and Prevention, Department of Psychology, University of Connecticut and the Department of Psychiatry, College of Medicine, University of Kentucky.

REFERENCES

AAP Committee on Sports Medicine and Fitness (1997). Athletic participation by children and adolescents who have systemic hypertension." *Pediatrics* 99(4): 637-8.

Balla, D. and E. Zigler (1971). "Expectancy of success and the probability learning of retarded children." *J Abnorm Psychol* 77(3): 275-81.

Bandini, L. G., C. Curtin, et al. (2005). "Prevalence of overweight in children with developmental disorders in the continuous national health and nutrition examination survey (NHANES) 1999-2002." *J of Pediatrics* 146: 738-43.

Committee on Sports Medicine and Fitness. (2001). "Medical conditions affecting sports participation." *Pediatrics* 107(5): 1205-9.

Crocker, P., Hoar, S., McDonough, M., Kowalski, K., & Niefer, C. (2004). *Emotional experience in youth sport. Developmental sport and exercise psychology: A lifespan perspective.* Morgantown

Dykens, E. M., B. A. Rosner, et al. (1998). "Exercise and sports in children and adolescents with developmental disabilities. Positive physical and psychosocial effects." *Child Adolesc Psychiatr Clin N Am* 7(4): 757-71, viii.

Erikson, Erik. *Identity and the Life Cycle.* New York: Norton & Co.1980

Ferreira, J. P., N. Chatzisarantis, et al. (2007). "Precompetitive anxiety and self-confidence in athletes with disability." *Percept Mot Skills* 105(1): 339-46.

Gabler-Halle, D., J. W. Halle, et al. (1993). "The effects of aerobic exercise on psychological and behavioral variables of individuals with developmental disabilities: a critical review." *Res Dev Disabil* 14(5): 359-86.

Greydanus D. E., D. R. Patel, et al. (2004). "Value of sports pre-participation examination in health care for adolescents." *Med Sci Monit* 10(9):RA204-214.

Health, C. o. S. M. a. F. a. C. o. S. (2006). "Active Healthy Living: Prevention of Childhood Obesity through Increased Physical Activity." *Pediatrics* 117(5): 1834-1842.

Hergenroeder A. C. (1997). "The preparticipation sports examination." *Adolescent Medicine* 44(6): 1525-40.

Johnson, W. R., B. R. Fretz, et al. (1968). "Changes in self-concepts during a physical development program." *Res Q* 39(3): 560-5.

Levy-Shiff, R., P. Kedem, et al. (1990). "Ego identity in mentally retarded adolescents." *Am J Ment Retard* 94(5): 541-9.

MacPhail, A., T. Gorely, et al. (2008). "Children's experiences of fun and enjoyment during a season of sport education." *Res Q Exerc Sport* 79(3): 344-55.

McCann, C. (1996). "Sports for the disabled: the evolution from rehabilitation to competitive sport." *Br J Sports Med* 30(4): 279-80.

Mharada, C. M. and G. N. Sipwestein (2009). "The sport experience of athletes with intellectual disabilities: a national survey of special olympics athletes and their families." *Adapt Phys Activ Q* 26(1): 68-85.

Minihan, P. M., S. N. Fitch, et al. (2007). "What does the epidemic of childhood obesity mean for children with special health care needs?" *J Law Med Ethics* 35(1):61-77.

Miracle League (2008) History of the Miracle League. Copyright © 2008 National Miracle League Association.. Retrieved from website June 02, 2009 at *http://www.miracleleague.com/history.html*

Molnar G, Alexander M. *Pediatric Rehabilitation.* Philadelphia: Hanley & Belfus, Inc.1999

Murphy, N. A. and P. S. Carbone (2008). "Promoting the participation of children with disabilities in sports, recreation, and physical activities." *Pediatrics* 121(5): 1057-61.

Ninot, G., J. Bilard, et al. (2005). "Effects of integrated or segregated sport participation on the physical self for adolescents with intellectual disabilities." *J Intellect Disabil Res* 49(Pt 9): 682-9.

Patel, D. R. and D. E. Greydanus. (2002). " The pediatric athlete with disabilities." *Ped Clin North America* 49: 803-8267.

Rimmer, J. H., J. L. Rowland, et al. (2007). "Obesity and secondary conditions in adolescents with disabilities: Addressing the needs of an underserved population." *J of Adolescent Health* 41: 224-229.

Scanlan, T. K., Carpenter, P.J., Lobel, M., & Simons, J.P. (1993). "Sources of enjoyment for youth sport athletes." *Pediatric Exercise Science* 5: 275-285.

Simpson, H. M. and C. Meaney (1979). "Effects of learning to ski on the self-concept of mentally retarded children." *Am J Ment Defic* 84(1): 25-9.

Weiss, J., T. Diamond, et al. (2003). "Involvement in Special Olympics and its relations to self-concept and actual competency in participants with developmental disabilities." *Res Dev Disabil* 24(4): 281-305.

Werner, H. (1957). *The concept of development.* Minneapolis, University of Minnesota Press.

Zigler, E., D. Balla, et al. (1972). "Developmental and experiential determinants of self-image disparity in institutionalized and noninstitutionalized retarded and normal children." *J Pers Soc Psychol* 23(1): 81-7.

In: Handbook of Sports Psychology   ISBN: 978-1-60741-256-4
Editor: Calvin H. Chang   ©2009 Nova Science Publishers, Inc.

Chapter 13

STRESS AND COPING AMONG YOUTH SPORT PARENTS

Camilla J. Knight, Nicholas L. Holt and Katherine A. Tamminen*
Child and Adolescent Sport and Activity Research Laboratory, University of Alberta,
Canada

ABSTRACT

Parents play important roles in the lives of young athletes, both in terms of facilitating their initial involvement in sport and influencing their on-going participation and development (Côté, 1999). But whereas parents often play a positive role in youth sport, inappropriate parental involvement can negatively influence child-athletes' experiences (Gould, Lauer, Rolo, Jannes, & Pennisi, 2008). Inappropriate involvement includes parents' holding excessive expectations for their children, criticising children during competitions, and exerting too much pressure on them to perform (Gould, Tuffey, Udry, & Loehr, 1996). There is little research examining *why* parents may engage in inappropriate behaviours in youth sport contexts. One promising line of research to help uncover more information about parents' behaviour in sport examines the *stressors* parents themselves experience (e.g., Harwood & Knight, 2009a). Therefore, the purpose of this chapter is to examine stressors parents may experience in relation to their children's sport involvement. Main issues discussed are: (a) general parenting stressors; (b) sport-related parenting stressors; (c) potential relations between sport parents' stressors and their behaviours; and (d) directions for future research.

INTRODUCTION

Parents' behaviours in youth sport have received scrutiny in the international media. In 2002, a father from the U.S. was sentenced to 6-10 years in jail for beating another father to death as their children played a pickup hockey game (Baum, 2002). The confrontation began

---

*Correspondence: Nicholas L. Holt, PhD, Faculty of Physical Education and Recreation, University of Alberta Edmonton, AB, T6G 2H9, Canada, Tel: 780-492-7386, E-mail: nick.holt@ualberta.ca

when the father became angry about slashing and body checking during what was supposed to be a non-contact game (CBS, 2002). In 2006, a father of two French tennis players was sentenced to eight years in jail for the manslaughter of one of his daughter's opponents. He had been drugging his children's opponents because he could no longer cope with watching his children compete (Litchfield, 2006). 2008 was a banner year for poor sports parenting in the U.K. Junior showjumping events were cancelled because officials received threats from parents (Bannerman, 2008); a report identified issues of intimidation, cheating, and arguing between tennis parents at tournaments (Gerard, 2008); and barriers were introduced at youth soccer games in an attempt to prevent parents abusing referees (Hughes & Sajn, 2008). Clearly, some sport parents' behaviours are problematic and a cause for concern.

Elite athletes often attribute their achievements to their parents' encouragement and financial, logistical, and emotional support (Duncan, 1997; Hellstedt, 1995; Wolfenden & Holt, 2005). However, empirical evidence also shows that inappropriate parental involvement reduces children's enjoyment of sport (Brustad, 1996; Gould, Tuffey, Udry, & Loehr, 1996; Hellstedt, 1990; Leff & Hoyle, 1995). For example, athletes who perceive greater parental pressure report lower self-confidence and higher sport anxiety than athletes perceiving less parental pressure (Norton, Burns, Hope, & Bauer, 2000; Ommundsen & Vaglum, 1991). Excessive parental pressure can even contribute to children burning out or dropping out of sport (Dale & Weinberg, 1990; Gould et al., 1996).

In attempts to improve parents' behaviours some sport organising bodies have introduced codes for parental involvement. For example, Hockey Canada (2008) introduced a parental code of conduct; the United States Tennis Association (USTA, 2005) produced guidelines for appropriate parental behaviour; and the English Football Association (EFA, 2008) introduced a code of conduct for parents and spectators to promote respect of players and referees. Although the efficacy and effectiveness of such programmes for improving parents' behaviours remains unknown, the fact they have been introduced by governing bodies of several sports and several countries reflects the issue that parents' behaviours in sport is an international concern.

This chapter is based on the assumption that to understand *why* parents may engage in certain behaviours in youth sport it is important to assess their perspectives and experiences. Research is starting to show that parents themselves appraise a range of stressors arising from their children's participation in sport; these stressors may provide a lens for understanding more about parents' behaviours in sport. Therefore, the purpose of this chapter is to examine stressors parents may experience in relation to their children's sport involvement. Main issues discussed are: (a) general parenting stressors; (b) sport-related parenting stressors; (c) potential relations between sports parents' stressors and their behaviours; and (d) directions for future research.

APPRAISAL AND COPING

There are competing terms and definitions in the stress and coping literature. Although a full historical discussion is beyond the scope of this chapter (see Fletcher, Hanton, & Mellalieu, 2006; Richards, 2004 for reviews), it is important to define the terminology that we will be using. We have used Lazarus' work as the basic conceptual framework underpinning this chapter (Lazaurs, 1999; Lazarus & Folkman, 1984). Indeed, this theoretical perspective has been most frequently used in the sport psychology literature (Hanton, Fletcher, & Coughton, 2005).

Lazarus (1999) proposed a cognitive-motivational-relational theory (CMRT) whereby stressors, emotions, and coping are connected in an ongoing transactional process that changes over time. A stressor is defined as an event or situation the individual appraises as taxing or exceeding his or her resources. Thus, stressors are identified via the individual's *appraisal* of the person-environment relationship. When faced with a demand or a situation, an individual engages in primary and secondary appraisals. Primary appraisal involves the individual's evaluation of whether what is happening is relevant to his or her goal commitments, values, beliefs about self and the world, and situational intentions. For example, if a parent places particular pride and importance on his or her child's performance, then a poor performance would threaten the parent's personal values. Primary appraisal may result in an evaluation of harm/loss (damage has already occurred), threat (damage may occur in the future), challenge (a 'positive' appraisal whereby the individual is enthusiastic about the forthcoming struggle), or benefit (where there is a possibility for gain; Lazarus, 1999).

Secondary appraisal is a cognitive evaluation of coping options (Lazarus, 1999; Lazarus & Folkman, 1984). Within the secondary appraisal process the individual compares his or her primary appraisals with the personal resources he or she has to manage these demands. This process involves an evaluation of blame/credit (who or what is responsible for the event?), coping potential (do I think I can cope with this event?), and future expectations (will this change for the better or worse?). Primary and secondary appraisals combine to form the individual's evaluation of the person-environment relationship, which gives rise to particular emotions and coping responses. In this way, appraisals of stressors, emotions, and coping are the interrelated components of Lazarus' (1999) CMRT theory of emotion.

Within the CMRT theory, coping is defined as a constantly changing cognitive, behavioural, and affective process individuals use to manage stressors that are appraised as taxing or exceeding their resources (Lazarus & Folkman, 1984). Coping can be used to manage emotions arising from stressor appraisals, and coping can also act as a mediator between an individual's appraisals and their emotional reactions (Lazarus, 1999). The two major functions of coping are to aid an individual in attempting to change the person-environment relationship (problem-focused coping) and to regulate the emotion associated with the situation (emotion-focused coping).

GENERAL PARENTING STRESSORS

Although families may face unique situations in youth sport that they do not experience much in other settings (e.g., the demands of competition), to fully understand youth sport parenting it is necessary to consider it within the wider social milieu of family life (Holt, Tamminen, Black, Mandigo, & Fox, 2009). Therefore, in the following section we briefly review some evidence from the general/developmental psychology parenting literature. Research shows that parents (whether their children are athletes or not) are likely to appraise stressors related to their parenting role (Crnic & Greensberg, 1990; Deater-Deckard, 2005). From the moment children are born they place complex demands on their parents (Alexander

& Higgins, 1993). For example, during children's earliest years parents must complete more chores (e.g., cleaning, cooking, and laundry) which can reduce their physical and emotional energy (Nomaguchi & Milkie, 2003). As children mature their basic demands change and parents must contend with meeting new expectations and the social roles of parenthood (Alexander & Higgins, 1993). Such expectations can include parents dedicating time to their children and their children's development (Nyström & Öhrling, 2004) and ensuring children are engaged in a range of activities (Sidebotham, 2001).

Parents face daily stressors relating to their children's life (e.g., preparing children for school, scheduling children's time and activities, ensuring children complete their homework, maintaining discipline; Coplan, Bowker, & Cooper, 2003). Such daily stressors may influence parents' behaviours and, in turn, parent-child relationships (Abidin, 1990; Deater-Deckard, 1998). Many parents also experience more general stressors (e.g., time and financial stressors) in their parenting role, which can influence their behaviours (Sidebotham, 2001).

Financial stressors can be a major concern (Jackson, Brooks-Gunn, Huang, & Glassman, 2000), particularly if parents place a great deal of importance on providing for their family and ensuring financial security (Gyamfi, Brooks-Gunn, & Jackson, 2001; McBride, Schoppe, & Rane, 2002). Parents' economic circumstances can also influence parents' behaviour towards their children (Webster-Stratton, 1990). For example, parents suffering financial hardship display more controlling behaviours and fewer nurturing interactions with their children than parents with more financial resources (Deater-Deckard & Scarr, 1996).

Time stressors also appear to be particularly pertinent for parents (Nyström & Öhrling, 2004). Parents report a constant feeling that there is too much to do, particularly in terms of balancing their childrearing responsibilities with the demands of work and domestic chores (Sidebotham, 2001). These stressors can lead to feelings of overwhelming role strain, exhaustion, guilt, resentment, and anger (Anderson, 1996; Horowitz & Damato, 1999; Nyström & Öhrling, 2004). Fulfilling multiple roles (e.g., as a parent, employee, or spouse/partner) can further result in role conflict and subsequent emotional exhaustion, reduced job and life satisfaction, and increased overall life stress (Frone, Yardley, & Markel, 1997; Parasuraman, Greenhaus, & Granrole, 1992; Piko, 2006).

In summary it is likely that parents experience stressors arising from the expectation that they should be spending time ensuring that their children achieve and develop appropriately (Sidebotham, 2001). The extensive emotional, financial, and logistical support that parents prioritise for their children may come at a cost with respect to the stressors parents themselves experience. Consequently, parental stressors carry risks to parents' psychological health and well-being and subsequently their children's development (Deater-Deckard, 1998).

PARENTING STRESSORS IN SPORT

Evidence briefly reviewed in the previous section indicates that parents have to cope with a range of stressors as they raise their children. Parents also play a key role in their children's sport participation. Fredricks and Eccles (2004) proposed that parents fulfill three fundamental roles in their children's sport experience. These are as 'provider' (of opportunities, finance, transport, etc.), as 'interpreter' (i.e., emotionally reacting in adaptive ways to competition) and as 'role model' of the sport experience (i.e., modeling ideal behaviours in sport). Parents may encounter various stressors in attempting to perform these roles.

A recent study surveyed 123 parents of junior tennis players from the U.K. to identify stressors they experienced in relation to their children's sport involvement (Harwood & Knight, 2009a). Parents reported seven types of stressors: attendance at competitive matches and tournaments; coaches' behaviour and responsibilities; financial concerns; time demands; sibling resentment and inequality of attention; inefficiencies and inequalities attributed to tennis organisations; and developmental concerns related to education and future tennis transitions. Broadly speaking, these stressors can be placed into three categories; competitive stressors, organizational stressors, and developmental stressors. Research relating to each category is discussed below.

Harwood and colleagues (Harwood, Drew, & Knight, 2009; Harwood & Knight, 2009b) conducted two follow-up studies to their original survey using interviews with parents of U.K. youth tennis players and focus groups with parents of U.K soccer players. In these studies parents reported competitive stressors including logistical factors, watching their children perform, issues of cheating or poor behaviour from opposing parents or opponents, and helping their children to deal with the outcomes of the match. These findings suggest that, to some extent, parents may 'share' or empathise with the stressors their children experience during competitions (also see Holt, Tamminen, Black, Sehn, & Wall, 2008).

Organisational stressors reported by parents include concerns regarding interactions with members of sport governing bodies along with financial and time constraints. For example, Harwood and Knight (2009b) found U.K. tennis parents perceived a lack of support and communication from the sport governing body, concerns about the organisation and structure of tournaments, problems with coaches and training, and a lack of support when children were injured. These stressors may be exacerbated because, on an almost daily basis, parents were required to arrange access to training facilities, interact with coaches, or obtain information from the organising body. In this sense parents were the managers or agents for their children's fledging sport careers and appeared to appraise stressors in relation to this role.

Time-related stressors may be particularly prominent for parents because they have implications for general family life, parents' social lives, and parents' work responsibilities (Wiersma & Fifer, 2008). For example, parents spend many hours transporting children to training and competition, watching matches, and waiting for training sessions to finish, which can reduce time for other aspects of their lives (e.g., work, family, and social) (Gould, Lauer, Rolo, Jannes, & Pennisi, 2006; 2008; Hoefer, McKenzie, Sallis, Marshall, & Conway, 2001). Time stressors may take on additional importance if parents have feelings of guilt regarding disproportional time allocation to different children (Andersonn & Andersonn, 2000) or if sibling rivalries arise (Gould et al., 2008). For example, if parents have one child who is heavily involved in sport while another child is not, they will likely spend far more time with their young athlete.

The financial commitment competitive youth sport places on families has been well documented (Baxter-Jones & Maffuli, 2003; Gould et al., 2006; 2008). Kirk et al. (1997a) surveyed 250 Australian families and completed follow up interviews with members of 27 families regarding the financial costs and consequences of their children's sports participation. One important finding was that the financial cost of sport reduced funds for parents' social lives, recreational activities, and payment of school fees. Parents may look at the financial cost of sport as an investment that will 'pay off' if children are successful in securing, in the U.S. for example, university scholarships. The pressure parents place on their children to succeed in sport may be because they see success and talent development as a means of justifying the financial and time investment they have made (Gould et al., 2008).

Finally, parents expressed stressors associated with their children's development, both within tennis and general life. These developmental stressors include making decisions regarding whether children should continue in full-time education or attend tennis academies; identifying the appropriate pathways to ensure their children achieve their future career and sport development goals (such as transitioning from regional to national and international levels of competition); and deciding if and when to specialise into a certain sport (Harwood & Knight, 2009b).

A DEVELOPMENTAL PERSPECTIVE

Sport talent development research shows parents' roles change as children progress in sport (Côté, 1999). Based on interviews with elite Canadian adolescent athletes and their families, Côté identified three stages of youth sport participation: sampling, specialising, and investment. In the sampling stage, children engaged in a range of activities and fun was of utmost importance. Parents played a central role in their children's development, devoting family time to sport, and fulfilling 'provider' roles by ensuring transportation and access to practices and competitions. In the specialising stage, children began to specialise in one or two sports and develop sport-specific skills through practice. Parents made an increasing financial and time commitment to their children as athletes and provided constant moral and emotional support. At the investment stage children pursued the aim of reaching an elite level in their chosen sport. Parents remained an important source of emotional support during this stage. However, parents' direct influence on their children's sporting career decreased as highly trained coaches were able to impart advanced knowledge of the sport that parents did not possess.

Some evidence shows parents experience different types of stressors in relation to the specific stage of sport in which their children are involved. Harwood and Knight (2009b) found parents of junior tennis players in the sampling stage were particularly susceptible to stressors associated with competitions (e.g., other parents' behaviour, their own children's behaviour and attitude, their children's performance, and the outcome of the match). These were unexpected findings given that Côté (1999) originally proposed the sampling stage to be associated with fun and play rather than competition. However, is it possible that children are increasingly engaging in higher levels of competition at younger ages (Strachan, Côté, & Deakin, 2009). In other words, the sampling stage may have become shorter as children are fast-tracked into the specialising and investing stages of sport to achieve high levels of performance. Young children may lack the maturity to understand the competitive process and therefore derive little enjoyment from it (McCarthy, Jones, & Clark-Carter, 2008). Children's lack of enjoyment may then be witnessed by parents.

Harwood and Knight (2009b) found that parents whose children were in the specialising and investment stages also identified competitive stressors. However, for some parents, competitive stressors were perceived to decrease during the specialising and investment stage because parents and athletes had more experience in the competitive sport environment. These parents reported more stressors associated with organisational issues (e.g., finances) and developmental issues relating to their child's achievements and career progress in sport. Consistent with the concepts presented in Côtè's (1999) model, some investment stage parents reported a slight decrease in certain day-to-day stressors (e.g., transporting children to training) they encountered due to their reduced direct involvement in their child's life and development as an athlete.

In a related study, Harwood et al. (2009) conducted six focus groups with parents whose children were in the specialising stage and attended soccer academies in the U.K. Parents reported stressors relating to a lack of communication from coaches and the academy, sport-family role conflict, and school support and education issues. Again, these soccer parents did report stressors relating to competition but the greatest discussion concerned organisational and developmental stressors. Interestingly, with the exception of developmental stressors, many of the stressors reported by parents in the studies reviewed above are similar to those experienced by elite athletes and coaches (e.g., Frey, 2007; Fletcher & Hanton, 2003; Hanton, Fletcher, & Coughton, 2005; Thelwell, Weston, Greenlees, & Hutchings., 2008).

RELATIONSHIP BETWEEN SPORTS PARENTS' STRESSORS AND THEIR BEHAVIOURS

There is an emerging body of research examining parents' behaviours during youth sport competitions. In a study of U.S. youth sport parents and athletes, 15% of 803 children reported that their parents get angry if they did not play well, 14% of 189 parents reported having yelled or argued with the referee, and 13% of parents acknowledged that they had responded angrily to their child following a sporting performance (Shields, Bredemeier, LaVoi, & Power, 2005). In a study of 101 tennis players and 45 of their parents, DeFrancesco and Johnson (1997) identified that 60.9% of players' reported their parents had embarrassed them by walking away from the court, 30.4% of players indicated that their parents have yelled at them or screamed out loud, and 13% of players disclosed that their parents had hit them following tennis matches. However, only 20% of parents reported that they had exhibited any inappropriate behaviours while they were watching their children compete. Kidman, McKenzie, and McKenzie (1999) created and used an observation instrument to document parents' comments during youth sport events. They established a range of categories through observation of 250 parents during youth sport games in New Zealand. Behaviours were categorized as positive (reinforcing, hustle), negative (correcting, scolding, witticism, and contradicting), and neutral (direct questioning, rhetorical questioning, extrinsic rewarding, social, 'what if' comments, nothing, and other). Kidman et al. reported that 42.7% of parents' comments were positive, 34.5% were negative, and the remainder were neutral.

Inappropriate or negative behaviours may arise when the stressors parents encounter result in emotional reactions such as anger, frustration, or anxiety. Research in the developmental psychology literature shows that stressors parents appraise influence the parenting styles and practices they use (Abidin, 1992; Belsky, 1984; Bonds, Gondoli, Sturge-Apple, & Salem, 2001; Deater-Deckard, 1998). For example, parents who appraise greater numbers of stressors consistently display more negative parenting styles such as higher levels of punitive punishment, more harsh interactions, and fewer interactions with their children than parents who appraise fewer stressors (Crnic & Low, 2002; Rodgers, 1998; Webster-Stratton, 1990). The behaviours that some parents display in youth sport, such as providing their children 'conditional love' based on outcomes, pressuring children to succeed, and punishing poor performances (e.g., Brustad, 1996; Gould et al., 2006; 2008; Murphy, 1999), are similar to certain parenting practices that emerge in parents who perceive high levels of parenting stressors (e.g., Deater-Deckard, 1998; Webster-Stratton, 1990).

Parents' behaviours may be related to psychological and social features of children's competitive sport performances. A study of Canadian parents' involvement in competitive youth soccer identified comments made by parents on a continuum from praise and encouragement to derogatory comments (Holt et al., 2008). In a two-part study, Holt and colleagues collected data using interviews and audio diaries from four families and observed parents' comments at youth soccer games over a four month period. Parents' comments were coded as being supportive and encouraging (praise/encouragement); attempting to improve child's performance (performance contingent feedback); direct commands or comments (instruction); a combination of negative followed by positive comments (striking a balance); negative comments; and derogatory comments directed at the children. Approximately 15% of the comments made by parents were negative or derogatory. Three factors that appeared to influence parents' comments were: 1) parents' empathy with their child, 2) the emotional intensity associated with a particular game, and 3) parents' perceived knowledge and experience of the sport. Hence, parents' comments appeared to change in relation to their personal factors and game circumstances. It could be that factors such as parents' empathy, knowledge, and emotional intensity have implications for their stressor appraisals and coping.

In fact, two of the main stressors that sports parents have expressed are related to watching their children compete (particularly when they are losing, appearing disappointed or not coping) and talking to their children after games (Harwood & Knight, 2009a; Wiersma & Fifer, 2008). Such stressors appear related to parents' empathising with their child during and after difficult games (Holt et al., 2008). Wiersma and Fifer (2008) found that issues associated with parental misconduct during games involved them failing to regulate their own behaviour when they saw their child struggling. Similarly, Goldstein and Iso-Ahola (2008) found parents' expressed greater feelings of frustration and anger when they were unable to vent their frustrations during children's match. Again, these findings suggest a relationship between stressors parents appraise in youth sport and their subsequent behaviours.

FUTURE RESEARCH DIRECTIONS

The emerging research in this area has focused on identifying stressors parents appraise in relation to their children's sport involvement (e.g., Harwood & Knight, 2009a) or the types of behaviours parents demonstrate during youth sport events (e.g., Holt et al., 2008). Although we hypothesise a relationship between the stressors parents experience and the behaviours they demonstrate toward their children, such a relationship has yet to be empirically examined. This represents an important area for future research.

To date researchers have yet to adequately examine the coping process among youth sport parents. Rather, discrete types of stressors have been identified (e.g., Harwood et al.,

2009; Harwood & Knight, 2009a; 2009b). Given that stressors are essentially appraisals central to a wider process of coping and emotion (Lazarus, 1999; Lazarus & Folkman, 1984), studies of coping as a process are required. Such process-oriented studies would implicate the need for longitudinal types of research designs. Recent developments in the literature to assess the stressors and coping strategies athletes report, such as the use of diaries (e.g., Nicholls, Holt, Polman, & James, 2005) could help advance the youth sport parenting literature.

Intervention research to assess the effect of parental education would represent an important addition to the literature. Simply providing codes of conduct in the absence of education may not be an effective means of optimising parental involvement in sport. Indeed, the efficacy and effectiveness of codes of conduct (such as those introduced by Hockey Canada, USTA, and EFA) remain unknown. Parents likely encounter many stressors they cannot control or change (e.g., financial costs, sport organisational issues) whereas they may be able to exert some control over their own emotional reactions during their children's performances. Training parents to use coping strategies to manage issues they can feasibly control could be a useful endeavour. In this sense, variations of the mental skills training programmes (relaxation/breathing techniques, positive re-appraisal, self-talk, etc.) sport psychology practitioners use could be delivered to parents and evaluated. Parents may also need strategies to cope with the organisational stressors they encounter. For example, teaching parents strategies to reduce time and financial demands (i.e., time management and budgeting) may reduce organisational stressors.

In conclusion, parents play important roles in the lives of young athletes. Although research shows that parents have both positive and negative influences on their children's sport participation, until recently little attention had been paid to understanding parents' perspectives and the issues that may underpin their behaviours. This review has shown that parents themselves report a range of stressors in relation to their children's sport, including organisational, competitive, and developmental concerns. We argued that the stressors parents appraise may influence the behaviours they display toward their children. Whereas this suggestion has been supported in the developmental psychology literature and there is some promising evidence in the sport psychology literature, it has yet to be empirically examined. Testing the relationship between the stressors parents appraise and their behaviours represents an important area for future research. Similarly, examining the coping strategies parents use and conducting intervention research to educate parents could be important future directions. Given the vital importance of parents in youth sport, it seems that more research devoted to understanding their experiences is an urgent requirement.

REFERENCES

Abidin, R. R. (1990). *Introduction to the special issues*: The stresses of parenting. Journal of Clinical Child Psychology, 19, 298-301.

Abidin, R. R. (1992). *The determinants of parenting behaviour*. Journal of Clinical Child and Adolescent Psychology, 21, 407-412.

Alexander, M. J., & Higgins, E. T. (1993). *Emotional trade-offs of becoming a parent: How social roles influence self-discrepancy effects.* Journal of Personality and Social Psychology, 65, 1259-1269.

Anderson, A. M. (1996). *Factors influencing the father-infant relationship.* Journal of Family Nursing, 2, 306-324.

Andersonn, C., & Andersonn, B. (2000). *Will you still love me if I don't win?* Dallas, TX: Taylor.

Bannerman, L. (2008, May 3). *'Pushy' pony parents reined in after one tantrum too many.* The Times, p.37.

Baum, G. (2002, January 26). *Dad sentences to 6 to 10 years for rink death.* Los Angeles Times, p. A10.

Baxter-Jones, A. D., & Maffuli, N. (2003). *Parental influence on sport participation in elite young athletes.* The Journal of Sports Medicine and Physical Fitness, 43, 250-255.

Belsky, J. (1984). *The determinants of parenting: A process model.* Child Development, 55, 83-96.

Bonds, D. D., Gondoli, D. M., Sturge-Apple, M. L., & Salem, L. N. (2001). *Parenting stress as a mediator of the relation between parenting support and optimal parenting.* Parenting, 2, 409-435.

Brustad, R. J. (1996). *Parental and peer influence on children's psychological development through sport.* In F. L. Smoll, & R. E. Smith (Eds.), Children and youth in sport: A biopsychosocial perpective (pp. 112-124). Madison, WI: Brown and Benchmark.

CBS (2002, January 11). *Hockey dad found guilty.* Retrieved March 3, 2009, from http://www.cbsnews.com/stories/2002/01/02/national/main322819.shtml.

Coplan, R. J., Bowker, A., & Cooper, S. M. (2003). *Parenting daily hassles, child temperament, and social adjustment in preschool.* Early Childhood Research Quarterly, 18, 376-395.

Côté, J. (1999). *The influence of the family in the development of talent in sport.* The Sport Psychologist, 13, 395- 417.

Crnic, K. A., & Greensberg, M. T. (1990). *Minor parenting stresses with young children.* Child Development, 61, 1628-1837.

Crnic, K., & Low, C. (2002). *Everyday stresses and parenting.* In M. Bornstein (Ed.), Handbook of parenting: Practical issues in parenting (2nd ed) (pp. 243-267). Mahwah, NJ: Lawrence Erlbaum Associates.

Dale, J., & Weinberg, R. (1990). *Burnout in sport: A review and critique.* Journal of Applied Sport Psychology, 2, 67-83.

Deater-Deckard, K. (1998). *Parenting stress and child adjustment: Some old hypotheses and new questions.* Clinical Psychology: Science and Practice, 5, 314-332.

Deater-Deckard, K. (2005). *Parenting stress and children's development: Introduction to the special issue.* Infant and Child Development, 14, 111-115.

Deater-Deckard, K., & Scarr, S. (1996). *Parenting stress among dual-earner mothers and fathers: Are there gender differences?* Journal of Family Psychology, 10, 45-59.

DeFrancesco, C., & Johnson, P. (1997). *Athlete and parent perception in junior tennis.* Journal of Sport Behavior, 20, 29-36.

Duncan, J. (1997). *Focus group interview with elite young athletes, coaches, and parents.* In J. Kremer, K. Trew, & S. Ogle (Eds.), Young People's Involvement in Sport (pp. 152-177). New York: Routledge.

Fletcher, D., & Hanton, S. (2003). *Sources of organizational stress in elite sports performers.* The Sport Psychologist, 17, 175-195.

Fletcher, D., Hanton, S. & Mellalieu, S. D. (2006). *An organizational stress review: Conceptual and theoretical issues in competitive sport.* In S. Hanton & S. D. Mellalieu (Eds.), Literature Reviews in Sport Psychology (pp. 321-373). Hauppauge, NY: Nova Science.

Football Association (2008). *Respect code of conduct.* Retrieved March 21, 2009 from http://www.thefa.com/NR/rdonlyres/7D2C1F35-7308-4B6C-B833-B0BED70B58F3/145335/Code_spectatorsFINAL.pdf

Fredricks, J. A., & Eccles, J. S. (2004). *Parental influence on youth involvement in sports.* In M. R. Weiss (Ed.), Developmental sport and exercise psychology: A lifespan perspective (pp. 145-164). Morgantown, WV: Fitness Information Technology.

Frey, M. (2007). *College coaches' experiences with stress: Problem solvers have problems too.* The Sport Psychologist, 21, 38-57.

Frone, M. R., Yardley, J. K., & Markel, K. S. (1997). *Developing and testing an integrative model of work-family interface.* Journal of Vocational Behavior, 50, 145-167.

Gerard, J. (2008, November 18). *Pushy parents poisoning junior tennis.* The Daily Telegraph, p. S20.

Goldstein, J. D., & Iso-Ahola, S. E. (2008). *Determinants of parents' sideline-rage emotions and behaviors at youth soccer games.* Journal of Applied Social Psychology, 38, 1442-1462.

Gould, D., Lauer, L., Rolo, C., Jannes, C., & Pennisi, N. (2006). *The role of parents in tennis success: Focus group interviews with junior coaches.* The Sport Psychologist, 22, 18-37.

Gould, D., Lauer, L., Rolo, C., Jannes, C., & Pennisi, N. (2008). *Understanding the role parents play in tennis success: A national survey of junior tennis coaches.* British Journal of Sports Medicine, 40, 632-636.

Gould, D., Tuffey, S., Udry, E., & Loehr, J. (1996). *Burnout in competitive junior tennis players: II. Qualitative analysis.* The Sport Psychologist, 10, 341-366.

Gyamfi, P. Brooks-Gunn, J., & Jackson, A. P. (2001). *Associations between employment and financial and parental stress in low-income single black mothers.* Women & Health, 32, 119-135

Hanton, S., Fletcher, D., & Coughlan, G. (2005). *Stress in elite sport performers: A comparative study of competitive and organizational stressors.* Journal of Sports Sciences, 23, 1129-1141.

Harwood, C., Drew, A., & Knight, C. (2009). *Parental stressors in professional youth football academies: A qualitative investigation of specializing stage parents.* Manuscript submitted for publication.

Harwood, C., & Knight, C. (2009a). *Understanding parental stressors: An investigation of British tennis-parents.* Journal of Sports Sciences, 27, 339-351.

Harwood, C., & Knight, C. (2009b). *Stress in youth sport: A developmental investigation of tennis parents.* Psychology of Sport and Exercise, 10, 447-456.

Hellstedt, J. C. (1990). *Early adolescent perceptions of parental pressure in the sport environment.* Journal of Sport Behavior, 13, 135-144.

Hellstedt, J. C. (1995). *Invisible players: a family systems model.* In S. Murphy (Ed.), Sport psychology interventions (pp.117-146). Champaign, IL: Human Kinetics.

Hockey Canada. (2008). *Policy and procedures manual.* Retrieved February 14, 2009, from www.hockeycanada.ca/index.php/ci_id/23656/la_id/1.htm

Hoefer, W. R., McKenzie, T. L., Sallis, J. F., Marshall, S. J., & Conway, T. L. (2001). *Parental provision of transportation for adolescent physical activity.* American Journal of Preventative Medicine, 21, 48-51.

Holt, N. L., Tamminen, K. A., Black, D. E., Mandigo, J. L, & Fox, K. R. (2009). *Youth sport parenting styles and practices.* Journal of Sport and Exercise Psychology, 31, 37-59.

Holt, N. L., Tamminen, K. A., Black, D. E., Sehn, Z. L., & Wall, M. P (2008). *Parental involvement in competitive youth sport settings.* Psychology of Sport and Exercise, 9, 663-685.

Horowitz, J. A., & Damato, E. G. (1999). *Mothers' perceptions of postpartum stress and satisfaction.* Journal of Obstetric Gynecologic and Neonatal Nursing, 28, 595-604.

Hughes, M., & Sajn, N. (2008, July 16). *Amateur football brings in barriers to keep pushy parents in line.* Retrieved January 31, 2009, from www.independent.co.uk/news/uk/this-britain/amateur-football-brings-in-barriers-to keep-pushy-parebts-in-line-868711.html

Jackson, A. P., Brooks-Gunn, J., Huang, C., & Glassman, M. (2000). *Single mothers in low-wage jobs: Financial strain, parenting, and preschoolers' outcomes.* Child Development, 71, 1409-1424.

Kidman, L., McKenzie, A., & McKenzie, B. (1999). *The nature and target of parents' comments during youth sport competitions.* Journal of Sport Behavior, 22, 55-68.

Kirk, D., Carlson, T., O'Connor, A., Burke, P., Davis, K., & Glover, S. (1997). *The economic impact on families of children's participation in junior sport.* Australian Journal of Science and Medicine in Sport, 29, 27-33.

Lazarus, R. S. (1999). *Stress and emotion:* A new synthesis. New York, NY: Springer.

Lazarus, R. S., & Folkman, S. (1984). *Stress, appraisal, and coping.* New York: Springer.

Leff, S. S., & Hoyle, R. H. (1995). *Young athlete's perceptions of parental support and pressure.* Journal of Youth and Adolescence, 24, 187-203.

Lichfield, J. (2006, March 10). *Obsessive father jailed for tennis player's death.* The Independent, p. 22.

McBride, B. A., Schoppe, S. J., & Rane, T. R. (2002). *Child characteristics, parenting stress, and parental involvement: fathers versus mothers.* Journal of Marriage and Family, 64, 998-1011.

McCarthy, P. J., Jones, M. V., & Clark-Carter, D. (2008). *Understanding enjoyment in youth sport: a developmental perspective.* Psychology of Sport and Exercise, 9, 142-156.

Murphy, J. (1999). *The Cheer and the tears:* A healthy alternative to the dark side of youth sports today. San Francisco: Jossey-Bass Publishers.

Nicholls, A. R., Holt, N. L., Polman, R. J. C., & James, D. W. G. (2005). *Stress and coping among international adolescent golfers.* Journal of Applied Sport Psychology, 17, 333-340.

Nomaguchi, K. M., & Milkie, M. A. (2003). *Costs and rewards of children: The effects of becoming a parent on adults' lives.* Journal of Marriage and the Family, 65, 336-374.

Norton, P. J., Burns, J. A., Hope, D. A., & Bauer, B. K. (2000). *Generalization of social anxiety to sporting and athletic situations: gender, sports involvement, and parental pressure.* Depression and Anxiety, 12, 193-202.

Nyström, K., & Öhrling, K. (2004). *Parenthood experiences during the child's first year: Literature review.* Journal of Advanced Nursing, 46, 319-330.

Ommundsen, Y., & Vaglum, P. (1991). *Soccer competition anxiety and enjoyment in young boy players. The influence of perceived competence and significant others' emotional involvement.* International Journal of Sport Psychology, 22, 35-49.

Parasuraman, S., Greenhaus, J. H., & Granrole, C. S. (1992). *Role stressors, social support, and well-being among two-earner couples.* Journal of Organizational Behavior, 13, 339-356.

Piko, B. (2006). *Burnout, role conflict, job satisfaction, and psychological health among Hungarian health care staff: A questionnaire survey.* International Journal of Nursing Studies, 43, 311-318.

Rodgers, A. Y. (1998). *Multiple sources of stress and parenting behavior.* Children and Youth Services Review, 20, 525-546.

Sidebotham, P. (2001). *Culture, stress and the parent-child relationship: A qualitative study of parents' perceptions of parenting.* Child: Care, Health and Development, 27, 1-18.

Shields, D. L., Bredemeier, B. L., LaVoi, N. M., & Power, C. F. (2005). *The behaviour of youth, parents, and coaches: The good, the bad, and the ugly.* Journal of Research in Character Education, 3, 43-59.

Strachan, L., Côté, J., & Deakin, J. (2009). *"Specialisers" versus "Samplers" in youth sport: comparing experiences and outcomes.* The Sport Psychologist, 23, 77-93.

Thelwell, R. C., Weston, N. J. V., Greenlees, I. A., & Hutchings, N. V. (2008). *Stressors in elite sport: A coach perspective.* Journal of Sports Sciences, 26, 905-919.

USTA (2006). *Recommended guidelines for successful junior tennis parenting.* Retrieved March 10, 2008, from www.playerdevelopment.usta.com/content/fullstory.sps?iNewsid= 146001&itype=7417.

Webster-Stratton, C. (1990). *Stress: A potential disruptor of parent perceptions and family interactions.* Journal of Clinical Child Psychology, 19, 302-312.

Wiersma, L. D., & Fifer, A. M. (2008). *"The schedule has been tough but we think it's worth it": The joys, challenges, and recommendations of youth sport parents.* Journal of Leisure Research, 40, 505-530.

Wolfenden, L. E., & Holt, N. L. (2005). *Talent development in elite junior tennis: Perceptions of players, parents, and coaches.* Journal of Applied Sport Psychology, 17, 108-126.

ACKNOWLEDGMENTS

During the preparation of this manuscript, Camilla J. Knight was supported by a FS Chia PhD Scholarship from the University of Alberta, Nicholas L. Holt was supported by a Population Health Investigator Award from the Alberta Heritage Foundation for Medical Research, and Katherine A. Tamminen was supported by a Doctoral Fellowship from the Social Sciences and Humanities Research Council of Canada.

In: Handbook of Sports Psychology
Editor: Calvin H. Chang

ISBN: 978-1-60741-256-4
©2009 Nova Science Publishers, Inc.

Chapter 14

EFFECTS OF A ONE-WEEK PLANNED PERIOD OF OVERREACHING TRAINING IN EXPERIENCED WEIGHTLIFTERS

Emidio E. Pistilli[*1], *David E. Kaminsky*[2], *Leo M. Totten*[3,4] *and David R. Miller*[4]

Department of Physiology and Pennsylvania Muscle Institute, University of Pennsylvania
School of Medicine, Philadelphia, PA[1]
AlphaBioCom, Radnor, PA[2]
Werksan Barbells, Moorestown, NJ[3]
East Coast Gold Weightlifting, Moorestown, NJ[4], USA

ABSTRACT

Introduction: As athletes train for competition, volume load and training intensity are specifically manipulated in an attempt to elicit gains in performance. The Theory of Periodization states that the planned manipulation of training variables over time can "peak" an athlete for competition while minimizing fatigue and preventing accommodation to training and/or overtraining. Overtraining can be defined as any increase in volume load and/or training intensity in which adaptation does not occur and results in long-term performance decrements. A milder form of overtraining, known as overreaching, can occur on a short-term basis in which athletes can easily recover over the course of a few days of reduced training. Daily manipulation of training variables can elicit changes either toward or away from a state of overtraining. If training and recovery periods have been planned correctly, a delayed increase in performance can occur upon the resumption of normal training. This delayed training effect should occur within approximately 2-5 weeks following the resumption of normal training.

Purpose: To determine the effects of a short-term planned period of overreaching on weightlifting performance and compare the training variables (volume load, total sets,

*Corresponding Author: Emidio E. Pistilli, Ph.D, University of Pennsylvania, Department of Physiology and Pennsylvania Muscle Institute, 3700 Hamilton Walk, A601 Richards Building, Philadelphia, PA 19104, 215-573-4549 (phone) 215-573-5851 (fax), epist@mail.med.upenn.edu

total repetitions) performed during the overreaching stimulus and the taper week immediately following the stimulus to normal training.

Methods: Members of a weightlifting team participated in a week-long training camp, in which volume load was double that which the athletes typically experience during normal training. At the completion of the training camp, athletes took part in a weightlifting competition. The results of the competition were compared to the athletes' self-reported best snatch and clean-and-jerk using a paired t-test, to determine the effects on weightlifting performance.

Results: Seven members of the weightlifting team were used in final analyses (age: 21y; height: 173.8cm; weight: 88.5kg; bodyfat: 15.2%; lean body mass: 74.7kg; systolic BP: 130.9mmHg; diastolic BP: 71.4mmHg; resting heart rate: 76.6bpm; weightlifting experience: 3.1y). Snatch performance following the overreaching stimulus was not significantly altered (Pre-camp = 103.9kg; Post-camp=99.6kg; -4.1%; p=0.27). A trend was noted in the clean-and-jerk following the overreaching stimulus, such that performance was reduced 5.25% (Pre-camp: 135kg; Post-camp=127.9kg; -5.25%; p=0.08). Training variables were also reduced 50%-80% during the taper week immediately following the week of overreaching.

Discussion: The results of this study indicate that weightlifting performance during a competition is not affected immediately following an overreaching stimulus. This work supports previous studies in which performance of a weightlifting-specific test battery in a group of junior weightlifters was not significantly affected by an overreaching stimulus. However, this study extends previous studies on the effects of short-term overreaching by analyzing the effects of the stimulus during an actual weightlifting competition.

INTRODUCTION

Training program design incorporates the principles of periodized training to plan and organize fluctuations in volume load (Weight x Sets x Repetitions) and training intensity (Percentage of 1 Repetition Maximum, 1RM) to elicit gains in qualities such as strength, power and rate of force development (4, 14, 16, 17). Periodization is defined as the planned manipulation of training variables over time, with the goals of periodized training being to "peak" an athlete for competition, minimize fatigue, and prevent accommodation to training and/or overtraining (1, 26, 31). During the course of training, planned periods of deliberate increases in volume load and/or training intensity can result in an increase in performance following a subsequent reduction in volume and intensity (3). Athletes can take advantage of this increase in performance capacity during subsequent periods of training; however, training must be planned appropriately to prevent maladaptation (ie, overtraining) and decreases in performance.

PERIODIZATION AND THE GENERAL ADAPTATION SYNDROME

The Theory of Periodization involves the manipulation and fluctuation of training variables to elicit specific training goals. Training is broken down into blocks of time, with discrete goals for each period of training (34). For example, the yearly training plan is termed the macrocycle, which is further broken down into mesocycles (ie,-months) and microcycles (ie,-weeks). Volume load and training intensity fluctuate periodically throughout the training year, and are manipulated based upon the scheduled competitions (26). This type of periodization is illustrated in the strength training model presented by Stone et al. (31). In this model, training is broken down into 4 basic phases with targeted training goals for volume load, training intensity, total sets, total repetitions, and the number of training sessions. As the athlete progresses through the phases of hypertrophy, basic strength, strength/power, and peaking, volume load is reduced while training intensity is increased to prepare the athlete for a competition. These fluctuations in volume load and training intensity allow for recovery and adaptation from one phase of training before initiating the subsequent phase of training.

In another example of periodization applied to weightlifting training, Andrey Matveyev described a periodized training program that consisted of 2 phases designed to prepare a weightlifter for a competition (14). The preparation phase was associated with a high volume load and moderate intensity of training. A typical training session would consist of 3-6 exercises with 4-8 sets per exercise and 4-6 repetitions per set (14). In this phase of training, the volume load in strength exercises, such as squats and pulls, could account for as much as 60%-70% of the total volume load (5, 20, 21). The second phase of training was termed the competition phase and was associated with a decrease in volume load and an increase in training intensity. A typical training session in this phase would consist of 1-4 exercises per session with 3-5 sets of each exercise and 1-3 repetitions per set (14). The total volume load of strength exercises in this phase would be reduced compared to the preparatory period, while the volume load of weightlifting-specific lifts would increase and comprise about 60% of the total volume load (5, 35). These phases were separated by what was termed a transition phase, as volume load was decreasing and training intensity was increasing (14).

Periodization of training is based on the General Adaptation Syndrome (GAS), originally presented by Hans Selye (28). Selye's GAS was broken down into 3 phases: the alarm stage, the resistance stage, and the exhaustion stage (2, 30, 31). During the alarm stage, the initial response to the stimulus is to recognize the stressor and mobilize the body's processes to deal with the stress. In the resistance stage, the body adapts to the stresses and improves its capacity to deal with the stress. The final stage, exhaustion, occurs if the stress becomes intolerable and the body is not able to adapt. Exercise training that results in positive adaptations is analogous to the resistance stage of the GAS, in which the body is able to adapt effectively to the stress of the exercise. In a similar fashion, periods of extreme exercise intensity or chronic periods of increased volume load without adequate rest can result in maladaptation and is analogous to the exhaustion stage of the GAS.

OVERTRAINING AND OVERREACHING

The phenomenon of overtraining has been the subject of considerable research (6, 29, 30) and is said to exist along a continuum (29). The relationships between the GAS, training, and overtraining are depicted in Figure 1. Overtraining can be defined as any increase in volume load and/or intensity of training in which adaptation does not occur and results in long-term performance decrements (6, 7, 30). A milder form of overtraining, known as overreaching, can occur on a short-term basis in which athletes can easily recover over the course of a few days of reduced training (6, 7). Along the continuum, overreaching can be further stratified into functional overreaching and non-functional overreaching. Functional overreaching can be used as a training stimulus to elicit improvements in performance if athletes are able to adapt to the increased training. In contrast, non-functional overreaching occurs when athletes cannot adapt to the training load and the first signs of overtraining may begin to appear (6, 22, 29, 30).

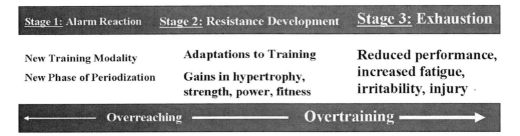

Figure 1. Relationships between overtraining, overreaching, and the General Adaptation Syndrome. It has been suggested that overtraining and overreaching exist along a continuum, that can be analogous to the stages of the GAS. When a new phase of training begins, the initial response is similar to the alarm stage of the GAS, in which the body prepares itself for this new "stress." If training is planned appropriately, this new phase of training can bring about positive adaptations, similar to the resistance stage of the GAS. At the far end of the continuum, chronic increases in training can lead to reduced performance, increased fatigue, and possible injury, and is similar to the exhaustion stage of the GAS.

The signs and symptoms of overtraining have been reviewed previously (30), and can include psychological factors, body composition changes, changes in hormonal levels, and decreases in performance. Daily manipulations in training variables can elicit changes either toward or away from a state of overtraining. It is often very difficult to diagnose whether an athlete is experiencing a bout of fatigue from an increase in training or progressing toward a state of overtraining. Moreover, there are no accepted diagnostic tools to accurately diagnosis overtraining in athletes (15). The key is that an athlete should be able to recover from mild, functional overreaching in a few days when volume load is reduced, while athletes that are near to or currently experiencing overtraining will take weeks to months to fully recover (6, 30).

If training and recovery periods have been planned correctly following a period of overreaching, a delayed increase in performance will manifest during these recovery periods. The fitness-fatigue model illustrates this effect (3). Following periods of increased training, both fitness and fatigue after-effects are maximized. However, the duration of the fatigue effects can be minimized while the fitness effects can be maintained. Upon resumption of "normal" training, athletes will be able to take advantage of the increase in fitness to train at a higher level. This delayed training effect should manifest within approximately 2-5 weeks upon resumption of normal training (26). Thus, athletes can maximize fitness gains through structured increases in volume load and/or training intensity, followed by a taper period to minimize fatigue after-effects.

Research on the development and consequences of a "true" state of overtraining in athletes has been difficult to complete. This is due in part to the fact that there are currently no diagnostic tests to definitively state whether an athlete is currently overtrained (15). In addition, it would be unethical to intentionally induce a state of overtraining in an athlete, for the sole purpose of studying this phenomenon (15). Instead, studies have been completed in athletes during short-term periods of intentional overreaching (10, 11, 29, 33). The effects of these overreaching training periods have been evaluated using various types of test batteries. However, to the authors' knowledge, there has not been a study analyzing the effects of short-term overreaching on actual weightlifting performance during a competition. Therefore, the primary purpose of this study was to determine the effects of a short-term planned increase in volume load (i.e. overreaching) on weightlifting performance, both during the overreaching stimulus and following the stimulus during a competition. A secondary purpose was to compare the training variables (volume load, total sets, total repetitions) performed during the overreaching stimulus and the taper week immediately following the overreaching stimulus to that performed during a week of normal training.

METHODS

Subjects

Seven members of a competitive weightlifting team volunteered for this study. Demographic data are presented in Table 1. Study participants were made aware of all aspects of the study and signed an informed consent document. This study was approved by the Institutional Review Board of West Virginia University.

Baseline Demographic Data

Height and body weight were measured using a standard tape and scale. Resting heart rate and blood pressure were measured prior to the start of training. Body fat percentage was calculated using skinfold calipers and a 7-site protocol (chest, mid-axillary, abdomen, triceps, subscapular, suprailiac, thigh). Fat weight was calculated as the product of body weight multiplied by body fat percentage. Lean body mass was calculated as the difference between whole body weight and fat weight (23).

Training Protocol

Data collection for this study took place during a 7-day training camp specifically designed to promote a state of short-term overreaching, as described previously (25). Volume load was elevated for one-week such that it was approximately 1-fold greater (i.e. double) than the volume typically experienced during a normal training week (24). Training intensity was increased above normal by performing 2-3 separate workouts each day, composed of a large number of single maximum attempts in the snatch and clean-and-jerk exercises. The number of workouts performed each day was adjusted to allow the athletes to recover for the following days training schedule. A total of 15 individual workouts were performed over the course of one week of training, with 2 workouts performed on days 1, 4, and 6 of the camp (Table 2), and 3 workouts performed on days 2, 3, and 5 of the camp (Table 3). On day 7 of the training camp, athletes competed in a weightlifting meet sanctioned by USA Weightlifting. A training log was completed by each athlete, which was used to calculate all training data (i,. volume load, number of sets,repetitions).

Table 1. Subject Characteristics

Subject	Age (yr)	Height (cm)	Body Mass (kg)	Body Fat (%)	Fat Mass (kg)	Lean Body Mass (kg)	Systolic BP (mmHg)	Diastolic BP (mmHg)	Resting HR (bpm)	Years Training (yr)	PR Back Squat (kg)
1	24	180.3	96.3	18.1	17.4	78.9	140	68	64	4	210
2	24	170.2	89.3	14.4	12.9	76.4	118	76	68	5	210
3	18	170.2	89.0	19.2	17.1	71.9	110	50	64	2.5	160
4	18	167.6	68.7	8.1	5.6	63.1	146	78	84	1.5	170.5
5	19	188	117.4	25.4	29.8	87.6	132	60	92	3	185
6	21	170.2	80.3	8.7	7.0	73.3	150	90	80	1.5	190
7	25	170.2	78.6	12.5	9.8	68.8	120	78	84	4	170
	21.3±3.0	173.8±7.5	88.5±15.6	15.2±6.2	14.2±8.3	74.7±7.7	130.9±15.3	71.4±13.3	76.6±11.2	3.1±1.3	185.1±19.7

Table 2. Example of a training day in which two successive workouts were performed.

Workout #1									
Snatch (FL)								-5% -5%	
Reps	2	2	2	1	1	T	T	1x2	2x2
20 Minute Rest									
Power Clean (FL)								-5% -5%	
Reps	2	2	2	1	1	T	T	1x2	2x2
Workout #2									
Power Snatch (FL)								-5% -5%	
Reps	2	2	2	1	1	T	T	1x2	2x2
Clean & Jerk (FL)								-5% -5%	
Reps	2+2	2+2	1+1	1+1	1+1	T	T	1+1	2+2

Table 3. Example of a training day in which three successive workouts were performed.

Workout #1									
Back Squat								-5% -5%	
Reps	5	4	3	2	1	T	T	1x2	2x2
20 MINUTE REST									
Snatch (FL)								-5% -5%	
Reps	2	2	2	1	1	T	T	1x2	2x2
Workout #2									
Clean & Jerk (FL)								-5% -5%	
Reps	2+2	2+2	1+1	1+1	1+1	T	T	1+1	2+2
20 MINUTE REST									
Clean Pulls						(100% 1RM C&J)			
	5	5	5	5	5				
Workout #3									
Power Snatch (FL)	(60%)	(70%)	(80%)	(85%)					
Reps	3	2	2	2x2					
Power Clean + Jerk								-5% -5%	
Reps	2+2	2+2	1+1	1+1	1+1	T	T	1+1	2+2
Snatch Pulls						(85% 1RM Snatch)			
Reps	3	3	3	3	3	3			

Statistical Analysis

All data were analyzed using the Prism software program (La Jolla, CA). Performance was analyzed using *t*-test to compare athletes' self-reported best snatch and clean-and-jerk to all lifts performed during the training camp and during the competition. One-way analysis of variance (ANOVA) was used to compare the training variables during the week of normal training, the week of overreaching, and the taper week immediately following the overreaching stimulus and for all comparisons of training variables. All data are presented as mean±SD.

RESULTS

Training Variables during the Overreaching Stimulus

Athletes completed training logs during the overreaching stimulus, which were used to quantify training variables, such as volume load and the number of sets and repetitions. Volume load was calculated for each workout and expressed as a normalized value relative to the athlete's body weight (Figure 2A). Volume load steadily increased and reached a maximal value on day 3 of training which was 55% greater than the initial day of training. Values were reduced on days 4 and 5 of training and were equivalent to the volume load on day 1 of training. On the final day of training, volume load was reduced 48% compared to the initial day of training.

The variation in volume load was due in part to the fluctuation in the numbers of sets and repetitions prescribed in the training plan and the athletes' level of fatigue as the overreaching stimulus progressed. For example, the number of sets performed during the first 3 days of training remained consistent, averaging about 50 sets per day. However, the number of sets was reduced by 28% on day 4, 11% on day 5, and 43% on day 6 of training (Figure 2B). The number of repetitions performed were the same on days 2 and 3 of training, which reflected a 34% increase from the initial day of training. On day 4 of training, the number of repetitions was equivalent to the number performed on the initial day of training, and was reduced 10% on day 5 and 45% on day 6 of training (Figure 2C).

Weightlifting Performance During the Overreaching Stimulus

Calculations for volume load and quantifying the numbers of sets and repetitions, as described above, is one way to track training progress. However, these numbers do not take into account the athletes' level of fatigue that may accumulate over the course of the overreaching stimulus. Performance of the snatch and clean-and-jerk exercises over the course of the overreaching stimulus may be a more sensitive measure of fatigue and thus, the ability to adapt to the increase in training load. Snatch and clean-and-jerk performance was analyzed 2 ways: 1) comparing the maximal weight lifted each day in these exercises to the athletes' self reported best snatch and clean-and-jerk performance (Figure 3); and 2) comparing the results of the weightlifting competition at the end of the overreaching stimulus to the athletes' self reported best snatch and clean-and-jerk performance (Figure 4).

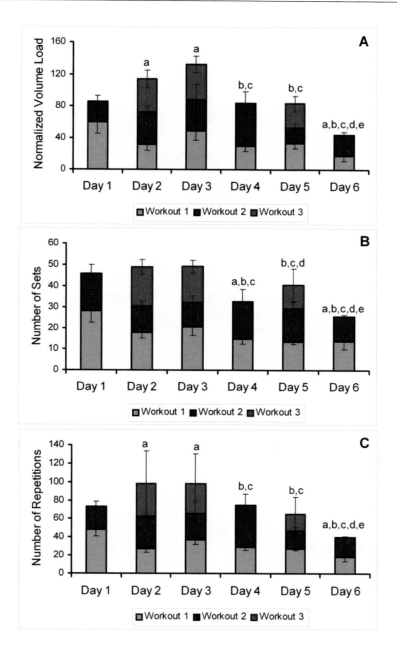

Figure 2. Training variables during a one-week overreaching stimulus. (A) Volume load is the product of weight lifted and the numbers of sets and repetitions performed. Volume load peaked at day 3 of training, with subsequent reductions during days 4, 5, and 6 of training to allow for recovery. (B) The number of sets performed remained relatively consistent during the first 3 days of training, with reductions during days 4, 5, and 6 of training. (C) The number of repetitions performed peaked during days 2 and 3 of training, with reductions during days 4, 5, and 6 of training. Statistical differences were noted when comparing variables to day 1 (a), day 2 (b), day 3 (c), day 4 (d), and day 5 (e).

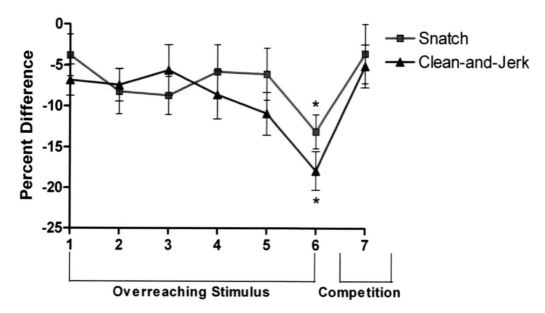

Figure 3. Weightlifting performance changes throughout the week of overreaching. Maximal attempts of the snatch and clean-and-jerk were performed everyday, and values were used to track the adaptation to training. Snatch and clean-and-jerk performance remained unchanged during the first 5 days of training. However, performance was significantly reduced on day 6 of training. This reduction was transient, as performance during a weightlifting competition was similar to the athletes' reported personal best lifts. *$P<0.05$.

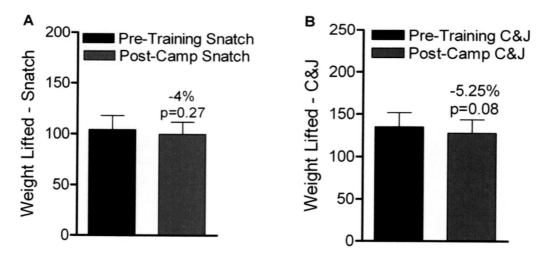

Figure 4. Affects of one-week of overreaching on weightlifting performance during a competition. (A) Snatch performance during the weightlifting competition was unaffected following the overreaching stimulus. (B) Similarly, clean-and-jerk performance during a weightlifting competition was unaffected following the overreaching stimulus. C&J – clean-and-jerk.

Snatch performance remained consistent during the first 5 days of the overreaching stimulus, with non-significant reductions averaging only 6% below the self-reported best snatch lift. However, snatch performance on day 6 was reduced 13% ($P=0.05$), suggesting an accumulation of fatigue from the prior 5 days of training (Figure 3, red line). Surprisingly, snatch performance during the weightlifting competition was not significantly different than the athletes' self-reported best snatch performance (-4%, $P=0.27$, Figure 4A).

Clean-and-jerk performance was not significantly different during the first 5 days of training when compared to the athletes' self-reported best clean-and-jerk. However, clean-and-jerk performance was significantly reduced 18% ($P=0.007$) on day 6 of training, again suggesting an accumulation of fatigue from the prior 5 days of training (Figure 3, blue line). Clean-and-jerk performance during the weightlifting competition was not significantly different from the athletes' self-reported best clean-and-jerk performance, although a statistical trend was noted as performance was reduced 5.25% ($P=0.08$, Figure 4B). These data suggest that although weightlifting performance was significantly reduced on day 6 of training, performance in an actual competition was not significantly affected and the athletes were able to adapt to the increase in training.

Overreaching Stimulus and Tapered Training Compared to Normal Training

As an additional method to compare training, volume load and the numbers of sets and repetitions were totaled during the weeklong overreaching stimulus and the taper week immediately following the overreaching stimulus, and compared to a normal week of training. In these comparisons, the values for the overreaching week and the taper week were expressed as a percent difference from the normal training values, which were set at a value of 1.0. The total volume load performed during the overreaching stimulus was 94% greater than normal training. During the taper week immediately following the overreaching stimulus, volume load was 74% less than during normal training (Figure 5A). The number of sets performed during the overreaching stimulus was 2.2-fold greater than normal training, while the number of sets was reduced 50% during the taper week (Figure 5B). The number of repetitions performed during the overreaching stimulus was 60% greater than normal training, while the number of repetitions was reduced 78% during the taper week (Figure 5C).

DISCUSSION

The primary purpose of this study was to determine the effects of a short-term planned increase in volume load (i.e. overreaching) on weightlifting performance, both during the overreaching stimulus and following the stimulus during a competition. Our data suggest that weightlifting performance during a competition is not negatively impacted immediately following a week of training in which volume load was 1-fold greater than normal. This effect was observed despite the fact that performance of the snatch and clean-and-jerk exercises was significantly reduced during the training sessions on day 6 of the training camp. We speculate that the level of experience of these athletes, which averaged 3.1 years of weightlifting training, allowed for a positive adaptation to the increased volume load. This speculation does not, however, underscore the need for the taper week immediately following the overreaching stimulus to allow for complete recovery from this type of training, both physically and mentally. Based on previous reports (3, 6, 29), it would be anticipated that following a taper period, these athletes would be able to train at a higher level due to the increase in fitness resulting from the overreaching stimulus.

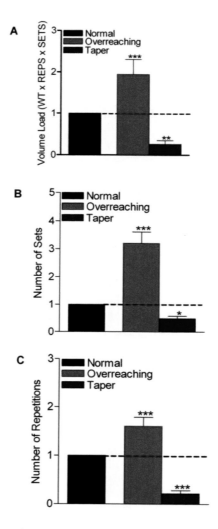

Figure 5. Training variable comparisons. (A) Compared to normal training, volume load was 1-fold greater during the week of overreaching and 74% less during the taper week. (B) The number of sets performed during the overreaching stimulus was 2.2-fold greater than normal training, while the number of sets was reduced 50% during the taper week. (C) The number of repetitions performed during the overreaching stimulus was 60% greater than normal training, while the number of repetitions was reduced 78% during the taper week. *$P<0.05$, **$P<0.001$, *** $P<0.0001$.

In general, signs of overtraining can be categorized into psychological factors, body composition changes, changes in hormonal levels, and decreases in performance (30). It is often difficult to determine if an athlete is exhibiting signs of an impending state of overtraining or simply experiencing fatigue due to an increase in training. In addition, research has shown that the physiological parameters altered in response to an increase in volume load are quite different in aerobic versus anaerobic athletes (10, 12, 18, 19, 32). To further complicate matters, it seems that the physiological parameters altered in response to high volume training are different than those altered in response to low volume high intensity training (8, 13). A consistent and necessary parameter to diagnose a state of overtraining is a decrease in performance in which long-term rest is required to resume training (13). Therefore, monitoring performance may be the most sensitive marker of an athletes' physiologic status. In the current study, performance of the snatch and clean-and-jerk exercises was unchanged until day 6 of the overreaching stimulus, suggesting a possible accumulation of fatigue from the previous 5 days of training. However, this accumulation was short-lived and did not impact subsequent weightlifting performance during a competition. Therefore, it is concluded that this overreaching stimulus did not result in a state of overtraining in this group of experienced weightlifters.

EFFECTS OF SHORT-TERM OVERREACHING IN WEIGHTLIFTERS

Studies have been performed in experienced weightlifters to determine the effects of planned periods of overreaching. The training programs used in these studies consisted of 2-4 workouts per day, a 100-200% increase in volume load, and exercise intensities between 70%-100% (11, 29, 33). In a study by Warren et al. (33), performance measures as well as blood indicators of overreaching were examined in a group of elite junior weightlifters following 7-days of a high volume load training camp. No immediate detrimental effects of increased volume load on subsequent weightlifting performance were observed in snatch performance following 7-days of overreaching. In addition, the changes in blood lactate and ammonia following 7-days of high-volume training also suggested no negative effect of training in the time immediately following the 7-day training period. In a follow-up study, Fry et al. (11) analyzed whether amino acid supplementation altered hormonal and performance measures to a similar 7-day overreaching training protocol. The results of this study support the previous study by Warren et al. (33), in that weightlifting performance was not altered following the increased volume of training. Furthermore, amino acid supplementation had no impact on performance, blood hormones (testosterone, growth hormone, cortisol) or blood lactate. Taken together, these data support the results of the current study and suggest that short periods of planned overreaching do not negatively affect weightlifting performance of experienced weightlifters in the period immediately following the stimulus.

In a study by Stone and Fry (29) in experienced weightlifters, a test battery was administered before the start of a week of overreaching, immediately after the overreaching stimulus, and 2 weeks following the completion of the overreaching stimulus. The test battery consisted of performance measures including snatch performance and vertical jump height, physiological measures including heart rate and blood pressure, and blood measures including hormones, lactate, glucose, and free fatty acids. Interestingly, athletes showed an improvement in performance measures immediately after the overreaching week and 2 weeks after completion, indicating a positive adaptation to the training stimulus. Resting heart rate and blood lactate were both lower at each test compared to the initial test. Positive changes were also noted in testosterone and the testosterone/cortisol ratio (T/C). The T/C has been used as a measure of the balance between anabolic and catabolic states (9), and an increase in this ratio would indicate a positive anabolic state. In summary, the test battery performed in this group of experienced weightlifters indicated a positive adaptation to the increase in training, both in performance and in physiology, which persisted for 2 weeks after the overreaching stimulus. This occurred despite the authors' stating that the training program was specifically designed to induce overreaching.

As suggested previously (11, 29, 33) and demonstrated in this study, prior exposure to periods of increased training volume and training experience seems to reduce the likelihood of detrimental effects of overreaching protocols in experienced weightlifters. Fry et al. (10) examined the effects of an overreaching stimulus in a group of weightlifters before and after one year of training, using similar methodology as their previous study (11). Interestingly, when the overreaching stimulus was performed by the weightlifters at the end of a year of training, testosterone concentrations were elevated immediately following the test. This was in contrast to reduced testosterone concentrations immediately following the test session that took place before the year of training. Although strength increased as a result of the year of training, strength was not altered immediately following the overreaching stimulus. These positive adaptations observed in the weightlifters may be a product of the weightlifting-specific training performed by these athletes as well as having experienced the overreaching stimulus previously. In summary, short-term overreaching performed by experienced weightlifters can lead to positive adaptations in anabolic hormones (10) as well as subsequent strength and performance (29) and, if properly planned, can be an effective training stimulus.

LIMITATIONS OF THIS STUDY

The results of this study on the effects of overreaching on weightlifting performance must be viewed in light of the following limitations. First, although having the athletes compete in a weightlifting meet immediately following the overreaching stimulus allowed us to determine the direct effects of overreaching on weightlifting performance, it is not recommended to have weightlifters train this way prior to competing. Second, the sample size of this study is relatively low when compared to other studies in weightlifters (11, 29, 33). Despite this, the statistically significant results on weightlifting performance indicate that the sample size was adequate. More importantly, this study only monitored training and weightlifting performance and did not analyze any physiologic and/or blood-borne markers that may be related to overreaching or overtraining. As stated above, numerous markers have been measured in an attempt to identify criteria to diagnose an impending or current state of overtraining. One consistent marker of overtraining status is a decrement in performance directly related to the sport or activity being investigated. Therefore, this study utilized the performance of the snatch and clean-and-jerk exercises as the sole measure of overtraining. Additional studies are required to determine the specific physiologic alterations to increased aerobic versus anaerobic exercise and high volume versus high intensity resistance exercise, as previously suggested (13).

CONCLUSIONS AND PRACTICAL APPLICATIONS

This study was performed in a group of experienced weightlifters to determine the performance-related effects of an increase in volume load. The results support previous studies (11, 29, 33) and suggest that this type of training paradigm is well tolerated by experienced weightlifters. The athletes in this study performed a week of training in which 15 individual workouts were performed over 6 days, with volume load 1-fold greater than during a period of normal training. The competition that took place on day 7 provided an ideal opportunity to determine the effects of this increase in training directly on weightlifting performance. In this group of athletes, performance of the snatch and clean-and-jerk during the competition was not statistically different from the reported personal best lifts. Therefore, the data and training program presented in this study can be used by weightlifting coaches to implement similar periods of short term overreaching into the training programs of their athletes.

When attempting to implement overreaching into a weightlifter's training program, the following points should be considered.

[1] This type of training is not recommended for beginning weightlifters. Previous research has shown that initially, a dramatic increase in volume load is associated with a reduction in muscular strength and power in resistance trained men (ie, not weightlifting athletes) (27). In addition, the study by Fry et al. (10) demonstrated different physiologic responses to overreaching in weightlifters after 1 year of weightlifting-specific training. Taken together, the data suggest that weightlifters with at least 1-3 years of training experience are able to tolerate and positively adapt to a short-term increase in training volume.

[2] The duration of the overreaching stimulus is an important consideration, as an extended period of time without proper recovery time can lead to decreases in performance and possible injury. The study by Stone and Fry (29) and the current study demonstrate that 1-2 weeks of overreaching is well tolerated by experienced weightlifters.

[3] When designing a short-term overreaching program, training variables can be manipulated such that volume load is increased, training intensity is increased, or both. In the current study, volume load was increased due to the performance of 15 individual workouts during the 6 days of training. In addition, training intensity was increased by having athletes perform maximal attempts in the snatch and clean-and-jerk everyday. Previous results (29) support this study and demonstrate that increases in volume load of approximately 100% are well tolerated in experienced weightlifters.

ACKNOWLEDGMENTS

The authors would like to thank the members of the East Coast Gold weightlifting team for their time and efforts in the completion of this study.

REFERENCES

[1]   Bompa TO. Periodization of strength: *The most effective methodology of strength training.* National Strength and Conditioning Association Journal 12: 49-52, 1990.

[2]   Brooks GA, Fahey TD, White TP, and Baldwin KM. Exercise Physiology: *Human Bioenergetics and its Applications.* Mountain View: Mayfield Publiching Company, 2000.

[3]   Chu LZF and Barnes JL. *The fitness-fatigue model revisited:* Implications for planning short- and long-term training Strength & Conditioning Journal 25: 42-51, 2003.

[4]   Dreschler A. The Weightlifting Encyclopedia: *A Guide to World Class Performance.* Flushing: A IS A Communications, 1998.

[5]   Ermakov AD, Abramyan MS, and Kim VF. *The training load of weightlifters in pulls and squats.* Soviet Sports Review 18: 33-35, 1983.

[6]   Fry AC. *The role of training intensity in resistance exercise overtraining and overreaching.* In: Overtraining in Sport. Illinois: Human Kinetics, 1998, p. 107-127.

[7]   Fry AC and Kraemer WJ. *Resistance exercise overtraining and overreaching: neuroendocrine responses.* Sports Medicine 23: 106-129, 1997.

[8]   Fry AC, Kraemer WJ, and Ramsey LT. *Pituitary-adrenal-gonadal responses to high-intensity resistance exercise overtraining.* J Appl Physiol 85: 2352-2359, 1998.

[9]   Fry AC, Kraemer WJ, Stone MH, Koziris LP, Thrush JT, and Fleck SJ. *Relationshipd between serum testosterone, cortisol, and weightlifting performance.* Journal of Strength and Conditioning Research 14: 338-343, 2000.

[10]   Fry AC, Kraemer WJ, Stone MH, Warren BJ, Fleck SJ, Kearney JT, and Gordon SE. *Endocrine responses to overreaching before and after 1 year of weightlifting.* Canadian Journal of Applied Physiology 19: 400-410, 1994.

[11]   Fry AC, Kraemer WJ, Stone MH, Warren BJ, Kearney JT, Maresh CM, Weseman CA, and Fleck SJ. *Endocrine and performance responses to high volume training and amino acid supplementation in elite junior weightlifters.* International Journal of Sports Nutrition 3: 306-322, 1993.

[12]   Fry AC, Kraemer WJ, van Borselen F, Lynch JM, Marsit JL, Roy EP, Triplett NT, and Knuttgen HG. *Performance decrements with high-intensity resistance exercise overtraining.* Medicine and science in sports and exercise 26: 1165-1173, 1994.

[13]   Fry AC, Schilling BK, Weiss LW, and Chiu LZ. *beta2-Adrenergic receptor downregulation and performance decrements during high-intensity resistance exercise overtraining.* J Appl Physiol 101: 1664-1672, 2006.

[14]   Garhammer J and Takano B. *Training for Weightlifting.* In: Strength and Power in Sport, edited by Komi PV. London: Blackwell Science, 1992, p. 357-369.

[15]   Halson SL and Jeukendrup AE. *Does overtraining exist? An analysis of overreaching and overtraining research.* Sports medicine (Auckland, NZ 34: 967-981, 2004.

[16]   Kawamori N and Haff GG. *The optimal training load for the development of muscular power.* Journal of Strength and Conditioning Research 18: 675-684, 2006.

[17]   Kawamori N, Rossi S, Justice B, Haff EE, Pistilli EE, O'Bryant HS, Stone MH, and Haff GG. *Peak for and rate of force development during isometric mid-thigh clean pulls and dynamic mid-thigh clean pulls performed at various intensities.* Journal of Strength and Conditioning Research 20: 483-491, 2006.

[18] Kuipers H. *Training and overtraining: an introduction.* Medicine and science in sports and exercise 30: 1137-1139, 1998.

[19] Lehmann M, Dickhuth HH, Gendrisch G, Lazar W, Thum M, Kaminski R, Aramendi JF, Peterke E, Wieland W, and Keul J. *Training-overtraining. A prospective, experimental study with experienced middle- and long-distance runners.* Int J Sports Med 12: 444-452, 1991.

[20] Medvedev AS, Frolov VI, Lukashev AA, and Krasov EA. *A comparative analysis of the clean and clean pull technique with various weights.* Soviet Sports Review 18: 17-19, 1983.

[21] Medvedev AS, Rodionov VI, Rogozyzn VN, and Gulyants AE. *Training content of weightlifters in the preparatory period.* Soviet Sports Review 17: 90-93, 1982.

[22] Meeusen R, Nederhof E, Buyse L, Roelands B, De Schutter G, and Piacentini MF. *Diagnosing overtraining in athletes using the two bout exercise protocol.* British journal of sports medicine, 2008.

[23] Nieman DC. *Fitness and Your Health.* Palo Alto: Bull Publishing Company, 1993.

[24] Pistilli EE, Kaminsky DE, Totten L, and Miller D. *An 8-week periodizedmesocycle leading to a national level weightlifting competition.* Strength & Conditioning Journal 26: 62-68, 2004.

[25] Pistilli EE, Kaminsky DE, Totten L, and Miller D. *Incorporating one week of planned overreaching into the training program of weightlifters.* Strength & Conditioning Journal 30: 39-44, 2008.

[26] Plisk SS and Stone MH. *Periodization strategies. Strength and Conditioning* Journal 25: 19-37, 2003.

[27] Ratamess NA, Kraemer WJ, Volek JS, Rubin MR, Gomez AL, French DN, Sharman MJ, McGuigan MM, Scheett T, Hakkinen K, Newton RU, and Dioguardi F. *The effects of amino acid supplementation on muscular performance during resistance training overreaching.* Journal of Strength and Conditioning Research 17: 250-258, 2003.

[28] Selye H. *The evolution of the stress concept.* American Scientist 61: 692-699, 1973.

[29] Stone MH and Fry AC. *Increased training volume in strength/power athletes.* In: Overtraining in Sport. Illinois: Human Kinetics, 1998, p. 87-105.

[30] Stone MH, Keith RE, Kearney JT, Fleck SJ, Wilson GD, and Triplett NT. Overtraining: *A review of the signs, symptoms and possible causes.* Journal of Applied Sports Science Research 5: 35-50, 1991.

[31] Stone MH, O'Bryant HS, and Garhammer J. *A hypothetical model for strength training.* Journal of Sports Medicine 21: 342-351, 1981.

[32] Urhausen A, Gabriel HH, and Kindermann W. *Impaired pituitary hormonal response to exhaustive exercise in overtrained endurance athletes.* Medicine and science in sports and exercise 30: 407-414, 1998.

[33] Warren BJ, Stone MH, Kearney JT, Fleck SJ, Johnson RL, Wilson GD, and Kraemer WJ. *Performance measures, blood lactate and plasma ammonia as indicators of overwork in elite junior weightlifters.* International Journal of Sports Medicine 13: 372-376, 1992.

[34] Wathen D. Periodization: *Concepts and Applications.* In: Essentials of Strength Training and Conditioning, edited by Baechle TR. Champaign: Human Kinetics, 1994, p. 459-472.

[35] Zatsiorsky VM. Training intensity: *Methods of strength training.* In: Science and Practice of Strength Training. Champaign: Human Kinetics, 1995, p. 98-99.

In: Handbook of Sports Psychology
Editor: Calvin H. Chang

ISBN: 978-1-60741-256-4
©2009 Nova Science Publishers, Inc.

Chapter 15

MEASURING SPORT SPECTATORS' COPING STRATEGIES: PRELIMINARY VALIDATION OF THE SPORT SPECTATOR IDENTITY MANAGEMENT (SSIM) SCALE

Iouri Bernache-Assollant[*1], *Patrick Bouchet*[**2], *Guillaume Bodet*[***3] *and Faycel Kada*[****4]

University of Franche-Comté[1]
University of Burgundy[2]
University of Loughborough[3]
University of Burgundy[4], France

ABSTRACT

Sport spectators' reactions to their favourite team's (athlete) defeat is a well studied phenomenon and several strategies used by sport spectators to cope with it have been previously identified in the literature. However, the conceptual distinctions between these strategies have not been empirically tested and no measure of spectators coping strategies has been elaborated so far. The current brief research attempted to fill this void. Based on the framework of the Social Identity Approach (Haslam, 2004) which postulated different categories of identity management strategies (i.e., individual mobility, social competition,

*Correspondence concerning the article can be addressed to Iouri Bernache-Assollant, Laboratoire de psychologie Recherches sur l'intentionnalité, représentations, croyances et subjectivité (EA 3188), Besançon, Université de Franche-Comté, IUT de Belfort-Montbéliard (Département techniques de commercialisations), bureau 302, 55, faubourg des Ancêtres, F-9000 Belfort, France. Tel: +33 (0)3 84 58 75 05. Fax: +33 (0)3 84 54 07 00. E-mail: iouri.bernache-assollant@univ-fcomte.fr.

**Patrick Bouchet, laboratoire SPMS (EA 4180), Faculté des sciences du sport, Université de Bourgogne, BP 27877, 21078 DIJON Cedex – France. Tel: +33 (0)3 80 39 67 46. Fax: (33) 3 80 39 67 02. E-mail: Patrick.Bouchet@u-bourgogne.fr.

***Bodet Guillaume, School of Sport and Exercise Sciences, Institute of Sport and Leisure Policy, Loughborough University, Loughborough, LE11 3TU, UK. Fax: +44-0-1509-226301. E-mail: G.S.P.Bodet@lboro.ac.uk.

****Faycel Kada, laboratoire SPMS (EA 4180), Faculté des sciences du sport, Université de Bourgogne, BP 27877, 21078 DIJON Cedex – France. Tel: +33 (0)3 80 39 67 46. Fax: +33 (0)3 80 39 67 02. E-mail: kf_kh@hotmail.fr.

and different social creativity strategies), the authors of this research developed a preliminary version of the Sport Spectator Identity Management (SSIM) scale which is made up of four subscales, and an empirical investigation was then conducted with one hundred and twenty spectators. Results of an exploratory factor analysis confirmed the four factors structure of the scale which accounted for 73.37% of the overall variance and revealed satisfying levels of internal reliability. In line with past research about this topic, the criterion related validity of the SSIM scale showed, as expected, that amount of identification with the team is significantly and positively related to all subscales. Finally, the study also supported a rather traditional picture of *rioters*: The spectators who demonstrate the highest levels of aggressive coping strategy are young males and tend to have the lowest socioeconomic status. Future directions to improve this instrument and to better track the condition of identity management strategy choices are discussed.

Keywords: Sport spectators, identity management strategies, social identity approach, team identification.

INTRODUCTION

From a contemporary sport-psychology perspective, the Social Identity Approach (SIA; Haslam, 2004), which refers to the integrated framework of Social Identity Theory (SIT; Tajfel & Turner, 1986) and Self-Categorization Theory (SCT; Turner, Hogg, Oakes, Reicher, & Wetherell, 1987), represents a relevant theoretical model to better understand the reactions of people who regularly follow sports--sport spectators--whose behaviour might otherwise seem quite irrational or pointless (Boen, Vanbeselaere, Pandelaere, & Schutters, 2008). According to SIA, individuals (1) define themselves to a large extent in terms of their social group memberships, and (2) seek to develop a positive social identity generally by comparing one's own group positively to other groups in a salient context. For sport spectators, one of the most relevant dimensions for social comparison, and consequently one of the most relevant dimensions of group threat value, is their team's (athlete) performance (Wann, 2006). In order to cope with a defeat and enhance a social identity, SIA research on sport spectators has identified several different *identity management strategies*. The use of theses strategies is strongly linked to the identification level to a team or athlete (for a complete overview, see Bernache-Assollant, in press; Wann, 2006).

Perhaps the most frequently studied strategy deals with the manipulation of one's association with a team. It has been shown that after a team (athlete) defeat, sport spectators can hide their connection with it to protect their social identity. This phenomenon, which is similar to the SIA's concept of social mobility, is known as Cutting of Reflected Failure--CORFing (Snyder, Lassegard, & Ford, 1986). CORFing is a corollary of BIRGing phenomenon which consists in accentuating the association with a team after a victory (see Cialdini *et al.*, 1976). The two terms are here conceptualized as bipolar endpoints along a continuum. For clarity purposes, the term *MATing* (Moving Away/Toward the Ingroup; see Stelzl, Janes, & Seligman, 2008 for a related conceptualisation) is used in the current research with lower levels indicating a spectator's desire to increase the distance between themselves and the team (or athlete) and higher levels indicating a spectator's desire to decrease this distance. The MATing phenomenon has been examined in various ways, including field studies (Byzman & Yinon, 2002; Cialdini *et al.*, 1976; Kimble & Cooper, 1992), class setting

(Wann & Branscombe, 1990), Internet studies (Boen, Vanbeselaere, & Feys, 2002; End, 2001; Joinson, 2000) and in fanzines (Bernache-Assollant, Lacassagne, & Braddock II, 2007). In regard with team identification, Wann and Branscombe (1990) found that the more sport spectators are highly identified to a team, the more they maintain their allegiance to it (i.e., display team loyalty in case of defeat and bask in its glory in case of victory).

Research on sport spectatorship suggests that highly identified spectators may use alternative strategies to restore a positive social identity, such as derogating the opponents and out-group fans in particular. This strategy, which referred to the social competition option of the SIA, has been labeled *blasting* (Cialdini & Richardson, 1980; see also Bernache-Assollant, Lacassagne, & Braddock II, 2007; Branscombe & Wann, 1994; End, 2001). Specifically, by acting in an hostile manner toward out-group members, highly identified spectators can feel as if they are better than the spectators of other teams.

Finally, highly identified spectators may use social creativity strategies to restore a positive social identity when threatened by their team's loss. Two kind of social creativity strategies have been identified in the literature on sport spectators. The first one includes creating new comparison dimensions between teams (*NCDing*; Lalonde, Mogaddam, & Taylor, 1987) that is maintaining the superiority of the team (or players) on dimensions that seemed to be relatively independent from performance (e.g., "our players are more talented than your players and we have the best supporters"). The second strategy is called *boosting* or indirect basking (Finch & Cialdini, 1989; see also Dechesne, Greenberg, Arndt, Schimel, & Solomon, 2000 for a similar strategy) and consists in re-evaluating negative comparison dimensions caused by a team defeat by accentuating the future success of the team (e.g., "even if we loose today, we are still the best and we will win lots of trophies this year"). This strategy can be closed to the social creativity strategy labelled temporal comparison and which consists, for group members, in referring to their past or future to boost the current status of their team threatened by a poor performance.

Although important steps have been made since about forty years in our understanding of sport spectator's identity management strategies using the SIA, the frameworks mentioned above suffered from at least two shortcomings. First, each strategy has generally been studied independently. Consequently, it is possible that respondents may have been forced to use a specific strategy in the context of the study which doesn't automatically correspond to the way they generally cope with a team's (athlete) defeat. Second, data have been collected using scales specifically constructed for the study, questioning the discriminant or construct validity of such a tool and making difficult the comparison of the results obtained in the different studies.

Given the theoretical and methodological shortcomings of these frameworks, it appears necessary to extend them in order to increase our understanding of identity management strategies used by sport spectators following a team (athlete) defeat. Hence, the aim of this research is to empirically differentiate the strategies identified in the literature and to test a preliminary version of a measurement scale.

METHOD

Participants and Procedure

We carried out the study in June 2008 and selected two French popular sport events broadcasted on French free-view TV channels: The 2008 international tennis tournament of Roland Garros and the 2008 final of the French football cup were selected. Questionnaires were administrated by email and a snow-ball strategy was used by the authors with sport management students as a starting point (see e.g., Boen, Vanbeselaere, & Swinnen, 2005; Boen *et al.*, 2008 for a similar strategy in a sport spectatorship context). Participants were 120 spectators with an average age of 29.46 years old ($SD = 6.75$). The proportion of men is about 75% which goes in line with previous studies on sport spectatorship (see Wann, Melnick, Russell, & Pease, 2001). On average, they physically attended 3.34 games ($SD = 4.14$) and watched 17.95 TV games ($SD = 9.93$) per year. Almost 65% of them spent on average less than €200 per year to attend games and 90% of them have an household comprised between €500 and €2000 per month.

Measures

The questionnaire was composed of a first question asking participants to mention the team or athlete they especially supported during the game they watched. Then, we measured team (athlete) identification using the Inclusion in the Self Scale (IIS) developed by Tropp and Wright (2001) in order to access the criterion validity of the scale measuring identity management strategies. The IIS is a single-item pictorial measure which uses Venn-like diagrams. In the present case, the diagrams depicted 2 circles (self vs. team or athlete) which progressively overlap following a 7-point scale (1 = separate circles, 7 = almost complete overlap). Participants thus rated their identification with their favourite team or athlete by selecting a specific degree of overlap. The greater the overlap, the stronger the identification. We choose to use the IIS scale instead of some existing team identification scales such as the Sport Spectator identification Scale (SSIS; Wann & Branscombe, 1993; see Bernache-Assollant, Bouchet, & Lacassagne, 2007 for the French validation) for several reasons. First, according to Tropp and Wright (2001), the pictorial measure designed to assess the level to which the team is included in the self reflects particularly well the essence of the connectedness to an in-group and can be adapted for a variety of group memberships (such as sport fandom). Second, as a single-item measure, the IIS can psychometrically be sound (see e.g., Kwon & Trail, 2005). Third, the IIS scale is strongly positively correlated with others measure of group identification such as the Collective Self Esteem Scale (Luhtanen & Crocker, 1992). Finally, previous research using community members in a French ice-hockey context (Bodet & Bernache-Assollant, 2009) and in an Australian soccer context (Lock, Darcy, & Taylor, 2009) has showed that the SSIS does not systematically perform well in non student context.

For the scale measuring identity management strategies, the item selection was guided by the theoretical implications of the Social Identity Approach (Haslam, 2004), previous studies on sport spectators identity management strategies (e.g., Bernache-Assollant, Lacassagne, &

Braddock II, 2007; Boen, Vanbeselaere, & Feys, 2002; Byzman & Yinon, 2002; End, 2001) and by existing scales (Blantz, Mummendey, Mielke, & Klink, 1998; Niens & Cairns, 2002) constructed in inter-regional and inter-religious contexts. Thus, we developed four scales measuring four different identity management strategies identified in the literature: Moving Away/Toward the Ingroup (MATing; 3 items), blasting (3 items), New Comparison Dimension (NCDing; 2 items) and boosting (3 items) (see table 1). Participants rated items by using a 7-point Likert response format anchored by the endpoints 1 (*strongly disagree*) and 7 (*strongly agree*). Participants completed the scale in a random assigned order and following a defeat of the team or athlete they watched compete.

Finally, participants completed several demographic questions regarding age, gender, socioeconomic standing, and sport involvement. Upon completion of the items participants were thanked and debriefed.

RESULTS

Preliminary Analyses

We performed a one-way univariate analysis of variance (ANOVA) across the two sports to compare the spectator's identification levels. Results revealed that tennis spectators ($M = 3.60$, $SD = 1.22$) and soccer spectators ($M = 3.97$, $SD = 1.36$), did not differ in their level of team (athlete) identification, $F(1, 119) = 2.40$, $p = .124$. Thus, all analyses were conducted across sport type (see e.g., Wann, Royalty, & Roberts, 2000 for a similar procedure).

Data Reduction and Factor Analysis

The sample was composed of 120 spectators which allowed the authors to conduct an EFA but not a CFA because SEM requires a minimum sample of 200 (Hair, Black, Babin, Anderson, & Tatham, 2006). An EFA with an oblique rotation (Oblimin) (using the maximum-likelihood solution (*ml*)) was first conducted on the sample because it allows correlated factors instead of maintaining independence between the factors (Hair *et al.*, 2006) (see Appendix 1). Items were deleted when they did not contribute enough to a specific dimension (i.e., factor loading inferior to .70 on any single component), when they cross-loaded and when a gap was too important between factor loadings of the same dimension (Hair *et al.*, 2006). Four factors, with eigenvalues of 3.609, 1.722, 1.459 and 1.282 were suitable for extraction based on the Kayser (1960) criterion and accounted respectively for 32.797%, 15.650%, 13.267% and 11.653% of the total variance (73.37% of overall variance explained) (see table 1).

Then, the Scree test criterion developed by Cattell (1966) was used and confirmed that four factors may be appropriate when considering the changes in eigenvalues (i.e., the "elbow" happens after the fourth factor) as well the eigenvalue-greater-than-one rule (see Figure 1). Finally, the MATing, blasting, and boosting dimensions kept three items and the NCDing dimension kept 2 items (loadings $\geq .77$ on their respective factors).

Appendix 1. *EFA for the sample,* **Total Variance Explained**

Component	Initial Eigenvalues			Extraction Sums of Squared Loadings			Rotation Sums of Squared Loadings(a)
	Total	% of Variance	Cumulative %	Total	% of Variance	Cumulative %	Total
1	3.608	32.797	32.797	3.608	32.797	32.797	2.355
2	1.722	15.650	48.448	1.722	15.650	48.448	2.535
3	1.459	13.267	61.715	1.459	13.267	61.715	2.540
4	1.282	11.653	73.368	1.282	11.653	73.368	1.951
5	.779	7.080	80.447				
6	.664	6.035	86.482				
7	.489	4.447	90.929				
8	.325	2.952	93.881				
9	.300	2.726	96.606				
10	.207	1.883	98.489				
11	.166	1.511	100.000				

Extraction Method: Principal Component Analysis.
a When components are correlated, sums of squared loadings cannot be added to obtain a total variance.

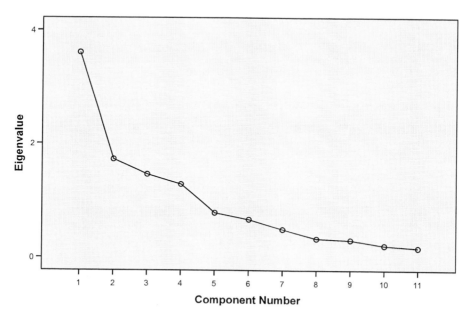

Figure 1. Scree test for the sample

Table 1. Items, factor loadings, eigenvalues and percent of variance accounted for the Sport Spectator Identity Management Scale (oblimin rotation)

	Factor 1 loading	Factor 2 loading	Factor 3 loading	Factor 4 loading
1. MATing (3 items)				
I want to support this team (athlete) for their next games	.823			
I want to publicly show my attachment to this team (athlete) (replica shirts, scarfs, posters…)	.909			
I want to communicate to others my support for this team (athlete)	.794			
2. Boosting (3 items)				
This team (athlete) should win at least one of the competitions that it is engaged in		.815		
I am pretty sure that this team (athlete) will be ranked ahead of its main rivals at the end of the season		.773		
I think that this team (athlete) will win more trophies in the future than in the past		.866		
3. Blasting (3 items)				
I strongly dislike all who support the main rivals of this team (athlete)			.767	
If I had to, I would not hesitate to insult the fans of the opposite team (athlete)			.890	
I would like to physically argue with the fans of the other team (athlete)			.835	
4. NCDing (2 items)				
Beyond the result, I think that the players of this team (this athlete) are (is) more talented than those of the opposite team				.868
Without any doubts, this team (athlete) has the best fans in the world				.839
Eigenvalue	3.608	1.722	1.459	1.282
Percent of Variance Accounted for	32.797	15.650	13.267	11.653

Note. Items were deleted when they did not contribute enough to a specific dimension (i.e., if it loaded less than .70 on any single component), when they cross-loaded and when a gap was too important between factor loadings of the same dimension. For ease of reading, only loadings above .40 appeared. $N = 120$.

Internal Consistency, Subscales Descriptions and Intercorrelations

Cronbach's alpha for the MATing, boosting, blasting and NCDing subscales were all satisfactory: .79, .75, .79 and .67 respectively (see table 2). In the current sample, the MATing and boosting strategies ($M = 4.45$) were the more used following by NCDing ($M = 3.95$) and blasting ($M = 1.75$). This result goes in line with those of Grieve, Shoenfelt, Wann, and Zapalac (2009) on North American hockey spectators which revealed that very few of their participants choose deviant coping strategies such as blasting.

Table 2. Descriptive statistics and reliability

Components	M	SD	Theorical scale range	Actual scale range	Cronbach Alpha
MATing	4.45	1.04	1-7	1.67-7	.79
Boosting	4.45	1.01	1-7	2.33-7	.75
Blasting	1.75	0.86	1-7	1-5	.79
NCDing	3.95	1.07	1-7	1.7	.67

All subscales were significantly and positively intercorrelated (see table 3): The MATing and boosting subscales, $r(120) = .33, p < .001$, the MATing and blasting subscales, $r(120) = .30, p < .001$, the MATing and NCDing subscales, $r(120) = .26, p < .001$, the boosting and blasting subscales, $r(120) = .22, p = .016$, the boosting and NCDing subscales, $r(120) = .20, p = .033$ and the blasting and NCDing subscales, $r(120) = .25, p = .005$.

Criterion-Related Validity

As expected, Pearson correlations showed that amount of identification with the team was significantly and positively related to the MATing, $r(120) = .24, p = .008$, the boosting, $r(120) = .43, p < .001$, the blasting, $r(120) = .32, p < .001$ and the NCDing subscales, $r(120) = .20, p = .028$, supporting past studies on this topic (see Bernache-Assollant, in press; Wann, 2006) (see table 3).

Table 3. Component correlation matrix

Components	Identification	MATing	Boosting	Blasting	NCDing
Identification	1.000				
MATing	.24**	1.000			
Boosting	.43***	.33***	1.000		
Blasting	.32***	.30***	.22*	1.000	
NCDing	.20*	.26***	.20*	.25**	1.000

Note. *p<.05; **p<.01; *** p<.001.

Discriminant Validity

In order to investigate the effect of various demographic characteristics on sport spectators' strategies, separate ANOVAs were conducted on gender (coded – 1 for male and +1 for female) and socioeconomic status (coded – 1 for household under €1000 per month, 0 for household between €1000 and €2000 per month and + 1 for household upper €2000 per month) with the identity management strategies scale and correlation analysis was performed for age (open ended question).

In regard with gender, results indicated that in comparison to females, males reported higher levels of boosting [Ms = 4.62 vs 3.96 for males and females, respectively, $F(1, 118)$ = 10.54, $p < .005$], blasting [Ms = 1.84 vs 1.47, $F(1, 118)$ = 4.03, p = .047] and NCDing [Ms = 4.07 vs 3.60, $F(1, 118)$ = 5.02, p = .036]. For the blasting strategy in particular, this result goes in line with past research on sport spectators' aggressive behaviors which revealed for instance that men where more accepting verbal aggression than women (Dimmock & Grove, 2003) and than men displayed more willingness to consider anonymous acts of hostile aggression than women (Wann, Haynes, McLean, & Pullen, 2003). In regard with socioeconomic status, no significant differences emerged between the three groups (all ps > .10). However, one way ANOVAs performed between each groups separately revealed a trend between the lowest socioeconomic group and the other two for the blasting strategy (p = .17 and p = .25), suggesting that a poor socioeconomic background may facilitate the use of aggressive behaviors (see Russell, 2003 for a complete overview; see also Zani & Kirchler, 1992 for a similar finding). Finally, concerning the age, results showed that it was negatively and significantly related to the blasting strategy (r (120) = -.22, p =.014): The older the spectators are and the least they use the aggressive strategy (all others ps > .10).

DISCUSSION

The purpose of this research was to empirically differentiate for the first time four identity management strategies potentially used by sport spectators to deal with their favourite team's defeat. In this regard, a preliminary version of a scale was developed and evaluated. Results from an EFA with oblique rotation (Oblimin) revealed a four factors solution (MATing, boosting, blasting and NCDing subscales) accounted for 73.37% of the overall variance which support our expectation that these strategies are related but distinct concepts. The subscales reliabilities were also satisfactory. Moreover, the criterion related to the scale's validity showed that the amount of identification with the team is significantly and positively related to all subscales, confirming previous studies on this topic (Bernache-Assollant, in press; Wann, 2006). Finally, the discriminant validity analysis supports a rather traditional picture of rioters highlighted in sociological and psycho-sociological research on hooliganism (see e.g., Russell, 2003; Zani & Kirchler, 1992): The spectators who demonstrate the highest levels of aggressive coping strategy are young males and tend to have the lowest socioeconomic status.

We felt that the development of this scale labelled Sport Spectator Identity Management (SSIM) scale increase our knowledge of spectators' reactions by providing to researchers a unique tool which covers a broad range of strategies. However, several limitations need to be addressed through further research. The first limit concerns the size of our sample which was quite modest (N = 120) and prevented us from performing a CFA analysis using SEM. Future research should thus be conducted with a larger sample. Additionally, a longitudinal design procedure with an interval between times of measurement should be used to access to the test-retest reliability of the SSIM. Moreover, it might be relevant to enrich the current version of the SSIM scale by adding an item to the NCDing subscale and by testing strategies not previously measured in the sport spectator literature. The taxonomy of identity management strategies proposed by Blantz *et al.* (1998) might be helpful in this way. Finally, it will be necessary in future inquiries to identify the antecedents of identity management strategies' choice. Therefore, the use of a multidimensional measure of team identification should be a positive step. Indeed, according to Tajfel and Turner's (1986) conception of social identification as cognitive, evaluative, and affective, recent research suggests that social identification with a group and a team in particular may be multidimensional (see e.g., Dimmock, Grove, & Eklund, 2005). This new theoretical frame seems attractive to analyze if specific dimensions of team identification contribute to particular identity management strategies' choices. Last, the investigation of potential moderating and mediating variables in the team-strategies link may represent promising avenues for future research.

REFERENCES

Bernache-Assollant, I. (in press). *Stratégies de gestion identitaire et supportérisme Ultra: une revue critique selon la perspective de l'identité sociale [Identity management strategies and ultra sport fandom:* A critical review based on the tenet of the social identity perspective]. Sciences & Motricité.

Bernache-Assollant, I., Bouchet, P., & Lacassagne, M.F. (2007). *Spectators' identification with French Sports Teams:* A French adaptation of the sport spectator identification scale. Perceptual and Motor Skills, 104, 83-90.

Bernache-Assollant, I., Lacassagne, M.-F., & Braddock II, J. H. (2007*). Basking in reflected glory and blasting: Differences in identity-management strategies between two groups of highly identified soccer fans.* Journal of Language and Social Psychology, 26, 381-388.

Blantz, M., Mummendey, A., Mielke, R., & Klink, A. (1998*). Responding to negative social identity: A taxonomy of identity management strategies.* European Journal of Social Psychology, 28, 697-729.

Bodet, G., & Bernache-Assollant, I. (2009). *Do fans care about hot dogs? A satisfaction analysis of French ice hockey spectators.* International Journal of Sport Management and Marketing, 5, 15-37.

Boen, F.,Vanbeselaere, N., & Feys, J. (2002). *Behavioral consequences of fluctuating group success: An internet study on soccer teams.* The Journal of Social Psychology, 142, 769-781.

Boen, F., Vanbeselaere, N., Pandelaere, M., Schutters, K., Rowe, P. (2008). *When your team is not really your team anymore: Identification with a merged basketball club.* Journal of applied sport psychology, 20(2), 165-183.

Boen, F., Vanbeselaere, N., & Swinnen, H. (2005). *Predicting fan support in a merger between soccer teams: A social-psychological perspective.* International Journal of Sport Psychology, 36, 1-21.

Branscombe, N. R., & Wann, D. L. (1994). *Collective self esteem consequences of out group derogation when a valued social identity is on trial.* European Journal of Social Psychology, 24, 641-657.

Byzman, A., & Yinon, Y. (2002). *Engaging in distancing tactics among sports fans: Effects on self-esteem and emotional responses.* The Journal of Social Psychology, 142, 381-392.

Cattell, R. B. (1966). *The scree test for the number of factors.* Multivariate Behavioral Research, 1, 245-276.

Cialdini, R. B., Bordon, R. J., Thorne, A., Walker, M. R., Freeman, S., & Sloan, L. R. (1976). *Basking in reflected glory: Three (football) field studies.* Journal of Personality and Social Psychology, 34, 366-375.

Cialdini, R. B., & Richardson, K. D. (1980).*Two indirect tactics of image management: Basking and blasting.* Journal of Personality and Social Psychology, 39, 406-415.

Dechesne, M., Greenberg, J., Arndt, J., Schimel, J., & Solomon, S. (2000). *Terror management and the vicissitudes of sports fan affiliation: The effects of mortality salience on fan identification and optimism.* European Journal of Social Psychology, 30, 813-835.

Dimmock, J.A., & Grove, J.R. (2003). *Relationship of fan identification to determinants of aggression.* Journal of Applied Sport Psychology, 17, 37-47.

Dimmock, J. A., Grove, J. R. & Eklund, R. C (2005). *Re-conceptualizing team identification: New dimensions and their relationship to intergroup bias.* Group Dynamics: Theory, Research and Practice, 9, 75-86.

End, C. M. (2001). *An examination of NFL fans' computer mediated BIRGing.* Journal of Sport Behavior, 24, 162-181.

Finch, J. F., & Cialdini, R. B. (1989). *Another indirect tactic of (self-) image management*: Boosting. Personality and Social Psychology Bulletin, 15, 222-232.

Grieve, F. G., Shoenfelt, E. L., Wann, D. L., & Zapalac, R. K. (2009). *The puck stops here: A brief report of National Hockey League fans' reactions to the 2004-2005 lockout.* International Journal of Sports Management and Marketing, 5, 101-114.

Hair, J. F., Black, W. C., Babin, B. J., Anderson, R. E., & Tatham, R. L. (2006). *Multivariate data analysis.* Upper Saddle River, NJ: Pearson, Prentice Hall.

Haslam, S. A. (2004*). Psychology in organizations*: The social identity approach (2nd ed.). London: Sage.

Joinson, A. N., & Harris, P. R. (2000). *Information seeking on the internet*: A study of soccer fans on the WWW. CyberPsychology & Behavior, 3, 185-190.

Kayser, H. F. (1960). *The application of electronic computers to factor analysis.* Educational and Psychological Measurement, 20, 141-151.

Kimble, C. E., & Cooper, B. P. (1992). *Association and dissociation by football fans.* Perceptual and Motor Skills, 75, 303-309.

Kwon, H., & Trail, G. (2005). *The feasibility of single-item measures in sport loyalty research.* Sport Management Review, 8, 69-89.

Lalonde, R. N., Moghaddam, F. M., & Taylor, D. M. (1987). *The process of group differentiation in a dynamic intergroup setting.* The ***Journal of Social Psychology, 127,*** 273-287.

Lock, L., Darcy, S., & Taylor, T. (2009). *Starting with a clean slate: An analysis of member identification with a new sports team.* Sport Management Review, 12, 15-25.

Luhtanen, R., & Crocker, J. (1992). *A collective self-esteem scale: Self-evaluation of one's social identity.* Personality and Social Psychology Bulletin, 18, 302-318.

Niens, U., & Cairns, E. (2002). *Identity management strategies in Northern Ireland.* The journal of Social Psychology, 142, 371-380.

Russell, G. W. (2004). *Sport riots: A social-psychological review.* Aggression and violent behavior, 9, 353-378.

Snyder, C. R., Lassegard, M., & Ford, C. E. (1986). *Distancing after group success and failure: Basking in reflected glory and cutting off reflected failure*. Journal of Personality and Social Psychology, 51, 382-388.

Stelzl, M., Janes, L.M., & Seligman, C. (2008). *Champ or chump: Strategic utilization of dual social identities of others.* **European Journal of Social Psychology, 38, 128-138.**

Tajfel, H., & Turner, J. C. (1986*). The social identity of intergroup behaviour*. In S. Worchel & W.G. Austin (Eds.), Psychology of intergroup relations (pp.7-24). Chicago, MI: Nelson Hall.

Tropp, L. R., & Wright, S. C. (2001). *Ingroup identification as the inclusion of the ingroup in the self.* Personality and Social Psychology Bulletin, 27, 585-600.

Turner, J. C., Hogg, M., Oakes, P. J., Reicher, S., & Wetherell, M. (1987). Rediscovering the social group: A self-categorisation theory. Oxford: Basil Blackwell.

Wann, D. L. (2006). *Understanding the positive social psychological benefits of sport team identification: The team identification-social psychological health model.* Group Dynamics: Theory, Research and Practice, 10, 272-296.

Wann, D. L., & Branscombe, N.R. (1990). *Die-hard and fair-weather fans: Effects of identification on BIRGing and CORFing tendencies.* Journal of Sport and Social Issues, 14, 103-117.

Wann, D.L., & Branscombe, N.R. (1993). *Sports fans: Measuring degree of identification with the team. International* Journal of Sport Psychology, 24, 1-17.

Wann, D.L., Haynes, G., McLean, B., & Pullen, P. (2003). *Sport team identification and willingness to consider anonymous acts of hostile aggression.* Aggressive Behavior, 29, 406-413.

Wann, D.L., Melnick, M., Russell, G., & Pease, D. (2001). *Sports fans: The psychology and social impact of spectators.* New-York (NY): Routledge.

Wann, D. L., Royalty, J., & Roberts, A. (2000). *The self-presentation of sport fans: Investigating the importance of team identification and self-esteem.* Journal of Sport Behavior, 23, 198-206.

Zani, B., & Kirchler, E. (1991). *When violence overshadows the spirit of sporting competition: Italian football fans and their clubs.* Journal of Community and Applied Social Psychology, 1, 5-21.

In: Handbook of Sports Psychology
Editor: Calvin H. Chang

ISBN: 978-1-60741-256-4
©2009 Nova Science Publishers, Inc.

Chapter 16

VIRTUAL REALITY FOR RESEARCH AND TRAINING IN SPORT: AN ILLUSTRATION WITH COPEFOOT

Cyril Bossard[1,2], Gilles Kermarrec [1,2], Romain Bénard [1], Pierre De Loor[1] and Jacques Tisseau[1]

Laboratoire d'Informatique des Systèmes Complexes[1], European University of Brittany, University of Brest, France, Faculty of Sport and Physical Education[2], European Centre for Virtual Reality, 25 rue Claude Chappe, 29 280 Plouzané,
E-mail: gilles.kermarrec@univ-brest.fr; {bossard ; benard ; deloor ; tisseau}@enib.fr

ABSTRACT

New possibilities for research and training in sport could be offered thanks to virtual reality simulations. The literature is examined, analysing the advantages and properties of current simulators. This paper aims to present an original experiment in virtual reality simulation design based on autonomy, interaction and evolving concepts. Our main suggestion is that believability of simulation for the user needs both regularity and surprises (in terms of virtual agents' behaviour). A naturalistic approach was used to study experts' decision-making processes in soccer settings. The decision-making model represented a guideline for choosing and implementing computational models. The advantages of virtual reality simulation are discussed in relation to training and research in sports science.

Keywords: Simulation, Virtual Reality, Sport, Design.

INTRODUCTION

The benefits of new technologies have led many researchers to develop research programmes relating to simulation design. Although simulations in the fields of driving, aviation and military or medical interventions is no longer questioned (Sebrechts et al., 2003), similar interest in the field of sport is much more recent (Ripoll, 2004). There is therefore very little information available about the benefits of simulations for research and training in high-level sports. Simulation, that is to say pretending, imagining or performing an action outside of its regular context, can serve many purposes in the context of high-level sports: preparing oneself for action, acquiring new technical skills, or studying particular techniques. In order to interact with a virtual environment, the validity of the simulation relies on the design approach and on the models of the virtual agents involved (Cobb et al., 2002).

Virtual environments (VE) can be used to immerse an individual or a team within a believable and interactive computer-generated environment. Users must be able to interact with autonomous agents and/or other human users. In order for the interaction to be effective, the virtual agents must also be able to influence the user, and be altered by the user's actions. The VE must be able to evolve due to these interactions. If the agents' behaviour evolves, it must be neither totally predictable, nor completely random. By making the virtual agents autonomous, we could expect more believable behaviours.

With a view to immersing high-level football players in a simulation, designing this believability depends on a balance between predictability and surprise in order to allow users to construct meaning in terms of their interaction with the VE. The aim of this paper is to present a multidisciplinary approach to designing simulations dedicated to sport. We will examine the methodological and scientific choices made in designing the CoPeFoot (Collective Perception in Football) virtual environment.

We will introduce our suggestion by a brief review of the simulators put forward up until now in the field of sports. We will show that these simulators respond poorly to the demands of autonomy, evolution and interaction. In our experiment, we will present four stages of a collaborative approach between sports science and computer science, with the aim of developing a believable simulation application for football. Finally, we will discuss the advantages of the simulation using virtual reality apparatus for sports research and training.

1. SPORT SIMULATION: A BRIEF OVERVIEW

According to Alessi (2004), three main aims can be associated with simulation for sports research and training: improving cognitive aspects of performance, improving the physical aspects of performance, and improving the affective aspects of performance (emotion and attitudes). Two main approaches are linked to these objectives and can be used to facilitate them: virtual reality simulation and realistic physical simulators. Within the approaches that use virtual reality simulations, we can identify the uses of simulations for strategic analysis of sports situations, and those relating to user-player immersion. The aim of the training in question imposes, or at least suggests the use of one or other of these approaches.

Realistic Physical Simulators for Studying Technical Movements

In physical simulators designed for studying technical movements, the aim is to recreate a more believable environment with regards to senses; mainly relating to sight, balance, touch and sound. The physical interaction between the user and the machine is an essential part of believability. In order to enhance the user's impression of immersion in these simulators, we use different mechanical systems to recreate the vibrations inherent to sports such as skiing or mountain biking, for example (Mester, 1999). Immersion through physical interaction is also linked to the scale (1/1) of the simulator. These very characteristics can be observed in *Peloton*, an environment which recreates virtual cycle races (Ensor *et al.*, 2000). Similarly, Bideau *et al.* (2003) suggest immersing handball goalkeepers by confronting them with virtual players; Huffman & Hubbard (1996), and Kelly & Hubbard (2000) also presented a virtual training environment for piloting Bobsleighs. One of the issues raised by these simulators is the evaluation of their value for completing the exercise in real-life situations. For example, Todorov *et al.* (1997) present a study based on the acquisition of technical moves in table tennis in a VE. They studied the transfer of these moves to real-life settings. Studies examining the transfer of acquisitions from the virtual to reality (Bossard *et al.*, 2008) show the need to think both about the alternation between real and virtual training sessions, and about the content of the desired acquisitions and the information provided by the virtual environment in response to the users' actions.

Finally, simulations for technical movements aim to optimize believability by focusing primarily on the physical interaction. Although these systems are tightly controlled, lacking autonomy and evolution, this type of simulation can be used to improve the physical aspects of performance.

Virtual Reality Simulation for Analysis and Strategic Assistance

The advantage of virtual reality simulations is that it is possible to conduct risk-free experiments and to be able to analyse the consequences of choices made by the players in different situations. The aim is not to use simulations to put the player in the thick of the action, but, on the contrary, to enable the player to take a step back from the action. In much the same way as for analysing parts of a game from video footage, the idea is to offer the player a number of different viewpoints. From a technical point of view; in order to generate a believable environment, this tool uses image processing and synthesis. For example, Ziane (2004) suggests that basketball coaches could be trained to analyse their team's actions. A model recreating scenes from the game based on a film was used to identify specific movements of both the players and the ball. A kinematic study of the action enables the coaches to graphically represent and to accurately interpret the different ways the teams positioned themselves on the court, the surface area occupied by each team, the distance between the players, the ball and the hoop, and the speed of the players and the ball. Other models (Bayesian networks) can be used in order to identify the most relevant viewpoint amongst all the possible points of view in order to study the correlations between the players' movement, the teams, and the ball. This tool has the advantage of being able to alter the view of the action and to identify the phenomena which are difficult to perceive through spontaneous observation. Metoyer & Hodgins (2000) also suggest a simulator with the aim of analysing the results of different combinations of movements in American football. These combinations are played by virtual agents. According to the authors, there is no point in modelling the virtual players to look realistic, as the illusion of reality is more likely to be lost if their *behaviour* is unnatural. Therefore, believability depends less on the appearance of the players than on their behaviour (their movements) in context. The aim is to test different movement strategies in order to evaluate the results before applying them to real-life settings. This type of simulation is therefore a useful tool in training high-level players.

Here, the believability of behaviours relies essentially on "visual" return from the images, or the conformity of the behaviours in the simulation compared to those from the knowledge base created by experts in the field. These approaches can be used to improve the strategic analysis of sports situations either outside of, or at a distance from the action. Furthermore, this type of simulator does not require the user to participate in the action but is rather concerned with the graphical quality of the environments or the conformity of the produced behaviours. The autonomy of the agents and the evolution of this kind of simulation are limited.

Virtual Reality Simulation for Immersion in Sports Settings

When the aim is to immerse the human user within a believable virtual environment, simulators attempt to produce virtual agents with a certain degree of autonomy. Video games can therefore provide very effective simulations. The TeamVision system from Konami, for example, is an adaptive artificially intelligent system for Pro Evolution Soccer 2008. The creators of the game FIFA 2008 (*Fédération Internationale de Football Association*) refer to a system evaluating up to thirty action options at any given time as an opportunity map. In the current state of affairs, the achieved behaviours are realistic, as they are due to the relative autonomy of the virtual players. The choices are made by each agent independently of a metamodel. However, these simulations often lack evolution in terms of behaviours, and interactions can be limited by the options programmed into the system. Sanza *et al.* (1999) present a football simulator called *NeViS (Networked Virtual Soccer)* enabling interaction between humans and virtual agents. The agents' behaviour is guided by a classifier system. The virtual agents can practice their interactions together in order to learn (to select) new winning strategies. The classifier system implements reinforcement learning from an "action-condition" set of rules. Each rule can be evaluated according to the quality of its attributes. The system inspects the environment, selects one of the applicable rules, and carries out an action as a result of these rules. The chosen rule may be reinforced, depending on the result (compensation). The rules can be combined using genetic algorithms to create new laws. This computational modelling allows for a good deal of evolution in the agents' behaviours. However, Sanza *et al.* (1999) highlight the fact that, as the new rules are generated randomly, they create valuable behaviours, but sometimes, these behaviours which are absurd in terms of suitability in sports settings. Research into the believability of behaviours is essential if these simulations are to be considered significant by experts in the field. Indeed, this requirement is crucial for players to be able to transfer real skills to virtual situations (Bossard *et al.*, 2008). Walls *et al.* (1998) present an experiment with a sailing simulator. The simulator reproduces the bridge of a boat, held up by two supports and dynamically controlled by the computer. The visual elements of the manoeuvres such as steering, or adjusting the sails, are extremely realistic. Having familiarized themselves with the simulator, competent sailors complete a 1km race into a headwind, aiming to complete the race in the fastest time possible. The ranking of each subject on the simulator was then compared to their ranking in other competitions. The results confirmed the possibility of transferring decisional skills from reality to the virtual and, as a consequence, they reinforce the believability of the environment.

Simulations aiming to immerse users in sports settings thus require autonomous agents whose behaviour evolves, in order to produce believable virtual situations.

2. A USER-CENTERED VIRTUAL REALITY SIMULATION: THE COPEFOOT PROJECT

We here present a user-centered design approach to virtual environments which is unique in that it is based on close collaboration between computer science researchers and researchers in sports science. This collaboration is founded on four stages, explained separately here, but which constitute an interactive process: 1) an analysis of the experts' activity is conducted in a naturalistic football setting (reality); 2) this analysis fuels the choice and implementation of computational models to improve the virtual agents' behavioural believability; 3) the result obtained, the VE, is used to engage in simulations (pairing subjects with the environment) and to improve the implemented computational model; 4) the believability of the virtual agents' behaviour and the simulator are evaluated using the simulation itself.

Modelling Tactical Decisions in Naturalistic Settings

Unlike "anthropomorphic" simulations (Burkhardt, 2007), the aim of our design approach to virtual environments is not to reproduce reality but to make the situation as believable as possible. In order for the simulation to be considered believable, agents need to be relatively autonomous, and the designer therefore needs a model for this autonomy. Each virtual entity must be able to make choices according to its past experience, its state, its perceptions and the possible actions it can execute, so that its behaviour appears coherent and unique. The role of the sports science researcher would be to participate in making these choices while this agent model is being defined. Although knowledge acquired from analyzing actions is starting to be utilized in the context of training settings (Ria *et al.*, 2006), their use in simulation settings making the most of virtual reality techniques remains largely unexplored. In order to simulate a counter attack in football, we wanted to model the tactical decision of players from a naturalistic study.

Using the NDM (Naturalistic Decision Making) approach, which examines the relationship between user and context, we considered the tactical decision to be a process of recognition of spatiotemporal configuration (Klein, 2008). This link can be described as a "cognitive package" (Ross *et al.*, 2006, p. 406), a set of elements relevant to the user. These elements are recognized as relevant and represent significant relationships as they are perceived from a background structure deriving from experience. From our hypothesis, this functional structure for recognizing and reacting seems to refer back to the concept of schemata (Piegorsch *et al.*, 2006).

In order to contribute to the empirical validation of this approach within the context of team sports, we tested a counter attack situation in football. Behavioural data was recorded from 12 national level football players (under 16s) supplemented by verbal data collected during self-confrontation interviews. Analyzing decision-making activity allows us to define activities and the most likely sequences (i.e. possible scenarios) of 16 schemata from experts in situations with tight time constraints. These schemata represent underlying structures which link perceptive and cognitive elements, and facilitate the recognition of situations during a counter attack.

Choosing and Implementing Computational Models

The second stage of the design process consisted of working on narrowing the gap between the decision-making model for tactical recognition of relevant configurations (Bossard, 2008) and computational models. In fact, two computational models were required in order to obtain what we refer to as a simplified analogy: a problem-solving model (Case Based Reasoning; Aamodt & Plaza, 1994) and a context representation model (Kokinov, 1995).

The CBR (Case Based Reasoning) model is based on the hypothesis that a perceived problem (development) can be solved successfully by referring to past experience. Finding a solution depends on identifying the experience which best fits the current situation, within all the cases encountered in the past (recall). Each case thus represents an action potential which is defined according to its context (adaptation). This ability to adapt is one of CBR's most encouraging features as the solutions found in the base are not applied directly but are rather adapted to fit a specific context. The base set of cases acts as a guide and does not dictate the responses. This model stems from frames theory (Minsky, 1975), which are similar to schemata concepts. The schemata can be adapted due to contextual representation.

Contextual representation originates from the model developed by Kokinov (1995). According to the dynamic theory of context, if the context of a decision is always general, we can distinguish its component dimensions through analysis and representation. He thus identifies internal and external context. External context refers to the physical properties of the situation, the elements that could be said to be objective from an exocentric point of view. Internal context is defined as the active state of an agent's cognitive system at a given moment t. These are the elements to which the agent will refer in order to make a decision: the context as perceived from an egocentric point perspective. From this initial distinction, the context of a CoPeFoot agent is then divided into a number of sub-contexts. The external, or environmental, context groups together all of the physical elements of the situation. Internal context is a representation of the agent's skills, or a representation of the agent's state, i.e. fatigue. Each sub-context is made up of a set of perceptions which, once assembled, form the context of the agent within the situation. This context-free representation has two roles. The first is to facilitate contextualised decision-making (figure 1); for each agent, the context is thus an active filter which generates the situation in progress. The second role is to authorise the graphical visualisation of each perception and context.

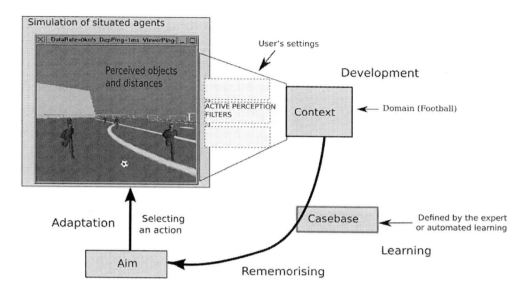

Figure 1. The computer-generated CBR and Context model (Bénard, 2007)

Using these two computational models, we can conduct a simplified analogy between a representation of the tactical decision, from a social-science perspective, and that of the autonomous virtual agents' decision-making, from a computer science perspective. Above all, we are trying to avoid contradiction between a tactical decision model in football and an autonomous virtual agent model.

Simulations and enhancing computational models

In order to improve the behavioural believability of the virtual agents, the computational model can be assigned evolution possibilities. We considered the evolution of the agents' behaviour according to three categories which can be positioned on three levels:

1. First level: the empirical model stemming from the analysis of human activity is used (applied) in order to enhance the set of cases and to define the agents' perceptions in context. In this respect, the description of expert footballers' typical schemata constitutes an information base for computer science researchers. The computer program limits actions: there is explicit learning or learning through instructions.
2. Second level: the computational model is enhanced through use. Within CoPeFoot, an interaction is proposed: the users click on the zones of the context they find relevant. Contextual information is reified by symbols indicating distance from the target, teammates and opposition players; symbols indicate whether or not teammates are marked or open.

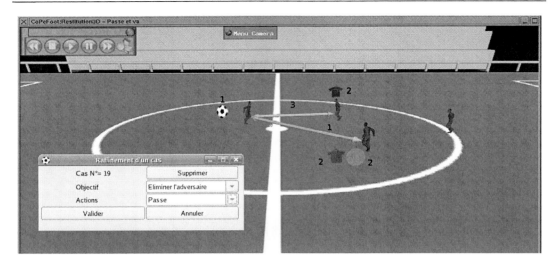

Figure 2. Representation of an agent's perceptions in context: exocentric perspective.

Thanks to the benefits offered by augmented virtuality, the user defines the action's significant elements. The information provided by the users, when they click on these elements, is used to revise the weighting associated with each contextual element according to an algorithm described in Bénard (2007). The computer program has only partial control of actions: learning is linked to the agents' imitation of the users' perceived behaviours.

3. Third level: enhancement is a result of the simulation. The computational model records the new cases which occur during interaction. The "case tree" expands in order to offer the virtual agents new possibilities in terms of actions. The computer program has very little control of actions: learning is implicit.

This stage of the design process of an interactive simulation demonstrates the importance of the models' evolution, which in turn enables the behaviours arising from that simulation to evolve.

Experimentation and Simulation Validation

The believability of a simulation is not easy to evaluate. Some simulators are tested in terms of skills transfer (for a complete review of these tests, see Bossard *et al.*, 2008). The transfer of skills from the virtual to reality is considered as a measure of the VE's success as a training tool. Some experimental studies have shown effective skills transfer (Rose *et al.*, 2000), while others have shown less significant results (Kozak *et al.*, 1993). These evaluations, which are carried out after the study, do not participate in designing the virtual environment and therefore are not used to modify the computational model. In order to rectify this shortcoming, we implemented an exploratory *in virtuo* study which aimed to evaluate the behavioural believability of CoPeFoot during the design process. Inspired by the Turing test (1950), this experimentation tested the ability of a user to distinguish between players controlled by humans and autonomous virtual players. This "decoy effect" was studied by comparing two groups of subjects (experts and novices) during three consecutive measurements. Results show a more marked decoy effect for novices when compared to experts, and an improvement for both groups over time. These results show that our virtual agents seem to demonstrate acceptable believability. They also show a reduction of this believability over time, and highlight the importance of the evolutionary nature of computational models in ensuring these simulations remain believable.

3. ADVANTAGES OF VIRTUAL REALITY SIMULATION FOR TRAINING AND RESEARCH IN SPORTS SCIENCES

Today, virtual reality provides a conceptual, methodological and experimental framework which is well adapted to imagining, modelling and experimenting complexity. Virtual reality simulations therefore allow real interaction with the modelled system. These simulations let us observe phenomena as if we had a virtual microscope which could be moved and oriented as we wish, with a choice of focal points. User can test the resistance of the implemented model (reactivity and adaptability). They become spectator-actor-creators as they can focus on observing a specific type of behaviour, a subsystem's activity or the overall activity of the system. The user can also interrupt the phenomenon at any time, accurately focus on the bodies present and the interactions underway, and then restart the simulation where it was stopped. This new kind of experiment is called *in virtuo* experimentation. Simulations in virtual reality allow the user to evolve with other users and/or virtual autonomous agents. Finally, users are "in situ" and "in action". Virtual reality fully involves the user in the simulation, which is closely akin to the participatory design approach preferring to consider users as human actors rather than human factors. Within this type of virtual environment, users must interact with autonomous agents and/or human team members. Various combinations of multiple human or virtual learners may be brought together for practice exercises.

Advances in virtual reality technologies can be used to enhance the acquisition of cognitive skills. As an example, to become progressively effective in a sport situation, the athlete must learn by acting. Putting the athlete into action can be expensive (in material terms) or risky (in human terms). This is the case when the aim is to learn how to act and react when faced with unpredictable events (like in team sports) or malfunctioning (material difficulties or psychological breakdown during competition). These problem-solving skills in dynamic situations are particularly difficult to deal with (uncertain, progressive and with strong time constraints) using the classical training approach of case studies, establishing general rules or instructions related to expected scenarios. On the contrary computer simulation makes it possible to immerse athletes in a VE where they can try things, choose, take initiatives, fail and try again. In virtual reality simulations, users can reconsider all previous research in order to study the operations induced by the sporting situation through the simulation. By confronting the athlete with more realistic environments than those traditionally used (i.e. pictures or videos), virtual reality allows, for example, to go from a mode of external or exocentric presentation to a mode of internal or egocentric presentation (Petit & Ripoll, 2008).

In conclusion, virtual reality simulations, as we developed them, allow the creation of game situations, which radically change the environments commonly used, in the perspective of both research and training. Of course, there is an obvious need for further investigation to acquire better and deeper understanding of the benefit of virtual reality simulations in sport. Loomis *et al.* (1999) have already highlighted the value of virtual reality technologies as a tool with high ecological validity that will greatly serve psychological research. We hope that, in view of this, sports science researchers will also be tempted by the new opportunities that virtual reality has to offer.

REFERENCES

Aamodt, A. & Plaza, E. (1994). *Case-Based Reasoning: Foundational Issues, Methodological Variations and System Approaches*. AI Commun, 7*(*1), 39-59

Alessi, S. (2004). *Five keys to successful simulations*. In Third International Sport Sciences Days, The analysis of elite performance in its contextual environment (pp. 141-143). Paris, INSEP.

Bénard, R. (2007). *Raisonnement en contexte pour la simulation participative et l'étude des situations dynamiques collaboratives. Une application au sport collectif.* [Reasoning in Context for Participatory Simulations and Studying Dynamic Collaborative Situations: An Application for Team Sports. (Doctoral thesis)] Thèse de doctorat, Université de Bretagne Occidentale.

Bideau, B., Kulpa, R., Ménardais, S., Fradet, L., Multon, F., Delamarche, P. & Arnaldi, B. (2003). *Real Handball Goalkeeper vs. Virtual Handball Thrower*. Presence: Teleoperators & Virtual Environments, 12(4), 411-421.

Bossard, C., Kermarrec, G., Buche, C. & Tisseau, J. (2008). *Transfer of learning in virtual environments: A new challenge?* Virtual Reality, 12, 151-161.

Burkhardt, J. M. (2007). *Immersion, Representation and Collaboration in Virtual Reality: discussion and empirical perspectives in cognitive ergonomics*. Intellectica, 45(1), 59–87.

Cobb, S. V. G., Neale, H. R., Crosier, J. K., & Wilson, J. R. (2002). *Development and evaluation of virtual environments in education*. In K. Stanney (Ed.), Virtual environment technology handbook (pp 911-936): Lawrence Erlbaum Associates Inc.

Ensor, J. R., Carraro, G. U., & Edmark, J. T. (2000). *Accommodating performance limitations in distributed virtual reality systems*. Computer Communications, 23(3), 199–204.

Huffman, R. K. & Hubbard, M. (1996). *A motion based virtual reality training simulator for bobsled drivers*. Dans Haake, S., (Eds), The Engineering of Sport, pages 195–203.

Kelly, A. & Hubbard, M. (2000). *Design and construction of a bobsled driver training simulator*. Sports Engineering, 3(1):13–24.

Klein, G. (2008). *Naturalistic Decision Making,* Human Factors, 50(3), 456-460.

Kokinov, B. (1995). *A Dynamic Approach to Context Modeling,* IJCAI'95 Workshop on Modeling Context in Knowledge Representations and Reasoning, IBP, LAFORIA 95/11, Paris.

Kozak, J.J., Hancock, P.A., Arthur, E.J., & Chrysler, S.T. (1993). *Transfer of training from virtual reality*. Ergonomics, 36(7), 777–784.

Loomis, J. M., Blascovich, J. J. & Beall, A. C. (1999). *Immersive virtual environment technology as a basic research tool in psychology*, Behavior Research Methods, Instruments, & Computers, 31(4), 557-564.

Mester, J. (1999). *Biological response to vibration load*. Abstract of the XVIIth congress of international society of Biomechanics, p32. Calgary,Alberta: ISB.

Metoyer, R. & Hodgins, J. (2000). *Animating athletic motion planning by example*. Graphics Interface, pp 61–68.

Minsky, M. (1975). *A framework for representing knowledge*. In Winston, P.H. (Eds), *The* Psychology of Computer Vision, pages 211–277. McGraw-Hill, New York.

Petit, J-P. & Ripoll, H. (2008). *Scene perception and decision-making in sport simulation: A masked priming investigation. International* Journal of Sport Psychology, 39(1), 1-19.

Piegorsch, K.M., Watkins, K.W., Piegorsch, W.W., Reininger, B., Corwin, S.J., & Valois, R.F. (2006). *Ergonomic decision-making: A conceptual framework for experienced practitioners from backgrounds in industrial engineering and physical therapy*. Applied Ergonomics, 37, 587–598.

Ria, L., Leblanc, S., Serres, G. & Durand, M. (2006). *Recherche et formation en « analyse des pratiques » : un exemple d'articulation*. [Research and Training in "practical analysis": an example of articulation.] Recherche et Formation, 51, 43–56.

Ripoll, H. , Le Troter, A., Baratgin, J., Mavromatis, S., Faissolle, M., Zmilsony, F., Poplu, G., Petit, J.P., & Sequeira, J. (2004). *The interest of simulation for research and training in sport: the exemple of football. Third International Sport Sciences Days,* The analysis of elite performance in its contextual environment, Paris, INSEP, pp. 147-148.

Rose, F.D., Atree, E.A., Perslow, D.M., Penn, P.R., & Ambihaipahan, N. (2000). *Training in virtual environments: transfer to real world tasks and equivalence to real task training*. Ergonomics, 43(4), 494–511.

Ross, K. G., Shafer, J. L. & Klein, G. (2006). *Professional judgments and "naturalistic decision making"*. In Ericsson, K. A., Charness, N., Hoffman, R. R. & Feltovich, P. J. (Eds): The Cambridge Handbook of Expertise and Expert Performance (pp 403–419). Cambridge University Press, Cambridge.

Sanza, C., Panatier, C., & Duthen, Y. (1999*). Adaptive behavior for cooperation: a virtual reality application.* In USA, I., Ed, RO-MAN'99, *8th IEEE International Workshop on Robot and Human Interaction, Pise, Italie, pages 76–81.*

Sebrechts, M. M., Lathan, C., Clawson, D. M., Miller, M. S., & Trepagnier, C. (2003). *Transfer of Training in Virtual Environments: Issues for Human Performance*. In Hettinger, L. J. & Haas, M. W. (Eds), Virtual and Adaptive Environments: Applications, Implications and Human Performance Issues (pp 67-90). Lawrence Erlbaum Associates, Mahwah: NJ.

Todorov, E., Shadmehr, R., & Bizzi, E. (1997). *Augmented feedback presented in a virtual environment accelerates learning of a difficult motor task*. Journal of Motor Behaviour, 29(2), 147–158.

Turing, A.M. (1950). *Computing machinery and intelligence*. Mind, 59, 433–460.

Walls, J., Bertrand, L., Gale, T., & Saunders, N. (1998). *Assessment of upwind dinghy sailing performance using a virtual reality dinghy sailing simulator*. Journal of science and medicine in sport, 1(2), 61–71.

Ziane, R. (2004). *Contribution à la formation des entraineurs sportifs, caractérisation et représentation des actions de jeu : l'exemple du basket-ball*. [A Contribution to Training

Sports Coaches, and to Characterising and Representing Actions from Sports: The Example of Basketball. (Doctoral Thesis)] Thèse de doctorat, ENS Cachan.

In: Handbook of Sports Psychology
Editor: Calvin H. Chang

ISBN: 978-1-60741-256-4
©2009 Nova Science Publishers, Inc.

Chapter 17

THE ROLE OF PHYSICAL ACTIVITY IN THE TREATMENT AND PREVENTION OF ANXIETY AND DEPRESSION IN CHILDREN: AN OVERVIEW

Patrick W.C. Lau and Erica Y.Y. Lau
Department of Physical Education, Hong Kong Baptist University
Kowloon Tong, Hong Kong

ABSTRACT

Anxiety and depression were the major mental health disease in worldwide (Zoeller, 2007). The prevalence of anxiety and depression in children and adolescents were accelerating at an alarming rate. Previous studies reported that 5.7% to 17.7% children were suffering form anxiety and 2% to 5% of them with diagnosed depression. Anxiety might lead to serious impairment to individual daily lives and depressed individuals were more likely to suffer from other chronic disease (i.e. diabetes, cardiovascular disease), health risk behaviors (i.e. drug abuse and alcoholism) and committed suicide.

Growing body of research indicated that physical activity (PA) was a protective factor of anxiety and depression and adopted it as a non-pharmaceutical for treating anxiety and depression in adults. However, issue in respect to the effectiveness, mechanism and the application of PA in the treatment and prevention of childhood anxiety and depression is still equivocal. Therefore, this chapter provided an overview on 1) the effect of PA in the treatment and prevention of anxiety and depression in children; 2) the mechanism of PA on anxiety and depression, and 3) PA recommendation for treating and preventing anxiety and depression treatment and prevention in children.

Keywords: physical activity, childhood anxiety and depression

INTRODUCTION

Physical activity (PA) has positive impacts on children's mental health. Regular PA was associated with improved mood and self-perception and reduced risk of two major mental disorders in children and adolescent: Anxiety and depression (Fox, 1999). Anxiety and depression are the major mental health diseases in worldwide (Zoeller, 2007). The prevalence of anxiety and depression in children and adolescents are also accelerating at an alarming rate. Previous studies reported that 5.7-17.7% and 2-5% of the children were suffering form anxiety and depression respectively.

Anxiety disorder could be categorized into panic disorder, obsessive-compulsive disorder, post-traumatic disorder, social phobia disorder, specific phobias disorder and generalized anxiety disorder. Although each disorder has its unique symptom but they all share the feelings of excessive apprehension, worry and fear (Barlow, 2004). Untreated anxiety may lead to serious impairment to individual's daily lives and interference their ability to establish and maintain relationship with others (World Health Organization, 2006). Moreover, it was associated with increased risk cardiovascular disease depression and suicide (Barlow, 2004).

Depression is a mood disorder which could be classified as depressive disorder (major depressive disorder (MDD) and dysthymic disorder) and bipolar disorder (bipolar I and bipolar II) (American Psychiatric Association (APA), 2002). Depressed individuals may have the following symptoms: depressed mood, loss of interest or pleasure, feelings of guilt or low self-worth, disturbed sleep or appetite, low energy, and poor concentration. These symptoms could be chronic or recurrent. Without appropriate treatment, depression might affect individual's ability to take care of his or her everyday responsibilities substantially (World Health Organization, 2006). Depression was associated with cardiovascular disease and diabetes (Mykletun *et al.*, 2007; Thakore, 2001), and other health risk behavior (i.e. drugs abuse, alcoholism, cigarette smoking and teen pregnancy) (Dunn & Weintraub, 2008). It was also the most frequent mental problem for people who committed suicide (Chan & Hung, 2006). These urged the needs for effective treatment.

In addition to treatment, prevention prior to the initial onset of the disorder is also important. Previous studies showed that children with a history of these disorders was at least 3 times more likely than those with no previous history to suffer from the disorders in their later life (Costello et al., 2003; Fergusson & Woodward, 2002). Moreover, prevention also plays an imperative role in reducing the prevalence if developing significant anxiety and depression. The reasons are that the symptoms of anxiety and depression are not easy to be recognized in children (Tomb & GHunter, 2004). Researchers believed that there may be a large proportion of children with undiagnosed anxiety and depression just because the extent did not reach to the diagnostic criteria. However, most of them were not receiving any treatment (Barrett & Turner, 2004). These evidences indicated the importance of early prevention or intervention.

CURRENT TREATMENT OF CHILDHOOD ANXIETY AND DEPRESSION

Currently, medication (i.e. Tricyclic antidepressants) and psychosocial treatments (i.e. Cognitive Behavior Therapy (CBT)) are the standard approaches in the treatment of anxiety and depression. However, medication showed little effect in children (Michael & Crowley, 2002). Importantly, it may lead to adverse effects to children's health such as weight gain, hyperlipidemia, elevated blood pressure and increased risk of suicidal behavior (Wipfli *et al.*,

2008). Although psychosocial treatment appeared to be an effective treatment (Cartwright-Hatton *et al.*, 2004), it requires certain level of cognitive ability which may not be well developed in young children. Therefore, its effectiveness was limited in older children. Moreover, psychosocial treatment may not be available in most communities (Cheung *et al.*, 2006). These evidences indicated that children with anxiety and depression were not treated effectively in the current state.

CURRENT PREVENTION OF CHILDHOOD ANXIETY AND DEPRESSION

Psychosocial therapy (i.e. cognitive reconstruction therapy) and education program were the approaches commonly used in the prevention of anxiety and depression in children (Clark, 1999; Garber, 2006; Merry et al., 2004). Previous studies showed that the effectiveness of these programs was modest (Barrett & Turner, 2004; Clark, 1999; Merry et al., 2004). In fact, majority of the prevention programs were secondary prevention that targeted to participants who were already experiencing the symptoms rather than before the onset of the disorders (Horowitz & Garber, 2006). That means the effectiveness of these approaches on preventing childhood anxiety and depression was remained unknown. Therefore, an effective, absence of unwanted adverse effects, and widely accessible and acceptable approach for treating and preventing anxiety and depression in children is warranted, and PA has considerable potential (Cartwright-Hatton et al., 2006; Dimeo et al., 2001; Dunn & Weintraub, 2008).

Several reviews studies (Dunn & Weintraub, 2008; Larun et al., 2008; Martinsen, 2007; Martinsen, 2008; Wipfli et al., 2008) provided evidences for adopting PA in the treatment and prevention of depression and some forms of anxiety disorder. These also concluded that PA may be a preventive factor of anxiety and depression in adults. However, issue in respect to the effectiveness, mechanism and the application of PA in the treatment and prevention of childhood anxiety and depression is still equivocal. Therefore, this chapter would discuss the role of PA in the treatment and prevention of anxiety and depression in children. As these reviews were all recent publication and have included most of the updated and relevant studies, this chapter would provide an overview in the following issues based on their findings:

1) the effect of PA in the treatment and prevention of anxiety and depression in children
2) the mechanism of PA on anxiety and depression
3) to provide PA recommendations for treating and preventing anxiety and depression in children

PA IN THE TREATMENT OF ANXIETY AND DEPRESSION

Anxiety

Few studies have been examined the treatment effect of PA on anxiety. Larun and colleague (2008) found that no randomized controlled trial (RCT) was conducted to investigate the effect of PA in the treatment of childhood anxiety in the last 20 years. Though, there was positive effect reported in recent non randomized controlled trial in clinical pediatric population. Kiluk and colleague (2009) found that children with Attention-deficit hyperactivity disorder (ADHD) who participated in three or more sports displayed significantly fewer anxiety or depression symptoms than those who participated in fewer than three sports. However, Strohle (2008) noted that the effect of PA in the treatment of childhood anxiety was difficult to justify because a specific type of disorder could not be generalized in other disorders as they are diverse in nature.

Depression

Comparatively, more studies have investigated the effect of PA on treating childhood depression (Dunn & Weintraub, 2008; Ströhle, 2008). Larun and colleague (2008) claimed that the treatment effect of PA on childhood depression was not confirmed by small number of study, although existing evidences showed that PA had a significant and positive effect in treating depressed children compared with no intervention control group. However, Dunn and colleague (2008) provoked that the positive finding in adults and animals model were strong enough to support the potential benefits of PA in the treatment of depression in children. This notion was supported by recent non randomized controlled trial. Stella and colleague (2005) conducted a 12-week PA intervention to reduce depression in 40 obese female adolescents. The result demonstrated that aerobic exercise produced significant reduction in the depression score. Similarly, Nabkasorn and colleague (2006) examined the effectiveness of an 8-week jogging exercise in 49 adolescent girls with mild-to-moderate depressive symptoms. The result indicated a significant decrease in depression scores and 24 hour excretions of urinary cortical and epinephrine level. In general, majority of the studies tended to illustrate positive impact of PA in the treatment of childhood depression.

PA IN THE PREVENTION OF ANXIETY AND DEPRESSION

Anxiety

Martinsen (2008) found that there was lack of longitudinal studies to support the prevention effect of PA on anxiety. Larun and colleague (2008) concluded that PA intervention has significant and positive effect on preventing anxiety compared to no intervention control group. Strohle (2008) studied 2548 adolescents found that people with regular PA had substantially lower incidence of any and comorbid mental disorder after 4 years and a lower incidence of somatoform- dynamic- and some anxiety disorder. Lindwall and Lindgren (2004) conducted a 6-month PA intervention program on physical self-perception and social physique anxiety in inactive adolescent girl. The result showed that the intervention significantly reduced the anxiety score after 6 months. The evidences regarding the positive effect of PA in the prevention of anxiety was relatively consistent.

Depression

In the study of Larun et al (2008), the result indicated that PA has a significant effect on preventing depression compared with no intervention or placebo control group. However, the prevention effect of PA on childhood depression is reserved. First, only small number of studies (n=16) were included. In addition, most of the include studies were targeted to older children aged above 12 years while the prevention effect of PA in young children was still equivocal. A longitudinal study (Harris *et al.*, 2006) in adults suggested that PA may have an indirect prevention effect on depression. It counteracted with medical conditions and negative life events.

Moreover, some studies (Dunn & Weintraub, 2008; Ströhle, 2008; Wipfli et al., 2008) argued that there was actually no study examined the preventive effect of PA on depression in healthy population. It is because majority of the participants in the previous studies were those who have previous episode of MDD. Therefore, these studies were in fact exploring the effect of PA on preventing the reoccurrence rather than the development of depression. The effect of PA in the prevention of depression was inconclusive.

In summary, existing evidences supported that PA appears to have significant and positive effect in the treatment of depression but inconclusive in anxiety. This only indicated that there was lack of consistent findings with respect to the treatment effect of PA on childhood anxiety. It is because the anxiety disorders are diverse in nature which limits the generalization of a significant result from a specific anxiety disorder to others. In contrast, PA seems to show consistent positive effect in the prevention of anxiety. However, no consensus exited in depression due to lack of pure prevention program (program intervene prior the initial onset t of the depressive symptom). Dunn and colleague (2008) suggested that this finding may be confounded by the floor effect. That is the intervention would not be able to produce further reduction in the depression level when participant's baseline level was very low.

MECHANISM OF PA ON ANXIETY AND DEPRESSION

Although none of the mechanism of PA on anxiety and depression was proven, a number of explanations were commonly accepted. From the biochemical perspective, PA increased the concentration of endorphin and serotonin that have been reported to affect mood (Dimeo et al., 2001; Nabkasorn et al., 2006; Sjoten & Kivel, 2006). Endorphin is a neuro-chemical substance that provides the euphoria sensation (Petruzzello et al., 1991). Serotonin is a neurotransmitter which is responsible for mood enhancement (Graeff et al., 1996). A deficit of endorphin and serotonin was found to be associated with anxiety and depression. These hypotheses were supported by the study in animal model (Russo-Neustadt et al., 2001).

Physiologically, increased in core body temperature, cerebral blood flow and muscle relaxation during and after exercising may also attributed to stress relaxation and mood improvement (Fox, 1999). Stathopoulou and colleague (2006) suggested that improved quality of sleep after performing PA may produce positive effect on ameliorating anxiety and depression, which is similar to certain types of antidepressant. To date, the findings were mixing. More studies are needed to investigate the impact of sleeping quality on anxiety and depression.

Furthermore, PA was associated with improved psychological outcome which may also reduce anxiety and depression. Self-esteem was closely related to anxiety and depression (Bragado et al., 2008). Self-esteem is the belief on how a person feels and thinks about themselves physically (i.e. body appearance), psychologically (i.e. self-efficacy) and socially (i.e. social skills) (Murk, 2006). PA offers a mean for improving and maintaining body appearance (i.e. fat loss and body shaping), enhancing one's self-efficacy (i.e. providing positive experience of mastering new tasks), and improving social skills (i.e. communication and cooperation with others). These may increase one's confidence on coping with anxiety and depression (Bandura, 2004; Fox, 1999; Stathopoulou et al., 2006)..

Operationally, PA was used as a medium to help distracting individual from negative and stressful aspects (Biddle et al., 2000; Stathopoulou et al., 2006). It was also adopted in the treatment to produce similar bodily sensation with anxiety like increases in heart rate, body temperature, respiration and perspiration. Anxious individual would expose to those anxiety reactions repetitively while engaging in PA. Individuals may be able to recognize and positively interpret those anxiety reactions as a normal sign of stress under the supervision of psychiatric and PA professionals (Borman-Fulk et al., 2003; Martinsen, 2008)

PA RECOMMENDATION IN THE TREATMENT AND PREVENTION OF CHILDHOOD ANXIETY AND DEPRESSION

The design of PA intervention should be varied in respect to different purposes (i.e. treatment and prevention) and several factors like severity of the illness, type, frequency, duration and intensity of PA should be considered.

For treatment purpose, PA intervention may produce greater effect in the treatment of childhood anxiety and depression in several population: 1) Inpatient with mild to moderate depression as they are not suffering from severe physical impairment (Martinsen, 2000; Sjoten & Kivel, 2006). 2) Children whom are conventional psychological intervention are less acceptable (Salmon, 2000). For instance, children who aged below 12 years-old may not possess sufficient cognitive ability to receive CBT. 3) Parents with children suffering in anxiety and depression disorders. Previous studies showed that parental involvement was positively associated with the success of anxiety and depression treatment (Beardslee et al., 2003), as well as PA intervention (Sharma, 2006).

Settings

Previous study in adult but not in children showed that supervised program was more effective than home-based self-help program (Ströhle, 2008). Therefore, a clinical-based treatment is suggested. For the prevention, school was suggested as the ideal setting for disseminating health promotion program because most of the children spend their day in schools (Sharma, 2006; van Sluijs et al., 2007). Compulsory basis was found to be an important determinant to the success of children's PA intervention (Lee, 2003; Palmer et al., 2005; Prochaska & Sallis, 2004; Winett et al., 1999).

Frequency and Intensity

Based on the experience from previous studies, at least 3 times per week with at least 20 minutes per session (Dunn & Weintraub, 2008; Larun et al., 2008). In respect to the intensity, some evidences indicated that mood improvement was associated with medium and long term moderate-intensity PA, while worsened mood was related with high-intensity which lasted for 10 days to a few weeks (Peluso & de Andrade, 2005). Considering anxious and depressed children may have lower physical fitness level than the general population (Martinsen, 2008), the exercise frequency should start at elementary level and progress gradually so as to minimize the risk of injury (Centers for Disease Control and Prevention, 2008). For instance, children with depressive and anxiety symptoms may start engaging in PA from the light-to-moderate PA from 2-3 times per week with 15-20 per day, then increase gradually according to individual condition.

Time

Previous studies demonstrated that an acute effect could be occurred even in one single session (Peluso & de Andrade, 2005). In general, the normal range of the intervention duration was 6- week to 20-week (Dunn & Weintraub, 2008; Larun et al., 2008). However, no study has been conducted to examine the optimal duration for reducing anxiety and depressive symptom in children. Indeed, there were strong evidences supporting the beneficial effect of PA to children's health (US Department of Health & Human Services, 2008). It seems harmless to adopt PA as a lifelong habit if no clinical condition was reported.

Types

In general, rhythmic aerobic exercise was agreed to be an appropriate types of exercise for alleviating anxiety and depression (Petruzzello et al., 1991). However, no significant difference was found between different aerobic (i.e. walking) and anaerobic exercise (i.e. weight training) in the treatment of depression (Larun et al., 2008). However, mixed results were found with respect to the treatment of anxiety (Peluso & de Andrade, 2005). From the exercise science perspective, positive experience was an important factor for repeated PA participation (Bandura, 2004). Therefore, activity like fun game rather than of harsh discipline and skill-dependent games are suggested. Also, exercise on individual and small group basis may be more appropriate than large collective activities to create enjoyable PA experience (Lagerberg, 2005).

In comparison, the PA recommendation for prevention program is much simpler. The Centers for Disease Control and Prevention (2008) recommended children to engage in at least 60 minutes PA per day. Three types of exercises are suggested: 1) moderate-to-vigorous-intensity aerobic exercise (i.e. brisk walking and running); 2) muscle strengthening (i.e.

gymnastics and push up) and 3) Bone strengthening (i.e. jumping rope or running). As children's PA pattern is spontaneous, activities could be divided into several 10- to 15-minute bouts. This guideline is certainly appropriate for all children in the general population to prevent and enhance both physical and mental health.

CONCLUSION

This chapter provided an overview in respect to the effect, mechanism and application of PA in the treatment and prevention of childhood anxiety and depression. PA appears to demonstrate certain extent of positive impact and no negative effect in treatment and prevention of childhood anxiety and depression. In addition, PA was associated with other health benefits to children's health physically (i.e. increase in fitness level, bone health, weight reduction and maintenance and stimulate brain development) (Warburton et al., 2006) and psychologically (i.e. increase in self-efficacy and self-esteem) (Biddle et al., 2000; Fox, 1999). Regarding to the implementation, PA seems to be more accessible than traditional approaches where psychiatric professionals may not presence. These evidences provide support for incorporating PA as a mean in the treatment and prevention of childhood anxiety and depression. However, the effect of PA in the treatment and prevention of childhood anxiety and depression should not be overstated. PA plays an imperative role in the prevention, but it only acts as an assistant in the pharmaceutical treatment, especially for those with severe anxiety and depression. Moreover, professional consultation should be conducted before starting any exercise treatment.

Research on the treatment and prevention effect of PA on childhood anxiety and depression is still on an early stage. More studies regarding the dose response and its effectiveness are needed to robust the evidences.

REFERENCES

American Psychiatric Association (APA). (2002). *Diagnostic and statistical manual of mental disorders* (4 ed.). Washington, D.C.: Author.

Bandura, A. (2004). *Health promotion by social cognitive means.* Health Education & Behavior, 31, 143-164.

Barlow, D. H. (2004). *Anxiety and its disorder*: The nature and treatment and anxiety and panic (2 ed.): Guilford Press.

Barrett, P. M., & Turner, C. M. (2004). *Prevention strategies.* In T. L. Morris & J. S. March (Eds.), A*nxiety disorder in children and adolescents* (2 ed.). New York, London: The Gulford Press.

Beardslee, W. R., Gladstone, T. R. G., Wright, E. J., & Cooper, A. B. (2003). *A family-based approach to the prevention of depressive symptoms in children at risk: Evidence of parental and child change.* Pediatrics, 112(2), e119-131.

Biddle, S., Fox, K. R., & Boutcher, S. H. (2000). P*hysical activity and psychological well-being:* An evidence based approach: Routledge.

Borman-Fulk, J. J., Berman, M. E., & Rabian, B. A. (2003). *Effects of aerobic exercise on anxiety sensitivity.* Behaviour Research and Therapy, 42(2), 125-136.

Bragado, C., Hernández-Lloreda, M. J., Sánchez-Bernardos, M. L., & Urbano, S. (2008). *Physcial self-concept, anxiety, depression, and self-esteem in children with cancer and healthy children without cancer history.* Psicothema, 20(3), 413-419.

Cartwright-Hatton, S., McNicol, K., & Doubleday, E. (2006). *Anxiety in a neglected population: Prevalence of anxiety disorders in pre-adolescent children.* Clinical Psychology Review, 26(7), 817.

Cartwright-Hatton, S., Roberts, C., Chitsabesan, P., Fothergill, C., & Harrington, R. (2004). *Systematic review of the efficacy of cognitive behaviour therapies for childhood and adolescent anxiety disorders.* British Journal of Clinical Psychology, 43(4), 421.

Centers for Disease Control and Prevention. (2008). *How much physical activity do children need?* Centers for Disease Control and Prevention.

Chan, P. M., & Hung, S. F. (2006). *Depression in children and adolescents.* The Hong Kong Particitioner, 28.

Cheung, A. H., Emslie, G. J., & Mayes, T. L. (2006). *The use of antidepressants to treat depression in children and adolescents.* CMAJ, 174(2), 193-200.

Clark, G. N. (1999). *Prevention of depression in at-risk samples of adolescents.* In C. A. Essau & E. Petermann (Eds.), *Depressive disorders in children and adolescents. Epidemiogy, risk factors, and treatment*: Jason Aronsaon Inc.

Costello, E. J., Mustillo, S., Erkanli, A., Keeler, G., & Angold, A. (2003). *Prevalence and development of psychiatric disorders in childhood and adolescence.* Arch Gen Psychiatry, 60(8), 837-844.

Dimeo, F., Bauer, M., Varahram, I., Proest, G., & Halter, U. (2001). *Benefits from aerobic exercise in patients with major depression: A pilot study.* British Journal of Sports and Medicine, 35, 114-117.

Dunn, A. L., & Weintraub, P. (2008). *Exercise in the prevention and treatment of adolescent depression: A promising but little researched intervention.* American Journal of Lifestyle Medicine, 2(6), 507-518.

Fergusson, D. M., & Woodward, L. J. (2002). *Mental health, educational, and social role outcomes of adolescents with depression.* Arch Gen Psychiatry, 59(3), 225-231.

Fox, K. R. (1999). *The influence of physical activity on mental well-being.* Public Health Nutrition, 2(3a), 411-418.

Garber, J. (2006). *Depression in children and adolescents:Linking risk research and prevention.* American Journal of Preventive Medicine, 31(6), 104-125.

Graeff, F. G., Guimarães, F. S., De Andrade, T. G. C. S., & Deakin, J. F. W. (1996). *Role of 5-ht in stress, anxiety, and depression.* Pharmacology Biochemistry and Behavior, 54(1), 129-141.

Harris, A., H.S., Cronkite, R., & Moos, R. (2006). *Physical activity, exercise coping and depression in a 10-year cohort study of depression patients.* Journal of Affective Disorder, 93, 79-85.

Horowitz, J. L., & Garber, J. (2006). T*he prevention of depressive symptoms in children and adolescents*: A meta-analytic review. Journal of Consulting and Clinical Psychology, 74(3), 401-415.

Kiluk, B. D., Weden, S., & Culotta, V. P. (2009). *Sport participation and anxiety in children with adhd.* J Atten Disord, 12(6), 499-506.

Lagerberg, D. (2005). *Physical activity and mental health in schoolchildren: A complicated relationship*. Acta Pædiatrica, 94, 1699-1705.

Larun, L., Nordheim, L. V., Ekeland, E., Hagen, K. B., & Heian, F. (2008). *Exericse in prevention and treatment of anxiety and depression among children and young people (review)*. The Cochrance Library(4).

Lee, W. (2003). *Fighting fat: With taf in singapore*. Diabetes Voice, 48(May), 49-50.

Lindwall, M., & Lindgren, E.-C. (2004). *The effects of a 6-month exercise intervention program on physical self-perceptions and social physique anxiety in non physically active adolescent swedish girls*. Psychology of Sport and Exercise, 6(6), 643-658.

Martinsen, E. W. (2000). *Physical activity for menatl health*. Tidsskrift for den Norske lægeforening, 230(25), 3054-3056.

Martinsen, E. W. (2007). *Themed review: Anxiety/depression*. American Journal of Lifestyle Medicine, 1(3), 159-166.

Martinsen, E. W. (2008). *Physical activity in the prevention and treatment of anxiety and depression*. Nordic Journal of Psychiatry, 62, 25.

Merry, S., McDowell, H., Hetrick, S., Bir, J., & Muller, N. (2004). *Psychological and/or educational interventions for the prevention of depression in children and adolescents*. Cochrane Database of Systematic Reviews(1), CD003380.

Michael, K. D., & Crowley, S. L. (2002). *How effective are treatments for children and adolescents depression? A meta-analytic review*. Clinical Psychology Review, 22(3), 247-269.

Murk, C. J. (2006). *Self-esteem research, theory, and practice:* Toward a positive psychology of self-esteem (3 ed.): Springer Publishing Company.

Mykletun, A., Bjerkeset, O., Dewey, M., Prince, M., Overland, S., & Stewart, R. (2007). *Anxiety, depression, and cause-specific mortality:* The hunt study. Psychosom Med, 69(4), 323-331.

Nabkasorn, C., Miyai, N., Sootmongkol, A., Junprasert, S., Yamamoto, H., Arita, M., et al. (2006). *Effects of physical exercise on depression, neuroendocrine stress hromones and physiological fitness in adolescent females with depressive symptoms*. European Journal of Public Health, 16(2), 179-184.

Palmer, S., Graham, G., & Elliott, E. (2005). *Effects of a web-based health program on fifth grade children's physical activity knowledge, attitudes and behavior*. American Journal of Health Education, 36(2), 86-93.

Peluso, M. A. M., & de Andrade, L. H. S. G. (2005). P*hysical activity and mental health: The association between exercise and mood*. Clinics, 60(1).

Petruzzello, S. J., Landers, D. M., Hatfield, B. D., Kubitz, K. A., & Salazar, W. (1991). *A meta analysis on the anxiety-reducing effects of acute and chronic exercise:* Outcome and mechanism. Sports Medicine, 11(3), 143-182.

Prochaska, J. J., & Sallis, J. F. (2004). *A randomized controlled trial of single versus multiple health behavior change: Promoting physical activity and nutrition among adolescents*. Health Psychology, 23(3), 314-318.

Russo-Neustadt, A., Ha, T., Ramirez, R., & Kesslak, J. P. (2001). *Physical activity-antidepressant treatment combination: Impact on brain-derived neurotrophic factor and beahvior in an animal model*. Behavior Brian Research, 11, 1495-1510.

Salmon, P. (2000). Effects of physical exercise on anxiety, depression, and sensitivity to stress: A unifying theory. Clinical Psychology Review, 21(1), 33-61.

Sharma, M. (2006). *International school-based intervention for preventing obesity in children.* Obesity Reviews, 8, 155-167.

Sjoten, N., & Kivel, S.-L. (2006). *The effects of physical exercise on depressive symptoms among the aged: A systematic review.* International Journal of Geriatric Psychiatry, 21(5), 410-418.

Stathopoulou, G., Power, M. B., Berry, A. C., Smits, J. A., & Otto, M. W. (2006). *Exercise interventions for mental health: A quantitative and qualitative review.* Clinical Psychology: Science & Practice, 13, 179-193.

Stella, S. G., Vilar, A. P., Lacroix, C., Fisberg, M., Santos, R. F., Mello, M. T., et al. (2005). *Effects of type of physical exercise and leisure activities on the depression scores of obese brazilian adolescents girls.* Brazilian Journal of Medical and Biological Research, 38(11), 1683-1689.

Ströhle, A. (2008). *Physical activity, exercise, depression and anxiety disorders.* J Neural Transm.

Thakore, J. H. (2001). P*hysical consequences of depression.* Peterfield, United Kingdom: Wrightson Biomedical.

Tomb, M., & GHunter, L. (2004). *Prevention of anxiety in children and adolescents in a school setting: The role of school-based practitioners.* Children & Schools, 26(2), 87-101.

US Department of Health & Human Services. (2008). 2008 *physical activity guidelines for americans.* Retrieved 18-05, 2009, from www.health.gov/paguidelines

van Sluijs, E. M. F., McMinn, A. M., & Griffin, S. J. (2007). *Effectiveness of interventions to promote physical activity in children and adolescents: Systematic review of controlled trials.* British Medical Journal, 335(7622), 703-.

Warburton, D. E. R., Nicol, C. W., & Bredin, S. S. D. (2006). *Health benefits of physical activity:* The evidence. CMAJ, 174(6), 801-809.

Winett, R. A., Roodman, A. A., Winett, S. G., WBajzek, W., Rovniak, L. S., & Whiteley, J. A. (1999). *The effect of the eat4 life internet-based health behavior program in the nutrition and activity practice of high school girls.* Journal of Gender, Culture, and Health, 4(3), 239-254.

Wipfli, B. M., Rethorst, C. D., & Landers, D. M. (2008). *The anxiolytic effects of exercise: A meta-analysis of randomized trials and dose-response analysis.* Journal of Sport & Exercise Psychology, 30(4), 392.

World Health Organization. (2006, 18-04-2006). *Diagnosing depression. Mental health and substance abuse.Facts and figures: conquering depression* Retrieved 15-04, 2008, from http://www.searo.who.int/en/Section1174/Section1199/Section1567/Section1826_8100.htm

Zoeller, R. F. J. R. (2007). *Physical activity: Depression, anxiety, physical activity, and cardiovascular disease: What's the connection?* American Journal of Lifestyle Medicine, 1(3), 175-180.

In: Handbook of Sports Psychology
Editor: Calvin H. Chang

ISBN: 978-1-60741-256-4
©2009 Nova Science Publishers, Inc.

Chapter 18

SUBJECTIVE SLEEP QUALITY AND STATE ANXIETY OF HIGH-SCHOOL STUDENTS PRIOR TO A FINAL SPORT EXAM

Daniel Erlacher
University of Heidelberg, Heidelberg, Germany

ABSTRACT

In this paper, changes of subjective sleep quality and state anxiety prior to a final sport exam have been investigated. Subjective sleep quality and state anxiety were psychometrically recorded from a group of high-school students one month prior, one week prior and the night before the exam. The high-school students showed higher state anxiety in the morning of the sport exam and for the night they reported less sleep quality, prolonged sleep latency and a higher number of nocturnal awakenings in comparison to the baseline measurement. Furthermore, a correlation between the feeling of being refreshed in the morning, cognitive state anxiety and self-confidence was found for the morning of the exam. It seems plausible that poor sleep quality and/or a feeling of not being refreshed in the morning might interfere with the performance during the sport exam. Future studies should correlate sleep parameters with performance to corroborate this assumption.

Keywords: Sleep, anxiety, exam, high-school students

INTRODUCTION

Numerous studies have shown that stressful events have a negative effect on sleep (overview: Partinen, 1994). In the field of sport, situational stress is caused by important events or competition (e.g. Spielberg, 1989) and therefore sleep might be disturbed prior to an important sporting event. In the literature it is anecdotally reported that excitement and anxiety about an upcoming competition often influence the athletes' normal sleep quality in a negative way (e.g. Shapiro, 1981; Morris, 1982, Shephard, 1984, Savis, 1994). Further anecdotal evidence comes from TV-interviews with athletes, e.g., during the Olympic Summer Games 2004 in Athens several German athletes complained after a competition in the interviews that they "couldn't close one eye during the night", or that they "had problems to get up in the morning" and "were still tired in the morning" (ARD, 2004).

Although there are numerous studies on state anxiety in the pre-competition time period (overview: Burton, 1998), surprisingly, research investigating sleep in the night before a competition is scarce. A study by Zimmermann (1996) investigated the ratio of noradrenaline (NA) and adrenaline (A) in members of eight different national teams. The morning NA/A-ratio can be seen as an indicator of either good recreation after sleep (high values) or poor recreation (low values). The results showed that the NA/A-ratio is decreased in the morning before a competition due to disturbed sleep compared to a morning before a usual training session. Furthermore low NA/A-ratios were followed by nervousness and low performance of the athletes during the competition. With a different approach using questionnaires, Savis, Eliot, Gansneder, and Rotella (1997) studied sport students (n = 65) regularly involved in sport competitions. The questionnaire involved several aspects of sleep habits (e.g. amount of sleep, sleep quality) before a competition and open questions about athletes' pre-competitive sleep. The results revealed a significant decrease in self-reported hours of sleep one night and two nights before a competition compared to the usual amount of nightly sleep. In the open questions the athletes often reported being "excited", "eager", or "anxious" before an important competition. Other statements differed in a wide range from "never getting over their anxiety, thus affecting both their sleep and performance" to "their sleep before their worst-ever performance was not any different than usual" (Savis et al, 1997, p. 167). Erlacher and Schredl (submitted) recorded the subjective sleep quality and the feeling of being refreshed in the morning with a standardized sleep questionnaire from a group of young female gymnasts (n = 16) one week prior, the night before and one week after the German junior championships. The results showed no differences for sleep quality but significant differences for the feeling of being refreshed in the morning were present, even the magnitude was within a normal range. For subjects who reported of having already experienced sleep problems prior to an important competition the changes were more pronounced.

However, in the study by Erlacher and Schredl no baseline measure in a sufficient distance prior to the competition has been carried out and one might speculate that the baseline level one week prior to the competition are seriously underestimated because of a heightened arousal caused by the upcoming competition.

The aims of the present study are twofold. First, subjective sleep quality and state anxiety will be elicited on three time periods prior to a final sport exam. The first measurement will be carried out in a sufficient time period before the exam to gain a baseline level. Second, correlations between the subjective sleep quality and the state anxiety will be analyzed. It is predicted that the sleep quality variables are reduced in the night before the exam in comparison to the prior measures and that both sleep measurements are correlated with the state anxiety variables.

METHOD

Participants

Twenty-three high-school students (4 women, 19 men) participated in the study. Their mean age was 19.7 years (SD = 0.9), ranging from 19 to 21 years of age. The high-school students were in their final high-school year of a sport-oriented high-school (Sportgymnasium). The sport exam was part of their final exam and included practical performance of individual sport (e.g. athletics, swimming) and sport games (e.g. soccer, basketball, etc.) in a competitive manner. Beside their curricular sport requirements for school all participants were engaged at least in one sport on a competitive level and practiced sport in average 9.5 hours a week (SD = 4.5). The participants as well as the teachers had given written informed consent to the study. Participation was not paid. Complete information was obtained from nine of the 23 high-school students.

Materials

For this study a questionnaire about "sleep and sport" was constructed. Additionally to sociodemographic variables the questionnaire comprised a series of questions assessing past sport experience (e.g. hours of practice per week), sleep (e.g. sleep habits) and occasions of poor sleep quality prior to a sport event.

The subjective sleep quality was elicited by a sleep questionnaire (SF-A; Görtelmeyer, 1986). The SF-A comprises 22 items measuring composite scores such as sleep quality (9 items) and the feeling of being refreshed in the morning (7 items) of the night before. The composite scores (averages) ranged from 1 to 5 since most scales of the SF-A followed this five-point format ranged from 1 = *none* to 5 = *very strong*. The sleep quality scale includes self ratings about sleep latency, frequency of nocturnal awakenings, duration of nocturnal wakefulness and psychological items anchored by a 5-point Likert scale about sleep quality, e.g. uniform, deep, restless (negative pooled). Sleep latency was measured by a six-point scale (1 = less than five minutes, 2 = 5 to 10 minutes, 3 = 10 to 20 minutes, 4 = 20 to 30 minutes, 5 = 30 minutes to one hour, 6 = more than one hour) and the frequency of nocturnal awakenings was measured by a five-point scale (1 = none, 2 = yes, once, 3 = twice, 4 = three times, 5 = more than three times). The duration of nocturnal wakefulness was calculated as sum of estimations in minutes for every awakening. The scale about the feeling of being refreshed in the morning composites psychological items anchored by a 5-point Likert scale (e.g. balanced, sleepy, and rested). The bedtime was calculated out of the going to bed time and the getting up time in the morning. The interitem consistency for the composite scores r = .89 was for the sleep quality and r = .91 for the feeling of being refreshed in the morning and the retest reliability (4 weeks) was r = .68 and r = 0.78, respectively (Görtelmeyer, 1986, 1996). Construct validity was shown in several factor analyses, and comparisons with expert ratings were satisfying, for example, r = -.67 between sleep quality and the degree of insomnia (Görtelmeyer, 1986, 1996).

State Anxiety was recorded by a German version of the revised competitive state anxiety inventory (CSAI-2g) adapted from Martens, Burton, Vealy, Bump, and Smith (1990). The

CSAI-2g is a 17-item inventory that measures cognitive state anxiety, somatic state anxiety, and self-confidence in a competitive setting. Evidence indicates that the CSAI-2g is an internally reliable instrument with demonstrated predictive validity. For the German version internal reliability coefficients of .83, .83, and .80 have been reported by Ehrlenspiel (2005). Each item on the CSAI-2g is anchored by a 4-point Likert scale (1 = *not at all*, 2 = *somewhat*, 2 = *moderately so*, 4 = *very much so*).

Design and Procedure

Data was collected on three pre-exam stages. The first recording was one month prior to the exam and served as baseline. The next recording was one week prior to the exam, and the final recording was in the morning of the exam. The high-school students were contacted by one of the authors prior to the one month pre-exam time period to distribute the set of questionnaires and the written instructions about "how" and "when" to fill out the SF-A and CSAI-2d. The questionnaire about "sleep and sport" was filled out during this session. To gain a higher response rate, in the morning of each pre-exam time period, the high-school students were reminded to fill out the questionnaires by an SMS message. In the morning of the final sport exam all questionnaires were collected. The exam lasted between 8.00 a.m. and 2.00 p. m.

Analyses of variance for repeated measures were carried out to analyze the differences between the three time periods. Greenhouse-Geiser corrections were used to adjust degrees of freedom. Since for subjective sleep quality variables and state anxiety the direction of the effect was predicted, one-tailed tests were applied. All other sleep parameters were tested two-tailed. Statistical analyses were carried out with the SPSS for Windows (Version 12.0) software package.

RESULTS

Table 1 shows the mean values and standard deviations for the sleep questionnaire variables. For the subjective sleep quality a significant difference over the pre-exam time periods was found, $F(2, 16) = 4.60$, $p = .02$. The post-hoc analysis revealed a significant difference between the baseline recording and the exam ($p = .01$) but failed to reach significance for the difference between the one week pre-exam time period to the exam ($p = .06$) and baseline to one week pre-exam time period (p = .09). No differences were found for the feeling of being refreshed in the morning, $F(2, 16) = 1.30$, $p = .15$, and bedtime, $F(2, 16) = 1.5$, $p = .27$. A post-hoc analysis revealed significant differences for sleep latency, $F(2, 16) = 4.0$, $p = .02$, and the frequency of nocturnal awakenings, $F(2, 16) = 4.9$, $p = 0.2$. The total duration of nocturnal wakefulness was not significantly heightened, $F(2, 16) = 0.4$, $p = .30$).

Table 2 shows the mean values and standard deviations for the factors of the CSAI-2d. Concerning state anxiety the analysis of variance showed a significant difference for the somatic state anxiety, $F(2, 16) = 5.82$, $p = .02$, but not for the cognitive state anxiety, $F(2, 16) = 1.87$, $p = .10$, and self confidence, $F(2, 16) = 2.02$, $p = .09$.

For the morning of the exam Pearson production-correlations for the subjective sleep quality parameters and the state anxiety factors are depicted in Table 3. Significant correlations have been found for the feeling of recovery after sleep and cognitive state anxiety (r = -.74) and for the feeling of recovery after sleep and self-confidence (r = .62).

Table 1. Mean values and standard deviation for variables of the sleep questionnaire for the three time periods

| | Time period | | | | | |
| | One month prior final exam n = 11 | | One week prior final exam n = 15 | | Morning of the final exam n = 14 | |
Variables	M	SD	M	SD	M	SD
Sleep quality	4.15 [a]	0.53	3.70	0.74	3.45 [c]	0.67
Feeling of being refreshed in the morning	2.62	0.86	2.50	0.85	3.23	0.44
Sleep Latency	2.27 [a]	0.91	2.67 [b]	1.35	3.00 [c]	1.41
Number of Nocturnal Awakenings	1.36 [a]	0.51	1.67 [b]	0.90	2.29 [c]	1.49
Duration of Nocturnal Wakefulness (minutes)	2.18	3.22	3.67	6.54	3.32	3.32
Bedtime (hours)	8.32	1.46	7.69	0.94	8.68	1.24

Note. [a] significant different from [c] ; [b] significant different from [c] ; calculation for n = 9.

Table 2. Mean values and standard deviation for the variables of the CSAI-2g for the three time periods

| | Time period | | | | | |
| | One month prior final exam n = 11 | | One week prior final exam n = 15 | | Morning of the final exam n = 14 | |
Variables	M	SD	M	SD	M	SD
somatic anxiety	12.73[a]	1.96	13.43[b]	2.95	18.06[c]	5.45
cognitive anxiety	16.18	4.85	16.27	3.85	18.14	4.33
self-confidence	31.36	4.95	27.60	5.03	30.86	7.00

Note. [a] significant different from [c] ; [b] significant different from [c] ; calculation for n = 9.

Table 3. Pearson correlations between sleep variables and state anxiety variables (n = 14).

Scale	sleep quality	feeling of recovery after sleep
somatic anxiety	.02	-.23
cognitive anxiety	-.05	-.74 **
self-confidence	-.02	.62 *

DISCUSSION

The findings of the present study indicate that the subjective sleep quality of high-school students is reduced during the night before an exam in comparison to the baseline night one month prior to the exam. In the morning of the exam the participants reported more somatic trait anxiety than in the baseline and the one week pre-exam time period. The feeling of being refreshed in the morning correlated with the cognitive state anxiety and self-confidence.

In this study a baseline was measured one month prior to the sport exam. The results showed that there is a decrease in sleep quality from the baseline measure to the one week pre-exam time period. Although the decrease is not significant, this finding indicates that a baseline recording in an appropriate distance before the sport event is essential. This finding might explain the small changes found by Erlacher and Schredl (submitted) in young female gymnasts, because the first measurement was one week prior to the competition.

As the results indicate that the upcoming sport exam affected the trait anxiety of the high-school students. Somatic state anxiety increased significantly in the morning of the sport exam in comparison to the baseline night and the time period one week prior to the exam. The increase in cognitive anxiety and the decrease in self confidence were not significant. The sport exam affected the high-school students' reports about their sleep quality. They reported prolonged sleep latency and higher frequency of nocturnal awakenings whereas the bedtime remained the same, e.g. the participants needed more time to fall asleep and had more awakenings during the night before the exam in comparison to the baseline night and the one week pre-exam time period. As reported in previous studies (e.g. Savis et al. 1997) the upcoming sport exam provoked poor sleep quality during the night.

The prolonged sleep latency and the frequent awakenings during the night might indicate a partial sleep restriction prior the sport exam. Other studies have shown that partial sleep restrictions have massive effects on the daytime performance (e.g. Van Dongen & Dinges, 2005). Future studies should collect objective sleep parameters prior the sport exam by using a portable sleep recording device and study whether sleep parameters affect the performance in a sport competition (c.f. Zimmermann, 1996).

For athletes having difficulties with sleep prior a competition or sport event it might be helpful to offer them specific interventions („sleep training") (e.g. Müller & Paterock, 1999). The same holds for sport events in different time zones. Here it seems to be important to plan their time schedule carefully to avoid sleep restrictions prior a competition due to jet lag (e.g. Smith, Guilleminault, & Efron, 1997).

The feeling of being refreshed in the morning was correlated to the cognitive state anxiety and self confidence in the morning of the sport exam. If the students did not feel refreshed in the morning they had more cognitive state anxiety and less self confidence regarding their sport exam. The low self-confidence and the higher cognitive state anxiety might interfere with performance in the sport exam. The sleep quality was not correlated to the somatic state anxiety in the morning prior the sport exam. In order to measure the effect of state anxiety on sleep quality it would be preferable to measure state anxiety in the evening.

To summarize, the present study demonstrated that the upcoming sport exam affected the subjective sleep quality of high-school students. It seems plausible that poor sleep quality and/or a lack of the feeling of being refreshed in the morning might interfere with the performance during the sport exam. Future studies should correlate sleep parameters with performance to corroborate this assumption. For athletes who have difficulties with sleep prior to a competition or sport event it would be beneficial to apply specific sleep interventions.

REFERENCES

ARD (2004). *Berichterstattung über die Olympischen Spiele 2004 in Athen. [Report about the Olympic Games 2004 in Athens].* Retrieved August 25, 2004, from http://olympia.ard.de/.

Burton, D. (1998). *Measuring Competitive State Anxiety.* In J. L. Duda (Ed.), Advances in Sport and Exercise Psychology Measurement (pp. 129-148). Morgentown, WV: Fitness Information Technologies.

Erlacher, D. & Schredl, M. (submitted). *Subjektive Schlafqualität bei Gymnastinnen vor dem Wettkampf* [Subjective sleep quality of female gymnasts prior to a competition].

Ehrlenspiel, F.(2005). *CSAI-2g. Eine deutschsprachige Fassung des Competitive State Anxiety Inventory 2 nach Martens, R., Burton, D., Vealy, R. S., Bump, L. A. & Smith, D. E. (1982) zur sportpsychologischen Messung von Angst im Wettkampfsport.* Retrieved April 6, 2006, from http://www.sport.uni-stuttgart.de/wettkampfangst/.

Görtelmeyer, R. (1986). Schlaf-Fragebogen A und B (Sf-A, Sf-B) *[Sleep questionnaire A and B (Sf-A, Sf-B)].* In Collegium Internationale Psychiatriae Scalarum (Eds.), International Skalen für Psychiatrie (3. Ed.). Weinheim: Beltz.

Görtelmeyer, R. (1996). Schlaf-Fragebogen A und B (Sf-A, Sf-B) *[Sleep questionnaire A and B (Sf-A, Sf-B)].* In Collegium Internationale Psychiatriae Scalarum (Eds.), International Skalen für Psychiatrie (4. Ed.). Weinheim: Beltz.

Martens, R., Burton, D., Vealy, R. S., Bump, L. A., & Smith, D. E. (1990). *Development and validation of the Competitive State Anxiety Inventory – 2.* In R. Martens, R. S. Veley, & D. Burton (Eds.), Competitive Anxiety in Sport (pp. 117-190). Champaign, IL: Human Kinetics.

Morris, A. F. (1982). *Sleep disturbances in athletes.* Physician and Sports Medicine, 10(9), 75-85.

Müller, T. & Paterok, B. (1999). *Schlaftraining. Ein Therapiemanual zur Behandlung von Schlafstörungen.* Göttingen: Hogrefe.

Partinen, M. (1994). *Sleep disorders and stress.* Journal of Psychosomatic Research, 38(Suppl. 1), 89-91.

Savis, J. C. (1994). *Sleep and athletic performance: Overview and implications for sport psychology.* The Sport Psychologist, 8(2), 111-125.

Savis, J. C., Eliot, J. F., Grasneder, B. & Rotella, R.J. (1997). *A subjective means of assessing college athletes' sleep: A modification of the morningness/eveningness questionnaire.* International Journal of Sport Psychology, 28(2), 157-170.

Shapiro, C. M. (1981). *Sleep and the Athlete.* British Journal of Sports Medicine, 15(1), 51-55.

Shephard, R. J. (1984). *Sleep, biorhythms, and human performance.* Sports Medicine, 1, 11-37.

Smith, R. S., Guilleminault, C., & Efron, B. (1997). *Circadian rhythms and enhanced athletic performance in the National Football League*. Sleep, 20, 362-365.

Spielberger, C. D. (1989). *Stress and anxiety in sports.* In D. Hackfort, & C. D. Spielberger (Eds.), Anxiety in sports: An international perspective (pp. 3-17). New York: Hemisphere Publishing Corporation.

Van Dongen, H. P. & Dinges, D. F. (2005). *Sleep, circadian rhythms, and psychomotor vigilance*. Clinics in Sports Medicine, 24, 237-249.

Zimmermann, E. (1996). *Leistung und Schlaf bei Sportlern [Performance and sleep in athletes]*. Wiener medizinische Wochenschrift, 13/14, 280-282.

In: Handbook of Sports Psychology
Editor: Calvin H. Chang

ISBN: 978-1-60741-256-4
©2009 Nova Science Publishers, Inc.

Chapter 19

SALIVARY CORTISOL AND MOOD REDUCTIONS IN AN OLYMPIC ATHLETE USING COGNITIVE-BEHAVIORAL METHODS

Henry Davis IV[*1], David Baron[2] and George Gillson [3]*

Suite 354, 401-9th Avenue SW, Calgary, Alberta, Canada T2P 3C5[1]

Chair, Department of Psychiatry, Temple University, Philadelphia, Pennsylvania[2], USA

President and Medical Director, Rocky Mountain Analytical, Calgary, Alberta[3]

ABSTRACT

Relaxation-enhanced, cognitive-behavioral coping methods (CBM) were taught to an Olympic athlete in mental skills training. In a controlled setting, salivary cortisol and mood were assessed in parallel at 4-minute intervals as the athlete repeatedly viewed a distressing competition video. After a baseline orientation (8-minutes) and mood provocation (12-minutes, immediately following baseline), the athlete was instructed to use CBM (8-minutes). Subjective distress was assessed together with cortisol secretion in a time sequence with eight saliva samples, collected over 28-minutes. Not until the final stage when the subject managed his subjective distress did mood and cortisol covary as commonly reported in the literature: During the CBM phase of the study, as the athlete reported reduced distress, his cortisol levels also reduced. It is suggested that in the case of negative mood, salivary cortisol secretions be assayed as an adjunct to psychometric assessment in multi-dimensional tracking during CBM training.

Keywords: cortisol, mood, negative mood, cognitive-behavioral, relaxation

[*] Corresponding Author: Henry (Hap) Davis IV, Ph.D., Suite 354, 401-9th Avenue SW, Calgary, Alberta, Canada T2P 3C5. 403-262-3737 (phone) hapdavis@gmail.com

Salivary Cortisol and Mood Reductions in an Olympic Athlete Using Cognitive-Behavioral Methods

Relatively few resources have been allocated to psychological, multimodal assessment and treatment of athletes relative to stress and mood. Likewise, clinical psychological research into the methods of managing stress in athletes rarely draws on physiologic measures. Still further, coaches are too often ill-equipped to address emotional issues arising from performance and training while their athletes rarely seek treatment (Ferraro & Rush, 2000). However, as recently reviewed by Johnson, Edmonds, Tenenbaum, and Kamata (2007), mood seen as a multidimensional entity has long been studied as integral to performance. Importantly, although the fundamental aims of CBT and mindfulness-based meditation are quite different (book), recent research using some element of mindfulness-based meditative practice with cognitive-behavioral methods (CBM) has shown efficacy in psychological management of mood among surgery, anxious, and depressive patients, athletes recovering from injury, and athletes seeking to enhance performance (Baer, 2006; Segal, Williams, & Teasdale, 2002; Gould, Greenleaf & Krane, 2002; Perna, Antoni, Baum, Gordon, & Schneiderman, 2003). Although endocrine responses have been known for some time to covary with relaxation, health, and emotional well-being (Davis, 1986) and have more recently been shown to relate to mood elevation following mindfulness-based stress reduction methods (Carlson, Speca, Patel, & Goodey, 2004), clinical sport psychology has been slow to integrate this work within applied settings.

Plasma and salivary levels of cortisol are among the most reliable biomarkers of stress and numerous studies over the past 30 years have examined the role of stress in athletes in a variety of sports using cortisol as a marker. Although the role of endocrine function in live sport performance is still being elucidated and conclusions are premature, there is an emerging literature in which salivary cortisol is monitored during competition and correlations with stress and performance are becoming evident (Doan, Newton, Kraemer, Kwon, & Scheet, 2007; Haneishi, Fry, Moore, Schilling, Li, & Fry, 2007; Hooper, Mackinnon, Howard, 1999). Two principal conclusions are possible: First, in the competitive environment, anxiety (one measure of subjective distress) frequently correlates with cortisol. Second, practitioners in applied, sport physiology settings have found benefit to assessing stress with cortisol measures.

Despite robust individual data sets on optimal mood, mindfulness, cognitive-behavior therapy, and endocrine function in stress, and emerging data on the utility of independently assessing subjective mood with cortisol in athletic settings, there has still been no comprehensive, multidimensional analysis of the psycho-physiologic effects of negative mood and cortisol in athletes in an applied, mental training context. It is widely believed that that hormonal regulation should play an important role in mental preparation for elite performance, covarying with mood during physical activity and sports training, but little is known of the actual interplay between mood and endocrine activity in applied, clinical settings (Kivlighan, Granger, & Booth, 2005; Hedge, Colby, & Goodman, 1987; Michael, Jenaway, Paykel, & Herbert, 2000). As stated, sport physiologists measure subjective mood and its physiological counterparts in their domain of practice but clinical sport psychology has not followed suit. It is only logical at this time that moment-to-moment mood assessment - in which a sport psychologist tracks mood multidimensionally and in real time, while an individual is task-engaged - (Johnson, Edmonds, Tenenbaum, & Kamata, 2007; Hanin, 2000; Lingjaerde & Foreland, 1998) should now become more standard.

The measurement of salivary cortisol is also standard in high performance labs and endocrine function tests cover the range of estradiol, estrone, estriol, progesterone, dehydroepiandrosterone (DHEA), testosterone and cortisol responses (Raff, Homar, & Skoner, 2003). Salivary cortisol samples are easily collected even on the playing field by coaches, trainers and researchers with little training. Salivary cortisol samples, unlike plasma samples, do not need to centrifuged and are relatively stable for short periods without refrigeration.

The purpose of our present case description is to illustrate the bi-dimensional assessment of mood and endocrine activity while an athlete is engaged in a CBM-based coping training method. We did not set out to demonstrate effects with our CBM; instead, our intention was to assess the utility and feasibility of employing multidimensional monitoring methods during mental training.

METHOD

Subject

The 30-year-old male Olympic athlete with extensive international competitive experience volunteered to participate and gave informed consent according to guidelines of the Helsinki Declaration, meeting also the ethics guidelines of the Canadian Psychological Association. He had failed to reach his goals at the 2002 Winter Olympic Games and, very upset, had returned from the Games before training in both mindfulness meditation, engaging in three, 10-day silent retreats, and 20-weeks of traditional cognitive therapy for depression (Beck et al., 1979).

Study Design

An 8-minute baseline orientation consisted of the athlete simply viewing other athletes from his own sport training at non-competitive venues.

Following baseline, mood provocation proceeded for 12-minutes. The athlete received the mood provocation in this period by watching a specific race video from his own Olympics. He watched critical aspects of the video repeatedly over the course of the case study.

For the last 8-minutes - while engaged in focused breathing and noting his subjective distress - he used cognitive-behavioral methods to re-frame his negative thoughts and to modify his dysfunctional thinking. In treatments which had preceded this case study, the athlete had been taught mindfulness-based meditative breathing (Kabot-Zinn, 2005; Teasdale et al., 2000) and cognitive-behavioral reframing strategies for facilitating coping in distressed persons (Clark, Beck, Alford, & Hoboken, 1999). Although he was practiced in meditation, we labeled this particular application of breathing as relaxation-based cognitive-behavioral method (CBM).

Mood ratings of subjective distress were taken every four minutes on a 1-7 Likert scale, with 7 indicating the highest distress. Saliva sampling occurred at each of these 4-minute markers.

- Mood provocation: After baseline, negative mood provocation was accomplished over a 12-minute period by having the athlete watch a key race from his Olympics. He had been instructed to "manage breathing while noticing what happens in the race and simultaneously allowing the experience of any feelings that arise." He was instructed further to "Watch the video passively with a focus also on your breathing. Use the meditative breathing that you have practiced." He had learned to identify cognitions that would develop with his feelings. Thus, in the 12-minute provocation phase of the study, as he continued to note his feelings without judgment, he simultaneously identified automatic thoughts corresponding to his mood, also without judgment. While noting this mood and related thoughts he volunteered aloud that he felt "desperate, scared, and alone".

- Active CBM coping: The study athlete was competent in using CBM, as described above. Therefore, for this phase of the study, he used focused breathing together with the cognitive-behavioral reframing strategies as taught. In the final 8-minutes of the study, while still viewing the personal video and attending to his even-paced, meditative breaths, he followed coping instructions: "Now, generate positive thoughts as alternates to your automatic negative ones. For example, to the word "scared" you might intentionally focus on phrases such as "I have nothing to be afraid of. I have done my own best. I am loveable. I am included. I am important to my team. I am happy for my teammates."

- Cortisol assessment: Salivary cortisol was collected eight times via passive drool at 4-minute intervals: 3 times during baseline orientation, 3 times during mood provocation, and 2 times during CBM. Saliva was collected in polystyrene tubes and frozen at -20C until assay. Concentrations were assayed at Rocky Mountain Analytical, Calgary, Alberta, Canada. The method of analysis was enzyme-linked immunosorbent assay (ELISA) using a kit designed for analysis of cortisol directly in saliva (Diagnostic Systems Laboratories, DSL-10-67100, Webster, TX). Samples were analyzed in duplicate. There were no conflicts between scientific and commercial interests. While the assay is not unique to Rocky Mountain Analytical its application in applied sport psychology – the focus of our study – is. The methods used in this study are widely available in both university and commercial labs. Most practitioners interested in pursuing a similar method will find it relatively easy to obtain the same assay in their setting.

RESULTS

The data showed mean salivary cortisol levels of 2.0 ng/ml, 1.7 ng/ml, and 1.2 ng/ml during over three periods: (A) baseline orientation, (B) mood provocation, and (C) active, CBM coping, respectively. The average subjective distress ratings of 2.0, 4.0, and 1.0 recorded for the three periods did not follow the same course as cortisol. Instead, while thinking distressing thoughts but maintaining a focus on relaxed breathing, the subject showed cortisol levels that steadily fell before period (C) when he used CBM coping and attained a level of subjective distress that matched his physiologic status. This mismatch in time course for the two measures identifies the disconnect between two tasks: On one hand, he permitted negative thoughts while, on the other hand, he simultaneously managed his breathing. The changes from (B) mood provocation to (C) active CBM coping were the principal focus for this study. Importantly, after baseline, there was a 30% reduction in average cortisol secretion between B and C that was mirrored by a comparable decline in average subjective distress from 4 to 1. Please see Figure 1.

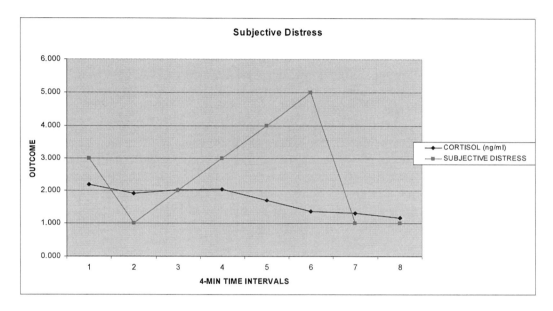

Figure 1. Ratings of subjective distress and cortisol over eight, 4-min periods.

As stated, during period (B), mood provocation, while maintaining focused and relaxed breathing the athlete spontaneously reported feeling "desperate", "scared", and "alone." In contrast, during period (C), active CBM coping, as cortisol levels continued to decline, the athlete spontaneously said, "I don't feel the same now. It would be hard to say that I am upset. I'm less stressed." In other words, during period (B) he did not feel relaxed as he was breathing, perhaps because he was *allowing* and not *managing* his subjective distress.

DISCUSSION

The principal purpose of the case study was to demonstrate the efficacy of multidimensional methods for tracking mood during mental training. In this feasibility illustration, there was a roughly 30-percent reduction in cortisol level over 28-minutes corresponding to roughly the same period of focused, relaxed breathing. During a period of active coping following mood provocation, using CBM, the cortisol reduction coupled with the corresponding reduction in subjective distress; each occurred within a period of 8-

minutes. This suggests a clinically significant aspect of our findings: A response to using CBM methods may be monitored with dual endocrine and psychological parameters while an athlete is engaged in mental training. It is important to note that although this athlete reported greater distress during provocation, his cortisol levels did not elevate beyond the hypervigilant state that was seen at baseline. This argues for using multidimensional methods: An athlete who claims verbally to be "better" and "worse" should simultaneously be evaluated with a biological measure. In this case the athlete's subjective sense of feeling "worse" was not consistently matched by an upregulation of cortisol while his impression of feeling "better" did correlate with the shift in cortisol. This is potentially very important information for the athlete in training.

Our case study was not a test of CBM and this demonstration of the covariation of cortisol with mood (during active coping) cannot be considered evidence for cause or effect. There were no experimental controls and the 8-point sampling procedure was too limited to permit meaningful t-tests or correlational analyses. Instead, the study is valuable for its clinical utility; sport clinicians may draw from two literatures – hormonal and affective - and apply this literature when assessing their applied interventions.

It is important to remember that although the important role of emotional stress in athletic performance is well documented in the extant sports psychology literature, the underlying mechanism by which stress may affect training, and competitive performance, is less well understood. Further, there is little agreement that cortisol levels can be used to predict performance. Finally, the elevation of cortisol has its limitations as a biomarker for stress and any variability in cortisol salivary levels must be considered in light of medical conditions and estrogens which could affect cortisol binding or HPAA activity (Hellhammer, Weist, & Kudielka, 2009).

The overall value of our results lies, therefore, not in the replication of a robust literature showing the covariation of cortisol with mood. Instead, it lies in the demonstration of a method of multidimensional assessment. Showing that a rapid reduction in the primary stress hormone, cortisol, may not mirror change in cognition - if the subject is permitted to feel distress but instructed to manage breathing - appears every bit as important as important as basic replication. Equally, when our subject finally worked to manage his negative mood (during relaxation-based cognitive coping) both mood and endocrine activity paralleled one another. This suggests the importance for measuring both the psychological and biological parameters of stress while tracking the progress of training in a CBM. Clinicians may, for instance, in using the simple assessment tools that we have demonstrated, employ competition videos to intentionally trigger negative mood and provide meaningful exposure to negative stress while tracking the client's coping responses. Undoubtedly, some athletes will not regulate their hormonal response to subjective distress as our own subject did using breathing (in most, subjective distress will likely increase with cortisol). The fact that our subject was essentially able to do these two things at once – allow distress while managing breathing - may be a unique finding, attributable to his unique training and intermediate experience in mindfulness meditation.

The twinning of mood ratings with a salivary cortisol assessment during CBM training will have important implications for practicing sports psychiatrists and psychologists who want ongoing multidimensional evidence for the efficacy of their individualized mental training protocols.

REFERENCES

Baer, R.A. (Ed.) (2007). *Mindfulness-based treatment approaches.* London: Elsevier.

Beck, A.T., Rush, A.J., Shaw, B.F., & Emery, G. (1979). *Cognitive therapy of depression.* New York: Guilford Press.

Carlson, L.E., Speca, M., Patel, K.D. Goodey, E. (2004). *Mindfulness-based stress reduction in relation to quality of life, mood, symptoms of stress and levels of cortisol, dehydroepiandrosterone sulfate (DHEAS) and melatonin in breast and prostate cancer outpatients.* Psychoneuroendocrinology, 29, 448-474.

Clark, D.A., Beck, A.T., Alford, B.A., Hoboken, N.J. (1999). *Scientific foundations of cognitive theory and therapy of depression.* Hoboken, NJ: John Wiley & Sons Inc.

Davis, H. (1986). *Effects of biofeedback and cognitive therapy on stress in patients with breast cancer.* Psychological Reports, 59, 967-974.

Doan, B.K., Newton, R.U., Kraemer, W.J., Kwon, Y.H., & Scheet, T.P. (2007). *Salivary cortisol, testosterone, and T/C ratio responses during a 36-hole golf competition. International* Journal of Sports Medicine, 28, 470-479.

Ferraro, T., & Rush, S. (2000). *Why athletes resist sport psychology.* Athletic Insight: Online Journal of Sport Psychology. 2, No Pagination Specified.

Gould, D., Greenleaf, C., & Krane, V. (2002). *Arousal-anxiety and sport behavior.* In: Horn TS, eds. Advances in sport psychology (2nd ed.) (pp. 207-236). Champaign, IL: Human Kinetics.

Hanin, Y.L. (2000). *Emotions in sport.* Champaign, IL: Human Kinetics.

Haneishi, K., Fry, A.C., Moore, C.A., Schilling, B.K., Li, Y., & Fry, M.D. (2007). *Cortisol and stress responses during a game and practice in female collegiate soccer players.* Journal of Strength Conditioning Research, 21, 583-588.

Hedge, G.A., Colby, H.D., Goodman, R.I. (1987) *Clinical Endocrine Physiology.* Philadelphia, PA: W.B. Saunders Company, 1987.

Hellhammer, D.H., Weist, S., Kudielka, B.M. (2009). Salivary coritsol as a biomarker in stress research. *Psychoneuroendocrinology, 34,* 163-171

Hooper, S.L., Mackinnon, L.T., Howard, A. (1999). *Physiological and psychometric variables for monitoring recovery during tapering for major competition.* Medical Science in Sports and Exercise, 31, 1205 -1210.

Johnson, M.B., Edmonds, W.A., Tenenbaum, G., & Kamata, A. (2007). *The relationship between affect and performance in competitive intercollegiate tennis: A dynamic conceptualization and application.* Journal of Clinical Sport Psychology, 1, 130-146.

Kabat-Zinn, J. (2005). *Bringing mindfulness to medicine*: An interview with Jon Kabat-Zinn. Advances in Mind Body Medicine, 21, 22-27.

Kivlighan, K.T., Granger, D.A., and Booth, A. (2005. *Gender differences in testosterone and cortisol response to competition.* Psychoneuroendocrinology, 30, 58-71.

Lingjaerde, O., & Foreland, A.R. (1998). *Direct assessment of improvement in winter depression with a visual analog scale: High reliability and validity.* Psychiatry Research, 81, 387-392.

Michael, A., Jenaway, A., Paykel, E.S., & Herbert, J. (2000). *Altered salivary dehydroepiandrosterone levels in major depression in adults.* Biological Psychiatry, 48, 989-995.

Perna, F.M., Antoni, M.H., Baum, A., Gordon, P., & Schneiderman, N. 2003. *Cognitive behavioral stress management effects on injury and illness among competitive athletes*: A randomized clinical trial. Annals of Behavioral Medicine. 25, 66-73.

Raff, H., Homar, P.J., & Skoner, D.P. (2003). *New enzyme immunoassay for salivary cortisol*. Clinical Chemistry, 49, 203-204.

Segal, ZV., Williams, J.M.G., & Teasdale, J.D. (2002). *Mindfulness-based cognitive therapy for depression*. New York: The Guilford Press.

Teasdale, J.D., Segal, Z.V., Williams, J.M., Ridgeway, V.A., Soulsby, J.M., & Lau, M.A. (2000). *Prevention of relapse/recurrence in major depression by mindfulness-based cognitive therapy*. Journal of Consulting and Clinical Psychology, 68, 615-623.

In: Handbook of Sports Psychology
Editor: Calvin H. Chang

Chapter 20

COPING, PERFORMANCE, AND ANXIETY SPORT PSYCHOLOGY RESEARCH: SOME THOUGHTS ON METHODS

Brett Smith[*1] *and Víctor Pérez-Samaniego*[2]

Loughborough University [1]
University of Valencia, Spain[2]

To date, research in sport psychology has predominantly used quantitative methods to understand coping, performance, and anxiety. For example, questionnaire scales are prevalent and readily available that measure anxiety -e.g. CSAI-2- (Martens et al., 1990), emotions -e.g. Sport Emotion Questionnaire- (Jones et al., 2005), and coping -e.g. Modified COPE- (Crocker and Graham 1995). Further, there have been calls for more work on quantitative methods. For instance, as Hanton, Neil, and Mellalieu (2008) put it in their erudite review of coping and anxiety work in sport psychology, future research should develop a measure that considers the stressors, appraisals, emotions and orientations, and behavior of the athlete "within the competitive environment. In the meantime, researchers should not tire of furthering our knowledge of the stress process through the adoption of a reductionist approach by combining instruments or rephrasing participant instructions to respond to specific demands" (p. 53).

Whilst sport psychology has predominantly relied on quantitative methods to understand coping, performance, and anxiety, there has however been a growing interest in qualitative methods to further our knowledge (for an excellent review see Neil, Mellalieu, & Hanton, in-press). For example, using the information that quantitative studies provided as a foundation, qualitative research has been conducted to further understand and explain swimmers anxiety symptoms, self-confidence, and the perceived effects of these components upon performance (Hanton & Connaughton, 2002). Qualitative procedures, strategies, and techniques (e.g. interviews) have also been used to explore the relationship between anxiety symptoms, self-confidence, and the directional interpretation of symptoms in athletes (Hanton, Mellalieu, & Hall, 2004).

---

*Correspondence to: Brett Smith. School of Sport, Exercise and Health Sciences, Loughborough University, Leicestershire, UK, LE11 3TU,E-Mail: B.M.Smith@exeter.ac.uk

Therefore, in our efforts to understand coping, performance, and anxiety both quantitative and qualitative *methods* (i.e. procedures, strategies, and techniques for the collection and analysis of data) have been used and heavily relied on. Importantly, often informing these methods, either implicitly or explicitly, are a set of assumptions. These assumptions might loosely be described as neorealist, or what some might term (post)positivist in nature (for detailed discussions see Smith, 1989, 1993; Smith & Deemer, 2000; Smith & Hodkinson, 2009). At the heart of neorealism is the assumption that there is a real world out there independent of our interest in or knowledge of that world, and we can gain access to that world and know it as it really is through method. That is, because methods properly applied are believed to be neutral/objective, they can be used to establish contact with an external reality beyond ourselves. One implication of this, which many sport psychologists have taken up, even if only implicitly, is the idea that methods can give researchers direct access to reality in a way that will allow them to claim reality can be accurately or objectivity depicted. Another implication that extends from this is that method is a marker of quality research. In other words, if methods can get at the reality and truth, then in principle they can sort out good research from bad coping, performance, and anxiety research. Sport psychologists can not only know coping and anxiety objectively through the appropriate use of procedures or techniques, but these methods will ensure that their work is valid.

However, the advancement of a central role for method as the way to establish contact with a reality independent of us and sort out quality from less quality research is, for some scholars, problematic. For example, in relation to establishing contact with a reality independent, as Hanson (1958), Putnam (1981), Smith (1993), and Sparkes and Smith (in-press) argued, there can be no separation between the researcher-researched or the observer-observed. As such, all observation is theory-laden and there is no possibility of theory-free knowledge. That is, who we are is crucial to how we see the world around us and we cannot cut ourselves loose from our own cultural, social and historical standpoint. Thus, establishing contact with a reality independent of our interests, purposes, and languages used, and achieving theory-free observation or knowledge of coping and anxiety, is a chimera. Quite simply, as Smith and Hodkinson (2009) put it, the problem is that there is no way to 'get at' the reality as it really is or to know if the reality has been mirrored correctly independent of us.

But, so the story goes for many scholars within sport psychology, this problem can be overcome by a researcher giving themselves over to method. This is because method itself is neutral and, properly applied, is the guarantor of procedural objectivity. This is captured well by Kerlinger (1979) when he said, "The procedures of science are objective—not the scientists....Scientists, like all men and women are opinionated, dogmatic, ideological...That is the very reason for insisting on procedural objectivity; to get the whole business outside of ourselves" (p. 264). Thus, methods are believed to be able to establish contact with a reality independent of our interests, purposes, and languages used. They can achieve theory-free observation or knowledge. Given this, for some sport psychologists, coping and anxiety can therefore be known objectively through the appropriate use of procedures or techniques. These methods can also sort out good coping and anxiety research from bad research. For quantitative research, one such method to do this includes questionnaires measures, like the CSAI-2. For qualitative research, as Sparkes and Smith (in-press) point out, the methods sport psychologists most often use are interviews coupled with the techniques advocated by Lincoln and Guba (1985) to achieve credibility: prolonged engagement, persistent observation, triangulation (sources, investigators, and methods), peer debriefing, negative case analysis, referential adequacy, and member checks (in process and terminal). Accordingly, methods become our saviour. Through them matters like coping and anxiety can be known, *at least in principle*, independent of our knowledge and as they really are.

However, for some scholars, this too is problematic (MacKenzie, 1981; Smith, 1993; in-press; Sparkes & Smith, in-press). This is because methods, it is argued, are not neutral or discovered, and cannot secure a procedural objectivity. They are something people have constructed in line with particular interests, purposes, and political/ideological commitments (MacKenzie, 1981; Smith, 1993; in-press; Sparkes & Smith, in-press). For example, MacKenzie (1981) contended that, even statistics, that seemingly most neutral/objective tool in our bag is itself a product of social and cultural influences. As such, he argued, the statistics that were developed in Great Britain from around 1865 to 1930, and which are still honoured by social science researchers, were not discovered, but rather socially constructed. Put differently, MacKenzie argued it is insufficient to hold that the concepts behind statistics and the mathematical working out of these concepts were somehow "out there" awaiting discovery; to the contrary the particular concepts and mathematical techniques were constructed within the context of certain value orientations to accomplish particular goals. Further, within sports research, Randall and Phoenix (in-press) suggested that, insofar as words and their comprehension are central to the utility of instrument and interview alike, there is no hard bottom of "objective reality" to be reached beneath either of them. For them, the Uncertainty Principle, so to speak, is inevitably at work: the very act of observation interferes with whatever we observe, including coping or anxiety and how they relate to human performance.

Furthermore, Smith (1993, in-press), Smith and Deemer (2000), and Smith and Hodkinson (2005, 2009) argued that methods are constructed in line with particular goals, values, and political/ideological commitments. One implication of this, they contend, is that methods cannot be neutral, the guarantor of procedural objectivity, or discovered. They cannot give researchers a direct access to a reality independent of their knowledge of that world and in a way that will allow them to claim reality can be accurately or objectivity depicted/described. Another implication is that methods cannot be relied on to sort out good research from bad research. We cannot call upon them to sort out the differences that inevitably arise amongst researchers over claims to knowledge about coping and anxiety. As Smith (in-press) argued.

There can be no theory-free knowledge or observation and we do not have a language, and have not the foggiest idea how to get a language, that would allow us to express the result of a theory-free observation. Those methods that have been and still are honored because they supposedly allow us to obtain the "clear-eyed gaze," to take a view from nowhere in particular, to keep our Cartesian mirror of the mind well-polished, or however one wishes to put it, are methods that people have constructed in line with their particular interests, purposes, political/ideological commitments, and so on. And, if this line of reasoning makes sense, then it is pointless to talk in terms of criteria, cut loose from particular times and particular places, for judging the quality of research studies. Research methods and the judgments about the quality of research studies always have been and likely always will be, contingent on who we are and what we think we can accomplish. (in-press)

Thus, to believe that we can gain access to a real world independent of our interests, purposes, and languages used via methods is problematic. Further, if we are intimately entangled with any claim we make to knowledge or to what counts as knowledge, then, by extension, this means we are intimately a part of any understanding we have of what counts as quality in research. That is, we all, researchers included, have a place in the world—an effective history (Gadamer, 1995)—that deeply influences how we see the goals of sport psychology research, how research on coping and anxiety should be undertaken, and, of course, how we should judge research quality. As such, the idea of method as a marker of quality research is seriously called into question. This is especially so since the existence of foundations, of a reality outside of ourselves that can be known objectively through the appropriate use of procedures or techniques has to be confirmed and, as Smith J. (1993, in-press), Smith and Deemer (2000), and Smith and Hodkinson (2005, 2009) emphasise, this assumption (the reality) has to be cashed in to do its work of adjudication. To date, however, the reality that is supposed to 'kick in' and adjudicate between trustworthy and untrustworthy interpretations has yet to do so in any published social science works to date. As Smith and Hodkinson (2009) pointed out, given the collapse of the empiricist distinction between subject and object,

The problem is that there is no way to 'get at' that reality as it really is. And, if one cannot capture that social reality as it really is, then that reality cannot be called upon to do the adjudicate-the-different-claims-to-knowledge work asked of it. This is the whole problematic posed by the idea that no matter how hard we try, we cannot achieve theory-free observation or knowledge. (p 10)

What can be concluded from this brief entry into methods?

Firstly, we accept, in a very common sense way, that there is a physical world out there independent of us—in other words, it is not a creation of our mind. However, while we accept that there are physical beings out there moving around in time and space and uttering what people calls words, we are aware that the interpretations/descriptions we or anybody else offers of these movements and utterances are not out there in the sense of being independent of our interests and purposes (Smith and Hodkinson, 2009). As an interpretivist, or what some might term non-realist, therefore, we collapse the empiricist distinction between subject and object. This being the case we reject any claims that we can gain access (via whatever method) to a psycho-social reality like coping and anxiety in ways that are independent of our interests, purposes, and languages used. However, in problematising the idea that there is a real world out there independent of our knowledge of that world and that we can gain access to that world and know it as it really is through method, we do not want to throw out methods. Nor do we want to suggest that methods, such as the CSAI-2 or member checks in qualitative interviewing, are of no value. They can and do have value. The point, simply put, is that methods are neither objective nor neutral. They cannot tap into the psycho-social realms of coping and anxiety in ways that are independent of us.

Secondly, methods are of value, but only under certain conditions and in certain situations depending upon the specific purposes of the inquiry. The choice about methods in any instance depends on what seems to be important at the time. In this view, methods cannot be used to establish contact with some external reality beyond ourselves. They are just the practical activities of those who engage in the practical tradition of coping and anxiety research with human beings. Thus, choices about which methods to use are practical in nature. These choices cannot, therefore, be predetermined or made in advance of any individual study that researchers engage in. Rather, these choices are made and worked out as part of the process of engagement as it develops over time.

Third, when making judgments about what constitutes good and bad coping and anxiety social science research, relying solely on criteria that speak to methods is problematic. This is not advocate research in which anything goes. That would be nonsense as all researchers make judgments and will continue to do so as far as one can see in the future. As Smith (1993) argued, it is impossible to imagine someone leading a life without making judgments or discriminations. Further, researchers who reject relying solely on criteria that speak to methods to make judgments about good from bad coping and anxiety social science research do not believe in abandoning criteria to judge research. On the contrary, they do believe in using criteria to judge research. They do believe in holding sport psychology research to very high standards. But, the point is that our criteria cannot be universal or determined in advance of any particular piece of social science inquiry. They cannot be grounded in an independently existing reality that can be known as it really is through methods. Instead, as Smith and Deemer (2000), Smith and Hodkinson (2009), and Sparkes and Smith (in-press) argued, our judgments are time and place contingent. Thus, the reality itself and method alone cannot provide a referent point for sorting out claims to knowledge – or 'good' and 'bad' coping and anxiety social science research related to performance. All we can do is appeal to time and place contingent lists of characteristics to sort out the good from the not so good coping and anxiety research.

REFERENCES

Crocker, P.R.E., & Graham, T.R. (1995). *Coping by competitive athletes with Performance stress: Gender differences and relationships with affect.* The Sport Psychologist, 9, 325-338.

Gadamer, H-G. (1995). *Truth and method.* (2nd rev. ed., J. Weinsheimer & D.G. Marshall, Trans.). New York: Crossroad.

Jones, M.V., Lane, A.M., Bray, S. & Caitlin, J., (2005). *Development and validation of the Sport Emotion Questionnaire.* Journal of Sport and Exercise Psychology, 27, 407-431.

Hanson, N. (1958). *Patterns of discovery.* Cambridge, UK: Cambridge University Press.

Hanton, S., & Connaughton, D. (2002). *Perceived control of anxiety and its relationship with self-confidence performance:* A qualitative explanation. Research Quarterly for Exercise and Sport, 73, 87-97.

Hanton, S., Mellalieu, S. D., & Hall, R. (2004). *Self-confidence and anxiety interpretation: A qualitative investigation.* Psychology of Sport and Exercise, 5, 379-521.

Hanton, S., Neil, R., & Mellalieu, S. D. (2008). Recent developments in competitive anxiety direction and competition stress research. International Review of Sport and Exercise Psychology, 1, 45-57.

Kerlinger, F. (1979). *Behaviorial research.* New York: Holt, Rinehart, & Winston.

Lincoln, Y., & Guba, E. (1985). *Naturalistic inquiry.* Thousand Oaks, CA: Sage.

Martens, R., Burton, D., Vealey, R. S., Bump, L., & Smith, D. E. (1990). *Development and validation of the Competitive State Anxiety Inventory*-2 (CSAI-2). In R. Martens, R. S. Vealey, & D. Burton (Eds.), *Competitive anxiety in sport* (pp. 117-213). Champaign, IL: Human Kinetics.

MacKenzie, D. (1981). *Statistics in Great Britain*: 1885-1930. Edinburgh: Edindurgh University Press.

Neil, R., Mellalieu., S. & Hanton, S. (in-press). The contribution of qualitative inquiry towards understanding competitive anxiety and competition stress. **Qualitative Research in Sport and Exercise.**

Putnam, H. (1981). *Reason, truth, and history.* Cambridge, UK: Cambridge University Press.

Randall, W. L. & Phoenix, C. (in press). *The problem with truth in qualitative interviews: Reflections from a narrative perspective.* **Qualitative Research in Sport and Exercise.**Smith, J. (1989). The nature of social and educational inquiry: Empiricism versus interpretation. Norwood, NJ: Ablex Publishing Corporation.

Smith, J. (1993). *After the demise of empiricism*: The problem of judging social and educational inquiry. Norwood, NJ: Ablex Publishing Corporation.

Smith, J., & Deemer, D. (2000). *The problem of criteria in the age of relativism.* In N. Denzin & Y. Lincoln (Eds.), Handbook of qualitative research (2nd edition) (pp. 877-896). London: Sage.

Smith, J., & Hodkinson, P. (2005). *Relativism, criteria and politics.* In N. Denzin & Y. Lincoln (Eds.), Handbook of qualitative research (3rd edition) (pp. 915-932). London: Sage.

Smith, J., & Hodkinson, P. (2009). *Challenging neorealism*: A response to Hammersley. Qualitative Inquiry, 15 (1), 30-39.

Sparkes, A. & Smith, B. (in press). *Judging the quality of qualitative inquiry: Criteriology and relativism in action.* Psychology of Sport and Exercise.

INDEX

B

D

E

H

I

J

N

O

P

Q

S

T